PETER
OF
SAVOY

PETER OF SAVOY

THE LITTLE CHARLEMAGNE

JOHN MARSHALL

PEN & SWORD HISTORY

AN IMPRINT OF PEN & SWORD BOOKS LTD.
YORKSHIRE · PHILADELPHIA

First published in Great Britain in 2023 by
PEN AND SWORD HISTORY
An imprint of
Pen & Sword Books Ltd
Yorkshire – Philadelphia

Copyright © John Marshall, 2023

ISBN 978 1 39906 566 5

The right of John Marshall to be identified as Author of this work has been asserted by him in accordance with the Copyright, Designs and Patents Act 1988.

A CIP catalogue record for this book is available from the British Library.

All rights reserved. No part of this book may be reproduced or transmitted in any form or by any means, electronic or mechanical including photocopying, recording or by any information storage and retrieval system, without permission from the Publisher in writing.

Typeset in Times New Roman 9.5/11.5 by SJmagic DESIGN SERVICES, India.
Printed and bound in the UK by CPI Group (UK) Ltd.

Pen & Sword Books Limited incorporates the imprints of Atlas, Archaeology, Aviation, Discovery, Family History, Fiction, History, Maritime, Military, Military Classics, Politics, Select, Transport, True Crime, Air World, Frontline Publishing, Leo Cooper, Remember When, Seaforth Publishing, The Praetorian Press, Wharncliffe Local History, Wharncliffe Transport, Wharncliffe True Crime and White Owl.

For a complete list of Pen & Sword titles please contact
PEN & SWORD BOOKS LIMITED
George House, Units 12 & 13, Beevor Street, Off Pontefract Road,
Barnsley, South Yorkshire, S71 1HN, England
E-mail: enquiries@pen-and-sword.co.uk
Website: www.pen-and-sword.co.uk

or

PEN AND SWORD BOOKS
1950 Lawrence Rd, Havertown, PA 19083, USA
E-mail: uspen-and-sword@casematepublishers.com
Website: www.penandswordbooks.com

Contents

Abbreviations vi
Pierre de Savoie Timeline ix
A Note on Names xii
A Note on Money xiii
Without Whose Help … xiv
Notable Savoyards in England xv
Family Trees xxiii
Maps xxvi
Introduction xxx
Prologue xxxiii

Chapter One 1
Chapter Two 12
Chapter Three 21
Chapter Four 36
Chapter Five 55
Chapter Six 72
Chapter Seven 92
Chapter Eight 116
Chapter Nine 140
Chapter Ten 153
Chapter Eleven 172
Appendix   Key Pierre de Savoie Estate Holdings in
            England and Savoy 189

Notes 206
Bibliography 310
Index 318

Abbreviations

Archives

ACV	Archives cantonales vaudoises, Lausanne, Switzerland
ADI	Archives départementales de l'Isère, Grenoble, France
ADS	Archives départementales de la Savoie, Chambéry, France
AST	Archivio di Stato di Torino, Italy
BNF	Bibliothèque Nationale de France, Paris
CAC	Calendar of Ancient Correspondence Concerning Wales
CFR	Calendar of Fine Rolls
CPR	Calendar of Patent Rolls
CCR	Calendar of Close Rolls
CChR	Calendar of Charter Rolls
CChW	Calendar of Chancery Warrants
CLR	Calendar of Liberate Rolls
CWR	Calendar of Welsh Rolls.
LF	Liber Feodorum (Book of Fees (Fiefs))
RG	Rôles Gascons
TNA	The National Archives of the UK

Collected and Published Primary Sources

Fœdera	Thomas Rymer. 1816. *Fœdera, Conventiones, Litteræ, et Cujuscunque Generis Acta Publica Inter Reges Angliæ et alios quosvis Imperatores, Reges, Pontifices, bel Communitates*. Vol 1, London.
La Finanza Sabauda	Mario Chiaudano. 1933–7. *La Finanza Sabauda* nel XIII sec. 3 Vols. Turin. Biblioteca Della Società Storica Subalpina.
Ridgeway	Huw Ridgeway. 2023. *An English Cartulary Roll of Peter of Savoy, Lord of Richmond (1240-1268): Archives, Interests and Servants of an Alien Favourite of Henry III* forthcoming publication of TNA C47/9/1 in a volume to be edited by Professors Nigel Saul & Nicholas Vincent for the Pipe Roll Society, London.
Wurstemberger	Johann Ludwig Wurstemberger. 1856–9. *Peter der Zweite, Graf von Savoyen, Markgraf in Italien*, Sein Haus und Seine Lande. Vols 1–4. Berne: Stæmpfle.

Chronicles

Ann. Cestrienses	Richard Copley Christie. 1887. *Annales Cestrienses*: or Chronicle of the Abbey of St. Werburg at Chester. The Record Society.
Ann. Dunstable	Henry Richards Luard. 1864. *Annales Monastici* vol III. London: Longmans, Green, Reader and Dye.
Ann. Londonsienses	Chronicles of the Reigns of Edward I and Edward II, pp. 3–252. DOI: https://doi.org/10.1017/CBO9781139343510.005. Publisher: Cambridge University Press. Print publication year: 2012. First published in: 1882.
Ann. Osney	Henry Richards Luard, 1869. *Annales Monastici* vol IV. London: Longmans, Green, Reader and Dye.
Ann. Tewkesbury	Henry Richards Luard. 1864. *Annales Monastici* vol I. London: Longmans, Green, Reader and Dye.
Ann. Thomas Wykes	Henry Richards Luard. 1869. *Annales monastici*, vol IV *Chronicon vulgo dictum chronicon Thomae Wykes* (1066–1289). London: Longmans, Green, Reader and Dye.
Ann. Trevet	Thomas Hog. 1845. F. Nicholai Triveti, *de ordine frat. Praedicatorum, Annales*. English Historical Society.
Ann. Waverley	Henry Richards Luard. 1865. *Annales Monastici vol II Annales Monasterii de Waverleia*. London.: Longman, Green, Longman, Roberts and Green.
Brut	*Brut y Tywysogion*, or the Chronicle of the Princes: 1955. Red Book of Hergest Version, edited and translated by T. Jones, History and Law Series, 16 Cardiff: Cardiff: University of Wales Press.
Cart. Lausanne	La Société d'Histoire de la Suisse Romande, 1851. Conon d'Estavayer. *Cartulaire du chapitre de Notre-Dame de Lausanne. Chronique des Évêques*, Librairie de Georges Bridel. Lausanne.
Chron. Flores	Henry Richards Luard. *Flores Historiarum*. 1890. London, HMSO.
Chron. Gloucester	William Alldis Wright, 1887. The Metrical Chronicle of Robert of Gloucester, Part II. London, HMSO.
Chron. Guisborough	Walter of Guisborough. 1848. *Chronicon domini Walteri de Hemingburgh*, vols 1 & 2. London.
Chron. Johannes de Oxenedes	Johannes de Oxenedes. Ed. Henry Ellis. 1859. *Chronica Johannes de Oxenedes*. Cambridge University Press. Cambridge.
Chron. Lanercost	Herbert Maxwell. 1913. The Chronicle of Lanercost, 1272–1346.
Chron. Langtoft	Thomas Wright. 1868. The Chronicle of Pierre de Langtoft: In French Verse from the Earliest Period to the Death of King Edward I, vol 2.
Chron. Majora Eng	John Allen Giles English translation. 1852–3. Matthew Paris's English History, vols 1–3. Henry G. Bohn. London.
Chron. Majora Lat	Latin text. *Matthæi Parisiensis*. 1880. *Chronica Majora*, vols 1–5. Henry Richards Luard (ed.). London: Longmans, Green, Reader & Dye.

Chron. Rishanger	James Orchard Halliwell. 1840. The Chronicle of William de Rishanger, Of The Barons' Wars. The Miracles of Simon de Montfort. London. The Camden Society.
Chron. Thedmar	Thomas Stapleton. 1844. Liber de Antiquis Legibus : cronica maiorum et vicecomitum Londoniarum. London : Societatis Camdenensis.
Giraldus Cambrensis	Giraldus Cambrensis, 1146?–1223?, George F. (George Frederic) Warner, James Francis Dimock & John Sherren Brewer. Giraldi Cambrensis Opera. London: Longman & co.; [etc., etc.], 1861–91.
Hist. Anglicana	Chronicles and Memorials of Great Britain and Ireland, 1859, Bartholomæi de Cotton, Monachi Norwicensus, Historia Anglicana.

Pierre de Savoie Timeline

1203	Probably born Susa, County of Savoy, now Italy
1223	Death of his brother, Humbert de Savoie
1224	Enters the written record witnessing a charter
1225	King Henry III of England reissues the *Magna Carta*
1226	Begins ecclesiastical career as a Canon in Lausanne
1229	Comes under the tutelage of Conon d'Estavayer
	Administrator of the See of Lausanne until 1231 during episcopal interregnum
1232	Boniface de Savoie elected Bishop of Belley and Prior of Nantua
1233	Death of his father, Count Thomas I de Savoie
1234	Chillon meeting to apportion the lands of Thomas to his sons
	Pierre granted castles in Bugey as part of a settlement within the County of Savoy
1236	Alianor de Provence, Pierre's niece, marries King Henry III of England
	Married to Agnès de Faucigny
	Guillaume de Savoie awarded the Honour of Richmond
1237	Birth of his daughter, Béatrice de Savoie
	Death of his brother, Aymon de Savoie, Lord of Chablais
	Thomas II de Savoie becomes Count of Flanders by marriage
	Guillaume de Savoie instrumental in Treaty of York which agrees Anglo-Scottish border
	Magna Carta and the Charter of the Forest reissued by Henry III
1239	Death of Guillaume de Savoie, Bishop of Valence and de facto Earl of Richmond
	Boniface de Savoie elected Bishop of Valence
	Birth of the Lord Edward, later King Edward I of England
1240	Acquisition of Romont by Pierre de Savoie, now Lord of Romont
	Battle of Lausanne and abortive attempt to have Philippe made Bishop of Lausanne
	Pierre d'Aigueblanche elected Bishop of Hereford
	Awarded the Honours of Richmond and the Eagle by King Henry III of England
	Death of Llywelyn Fawr in Gwynedd, succeeded by Dafydd ap Llywelyn
1241	Knighted by King Henry III of England
	Appointed Castellan of Dover Castle and Keeper of the Coast, both until 1242
	Treaty of Gwerneigron with Gwynedd
	Philippe de Savoie elected Bishop of Valence
	Boniface de Savoie elected Archbishop of Canterbury
	Diplomatic mission to France with Pierre d'Aigueblanche to build southern alliance
1242	Diplomatic mission to Poitevin rebels
	Battle of Taillebourg and abortive Poitevin campaign by King Henry III
	Acquired the fief of Aubonne in Vaud

Peter of Savoy: The Little Charlemagne

1243	King Louis IX of France begins construction of Saint Chapelle in Paris
	Richard, Earl of Cornwall marries Sanchia de Provence
1244	Death of Countess Jeanne de Flandres; no longer Count, Thomas II returns to Savoy
1245	Death of Ramon Berenguer V, Count of Provence
1246	Granted Pevensey Castle in Sussex
	Count Amédée IV de Savoie enfeoffes the castles of Bard and Avigliana, the palace of Susa and the town of Saint Maurice to King Henry III of England
	King Henry III grants land by The Strand in London to Pierre de Savoie
1247	First arrival of the Lusignans in England
1249	Granted the Honour of Hastings including Hastings Castle in Sussex
1250	Renewed successful hostilities with Count of Geneva and the Lords of La Tour du Pin
1252	Death of his mother, Countess Marguerite de Genève
	Thomas II de Savoie remarries, to Béatrice de Fieschi, niece of Pope Innocent IV
1253	Death of his brother, Count Amédée IV de Savoie; he is succeeded by his son Boniface (not to be confused with the Archbishop of Canterbury)
1254	Campaigns in Gascony with King Henry III, Duke of Aquitaine
	Meets Jean de Mézos at the siege of Benauges
1255	Appointed Protector of Berne and Morat
	Acquired land holdings in Valais and Chablais along with the Château de Chillon
	Pierre de Savoie hires Jean de Mézos to strengthen castles in the Valais and Chablais
	King Henry III's son Edmund declared King of Sicily
	Thomas II de Savoie is imprisoned in Turin whilst campaigning in Piedmont
1256	Pierre and Philippe de Savoie lead an army to Turin attempting to free Thomas
1257	Thomas II de Savoie freed from Torinese captivity
	Richard, Earl of Cornwall elected King of the Romans, de facto King of Germany and Suzerain of the Holy Roman Empire including the County of Savoy
	Pierre founds the village of Versoix on the frontier of Vaud and Geneva
1258	One of the oath-takers promising mutual support in reforming the realm of England
	Oath-takers led by Roger Bigod, likely including Pierre de Savoie, begin pressing reform of the realm on Henry III at Westminster
	Provisions of Oxford
	Lusignans expelled from England
1259	Death of his brother, Thomas II de Savoie, formerly Count of Flanders
	Treaty of Paris, negotiated in part by Pierre de Savoie, recognises Henry III as Duke of Aquitaine as vassal of King Louis IX of France in return for the Plantagenets giving up claims to Anjou, Maine, Normandy and Poitou
	Provisions of Westminster
1260	Break with the reform movement
	Pierre allied with Richard of Cornwall, John Mansel and Robert Walerand presses for a return of the king's authority
	Acquires land at Yverdon to build a new town and castle
	Acquires temporal authority in Lausanne
1261	Hires Maître Jean and Maître Jacques to build Yverdon castle
1262	Pierre leaves England for the last time in June
	Count Boniface de Savoie unexpectedly dies in the autumn

Pierre de Savoie Timeline

1263	Becomes Count of Savoy upon the death of his nephew Boniface de Savoie
	Death of Hartmann V von Kyburg threatens a war for Western & Central Helvetia
1264	King Louis IX of France nullifies the Provisions of Oxford by the Mise of Amiens
	Reforming rebels under Simon de Montfort defeat King Henry III and the Lord Edward at Lewes
	Siege of Pierre's castles at Pevensey and Richmond begin
	Simon de Montfort leads government in England, King Henry III a puppet king
	Alianor de Provence and Pierre de Savoie assemble an army in Flanders to free Henry and Edward
	Death of Hartmann IV von Kyburg, childless renders succession crisis in Western & Central Helvetia between rivals Rudolf I von Habsburg and Pierre de Savoie
1265	Simon de Montfort calls a Parliament that is seen as an important milestone in English parliamentary history by summoning representatives from towns
	The Lord Edward escapes Montfortian captivity and defeats Montfort at Evesham
	Pierre and Alianor's army in Flanders is disbanded
	Pierre's castles at Pevensey and Richmond withstand siege and are relieved
	The Bishop of Sion invades the Valais, Pierre de Savoie returns from Flanders
	Pierre de Savoie defeats the Bishop of Sion, a truce is agreed
	1265–7 Legal and administrative reforms in Savoy, reflecting *Magna Carta*, Provisions of Oxford and English practise
1266	Expiry of 1265 truce with the Bishop of Sion brings a resumption of war in the Valais
	Pierre de Savoie once more defeats the Bishop of Sion
	War with Rudolph I von Habsburg which results in a stalemate
	Dictum of Kenilworth
1267	Death of his sister, Béatrice de Provence, mother of Alianor de Provence
1268	Pierre II de Savoie dies at Pierre-Châtel, County of Savoy, now France
	Death of Pierre d'Aigueblanche, Bishop of Hereford
1270	Death of King Louis IX of France
	Death of Archbishop Boniface de Savoie
1272	Deaths of both King Henry III and Richard, Earl of Cornwall
1274	The Lord Edward crowned as King Edward I of England
1285	Death of Count Philippe I de Savoie
1291	Death of Alianor de Provence

A Note on Names

It was normal in previous years to anglicise the names of people and places of other lands for English-speaking readers, thus Welsh Dafydd became David and francophone Jacques became James, similarly place names like Conwy became Conway and Caernarfon became Carnarvon. In deference to the people involved in this story and modern readers who are by now more used to place names expressed in local languages we will use names, as far as is reasonably possible, with which they would have self-identified, that is called themselves.

The main protagonist of the story is known today in the UK as Peter of Savoy, but he was known in his own time and was referred to by King Henry III of England in Anglo-Norman French as *Monsire Pirres de Savoye nostre chier uncle*. In French he's known nowadays as Pierre de Savoie and as his land today is mostly French-speaking and that is how I first came to know of him then that is how this book will generally know him. Similarly, with Eleanor de Provence we will use the Provençal form of her name which she herself used in correspondence, Alianor.

Place names in Wales will use Welsh names, not anglicised versions. When quoting directly from previous authors who used anglicised or latinised versions of these names we will quote the authors directly.

There is no right or wrong way in this regard but, within reason, I've tried to honour people and places with names as close to those they used themselves.

A Note on Money

The main money in use in Savoy, France and the British Isles, and so the substance of this book, were *Livre*, *Sol* and *Denari*, varying in value by the issuing mints' silver content. In Latin this would be expressed as *Libra*, *Solidus* and *Denarius*, rendered in French as *Livre*, *Sou* and *Denier* and lastly rendered into English as Pounds, Shillings and Pence – shortened in all three languages as L, s and d. No *Libra, Livre*, Pound or *Solidus, Sou* or Shilling coins were ever issued: they were simply a convenient accounting form.

There were twelve (12) *Denarius, Denier* or Pence in one (1) *Solidus, Sou or Shilling*. There were twenty (20) *Solidus, Sou* or Shillings in one (1) *Libra, Livre* or Pound. And so, there were two hundred and forty (240) *Denarius, Denier* or Pence in one (1) *Libra, Livre* or Pound.

A further accounting form in use in England was the Mark which represented two-thirds of a pound, and so thirteen (13) shillings and four (4) pence or one hundred and sixty (160) pence.

To help, on occasion, to give some meaning to quoted numbers, we have used the UK National Archives currency converter. This has been done as a helpful guide and is in no way intended to be a statement of fact. The converter can be found online at www.nationalarchives.gov.uk/currency-converter/ – hereinafter abbreviated as TNA currency converter.

Without Whose Help …

A stranger in a strange land, I am indebted to the help of many in the preparation of this book. In no particular order: Jean-Luc Rosset whose patient explanation of Medieval Latin, of its origins and difference from Classical Latin was quite simply invaluable.

Thanks to the herculean efforts of research carried out by the first biographer of Pierre de Savoie, the Swiss historian Johann Ludwig Wurstemberger, particularly his fourth volume in which was printed a good deal of the necessary primary sources for this book. Many thanks for the help and encouragement of historian Huw Ridgeway, in particular an advance copy of his paper for the Pipe Rolls Society on and including Pierre de Savoie's English cartulary. Thanks also to historian Michael Ray for his help and encouragement.

Thanks to Monsignor Jean-Pierre Voutaz of the Hospice of the Grand Saint-Bernard who was kind enough to let me see the treasures of their archive, including being able to hold the seal of King Edward I.

Thanks to Roy Porter of English Heritage in whose care is the castle at Pevensey. Particularly for his encouragement in the preparation of this book and interest in Pierre de Savoie and the defenders of Pevensey that winter of 1264–5. Also many thanks to Colin Torode of the team at Pevensey for showing us around the castle and pointing out the peculiarities of some of the architecture on what was perhaps the hottest day in England on record in July 2022.

Thanks to the monks of Hautecombe Abbey for granting access to the still-active monastery that bears the tombs of the comital family of Savoy, a reminder that despite the desecrations of the French Revolution those interred there were real people deserving of respect.

Thanks to my son, Sean, for spending his holiday time in Switzerland delving deep into the byways to seek out long-gone castles in the undergrowth, and for adding his own insight to the developing story; particularly at Aiguebelle searching for the remains of the castle of Thomas I de Savoie, Pierre de Savoie's father, in the undergrowth of the steep-sided hill above the village.

And lastly, and mostly, thanks as always to my partner, Mary-Claude Dennler, without whose many hours of patience and fortitude trekking the wilds of the Viennois, the archives in Lausanne, Chambéry, Grenoble and Kew, and castles too numerous to mention, this book would simply not have been possible. Her particular help in trying to make sense of Old French texts should be noted. Also of particular note is Mary-Claude's eye for detail in noticing the architectural links that have thus far escaped notice that link Pierre's castles at Pevensey and Yverdon.

Notable Savoyards in England

The Comital Family

Pierre II de Savoie (1203–1268), Count of Savoy
The seventh son of Count Thomas I de Savoie and Marguerite de Genève, uncle to Queen Alianor de Provence of England and so great-uncle to King Edward I of England. He was likely born in Susa. In January 1236, Alianor de Provence, Pierre's niece, married King Henry III of England. On 20 April 1240 Peter was given the Honour of Richmond by Henry III who invited him to England about the end of the year and knighted him on 5 January 1241, when he became known popularly as Earl of Richmond, although he never assumed the title of Earl, nor was it ever given to him in official documents. From 1241 until 1242 he was Castellan of Dover Castle and Keeper of the Coast. In February 1246 he was granted land between the Strand and the Thames, where Peter built the Savoy Palace in 1263, on the site of the present Savoy Hotel. It was destroyed during the Peasants' Revolt of 1381. When Pierre's nephew, Count Boniface de Savoie died without heirs in 1263, he became Count of Savoy and largely withdrew from English affairs.

Alianor de Provence (1223–24/25 June 1291), Queen of England
The sister of Marguerite de Provence, Queen of France, Sanchia de Provence, Queen of the Romans and Béatrice de Provence, Queen of Naples. Born in Aix-en-Provence or Brignoles, she was the second daughter of Ramon Berenguer V, Count of Provence (1198–1245) and Béatrice de Savoie (1198–1267), the daughter of Thomas I de Savoie and his wife Marguerite de Genève. She was well educated as a child and developed a strong love of reading. Her three sisters also married kings. Like her mother, grandmother and sisters, Alianor was renowned for her beauty. She was a dark-haired brunette with fine eyes. Although she was completely devoted to her husband, and staunchly defended him against the rebel Simon de Montfort, 6th Earl of Leicester, she was disliked by the Londoners. Responsible for introducing many Savoyards to the English court.

Sanchia de Provence (1225 – 9 November 1261), Queen of the Romans
A sister to Queen Alianor de Provence of England, sister-in-law of King Henry III of England and King Louis IX of France, aunt to King Edward I of England and wife to 1st Earl Richard of Cornwall King of the Romans.

Guillaume de Savoie (unknown – 1239), Bishop Elect of Valence
A son of Thomas I de Savoie and Marguerite de Genève, another uncle of Queen Alianor de Provence of England and so great-uncle to King Edward I of England. When already a Dean of Vienne, he was elected Bishop of Valence in 1224. He negotiated the weddings of Queens Marguerite and Alianor de Provence and was an advisor to Henry III of England. Between his religious roles and his family relations, his influence was noted from London to Rome.

Boniface de Savoie (1217–18 July 1270), Archbishop of Canterbury
A son of Thomas I de Savoie and Marguerite de Genève, yet another uncle of Queen Alianor de Provence of England and so great-uncle of King Edward I of England. He is not to be confused with his nephew and fellow member of the House of Savoy, Count Boniface de Savoie, the son of Amedée IV. Boniface was the Prior of Nantua in 1232 along with the Bishopric of Belley in Savoy. After the marriage of his niece, Alianor de Provence, to King Henry III of England, Henry attempted to have Boniface elected Bishop of Winchester, but was unable to get the cathedral chapter to elect Boniface. On 1 February 1241, he was nominated to the See of Canterbury, and was enthroned at Canterbury Cathedral on 1 November 1249. He clashed with his bishops, with his nephew-by-marriage, and with the papacy, but managed to eliminate the archiepiscopal debt that he had inherited on taking office. During Simon de Montfort's struggle with King Henry, Boniface initially helped Montfort's cause, but later supported the king. After his death in Savoy, his tomb became the object of a cult, and he was eventually beatified in 1839.

Philippe I de Savoie (1207–16 August 1285), Archbishop of Lyon then Count of Savoy
The eighth son of Thomas I de Savoie and Marguerite de Genève, once more, another uncle of Queen Alianor de Provence of England and so great-uncle of King Edward I of England. Philippe was born in Aiguebelle in Savoy. His family prepared him for a clerical career. He followed his brother Guillaume as Dean of Vienne and Bishop Elect of Valence. In 1244, Pope Innocent IV fled from Rome, and Philippe convinced his brother, Amedée IV, Count of Savoy, to let the Pope pass through Savoy. Philippe escorted the Pope to Lyon, and then remained with him to ensure his safety. Pope Innocent ensured Philippe's election as Archbishop of Lyon in 1245. When, against expectations, Philippe became the next heir for the County of Savoy, he gave up his church offices and married Adelaide, Countess Palatine de Bourgogne, on 12 June 1267. He became Count of Savoy in 1268, and in 1272 he also acquired Bresse.

Amédée V de Savoie (4 September 1249–16 October 1323), Count of Savoy
A son of Thomas, Count of Flanders, and household knight of King Edward I of England, he was married to Sibylle de Baugé, bringing Bresse into Savoy. He was with the English army at Montgomery in 1277 in the First Welsh War before, in the Second Welsh War, leading the English army that relieved the siege of Rhuddlan in 1282. A son, Edward, born in 1284 and named after Edward I of England, would go on to be Count Edward de Savoie in 1323.

Louis I de Vaud (1249–1302), Baron de Vaud
Son of Thomas, Count of Flanders, household knight of King Edward I of England and Dean of St. Martin's Le Grand in London. His barony was created at the time of the succession of his brother Amédée V as Count of Savoy with the help of Queen Alianor de Provence of England and King Edward I of England.

Savoyard Knights

Sir Othon de Grandson (1238–1328), *Seigneur de Grandson*
Othon was the most prominent of the Savoyard knights in the service of Edward I, King of England. He was a close personal friend of Edward, a career diplomat and envoy of the

Crown. The son of Pierre, Lord of Grandson, the young Othon travelled to England, probably in the company of Pierre II de Savoie around 1252, certainly not later than 1265. There he entered the service of King Henry III and by 1267 was placed in the household of the Lord Edward. By 1267 he had been knighted, and in 1271, he accompanied his lord on the Ninth Crusade, where he served at Acre. Returning to England, he was a key household knight of King Edward I in his campaigns in Scotland and Wales, where he served as Justiciar of North Wales, based at Caernarfon Castle from 1284 to 1294. In 1278 he served as Lieutenant of Gascony, along with Robert Burnell, Bishop of Bath and Wells, hiring Jean de Grailly as Seneschal and laying the foundations of the Treaty of Amiens (1279) which returned the Saintonge and Agenais to the Crown. During the second invasion of Wales in 1282–3 he narrowly escaped death at the Battle of Moel-y-don before, in April 1283, taking the town of Harlech at the head of 560 infantry. He was appointed governor of the Channel Islands and in 1290 appointed a bailiff for each of the bailiwicks of Guernsey and Jersey, giving them civil powers to administer the islands.

Pierre de Champvent (unknown–c. 1303), Steward to King Henry III and Chamberlain of the Royal Household to Edward I
Son of Henri de Champvent and Helviz, brother of Guillaume and Othon de Champvent, both Bishops of Lausanne, a cousin of Othon de Grandson. Steward to King Henry III, he was knighted in 1259, serving as a knight of the royal household, then in 1269, Sheriff of Gloucestershire and Constable of Gloucester Castle. Later under Edward I he was again a steward before becoming a Chamberlain of the Royal Household to King Edward I. He fought in the Welsh Wars and later in Scotland.

Pierre de Genève (before 1220–1249), Constable of Windsor Castle; also Ebal de Genève
Peter of Geneva or Pierre de Genève was the son of Humbert de Genève, Count of Geneva. Humbert de Genève had been the Count until 1220, but when he died, the County did not pass to his sons Pierre and Ebal but to Humbert's younger brother Guillaume de Genève, who was now established as the Count of Geneva. It has been suggested that either Pierre de Savoie arranged for Pierre and Ebal to find preferment in England in return for their rights on the north shore of Lake Geneva or more generously that he befriended them and offered them a life in England as a good uncle to nephews in need – either way, they arrived in England between 1240 and 1241 and feature in English records in the early 1240s.

Once in England, they joined Pierre's staff; he was able to find Pierre de Genève a good marriage match, Maud de Lacy, youngest daughter of Gilbert de Lacy, who claimed descent from the great William Marshal. The family held the castle in the Welsh Marches at Ludlow, and for a time Pierre became Lord of Ludlow through Maud before succeeding Bernard de Savoie, becoming a Constable of Windsor Castle itself, before dying in 1249. His English bride would find another Savoyard match in Geoffroi de Joinville (known in England as Geoffrey de Geneville), the brother of Saint Louis' biographer and famed chronicler of the Crusades' Jean de Joinville. Pierre de Genève spent much time in Pierre de Savoie's employ, attending, for example, Henry's grant to Pierre de Savoie of the Honour of the Eagle.

His brother Ebal de Genève, meanwhile, found a good marriage match in Ireland, Christiana de Marais, the daughter of Robert de Marais (himself a son of John's Justicier in Ireland who received large grants of land in Munster). Henry III's grant of marriage bestowed all lands inherited by Christiana on Ebal. He would later accompany the Lord Edward in

Peter of Savoy: The Little Charlemagne

service to Gascony before leaving his entire estate to, unsurprisingly, Pierre de Savoie, his benefactor.

Gefferoi de Geneville [Joinville] (c. 1226–21 October 1314), 1st Baron de Geneville
The middle son of Simon de Joinville and Béatrice d'Auxonne. Béatrice had earlier married Aymon de Faucigny and was the mother of Agnès de Faucigny the wife of Pierre de Savoie. This made Gefferoi the half-brother-in-law of Pierre de Savoie. His two other brothers are well known to history, Jean de Joinville as the biographer of King Louis IX of France and Simon de Joinville, Seigneur de Gex et Marnay. Some time between 1249 and 8 August 1252, Henry III arranged Geoffrey's marriage to Maud de Lacy, widow of another Savoyard, Pierre de Genève. Maud had been co-heiress to vast estates and lordships in Ireland, Herefordshire, and the Welsh Marches. He was appointed Baron of Trim in Ireland and, subsequently, a staunch supporter of King Edward I, serving as Justiciar* of Ireland. Like his younger brother Simon, he had been implicated in the escape from Montfortian imprisonment of Edward in 1265. Edward escaped to Gefferoi's castle in the Welsh Marches at Ludlow.

Simon de Joinville (c.1231 - 3rd June 1277), Seigneur de Gex et Marnay
The youngest son of Simon de Joinville and Béatrice d'Auxonne. Béatrice having earlier married Aymon de Faucigny and was the mother of Agnès de Faucigny the wife of Pierre de Savoie. This made Simon the half-brother-in-law of Pierre de Savoie. His two elder brothers are well known to history, Jean de Joinville as the biographer of King Louis IX of France and Gefferoi de Geneville (as he was known in England) who became Henry III's Seneschal in Ireland. Like his elder brother, Geoffroi, he was heavily involved in English affairs, including Henry III's Gascon campaign of 1253-4 and aborted Welsh campaign of 1258. He is also implicated in the successful plot to free the Lord Edward (later Edward I) from Montfortian imprisonment in 1265, again along with his elder brother Gefferoi. We can lilkely attribute a number of knights service in or for England, such as Guillaume de Pesmes and Richard de Montbéliard to the relationship between Joinville and Pierre de Savoie.

Guillaume de Pesmes
Of the Famille de Pesmes, vassals in the Free County of Burgundy of both Béatrice d'Auxonne and her son Simon de Joinville as Dame and Seigneur de Marnay. Almost certainly to be identified as Guillaume VI de Pesmes the brother of Guillaume V de Pesmes, Seigneur de Pesmes. Pesmes took part with Joinville in Henry III's Gascon campaign of 1253-4 and aborted Welsh campaign of 1258. He then became a household knight of the Lord Edward, later King Edward I. When the grandson of Guillaume V dies in 1327 without a male heir the Seigneury de Pesmes will pass to the nephew of Othon de Grandson of English fame, Othon II de Grandson. Thus the Famille de Pesmes will become the Famille de Grandson Pesmes in the 14th century. But unknown to Swiss historians the two families had been linked earlier by Guillaume Vi de Pesmes and Othon I de Grandson being household knights in England in the 13th century.

Jean de Dornay, Seigneur de Dornay
Seigneur de Dornay, now Durnes in the Franche Comté de Bourgogne, was another of Henry III's Burgundian knights recruited likely at the behest of Simon de Joinville, Seigneur de Gex et Marnay and thus Pierre de Savoie to serve in the aborted Welsh campaign of 1258.

Notable Savoyards in England

Richard IV de Montbéliard
Of the Famille de Montfaucon, the son of Richard III de Montfaucon and Agnès de Bourgogne-Auxonne, and younger brother of Amédée III de Montfaucon, Seigneur de Orbe et Echallens.. It would be his brother Amédée who ceded rights to Pierre de Savoie to build the castle of Yverdon in 1260. Montbéliard had earlier taken part, alongside Pierre de Savoie, in Henry III's Gascon campaign of 1253-4 and called to Oxford to take part in Henry's aborted 1258 campaign in Wales, each time alongside both Guillaume de Pesmes and Simon de Joinville.

Guichard I de Charron (1210–1268), Seneschal of the Honour of Richmond
Born in Charron in the Valromey district of Bugey in Savoy to Guichard Charron de Sabaudia, a cleric, he moved to England with Pierre de Savoie; he married an English woman, Mary de Sutton, in 1237. Guichard would be unkindly described by English chronicler Matthew Paris as "a beastly clerk" with a "belly ... like a bladder in frosty weather, and whose body would load a waggon".

Guichard II de Charron (1242–1297), Seneschal of the Honour of Richmond
Son of Guichard I de Charron and Mary de Sutton, he in turn married Isabel de Horton, another English woman. Charron followed his father as Seneschal, Constable and/or Bailiff for Pierre de Savoie of the Honour of Richmond. He successfully held Richmond Castle for Pierre during the Second Baronial War, 1264–5.

Nantelme de Cholay
Of the family of the Lords of Cholay, now Choulex, near Geneva, then vassals of Faucigny, Cholay is the one named defender of Pevensey Castle during the year-long siege of the Second Baronial War. The Savoyard records suggest he had "kindred" or "allies" but does not name them.

Bernard de Savoie, Constable of Windsor Castle
Brother of Guichard I de Charron and Stephen de Charron, he moved to England with Pierre de Savoie in 1241. He was appointed Constable of both Reigate and Windsor Castles.

Jean de Grailly (unknown–1301), Seneschal of Gascony
Jean was born at Grilly near Gex on the shores of Lac Léman in the County of Savoy. He probably travelled to England during the reign of Henry III of England in the entourage of Pierre II de Savoie, In 1262 he was already a knight in the household of Prince Edward, the king's heir and future King Edward I of England. In 1263 he had attained the status of a counsellor of the young prince. He was made Edward's Seneschal in Gascony from 1278. In 1279, Jean travelled to Amiens and to England to negotiate the Treaty of Amiens, which ended the state of war between Edward of England and Philip III of France and returned the Agenais to English control. Jean de Grailly eventually fell short of funds for his activities, since his expenses needed approval from the Exchequer before he could receive his salary. He took to exploitation and illegal exactions from the peasants, whose complaints eventually reached the ears of Edward I. He was removed from office sometime between June 1286 and spring 1287. He led a French force alongside the English under Othon de Grandson at the Fall of Acre in 1291.

Ebal II de Mont (unknown c. 1230–1268), Constable of Windsor Castle
Born as a younger son of Ebal I de Mont and his wife, Béatrice, Ebal II was first noted in 1237. Better known in English records as Ebulo de Montibus, Ebal II de Mont had travelled

to England by 1246. A household steward and knight of King Henry III of England, he was granted much land in England. By 1256 he was part of the Savoyard circle of the Lord Edward (possibly steward), later King Edward I. A witness for King Henry at the Mise of Amiens, where he swore for the king's good conduct in accepting King Louis XIVs arbitration. He left England with Queen Alianor and Pierre II de Savoie and was active in attempting to raise an army loyal to the Crown. Rewarded for his loyalty by being made Constable of Windsor Castle.

Pierre d'Estavayer (unknown–1322), Lord of Tipperary
Nephew of Othon de Grandson, he was in the service of King Edward I as a household knight. He was given the Lordship of Tipperary in 1290 by his uncle with whom he served at Acre in 1291. His brother, Guillaume d'Estavayer, became Archdeacon of Lincoln in 1290.

Imbert Pugeys, (unknown–1262), Steward to King Henry III and Castellan of the Tower of London
Imbert Pugeys, or Imbert de Savoie, was a valet in the king's chamber who became Constable at Hadleigh Castle in 1244 and Oxford Castle in 1253. Advancing further, from 1257, the Savoyard became a steward of the royal household of King Henry III of England and castellan of the Tower of London. His influence at court in 1262 is evidenced by his joining the Savoyard witness list for a charter relating to Queen Alianor's dowry. Imbert married Joan de Aguillon; their son gave the family name to what became Stoke Poges in Buckinghamshire.

Savoyard Clerics

Pierre d'Aigueblanche (unknown–1268), Keeper of the King's Wardrobe then Bishop of Hereford
Born at Aigueblanche, of the *Famille de Briançon*, Lords of Aigueblanche, in Savoy, he was initially a clerk to Guillaume de Savoie and came to England with the wedding party of Alianor de Provence. He entered the service of King Henry III, becoming first Keeper of the Wardrobe in February 1240 then Bishop of Hereford in 1241. As a diplomat and envoy, he was in regular employment by the English Crown; he helped to arrange the marriage of Earl Richard of Cornwall to Sanchia de Provence and later the Lord Edward to Leonor of Castile. He became embroiled in King Henry's attempts to acquire the kingdom of Sicily for Henry's son Edmund. During the anti-Savoyard period of the Second Barons War, he was arrested briefly in 1263 by the said barons, before being mostly restored to his lands after the Battle of Evesham.

Guillaume de Champvent (c. 1239–1301), Dean of St. Martin's Le Grand in London then Bishop of Lausanne
Son of Henri de Champvent and Helviz, brother of Pierre de Champvent, in the household of both King Henry III and Edward I of England, he was also brother of Othon de Champvent. From 1262 he was the Dean of St. Martin's Le Grand in London, before election as Bishop of Lausanne in 1273. He would maintain diplomatic service for King Edward I.

Gerard de Vuippens (c. 1260–5–17 March 1325), Pastor of Greystoke in Cumbria, Canon in York then Bishop of Lausanne
Son of Ulrich de Vuippens and Agnès de Grandson, sister of Othon de Grandson, he was accordingly his nephew. He moved to England to become first a sub deacon at the Priory of

St. Leonard in Stamford, then a pastor at Greystoke in Cumberland. He went on to become a sub deacon in Richmond and Canon at York before taking on a key diplomatic role with King Edward I during the difficult negotiations with King Philippe IV of France over Gascony. He left England to become first Bishop of Lausanne from 1301 until 1309 when he moved on to become the Bishop of Basel until his death in 1325.

Anthelme de Clermont (unknown–1269), Dean of Hereford Cathedral then Bishop of Maurienne
Anthelme de Clermont was the son of the noble *Famille de Clermont* of the Viennois. He moved to England, along with the Savoyard migration, at the behest of Pierre de Savoie. By 1250 he had been elected Dean of Hereford Cathedral, before being elected Bishop of Maurienne in 1262, a position he held until his death in 1269.

Aymon de Miolans (unknown–1300), Chapter of Hereford then Bishop of Maurienne
Aymon de Miolans was of one of the most distinguished and noble families of Savoy, the *Famille de Miolans* of the castle of Miolans located "at the gates" of the Maurienne and Tarentaise valleys between Montmélian and Conflans. A member of Pierre d'Aigueblanche's Chapter at Hereford Cathedral before being elected Bishop of Maurienne in 1273, a position he held until his death in 1300.

Stephen de Charron (unknown–1248), Prior of Thetford
Brother of Guichard I de Charron and Bernard de Savoie, he moved to England with Pierre de Savoie in 1241. As cleric he was made Prior of Thetford in the county of Norfolk. He was murdered in 1248. Matthew Paris suggested the murder followed a bout of drunken debauchery.

Jacques d'Aigueblanche, Keeper of the Wardrobe to Alianor de Provence, Archdeacon of Hereford Cathedral
Jacques d'Aigueblanche was a nephew of Pierre d'Aigueblanche, Bishop of Hereford, likely the son of Hugh d'Aigueblanche. He was a member of the Chapter of Hereford Cathedral. Like his uncle Pierre d'Aigueblanche he would be an Archdeacon of Shropshire, then partly within the See of Hereford.

Jean d'Aigueblanche (unknown–1320), Dean of Hereford Cathedral
Jean d'Aigueblanche was another nephew of Pierre d'Aigueblanche, Bishop of Hereford. Like his nephews he found preferment within the largely Savoyard Chapter of Hereford Cathedral, becoming Dean there in 1262, a position he would hold until his death in 1320.

Guillaume de Conflans (unknown–1294), Archdeacon of Hereford Cathedral, Bishop of Geneva
Guillaume de Conflans was of the noble *Famille de Duin* or *Duyn*, the son of Raymond de Duin and Anne de Conflans, the family basing themselves in the Châtel de Conflans and thence taking the name. Conflans was another Savoyard member of the Chapter of Hereford Cathedral who rose to become Archdeacon from 1255. He remained in England after the Second Baronial War before returning to Savoy to become Bishop of Geneva from 1287 where he remained until his death in 1294.

Guy de la Palud, Keeper of the Wardrobe to Alianor de Provence
Guy de la Palud, originated in Châtillon-la-Palud in the Dombes region; he was the noble son of Guillaume de la Palud of the *Famille de la Palud*. He was, from 1242 until 1258, a Keeper of the Wardrobe to Queen Alianor de Provence. He later returned to Savoy where he became an Archdeacon at Lyon. An ancestor, Guillaume, had been Bishop of Aosta, and another, Pierre de la Palud, would later be Patriarch of Jerusalem.

Pierre d'Ugine, Chapter of Hereford
A long-term clerk to Pierre d'Aigueblanche, he was appointed to the Chapter of Hereford upon his arrival in England. His origin of Ugine, on the road from Annecy to Conflans, was the fief of Archbishop Boniface de Savoie. His close relationship with Aigueblanche meant diplomatic service on behalf of the English Crown; in 1254 he was negotiating on behalf of both Aigueblanche and Henry III with Albert de Palma, the apostolic notary and legate in France.

Savoyard Builders, Masons and Artisans

Maître Jacques de Saint-Georges, Master of the King's Works in Wales
He is documented as the son of a master stonemason, Jean, very likely to be identified as Jean Cotereel, the Master of Works for the Cathedral of Lausanne and town of Saint-Prex. His recorded work in Savoy includes castles at Yverdon, Voiron, La-Côte-Saint-André, Saint-Laurent-du-Pont and Saint-Georges-d'Espéranche in addition to works at Romont, Gümmenen, Salins, Châtel Argent, Montmélian and likely Chillon. But his worldwide renown is a product of the work he carried out in North Wales for King Edward I of England, the UNESCO-listed castles of Caernarfon, Harlech, Conwy and Beaumaris, plus Aberystwyth, Flint and Rhuddlan and amongst other likely works at Caergwrle, Denbigh, Dolywyddelan and Criccieth. He came to England with his wife, Ambrosia, where they were later joined by their likely son, Giles.

Family Trees

Counts of Savoy

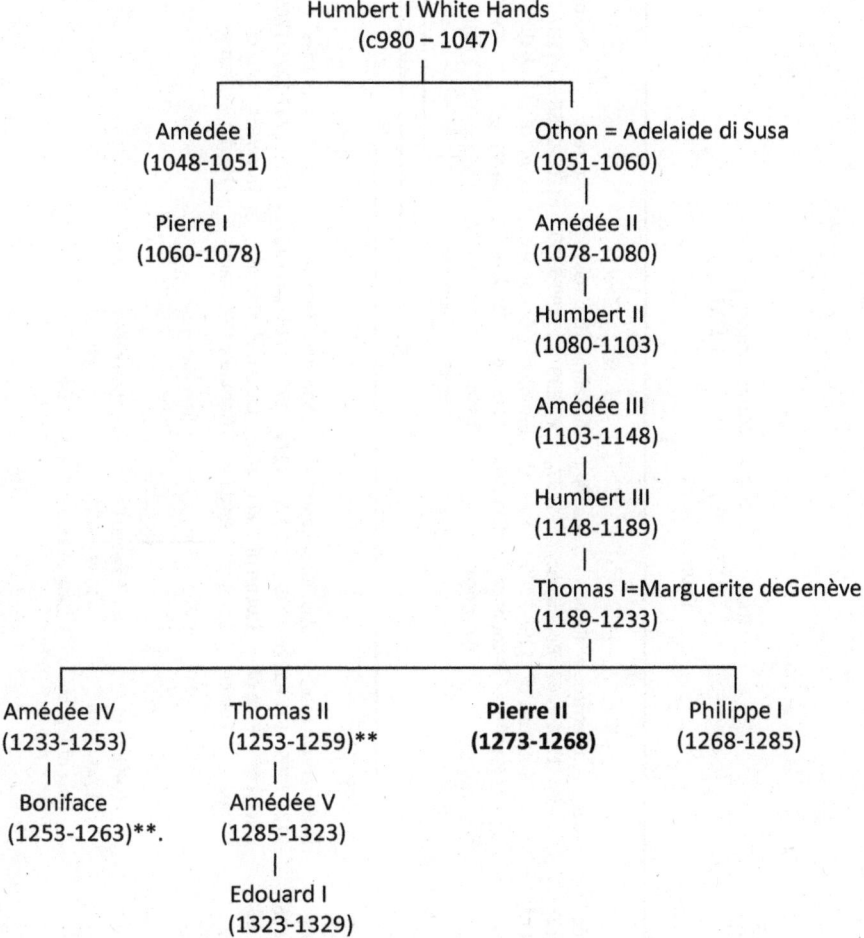

** Count Thomas II of Flanders ruled as Regent 1253-1259 to Boniface.

Peter of Savoy: The Little Charlemagne

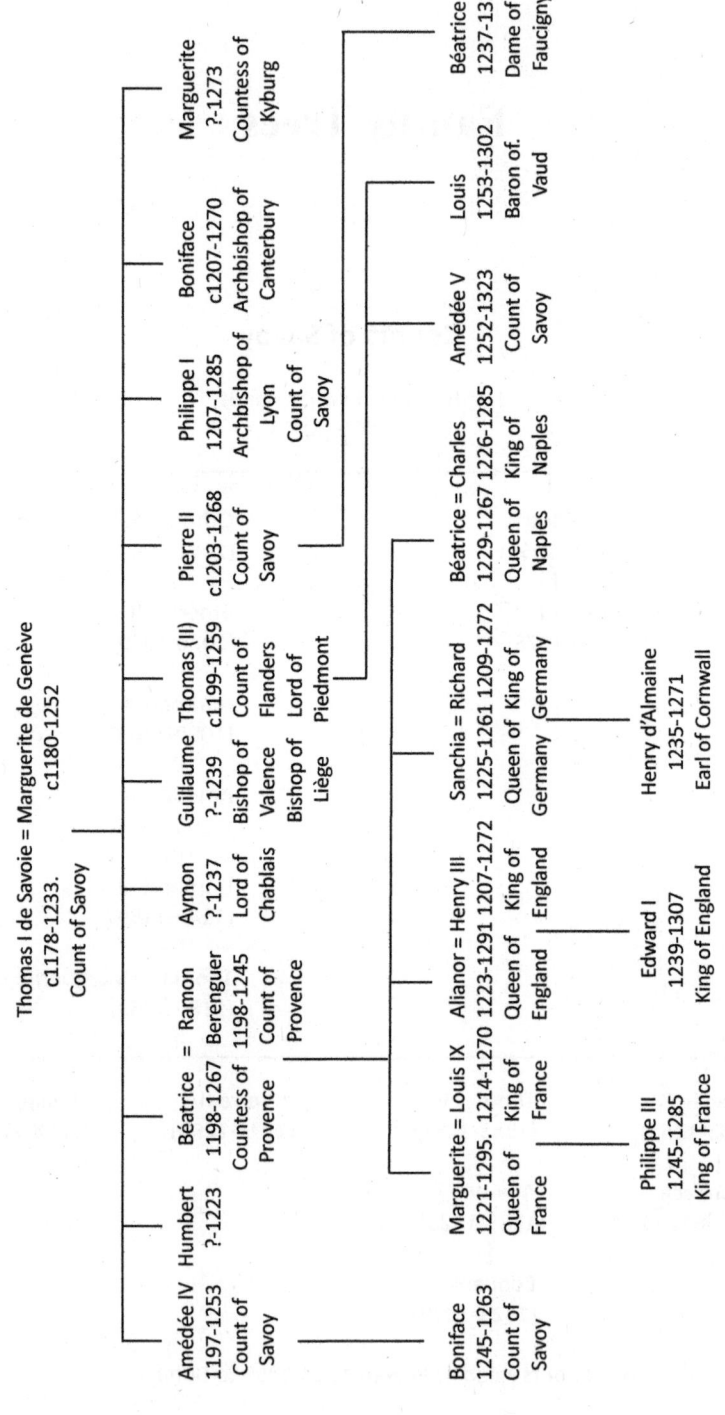

Family Trees

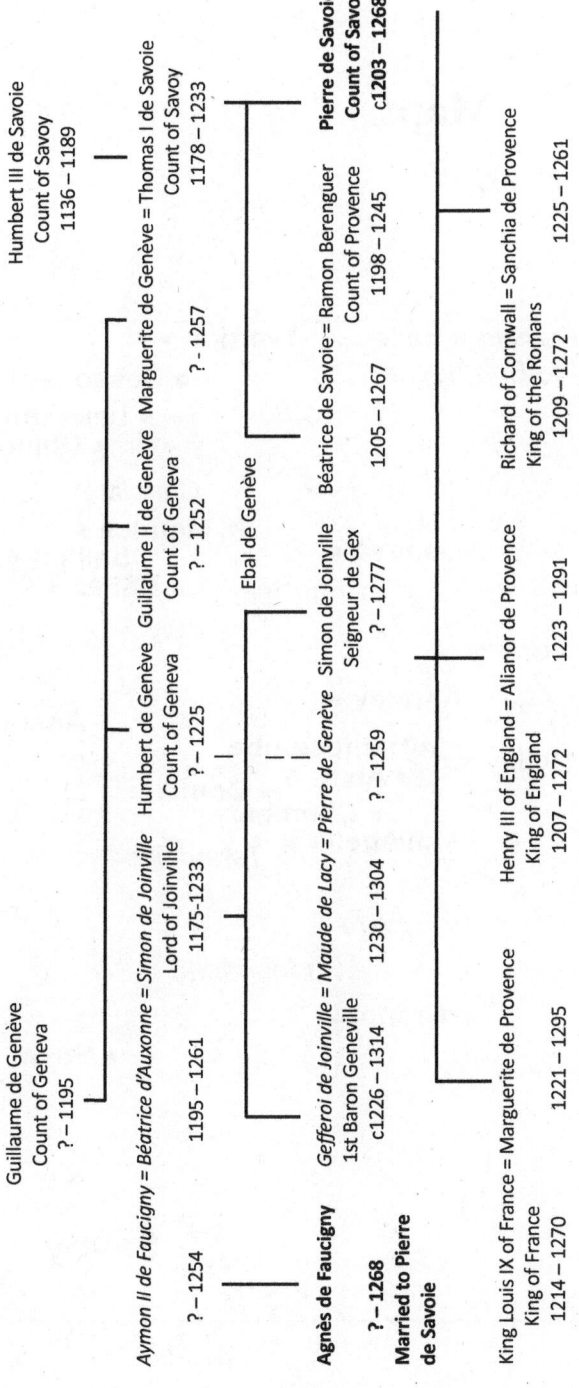

Beatrice d'Auxonne is first married to Aymon II de Faucigny, then to Simon de Joinville. Maude de Lacy is first married to Pierre de Genève, then to Gefferoi de Joinville.

Thus, when the Lord Edward sought refuge at Ludlow Castle, the home of Maude de Lacy, this was the same Maude de Lacy who had been previously married to the kinsman of Pierre de Savoie, Pierre de Genève. The same Maude de Lacy who was now married to the kinsman Gefferoi de Savoie by marriage Gefferoi de Geneville who was also the brother of Simon de Joinville, Seigneur de Gex et Marnay a vassal and half-brother-in-law of Pierre de Savoie. The Simon de Joinville of Gex who would be referred to by Agnès de Faucigny, wife of Pierre de Savoie, as "her brother" and remembered accordingly in her will of 1268. Indeed, the Joinvilles might be said to "*durent leur fortune aux relations que le mariage d'une de leurs sœurs utérines, Agnès, leur donnait avec la maison de Savoie*" that is that they "owed their fortune to the relations which the marriage of one of their uterine sisters, Agnès, gave them with the house of Savoy".

xxv

Maps

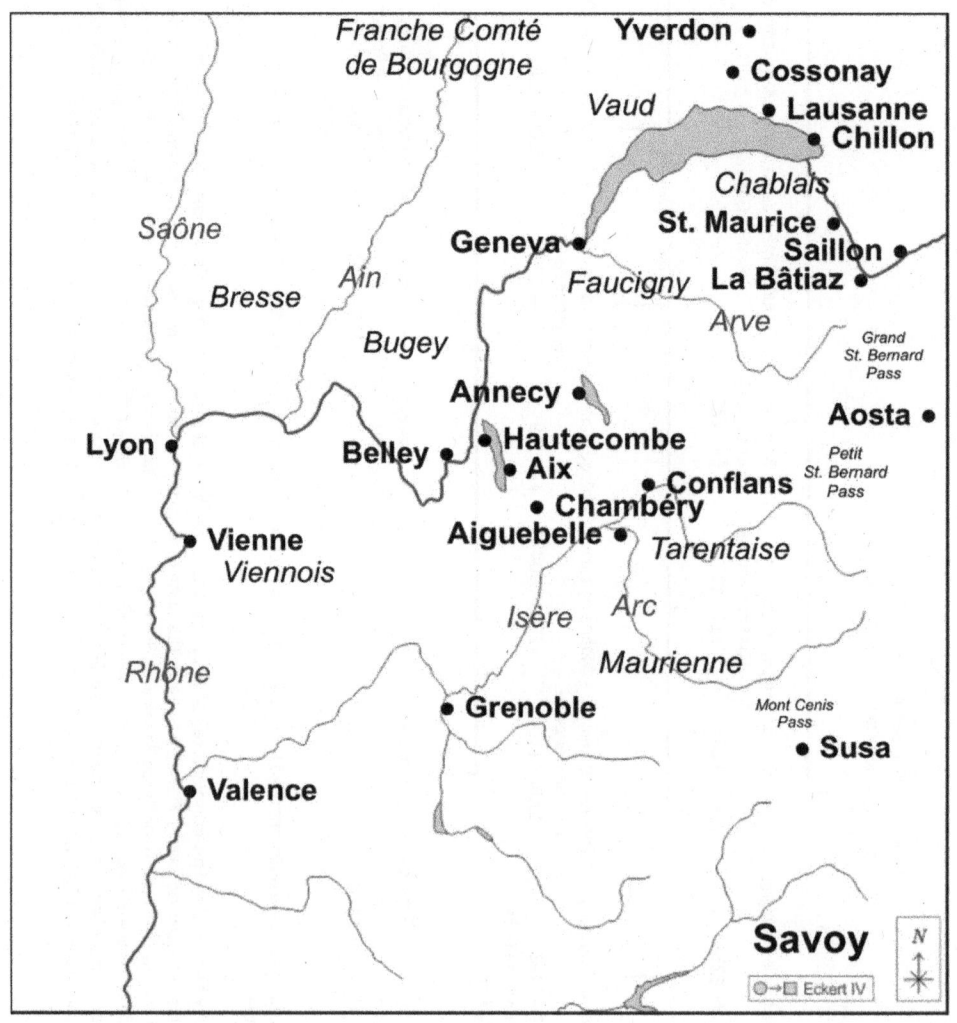

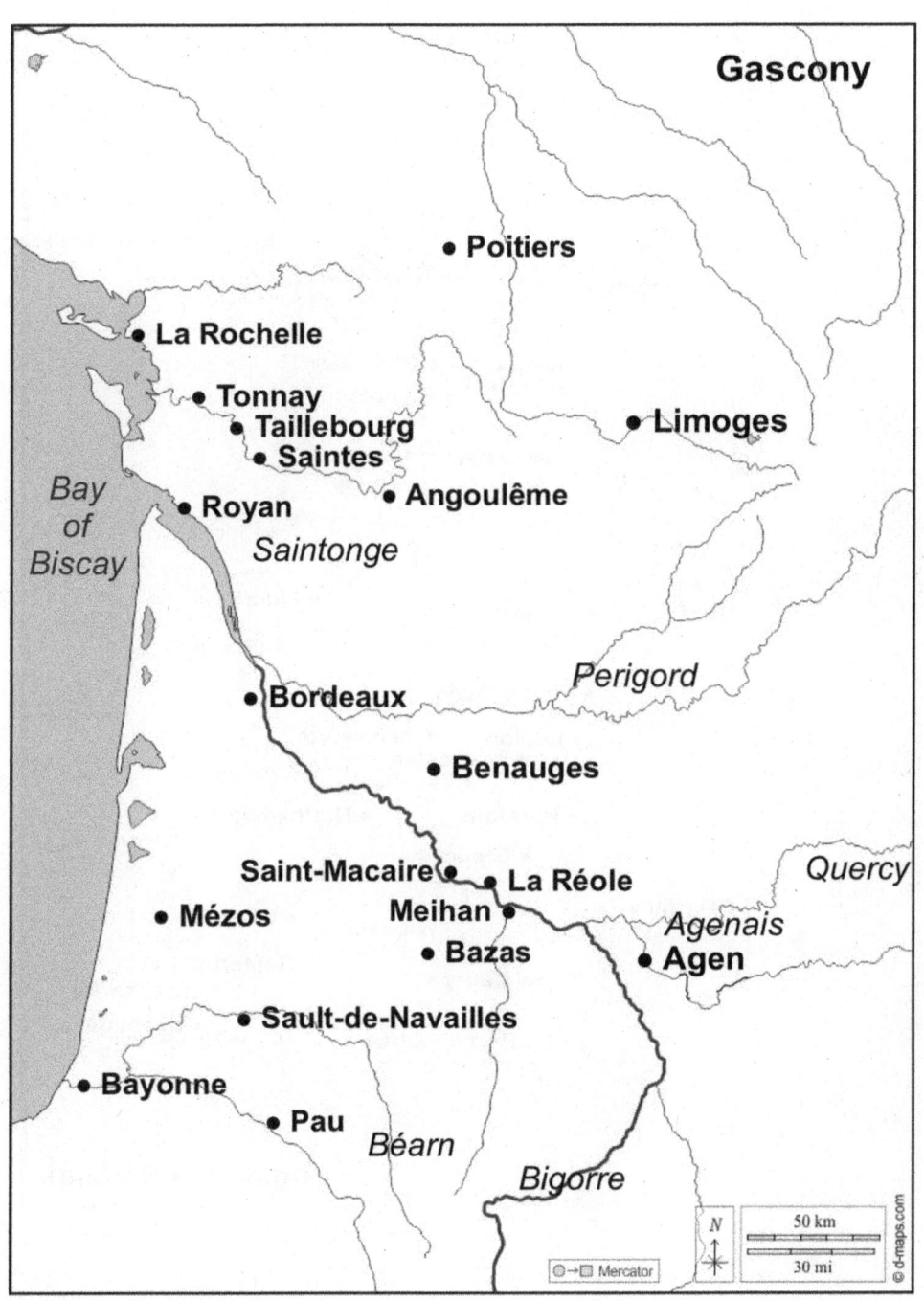

Peter of Savoy: The Little Charlemagne

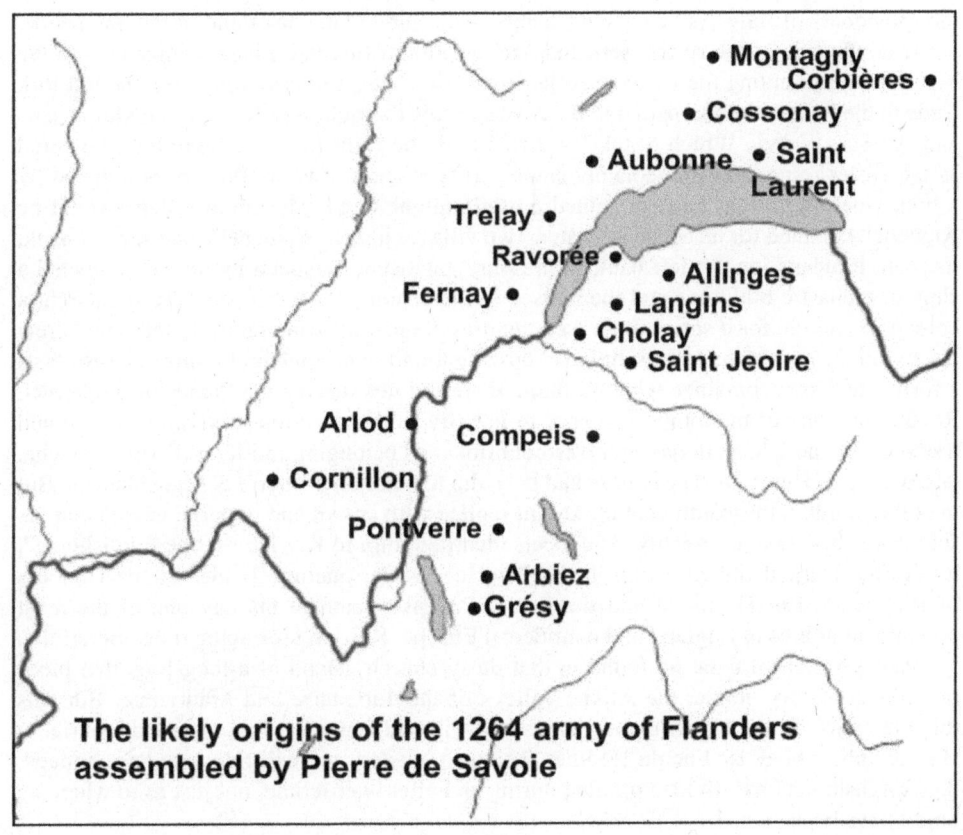

The likely origins of the 1264 army of Flanders assembled by Pierre de Savoie

Introduction

In 1771 the English antiquarian Thomas Kerrich was travelling through Savoy on his way to the splendours of Italy. As he passed Chambéry he came to the heartland of the Savoyards, to the confluence of the rivers Isère and Arc, where the Tarentaise parts company with the Maurienne, presenting the weary traveller with two routes to Turin and Italy. The left fork leads to the Petit-Saint-Bernard and the Aosta Valley, the right fork leads to the Mont Cenis and the Susa Valley. Which to take? Kerrich took the right fork, the route long favoured as the easier route, and immediately came across a small town by the Arc dominated by a rock where he might have imagined a castle might stand. The small village would be Aiguebelle, named for its beautiful water. Two villages in fact: Aiguebelle on the right bank, its twin, Randens, on the left bank. A masonry enclosure defended by towers protected a church, monastic buildings and the houses of the canons. Indeed it was a large church, a collegiate church, for it served both communities: Saint-Catherine sat in Randens and drew his attention. Within the large religious house he found two sepulchral tombs. It was for us a fortunate discovery, since what he found there did not survive the flames of the French Revolution. One of the tombs was easy to identify, and indeed his surviving last will and testament in the UK National Archives confirms it as belonging to Pierre d'Aigueblanche, late Bishop of Hereford. The church had been the foundation of Pierre d'Aigueblanche. But the other tomb, a thirteenth-century knight replete with crown and imperial eagle upon his shield was less easy to identify. The locals identified him to Kerrich as "the Englishman", a man the learned traveller took to be Peter of Savoy, onetime holder of the Honours of Richmond, Eu (Hastings) and the Eagle (Pevensey) and in his day one of the most preeminent nobles in England and continental Europe. Kerrich took some time, mercifully, to make a sketch of what he found in that dusty church, island of a long-forgotten piece of English history amidst the Alpine valleys of the Tarentaise and Maurienne. But was this the tomb of "the Englishman", as his last will and testament had recorded a burial at Hautecombe Abbey by Lac du Bourget. This is a mystery we will return to later. Indeed, the "Englishman" has divided opinion during and after his lifetime, not just as to where he might have been buried.

Writing in 1419, the French chronicler Jean d'Oroville[1] said of Pierre de Savoie:

> *Pierre de Savoie, le sixième fils du comte Thomas était un homme très sage, fier et hardi, terrible comme un lion; il soumit à son autorité un grand nombre de territoires et, en raison de ses prouesses, fut appelé le Petit Charlemagne.*[2]

Pierre de Savoie, the sixth son of Count Thomas was a very wise, proud and bold man, terrible as a lion; he submitted a large number of territories to his authority and, because of his prowess, was called the Little Charlemagne.

Introduction

Oroville was then the source of the Charlemagne comparison. But the English chronicler Matthew Paris writing in the thirteenth century of Pierre and his family and their time in England, had written often of a different opinion:

> He [Henry III] also allowed foreigners … to fatten themselves on the good things of the country, to the injury of the Kingdom.³

> Our English king [Henry III] … has fattened all the kindred and relatives of his wife [Alianor de Provence] with lands, possessions, and money … and England becomes, as it were, a vineyard without a wall, in which all who pass along the road gather the grapes.⁴

In the first regard Paris was talking of Pierre's brother Guillaume who held the same title and influence in England that Pierre would hold, and so we can imagine his view of Pierre would be likewise xenophobic.

If the medieval chroniclers were divided then so too contemporary historians who have taken widely different views: Darren Baker described him as an "ingrate"⁵: Andrew Spencer, more widely, took up again the "vineyard without a wall"⁶ theme bemoaned by Paris. Whereas Savoyard historian André Perret described the "*bon conseil*" given by an "*homme de guerre de valeur et diplomate*" and the "*grands services*" he rendered King Henry III of England, his nephew.⁷ The Swiss historian went further, writing:

> *se profile naturellement la grande figure du diplomate influent et du brillant homme d'Etat, celui du lien vivant entre la Savoie et l'Angleterre à l'époque, nous l'avons nommé Pierre de Savoie.*⁸

> The great figure of the influential diplomat and brilliant statesman naturally emerges, that of the living link between Savoy and England at the time, we have named him Peter of Savoy.

Is it a coincidence that those especially critical of Pierre de Savoie are anglophones? And those most in praise francophones? Does your view of Pierre de Savoie depend upon whether you're an anglophone or a francophone, or as we shall see a Montfortian or a Royalist? A "wise man, proud and bold, a lion", or an "ingrate" and gatherer of English "grapes"?

More recently English historiography has perhaps aligned more closely with francophone historiography of Pierre. Huw Ridgeway in his 2023 publication of Pierre's English cartulary wrote:

> "Peter appears here in a new light: less grasping foreigner, more a councillor with interests of the Crown at heart;"⁹

The reputation of Pierre de Savoie has been mixed; he lived a life with one foot in England, a de facto regent of England and one foot in Savoy, a Count of Savoy. But who was Peter of Savoy, Pierre de Savoie, this little Charlemagne? Perhaps it is time to break free of our tribal prejudices and assess the life, times and career of a man who left a legacy on both sides of the Channel.

Peter of Savoy: The Little Charlemagne

David Carpenter, the definitive biographer of Pierre's friend and kinsman by marriage, King Henry III of England, noted of Henry and his brother-in-law Louis IX of France, that "there have been few thirteenth-century historians equally at home on both sides of the Channel. French, British, and American scholars alike have tended to concentrate either on France or on Britain".[10] The same might well be said of the career of Pierre de Savoie, the "Englishman" from Savoy. His definitive biographer thus far, Johann Ludwig Wurstemberger, divided his life into separate Alpine and English volumes. Swiss and French historians have naturally concentrated their efforts on his role in Swiss and Savoyard history, British historians on his role in Britain. But Jean-Pierre Chapuisat rightly described him as the "living link" between Savoy and England. A notable exception to this division of his life was the American historian Eugene Cox who wrote the definitive anglophone history of thirteenth-century Savoy, but his work takes in *all* the children of Thomas I de Savoie, not just Pierre. The aim of this book is to hopefully reunite the two sides of Pierre II de Savoie, his pivotal role in both English and Alpine lands, because the *Petit Charlemagne*'s career transcended national stories; his was a life where family mattered more than nascent nations, and sadly his story has fallen between the cracks in the pavement of history, not fitting well into the *mythe nationals* of England, France or Switzerland.

Prologue

There is a story of the mountains, which may or may not be true.[1] It was the year of our Lord 1159, and the new Angevin King of England, Henry the second of that name, also Duke of Normandy, Duke of Aquitaine and Count of Anjou, Maine and Nantes, was intending to extend yet further his French lands by making war upon the Count of Toulouse. However, the French king, Louis the Seventh of that name, had his own designs on the southern county. The two kings, both Frenchmen, but of the rival Plantagenet and Capetian dynasties, needed an alliance with the emperor, or at least his acquiescence in their scheming. To this end envoys were sent from Henry's court in Normandy to sway the emperor, the renowned Frederick Barbarossa, who was then making war himself upon the Italian cities in Lombardy. The route taken by Henry's ambassadors would take them across France into Burgundy, thence across the Jura mountains and to Lausanne, skirting the great lake and into the mountains, pausing at the confluence of valleys that is now Martigny in Switzerland. Ahead of the diplomatic party lay the forbidding mountains of the Alpine massif; they would have to take the old pilgrimage route, the *Via Francigena*. As the snow and wind blinded their eyes, they made their way into the hellish peaks.

Altitude sickness began to overcome them, and the way ahead was not clear; like many before them and many after, they were ill-prepared for this journey. Snow blindness and frostbite began to take their toll, numbing their senses, beards frozen to their faces; they feared for their souls and took shelter high in the mountains to rest. As the blizzard raged outside the little cabin, the wind howling and terrifying all those inside, it seemed their envoy would end in disaster. These mountains might take yet more victims. The Englishmen succumbed to sleep; surely things would be better if only they could sleep, and yet if they slept death would surely overtake them.

And there in that cabin they slumbered, but it was not the grim reaper that came calling but a group of brothers from the nearby Hospice of St. Nicholas and St. Bernard, for here upon the Mount of Jupiter himself there was help at hand. The brothers awoke the envoys and helped them the few miles to the light and warmth of their hospice: they'd been rescued. Nursing them back to health, the brothers related that many had fallen amongst the snows of these impenetrable mountains, but by the grace of God they'd now show them the way off these jagged peaks and into Italy.

When the envoys returned to Henry, he was so grateful for the brothers' help he granted them a church in his manor of Havering in Essex that they might be further sustained in shining a light for travellers in the mountains. The hospice lay in the lands of the Humbert III de Savoie, Count of Savoy, and thus began in 1158 or 1159 the entanglement between the Plantagenets and the Savoyards.[2]

Peter of Savoy: The Little Charlemagne

Nuncii quoque Ludovici regis Francorum et Henrici regis Angliæ, cum post unos mox alii supervenissent uterque Fridericum in partem ac favorom sui principis inclinare multis verborum delinimentis atque muneribus concertabant.

Muratori, Rerum Ital. Scriptores vi. 804.

Henricus dei gratia .Rex Anglorum, et Dux Normannorum et Aquitannorum et comes Andegavorum, archiepiscopis, episcopis, abbatibus, comitibus, baronibus, justiciariis, vicecomitibus, ministris, et omnibus fidelibus suis Francis et Anglis totius Anglie salutem. Sciatis me concessisse et cledisse et presenti carta confirmasse ecclesie sancti Bernardi de Monte Jovis et fratribus ibidem deo servientibus ecclesiam de Havering cum omnibus pertinentiis suis ad faciendum sibi ignem et pauperibus. Et ideo volo et firmiter precipio quod predicti fratres prefatam ecclesiam habeant et teneant cum omnibus pertinentiis suis bene et in pace, libere et quiete, plenarie et integre et honorifice cum omnibus libertatibus (et) consuetudinibus suis. Et prohibeo nequis super hoc eis inde injuriam facere presumflt vel contumeliam. Testibus: comite Gaufrido de Mandevilla; Ricardo de Lucy; Reginaldo de Sancto Walerico; Gocelino de Baliol, et Willelmo Oade, apud Berchamstede.

> William Dugdale. *Dugdale's Monasticon Anglicanum: a History of the Abbies and other Monasteries, Hospitals, Frieries, and Cathedral and Collegiate Churches, with their Dependencies, in England and Wales.*

Chapter One

Savoy is a land of lakes, glaciers and tall mountains, towering peaks and glistening blue waters. Set amidst the high Alpine passes, it sits astride the ancient routes from the balmy Mediterranean lands of the classical world of the South, to the colder, darker world of the North. The name Savoy, in French Savoie, in Italian Savoia, in the local Arpitan Savouè, comes from the late Latin Sapaudia – which came from a Celtic name for the *Pays de Sapins* – Land of the Fir Trees.[1] Mountain passes were the raison d'être of Savoy, the source of its wealth and therefore the very essence of its being. The *Col du Mons Jovis* or Grand-Saint-Bernard, the *Colonne de Jovis* or Petit-Saint-Bernard, the Mont Cenis – these were the routes of pilgrims to Rome since classical antiquity, including the *Via Francigena*. During the time of the failing Kingdom of Arles, or Second Kingdom of Burgundy as it's otherwise called, the Great St. Bernard Pass had been held for a time by Saracens. A Christian leader, Bernard of Aosta (also known as Bernard de Menthon), was given the task of restoring the sacked monastery at Bourg-Saint-Pierre but chose to found a new hospice at the summit of the pass, still given the Roman name of *Mons Jovis* around 1050.[2] A century later the pass, and much later the rescue dogs that were trained there, were named after him. The mountain passes lead quite literally to heaven, not so much passes as cracks in the mountain wall that separated Italy from Europe. If you needed to travel between where men spoke French and where men spoke Italian then you needed to travel through the lands of Savoy.

Savoy stretched across the Western Alps in an arc from the Mediterranean to the Gotthard central massif of what is now Switzerland. Spilling down from the high mountains to stretch tentacles of power and influence to Turin and Piedmont in latter-day Italy, down to Provence and the blue-green waters of the Mediterranean, west through the Dauphiné and Bresse on the valley of the River Rhône, now France, north down the Grand-Saint-Bernard to the valley of the Rhône in modern Switzerland along Lake Geneva (hereinafter referred to by the local French name Lac Léman[3]) to the fertile *Pays de Vaud* and Burgundy – a fief bounded by the territorially expansive Kingdom of France to the west and north-west, by the quarrel between Holy Roman emperors and popes to the north, south and east. There was contrast between the fertile lands of Provence, the Rhône valleys, the Pays de Vaud and the high mountain passes covered for much of the year in snow and ice. Whatever the fertility of the land, it is noted throughout for its stunning natural beauty, vineyards producing the most wonderful wines, pasture supporting livestock in abundance. Today it might be said of Savoy that it encompassed a garden of Eden.

The County of Savoy had grown from the wreckage of several post-Western Roman Empire kingdoms that had established their rule of the lands of the Jura and Alps. Originally the Francs had dominated, conquering the First Kingdom of Burgundy[4] in 534 only to see what had become by then the Carolingian Empire divided into three by the Treaty of Verdun in 843. The westernmost kingdom would become West Francia and later still France, the easternmost kingdom ultimately the German lands of the Holy Roman Empire. But the Middle Kingdom would be Lotharingia, named after its founder. There would be a temporary reuniting of the Frankish lands, but in 888 the last Carolingian, Charles the Fat, fell and with him the Carolingian Empire was finally laid to rest. West Francia would take what became the Duchy of Burgundy, that is Burgundy north and west of the Saône, with it; meanwhile, the remainder of Burgundy formed itself anew into a kingdom. Henceforth the Saône would mark the frontier. At the abbey of Saint-Maurice, the last margrave of Transjurane Burgundy, Rudolf I was elected king of one of the successor states, Upper Burgundy, centred on the lands of the Jura mountains and Alpine foothills, the former Carolingian Margraviate of Transjurane Burgundy. His son, Rudolf II, extended the kingdom, reuniting it in 933 with Lower Burgundy the lands of Cisjurania and Provence. The united kingdom of upper and lower Burgundy has been known by a number of names: the Kingdom of Arles, the Kingdom of Arles and Vienne, the Arelat and lastly the name we shall use, the Second Kingdom of Burgundy (see figure 1.0). Geographically, it encompassed mostly the course of the River Rhône, ethnically it was a Romance kingdom, linguistically it spoke what we now call Arpitan in the mountains and a form of Occitan further south.[5] This Second Kingdom of Burgundy remained independent until 1033 when it was absorbed into the empire; the dying last king of Burgundy, Rudolf III, sent his crown and regalia to the Emperor Konrad II. Rudolf had been forced to sign a succession treaty with Henry II, the future emperor in 1006 which granted his lands to the empire. Although Henry II did not see this come to fruition, reigning until 1024, his successor Konrad did. It was henceforth generally accepted that the emperor was king of three kingdoms: of Germany, of Italy and of Burgundy.[6] Konrad had himself crowned King of Burgundy at Payerne in 1033. Frederick I, known to history as Frederick Barbarossa, had himself crowned king of Burgundy at Arles in 1178. The independent Burgundian kingdom failed ultimately for want of a centralised state, Saracen incursion[7] and the failure of Rudolf III to provide an heir.[8]

Charles Previté-Orton found little to challenge the conclusions of the chroniclers,[9] that the last king of Burgundy was a "sluggard".[10] He'd earlier highlighted this failure of centralised state control, and power taken assumed by Counts, noting that "the expulsion of the Saracens, was accomplished not by the King, but by the local barons".[11] The Saracens based in Provence had made war upon the Jura and Alpine regions for more than eighty years in the ninth and tenth centuries, sacking the great monastery at Saint-Maurice, holding the key Alpine passes such as the Grand-Saint-Bernard, Petit-Saint-Bernard and Mont Cenis and laying waste to valleys such as that of the Susa. Their power base had been the fortress Fraxinetum on the heights overlooking the current village of Garde-Freinet, about twelve miles (twenty kilometres) north-west of St. Tropez. From this impregnable fortress, the Saracens raided the Rhône Valley, the Jura and the Alps until 973 when Count Guillaume de Provence, the Liberator, defeated and expelled them. The effect upon the region may be said to be analogous of that of the Vikings upon England. Still today the people of the Tarentaise describe bad weather as *temps de Sarrasins*. That it was not the king but the barons that liberated the region is vital to understanding the end of the Second Kingdom of Burgundy and the emergence of Savoy. Nature, they say, abhors a vacuum and so into the power vacuum of the failed Second Kingdom of Burgundy strode the Savoyards (see figure 1.1). They say "to the victor go the spoils": the origins of the successor powers in the region to the failed Burgundian kingdom, that is the counties of Albon, Provence and of Savoy, lay in the extirpation of the Saracen pest.[12]

Chapter One

By the thirteenth century the County of Savoy was thus a fief of the Holy Roman Empire – it was not to become a Duchy until 1310[13] – the Empire that, in the view of Voltaire, was neither Holy, nor Roman, nor an Empire[14] – therefore the Count of Savoy was a vassal of the Holy Roman Emperor, but as Voltaire might have understood, that gave the Count a high degree of latitude for movement and independence. This means, for example, a Count of Savoy would be able to develop his own international foreign policy and alliances independent to a large extent of imperial policy. So within the titular Kingdom of Burgundy, itself now within the empire, the County of Savoy enjoyed considerable freedom; as an example, Provence to the south-west went so far as to leave the empire in 1246 when acquired by the Angevins.[15] As we shall see, the Counts of Savoy were more than free to conduct their own foreign relations outside of any imperial relations, such as those they developed with the Plantagenet lands that will form the basis of this story.

The founder of the House of Savoy was Humbert I de Savoie. He had been an ally of Rudolf and likely held lands in Burgundy, his family holding interests in the Viennois, Belley and Savoy.[16] Counts and counties had grown to prominence from the time of the decline of the Carolingian state; *"comes"* or companions of the emperor would be granted land in return for service in place of paid officials and administrators.[17] So it was with Savoy, Humbert being granted lands as a reward for service, lands in Maurienne, the Aosta Valley, the Chablais and the Upper Rhône Valley by the emperor Konrad II when he'd inherited Burgundy in 1033. Humbert had supported Konrad in his campaigns against Eudes II, Count of Blois, who had contested the emperor's rights in Burgundy. On 2 February 1033, at Payerne, Konrad had himself elected and proclaimed titular King of Burgundy, thence to Zurich where he received the homage of Rudolf's late queen, Ermengarde,[18] along with Humbert I de Savoie.[19] Thus began the comital family of Savoy, vassals of the Holy Roman Empire.

Before Humbert and his descendants began styling themselves Counts of Savoy they had been known as Counts of Maurienne, being first styled as such in 1046, then Counts of Maurienne and Savoy before finally of Savoy. The centre of Maurienne was Aiguebelle, the beautiful water, the beautiful waters being the River Arc. Aiguebelle sat not far from the confluence of the Arc and its valley, the Maurienne, and its route to the Mont Cenis Pass and the Isère and its valley, the Tarentaise, and its route to the Petit-Saint-Bernard Pass. From Aiguebelle two key mountain passes could be controlled. In a charter of 1044, Aiguebelle is known for the castle that had been built atop a *verrou glaciaire* (a rock protrusion into a glacial valley), Charbonnière. The castle itself is no more, but its rock can be climbed and its overgrown walls discerned, the deep imperial connections of Humbert and later Thomas and Pierre de Savoie are proclaimed by the flying to this day of a flag bearing the black eagle upon a yellow background that signified high imperial office. Humbert died in 1048 and was buried at the cathedral in Saint-Jean-de-Maurienne, where he lies today in a magnificent tomb located in the much later façade, the inscription reading: *"Humbert Aux Blanches Moins, Comte de Maurienne, Fondateur de la Dynastie de Savoie."* Perhaps the local highway authorities express it best when a large brown tourist sign by the motorway betwixt Saint-Jean and Aiguebelle lauds the Maurienne Valley as the *"Berceau de la Maison de Savoie"* or Cradle of the House of Savoy.

Maurienne and with it the acquisition of imperial grants by a loyal supporter secured key passes through the Alps, controlling trade between Italy and Western Europe, which would be the core of Savoyard power for centuries. For English readers Previté-Orton suggested that we might consider "Count Humbert … not much the inferior to a contemporary Duke of Aquitaine".[20] That Konrad appears to have granted Humbert almost sovereign status in these new lands speaks to the importance he attached to such vital trade routes being held in the possession of a man he could trust; we have here the seeds of the tremendous power that would accrue to the House of Savoy in international affairs.

Humbert I, also known as "White Hands",[21] had had what is perhaps the earliest contact between Savoy and the English, albeit a brief one. Humbert had travelled to Rome as the Conte d'Aoste in 1027 for the coronation, as emperor, of Konrad. Also travelling to Rome that summer was the King of England and Denmark, Cnut or Canute as the English know him (he of the waves coming in).[22] Since the days the Saracens had held the pilgrim routes across the Alps, the way from the Upper Rhône Valley to Italy had been plagued by brigands robbing and massacring travellers. Canute wanted order restored. We have his letter from Rome:

> I spoke with the Emperor himself and the Lord Pope and the princes there about the needs of all people of my entire realm, both English and Danes, that a juster law and securer peace might be granted to them on the road to Rome and that they should not be straitened by so many barriers along the road, and harassed by unjust tolls; and the Emperor agreed and likewise King Robert who governs most of these same toll gates. And all the magnates confirmed by edict that my people, both merchants, and the others who travel to make their devotions, might go to Rome and return without being afflicted by barriers and toll collectors, in firm peace and secure in a just law.[23]

One of those "magnates" was Humbert, and Canute's concern for the English route to Rome would directly concern his mountain passes.[24] The passage of them would bring England and Savoy ever closer over the coming centuries. As we saw earlier and in response to Canute's concern, the Church would ask a cleric, Saint Bernard de Menthon, from Aosta to refound the monastery at Bourg-Saint-Pierre. In 1050, the cleric began a hospice at the very summit of the pass that would one day carry his name.

We have circumstantial evidence that the route through Savoy to Rome was well known to Englishmen since the days of the sixth century when Saint Augustine had brought the Church back to what would later become England. Several pilgrims and travellers to Rome had likely made the journey, amongst them Theodore, Archbishop of Canterbury from 668, Caedwalla, King of Wessex from circa 685[25] and Æthelhard, Archbishop of Canterbury from 793.[26] The young King Ælfred is said to have accompanied his parents on pilgrimage to Rome on two occasions before he was 7; the route is unknown but likely to have been the *Via Francigena*. But the best evidence comes from the late Anglo-Saxon Archbishop Sigeric who kindly left us his itinerary for his journey to Rome in 990 AD, which followed the familiar road through Besançon, Pontarlier, Lausanne, Saint-Maurice, Martigny, the Grand-Saint-Bernard Pass thence to Aosta and eventually Rome.[27] Another Archbishop of Canterbury, Saint Anselm, holder of the see from 1093 until 1109, had been a native son of Aosta before moving to Normandy then England.

John of Salisbury, Secretary to the Archbishop of Canterbury and later Bishop of Chartres, spoke for many Englishmen of the perils of crossing the Grand-Saint-Bernard, writing:

> Pardon me for not writing. I have been on the Mount of Jove; on the one hand, looking up to the heavens of the mountains, on the other shuddering at the hell of the valleys ... Lord, I said, restore me to my brethren, that I may tell them that they come not into this place of torment.[28]

Chapter One

And went on to add:

> Where the ground is covered with stones and marbles of glaciers, where it is not possible to fix a foot, nay, not to place it without danger, and in a strange way, when you cannot stand on slippery ground, you fall to your death if you slip.[29]

As we saw earlier, in the winter of 1158/9, King Henry II sent envoys to the Emperor Frederick Barbarossa by way of the Grand-Saint-Bernard. However, it seems the English envoys got lost in the Alps beyond Martigny, only to be rescued by the monks of the hospice crowning the pass. A grateful Henry gave the monks land at Havering in Essex to build a church for themselves; it stands to this day, now parish church of St. Andrew's.[30] The canons of Mont-Joux, the Mount of Jupiter, of the Grand-Saint-Bernard Pass came from Salins, Vevey and Lausanne amongst others, the reach of the first Plantagenet king following the pilgrim road to Rome. The Grand-Saint-Bernard and the Mont Cenis were well known to English travellers, those documented being likely only a fraction of those who made the hazardous journey. Savoy was not unknown to the English.[31]

We need perhaps at this point to describe the lands bequeathed by the failed Burgundian state to what would become the County of Savoy, and not be troubled yet by the precise nature of Savoyard tenure. The centre of the Savoyard lands would be said then to encompass the Tarentaise and Maurienne, leading to the Petit-Saint-Bernard and Mont Cenis passes. Across the Alpine peaks these routes would lead to the Aosta Valley and the Susa Valley, both leading to Lombardy and Italy. The Aosta Valley would not be linguistically or ethnically Italian but be more akin to their brethren on the other side of the Petit-Saint-Bernard. The ancient Roman town of Aosta[32] would itself form a junction with the route across the classic Grand-Saint-Bernard leading into the Upper Rhône Valley at Martigny. Turning left one would pass the great monastery of Saint Maurice at Agaunum before meeting the headwaters of Lac Léman. The eighth-century abbey of Saint Maurice memorialised the site of the martyrdom of the Theban Legion under the command of Saint Maurice in and around 285 AD, martyred for refusing to forsake their Christian faith. Saint Maurice would become the patron saint of Savoy. From the head of the lake, to the left the narrow way would take the southern shore skirting the Chablais, but the easier way would be the northern shore by way of the Pays de Vaud and Lausanne to the westernmost tip of the lake at Geneva. Following the Isère west from the Tarentaise and Maurienne would bring travellers to the foothills of the Alps and *Savoie Propre*. Savoy itself encompassed lands toward Montmelian and Aix-les-Bains, the beautiful Lac du Bourget and the lowlands to its south. Thence from *Savoie Propre* further west through Bugey and the episcopal See of Belley to the Viennois and environs of Lyon and the Rhône at the confluence with the Saone. Lyon, Vienne, Geneva and Lausanne had been major centres of Roman government, and this survived into the high Middle Ages in the form of important seats of the Church. The scope of the Savoyard lands stretched over much of the modern-day French departments of Savoie, Haute Savoie and Ain, sharing Isère with the County of Albon, and the Italian Aosta and Susa valleys, and lastly the Swiss cantons of Valais and Vaud.

Surrounding Savoy were its Germanic neighbours to the north, its Italian neighbours to the south and francophone neighbours to the west. To the north, the House of Zähringen was a dynasty of Swabian nobility. Their name is derived from Zähringen castle near what's now Freiburg in south-western Germany. By the early thirteenth century they had developed a fiefdom within the empire that had spread southward, adding much of what's now German-speaking Switzerland to their lands in Germany. Their Swiss lands were principally the area around the growing city of Bern, to Solothurn in the north and Freiburg in the south. Their German heartland within the Duchy of Swabia would also give rise to the Hohenstaufen dynasty. The eastern area of what's now German-speaking Switzerland were the lands around Zürich and the Counts of Kyburg. But, for the Zähringen, their power was waning; the ducal line ended in 1218, the Hohenstaufen Emperor Frederick II withdrew the ducal and most of the imperial rights, their lands being divided up by the Counts of Urach (subsequently Freiburg) and the Counts of Kyburg.[33] But mid-century the line of Kyburg would also end and into the vacuum the Zähringen and Kyburgs left would step the Savoyard from the south and the Habsburgs and Swiss Cantons from the north and east. Such was the shifting sands of the German-speaking aristocratic lines north of the Savoyards: the Zähringen, the Kyburgs, the Habsburgs and the nascent Swiss cantons. An independent buffer of sorts between the Zähringen and Savoy was the small independent County of Gruyère, centred around the castle and small town beneath it in the upper Saanen valley.

To the south lay the Italian city states of the Lombard League, including Milan, which spent much of the period (supported by the Pope) at war with the emperor of the empire of which they were a part. West of the Lombard League, but still on the Italian side of the Alps, lay the Lordship of Piedmont, a Savoyard appanage, and the Marquisate of Saluzzo, a Savoyard vassal. Saluzzo would become important to Savoy as it provided a direct land border with the County of Provence and its access to the Mediterranean. Nestled between the Lombard League and Savoy was the important city of Turin. Otto, Count of Savoy had acquired Turin by marriage to Adelaide di Susa in 1046, as she was the last of the line of the Marquisate of Susa, also known as the Marquisate of Turin.[34] However, with her death in 1091, the city itself had become the fief of the Prince Bishop of Turin. The Italian city and its bishop would be a thorn in the Savoyard side until control of Turin was established in the late thirteenth century. Ultimately Turin would become a seat of power of the successor Duchy of Savoy and today boasts many fine buildings bearing the Savoyard arms; however, in the thirteenth century that was far away in the future and in the meantime the city would be a source of conflict.

To the north-west lay the francophone Franche Comté de Bourgogne or Free County of Burgundy, also a part of the empire. To the west lay the Lords of Bâgé and the flatlands of Bresse and the foothills of the Alps of the Dauphin in the Dauphiné (not yet then France). The Dauphiné had been the County of Albon. By the twelfth century, the local ruler was wearing a dolphin on his coat of arms and was nicknamed le Dauphin (dolphin). By the thirteenth century the Dauphin held the former County of Albon and to the east the Bailliages of Grésivaudan and Briançonnais and the Margravate of Cesena. Between Savoy and the County of Albion lay what was called the Manche des Coligny, a long sliver of land that comprised Lons-le-Saulnier in the north up by the Franche Conte de Bourgogne to Albon in the south. The Manche was made up of a loose collection of lordships which were in the process of breaking up due to split inheritance, the Lordship of Coligny and the Lordship of La Tour du Pin being the most notable. This wedge of land blocked Savoyard advance to the southwest, where lay the Mediterranean and Provence which now was held by counts from Barcelona, and so would be the setting for a south-westward and westward advance on behalf of the Savoyard as the thirteenth century progressed.

A number of troublesome enclaves lay within the County of Savoy, principally the Bishopric of Lausanne and the County of Geneva. Since 1011 the See of Lausanne had been

Chapter One

a Prince Bishopric within the Holy Roman Empire, having temporal as well as spiritual power within the important city of Lausanne by Lac Léman. The bishops' enclave within Savoyard lands would prove a continuing source of conflict. To the west of Lausanne lay the County of Geneva, another fief of the empire. The Counts of Geneva struggled to retain their independence from Savoy (ultimately, they'd fail)[35] as the Savoyards controlled all the trading routes into the county which would find itself continually squeezed. It was in itself divided to some extent too, in that Geneva itself was the home of the Bishop of Geneva whilst the Count of Geneva resided in Annecy. As the thirteenth century dawned, Geneva held the northern coast of Lac Léman as far as the Bishop of Lausanne's lands, Geneva itself, the lands around Annecy and its lake, and the vassal of the Lordship of Faucigny.

"Thomas I, Count of Savoy ... was the author of it all."[36] So began definitive historian of Savoy, Eugene Cox, and indeed he can be said to be the beginning of the Savoyard golden age, and this story too, except before we begin, we must record a "false start", a prequel if you will. Until Thomas and since Humbert I the White-handed, the counts had normally styled themselves Count of Maurienne and Savoy. From 5 March 1200 Thomas began simply calling himself Count of Savoy. The story of the Savoyard and the English that begins with Thomas nearly began with his father, Humbert III de Savoie.[37] It had been Humbert III who had settled upon the white cross on a scarlet red field as the heraldic device by which the family would later be known and to this day, the cross perhaps evidencing his wish once to be a monk.[38] Across the Rhône from Savoy was the County of Toulouse, and specifically Count Raymond V of Toulouse, with whom the Savoyard did not see eye to eye: they were rivals. Also, across the Rhône, but to the north, was Henri Duc d'Aquitaine, who also happened to be King Henry II of England. Humbert III had a marriageable daughter, little Alais, and he thought that an alliance with Aquitaine and England would strengthen his position vis-à-vis the County of Toulouse. Humbert travelled the eighty miles (130 kilometres) or so west of his lands to meet with Henry at Montferrand in the Auvergne, then a part of Aquitaine.[39] For Henry, the Angevin ruler of lands from the Scottish border to the Pyrenees, an alliance with the County of Savoy would help prevent the southern expansion of Capetian France and give him access to the valuable transalpine passes to Italy and the Pope. Both Henry Plantagenet and Humbert of Savoy had common cause in eying the acquisitive Capetian Kingdom of France with suspicion. The thirteenth-century Anglo-Savoyard alliance would, at its core, be an alliance of francophone families who'd rather not be a part of the Kingdom of France if they could help it.[40] Accordingly, he offered his youngest son in marriage, the boy John. In February 1173, they were betrothed. Benedict of Peterborough recorded the marriage contract between "*De Rege et comite Maurianæ*" of "*Aalis filiam suam majorem*" to "*Johannis filii sui junioris*": of Alais, eldest daughter of Humbert, to John, youngest son of the king. The contract provided that the whole County of Maurienne should pass to John should Humbert die without an heir "*cum toto comitatu de Mauriana.*"[41] Alais travelled to Henry's court, not in England, but to Chinon, on the Loire, for Henry was a decidedly French-English king. To cement the match, Humbert offered Henry the castles of Rossillon and Pierre-Châtel; in return Henry transferred to the 5-year-old John the the castles of Chinon itself, Loudun and Mirebeau[42]. Sadly, for Henry, John, Humbert and mostly Alais, the plan backfired spectacularly. Angered at the favour being bestowed upon John, his elder brothers, Henry the young king and Richard (later *Cœur de Lion*) flew into rebellion against their father and allied themselves with the French King Louis VII, and poor Alais, barely 8 years old, passed away at Henry's court. This left neither Humbert nor Henry with their alliance, and Henry with a rebellious family to bring to terms with whom relations would now be permanently strained. But the idea of an Anglo-Savoyard alliance was passed from Humbert to his son Thomas and in turn to his sons, Amédée, Guillaume and Pierre.

Thomas was born in 1189 at Aiguebelle in the Savoyard heartland, and named as was the fashion after the shocking murder at Canterbury in 1170, after Archbishop Thomas Becket[43] – Thomas reigned for forty-four long years, as long life was the custom amongst those raised in the alpine mountain peaks. Thomas was a courageous warrior and rightly reputed to have expanded Savoyard power and fiefdom from the mountain valleys of the Maurienne and Tarentaise into the fertile plateau of Vaud by Lac Léman to the north, Piedmont to the east and the Jura foothills to the west of Bugey. However, it is for his offspring he is most known to history, a brood of children that would spread Savoyard power and influence to the four corners of Europe.

At the time Thomas became Count of Savoy, his territories encompassed land north and west of the Alps and down to Italy. The lands he bequeathed to later Counts of Savoy included in Savoie Propre: Montmélian, Aiguebelle, Tournon, Ugine and Le Chatelar-en-Bauges; in the Tarentaise and Maurienne, Salins and the Val d'Isère; in Novalaise, Les Échelles, Saint-Laurent, Saint-Genix, Pierre-Châtel; in Bugey, Rossillon, Lompnes, Seyssel, and the Valromey; in the Val di Susa, Susa and Avigliana; in the Valle d'Aosta, Aosta and Châtel-Argent; in Chablais, Chillon and Saint-Maurice d'Agaune; and some lands in the Viennois and Piedmont. So, in addition to Savoy and Maurienne there was also Chablais, assorted lands around Lac Léman and in the Viennois-Lyonnais region; in Italy he was the Count of Aosta and the Marquis of Susa, and finally he held lands extending down to the fertile plains of the Po.[44]

Thomas acquired a bride to sire his brood in a most unconventional manner: he kidnapped her.[45] The *Chronique de Savoie*, written in the middle of the fifteenth century, related the colourful and perhaps romantic tale.[46] The chronicler was writing some two centuries after the reported events, but his words have a ring of truth about them, if not Gallic romance. Thomas gathered a group of knights and lay in wait for Marguerite de Geneva (daughter of the Count of Geneva), who was being transported to France for her forthcoming marriage to King Philippe II Auguste. Marguerite was by all accounts a beauty of some distinction; no doubt she would have had to have been to embolden a Count of Savoy to attempt the kidnap of a future Queen of France. Struck so assuredly by Cupid's bow, the Count and his knights hid themselves in the Albarine valley for the beauteous Marguerite to pass. Upon kidnap, Marguerite went willingly with the Count the short distance to the little parish church at Rossilon in the Cluse de Hopitâux by the fast-flowing Furans, where the two were immediately made Count and Countess. Philippe Auguste acquiesced to the kidnap of his bride-to-be, convinced that Thomas and Marguerite were in love and that Thomas had prior rights to the lady.[47] Marguerite is also called Beatrix in some later sources. There is no explanation that has yet been found for these dual names. The fact that "Beatrix" appears in a seal shows that it was not a transcription error.[48]

Beauty and indeed feminine beauty are in the eye of the beholder, and attempting to talk of notable beauty at the distance of so many centuries is to attempt almost the impossible. However, the story of young Thomas de Savoie so struck by the beauty of Marguerite de Genève is important because it carries echoes that will be important to our story. Her daughter Béatrice de Savoie was described by Matthew Paris,[49] no lover of the Savoyards, as being a woman of some beauty.[50] Béatrice would be of such beauty that the troubadour Guillaume

Chapter One

de Saint Grigori sang: "Courageous Countess of the highest lineage, we hold you to be the most beautiful we have ever seen in the world: for the pure fountain from which spring all virtues."[51] This pure fountain would give rise to four daughters of legend, all to become queens: Marguerite, Alianor, Sanchia and Béatrice who were in turn also the subject of stories surrounding their great beauty. Paris described Alianor as being possessed of both *"décor"* and *"venustissima"*, that is to say a very attractive beauty.[52] Notwithstanding the flattery of the *Chronique de Savoie* or the often-backhanded compliments of Matthew Paris, the simple physical attractiveness of the ladies of Savoy should not go unremarked in understanding how the comital family was able to extend its influence far beyond the mountains to England – feminine charm played no small part (see figure 1.2).

Poor Philippe Auguste had needed a wife following the death of his first spouse, Isabelle de Hainault and had married Ingeborg of Denmark on 15 August 1193. On the day after his marriage to Ingeborg, King Philippe changed his mind, wished to obtain a separation and attempted to send her back to Denmark. Hence Philippe's attempt to wed Marguerite in 1195. Meanwhile, outraged, Ingeborg fled to a convent in Soissons, from where she protested to Pope Celestine III. Poor Ingeborg protested that Philippe was using a spurious family tree to get out of the marriage and so the Danes sent a delegation to meet the Pope. They convinced him that the dodgy French family tree was false, but the Pope merely declared the annulment invalid and prohibited Philippe from marrying again. Philippe ignored Celestine's verdict. Ingeborg spent the next twenty years in virtual imprisonment in various French castles. Philippe rejecting Ingeborg, and losing Marguerite, married Agnès von Merania in 1196.

So off into the Alpine sunset rode Thomas and his bride Marguerite to sire a family of children who would bring untold riches and power to their family. The great Carthusian Saint Anthelme of Belley had blessed Humbert III and his son Thomas with many children, and this blessing appears to have done the trick.[53] The multitudinous family of Thomas and Marguerite comprised no less than at least eight sons and two daughters, perhaps more. In order of appearance Marguerite would give birth to the boys Amédée at Montmélian in 1197, Humbert circa 1198, Aymon circa 1200, Guillaume circa 1201, Thomas at Montmélian in 1202, Pierre at Susa in 1203, Philippe at Aiguebelle in 1207 and Boniface at the Château de Sainte-Hélène du Lac circa 1207, and the girls Béatrice at Les Echelles circa 1205 and Marguerite circa 1212. Giving birth to the Savoyard dynasty was for Marguerite no doubt a full-time occupation.[54] As Cox said, "genealogical charts for the medieval House of Savoy are as trustworthy as they are numerous"[55] – there are claims to many other children, legitimate or otherwise, but we can at least be sure of these eight sons and two daughters.[56]

Count Thomas and Marguerite did not live in one place, as evidenced by the documents issued in their name, but ran an itinerant court, travelling from place to place, and so we must assume at some stage so too did the children, including Pierre. Their favourite calls appear to have been their castles at Aiguebelle at the mouth of the Maurienne, Montmélian in the heart of Savoy, Chillon by Lac Léman, Pierre-Châtel by the Rhône and Les Echelles on the road from Chambéry to Lyon and the Viennois, but also religious houses such as Saint-Maurice d'Agaune and the houses of Templars and Hospitallers in Chambéry.[57] According to legend, but no more, Pierre de Savoie was born in the palace castle at Susa in the Susa Valley leading from the Maurienne to Turin. There are two castles in Susa, and we should not confuse them; there is the Castello San Giorio di Susa but the more likely haunt of Thomas and his family would have been the Castello della Contessa Adelaide. The former was a castle, the latter was more of a palace than a castle. The palace is named for Adelaide of Turin, whose eleventh-century marriage to Othon de Savoie, the younger son of the Savoyard dynasty founder, Humbert I, first brought the Savoyards to the Susa Valley.

Thomas and Marguerite were blessed with a good deal more offspring than previous generations of the comital family, and Thomas had no wish to divide his legacy. Accordingly, the first son Amédée would go on to be Thomas's heir as Count of Savoy (Amédée IV), and Aymon would be Lord of Chablais.[58] But what of the others? A church career beckoned. Thomas became Comte de Flandres, but not before a time in the clergy, and Guillaume became Bishop of Valence before going on to a key role at the court of King Henry III and having the Honour of Richmond bestowed upon him. Philippe went on to be Archbishop of Lyon before in turn also becoming Count of Savoy (Philippe I) and lastly Boniface would become Archbishop of Canterbury. Humbert would die young in 1223.[59] Of the sisters, Béatrice would become perhaps the most influential of all, marrying into the County of Provence. So many brothers would go into the church in response to the perennial feudal problem; you needed a male heir and, preferably, given the many ways one might die in the thirteenth century, spare heirs – but what to do if the premier heir didn't die?

It would be the sixth-born son, destined seemingly for a career in the church, that will be the focus of our story, and perhaps the most famous of the sons of Thomas and Marguerite. His father had been occupied in a brief engagement with Piedmontese politics as Pierre was born, and, as we've seen, it was, according to the fifteenth-century chronicler Jean d'Oronville in *La Chronique de Savoie,* that the *Petit Charlemagne* entered this world in the palace castle at Susa in 1203.[60] The Val di Susa formed the Italian half of the route from the Savoyard heartland in the Maurienne to Turin, by way of the Mont Cenis Pass. Piedmontese politics were notoriously complicated as the rival communes sought to exercise authority and control one over the other, chief of which were Turin, and around thirty miles (forty-nine kilometres) to the east, Asti. Thomas sought to exploit political divisions within the region to extend Savoyard rule to Turin, something that his far-distant progeny would eventually succeed in. But as the thirteenth century dawned Thomas contented himself with dabbling in Italian waters and ensuring his position in Susa, hence Pierre's entry into this life in the steeply sided valley.

As for the daughters of Thomas and Marguerite, their marriages could be used in the quest for territorial expansion and/or allies. The younger daughter, Marguerite, was married in 1218 to Hartmann,[61] the second son of Ulrich III, Count of Kyburg, and Anna von Zähringen. Marguerite was to be a pawn in Thomas's expansion into western Helvetian lands to the north of Lac Léman, long the fief of the Dukes of Zähringen. That dynasty was waning as the last duke, Berthold V, had just died (18 February 1218) without an heir, and as a result his territory divided; the southern half in the Pays de Vaud had passed to Ulrich's wife, Anna von Zähringen. Marguerite's marriage to their son Hartmann brought an end to Zähringen–Savoyard rivalry.[62] Cox wrote, "The friendship of Hartmann of Kyburg would be an important factor in the Savoyard 'conquest' of the Pays de Vaud over the next fifty years."[63] Earlier there had been a decisive war between Thomas and the last Zähringen Duke, Berthold V, founder of Bern and Bishop of Neuchatel. Details of the war, which lasted from 1201 until 1207, are unclear; the castle of Roger de Vico-Pisano, the Bishop of Lausanne, the Château de Lucens, was burned by Thomas, along with his tower near Ouchy on Lausanne's lakefront.[64] There is talk in one chronicle account of a great battle between Thomas and Berthold by Chillon itself, at which Berthold was himself taken prisoner.[65] The ever-persistent Berthold subsequently tried again, this time in the Valais, by way of the

Chapter One

Grimsel Pass, but defeated at Ulrichen, he signed, at Hautcrêt Abbey on 19 October 1211, a treaty that forced him to concede Savoyard suzerainty there.[66] Later, after the Treaty of Burier of 8 July 1219,[67] Thomas had established a Savoyard power base in the centre of Vaud. He held from the Bishop of Lausanne the castle and town of Moudon in the rich lands between Lausanne and Fribourg; as Roman Minnodunum it had sat astride the road to Aventicum (now Avenches).[68] Cox thought that nearby Romont had been ceded at this time to Savoy by the Zähringen.[69] Linguistic boundaries between French and German speakers that last until this day were being set. However, the main regional obstacles to the Savoyard would appear to have been the bishops Lausanne and Sion, the former in the Pays de Vaud and the latter in the Valais. More recently than Cox, Florian Defferrard, writing in the Swiss *Historiches Lexikon*, has shown that at Romont it was Pierre who acquired the rights to what had been described in 1177 as a wooded hill, from the lesser Vaudois *Famille de Billens*, specifically Nantelme de Billens. The fief of Romont, meanwhile, appears to have belonged until then to the Bishops of Lausanne. Pierre built a castle upon the hill, and installed a castelain. A guarantee of rights addressed to the prior of nearby Payerne of 1240 by Pierre carries the title "*dominus Rotundi Montis*".[70] This established that immediately before his move to England, Pierre de Savoie was styling himself Lord of Romont – it would be some leap from the Round Hill or Romont, on the way from Lausanne to Fribourg to the Strong Hill, or Richemont, of Yorkshire as we shall see later. His acquisition of Romont would be consolidated by the later Peace of Evian between the Savoyards and the See of Lausanne in 1244.[71]

The use by Thomas of the Imperial Eagle as his heraldic device, as opposed to the white cross on a red field of his father, dates from his support for Philip of Swabia and the contested German throne at Basel in 1207.[72] Thomas would be given the title *vicarius* in Lombardy by Emperor Frederick II.[73] The black eagle with scarlet claws would be carried on the shield of the knight whose sepulchral tomb Kerrich took to be Pierre de Savoie in 1771.[74] The straight-clawed eagle he drew from Aiguebelle is certainly consistent with the imperial eagles used in the thirteenth century. Meanwhile, Thomas, having secured the way to expansion in the north, looked toward the south.

Chapter Two

The County of Provence bordered Count Thomas's lands to the south. Provence (named as the first Roman province in Gaul) was by now the fabled land of the troubadours, of wine, song and courtly love.[1] The county was largely agrarian in nature and sparsely populated, its principal towns being those on the Rhône, Avignon and Arles, the latter giving its name to the entire, now only titular, Kingdom of Arles, which also comprised Savoy and Burgundy. The beauty of the landscape attracted most of the troubadours, those roving players who gave the county the title by which it was known across Europe – the Land of Song. To the west of Provence lay the troubled County of Toulouse whose Count Ramon VI de Toulouse had recently experienced excommunication, and the murderous Albigensian Crusade against the religious heretics, the Cathars, within his county. The crusade was led by one Simon de Montfort, father of the boy of the same name who would bring so much trouble to England later in the story.

Count Thomas was looking for a southern ally in his fight to secure more land in the Piedmont and his rivalry with the County of Albon and its Dauphin, therefore the marriageability of his daughter Béatrice in pursuance of that goal came to the fore. On 5 June 1219[2] he met at Dronero with interested bishops[3] and the Provençal council to discuss the betrothal of his daughter to the Count of Provence, Ramon Berenguer V.[4] The County of Provence lay to the west of Piedmont and Saluzzo and to the south of Albon. Indeed, the Count of Provence claimed suzerainty over the County of Forcalquier that bordered Albon; an alliance with Provence would sandwich the lands of the Dauphiné. As with her father, with her mother, 14-year-old Count Ramon Berenguer was bewitched by the beauty of 12-year-old Béatrice. English chronicler Matthew Paris,[5] not given to flattery where Provençals and Savoyards were concerned, described Ramon as "brave in battle" and Béatrice as "a woman of remarkable beauty".[6] They married not long after the betrothal,[7] thus uniting the ruling families of Savoy and Provence.[8]

The young Ramon Berenguer was the son of Alfonso II, Count of Provence, the name rightly implying the Catalan origins of the family, the House of Barcelona. When his father had died in 1209, Ramon had been away living in the Templar castle at Monzón in the Kingdom of Aragon. His mother was Garsende de Forcalquier, whose marriage to Ramon had united her county with Provence. She was a great patron of the troubadour culture that would fill the lives of her daughters. Reputedly Ramon was "a lord of gentle lineage" and "a wise and courteous lord was he, and of noble state and virtuous, and in his time did honourable deeds".[9] The ongoing Albigensian Crusade against the Cathars in southern France had taken their toll on Ramon's resources, as had a growing family. It had not taken long for a family to appear, sons not surviving long,[10] before a string of daughters was born by Béatrice for the Count of Provence: Marguerite was born in 1221, Alianor in 1223, Sanchia in 1228 and lastly Béatrice probably in 1231.[11] The girls spent their childhood moving between the principal

Chapter Two

castle at Tarascon on the River Rhône midway between Arles and Avignon and the summer residence at Aix-en-Provence, and also at Ramon's newly built castle at Brignoles, built in the year of Alianor's birth.[12]

The daughters were of such fame that Dante Alighieri would later write of them in his *The Divine Comedy: Paradise Canto IV*. Ramon and Béatrice had appointed troubadour and poet Romeo de Villeneuve as their tutor.[13] Dante encountered Justinian in the sphere of Mercury, who described Romeo de Villeneuve as "the shining light" responsible for their good fortune in life, saying:

> *Quattro figlie ebbe, e ciascuna reina,*
> *Raimondo Berlinghieri, a cio le fece*
> *Romeo, persona umile e peregrina.*[14&15]

> Four daughters had Count Ramon Berenguer,
> Each of them a Queen, thanks to Romeo,
> This man of lowly birth, this pilgrim soul.[16]

With their grandmother Marguerite de Genève and mother Béatrice de Savoie[17] being noted for their charm and beauty, we can't be entirely astonished that the four daughters growing to maidenhood in the Land of Song and courtly love would become the most eligible young ladies in Christendom. Matthew Paris, again, did not spare the eulogies, in later (1254) describing their mother Béatrice as Niobe and suggesting that "among the female sex throughout the world, no other mother could boast of such illustrious fruit of the womb as could she in her daughters".[18] He would later, in 1257, return again to the same theme, remarking upon the "fecundity of Béatrice, Countess of Provence".[19] In commenting on the passing of Ramon Berenguer, in 1245, he would write that he had left an "unusual source of wonder to all the ages in the excelling beauty of his daughters".[20] Not surprising then that very soon the crowned heads and hearts of Europe would come a calling in Provence.

Ties between the Maison de Savoie and the English were renewed in 1220 when Henry III had promised the next available benefices to become available,[21] by 1226. Guillaume de Savoie had been granted two benefices,[22] those at *Sancti Michaelis super Wer* (St. Michael's on Wyre) in Lancashire just south of Lancaster[23] and at *Byngham* (Bingham) in Nottinghamshire.[24] These benefices granted upon the request of Count Thomas by Hubert de Burgh the young Henry's Chief Justiciar in favour of the young Guillaume de Savoie represent the earliest Anglo-Savoyard dealings involving the sons of Thomas. The 1220 letter suggests that the potential Anglo-Savoyard alliance of 1173, had not been filed away in some diplomatic drawer but was an ongoing project to be realised.

So, in beginning the story of the entanglement of the Houses of Savoy and Plantagenet England we must focus firstly on the career of Guillaume de Savoie. It might seem that whilst his elder brother Amédée focused on running Savoy itself, it would Guillaume who busied himself with foreign relations. Meanwhile, in 1225, already a Dean of the Chapter of Vienne[25] and acting as a procurator for Valence, Guillaume was elected Bishop of Valence, the old Roman town centred upon the Romanesque cathedral and just south of the confluence of the Rhône and the Isère. Cox was of the opinion that the See of Valence had been the gift of Emperor Henry III in response to a request by Guillaume's father Count Thomas I, thus extending Savoyard influence to the Rhône – this idea seems very plausible.[26] Guillaume's brother Thomas, who was already a canon at Lausanne,[27] then also became a provost at Valence.[28] Guillaume contested temporal authority there with the Count of Valence, eventually securing both temporal and spiritual authority following a treaty of 1231, confirmed by charter in 1238. Subsequently he paid much attention to securing a firmer financial footing for Valence.[29] Next, Guillaume de Savoie sitting astride the Rhône looked for favourable marriage matches for his beautiful nieces that might advance the family's fortunes. Through Guillaume the family that controlled the Alpine passes now also controlled the great river that flowed south from France to Provence and for much of its length a frontier between France and the Empire – the Savoyard were nothing if not good at being in positions of strategic European importance. Matthew Paris described the Bishop of Valence, sitting astride the wide Rhône, as a "spiritual monster and a beast with many heads"[30] – if this be so, his tentacles would soon reach northward. He looked firstly at the kingdom across the Rhône, that of France, and then to the north of France, to England.

But whatever Guillaume's ambitions may have been, closer to home, in Savoy, the Savoyard began their expansion into the plateau lands of western Helvetia, modern-day Switzerland, upward from Lac Léman toward the Jura and Lac de Neuchâtel. Lac Léman, one of Europe's largest, is a crescent-shaped, crystal-clear lake formed by inflow from the Rhône at its eastward point, to the onward outflow to the Rhône again at Geneva on its westward tip. Toward the south of the lake the Chablais Alps reach almost to the lakeside; only here and there, as at Evian, is limited development made possible by the towering mountains. On the northern shore, only, betwixt the Alps and the Jura, is there sufficient extended land available for agriculture. The Romans had developed the region, establishing *Colonia Iulia Equestris* (modern-day Nyon) as a colony, *Viviscus* (modern-day Vevey) and founding the city of Lausanne as *Lousonna*, a Gallo-Roman trading port. This verdant countryside was (and is) home to significant wine production. The northern shoreline carried the *Camino de Santiago* east–west toward France and at Lausanne it formed a junction with the *Via Francigena* coming down from England and France en route to Italy via the Grand-Saint-Bernard Pass.

Then, as now, this crossroads, Lausanne, would be the key focus of human activity and development in the region. The Merovingian Franks and then the Burgundians had dominated the region following the waning of Roman power, and they had in turn been replaced by the Zähringens from Germany – then as now the *Pays de Vaud* sat on the linguistic European fault line, Latin speakers to the south and west, Germanic speakers to the north and east.

As we saw earlier, Guillaume's younger brother Pierre had been born in 1203, and like his elder brother he'd been marked out for a career in the Church since the eldest brother of all, Amédée, would become Count. Thomas had been blessed with as many as eight sons, perhaps more if the rumours of illegitimate offspring are considered. Such a brood of sons could be a curse – what to do with them all? How to stop them fighting? Thomas would be well aware of the dynastic struggles of the Plantagenets. He would be succeeded as Count by his eldest son Amédée, but what of the others? Well, judging by the grant of appanages, land would be provided for the next two, Humbert and Aymon, but the remainder, Guillaume, Thomas, Pierre, Philippe and Boniface, would be marked out for a career in the Church. Count Thomas had begun Pierre's ecclesiastical career, enabling his being a canon in Lausanne, and provost in Aosta[31] and Geneva.[32] In 1229, at Lausanne, Pierre began a career that would lead eventually to being one of a council ruling England and Count of Savoy, under the tutelage of the provost, Conon d'Estavayer.[33] This is a relationship we should not overlook. Estavayer had been to the university in Paris, and his education of Pierre will have included administration,

Chapter Two

something for which the young Savoyard would later become particularly known. For those in search of the origins of Pierre's talent for administration, both in England and Savoy, the origin would appear to be the University of Paris.[34] Conon d'Estavayer is perhaps best known for his Cartulary of Lausanne which provides a written record begun in 1202 and lasting until 1235 that, apart from providing a unique insight into the construction of Lausanne Cathedral, is the oldest document of record in Savoy. The *Famille d'Estavayer* are also related to the Champvents and Grandsons who by way of Pierre de Savoie would influence English history.

A charter dated 1224, when Pierre had most likely turned 21, marks the entrance of Pierre de Savoie into the written record, bearing witness to an agreement between his father and the Bishop of Sion, Landry de Mont.[35] In November 1226, he is cited as the twentieth of the twenty canons of Bishop Guillaume de Ecublens at Lausanne,[36] the next year as Provost of Aosta without having given up being canon on the other side of the mountain; this is the beginning, in a modest way, of a gathering of titles by which the young Pierre will be later well known.

The original pathway laid for Pierre by his father was to ultimately become himself the Bishop of Lausanne, thus cementing the Savoyard position north of the Léman. The Bishop of Lausanne was both temporal and spiritual authority in Lausanne, a Prince-Bishopric within the Empire since 1011. When Bishop Guillaume died in 1229, the way seemed to open, especially when Pierre became the administrator of the see, but the door closed with the appointment of a new bishop, Boniface de Bruxelles, in 1231.[37] Although only one document survives from his time as administrator of Lausanne, we do know from Conon d'Estavayer that Pierre had held the keys of the episcopal palace by the nearly finished cathedral, allowing admittance to only those of his choosing.[38] So, for the moment, his upward career path was blocked.

Thomas, Count of Savoy, died on the first day of March 1233,[39] whilst laying siege to Moncalieri in the Piedmont and contracting *moult griefve maladie*.[40] For all his success north of the mountains he was singularly unsuccessful in furthering Savoyard lands in Italy. He was laid to rest at the Abbaye Saint-Michel-de-la-Cluse on Mount Pirchiriano at the entrance to the Val di Susa. He would be survived by the Contesse Marguerite de Genève by nearly twenty years: she died in Paris in 1252. Thomas was succeeded as the Count of Savoy by Amédée who became Count Amédée IV from 7 March 1233.[41] The succession of Amédée was not necessarily straightforward, primogeniture not yet being established in the House of Savoy. Guillaume was the key figure in ensuring a succession and "rescuing the family from internecine strife in 1233–35".[42] A vital confirmatory succession conference had been held at Chillon in July 1234 (see figure 1.3) to apportion the lands of Savoy amongst the many sons of Thomas.

So his father having died, it was his influential brother Guillaume who was instrumental in arranging a marriage of much convenience for Pierre – that to Agnès de Faucigny. Betrothal took place at the castle of Châtillon-sur-Cluses in Faucigny in February 1234.[43] His powerful new father-in-law would certainly have been well known to the young Pierre from his time as a member of the Lausanne chapter. The match was advantageous in several ways: first, Agnès was a rich heiress, thus enabling Pierre to abandon entirely his blocked pathway within the Church for a secular career; second, Faucigny had extensive land holdings in the Léman region. Agnès brought with her the rich fertile *seigneuries* of Faucigny and Beaufort, both to the south-east of Geneva, as her dowry. Agnès was the daughter of Aymon II de Faucigny, an erstwhile fief of the County of Geneva; the marriage into the family of a lord without a male heir would bring Faucigny, sandwiched between Savoyard Chablais and the County of

Geneva on the southern shore of Lac Léman, into alliance with the House of Savoy. Agnès would never join her husband on his travels in life, likely preferring the family castle of Châtillon-sur-Cluses in Faucigny. Aymon rewrote his will, ascribing his lands to Agnès should he die without an heir; if he should produce a boy then a dowry would go with Agnès. No male heir was forthcoming.[44] The will links, in its provisions, for the first time, Pierre de Savoie and the *Famille de Grandson*, in the form of Henri de Champvent – the links between the Savoyards and the Grandsons will become fundamental to our story.[45]

We do not know the point at which Pierre de Savoie began to think of renouncing his ecclesiastical career, but the death of Thomas I de Savoie and subsequent marriage formally marked the beginning of a secular path. Having lost his father and seen his elder brother Amédée succeed as Count of Savoy, he was thus freed from his father's wishes for a career in the Church, something not made easier by the recent appointment of a new Bishop of Lausanne. Therefore, the newly married Pierre wasted little time in beginning his conquest of the lands surrounding the lake, beginning with inducing the Lord of Gex (in the foothills of the Jura above Geneva) to became his fief, including the castle at Gex and lands around nearby Divonne.[46] The castle and its land provided access from the west, via the Col de la Faucille, to the north of the Jura. The acquisition of Gex would have far-reaching consequences for England and its monarchy as we shall see much later, but suffice at this point to note its acquisition by Pierre. This move, since the Lord of Gex had been (and technically still was) a fief of the usurper Count Guillaume II de Genève, signalled the opening of hostilities on the part of Pierre against the House of Geneva – from whom Pierre intended to carve out a territory of his own. We should remember at this point that Pierre's maternal family was the comital house of Geneva, therefore the ensuing battles would have the characteristics of a familial civil war as much as any wish on the part of Savoy to acquire Geneva. Guillaume had seized Geneva upon the death of his brother Humbert in 1225 and the sons of Humbert who should have inherited would become allies of Pierre in England. From events that will follow we can be reasonably certain that Pierre was less than approving of his Uncle Guillaume becoming Count of Geneva.

At this point Pierre allied himself with his brother Aymon in seeking a better share of their paternal inheritance from the now Count Amédée IV. Guillaume de Savoie acted as a mediator in the dispute and chaired the aforesaid gathering at Chillon of July 1234. Aymon would receive his appanage, and become Lord of Chablais, that is the lands of the Upper Rhône Valley abutting those of the Bishop of Sion. Boniface, despite a church career, received the castle at Ugine to the south of Lac d'Annecy on the borders of the County of Geneva.[47]

But it was by the charter of 23 July 1234 that Pierre received the Château d'Angeville at Lompnes and the Château de Cornillon at Saint-Rambert (see figure 1.4).[48] In this modest way begins the long association of Pierre de Savoie with castles, at Lompnes (now a nursing home) and at Saint-Rambert-en-Bugey (now in a ruinous state above the town). Both these castles in Bugey guarded approaches to Geneva from Lyon. Pierre had Geneva now surrounded and in his vice-like control. Lompnes sits high on the Plateau de Hauteville, not far from the source of the Albarine, famous for its marble which would later grace the Empire State Building amongst others; the castle dominated the plateau with views for tens of kilometres around. Saint-Rambert-en-Bugey, then Saint-Rambert de Joux, sits deep in the Albarine Valley as it flows westward out of Bugey. In 1196 Thomas had acquired the castle following a request from the abbot of the nearby abbey for protection. The Albarine Valley had long been an invasion route, both into and out of the Lemanic region. Indeed, the valley had also been the scene of the kidnap of Marguerite de Genève by Thomas I de Savoie and so it was oddly appropriate that Pierre now gained the associated

Chapter Two

fiefs. Furthermore, Bugey had been the first expansion of territory undertaken by Thomas, so the grant to Pierre was thus notable.[49] So, Faucigny, Beaufort, Gex, Saint-Rambert and Lompnes, the little Charlemagne was making a beginning in the secular world. Bugey represented the cork in the Genevois bottle, since it blocked or controlled access to the city from Lyon and the west – Savoyard domain in Bugey represented a direct threat to Geneva.

Indeed, conversely, the House of Geneva represented the primary challenge to Savoyard authority since it initially controlled the bishoprics of both Geneva and Lausanne, albeit this authority was being increasingly challenged by a Church attempting to reinstate its independence in light of the conflict between Pope and emperor. The revival of episcopal independence weakened the House of Geneva, therefore further encouraging Pierre. As we saw earlier, a little of the recent past of the House of Geneva will perhaps explain some of the enmity between Pierre and Geneva that now begins to boil over, so to speak. We met Guillaume I de Genève earlier, as the father of the kidnapped Marguerite de Genève and so Pierre's maternal grandfather. Guillaume de Genève had married Béatrice de Faucigny, and their daughter was aforesaid Marguerite, and so Pierre could trace his lineage to both Geneva and Faucigny. Guillaume I had two sons, Humbert and Guillaume. Humbert duly succeeded his father, but when Humbert died in 1225 the succession did not pass to either of his sons, Pierre or Ebal (whom we shall meet later in England) but to Guillaume II – he had usurped the comital throne. What's more, Aymon de Faucigny, Pierre's new father-in-law had been in a state of much enmity with Geneva for some time. The signal for the conflict appears to have been Aymon making himself the protector of the priory at Chamonix, disregarding the previous rights there of the Count of Geneva.[50] So we have a usurper in Geneva and a father-in-law harbouring a grudge. The writer of the *Chronique de Savoie* gives us an apocryphal story, but one that, given its colour is worth repeating. Later in life when asked to explain the enmity between himself and the Count of Geneva by his niece Alianor, Pierre replied:

> à l'epoque où nous étions enfants, le comte de Genève et moi, nous avians l'habitude de jouer aux échecs; une fois, pour rire, je lui donnai un coup de poing au visage et lui répliqua alors en me frappant sur la tête avec l'échiquier; depuis jour-là, nous ne nous sommes guère aimés.[51]

> When we were children, the Count of Geneva and I used to play chess; once, for fun, I punched him in the face and then he replied by hitting me on the head with the chessboard, since that day we have not loved each other much.

The chronicler may not give us the politics of the enmity, but he does give us a more colourful, and perhaps, who knows, a truthful origin for the quarrel of the cousins.

Of the war that followed nothing has survived in the way of history, save for the terms of the peace (more a truce) of 1237 that followed it. We know that in the end the Savoyard seems to have had the better of things and bested the Count of Geneva. Count Amédée IV was able to extract land and money (20,000 silver marks) from the declining power by the lake – also adding the strategic fortress of Arlod by the Rhône.[52] But one event that does seem to have occurred interests us in this story of the life of Pierre de Savoie. Apparently, Raoul, the son of Guillaume de Genève, and a man described as most "quarrelsome", ambushed Pierre, much in the same way an earlier ambush had been staged by Thomas de Savoie. The mountain passes and deep valleys of the Trans Jura and Savoie clearly lend themselves to ambush. But in this case, it was not a fair damsel who was taken but the young Pierre de Savoie and, it seems, this time there had been a fight, and Pierre was injured. Wurstemberger talks of him being "beaten, wounded and thrown into a dungeon".[53] An accomplice of Raoul de Genève was Rudolphe de Rue, and subsequent events might suggest the Château de Rue as a place of imprisonment. Jean-Daniel Morerod writes that

> an ambush ... was laid for Pierre, during a truce, by Rodolphe de Rue, lord vassal of the counts of Geneva, and by Raoul de Genève, son of Count Guillaume. Pierre lost men and was held prisoner at the Château de Rue. A coalition – his brothers Amédée and Thomas, his father-in-law Aymon [de Faucigny], the lords of Chalon and Kibourg – was then formed and besieged Rue twice. The kidnappers were defeated, the castle destroyed.[54]

The castle would be rebuilt at Rue and come to Pierre a decade later. He would install as his castellan one Henri de Bonvillars, the father of the future constable of Harlech Castle, Deputy Justiciar of North Wales, Jean de Bonvillars. That Pierre was ambushed and imprisoned by Rudolphe de Rue would seem to indicate that the conflict was not confined to the environs of Geneva, the Pays de Gex or Bugey but encompassed the *Pays de Vaud* also. In any case a peace was signed on 13 May 1237, by which point, from the terms of the treaty, the Genevois had clearly lost.[55]

The previous year, 1236, Aymon de Savoie had decided to found a hospice at the head of Lac Léman, at what would become Villeneuve. Accordingly, he called for a reunion of the brothers and their widowed mother Marguerite de Genève at the Château de Chillon. The castle by the lake had become his favoured residence as Lord of Chablais since the family meeting of 1234. The family rendezvous of 1236 would be the last at which the seven surviving sons[56] and their mother were all present. Aymon would die, it is rumoured of leprosy, leaving no heir, in the summer of 1237.[57]

The truce between the Genevois and Savoyards would last through 1238. As we shall see later there were distractions in Italy that drew the Savoyards away, but in the summer of 1239 the See of Lausanne became vacant once more with the resignation of Bishop Boniface. Back in 1234, just before the recent unpleasantness with Pierre, Guillaume de Genève had managed to get the other of his sons, Amédée, installed as a canon of Lausanne. Pierre, meanwhile, saw the opportunity of a Savoyard Bishop of Lausanne, in his younger brother Philippe, the Dean of Metz Cathedral.[58] Having himself been thwarted in his own ambitions in Lausanne, an opportunity for family advancement had presented itself. So now the Genevois–Savoyard struggle would continue in a proxy war for the See of Lausanne.

Lausanne, then as now, was split into two parts: the *Cité* and the *Bourg* – the *Cité* sat atop the highest hill centring upon the towering cathedral and the accompanying Bishop's Palace, the *Bourg* a minor hill to the west containing the commercial market elements of the town. The fast-flowing Flon and Louve rivers came either side of the *Cité* to a confluence before continuing onward to Lac Léman. The *Cité* could be reasonably approached from one direction only, that by the Gate of Saint Maire from the north, the other three elevations of the hill being increasingly precipitate, especially the southern beneath the palace which took the form of a rocky cliff. Likewise, the Chapter of Lausanne was split into two parts: the pro- and anti-Savoyard factions. The anti-Savoyard faction, backed by the Count of Geneva, was principally made up of local nobility who feared the growing power of the House of Savoy –

Chapter Two

coalescing around Amédée de Genève were Guillaume de Gruyères and the precentor of the chapter, Jean de Cossonay; meanwhile, the leader of the pro-Savoyard party was Conon d'Estavayer. It is from Conon d'Estavayer that we have the only eyewitness accounts of events; however, his record in the Lausanne Cartulaire is fragmentary and frustratingly vague. During his time with Pope Gregory IX, the resigning Bishop Boniface had warned the Pope that the succession may well be difficult, and so it proved.

On 18 July 1239 the Pope offered the bishops Besançon and Langres as arbiters, should the chapter not be able to choose a successor to Boniface. The canons of the chapter argued, the anti-Savoyard for Jean de Cossonay, the pro-Savoyard for Philippe de Savoie. Neither party was able to get the required two-thirds of votes to be elected bishop – the three months allotted to the election passed with deadlock. Thus, the appointment transferred to the papally authorised bishops of Besançon and Langres – Geoffroi and Robert. The bishops set the twentieth day after Christmas 1239 and either Besançon or Dole as the venue for the election.

No such election took place, because events moved more quickly: the pro-Savoyard party unilaterally declared Philippe de Savoie as Bishop of Lausanne. They announced the decision to the bishops and sent a messenger with the news to the Pope. In the meantime, however, the anti-Savoyard faction had gained the bishops' approval for their choice Jean de Cossonay, and so he was solemnly also elected Bishop of Lausanne. Now of course, there couldn't be two bishops, so Lausanne was set upon a collision course for war.

Jean de Cossonay exploited the fear of an overbearing House of Savoy, wielding the military, judicial and administrative power of the bishopric. Accordingly, the merchants of the *Bourg* favoured Cossonay. On 20 April 1240 the supporters of Cossonay arrived at nearby Pully to attempt to negotiate their way into the *Cité* by peaceful means. The attempt failed, so Cossonay occupied the *Bourg* as it was friendly to him, and laid siege to the *Cité* occupied by Pierre's father-in-law, Aymon de Faucigny.

Within a short time Aymon had "*fecit dirui domos prope muros*", that is, demolished buildings beneath his walls opposite the *Bourg* to aid his defence of the *Cité*. In retaliation those of the town "*molendina ciuitatis*", that is, the mills outside the *Cité* were set afire. The *Bourg* sat immediately to the south and west of the *Cité* and many of the mills sat by the Flon River to the east, so we can imagine that the *Cité* was more or less besieged. Pierre de Savoie then entered the fray with no less than 6,000 men; soldiers came from Moudon, which he'd recently acquired from his brother Aymon, his own fief of Romont, and as far away as Bern and Morat (we are not sure on which side the latter fought). As the siege got under way, mangonels and likely trebuchets too – the heavy artillery of medieval warfare – were constructed and the air was soon thick with flying missiles of heavy rock – this to decide who should be bishop![59] Conon d'Estavayer, writing of the ensuing battle, recounts "the attacks, the fires, the damage which was caused by both sides can hardly be described."[60] The account in the *Cartulaire* is a little loose, but it would seem the attack on the *Cité* atop its hill came from the north by way of the Gate of Saint Marie (not to be confused with the Blessed Mary after whom the cathedral takes its name).[61] Estavayer talks of projectiles being thrown to and fro from the monastery, likely the Dominican house of Mary Magdalene or "*beate Marie*" of 1234 that once stood where today where we find the Place de la Riponne and Place de la Madeleine. Apparently, around thirty people were killed and 300 wounded determining the episcopal succession.[62] The attack on the *Cité* was repulsed and since no outcome could be forced, a truce was agreed.[63] Cossonay, not taking any chances, refortified himself within the episcopal castle of Saint Maire.[64]

The Pope then took matters into his own hands and removed authority from the bishops of Besançon and Langres and gave it to the prior of Ainay and the sacristan of St. Paul de Lyon, along with a letter that said that the "*major et senior pars*" of the Chapter of Lausanne had in fact chosen Philippe de Savoie "our beloved son ... the Dean of Metz, a noble, prudent and upright man", whereas the "*minor et inferior pars*" had chosen Jean de Cossonay "in a place exceedingly suspect".[65] All seemed up for Jean de Cossonay and those wanting to resist Savoyard encroachment.

However, for reasons lost to us, the papal letter and its Savoyard preference seems to have been disregarded, leaving Jean de Cossonay as Bishop of Lausanne and the House of Savoy thwarted for the moment in their ambitions. American historian of Savoy, Cox, whose own account comes from Conon d'Estavayer and the Cartulaire of Lausanne, suggests correctly that the explanation for the House of Savoy not pressing its claim is that "the Savoyards were distracted by other developments in 1240 and that they had found other means of achieving their objectives".[66] Instead of Lausanne, Philippe would follow his brother Guillaume as Dean of Vienne before becoming Bishop of Valence in 1241, and Pierre as we shall shortly see was bound for a career in England. Even as Pierre was marching toward Lausanne that spring and summer of 1240, away in London, he was being granted the Honour of Richmond. In the meantime, Lausanne would, for now, remain a block to Savoyard expansion in the *Pays de Vaud*.

The Lausanne setback notwithstanding, with the acquisition of Moudon from his ailing brother Aymon (he would die of leprosy in 1242) and his own fief of Romont, Pierre began the conquest of what is now the French-speaking portion of Switzerland; indeed, it is widely believed that it is thanks to Pierre that the modern-day inhabitants of the region speak French and not German. Unlike his previous acquisitions in the hinterland of Geneva, the new fiefdoms – Moudon, on the road from Lausanne north to Avenches, and the former episcopal land at Romont (see figure 1.5), not far to the north-east, sitting atop a wooded hillside commanding the way to Fribourg and Bern – established a foothold in the *Pays de Vaud*. Moudon, once a fief of the Counts of Geneva, would become the centre of Savoyard Vaud for centuries to come. Although some of the conquest of Vaud, which he was to have attributed to him, was that of his father Thomas, such as Moudon itself, the epithet "*Petit Charlemagne*" is one that became firmly attached to him. Previté-Orton concluded that the Savoyard expansion into Vaud ultimately prevented French expansion into the French-speaking region of Switzerland and thus helped to create the multilingual state that is today Switzerland[67] – if inadvertently, this can be seen as Pierre de Savoie's most significant legacy in the modem world.[68]

Nonetheless, the failure to acquire the See of Lausanne was seen as a setback, but we should also see that at this time other more lucrative opportunities for advancement presented themselves to both Pierre and Philippe in more distant lands. For Philippe this would be in the sunnier climes of the Lyonnais and for Pierre his eyes turned toward the distant shores of England. To explain how and why this might be we will have to backtrack the story a little and concern ourselves with his niece Alianor de Provence and his brother Guillaume.

Chapter Three

In England, King Henry III, named for his illustrious grandfather Henry II, had been crowned in Gloucester in October 1216 amidst the wreckage of the kingdom left to him by his unlamented father, John. Henry had come to the throne at the tender age of but 9 years, meaning that a regent had been running the kingdom; first that man would be the redoubtable knight William Marshal, 1st Earl of Pembroke until his death in 1219. Thereafter several figures dominated the realm, first Hubert de Burgh as Justiciar and then Bishop Pierre des Roches; both had been servants of his late father. Roches was born in Touraine and was Archdeacon of Poitiers before becoming Bishop of Winchester and Lord Chamberlain of England; he would become a key influence in the young Henry's life. In light of what would come later, that Pierre des Roches was a Frenchman more loyal to the dynasty than to England might not come as a total surprise; it is a pattern that would repeat itself.[1] Meanwhile, across the Channel the younger King of France, the future Saint Louis, had been crowned in Reims ten years later in November 1226. In the way of the tangled relationship between the Plantagenet family ruling England and the Capetians ruling France they were both branches of the same tree, King Henry II of England being both grandfather to Henry and great grandfather to Louis.[2] Soon the two would also become brothers-in-law.

We described earlier how Thomas I de Savoie had sought an alliance with Provence, the most southerly remnant of the Second Kingdom of Burgundy, as he looked for allies in his struggles with the County of Albon, the Dauphiné between them. Pierre's younger sister, Béatrice, had been married to Count Ramon Berenguer V de Provence and the couple had been blessed with four beautiful daughters, Marguerite, Alianor, Sanchia and Béatrice. Such beauty and the attractiveness of an alliance with both Provence and Savoy made the young girls some of Christendom's most desirable matches.

First, the Provençal daughters came to the attention of the French royal court, and it is they who would have first pick of the daughters, as an unknown Reims chronicler of 1260 would write: "Now will we ... tell you of the King of France, who was now twenty years of age. And the Queen had a mind that he should marry ... so he took to wife the eldest of the daughters of the Count of Provence, of whom there were four."[3] The King of France would be Louis IX, the mother would be Blanche de Castille and the daughter Marguerite de Provence. The marriage took place at Sens on 27 May 1234, but it would not be Ramon Berenguer V, Count of Provence giving Marguerite away, it would be her uncle, Guillaume de Savoie, Bishop of Valance.[4] Accompanying Guillaume to Sens was his brother Thomas, who like Pierre had also recently given up on a church career, having been a canon at Lausanne and Lyon, and provost of Valence. There he was encouraged, by either Louis or perhaps more likely Blanche, to marry the eligible Countess of Flanders and Hainaut, Jeanne. Intriguingly Jeanne had the young Simon de Montfort in mind as a match. It's worth pondering how this story and indeed the history of England might have differed if Simon de Montfort had indeed become the Count of Flanders and Hainaut.[5] Indeed, Jeanne was not the first lady at which the young Montfort had set his cap, having earlier pursued the Countess of Boulogne.[6] Blanche has been described as "the mother-in-law from hell" and wasn't about to have the new queen's Savoyard uncles at court, so the brothers' attempts to ingratiate themselves in Paris failed, Guillaume to return to Valence and Thomas to be deflected to Flanders. His installation there as Count of Flanders by marriage would, however, place him directly in a position of influence in English affairs, since Flanders and England were engaged in a mutually advantageous relationship centred upon England growing the sheep for wool that would feed Flanders' thriving tapestry business.

But returning to the marriage of Louis and Marguerite, the alliance between the Kingdom of France and a county nominally belonging to the Empire to the south of France would foreshadow and further French territorial expansion toward the Mediterranean at the expense of imperial Holy Roman lands. The Capetian monarchy accepted as part payment of the dowry the important fortress of Tarascon, thus encroaching upon the imperial side of the Rhône.[7] Marguerite would be the first of the nieces of the *Maison de Savoie* to become a queen; she would not be the last, and the French court would not be the last to see Savoyard uncles in search of a career.

We must see what happens next in terms of how the Plantagenet ruling family of England saw its rivalry with the Capetian ruling family of France, for it is the prism through which we must look to see England's actions toward France.[8] King Philippe Auguste of France had stripped King John and the succeeding Plantagenet family of most of their French possessions earlier in the century and much of England's King Henry III's actions on the European continent had recovery of these ancestral lands as an ultimate goal.[9] Matthew Paris described Henry's recovery of Poitou as being the subject of "the irrevocable determination of his heart."[10] Poitou had been a part of the Duchy of Aquitaine, of which his grandmother Alianor d'Aquitaine had been heiress. The Angoulême of his mother had also been a vassal county of the Duchy of Aquitaine. What's more, Anjou had been the birthplace and fief of his grandfather Henry, and Normandy of his great-grandmother Mathilde. Henry and his family were heirs to Poitou, Anjou and Normandy and wanted it back from what they saw as the usurpers from the Capetian family.

Henry still held a part of Aquitaine, Gascony in south-west France; French territorial expansion southward could be thwarted much in the same way as one might move chess pieces on a board, Blanche and France had moved to take the Provençal leading lady, and blocked his earlier attempts to marry Jeanne de Ponthieu, so Henry and England might move to counter that move by taking another Provençal daughter.[11] Björn Weiler rightly sees Henry's interest in Provence as a consequence of his attempts at a "reconquest of Poitou and Normandy".[12] The negotiations began in June 1235, with the Count of Provence, but also with the uncles of the bride, Amédée and Guillaume de Savoie.[13] Henry reminded them that earlier his father John had been betrothed to a lady of the House of Savoy, Alais daughter of Humbert III in 1173, now was a time to begin the alliance of England and Savoy a new. Henry wrote:

> which induces us to enter into a league of friendship between us and you, just as there has always been a mutual affection between our predecessors and yours, we will pursue your sincerity with pious thanksgiving; desiring, as much as is in us, that a friendship long ago contracted between our ancestors would not fail in our time, but would rather accept an increase.[14]

Chapter Three

We also saw that a letter from 1220 promised English benefices to Thomas I de Savoie for his son, and that from 1226 that son would be Guillaume. We should also then note that the contracting Savoyard brothers were Amédée as Count, but also Guillaume, a reminder that at this stage Pierre was not involved in matters of family strategy. So, the broad picture was that Henry's marriage would be a fulfilment in 1235 of a closer relationship between the Plantagenets and the Savoyards that had been developing for some time. By 10 October, Henry sent two envoys to Provence, Richard le Gras, the Abbot of Evesham and later Keeper of the Great Seal, along with John de Gatesden.[15]

Blanche and France perhaps considered Provence (and Savoy) as far enough away from Plantagenet lands not to be a threat – and both counties lay within the Holy Roman Empire, and not within the Kingdom of France, well at least not yet. No, at this point both Provence and Savoy remained with the Empire; it would be the Emperor Frederick II that had dubbed Ramon Berenguer a knight, the ruling families of France and England considering it beneath them to marry the daughters of a man not yet a knight – but the knighting confirms imperial suzerainty of Provence in 1235.[16] Henry had also acted, in 1235, to marry his sister Isabelle to the much-excommunicated Holy Roman Emperor Frederick II to pursue an Anglo-Imperial alliance so much dreaded by generations of the French. The marriage to Alianor would also be looked upon favourably by the Emperor, the Count of Provence's suzerain who might equally fear the Kingdom of France moving toward the Alpine passes that linked his northern and southern lands. Despite losses of territory further north, the Plantagenet dynasty still held extensive lands in the south of Aquitaine and in Gascony; a marriage to the House of Provence and links to the House of Savoy would strengthen Henry's position to the south of the Capetians – a southern alliance. So in the medieval game of power chess the next move would be that of English King Henry III for the next daughter in line, Alianor de Provence.[17]

Matthew Paris described the young Alianor as *"Decoris Expectabilis"*[18] and of the anticipated arrival of beauty and *"speciei venustissimae"*[19] or "species of beauty" – in short, graceful, charming and elegant.[20] In the same passage Paris described Guillaume de Savoie as being *"viri praeclari et elegantis"*, which Giles translated as "a man of distinction", but perhaps we should take Paris at his word and more descriptively "a distinguished and elegant man".[21]

Paris described the nuptial negotiations:

> Anno Domini 1236, which was the twentieth year of the reign of King Henry the Third, he held his court at Winchester at Christmas, where he observed that festival with rejoicings. He was at this time anxiously looking for the return of special messengers, whom he had sent into Provence to Ramon, count of that province, with letters containing his inmost thoughts about contracting marriage with his daughter Eleanor. This said count was a man of illustrious race and brave in battle ... He had married the daughter of Thomas, the late Count of Savoy, and sister of the present count, Amédée, a woman of remarkable beauty, by name Béatrice. This lady had issue by the aforesaid count, two daughters of great beauty, the elder of whom, named Margaret, was married to Louis, the French king ... and the King of England had now, by the aforesaid messengers, demanded the younger one, a young lady of handsome appearance in marriage ... These messengers were received by the count on their arrival in Provence with the greatest honour and respect, and

from his hands received his daughter Eleanor for the purpose of being united to the King of England; she was also attended by her uncle, William, bishop of Valentia, a man of distinction, and by the count of Champagne, a relation of the English king.[22]

After some negotiation the dower was set at 10,000 marks, the same sum as had been agreed for her sister Marguerite, and with that, as we saw Alianor set off for a new life as the Queen of England, accompanied by her uncle, Guillaume de Savoie and her personal maid, the Lady Guillelma de Attelis.[23] Her father, Count Ramon, accompanied her by way of Vienne, as far as Champagne, where they'd been entertained by Theobald IV "The Troubadour", who'd also recently become the King of Navarre, before returning to Provence. Whether Theobald treated the Savoyard party to a song or poem is not known; neither do we know of the certainty behind the rumours that he'd had an affair with Blanche de Castille behind the back of Louis VIII – a colourful man Theobald. Illustrating the web of intermarriage in thirteenth-century Europe, Alianor, on her way to England, was of course the niece of Guillaume and Pierre de Savoie. Her host in Champagne, Theobald, had a daughter, Blanche, who'd also be married in 1236, to Jean I de Bretagne. The ruling house of Brittany had only recently had its lands in England, the Honour of Richmond, confiscated and would continue to contest them with first Theobald's guest, Alianor's uncle, Guillaume de Savoie and then his brother Pierre. But that would be for the future; for the meantime the Count of Champagne, King of Navarre, escorted them to the French border whence they were conducted to the French coast, at Wissant, by King Louis IX himself, along with his mother Blanche de Castille and of course Alianor's sister Marguerite.[24] With the safe conduct of the party across France, the royal accompaniment tell us that Blanche was happy that Henry in England had found a bride other than the potentially dangerous match, as she saw it, of Jeanne de Ponthieu. The French were in effect giving their blessing to the marriage, perhaps a hope for a Savoyard-brokered thawing of Anglo-French relations? Not yet, but perhaps in the future.

And so was Alianor de Provence married to King Henry III of England amid great fanfare and pageantry. "*Henricus Rex Anglie duxit in uxorem filiam comitis Provincie nomine Alienoram.*"[25]

Alianor's uncle, Guillaume de Savoie, had also been, according to Matthew Paris, attending upon his sister Béatrice at the point of her daughter's betrothal to King Henry III of England – more than that he'd been a guiding influence in favour of the match.[26] Letters from Henry attest to Guillaume being the prime mover in the marriage. Guillaume escorted her along with a retinue of 300 horsemen through France, by way of his cathedral at Vienne.[27] The terms of the marriage contact itself had been confirmed at his cathedral above the Rhône at Vienne. Once the Savoyard had reached London, and within a mere four months of his arrival, he became so influential that he soon led King Henry's council.[28] Historian N. Denholm-Young described him as "virtually Prime Minister".[29] The expression "*per electum Valentinium*" found its way to the end of many instruments of royal patronage.[30] Henry had been in want of a chief advisor since the demise of Pierre des Roches a few years earlier. Perhaps Henry had been impressed by the way he'd secured autonomy within the empire for Valence and his financial acumen in improving its finances, the latter something he'd always be in need of. He would be the first of what would become a veritable flood of Savoyards crossing the Channel. Paris is critical of Guillaume and the way, through him and his niece Alianor, the Savoyard came to influence the English court. Some might even go so far to accuse the St. Albans monk

Chapter Three

of xenophobia – Paris would later charge Guillaume of directing his steps toward Dover with the "packsaddles of his beasts of burden full of gold, silver, and divers royal presents".[31] One of the "divers royal presents" falling into the hands of the Savoyard would be the lands previously held by Henry's former ally, the Count of Brittany,[32] the Honour of Richmond, granted on 22 August 1236.[33] The latter was a tremendous decoration for someone so new to the country, and Guillaume would not be the last of his brothers to hold it; we will go further into its bounteous rewards when it would be later held by his brother Pierre. However, one is bound to agree with Cox: we must view the St. Albans monk's "malicious insinuations" as to Guillaume's character as that of a partial witness.[34] In the chronicle entry blackening Guillaume, Paris also goes on to wail against the wider influence of "foreigners – Poitevins, Germans, Provençals, and Romans".[35] Certainly, when electing him Bishop of Valence, the electorate there thought highly of him, with only one dissenting voice. Certainly, King Henry III of England thought highly of him, despite Matthew Paris's protestations and accusations of seizing illegitimate power and influence, to bestow upon Guillaume an annual income estimated to be £1,200 which would be more than £750,000 in today's money.[36]

Indeed, Matthew Paris has long been considered a partial witness when it comes to the foreign influences upon the English court. Swiss historian Chapuisat offers an explanation for his *"traces d'un nationalisme naissant"*, suggesting that Paris, a Benedictine monk, may well have held a deep prejudice against those connected with other religious orders, specifically in the case of the Savoyard who had Franciscan connections – that is, he explains his xenophobia in terms of religious rivalry long past.[37] The late twelfth century had seen the rise of the Franciscans set against a decline of the Benedictines, something that would also see the breakaway of the Cistercians. Indeed, in his *The Life of St. Edmund* (late Archbishop of Canterbury) Paris wrote, "Had [Edmund] been a real saint, he would not have cared to be buried in a Cistercian house. Almost all the glorious saints lie in houses of Black Monks, few or none in Cistercian ones," with Paris exhibiting the prejudice Chapuisat speaks of.[38] Henry had actually confessed shame to Amedée in Savoy for attacks on foreign clerks, so the views expressed by Paris might be seen as not unusual at this time.[39] Indeed, the fall of Henry's onetime tutor, Bishop Pierre des Roches, in 1234 was in no small way due to him being a Poitevin.

Historian Baker characterises the traditional view of Guillaume de Savoie, describing him as a "glorified parasite" before acknowledging him as "handsome, urbane and worldly wise". He goes on to give his explanation for King Henry's interest in Guillaume, that he needed someone to "reform his financial administration" and his attributes as "newness to the land", by which he meant a lack of any attachment and therefore loyalty to a baronage Henry distrusted.[40] In late 1236, Guillaume was instrumental in Henry calling a great council of the knights, barons, magnates and burgesses of the realm. They met in early 1237, a council given the name *parliamentum generalissimum*, the first time the name parliament had been used in this connection – importantly the Savoyards were in at the very birth of what would eventually become English democracy. Henry reconfirmed that other foundation of English liberty, the *Magna Carta*,[41] all this Guillaume had crafted in return for something Henry wanted and needed, a tax of a thirtieth on movables. The connection between the *Magna Carta* and the foundation of Parliament stems from the clause in the charter that insisted that kings could only raise taxation with the common consent of the kingdom, hence the reconfirmed charter and the resulting grant of taxation. Guillaume de Savoie had helped raise some £22,500 for Henry – this helps to explain his sudden rise in England, and why

Henry became so enamoured of Alianor's uncles – the same administrative and diplomatic competence that had once been applied to the See of Valence was now deployed on the far wider stage of the Kingdom of England.[42]

Henry's distrust of the English barony and favour of foreigners like Guillaume would mark his reign and to some extent that of his successor, Edward. The English barony had after all made war on his father, John, extracting the *Magna Carta*[43] from him and then encouraged his father's dispossession in favour of the son of the French king – hardly actions that would breed a feeling of trust and loyalty within Henry. Later in Henry's reign, this disloyalty on the part of the barons would spill over once more into open rebellion.

Along with Guillaume came a clerk and steward, Pierre d'Aigueblanche, from the small village, lying in the narrow Tarentaise Valley that runs from the Petit-Saint-Bernard Pass to Chambéry, near Moûtiers.[44] He was of the *Famille de Briançon*,[45] Lords of Aigueblanche, perhaps a younger brother[46] since the Church was the traditional path for those unlikely to inherit. He had come to prominence in Savoy under Archbishop Herluin of Tarentaise before working for the comital family and in particular Guillaume. Pierre was Guillaume's treasurer,[47] who then served as Keeper of Henry's Privy Wardrobe, and had been made an Archdeacon of Shropshire,[48] before being elected Bishop of Hereford on 24 August 1240[49] and consecrated there later that year on 23 December at St. Paul's Cathedral by Archbishop of York, Walter de Gray.[50] The ceremony in London was conducted in the presence of the Papal Legate, Otto di Tonengo, whose own origins lay in the Piedmontese Marquisate of Montferrat, whose ruling house were closely related to and allies of the Savoyard comital family – these connections remind us of the political advantages to Rome of the Anglo-Savoyard relationship.

Like Guillaume, Pierre d'Aigueblanche, or Peter as he would be known to the English, became another Savoyard favourite of Henry. At one point the king attempted to move him to the richer See of Durham, but this venture failed. Amongst Pierre's first acts in England was an involvement in the 1241 Treaty of Gwerneigron with Gwynedd, perhaps the first Savoyard involvement in Welsh affairs – it would not be the last. Building upon papal connections, Pierre would become a key diplomat working for Henry in later years, including the Sicilian affair and the marriage negotiations of his brother and children.[51] Though, as you might imagine, Matthew Paris was not a fan, suggesting that he "exudes a sulphurous stench".[52] More recently, church historian W. N. Yates was more generous, ascribing to him an "extraordinary ability".[53]

That he maintained amicable relations with the cathedral chapter in Hereford is perhaps unsurprising since he packed it with so many Savoyards: twenty in total, including his nephews: Jean, dean from 1262, Jacques, a keeper of Queen Alianor's wardrobe, Aymon, precentor by 1268, and Aimeric, chancellor by 1268.[54] Aigueblanche would attract much criticism in his diplomatic role for Henry, but he would be better known perhaps in Hereford for his tenure there, overhauling the cathedral's liturgy and establishing its first statutes[55] – administration is something it seems at which the Savoyards excelled. Savoyards not only dominated his chapter, but his household too. Excellent research by Julia Barrow has shed light on lower levels of Savoyard migration hitherto unrecorded in England; she noted from the family names of his household that eighteen appear to have been Savoyards, from senior clerks to kitchen staff.[56] Barrow gives us the name of one of the senior clerks, the bishop's official, Pierre de Sollières, who'd originated in the Maurienne Valley, a place named for a "sunny place" – one hopes he found Herefordshire equally sunny. One of his tasks concerned Englishmen of the locale who'd not been to church within the prescribed forty

Chapter Three

days, something that will no doubt have made him popular. Chapuisat adds the name of Aigueblanche's physician, Maître Jean Cantorin, who appears in several documents before likely returning to Savoy following the passing of his master.[57]

But along with the nephews of the Bishop of Hereford, and his attendants, came noblemen from Savoy in search of a church career in England, men whose advance in England would also cement Pierre's position in Savoy. A long-term lieutenant of Aigueblanche would be Pierre d'Ugine, who was entrusted with negotiations upon the bishop's behalf. Evidence of Ugine being sustained by income from nearby Dore Abbey dates his English endeavours to at least before 1247.[58] Ugine itself, on the road from Annecy to Conflans, was since 1234 a fief of Pierre's brother, Boniface de Savoie. Yates gave us the name of a Savoyard chapter member at Hereford in the service of Aigueblanche, Guillaume de Gruyères. Guillaume's presence in Herefordshire is undoubtedly related to Gruyère becoming a fief of Pierre de Savoie in 1244. An archdeacon at Hereford from 1255 would be the Savoyard Guillaume de Conflans, who would, from 1287, rise to become the Bishop of Geneva. Conflans was a fortified town at the entrance to the Tarentaise, which today lies high above the commune of Albertville.[59] Guillaume de Conflans was of the noble Duin or Duyn family that had made its base in the Châtel de Conflans which held a strategic position in the Tarentaise. His introduction to a thirty-year church career in England which led eventually to the See of Geneva, has been rightly attributed to Pierre de Savoie. Dean of Hereford under Pierre d'Aigueblanche would be Anthelme de Clermont of the noble *Famille de Clermont* which had originated in the tiny village of Clermont in the Viennois, now attached to the commune of Chirens. The lords of Clermont's castle and lands lay just to the north of Voiron where Jacques de Saint-Georges would later build a castle for Philippe de Savoie. We can see in the career of Clermont, the hand of Pierre de Savoie once more, to ally the Lords of Clermont with Savoy in their expansion into the Viennois. In 1262 Anthelme de Clermont would be rewarded with the key Savoyard bishopric of Maurienne, which he held until his death in 1269. As his mentor, Pierre d'Aigueblanche had been responsible for the statutes at Hereford, so Anthelme de Clermont would be responsible for the statutes at Maurienne in 1267. Remarkably, the Chapter of Hereford Cathedral would provide a second Bishop of Maurienne when Aymon de Miolans, a former chapter member in Herefordshire, was also elected bishop in Maurienne in 1273.

Along with Conflans and Anthelme de Clermont, Guillaume de Champvent and Girard de Vuippens would also find a church career in England a stepping stone to a bishopric in Savoy. Gruyères, Conflans and Clermont give us significant examples of Pierre de Savoie's coming position in England aiding the acquisition or consolidation of allies in Savoy. Again, we see that we cannot view Pierre's career in England and Savoy in isolation: one begat the other. Other than the names of Pierre de Savoie's stewards in England, also Savoyards, we don't know of his attendants, but given what we know of what would become the household of Alianor and Pierre d'Aigueblanche, it's more than likely too that Richmond, Pevensey and the house in London were also populated at least in part by men and women from the Alps.

Swiss historian Chapuisat gave us a revealing picture of the Savoyard Chapter of Hereford Cathedral as it had been in 1255:[60]

Dean	Anthelme de Clermont
Archdeacon of Hereford	Guillaume de Conflans
Archdeacon of Shropshire	Jacques d'Aigueblanche
Precentor of Hereford	Aimeric d'Aigueblanche

Peter of Savoy: The Little Charlemagne

If we imagine the Second Baronial War might have purged the Savoyard presence in Herefordshire and that the death of Bishop Pierre d'Aigueblanche and the new reign of Edward brought change then alas no, Chapuisat gave a breakdown for 1275:[61]

Dean	Jean d'Aigueblanche
Archdeacon of Hereford	Guillaume de Conflans
Archdeacon of Shropshire	Jacques d'Aigueblanche
Chancellor	Aimeric d'Aigueblanche

The Savoyard presence in Hereford would be resilient and long-lasting; its survival of the traumas to be recounted later in Henry's reign into that of his son, Edward, will be a theme we shall return to. (For a full list of the Savoyards at Hereford see appendix.)

Meanwhile, returning to Henry's earlier reign, accompanying Alianor to England and serving in the role of one of the young queen's ladies was Willelma d'Attelens, along with her daughter Isabel.[62] Savoyard Attalens in the Veveyse district above Vevey and Lac Léman had been home to its castle since the twelfth century – that Willelma would find her way to England with the young queen from Provence as a *dame d'honneur* tells us something of the reach of the House of Savoy into the comital court of Provence and a reminder that young Alianor was as much Savoyard as Provençal. Willelma d'Attelens would remain long in Alianor's service; indeed, Isabel's brother Pierre d'Oron would soon be one of the Savoyards receiving royal favour for "his constant, faithful and devoted service to the queen".[63]

Henry and Alianor had been married by proxy at the castle of Tarascon in Provence, on 23 November 1235.[64] As we saw, her uncle, Guillaume de Savoie, Bishop of Valence had led her party to England, and on 15 December they had reached his Romanesque cathedral at Vienne where the terms of contract of marriage were confirmed before they travelled on to England. The party made the difficult winter crossing of the Channel, landing at Dover. We should remember for little Alianor, she was arriving in a strange country, known mostly to her through the popular Arthurian legend, to marry a man born the same year as her Uncle Philippe. They made their way to ancient Canterbury, there on 14 January 1236, to be married by Archbishop Edmund Rich.

Alianor was crowned amid much pomp and circumstance at Westminster Abbey five days later. This would not be the Westminster Abbey we know today; that was very much the work of her new husband Henry, The ceremony would have been in the old Confessor's church as Henry III did not start his rebuilding of the Abbey until 1245. Edward's church had become known as the West Minster to distinguish it from St. Paul's in the city itself. Alianor would have processed between the rounded Romanesque arches of the Confessor before being crowned beneath the tower astride the transept. England had once more a King Henry and a Queen Eleanor on the throne. Contemporary chronicler, the Benedictine St. Albans monk Matthew Paris, relates the story in his *History of England*:

> There were assembled at the king's nuptial festivities such a host of nobles of both sexes, such numbers of religious men, such crowds of the populace, and such a variety of actors, that London, with its capacious bosom could scarcely contain them. The whole city was ornamented with flags and banners, chaplets and hangings, candles and lamps and with wonderful devices and extraordinary representations, and all the roads were cleansed of mud, and

Chapter Three

dirt, sticks and everything offensive. The citizens too, went out to meet the King and Queen, dressed out in their ornaments ... they proceeded thither dressed in silk garments, with mantles worked in gold and with costly changes in raiment, mounted on valuable horses, glittering with new bits and saddles and riding in troops arranged in order.

They carried with them three hundred and sixty gold and silver cups, preceded by the kings' trumpeters and with horns sounding, so that such a wonderful novelty struck all who beheld it astonishment. The Archbishop of Canterbury,[65] by the right especially belonging to him, performed the duty of crowning, with the usual solemnities, the Bishop of London[66] attending him as dean ... The ceremony was splendid with the gay dresses of the clergy and knights who were present ... The Earl of Chester carried the sword of St. Edward, which was called "Curtein" ... The Earl of Leicester [Simon de Montfort] supplied the king with water in basins to wash before his meal ... Why should I describe all those persons who reverently ministered in the church as was their duty? Why describe the abundance of meats and dishes on the table? The quantities of venison, the variety of fish, the joyous sounds of the glee-men and the gaiety of the waiters? Whatever the world could offer in pleasure and magnificence was there brought together from every quarter.[67]

The choir singing *Christus vincit, Christus regnat, Christus, Christus imperat* implored the almighty to give good health and long life to the Queen of the English.[68] So amidst the splendour described by Paris, joined together – for the two strands that will make up this story – the mountain county of Savoy and the Kingdom of England. Although Alianor's welcome to England was also of great tradition in another way – it rained throughout the next January, February and much of March, so much so that the Palace of Westminster flooded.[69] For the young girl from Provence and her uncle from Savoy who had travelled far, it was no longer the steady continental climate they knew well; on this island all four seasons could be had in a single morning.

Guillaume had been so liked by King Henry of England that he had invited him to stay on in England following his marriage to Alianor. If Guillaume missed the sun of the south, he didn't show it. In England he was as zealous in pursuit of financial reform as he had been in Valence, reforms of the sheriffs of the counties that brought Henry a much-needed extra £1,500[70] revenue per year. Such acumen soon elevated the Bishop Elect of Valence to, in effect, Henry's chief counsellor. In January 1237, Guillaume attended, at Westminster, the first English assembly to be called a parliament and the latest confirmation of the *Magna Carta* along with the Charter of the Forest – a key period in the development of English political life.[71] The Dunstable annalist described the Bishop Elect of Valence as "*consiliarius regis principalis*", the king's chief counsellor.[72] Henry had employed Guillaume in a much-needed reorganisation of the realm's finances. Not beholden to the barons as he was, Guillaume had gone on to make enemies amongst the local aristocracy who, unsurprisingly, resented such foreign interference. Matthew Paris was not happy and began to report discontent amongst the local nobility almost as soon as Guillaume had arrived in England, writing that at the 28 April council of state the barons had wondered why they'd been saddled with a Savoyard uncle when the French court was not similarly encumbered.[73] Alianor's biographer Margaret Howell suggests this may well have been unfair, that the xenophobia was a misdirected response to reforms not to the barons' liking, and that Henry's Chief Justice, native-born William Raleigh, was the "guiding intelligence" behind the reforms – as always it was easier to lay the blame at the door of the incoming foreigner.[74]

With the death on 9 June 1238 of Henry's former mentor and favourite, Pierre des Roches, the richest see in England, the bishopric of Winchester became vacant.[75] Henry let it be known that his chosen man was Guillaume, Henry's choice carrying the extra weight in Winchester as the place of his birth. However, the monks of Winchester decided that their choice was Ralph Neville, the bishop of nearby Chichester and holder of the King's Seal. Alas, Henry was not enamoured of the monks' choice, going so far as to remove the Great Seal from Neville's possession, before getting Rome to annul the appointment of Neville as bishop.[76] There does seem to be no little politics in all this Ralph Neville matter, as Lord Chancellor was a part of Henry's former regime that he and/or Guillaume may well have wanted to see the back of in their attempts to reform the realm. Henry's preference for Guillaume over Neville for the See of Winchester ought to be seen in this light. The monks of Winchester appealed to the Pope for the right to choose themselves and the matter ran for some years. Guillaume de Savoie was not to be Bishop of Winchester, nor was Ralph Neville, nor was he long for the world, dying in February 1244, restored as Chancellor but without the Great Seal.

Given Henry's difficulty appointing the Savoyard to the See of Winchester, one might also contrast and ponder the readiness of the English court to accept Alianor's extended family into court with the relative reluctance of the French court to accept Marguerite's. There was no little misogyny in Matthew Paris bemoaning the Savoyard influence in England and contrasting it with that across the Channel; he wrote of the "careful king of France who did not permit their backs to be trodden on by their wives and their relatives and countrymen".[77] The answer lies with the respective mothers-in-law: in France Blanche de Castile and in England (or rather in France as that's where she'd remarried and lived) Isabelle d'Angoulême. Blanche dismissed the Savoyard uncles from Fontainebleau with polite courtesy in the form of gifts, but no power or influence – a gift of 236 *livres*, no more.[78] Blanche was very protective of Louis; his biographer Jean de Joinville wrote that she "would never, if she could help it, suffer her son to be in his wife's company, unless at night, when he went to bed with her".[79] Whereas young Henry had come to the throne of England with the early death of his father John, leaving his mother to remarry the Poitevin Hugues X de Lusignan. The absence of an overbearing mother-in-law at the English court – no Blanche de Castile – allowed room for the Savoyard uncles to wield influence. The role of Blanche de Castile in channelling Savoyard influence to London and away from Paris is one of the thirteenth century's more unintended consequences.[80] So it wasn't so much the "careful king of France" as the careful mother of the king of France, and the want of a mother-in-law in England.[81]

However, in addition to English affairs, Guillaume had family interests to attend to, which took him away from England, namely the marriage of his brother Thomas to Jeanne, Countess of Flanders and Hainaut, widow of Ferdinand, Count of Flanders and daughter of the Latin Emperor Baldwin I.[82] This marriage had brought Flanders into the Savoyard orbit and the involvement of the King of France and Latin Emperor of Constantinople illustrate well the influence Henry sought by his counsel, the influence of the House of Savoy.

In 1237, when Henry made peace with Alexander II of Scotland, Guillaume de Savoie would be one of the negotiators for Henry alongside the mediation of the Papal Legate, San Nicola. The resulting treaty bears Guillaume's seal as witness.[83] When Henry's sister, Joan, Queen of Scots, died on 4 March 1238, Guillaume was to be an executor of her will.[84]

Chapter Three

Matthew Paris, so quick to criticise Guillaume, makes no mention of him in connection with the Scottish treaty.[85] Which is a pity because what would become known as the 1237 Treaty of York affirmed that Northumberland, then also encompassing Cumberland, Durham and Westmorland, would be a part of England – something that remains true to this day. Guillaume was also instrumental in negotiating with his brother Thomas for the peaceful resumption following disputes of good trading terms between England and Flanders.[86]

However, we should balance these pluses with the controversy that surrounded the marriage of Henry's sister Eleanor to none other than the knight to which Jeanne, Countess of Flanders had shown a marital interest, Simon de Montfort. Thus enters our story the Earl of Leicester, son of the leader of the Albigensian Crusades of the same name[87] and a central figure in the life of Pierre de Savoie. Montfort had inherited a claim to Leicester through his grandmother, Amice de Beaumont,[88] who had been the sister of the childless Robert de Breteuil, 4th Earl of Leicester. The claim had passed by way of his father thence at first to Montfort's elder brother, Amauri[89] but he would pass his rights on to Simon, the third son. Simon the Elder had been a man of religious fervour, hence the deaths of so many Cathars, and as with the father so it was with the son.[90] Simon de Montfort had travelled to England in 1230[91] in search of his inherited lands of Leicester, rights to which, remarkably, Henry had granted.[92] As Montfort later said, "*E je alai en Engleterre, e priai mon seigneur le Rai q'il me vousist l'eritage mon pere rendre*,"[93] that is "And I went to England, and prayed to my lord the King that he would give me my father's inheritance." And so begins a fatal encounter. Later in his career Montfort would rail against aliens being granted riches in England, and yet he himself began life in England as an alien in receipt of Henry's generosity. Simon de Montfort was not one to be given to irony. Yet unbeknownst to Simon, or indeed to Henry and their contemporaries, Simon de Montfort was a great-great-great-great-grandson of William the Conqueror; as such he was of that aristocracy with a foot set either side of the Channel, the brother of a Constable of France, yet descended from a Duke of Normandy and King of England.[94] It has only recently become increasingly apparent that Henry's preferment of aliens had one thing chiefly in mind, not a weak-minded character as was traditionally supposed, but the return of his ancestral lands. So, in many ways the young Henry and the young Simon shared similar goals, the return of what they saw as their birthright. Simon de Montfort was recruited into Henry's favour and service immediately before what would prove to be an unsuccessful venture into Poitou; that Montfort came from such an illustrious military family with much influence in northern France is likely to have influenced Henry greatly. This preference for influential francophones would be the mark of Henry's reign; it would influence him successively with Montfort, the Savoyards and as we shall see later, with the Lusignans.[95] We should see this preference for francophones at court through one prism – that of Henry's yearning for the return of his *patrimoine* in France.

Eleanor, meanwhile, had been previously married to William Marshal, 2nd Earl of Pembroke, he the son of THE William Marshal, 1st Earl and onetime Regent of England, and saviour of Henry's reign. But Eleanor's husband, the 2nd Earl, had died in 1231 and she was in need of a new husband, having been only a girl of some 16 years at the time. According to Paris the beauteous Eleanor and Simon met and had fallen in love and married secretly on 7 January 1238 in the king's small chapel at Westminster Palace.[96] The match was, however, controversial since Eleanor had taken a vow of chastity and her hand, as Henry's sister, would confer much power and influence upon the man lucky enough to win it. The hand of the sister of the King of England might offer much to the realm in terms of an advantageous alliance, and now it was to be squandered on a foreign arrival at court "on the make". Against the marriage would be Archbishop Edmund of Canterbury who had administered her vow, and Gilbert Marshal. Her vow had been used to reconcile the Marshal family to the Crown a number of years earlier, but worse was that Henry had not consulted his and Eleanor's brother, Richard, Earl of Cornwall.[97] We don't know the extent to which Guillaume played a part in advising Henry to consent to the marriage, Matthew Paris in his prejudiced account includes another swipe at "foreigners", which may indicate Guillaume, but it at least seems certain that some advice may have been given.[98] If so, then the advice of a recently arrived Savoyard to court was a misstep and showed a perhaps understandable ignorance of the English court. However, it's also possible that Guillaume may have played little part in the marriage, as he was away from the country a while.[99] We do know, however, that he returned to at least play a role in the mediation that resolved Richard's opposition.[100] The marriage, however, elevated Montfort to the status of Henry's brother-in-law, but one with a sense of insecurity. When acquiring Leicester, Montfort had acquired the £500 annual income, a tidy sum in the thirteenth century, but in marrying Eleanor he'd doubled that with the addition of her £550 annual income from the Marshal estate. However, there was a catch: this £550 annual income would only last whilst Eleanor lived and could not be passed on, so Montfort was rich, but these riches carried an expiry date.[101] The irony in all that would follow is that Montfort's marriage was frowned upon because he was an alien newcomer to court.

And yet as the Bishopric in Lausanne was becoming vacant, so unexpectedly did the See of Valence: Pierre's brother, Guillaume de Savoie, was dead. Guillaume had left England in May 1238, at Henry's behest, to lead a party of knights from Gascony, along with the seneschal Henry de Turberville, as part of an imperial invasion of Italy. Amongst the English knights sent by Henry was John Mansel who would later become his Keeper of the Seal. Mansel would become a key ally for Pierre de Savoie throughout his time in England and it may well be that their paths crossed for this first time in 1238 in Lombardy as it is likely that Pierre supported his brother Guillaume.[102] The emperor, the much-excommunicated Frederick II, was Henry's brother-in-law, having married Isabella of England in 1235. The County of Savoy also lay within the empire and Guillaume's assistance, particularly in leading the knights through the alpine passes, doubled as the fulfilment of a vassal's obligations. The Emperor and the Pope, following a brief peace, were once more at loggerheads; Frederick again, for the fourth time (he may have been getting used to it by now) would be excommunicated. The insults had been flying too: Frederick called Gregory a "Pharisee seated on the chair of pestilence", Gregory called Frederick "a forerunner of the antichrist" – such was an imperial papal dispute in the thirteenth century.[103] Lombardy had flown into rebellion against the Hohenstaufen emperor. Guillaume joined the imperial army in Turin, and then went on to participate in the siege of Brescia. His prowess during the siege was widely noted. Philippe Mousket recorded that he led his troops on 23 August to drive off a force coming in from Piacenza to help Brescia. Guillaume stayed in Italy in 1239, following a stay with the Pope in Rome. This visit to Rome shortly after leading an army in support of the emperor reminds us of the narrow diplomatic as well as Alpine paths the Savoyards had to tread. His brother Thomas had lobbied for him to become Prince Bishop of Liege, which necessitated a trip to Rome for confirmation. Paris records that he'd been given permission by the Pope in regard to both Liege and Winchester, but alas, as he was heading northward, he was taken ill on the slopes of Mount Cimini at Viterbo.[104] There were rumours of foul play, of poison;[105] however, whatever the cause, Guillaume de Savoie passed away on or around 1 November 1239. The man described by Matthew Paris as being "a beast with many heads",[106] the man who had managed the Savoyard succession, the man who'd arranged the marriage of the two Provençal daughters to the kings of France and England, the man who'd become King Henry III of England's principal adviser was no more. The Savoyard chroniclers called him "*Le petit Alexandre*"; they spoke of Valence never having been better run, of his generosity and bravery, but noted that perhaps he had been too trusting and had indeed been poisoned.[107] However, Matthew Paris wrote less charitably and with some satisfaction:

> As the feast of All Saints drew near [1 November 1239], William, bishop elect of Valentia … closed his life at Viterbo, having as was said, been poisoned at the instigation of Master Lawrence, an Englishman, but was afterwards entirely cleared himself of the charge. When the pope heard of this event, he was much grieved, for he had purposed to make him the commander of his army in his war against the emperor, and thus made him a spiritual monster and a beast of many heads; for he knew that he was strenuous in slaughter, prone to bloodshed, and wanton in incendiarism; that he was master of the English king, a friend of the French monarch, a brother in law of both them, an uncle of their queens, a brother of the Count of Savoy, and allied to many others by kindred or blood; his unexpected death, however, disconcerted his whole scheme.[108]

Paris then records that Henry was apparently so grief stricken at the news that he "could not restrain himself for grief, but tore his clothes and threw them into the fire and, giving vent to loud lamentations, refused to accept consolation from anyone".[109] In our assessment of Matthew Paris as a witness of the life and times of Pierre de Savoie, we should place less trust in him as an impartial witness than has been the case traditionally in England. His view of Guillaume de Savoie, for example, of being a "monster" is entirely at variance with the later Savoyard chronicler description of "bravery" and "generosity". In the end, perhaps the truth lies somewhere in between. Wurstemberger called Paris "spiteful" in his picture of Guillaume, and as a historian pointed to a complete lack of evidence upon the part of the English monk.[110] Far from Baker's "parasite", historian Huw Ridgeway, perhaps with more consideration, wrote of his arrival at court with Alianor "as one of her brilliant uncles" and "William was no Peter des Roches, for he cultivated men from all factions, supported the jurist and administrative reformer William of Raleigh, and promoted few foreigners".[111] Ultimately, your view of Guillaume de Savoie, indeed of Savoyards in general, will depend upon the store you set by Matthew Paris. The Savoyard Chronicles note that Pierre went to Italy to recover the body of his slain brother, and that he was laid to rest at Hautecombe Abbey by the shores of Lac du Bourget in Savoy.[112]

Meanwhile, happier news, England had been rejoicing in the birth of a son to King Henry and Queen Alianor – that thing to which all monarchies of the time aspired above all others – a royal baby, a boy, an heir. Our faithful English chronicler Matthew Paris recorded events in London:

> On the night of the 16th of June[113] [1239], a son was born at Westminster to the king by his wife Eleanor. At this event all the nobles of the kingdom offered their congratulations, and especially the citizens of London; and

they assembled bands of dancers, with drums and tambourines, and at night illuminated the streets with large lanterns. The Bishop of Carlisle initiated the infant, and the legate baptised him, although he was not a priest, but Edmund Archbishop of Canterbury, confirmed him, and at the wish of the king the name of EDWARD was given to him.[114]

The young prince was to be the first king of England since 1065 to carry an English name, named for the saintly penultimate Anglo-Saxon king of England, Edward the Confessor. Perhaps we shouldn't be entirely surprised by Henry's veneration of Edward, obviously because they shared a sincere piety but also because Henry was the first English king since Edward's time to be raised exclusively in England.[115] Edward would be a break with the recent past for the French-speaking Anglo-Norman Plantagenet – harking back to an earlier age, an English king of England, a new Arthur. At his baptism the king's brother, Richard, Earl of Cornwall and then best friend, one Simon de Montfort, would be godfathers. As we saw earlier, the latter had come to England to regain his familial lands in Leicestershire, which he'd been granted back in 1231. He would go on to be a rising star at court and close to Henry, hence his being Edward's godfather.

That summer of 1239 another Savoyard brother, Thomas, the Count of Flanders (see figure 1.6), visited London. Matthew Paris again wrote disapprovingly:

> About the feast of the Assumption of the blessed Mary, Thomas Count of Flanders, the queen's uncle, came to England, landing at Dover. When the King was informed of his arrival, he, in a way not becoming him, went in his joy to meet him; and ordered the citizens of London, on his approach, to remove all stems and dung, mud and everything offensive from the streets.[116]

You can almost hear Paris's "Oh no not another Savoyard uncle" in his admonition of Henry acting in a way "not becoming of him". Thomas had come, in 1239, to pay homage in return for the usual pension[117] and regarding a debt owed to him by Simon de Montfort, who'd given Henry's name as surety. Simon was now Henry's brother-in-law, having married his sister Eleanor Marshal in 1238, but he had not received a dowry and incurred expense acquiring the Earldom of Leicester. Simon no doubt figured the king owed him, and indeed this episode betokens Montfort's financial vulnerability. Montfort had originally borrowed 2,800 marks from Pierre Dreux of Brittany, likely to buy out his brother Amauri's share in Leicester; we don't know how but the debt had been taken on by Thomas, Montfort displaying his financial weakness had named Henry as guarantor – not his best move.[118]

Understandably Thomas asked that as Henry was given as the guarantor of Simon's now 2,000 marks (£1,320) debt,[119] would he mind paying up? The resulting furious argument between Henry and Montfort would lay the stones for the subsequent baronial conflict that would later engulf Henry's reign. On 9 August 1239, when Montfort and his wife were in London for Alianor's churching, the storm broke. The account related to us by Paris has Henry hurling insults at Montfort: "You seduced my sister before her marriage" and "when I discovered this I gave her to you, though unwillingly, to avoid a scandal."[120] Henry would have thrown him into the Tower had it not been for the intervention of Richard, allowing Simon and Eleanor to sail "in all haste" for France.[121] Thomas returned in the spring of 1240 to collect once more: Henry gave him 500 marks (£330), his yearly pension of 500 marks and

Chapter Three

the remaining 1,500 marks (£990) by levying against Simon's English possessions. In return Thomas again paid homage to Henry. In view of England's trading relationship with Flanders, having the Count as "your man" was always good business, quite apart from his being family. Indeed, we should add that Thomas honoured his feudal commitment to Henry, arriving at the head of sixty knights to his aid when war with Scotland threatened in 1244, a war averted by the Treaty of Newcastle of that year that settled the border between England and Scotland.[122] Matthew Paris, so quick to criticise the uncles of the queen for their apparent rewards without service, dismissed this particular service by suggesting his coming to Henry's aid "excited great indignation and derision" as "England was capable of utterly uprooting Scotland without him".[123] One is bound to suggest that Alianor's uncles could not win either way.

With the departure of disgraced Simon de Montfort, who left on crusade in the summer of 1240, and with the death of Guillaume de Savoie in 1239, there was a vacancy for a court favourite, so to speak, in London. What's more, there was a political vacuum too, since Henry's brother Richard, Earl of Cornwall had also left England to lead the so-called Baron's Crusade, his first wife Isabel Marshal having died. Therefore, Henry had also sent Thomas on his way with an offer to his Savoyard brothers from Henry and Alianor, an offer of preferment in return for service.[124]

Chapter Four

From the death of his brother Guillaume and the invitation to England likely extended by Alianor through Thomas, the career of Pierre de Savoie takes, as Wurstemberger said, "widely divergent directions" as he sought to balance a life in England with a life in Savoy. Wurstemberger chose to treat these two paths separately, suggesting that a "chronological account of his life would furnish a long series of fragments".[1] This is no doubt true, and yet we will attempt a more chronological story, if only to show the way these fragments interacted with one another, and that to truly understand Pierre de Savoie we need to knit back together the Savoyard Pierre de Savoie with the English Peter of Savoy. It is the international nature of his career, not fitting easily into a "national story" that makes him such an interesting character and a man of his times. This will be no easy task, as we shall see the Savoyard clocked up an enormous amount of horse miles in the three-week journey to and from England and Savoy. A good example, as we shall see, of the Machiavellian ways Pierre sought to further the affairs of both England and Savoy simultaneously can be seen in the marriage of Richard, Earl of Cornwall and Sanchia de Provence. The match suited both English and Savoyard interests and illustrates the way we cannot see Pierre's life as neatly fitting into either an English or an Alpine box.

Pierre de Savoie, lately struggling with the House of Geneva in the *Pays de Vaud* and fighting the Battle of Lausanne, had indeed been distracted, as Cox said, by riches elsewhere. Pierre, by now nearly 40 years of age, responded to advice from his brother Thomas, Count of Flanders, that preferment awaited in England for those Savoyard prepared to serve King Henry. The conduit of the life-changing advice to move to England was almost certainly Thomas, who'd visited London again around the Easter of 1240,[2] following news of the death of Guillaume on 1 November 1239. Cox suggests, what was in effect a job offer, reached Pierre by means of Thomas and Philippe later in 1240.[3]

On 20 April 1240, at Westminster, the Calendar of Charter Rolls for Henry III records, "Gift to Pierre de Sabaudia and his heirs in the honor of Richemund, with its free liberties and customs, to hold by the service therefrom."[4] It is almost certain that Henry awarded Pierre the Honour of Richmond before having met him.[5] This speaks volumes for the trust he'd placed in Guillaume, and continued to place in Alianor and Thomas, but would no doubt raise eyebrows then and now as to it being a wise course for a king to take. For sure Henry was in need of a trusted adviser, something he'd grown accustomed to with the services of Burgh, Roches and lately Guillaume de Savoie, but I think the one in real need was young Alianor who'd also been content to reside in a foreign court accompanied by one of her uncles who might help her to navigate the perilous waters that might surround a medieval queen.

And so Pierre de Savoie set forth for England, a journey not described, but perhaps we can follow the earlier journey of Archbishop Sigeric two centuries earlier, which was documented for most of the way. Setting out from his fief at the castle of Moudon, he would have likely

Chapter Four

crossed the low hills of the Gros-de-Vaud before coming to the shores of Lac de Neuchâtel. Passing the site of the former Roman *Eburodunum*, he may well have reflected upon its suitability for the *ville neuve* he would later build there. Passing by the castles of Grandson and Champvent, home to his loyal allies Pierre de Grandson and Henri de Champvent, he would come to the town Sigeric called *Urba*, today's Orbe, and then followed the winding River Orbe up into the Jura mountains to take the Col de Jougne over into the Free County of Burgundy, passing the Château de Joux guarding the narrow gorge on the approach to the town Sigeric called *Punterlin*, today Pontarlier. Thirty years hence Count Othon de Bourgogne would pay homage to King Edward I of England for castle and town, both sitting astride the *Via Francigena*. Once north of the Jura multiple routes presented themselves to the English-bound traveller, but perhaps the *Via Francigena* trod by Sigeric is the most likely to have been taken by Pierre. First, the Burgundian town of Besançon, Sigeric's *Bysiceon*, for a crossing of the Doubs, thence northward to Langres, crossing the Marne at Châlons-en-Champagne, where Attila the Hun was once defeated, before reaching the great cathedral city of Reims, where French kings were crowned. From there he likely made for Artois and what Sigeric called *Atherats*, modern-day Arras and the Channel at Wissant which was a commonly documented crossing point where boats for England might be obtained. As the French coast retreated behind him and the white cliffs of Dover beckoned, we can only imagine the thoughts of this son of the mountains as he arrived on the island kingdom where his niece reigned as queen.

Matthew Paris sniffly commented:

> About the same time [1240] Peter of Savoy, the queen's uncle, on whom the king had bestowed the earldom of Richmond, came to England, as he perceived that it was such a profitable country. The king went to meet him on his arrival and received him the inexpressible joy, entrusted himself and his possessions to his counsel, and also enlarged his lands by the gift of several more.[6]

You can have some sympathy for poor Matthew Paris; perhaps he'd thought that with the departure of Guillaume and his full saddle bags he'd seen the last of the Savoyards. Alas, it was not to be. Spencer echoed the spiteful comments of the monk who'd described Guillaume as a "beast of many heads"[7] by describing the comital family of Savoy as "the Hydra".[8] Matthew Paris, in introducing Pierre de Savoie to his chronicle, immediately disparaged him, as he had his late brother, as one in search of a "profitable country", making no attempt to consider why Henry or Alianor might be in need of counsel. That having been said, giving Paris the benefit of the doubt, perhaps Giles is translating a little liberally. Paris used the word "*fructuosam*" which might more charitably be translated as "fruitful" and attached it to the act of coming to England, that is "he came to England, which he felt fruitful for him". The English word "profitable" is more specifically, according to the OED, related to financial gain, whereas "fruitful" has a wider meaning.

Either way, the reasons for Henry's preference for Pierre's counsel remained as they had been earlier for Guillaume: the Savoyard could be trusted to serve him in ways that the English nobility could not. In the words of Simon the Norman, a former steward to Henry III, to the Pope "there is at this time not one Englishman of approved fidelity that the king can trust".[9] Furthermore, the Savoyards were a well-connected family that could serve him in providing a reliable conduit between himself, the empire and the papacy – but most importantly for a

Plantagenet, one who could assist in his rivalry with the Capetian French. Henry had been bereft at the death of Guillaume, but now he had a ready replacement. In summary, since the days of his minority, he had grown accustomed to ruling with the help of wise counsel: there had been William the Marshal, Pierre des Roches and Hubert de Burgh before the lately departed Guillaume de Savoie. The well-connected comital family of Savoy provided a ready source of expertise but also, importantly, they were family. This would be doubly true for Alianor who valued an uncle at court, but for Henry he simply offered something that had belonged to one member of the family to another, with the hope he might prove as effective as the departed and much-lamented Guillaume. As for Pierre, he saw the need to dutifully represent the family in London whilst maintaining the ability to generate wealth for himself in pursuing his thwarted expansion plans in the *Pays de Vaud*. King Henry did indeed meet Pierre with "inexpressible joy", and we know of some of the sumptuous banqueting that the newly arrived Savoyard would have partaken of that Christmas of 1240. The feasting included 1,500 lambs, 5 bulls, 7,000 hens, 80 porkers, 500 rabbits, 150 salmon pies, 200 kids, 40 roes, 312 pheasants, 1,290 partridges, 90 peacocks, 900 hares, 60 herons, 68 boars and that most magnificent of medieval dishes, as many swans as could be had.[10] Pierre de Savoie had arrived at one of the richest courts in Europe and it would not do for the king's uncle and future envoy of the King of England not to be of the knightly class and so it was not long before he bestowed upon him the honour of knighthood. Matthew Paris again writes:

> On St. Edward's day [5 January 1241],[11] which the king makes a practise of observing with extraordinary veneration and honour, he, in order to give still more religious character to the day, conferred the honour of knighthood on the aforesaid Peter of Savoy and fifteen other illustrious youths, in the church of St. Peter at Westminster. And on the day after, which was the day of the Epiphany, in honour of the said Peter, he, together with a great number of guests, celebrated their initiation with a rich and costly banquet. The citizens of London, too, were summoned by royal warrant to be present, and some, who were called the mayors of the city, were compelled, under penalty of a fine of a hundred shillings, to come there dressed out for a feast, or as if to celebrate a marriage.[12]

Pierre, knighted that day in 1241, is unlikely to have worn the heraldry of his grandfather, the now familiar white cross on a red field, but rather that worn by his father Thomas, the black eagle on a yellow field. We can surmise this from the now destroyed tomb ascribed to Pierre de Savoie at Aiguebelle, drawn for us by Thomas Kerrich. Kerrich was a clergyman, draughtsman, antiquarian and gifted amateur artist, but also a librarian at Cambridge University. Thankfully, for us, he visited the now destroyed tomb Pierre de Savoie at Aiguebelle and made a detailed drawing which was published in 1817 in the review *Archaeologia*.[13] The attribution is not certain, as Kerrich took the tomb to be that of Pierre upon the advice of the locals that it was the tomb of "the Englishman". As we shall see later, Pierre's final will and testament sought burial at Hautecombe Abbey, but this does not preclude, as was much the thirteenth-century habit of viscera finding burial in one place and the body in another. Certainly, Kerrich found alongside "the Englishman" the second tomb of Pierre d'Aigueblanche, Bishop of Hereford, whose other tomb remains to this day in Hereford Cathedral. Sadly, for us, both the tombs of Hautecombe and that found by Kerrich at Aiguebelle have been destroyed, along with the records that went

Chapter Four

with them, in the French Revolution. Nonetheless, the drawing by Kerrich is the closest we will ever get to a "from life" image of Pierre de Savoie. Kerrich drew a tall, handsome knight, dressed in a coat of mail, as befitting a thirteenth-century knight with no plate armour. He lay beneath his shield, but the heraldry of the tall kite-shaped shield was not that of the white cross on a red field, but the black eagle on a yellow field which displayed his father's 1207 allegiance to Philip of Swabia and the empire.[14] So we must assume that as Pierre knelt before Henry to be dubbed a knight, he was adorned with the imperial eagle of Henry's brother-in-law Frederick II.

The ceremony of enoblement, of dubbing Pierre de Savoie a knight, was a very prescribed affair and rich in ceremony. An explanation of the language is helpful; the word we find in sources, "*addobatorum*", was a Latinised rendering of the Old French "*adober*" which meant to dress with armour or adorn. The act of dubbing would also be known by its Old French origin of "*adoubement*". This confirms that the origins of knighthood and chivalry lay deeply rooted in Pierre's francophone culture. The ceremony itself later gave rise to the English word "accolade" which gives us a graphic picture of the ceremony from its Occitan origin "*acolada*", literally "to the neck" which in Occitan meant "embrace". It had been thought for a time by some historians that thirteenth-century English knighting ceremonies did not include the ritual bathing; the archive in Turin, for a subsequent enabling of Savoyards in Darlington decades later, confirms that it very much did.[15]

Geoffroi de Charny[16] described the ceremony of enrolment as:

1. The day before the ceremony (4 January 1241 in this case) the knights to be would bathe for some time, the idea being not to physically cleanse but to spiritually cleanse.
2. The night would have been spent in a new bed with clean linen.
3. The following morning (5 January 1241 in this case) the squires would have been dressed by knights: a red tunic to show a willingness to shed blood for the faith, black stockings as a symbol of mortality, a white belt symbolising purity and chastity and finally a red cloak to show humility.
4. The squires would then go to church to hold a vigil.
5. Finally, the ceremony itself saw the affixing of golden spurs, the belt of knighthood, followed by Henry III (as is likely in this case) passing the sword of knighthood along with either a blow (across the cheek) or a tap with the sword (as today).

Edward the Confessor was a hero to Henry, who would soon rebuild Edward's Westminster in an act of veneration. The greatest honour he could bestow upon Pierre was not only to knight him, but to raise him to knighthood upon St. Edward's Day – Edward then being patron saint of England. Poor Matthew Paris looked on with disapproval – the citizens "were compelled" to attend he sniffed "as if to celebrate a marriage". In the wake of Henry's attachment to Guillaume this new attachment to Pierre was too much for the monk from St. Albans.

The son of Thomas, Count of Maurienne and Savoie, was now Sir Pierre de Savoie. He had very much arrived in England. It would have been considered normal for Henry to dub his uncle a knight if he were not yet ennobled. Such a gesture would be looked upon happily by Alianor as a sign of the joining of their two families, but also at court, Pierre had to "join the club" so to speak: to be an important member of Henry's court he really needed to be of the knightly class. But Henry was to not stop there – his benevolence continued.

Paris wrote at this time that the newly arrived Pierre arranged for a tournament to be held that would have pitted foreigners against Englishmen, only for it to be cancelled by Henry.[17]

If we take Paris at his word this would have been a misstep, as with Guillaume and his advice on the Montfort marriage, it would have been evidence of a naivety on Pierre's part on the sensitive political environment into which he'd arrived. As we shall see, Pierre was nothing if not a quick learner and his future conduct would bear English sensitives in mind.

Nonetheless, further examples of Henry's benevolence toward Pierre are found in the Close Rolls of Henry's reign, for example, "Deer in the forest of Wichewud for Peter of Savoy, a gift of the king."[18] There was much too much *de dono regis* for Matthew Paris to abide happily in St. Albans. On 6 May 1241 Pierre received confirmation from Henry of the Honour of Richmond[19], an Honour being a collection of lands granted by the king to a follower who in turn would subinfeud to his followers. This grant of land and sub-granting of land was the very foundation and creation of the feudal system in England. The Honour of Richmond had previously been held by his late brother Guillaume, so this was perhaps merely keeping it in the family. The Honour of Richmond, a name first coined in 1203, comprised a vast and wealthy landholding of 199 manors in 1086, centred upon the "good castle, fair and strong" built then on land granted to him by William the Conqueror by Alain Le Roux, that is Alan Rufus.[20] The castle itself was built upon a high rocky promontory, a *Richemont*,[21] above the River Swale, offering excellent protection in a hostile land (see figure 1.7).

Rufus had been a Breton nobleman and kinsman, second cousin, to the Conqueror, the son of Count Eudo de Penthièvre, the Regent of Brittany.[22] As a descendant of Duke Richard I de Normandie, Alain would share kinship with several of the new nobility of England whose lands would also find their way into Pierre de Savoie's portfolio. Robert de Mortain, a great-grandson of the Norman, would be Lord of Pevensey, Guillaume de Eu, a grandson, would be Lord of Hastings, and also related through Richard's wife Gunnora would be Guillaume de Warenne, the Lord of Lewes. This illustrates a number of points: first, the close kinship of the Norman invaders of 1066, but also their being granted key defensible territories on the English borders. That they came into the possession of Pierre de Savoie also illustrates both the rupture of the Anglo-Norman realm wrought by Philippe Auguste, which returned these lands to the English Crown and also the way Henry simply trusted Pierre with the defence of his realm.

The Honour of Richmond would pass variously between the ruling house of Brittany and the Crown until it was awarded to Guillaume de Savoie. The Dukes of Brittany lost their hold on Richmond in return for their backing the Capetian kings of France, a reminder that the confiscation of Plantagenet lands in France could also mean the loss in return of their vassals' lands in England. Philippe Auguste's seizure of Normandy, Anjou and Maine had in this case led to the loss of lands in England long in the possession of the Dukes of Brittany.

Much of what would later become the Honour of Richmond had belonged hitherto to the Saxon, Edwin of Mercia, the elder brother of Morcar, Earl of Northumbria. Rufus, now one of the wealthiest men in England, would settle forty followers on the lands he'd gained in England and all but two of them would be Bretons – conquest was clearly a profitable business.[23] Richmond, the splendid hill, had been previously known as Hindrelag. The newcomers not only took the land, they gave it new names too.[24]

The Norman Conquest decapitated the former Saxon aristocracy, replacing it with a French one, the Honour of Richmond being the legacy of perhaps the most momentous regime change in English history. The land granted to Rufus, according to the Domesday Book of 1086, was centred on a goodly portion of what is now North Yorkshire, called Richmondshire with the castle of Richmond at its heart, but also valuable land scattered across the length and breadth

Chapter Four

of eastern England, in Lincolnshire, Cambridgeshire, and Norfolk and Suffolk.[25] The lands in Yorkshire formed a group some thirty-seven miles (sixty kilometres) from east to west by twenty-eight miles (forty-five kilometres) from north to south. The County of Richmondshire was divided into the wapentakes of Gilling, Hang and Hallikeld[26] – a wapentake being the Norse equivalent of the Saxon hundred, a reminder that before Edwin had held the land, it had once formed lands within the Viking-held Danelaw.[27] The territory spread out across the bleak high moorland of the North Riding of Yorkshire as far west as Dent and Sedbergh. The lands encompassed then, as it does to this day, two of the key routes through northern England; whilst not perhaps as important in themselves as the mountain passes ruled by the Savoyards, they were nevertheless of strategic importance. The Great North Road, Roman Dere Street, made its way from York to Newcastle, skirting just to the east of Richmond itself, the route followed today by the A1, then the principal route between the English and Scottish kingdoms. Leaving this road in Richmondshire, at a junction now known by the name of the hotel built there, Scotch Corner, was the old Roman route west across the Pennines by way of the Stainmore Gap to what became Westmorland and Cumberland, a vital east–west artery in a land when there were but few. Sitting astride this westward road would be Bowes Castle, an important guardian held by the holders of the Honour of Richmond. The castle at Bowes had been raised within the ruins of the Roman fort of *Lavatrae*, much as had the castle at Pevensey. It guarded the important Roman road from *Eboracum* or York to *Luguvalium* or Carlisle. At the westward end of the Stainmore Gap lay the castle at Brough, itself within the ruins of the Roman fort of *Verteris*.[28]

So, in England, as his family had in Savoy, Pierre found himself sitting astride ancient and key trade routes. To his north lay the lands of the prince bishops of Durham, to his south the greatest city of northern England, the Archbishopric of York, onetime capital city of Saxon Northumbria and later its Viking successor. That the Honour of Richmond was well known to be of strategic value to the Crown is evidenced by the incursions southward by the Scots, not least the siege of Bowes Castle of 1173.

Historian Ridgeway estimated Pierre de Savoie's English income to have been of the order of £3,000,[29] nearly triple that Guillaume had had in England, or nearly £2.2 million in today's money – so what made up such a king's ransom? First, the Honour of Richmond, reputed to have been one of the most profitable in all England, having an annual value of some £1,811 from demesne lands alone,[30] which in modern terms is £1.3 million.[31] Having said that, this represented only a third of the Honour's annual value of £5,609 or nearly £4.1 million in today's money. Between 1086 and the thirteenth century around three-quarters of the Honours demesne lands had been alienated or sub-let.[32] Early in 1242, Pierre's bailiffs were asked to investigate the specific nature of what was and wasn't held by the Honour of Richmond.[33] The fifteen residual manors actually granted to Pierre as demesne lands included Catterick,[34] Moulton,[35] Gilling[36] and Forcett[37] in Yorkshire; Frampton,[38] Wykes,[39] Washingborough[40] and the Soke of Boston in Lincolnshire; Swaffham[41] and Costesy[42] in Norfolk; Wisset,[43] Kettleburgh[44] and Nettlestead[45] in Suffolk; Cherry Hinton[46] in Cambridgeshire; and Cheshunt[47] in Hertfordshire.[48] So, given that the Honour represented only fifteen manors that had been demesne lands in 1086, how might the newly arrived Savoyard derive further income?[49]

First, this subinfeudation had originally created a band of followers loyal to the holder of the Honour, politically and militarily. But by the thirteenth century military service was more often exchanged for a financial substitute, scutage. There is a remarkable document dating from around 1400 that illustrates the castle at Richmond, and how the knights of the Honour might defend the castle, detailing which knights were responsible for defending which parts; although it dates from more than a century after Pierre's time, given the hereditary nature of their holdings, the names would have been familiar to him. We have the Lords of Middeham, a castle that would later pass to the Neville family of Kingmaker fame, the Lords of Constable Burton, of Ravensworth, of Kelfield, of Mansfield, of Cowton. These knights owed military service, typically forty days, to their lord, in this case Pierre de Savoie, but could exchange this service for payment of a fee known as scutage.[50] Hugh Thomas wrote that by the thirteenth century, although those named above might still defend the castle at Richmond, but that holders of the honour "no longer received active service from their tenants", going on further to add Pierre de Savoie's followers were "foreign and he had to provide for them from the resources of his demesne lands".[51] This would certainly explain Savoyard knights from the *Pays de Vaud* serving with him in Gascony as we shall see later, and as we shall also see, the Charron family acting as stewards in Yorkshire. However, scutage for the castle guard at Richmond, illustrated as above in 1400, would only attract another £62 or £45,249 in today's money.[52]

Another means was the patient recovery of demesne lands; in 1247 he recovered the manor of Aldbrough (today Aldbrough St. John) some seven miles from Richmond.[53] The manors of Long Bennington and Foston in Lincolnshire were reacquired from the estate of Clemencia, the widow of onetime holder of the honour, Earl Ranulf of Chester.[54] Of some strategic interest, these two manors sat hard by the Great North Road linking London to Pierre's estates in Yorkshire. Long Bennington was the home of a priory, daughter house to the Cistercian monastery of Savigny in northern France.

Reacquired in 1250 were the Lincolnshire manors of Fulbeck and Leadenham; Ridgeway is almost certainly right to highlight their proximity to Ermine Street and the roads to Yorkshire and Boston. There is more than a suggestion of strategic thought in Pierre's acquisition of manors for the Honour of Richmond, something which the lesser nobles and people of Vaud and Bugey would no doubt have been familiar with.[55] An acquisition, and not without some considerable legal wrangle, would be that of Redenhall Manor in Norfolk in 1257. Roger Bigod, Earl of Norfolk had been disputing the ability of Sir Nicholas de Lenham to hold the manor from Alianor, the Queen. Eventually Lenham sold out to Pierre de Savoie who settled the manor on Ingeram de Feynes and his wife Isabel. By 1261 Redenhall Manor was passed by Pierre to the Lord Edward, which was almost certainly the design all along.[56]

Other demesne lands, which Pierre was reacquiring for the Honour, included what might be best described in modern parlance as sheep ranches. A case in point is the manor of Bainbridge in Wensleydale, which was also recovered in 1247,[57] today a village of fewer than 500 souls, but in the thirteenth century this manor alone was worth £214 annually in wool production, over £150,000 in today's money.[58] The mid-thirteenth-century "high farming" on large estates in England, such as Bainbridge, reached almost industrial-scale production. The manor of Bainbridge was only newly pastoralised – only the previous century it had been forest land overrun by wolves.[59]

As Eileen Power wrote:

> In these reeve's or bailiff's accounts the long round of the shepherd's year unrolls itself like one of those horizontal Chinese scrolls ... We see the shepherd at the lambing season in the dark sheephouse, for which he lays in a stock of candles, for he must sit up all night. We see the pails of milk carried

Chapter Four

down from the dairy for the weakly lambs, and the great earthenware pots in which it was heated; and we know how many were born and how many survived, which ewes twinned, and which disgraced themselves by remaining sterile. Then comes the ewe-milking when the dairymaids are busy … Even greater is the hustle when the time for washing and shearing comes round. The shepherd himself hardly ever does it. Sometimes the tenants have to do the work as a customary service, sometimes gangs of clippers are hired, and often enough it is a woman's job. The sheep are driven in from outlying manors to the washing place … From there they go to the shearing shed, and the shearing and winding of the wool is the great moment of the sheep farmer's year. On a big estate the steward or stock-keeper is always there to supervise it, sometimes accompanied by the lord's chaplain, or if it is an abbey farm, by the cellarer or one of the monks. When the wool has been sold on contract the merchant's agent is often there too, to see that it is up to sample. And at the end there is the sheep-shearing feast immortalised in The Winter's Tale.[60]

These medieval manors, such as Bainbridge, pretty much created the Yorkshire Dales we know today, the drystone walls, the hay meadows, the isolated stone field-barns. In the shepherds and upland meadows of Wensleydale did the noble born in the Susa Valley find great riches.

But much larger sums, and an example of how the interests of the Savoyard brothers might line up, can be found in the port of Boston in Lincolnshire, which was attached to the Honour of Richmond by what was known as the Richmond Fee. In the reign of King John, we know that it was second only to London in its importance as a port of export.[61] By the time of Pierre's acquisition of the honour, Boston was exporting over a third of England's wool exports, much of it from Yorkshire estates including Pierre's, to destinations including Flanders. Merchants from Flanders, from Ypres, Arras and Ostend permanently occupied houses in Boston.[62] Ypres was one of the triumvirates of cloth-producing giants, along with Ghent and Bruges, that was beginning to demand ever more imported wool to transform into finished cloth.[63] If these centres produced the finest cloth in Europe, then England was its largest and most important source of fine wool.[64]

If the comital family of Savoy held over a third of the exports of the finest wool in Europe, then the same family would also preside as Count over its largest customer, and in turn a dominant centre for the resulting production of fine cloth. The Count of Flanders had been since 1237, Pierre's brother Thomas, and since 1239 Thomas had recognised Henry as his suzerain. Thomas had been granted a *tonlieu*, a feudal toll, of four *deniers*, or pence, on each sack of English wool transiting his lands.[65] Boston was the single highest source of revenue for Pierre de Savoie in England. A goodly portion of Pierre's entire Honour of Richmond income came from Boston, some £333[66] or nearly £250,000 in today's terms.[67] The largest portion of this income derived from the Boston Fair, which attracted merchants from the length and breadth of Europe, but it would be the resident merchants of Flanders who provided the link in the Savoyard chain. Thomas confirms that Pierre de Savoie was "certainly promoting the interests of the town [Boston] as well as protecting his own".[68] The fair of St. Botolphs at Boston played a key role in Englands's international trade; in 1257 Henry granted Pierre and the merchants coming to the Easter fair seven years quittance from royal purveyance.[69] Pierre's income from the fair would come specifically in stall rents, court fines and tolls. The principal trades were of course wool and cloth, Pierre's interest, but also a wide-ranging selection of wares: chests, knives, spices, medicines, cattle, sheep, pigs, fish, cheese, butter, grain, furs and wax. In addition to Pierre's estates interests in the wool trade at Boston, we should add that the great Cistercian monastery at Fountains with its many sheep granges also maintained property in the booming Lincolnshire port. So we have wool grown on Savoyard estates shipped through a Savoyard port to another Savoyard to make into expensive tapestries and sell throughout Europe – good business. If we want to find the most important source of the English riches that will accrue to the Savoyard in England, then we must look to the Lincolnshire coast and the trade with Flanders.

An interesting footnote to the award of the Honour of Richmond to Pierre de Savoie is to be found in the English archives, which relate an order from Henry to the Abbot of Jervaulx Abbey near Ripon to answer for the manor farm of East Witton, henceforth to the Savoyard. Jervaulx Abbey had been founded back in 1145 by the Savignacs from Normandy but had latterly become a Cistercian house. The name Jervaulx came from the French *Jorvalle*, itself a rendering of the English Ure Valley – which today we call Wensleydale. Jervaulx Abbey was the original home of Wensleydale cheese – Pierre de Savoie had in some small way become responsible for what would become a Yorkshire icon.[70] Relations between the abbey and the new holder of the Honour of Richmond do not seem to have been harmonious, Matthew Paris grumbled on behalf of the Cistercians in 1252, and matters deteriorated to such an extent that the previous holders of the honour, the House of Brittany, intervened in the person of Duke Jean.[71]

There would soon not be just one Savoyard uncle for Paris to be concerned with, but two. Upon Guillaume de Savoie's rejection by the Chapter of Winchester as bishop and subsequent death, King Henry III had settled upon another Savoyard brother as his choice for the see – Boniface. However, much to Henry's fury, the monks of Winchester were not to have a Savoyard foisted upon them as bishop.[72] So, when on 16 November 1240, Edmund, Archbishop of Canterbury left this mortal coil at Soisy-en-Brie in France en route for Rome, Henry saw his chance to replace Edmund in England with Boniface. Edmund made a point to Henry by choosing to have his body taken to the abbey at Pontigny for burial, the retreat for Thomas Becket during his exile from Henry's grandfather. The monks of Canterbury acquiesced with the king's choice since the former archbishop, Edmund, had had a strained relationship with them. Boniface was actually elected twice to the See of Canterbury, first on 1 February 1241[73] and again in May, the reason being that relations between Edmund and Canterbury had grown so strained that the archbishop had excommunicated the monks there, and they'd elected first whilst still under interdict, hence the reelection when the Pope had released them from excommunication – such were Church politics in the thirteenth century.[74]

Boniface, from the Latin Bonifatius, meant one of "good fate" and indeed this would be true of Boniface de Savoie. He was by accounts a good-looking man, so much so that "many ladies and women made demands upon him out of lust for his beauty" but Boniface was not likely to inherit much if anything in the way of land; with so many elder brothers, he was bound for a career in the Church. It seems, at first, it would be a monk's life for young Boniface – he became a novice at a Carthusian daughter house of the Grand Chartreuse, at Portes. However, by the 1230s several religious houses to the west of Savoy were looking for Savoyard protection, not least the See of Belley and the Priory of Nantua on one of the key roads from Geneva to Lyon and Bresse. They had good cause to seek protection: the strategically placed priory had long been the target of those wanting to sack and pillage. Founded in 671 AD as a Benedictine monastery by Saint Amand, it had been raided first by wandering bands of Magyars and

Chapter Four

more lately it had been burned in 1230 by Etienne I de Thoire-Villars. Accordingly, Boniface was elected both Bishop of Belley and Prior of Nantua in 1232.[75] Following the death of his brother Guillaume in 1239, he had then succeeded him as Bishop of Valence. The election, then, of Boniface to the See of Canterbury marked the culmination of the meteoric rise of Boniface from Prior of Nantua to Bishop of Belley thence Bishop of Valence. Good looks running in the family and younger than his brothers, Boniface was close to King Henry's age. Henry, and more so Alianor, had grown accustomed through Guillaume to the advantages of a suave, debonair Savoyard at court to help them pursue their interests. Boniface wasn't the first Savoyard Archbishop of Canterbury; he was following in the hallowed footsteps of Aosta-born Saint Anselm, but he was the first of the Savoyard comital family. Boniface would not, however, arrive in England until 1244, likely delayed by the long-standing Savoyard rivalry with Etienne II de Thoire-Villars who continued to menace his priory and town of Nantua.[76]

So, why had Henry sought to bring Boniface to England, alongside his brother Pierre? The answer is given in a letter he wrote to Dafydd ap Llywelyn in Gwynedd in 1241.[77] In the words of Carpenter, "Boniface would give security to both king and kingdom and protect the infant Edward from danger in the event of Henry's death."[78] This is why Henry brought the brothers to England, but we can also turn the telescope around: for the *Famille de Savoie*, the protection of Alianor and Edward was seen as paramount.[79] The joint project, so to speak, of Henry, Alianor, Pierre and Boniface was Edward. Events centuries later, with the death of the Plantagenet King Edward IV and the peril this placed his surviving queen and children in, illustrate that this was no imagined danger. It would seem for the *Famille de Savoie* two brothers in London were better than one. King Henry was then a deeply pious man, but not in the terms of a medieval monarch, a strong man. It was said of him that he held the opinion of the last man (or woman) to talk to him – and it was suggested that woman would most often be his wife, Alianor de Provence, and the men her uncles from Savoy. The English nobility would, in part, come to resent the Savoyard influence at court and go some way to alienate Henry's barony and ultimately lead to bloody revolt. However, despite the ups and downs to come, the project would in the end be a successful one, Edward succeeding his father peacefully and going on to be one of England's greatest monarchs.

However, for now, resentment would attach to Pierre as it had to Guillaume. Following the Honour of Richmond in April 1240,[80] he was granted the Honour of the Eagle, also known as the Honour of Pevensey, in September 1241, the lands of the late Earl Warenne in Surrey and Sussex including the wardship of the young Jean de Warenne, the castle at Lewes.[81] When a baron came into his inheritance before he'd reached his twenty-first birthday, being underage the king would take his revenues to himself until he came of age. The king might bestow this wardship upon a favoured baron as an act of patronage, as Henry did so with Warenne in favour of Pierre. He was also made Warden of the Cinque Ports, these being literally the five ports [82]: Hastings, New Romney, Hythe, Dover, Sandwich and Rye were collectively the most important ports in England. Their origin can be found in Anglo-Saxon England but by 1155 their main importance lay in a charter requiring them to provide ships for the Crown in case of need. In return they were granted some autonomy, legal and financial advantages. Pierre was also conferred temporary custody of the castles of Dover and Rochester from November 1241 until March 1242.[83] It's no understatement to suggest that within a few short months Pierre de Savoie now possessed the very keys to England.

It's understandable that such rapid preferment would attract envy. Matthew Paris had been unhappy at Guillaume's "full saddle bags", now he was as beside himself as it was possible for a monk to be. The debate as to the pros and cons for England in having the Savoyards at court has been a long one. Historian Nancy Goldstone writes an eloquent defence of Henry's preferment of the Savoyard: "The uncles from Savoy were the medieval equivalent of a world-renowned firm of international consultants or investment bankers."[84] Perhaps drawing upon Savoyard historian André Perret who described Pierre de Savoie as "a thoughtful man of good advice, a soldier of valour and a skilful diplomat, who rendered great services to his royal nephew".[85] Ridgeway agrees on the overall point, saying that "outside the king's household, the work of the Savoyards at court was confined exclusively to two areas: royal diplomacy, and the affairs of the Queen and the Lord Edward".[86] Taking the contrary view, in the spirit of Matthew Paris, would be historian Andrew M. Spencer who complained of "the open purse of England's king".[87] Lisa Hilton helpfully noted that the attractiveness of Ramon Berenguer's daughters lay not in the value of Provence as an ally, but that of Savoy.[88]

Julia Barrow, in reviewing the career of Pierre d'Aigueblanche, makes an excellent point, and one I've not found made elsewhere: that of language. Aigueblanche, she suggests, spoke Franco-Provençal, a language now known as Arpitan.[89] As a form of French it differed markedly to both the Anglo-Norman French of the English and the Old French of the Capetians, both northern forms of French. Franco-Provençal or Arpitan speakers would be comfortable dealing with other southern French forms, such as the Occitan of Gascony and the straight Provençal of Provence; furthermore, its southern form gave them an advantage with Italian (Papal Curia) and Castilian (Gascony's southern neighbour), both vital to English interests.[90] What was true of Aigueblanche's mother tongue would be equally true of Pierre de Savoie.

The advantages of Savoy to Henry's hopes of restoring his ancestral lands and a southern alliance is something that many English authors, from Matthew Paris to Spencer, in their eagerness to dismiss Henry's promotion of his wife's maternal family, have neglected to value. In the end your view of Henry's policy of seeking continental alliances through preferment will be coloured by whether you see Henry as primarily a King of England, or as something I think he viewed himself as, the holder of the familial banner of his father John, his grandfather Henry II and grandmother Alianor d'Aquitaine. Although Spencer draws attention to the ultimate failure of the alliance with Savoy in furthering Henry's cause in southern France, he neglects to mention that in this policy Henry was merely following his grandfather, Henry II, who'd sought to ally himself with Savoy through a marriage between John and Alais,[91] and as Ridgeway reminds us, learning from the mistakes of his father, in that it was the want of continental allies that helped bring about the loss of Plantagenet lands in France in 1204.[92] Perhaps Henry was guilty of learning from the mistakes of his father and following the pattern of his grandfather; in that we can hardly condemn him.

That the policy might ultimately prove unsuccessful and Provence would fall into Capetian hands was not known at the time to either Henry or his grandfather. But, the alliance did at least provide the Plantagenets with support upon which Henry and Edward would come to rely upon.[93] Savoyards from Pierre de Savoie in Henry's time through to the men who built the castles of Wales for his son Edward would be constant in their support of Henry, Alianor and Edward because they were kin, they were family. Amidst the turmoil of the Baronial War, it would be the support of Pierre de Savoie upon which Henry and Edward could rely. As we shall see, it was Pierre's castles that held out against the Montfortians, and the likely plans of Alianor and Pierre that would free Edward from captivity. Edward certainly learned at this time upon whom he could rely when "the chips were down" – in his day he would trust the counsel of the Savoyard Othon de Grandson above almost all others.

Chapter Four

If Henry's marriage to Alianor had been a counter move to Louis' marriage to Marguerite in the Great Plantagenet Capetian chess game being played across Europe, then Henry was about to make another move, using his brother Richard as the next chess piece by which to strengthen the Anglo–Savoyard alliance.[94]

Richard, 1st Earl of Cornwall, was Henry's younger brother, who had been given Cornwall as a gift by Henry when he was but 16 (1225) and had been so taken with Arthurian myths and legends current at the time that in 1233 he'd built a castle at Tintagel. A motivation for Richard in building Tintagel was to co-opt the Celtic Arthurian myths of the Cornish population in an attempt to buy loyalty – he would not be the first Anglo-Norman prince to do so. Cornwall had reputedly helped make Richard one of the wealthiest men in Europe, but sibling rivalry had also meant that Richard was a Plantagenet in search of a role. Richard had been married to Isabel Marshal but upon her death in 1240, he was not only in need of a role, he was in need of a bride.

Shortly after Isabel's passing Richard went off on crusade, the so-called Barons' Crusade. Little of note was achieved, but his return journey did provide pointers toward his future; first, he travelled to the Holy Roman Empire, meeting his sister the Empress Isabella and her husband Frederick II. But beforehand he'd called in on the queen's father, Ramon Berenguer V, Count of Provence – where he'd met the beautiful Sanchia, the queen's sister. The beauty that had drawn Count Thomas de Savoie to Marguerite de Genève, that had drawn Ramon to Béatrice de Savoie, that had drawn Henry to Alianor de Provence would find another admirer – reputedly Richard was struck by Cupid's arrow on crusade not by a Saracen arrow.

Henry had begun to see a new way to outflank the Capetians, Alianor a new way to strengthen her position at court: another Savoyard would be heading to England. Henry had been eyeing an alliance with the powers of the southern regions of France against Capetian encroachment from the north. To this end, in June 1241, he'd sent Pierre d'Aigueblanche alongside Pierre de Savoie, on perhaps the latter's first diplomatic mission for Henry, to the francophone parts of the empire, the Franche Comté and the Viennois, to see if Guillaume de Vienne and Jean de Chalon could be tempted into alliance.[95] This would be the beginning of a long and distinguished diplomatic career for Pierre in the service of the Crown. Indeed, it would be one that he'd share with the Savoyard Bishop of Hereford, Pierre d'Aigueblanche. What's more, the two Pierres would be succeeded by yet more generations of Savoyards operating as envoys for the Crown, in Othon de Grandson and Gérard de Vuippens going on to serve Henry's son Edward. But in Henry's time the Savoyard web involved in the potential alliance is evidenced by the destination of Pierre's letters of accreditation: Thomas de Savoie, Count of Flanders, Amédée IV de Savoie, Count of Savoy, Boniface de Savoie, Archbishop of Canterbury still in Belley, Philippe de Savoie, now Archbishop elect of Lyon and to Béatrice de Provence, nee Béatrice de Savoie, Countess of Provence. If we are to imagine why Henry was so keen to develop ties with Alianor's family, these letters of accreditation show us the network into which he'd hopefully plugged England.

Henry seems to have been happy with the result, since on Pierre's return in September 1241, the king rewarded him with the Honour of the Eagle. The award recorded in the Calendar of Patent Rolls and *Fœdera* as 25 September 1241 at Westminster,[96] was later confirmed by charter of 20 July 1246.[97] In attendance would also be a member of Pierre's coterie, Pierre de Genève.[98] The origins of the Honour, like Richmond, lay in the Norman Conquest of England. Engenulphe de l'Aigle had been another well-known follower of the Conqueror, but unlike Alan Rufus, he was a Norman who perished along with Harold at Hastings. The ill-fated

Engenulphe hailed from the Château de l'Aigle by the River Risle in Normandy, so named as an eagle's nest was reputedly found on the land upon which the castle was built. Curiously the commune of l'Aigle in Normandy today is twinned with Aigle in Switzerland, once Savoy. The Aigle lands in England were created by William for the descendants of Engenulphe, and held by the family until the early thirteenth century, when, like the Dukes of Brittany, they were made to choose between English and French allegiances and chose French. Accordingly, their English lands, like Richmond, passed into the hands of the Crown. Originally the castle at Pevensey itself had not been a part of the Honour, as it had gone to the Conqueror's half-brother Robert, Count of Mortain. However, by the mid-thirteenth century, the castle had been joined to the rape, Gilbert de l'Aigle II having acquired it when the incumbent Montain had rebelled against Henry I. The *Rapus de Peuenese* or Rape of Pevensey, a rape being in this case a subdivision of land in the county of Sussex, were the lands lying between the Rapes of Lewes and Hastings. The Honour of Hastings would come to Pierre in 1249, thus uniting the lands of the Sussex coast under his title (see figure 1.8).

Witley Manor near Haselmere in Surrey came to Pierre as part of the Honour of the Eagle and may well have become a favoured residence for Pierre. The manor had belonged to Earl Godwin before the conquest before being granted to the grandson of the aforementioned Engenulphe. He was building at Witley for as long as he lived in England[99] and appointed his Savoyard clerk, Simon de Vercelli, as parson there.[100] The refusal of some of his tenants there to pay the necessary homage as xenophobia gripped England during the Baronial War and Pierre's subsequent raising of rents became a weapon in the hands of the Montfortian regime. Witley was just over thirty miles from Windsor (50 kilometres), a day's horse ride, and so conveniently close to Henry and Alianor. Following Pierre's death the manor passed to Alianor who caused the church at Witley to offer prayers at a yearly service for the departed souls of Henry and Pierre.

Alongside the Honour came the ward of Jean de Warenne, the young 6th Earl of Surrey. Jean's father Guillaume, the 5th Earl, had died in 1240 with Jean not yet 10 years of age. Guardianship of the lands of the young Earl of Surrey brought with it custody of the castles at Lewes and the Rape of Lewes,[101] adjacent to Pevensey, and castles at Reigate, Castle Acre in Norfolk and Conisborough in Yorkshire. As will be familiar now, the Earldom of Surrey went back to the Norman Conquest of England and had been in the Warenne family since the 1st Earl, Guillaume de Warenne, had ventured across the Channel with the conqueror. The name came from the family's ancestral castle in Normandy, at Bellencombre, by the River Varenne. The ward of such an influential earldom would ensure Jean de Warenne was loyal to both the Crown and the queen for life, brought up as he was, at court.

Returning to the southern alliance and a bride for Richard, Henry's younger brother, the strengthening of Alianor's position at court may have been the overarching Savoyard interest in a match. But also, Alianor and Pierre may also have been acting in the direct interests of Savoy. Sanchia de Provence had been betrothed to Guigues VII, the Dauphin of the Viennois, a perennial Savoyard rival. In marrying Sanchia to Richard, he was not only able to bring Richard into the Anglo-Savoyard circle, but also forestall any Provençal Dauphiné match – a double virtue. Suspicions that this might have been the root cause, rather than just Cupid's arrow, are heightened when we note that Guigues was then, in 1241, betrothed not to Sanchia but to Pierre's own daughter, the very young Béatrice de Savoie, dame de Faucigny. Béatrice would not marry Guigues until 1253, which for the time being nullified any threats to Pierre's lands from the Dauphin. It's an interesting example of the Machiavellian ways Pierre was

Chapter Four

capable – one might observe that both Alianor and Henry were wise in employing such a mind in their cause. Accordingly, Henry, Alianor and Pierre met Richard returning from crusade at Dover on 7 January 1242. There had been fears that he might bring renewed rivalry with him, but as we've seen, Cupid's arrow had struck, and he was soon persuaded of the advantages of a marriage alliance and, as we shall see, an expedition to Poitou. In this conversion of a former Savoyard rival to a Savoyard ally of Richard, Earl of Cornwall, we can see that the diplomatic reputation of Pierre de Savoie was not without foundation.

In attempting a southern alliance, Henry was engaging in another under-resourced and futile attempt to regain lost ancestral territory in France. Having tried and failed over a decade earlier in 1230, Henry would try once more to recover Poitou. The southern alliance encompassing Toulouse, Provence and Savoy would rely upon coordinated action and Poitevin rebellion. The Count of Toulouse, Raymond VII, was Henry's cousin, being the son of Joan of England, and so a grandson like Henry of Henry II and Alianor d'Aquitaine. Poitou had been the northernmost part of Henry's grandmother's Duchy of Aquitaine, the southernmost part being Gascony. Indeed, the ducal palace had been in Poitiers, in Poitou not in Gascony. The Poitevins, of whom Henry's brother Richard was still a titular count, attempted revolt against Capetian rule, but sadly the premature revolt would be singularly unsuccessful. The revolt was led by Hugues X de Lusignan in concert with his wife, Isabelle d'Angoulême, Henry's mother.[102] In June 1241, Louis had awarded the county to his younger brother Alphonse, whom Isabelle d'Angoulême regarded as a usurper. Isabelle had felt deeply slighted at the ceremony to invest Alphonse with lands she felt belonged to her family.[103] As with all things of the period this was deeply personal; Blanche de Castille, as we saw earlier who'd rejected the inclusion of Marguerite de Provence's Savoyard family at the French court, slighted Isabelle as a lesser noble, when in Isabelle's mind she remained a Queen of England. Hugues, putting together an alliance of disaffected nobles, had reputedly said, "The French have always detested us … They will treat us worse than the Normans and Albigeois." A reminder that many in Poitou did not yet consider themselves French, and that Alphonse was considered an imposition. At Christmas 1241 at the court of the newly installed Alphonse, Hugues formally renounced his homage.

So in February 1242, Pierre de Savoie was dispatched from London to make contact with the Poitevin rebels and also to move south to negotiate a marriage between Richard and Sanchia de Provence. He was accompanied again by his compatriot, Pierre d'Aigueblanche, Bishop of Hereford. Pierre de Savoie narrowly escaped an "ambuscade" before returning to London, according to Paris, "sound in body, but not without loss".[104] Some think the ambush was an attempt by French King Louis to forestall the match.[105] Pierre de Savoie returned to England by Easter of 1242. Pierre d'Aigueblanche, meanwhile, continued on to Provence to successfully perform the nuptial negotiations.[106] Shortly before the conclusion he was joined by way of Gascony, by Pierre de Savoie. On 17 July at Tarascon the marriage contract between Richard, Earl of Cornwall and Sanchia de Provence was sealed. If Alianor's marriage contract to Henry had Savoyard fingerprints all over it, then that of Sanchia even more so – it bore the seals of Ramon Berenguer V, Count of Provence, but also her mother Béatrice de Savoie, her uncles Pierre and Philippe de Savoie, along with the Savoyard Bishop of Hereford.[107]

Meanwhile, in support of the Poitevin rebellion, on 9 May 1242, Henry had led an English expeditionary force from Portsmouth to France, landing at Royan, on the northern bank of the Gironde, on 13 May. At this point Simon de Montfort re-enters the story, having left the Holy Land in the autumn of 1241; he was summoned to the king's colours from Burgundy to join the campaign. Henry marched inland to Pons, on the road north from Bordeaux to Saintes, where he met again, for the first time since he was a boy, his mother, Isabelle d'Angoulême. However, Louis IX, unlike the uncoordinated alliance, had moved quickly, sweeping through Poitou from Chinon, ravaging the land and taking the castles; Poitevin support quickly melted, Henry's plans were unravelling before his eyes. On 7 June Henry advanced to the capital of the Saintonge, to Saintes, where he then paused for two weeks, before marching on to Tonnay on the Charente where he arrived on 23 June. But Henry's thoughts of advancing into Poitou were soon to change to ones of preventing Louis marching into the Saintonge and Gascony. Matthew Paris talks of a French army of "four thousand knights" along with "twenty thousand retainers and crossbowmen".[108]

From Saintes Henry first moved the twenty-two miles (thirty-five kilometres) downstream on the Charente to the bridge at Tonnay before returning the twenty-two miles upstream from Tonnay to Taillebourg. There the two armies met at another bridge over the Charente by a loop in the river, on 21 July. Louis had advanced south with an army behind the *oriflamme*, counting over twice as many knights as Henry's.[109] Louis had made the castle on the north bank of the river his base, probably from 19 July, its Lord Geoffrey de Rancon being no lover of Henry's stepfather Hugues X de Lusignan. The Charente was an unfordable river and so the bridge became the key for either side. Paris assessed the English arm comprising "sixteen hundred knights, twenty thousand foot-soldiers and seven hundred crossbowmen".[110] The French brought up a wooden bridge and wooden boats to effect a crossing. The smaller army looked doomed and there followed a skirmish more than a battle, in which Simon de Montfort appears to have distinguished himself. Both sides retired thinking they had the victory. Back in Saintes Henry asked his stepfather where the promised Poitevin support had gone.[111] An indignant Simon de Montfort suggested that Henry was so incompetent a martial king that he ought to "put away somewhere" in the manner of French Carolingian King Charles the Simple in 923 AD after the Battle of Soissons – this was not an insult that Henry would forgive or forget.[112] In an untenable position at Saintes, Henry then withdrew and so Henry's brother, Richard, had to intervene in guise of a pilgrim to seek a truce with Louis to enable an English withdrawal in some semblance of order. The account of the Battle of Taillebourg comes from Jean de Joinville, whose brother Simon would be a vassal of Pierre de Savoie at Gex, whom we shall meet later as he may well have played an important hidden part in English affairs. Joinville wrote:

> The King of England came into Gascony to make war on the King of France. Our holy King, with as many men as he could raise, rode forth to give him battle. Thither came the King of England and the Count of La Marche to do battle before a castle called Taillebourg, which lies on a dangerous river named the Charente, where there is no crossing save by a very narrow stone bridge. No sooner had the King reached Taillebourg, and the armies were face to face, than our men, (who had the castle on their side) pushed on at great cost, and crossed over most hazardously by means of boats and the bridge, and rushed upon the English; and there began a general hand-to-hand engagement stiffly contested. The King perceiving this, adventured himself into the thick of it along with the rest, for the English had four men for every one that the King had after he had crossed. Howsoever it so happened by God's will, that when the English saw the King cross over, they lost heart, and retired into the city of

Chapter Four

Saintes; and some of our men entered the city mixed up with them, and were taken prisoners."[113]

Delacroix later immortalised at Versailles the battle in French history in his painting of a valiant Louis riding down the English defences on the bridge at Taillebourg. The Capetians would extend the idea of a reconquest of Aquitaine; the Plantagenets might have called it a conquest – such are the national myths that abound. The rebellion was defeated by a triumphant Louis and the Capetians were victorious, thus ending forever Poitevin independence and Plantagenet dreams of recovering their ancestral lands in Poitou. The stitching together of a southern alliance with the help of Pierre de Savoie had come to naught. On 12 March 1243 a five-year truce was agreed: Henry would hold Gascony but Poitou was now irrevocably lost. Thomas, Philippe and, of course, Pierre de Savoie had all played a hand in constructing Henry's southern anti-Capetian alliance. That it had foundered at Taillebourg was not of their making; their ability to provide a diplomatic entrée into the affairs of southern magnates had proven as useful as Henry had hoped it might. The failure of the Poitevin campaign of 1242–3 has been laid at the door of a militarily inept Henry, but it can equally be laid at the door of the premature renunciation of homage by Hugues X de Lusignan and the fiery Isabelle d'Angoulême, which alerted Louis to the impending crisis earlier than might have been wished. And so it was that a truce came to pass between the Plantagenets and Capetians, Henry's ancestral lands in Poitou, Anjou and Normandy remaining lost.[114] Henry's mother Isabelle, having failed to aid her son in the recovery of Poitou, sought refuge in the ancestral Fontevraud Abbey, dying there on 4 June 1246. The death of Count Raymond VII de Toulouse in 1249 marked the end of Henry's southern alliance; upon his death, the County of Toulouse passed to Capetian France. Raymond, the son of Joan of England, herself a daughter of Henry II and Alianor d'Aquitaine, chose burial also at Fontevraud Abbey alongside his mother. Henry's French relatives were being buried along with his French ambitions in the family necropolis in Anjou.

Pierre was fortunate enough to miss the debacle of Taillebourg. Having been at the court in London, at the Easter of 1242, he had set sail for Gascony with Henry. But on 25 May had been given leave of the army at Pons to run a diplomatic errand, as we saw earlier, regarding the marriage of Henry's brother, Richard. Heading south-east through Perigord and Quercy, the eastern lands of Aquitaine disputed with the French king, passing through the lands of the Counts of Toulouse, he made for the Provençal court at the castle of Tarascon on the Rhône, where he was noted on 19 July 1242 negotiating for Richard, Earl of Cornwall to marry his niece, Sanchia de Provence, alongside his brother Philippe and Pierre d'Aigueblanche.[115]

Before leaving England, he had requested his vassals of the Honours of Richmond and the Eagle "make a competent aid, as he [Pierre] is about to cross with the King, where he will have expenses of every kind".[116] Sailing with them was Pierre de Genève,[117] son of Humbert, former Count of Geneva, Pierre having been deposed by his uncle Guillaume. Pierre de Genève, along with his brother Ebal, would become followers of Pierre de Savoie and would find preferment in England as a result.

Alongside them was Pierre's long-time Savoyard physician, Pierre de Mont,[118] who'd come to England with Pierre, having previously taken care of the ailing Aymon de Savoie, and was also noted as being with the army. John Mansel, whom Pierre had almost certainly met back in 1238 in Lombardy when Mansel was pay-keeper of English knights led by Guillaume de Savoie, was badly injured. French rebels had holed up in the monastery of Vérin near Bordeaux, Mansel took it upon himself to courageously scout an entrance when he was assailed on high by a defender throwing rocks, one of which crushed his leg. Pierre de Mont's care of Mansel at Pierre de Savoie's urging healed Mansel sufficiently enough for him to walk again, albeit with a limp. This episode, taken together with their likely serving together in Lombardy explains somewhat the ongoing alliance between the Savoyard and the Englishman who would become Henry's keeper of the great seal and loyal and trusted adviser.[119]

Pierre de Mont was thus certainly of the entourage that had come to England with Pierre de Savoie. Unsurprisingly, Pierre had brought to England his physician; equally unsurprising is that he brought with him men who could manage his estates in England during his absences overseas.[120] Three of Pierre's entourage would be the three brothers Charron, Charron being still today a small village in Bugey, twelve miles (nineteen kilometres) east of Pierre's Château d'Angeville at Lompnes (see figure 1.9). The three, a knight, a cleric and a Cluniac monk, included a Bernard, Guichard and Stephen. Bernard is thought to be the Bernard de Savoie, along with his wife Douceline, who became a key part of Henry's court, being constable of Reigate then Windsor Castle and whom we met earlier; he is elsewhere thought to be an illegitimate brother of Pierre de Savoie.[121] Stephen became prior of St. Mary's, Thetford in Norfolk until he was murdered by his monks in 1246.[122] As we saw earlier Matthew Paris took great delight in describing his drunken debauchery and reporting his Savoyard origins. It would be Guichard that would carry the Charron name in England, with Guichard becoming Pierre's seneschal up in Yorkshire. Guichard de Charron married a Mary de Sutton[123] in England, having a son of the same name who in turn had a son also of the same name.[124] As mentioned, Guichard was described by Paris unkindly as "a beastly clerk" with a "belly ... like a bladder in frosty weather, and whose body would load a waggon".[125] As we shall oft times find, identification of all the Ebals de Mont, Othons de Grandson and Guichards de Charron can confuse us poor historians, the habit of fathers naming sons after themselves being obviously rigorous in Savoy. It would be a Guichard de Charron, likely the son of the first, who would play a key role in protecting Richmond from Simon de Montfort later in our story. So, with his English possessions left in the hands of lieutenants, Pierre left the army at Pons and made for Tarascon before he then returned to Savoy to put his Alpine affairs in order.

As he moved on from Tarascon, thoughts no doubt began to turn to potential acquisitions at home. In December 1241, he had received Count Amédée IV de Savoie's permission to acquire further fiefs in the County of Savoy to support his interests.[126] In March 1242, he acquired the liege-homage of Jacques d'Aubonne.[127] He would be ceded his brother's share of the fief Guerry d'Aubonne in 1255,[128] definitively in 1261.[129] The castle, town and lands of Aubonne lay at the midway point of the road from Geneva to Lausanne.

In the peace of 1237 with Guillaume II de Genève, the strategic castle at Arlod was supposed to have been surrendered to Pierre. That a brief war appears to have flared on Pierre's return in 1242 suggests that Guillaume had been less than forthcoming in the matter. On 26 August 1242 a new peace "in front of Arlod" compelled Guillaume to surrender the castle to Pierre.[130] Pierre strengthened the castle, very much Geneva's front door, which sat hard by a fortified bridge over the Rhône, twenty-five miles (forty kilometres) downstream of Geneva, a veritable knife to Geneva's throat, so perhaps it's understandable why Guillaume was reluctant to relinquish it.[131] Today the ruins of the once-important castle sit beneath the waters of the Genissiat Dam of the Rhône. As always with Pierre, Savoyard and English affairs are inextricably linked; his return to Savoy in the late summer of 1242 is followed by an April 1243 record in the English Calendar of Patent Rolls that has Bouchard, the Abbot of Hautecombe Abbey, travelling to Rome for papal negotiations regarding the confirmation of

Chapter Four

Boniface as Archbishop of Canterbury on behalf of King Henry III of England. That the abbot of the principal Savoyard abbey would appear in an English archive for Bordeaux can surely be attributed to a visit by Pierre de Savoie to Hautecombe and Belley whilst dealing with the Count of Geneva.[132] Bouchard wasn't the last abbot of Hautecombe to be used by Henry as an ambassador to the papal Curia: he would be followed by Pierre de Soleriis in the role.[133]

Pierre's intriguing in the affairs of the County of Geneva extended to Guillaume II de Genève's deposed nephews, Pierre and Ebal. Pierre de Geneve's father had been the Count of Geneva, Humbert de Genève; he was the brother of Marguerite de Genève and so Pierre de Savoie's uncle. Humbert had been the Count of Geneva until 1225, but when he'd died, the county did not pass to his children Pierre and Ebal but Humbert's younger brother Guillaume II de Genève. The Genevois held not only the lands between Annecy and Geneva but still had lands on the northern shore of Lac Léman, as far as Lausanne – and these fertile (now inordinately expensive) lands were coveted by Pierre de Savoie. The Savoyard who'd subsequently been engaged in wars with Guillaume was looking for ways to carve out a niche for himself in the *Pays de Vaud*, at Guillaume's expense. It has been suggested that either Pierre de Savoie arranged for Pierre and Ebal de Genève to find preferment in England in return for their rights on the northern shore of Lac Léman or more generously that he befriended them and offered them a life in England as a good uncle to nephews in need – either way they arrive in England between 1240 and 1241 and feature in English records in the early 1240s.[134] Once in England they joined Pierre de Savoie's staff, following an interest in the widow of Hugh d'Aubigny, 5th Earl of Arundel, Isabel de Warenne.[135] Pierre de Savoie was able to find Pierre de Geneve a good marriage match, Mathilde de Lacy, youngest daughter of Gilbert de Lacy who claimed descent from the great William Marshal. The family held the castle in the Welsh Marches at Ludlow, and for a time Pierre became Lord of Ludlow through Mathilde, before succeeding Bernard de Savoie, becoming a constable of Windsor Castle itself, before dying in 1249. His connection, and therefore Pierre de Savoie's ongoing connection with the Lord Edward and the protection of Savoyard investment in the heir to the throne, is further evidenced by Pierre de Geneve's administration of the castle at Tickhill, on the Yorkshire–Nottingham border, on behalf of the prince; that he should follow his compatriot Bernard de Savoie, and be followed by Pierre de Savoie himself in this is instructive.[136] His death shows, once more, how Matthew Paris could get very confused with all these incomers from Savoy, Paris describing the son of a Count of Geneva as "Peter de Geneure, a Provençal ... of humble origin".[137]

Pierre de Genève's English widow would find another Savoyard match in Geoffroi de Joinville (known in England as de Geneville), the brother of Saint Louis' biographer and famed chronicler of Taillebourg and the crusades, Jean de Joinville. Maud de Lacy held Windsor Castle for a short while, before a third successive Savoyard was appointed Constable, Aymon de Thurumberd – Windsor Castle, that most powerful symbol of English identity, had constables from Savoy for twenty years, between 1242 and 1261. Even then, following the hiatus of the Baronial War, another was installed in 1266, Ebal II de Mont. The reason for this Savoyard control of Windsor will become quite clear: it was the home of the royal household, the queen and her children, and so needed the protection provided by Pierre de Savoie. But we should also note that the important descendant of the great William Marshal and holder of key lands in the Welsh Marches, Mathilde de Lacy, should find herself married successively to men in the service of Pierre de Savoie. Indeed the evidence of Pierre's protection of Alianor by way of Edward using his coterie of followers from Vaud is definitively concluded by Ebal II de Mont being appointed Steward of the Household of the Lord Edward from 1251 until 1257, shown as having been knighted by 1252,[138] before becoming Steward of the King's Household from 1261 until 1263, before that aforementioned appointment as Constable of Windsor Castle from 1266 until his death in 1268.[139] Ebal II de Mont was by Edward's side throughout his life until his passing, so we should not be surprised then to find one of the squires entrusted to what would become Harlech Castle some twenty years later being Ebal IV de Mont, his son. Those, such as Spencer, who query the loyalty of the Savoyards in royal service disregard the service of those such as the *Famille de Mont*, something neither Henry nor Edward did.

Meanwhile, Pierre de Genève's brother Ebal was found a good marriage match in Ireland, Christiana de Marais, the daughter of Robert de Marais (himself a son of John's Justiciar in Ireland who'd received large grants of land in Munster). Henry III's grant of marriage bestowed all lands inherited by Christiana on Ebal.[140] Ebal would later accompany the Lord Edward in service to Gascony, then being granted custody of Hadleigh Castle until his early death in 1259.[141] He left his entire estate, perhaps unsurprisingly, to Pierre de Savoie, his benefactor.[142] It would be this last action that would reverberate in Savoy, helping to bring about further hostilities between Pierre and the Count of Geneva.

Supporting the Machiavellian view that these Genevois in England played a part in furthering Pierre de Savoie's Vaudois interests are documents that show the grateful Genevois renouncing their claims in the County of Geneva. They were drawn up in London, in favour of Pierre de Savoie – and sealed by those other Vaudois in England or related to those therein, Gerard de Grandson (a canon in Lyon), Ebal II de Mont, Pierre de Champvent and Simon de Joinville:[143] a prima facie case of Pierre de Savoie using his position in England to gain advantage in Vaud.[144]

The link between the Joinvilles and Pierre de Savoie had come from his marriage to Agnès de Faucigny – her father had of course been Aymon de Faucigny, his ally in the Battle of Lausanne, but her mother was Béatrice d'Auxonne. Following marriage to Aymon, Béatrice was married to the senior Simon de Joinville, their offspring being Gefferoi, Jean and the younger Simon – Pierre's wife was half-sister to the Joinville brothers who were Pierre's half-brothers-in-law. If Pierre de Savoie was using Geoffroi de Joinville as a chess piece in his English game, then his brother Simon de Joinville would be used in his Savoyard game. When Amédée, *Seigneur de Gex*, already a vassal of Pierre's from his first conflict with the Counts of Geneva, died without a male heir, his surviving daughters, Léonette, Marguerite and Isabelle, offered the chance to consolidate his position in the strategic lordship of Gex. When in January 1252, Léonette was married to Simon de Joinville, the younger brother of Gefferoi and Jean, Gex came as her dowry.[145] The link is also suggested by Nicholas de Joinville and Martin de Gex being members of the Chapter of Hereford Cathedral, most of whose members were introduced to England by Pierre de Savoie (see appendix). The bond between Pierre and the Joinvilles would remain until his death in 1268; upon her death, also in 1268, Agnès de Faucigny would make Simon de Joinville a benefactor.[146] Within a year of Joinville acquiring through Léonette Gex to his Lordship of his mother's Marnay in Burgundy, he'd be off fighting in Gascony on Pierre's behalf for Henry of England.

That one member of the Joinville family might be a part of the Savoyard web in England, another a vassal of Pierre's in Savoy and another trumpeting the achievements of the French against England also illustrates the tangled web of family relationships in the francophone world of the thirteenth century. The links between the family's Joinville, Genève, Faucigny and Savoie are best explained by a quick examination of their family tree illustrated in the appendix. The links between Faucigny, Gex, Ludlow and the Savoyards will play a vital role in later affairs as we shall see.

Chapter Five

Meanwhile, grateful for his help, after Taillebourg, Henry had promised Gascony to Richard, which directly cut across the ambitions of both Alianor and Pierre de Savoie for the young Edward. Alianor had also feared the power of Richard if Henry had died in the ill-fated Poitevin expedition, and so had circled the Savoyard wagons around herself and her son Edward, the all-important heir and source of her power. On 17 August 1243, whilst Henry and Alianor were still in Gascony, the county of Cheshire, amongst other things, was assigned to the queen as replacement for other manors of her 1236 dower. The move was to prevent Richard from gaining Cheshire; the first two witnesses of the Cheshire dower provision are revealing – Savoyards, Pierre d'Aigueblanche and Philippe de Savoie.[1] Cheshire, as we shall see later, was to become a key component of Edward's appanage. Its move, temporarily to Alianor, is a key example of not only the queen but also her extended family from Savoy acting on Edward's behalf at an early stage. It's also worth noting that the Savoyards would inadvertently set events in motion, that is establishing Edward as future neighbour of the Princes of Gwynedd, that would ultimately lead to their own participation decades later in the Edwardian castles of North Wales – very much the law of unintended consequences.

So for Henry the forthcoming arrival of Alianor's sister Sanchia was a way of strengthening the Plantagenet position in relation to the Capetians, but for Alianor the marriage would bring an ally, in her younger sister, to England, but also it would bring Richard into the Savoyard family and nullify any threat he might be to her or Edward. Meanwhile, our monkish chronicler from St. Albans gave vent once more to his displeasure at the impending marriage giving him yet another Savoyard to suffer at court, writing in an admonishing tone:

> At this the whole community in England were much excited and began to fear that the whole business of the kingdom, would be disposed of at will of the Queen and her sister, the said Cincia about to become the wife of Earl Richard, who would be, as it were, a second Queen.[2]

Philippe de Savoie accompanied the bride-to-be on her journey to the English court in Gascony, and be paid handsomely for his expenses, 1,000 marks.[3] Philippe de Savoie, who'd been blocked in his ambition to be the Bishop of Lausanne, had become, in the meantime, the Bishop of Valence (succeeding his brothers Boniface and Guillaume). He was rewarded for his labours with the benefice of the churches at Reculver and Wingham in Kent.[4] Richard, then Henry returned to England to prepare for the wedding. Before Alianor, her sister Sanchia and mother, Béatrice de Savoie also sailed for England, making safe landfall at Dover on 14 November. Earlier in February 1243, Béatrice had been awarded the lifelong possession of the manor at Feckenham in Worcestershire, surrounded by a favourite royal forest[5]. Henry's marriage settlement for Richard and Sanchia centred upon Cornwall where Richard had since

1225 been its first Earl. Today the Earldom, now a Duchy remains in royal hands. In so doing, Alianor had succeeded in ensuring Cheshire would be Edward's – the way was now clear for Edward's appanage.[6]

The wedding had occasioned the first time Alianor had met her mother and sister since leaving for England nearly a decade before. Richard, 1st Earl of Cornwall, was then married to Sanchia[7] de Provence on 23 November 1243 at Westminster. The royal wedding would be the flowering of the Plantagenet Savoyard alliance.

Paris chronicled the arrival of Béatrice:

> About the same time, viz the 1st December, Béatrice, countess of Provence, mother to the queens of England and France, a woman of a gracious mien, prudent and civil, landed at Dover; by the King's invitation, who paid the expenses of her journey. She came in great state, and with very pompous pageantry ... the king ordered that the city of London should be decorated with hangings, curtains and divers other ornaments, from the bridge to Westminster, and they should put out of the sight of those who passed through the city, blocks of wood, mud, dirt and all obstacles. She brought with her daughter Cynthia, to be united to Earl Richard.[8]

Whilst in London, Béatrice negotiated with Henry for a loan to Provence of 4,000 marks[9] in return for the surety of five Provençal castles. Despite his recent Poitevin reverse and to the dismay of his own nobility, Henry still harboured ambitions in France.[10] Historian Goldstone suggests that one of these castles was the key – Tarascon – where his marriage to Alianor had been agreed.[11] Wurstemberger, citing Guichenon, lists the others as Forcalquier,[12] Volonne,[13] Medes[14] and Obsede.[15] Ramon Berenguer V and Béatrice were perennially short of money,[16] with all those dowries and hostile neighbours, and the English loan was a most welcome addition to the comital coffers. So, perhaps with the need for family reconciliation and of a consciousness of the financial needs that dowries might involve, Béatrice persuaded Henry to grant the Montforts 500 marks as a marriage portion, lacking since their controversial marriage.[17] Indeed the marriage portion was not the only example of Henry's largesse toward the Montforts in the aftermath of Richard and Sanchia's marriage: Henry would pardon some £1,834 of their debts and grant them custody of the great castle at Kenilworth, thereafter their main home.[18]

But, as she left England, Béatrice learned that her husband, who'd remained in Provence, was seriously ill, and indeed he would not recover.[19] It may well be that the much-criticised loan with the castles as security was intended to strengthen Henry's position in southern France. One of two proctors sent by Henry to take possession of the castles was the Savoyard Guy de Rossillon.[20] Rossillon, on the onetime frontier between Savoy and Bugey, was the town where Count Thomas de Savoie had taken Marguerite de Genève to be his wife half a century earlier. As the brother of Pierre de Savoie's chancellor, Thomas de Rossillon,[21] he'd come to England along with the Pierre-inspired Savoyard migration in 1241, and he'd received clerical benefices in Rothwell, Preston, Wrotham and Lichfield, before being given the "*Maison de Cantorbéry*" for a short while.[22] Once having taken hold of the castles, they were given to the Archbishop of Embrun[23] and the canonist and friend of Henry, Henri di Susa[24] – both Savoyards. Their oaths on taking possession were to keep the castles for the use of "the king and queen" – Henry and Alianor.[25]

Chapter Five

Meanwhile, Philippe de Savoie's rise to prominence continued. In June 1243 a new pope had been elected, Innocent IV. Gregory IX, exhausted no doubt by the struggle with Frederick II and all that excommunicating, had given up his ghost on 22 August 1241. Goffredo da Castiglione had come to the papacy as Celestine IV in the October of 1241 but had yet to reign for a month when he too passed away on 10 November. There had then followed an interregnum until 25 June 1243 when Sinibaldo of the Genoese Fieschi clan came to the throne of Saint Peter as Innocent IV. However, the enmity between Holy Roman Emperor Frederick II and the papacy rolled on, to such an extent that this latest pope, fearing for his life amidst imperial-inspired enmity, fled Italy. The papal rhetoric had soared to new heights in May 1239 when then Pope Gregory IX had described Emperor Frederick II in these terms: "There has risen from the Sea a Beast full of Blasphemous Words which, with the Feet of a Bear, the Jaws of a Raging Lion, and its Limbs resembling those of a Panther, opens its Mouth in Curses against Gods name." With this Gregory had excommunicated Frederick.[26] With the accession of this new pope, Innocent IV, relations had not improved – so on his travels went his holiness. His destination, after negotiation with Count Amédée IV de Savoie and Philippe, was Lyon. Innocent arrived in Lyon accompanied by Philippe, on 2 December 1244.

That next summer, in June 1245, what became known as the first Council of Lyon took place, the first in thirty years. Church reform was on the agenda, as well as the fall of Jerusalem to Khwarezmian Turks in 1244 and, most importantly for Innocent, an opportunity to announce the "deposition" of Frederick. This was perhaps more than a little unjust, since it had been Frederick, on 17 March 1229, who had peacefully retaken Jerusalem by agreement with Sultan al-Kamil. Nonetheless, on 17 July 1245 Frederick was announced to be deposed and excommunicated, leaving a vacancy amongst other crowns in the realm of Sicily, of which much more anon. In the meantime, the Savoyards (as indeed the English too) attempted to walk a line between the empire and the papacy, controlling as they did the Alpine passes betwixt the two.[27] This feud between emperor and pope would continue, Frederick simply ignoring his deposition, Innocent attempting to promote rival kings and even the emperor's assassination exhausting papal coffers in the process.[28] The Pope, grateful for his sanctuary, and with the less than wholehearted blessing of Aimery de Rives, Archbishop of Lyon, arranged for the resignation of Aimery and the election in his stead of Philippe.[29] Thus Philippe de Savoie, thwarted in his attempt to gain the See of Lausanne, and only recently having become Bishop Elect of Valence, was now Archbishop Elect of Lyon – like his brother Boniface, a meteoric rise to an archbishopric. Philippe was unusually allowed to keep all his previous benefices in addition to his new income as Archbishop of Lyon, which would make him a wealthy man indeed – and this considerable church income came without ever being even a priest. The most likely reason for Innocent's generosity was his sanctuary in Lyon, but also buying at least the neutrality of the Maison de Savoie in his quarrels with the emperor.[30]

Meanwhile, the papal interregnum between the reigns of Celestine IV and Innocent IV,[31] from November 1241 until June 1243, delayed the process of confirming the election of Boniface de Savoie as Archbishop of Canterbury. No lover of Savoyards, Matthew Paris wrote of the confirmation:

> At that very time, Boniface, elect of Bellay, uncle to the queen, and by nation a Provençal, was confirmed by the pope in the archbishopric of Canterbury, through the strenuous exertions of the king, to the astonishment of many. In fact the king, that he might more easily raise Boniface to the Archbishopric of

Canterbury, wrote a book, at the instigation of the Queen, in which he lavished praises on the manners, science, and generosity of the said Boniface ... The abbot of St. Albans was the only one who, by cautiously declining, avoided this false testimony.[32]

One can't help but feel a little sorry for Matthew Paris. First, he'd had Guillaume, then Alianor, then Pierre, Philippe and Béatrice had visited, then Sanchia. Was there no end to this train of Savoyard heading northward? No doubt to Paris's satisfaction and despite the new pope's urging, and that of King Henry, it would not be until 1244 that Boniface finally ventured north to Albion. So it was, in April 1244, when the weather made for easier travel, he crossed the Channel, taking up residence at a newly refurbished Lambeth Palace. He was met at Dover by fellow Savoyard, Bishop of Hereford, Pierre d'Aigueblanche, along with his pallium, the symbol of an archbishop's authority. Aigueblanche had been acting on Boniface's behalf in England before his belated arrival. Upon arrival at Westminster, he paid homage to the king – Archbishop Boniface was Henry's man.[33]

For Pierre de Savoie, England began to be more of a home than Savoy, given the increasing conflict between Emperor Frederick II and Pope Innocent IV. This is perhaps understandable – the island on the edge of Europe being a moat defensive against unhappier lands as Shakespeare went on to opine. But more than a refuge, England was now the source of much of Pierre's wealth, the Honour of Richmond especially, allowing him to build a war chest for his continued ambitions in Savoy. Eventually his absences from Savoy in England would grow so lengthy that he would delegate his authority to his brother, Philippe, when he was away north of the Channel.[34] The ability of Pierre to play a role both in English and Savoyard politics simultaneously is something often overlooked, especially in English histories.

The war chest was used on 9 May 1244 to obtain the submission of Gruyères, to the north of Lausanne.[35] The Count of Gruyères appeared before Pierre at Romont,[36] where Pierre had recently (1240) begun construction of a castle, to surrender *"in merum lignum et francium"* his ancestral castle and its fertile land. Gruyères was (and still is) a commanding castle that dominates its hinterland to the north of Vaud, land whose rich pasture produces Gruyère cheese to this day. The extension of Pierre's interest into the lands of the Saane Valley brought yet more vassals into his orbit, such as that of the Vuippens family, but also into an important seat of power for the Bishops of Lausanne at Bulle. A network of castles and vassals now extended north from Lausanne to Moudon, Romont and Gruyères. The Count of Gruyères had also been a supporter of Jean de Cossonay in the bishopric dispute at Lausanne, and his transfer to the Savoyard helped isolate the bishop further. The castle at Romont had been Pierre's first new-build construction, and the first to incorporate round towers in its defences.[37]

Jean de Cossonay's isolation in his bishops' palace above Lausanne drove him to an accommodation with the Savoyards. On 29 May 1244 the bishop was summoned to cross the lake to the Savoyard castle at Evian.[38] There Count Amédée IV, along with Pierre, made the bishop pay the price for his accession to the see.[39] The bishop was forced to cede all the church possessed at Romont (including the profitable market rights there). Also ceded was church land between the rivers Glâne[40] in central Vaud, along with the district of Boussens and the castle by the Lac de Neuchâtel at Estavayer. Pierre then went on to take into his fiefdom supporters of the Cossonays – Richard of St. Martin and Guillaume and Nicolas de Fruence. Pierre's conquest of Vaud was not so much a military one, as one achieved by purchasing the liege-homage of key castles and their families. The struggle for supremacy north of Lac Léman was being settled in

Chapter Five

favour of the House of Savoy, and so it was that the Gruyères and the Cossonays also became fiefs of the Savoyard.[41] One of the brokers of the rapprochement with the Savoyards was Ulrich de Vuippens, the husband of Agnès de Grandson, the daughter of the Lord of Grandson, Pierre and Agnès de Grandson. The sons of both Pierre and Agnès de Grandson and Ulrich and Agnès de Vuippens would play a key role in English affairs later in our story – both would benefit from their new links with the Savoyard ruling family and its relatives, the English ruling family: yet more examples of the way Pierre de Savoie wove the destinies of Vaud and England together. The peace of Evian also regularised Pierre de Savoie's acquisitions in Vaud in the four years since 1240, including those of Romont and Moudon.

The early years of the 1240s would see what Cox called the "years of the migration" of Savoyards to England.[42] The migration had begun with the arrival of Alianor de Provence and her followers from Provence, who included some from Savoy. It would be natural for the young queen to surround herself with familiar places from home, both for comfort and for protection. This had then led first to the arrival of her uncles, first Guillaume then, following his death, of Pierre de Savoie – but it is with Pierre and his weaving of advancement in Vaud and England that the Savoyard migration to England went into overdrive.[43]

First, Alianor would see that Prince Edward, and the ensuing royal children, were heavily influenced and raised by Savoyards like Bernard de Savoie, who in addition to being constable at Reigate Castle from June 1241,[44] became constable[45] of Windsor Castle in December 1241.[46] Only the best would do for the young prince, Henry wrote to Bernard in October 1242, having earlier granted him one *tun* of wine a year,[47] asking that better wine be served, the best wine to be found in the castle no less, for a boy of 3 years.[48] Bernard was rewarded for his service in 1244 by award of the manor of Berminton.[49] He was joined in England by his wife, Douceline, who was responsible for the young prince, Chapuisat noting the name being of Provençal origin.[50] In 1244, he was also given the administration of the castle at Tickhill on the Yorkshire–Nottingham border for "the use of Edward, the king's son".[51] That Bernard was in Pierre's coterie is shown by the position of his brother, Guichard de Charron, at Richmond, and that Bernard's position at Reigate came within Pierre's responsibilities holding the ward of Jean de Warenne.[52] Bernard would be followed, at both Windsor and Tickhill, by another Savoyard, Pierre de Genève, both men being in the service of Pierre de Savoie. Eventually in 1252 Tickhill would come for a short while to Pierre de Savoie himself, until he finally passed it to the Lord Edward in 1254.[53] As we shall see repeatedly, Pierre's position in England, from a Savoyard perspective, was principally as Alianor's protector, and protection of Alianor chiefly involved protection of her prized asset, the heir to the throne. Walter de Dya, formerly a clerk of Guillaume de Savoie, was another Savoyard guiding the royal children, this time in the role of tutor.[54] Others included Henry and Alianor's stewards, Pierre de Champvent, the Burgundian Stephen de Salines, and Imbert Pugeys or Imbert de Savoie,[55] valets in the king's chamber. We will discuss the long-serving Champvent who was the first of the *Famille de Grandson* to find favour in England later. Imbert Pugeys moved from the position of valet to household knight and would become constable at Hadleigh Castle in 1244 and Oxford Castle in 1253. Advancing further, from 1257, the Savoyard knight became a steward of the royal household[56] and later castellan of the Tower of London, before eventually passing away in 1262. Imbert married one Joan de Aguillon, and, as mentioned, their son gave the family name to what would become Stoke Poges in Buckinghamshire.[57] Another Savoyard would be Imbert de Montferrand, from Bugey, not far to the north-west of Boniface de Savoie's See of Belley. Montferrand had come to England with Pierre d'Aigueblanche. He had a long career in England and became keeper of Edward's castle at Montgomery from 1254 until 1257, almost certainly a part of Pierre's policy of surrounding the heir with Savoyards. Imbert de Montferrand became Marshal of the King's Household from 1258 until 1274, thus serving both Henry and Edward, before retiring into the service of the widowed Alianor from 1275 until 1279. Amongst those in Alianor's service from the beginning would be her valet Guillaume de Valereys, a Vaudois, originating from lands in the immediate vicinity of Champvent and Grandson.[58] That Valereys was in Pierre's coterie will be evidenced later in his role as messenger for him. Another in Alianor's service was Matthew Bezill, often reported as a Savoyard but in fact a native of Touraine, although I suspect the niceties of which part of the francophone world one called home were lost in Matthew Paris.

Unlike France, whose court remained under the control of Blanche de Castile, the English court, to the chagrin of Matthew Paris, would fall heavily under Savoyard influence.[59] Thinking of his grandfather's grant to the monks of the Grand-Saint-Bernard, and reminding us again that the *Via Francigena* was never far from the mind of English monarchs, Henry granted protection without term to the "brethren of the Hospital of St. Bernard of Montjoux".[60]

For Alianor, the influx of Savoyards, which turned from a trickle into a flood, provided people she could rely on, a strong attraction, as historian Goldstone writes:

> The simplest way of expanding royal influence, of course, is to recruit intimates who are entirely dependent upon the goodwill of their sovereign, and so it was that Alianor, aided by her ever-present Savoyard uncles, began encouraging trusted friends and subordinates from Provence and Savoy to immigrate to England. This was not difficult to do, as the king and queen of England had a reputation for easy generosity; accordingly, over the next decade or so, approximately three hundred of Alianor's and her uncles' countrymen – and women, elected to relocate. Some of these people secured administrative positions at court, some served the august Archbishop of Canterbury [Uncle Boniface] or the equally powerful Earl of Richmond [Uncle Peter]."[61]

The source for Goldstone, although her work does not carry citations, was the extraordinarily diligent work of Swiss historian Chapuisat who spent much time in the 1950s in the London archives of the Public Records Office looking for family names of Vaudois, and more widely Savoyard, relevance and descent. Chapuisat wrote : "*Six mois de recherches à Londres m'ont fait rencontrer, enregistrés dans les archives de provenance royale ou épiscopale, les noms de plus de cent famillles diverses provenant de nos régions et représentant près de trois cents individus.*"[62] Which translates as "Six months of research in London made me meet, recorded in the archives of royal or episcopal provenance, the names of more than one hundred diverse families from our regions and representing nearly three hundred individuals." Lower numbers have subsequently been ventured by Carpenter, who estimated that between 1236 and 1272 lands in England were granted to thirty-nine Savoyards; additionally, forty men received money pensions, and an overall total of 170 individuals.[63] Ridgeway pointed toward a possible explanation of the discrepancy, that is that many of the names Chapuisat saw were absentee beneficiaries. Ridgeway went on, however, to note that given the coming and going betwixt Savoy and England, it's "truly difficult" to arrive at a definitive total[64] – suffice to say, it was a significant number, certainly over a hundred, likely over two hundred.

The protection afforded to Alianor by the presence of her uncles in England is made clear when King Henry went to war, as illustrated in 1242 during the ill-fated Poitevin campaign.

Chapter Five

In November 1241, Pierre had been granted custody of Dover Castle, relinquishing it the following spring in time for the French expedition to the Sheriff of Kent, Bertram de Cryoyl. Matthew Paris saw in this ceding of the castle a need to placate the returning Richard.[65]

However, shortly after, Cryoyl was instructed that he should surrender the castle to no one but the king, and upon his death, only to Alianor and, importantly, should she not be able to come to the castle herself, then Cryoyl was to surrender the castle only to one of Alianor's Savoyard uncles. No mention is made whatsoever of Richard, Earl of Cornwall.[66]

If the entourage of Alianor had brought one migration, then the techniques employed by Pierre in his expansions in Vaud had brought another. First, he enfiefed key commercial and trading centres or the routes between them – thus taking a strong hold of the region and increasing his incomes yet further – such as at Romont and Moudon. But his second technique was to have radical impacts upon the story of not only the *Pays de Vaud*, but also faraway England. Pierre would metaphorically travel Vaud, approaching financially challenged nobles with the promise of English gold and preferment to those who would take him as their suzerain. Many an impoverished lord of Vaud would succumb to the offer of money and advancement in England for their sons in return for allegiance to the House of Savoy. Thus, Pierre's advance in England fed his advance in Vaud, which in turn fed his advance in England, and so on and so on – Pierre had discovered a virtuous circle indeed.[67]

Bernard Andenmatten describes this acquisition of Vaudois nobility as vassals of Savoy, as solving *"les problemes d'une petite aristocratie en mal de numéraire"*[68] – a sickness of financial resources experienced by a small aristocracy.[69] Pierre often took with him the second eldest male child who, not inheriting an estate, was a perennial problem in the days of primogeniture. Traditionally, as had been mapped out for Pierre himself, a career in the Church was a solution, but England and the opportunities it presented was a more attractive proposition. A good example would be young Ebal II de Mont, second son of Ebal I de Mont and his wife Béatrice who held the castle at Mont-le-Grand, today's Mont-sur-Rolle on the road from Lausanne to Geneva, above Lac Leman.[70] The castle had been high above Lac Léman since at least 996 AD in the dying years of the old Kingdom of Burgundy, a very early example of a castle in the region. The eldest son Henri stood to (and indeed did) inherit the family castle, while Ebal was taken to England with Pierre, along with the young Othon de Grandson and his cousin Pierre de Champvent, to enter service with the English court, becoming a steward in the royal household from 1251.

Cox cited Estavayer as an example of the son of a lord becoming a vassal of Pierre de Savoie, often after the castle had passed to the son's control.[71] Mention of the Estavayers, Champvents and indeed Grandsons will bring us neatly to the arrival in England, courtesy of the feudal ambitions in Vaud of Pierre de Savoie, of a family that will provide yet another key wave of migrants – the *Famille de Grandson*, a family that would become enormously influential, not only in the reign of Henry III but perhaps more so in that of his son Edward I. The introduction to England of the *Famille de Grandson* may well be the single greatest legacy to Anglo-Savoyard history of Pierre de Savoie, and eventually lead to his legacy in Britain extending to the Edwardian castles of North Wales that would be constructed after his death.

Pierre went on to widen his net of vassalage to encompass the lords of Grandson, Belmont, La Sarraz and Cossonay, whose territories also lay across the roads from the west.[72] The castle at Grandson lay at the southernmost point of Lac de Neuchâtel, on the Neuchâtel side, in the shadow of the Jura. The castle itself had been constructed on a rectangular ridge of glacial moraine overlooking the lake. Ebal IV de Grandson had been Lord of Grandson until his death in 1235, his fief also including Belmont and La Sarraz. He had been granted the lands by Emperor Frederick Barbarossa to *"construire dans le territoire des Noires-Joux, maisons, villages, bourgs et châteaux, sans autre réserve que celle de suzeraineté immédiate de l'empire"* or "to build in the territory of the Noires-Joux, houses, villages, towns and castles, without any other reserve than that of immediate suzerainty of the empire". However, the family title to the lands predated the empire. Lambert I de Grandson is mentioned in 994 alongside the Archbishop of Lyon and Rudolf III the King of Burgundy – so it looks almost certain that the family association with the Lac de Neuchâtel dates from the dying days of Arelat. Indeed, there is a strong possibility it dates from 981–3 and his predecessor, Adalbert I de Grandson[73] – in so doing, this would place the Grandson line as beginning contemporaneously with that of the House of Savoy and a cause of the collapsing state of the Second Kingdom of Burgundy.[74] Ebal's grandfather, Barthélémy de Grandson (1110–58/9), had been a crusading knight, accompanying Count Amédée III de Savoie on the Second Crusade, passing from this world in Jerusalem. Ebal had divided his lands into three amongst his first three sons;[75] Henri received Champvent (only five miles from Grandson), Girard got La Sarraz and finally Pierre, Grandson itself. Pierre[76] would have a son, Othon, Henri a son, Pierre – both would be taken up by Pierre de Savoie to England to go into the service of the English monarchy.[77] Pierre de Grandson and Henri de Champvent had both been friends of Pierre de Savoie since at least 1234 and acted on his behalf in the region.[78] We're not certain of Othon's date of birth, but Swiss academics have speculated with some accuracy the year 1238 or soon thereafter,[79] making him around the same age as England's Prince Edward.[80]

And so, the two cousins travelled the road northward through the Jura and Burgundy to England and fortune, very soon after their fathers became vassals of Pierre de Savoie. The move followed Pierre's usual modus operandi (notwithstanding his manipulation of Pierre and Ebal de Genève noted earlier) in terms of extending his vassalage in the *Pays de Vaud*. Approaching a family in need of money and protection with the offer of same in return for becoming his vassal – part of the deal would be the chance for the new vassal's children to enjoy advancement in England using Pierre's royal patronage.[81] This acquisition of allodial[82] tenure as a means of extended fiefdom began in France during the tenth century, spread south of the Loire in the eleventh and would now be practised by the Savoyard in Vaud.[83]

So not only did Alianor strengthen her position at court, so too did Pierre and Boniface. The road north from Savoy through Burgundy and then on through France to the Channel ports was becoming very worn indeed – a veritable medieval migration, birds flocking north for riches and advancement. Alianor's position at court, strengthened by the birth of an heir in 1239, was further solidified in January 1245 with a spare heir. She gave birth to a second boy, Edmund, who'd grow to be a loyal supporter of his elder brother and the 1st Earl of Lancaster. It was around this time too that Alianor appointed the Savoyard Guy de la Palud as a guardian of the Queen's Wardrobe. He had accompanied her sister Sanchia to Gascony for her to marry her brother-in-law Richard, and would later become an archdeacon at Lyon under her uncle Philippe as archbishop there.[84] His origin isn't certain, but most likely to be that of Châtillon-la-Palud in the Dombes region just north-east of Lyon. Another Keeper of the Queen's Wardrobe, following Guy de la Palud, would be Jacques d'Aigueblanche, a nephew of the Bishop of Hereford and member of the chapter there, who served from 1254 until the Baronial War.[85] For most of her time in England, Alianor's Wardrobe would be looked after, not unnaturally, by a Savoyard.

When Guillaume de Warenne, 5th Earl of Surrey had died in 1240, his son Jean was but 9 years of age. He was made a ward of Pierre de Savoie and his lands and holdings awarded

Chapter Five

to the Savoyard as guardian. Later still, in 1246, Pierre was awarded the castle at Pevensey, originally a Roman Saxon Shore Fort which had latterly had a Norman *donjon* added to its defences. The Romans called their fort *Anderitum*,[86] but later the Saxons had developed this into *Andredesceaster* before attaching the name Pevensey which alluded to the site being on the marsh of *Pefen*. That Pevensey was once almost an island, now a peninsula, explains its attraction as a site to dominate Pevensey Bay and the coastline. Pierre's tenure of the castle was reinforced in 1252 by the grant of "free warren" of adjacent lands, "free warren" being the privilege of hunting certain beasts and fowls—the pheasant, partridge, hare and rabbit.[87] In addition to aforesaid "free warren", his landholding increased yet further. As with Richmond Pierre sought to acquire once associated lands in Sussex, with the grant of the manor of Burne [Eastbourne] "by the castle of Pevenesey", "late of Peter de Croun".[88]

Having, in 1249, been instructed by Henry to fortify once more the castle at Hastings, Pierre sought to address the castle at Pevensey. The castle itself had been neglected in the reign of King John and so Pierre wasted little time in constructing a curtain wall within the Roman walls to encompass the donjon providing an inner ward.[89] The gatehouse he found there is one of the earlier examples in England, being built around 1200 and incorporated into the Norman wooden palisade that formed the inner bailey. The upkeep of the castle had been undertaken by a local tax known as "heckage".[90] Pierre monetised this to finance the replacement of the wooden palisade with a stone curtain wall and towers that make up the castle to this day.[91] It is the 1254 compounding of "heckage"[92] that allows us to date and attribute the stone walls of Pevensey to Pierre since the "ancient stockade had been replaced by stone walls".[93] Indeed we may even be able to be more precise, Ridgeway highlights a reference to Pierre being "somewhere in Sussex" in June 1252 and January 1253; he suggests and I would agree that this is the likely beginning of works at Hastings and Pevensey.[94]

The keep at Pevensey sat against the former Roman eastern wall. Pierre raised a curtain wall of three sides to surround it, with three D-shaped towers and the aforesaid earlier twin-towered gatehouse. These defences would be tested within the decade.[95] We also have a deed in Pierre's recently published cartulary whereby the Bishop of Chichester is giving licence to the Savoyard to transfer the chapel at Pevensey within "the ancient walls of the vill", so that the parishioners may have access both in peacetime and war, the move to be conducted "at his own expense."[96] The stone structure of the castle, incorporating the fortified gatehouse and towers, became Pierre's second castle construction after Romont circa 1240. Pevensey Castle, and to some extent Hastings, thus represent an often-missed link in the Little Charlemagne's castle-building career between Romont of 1240 and Yverdon of 1260, both in Vaud. The importance of which comes to the fore when we remember that Yverdon was the first castle to engage the services of Maître Jacques de Saint-Georges who would later build the great Edwardian castles of North Wales. Nicola Coldstream in her critique of Maitre Jacques' design of these later Welsh castles has been that he had "never seen" a twin-towered gatehouse, and "can certainly never have designed or built one" and a critique that overlooks the common patronage of Pierre de Savoie at Pevensey, Hastings and Yverdon.[97] Twin-towered gatehouses were becoming a common form in England but remained unknown in Savoy. Whilst this may be true, the evidence of Pierre de Savoie's patronage of the castle building at Pevensey and the rebuilding at Hastings, then the building of Yverdon, suggests that the builder of Yverdon was working for a man who was most certainly familiar with twin-towered gatehouses. The critique emphasises the unfamiliarity of Savoyard builders with new English castle-building ideas, but the critique entirely overlooks Pierre de Savoie having, as we can say, feet planted both in England and

Savoy. Thus, the works at Pevensey and Hastings has been consistently overlooked in studies of the evolution of Savoyard castle design and its implications for the later castles of north Wales. It seems that if Amédée IV would give Henry the keys to the front door of Savoy in terms of Bard and Avigliana then Henry returned the compliment by granting Pierre the keys to the first castles built in England by William the Conqueror – England's front door.

Further research we have undertaken at Pevensey and Yverdon shows that Pierre's patronage may well have brought about architectural similitude between the earlier castle in Sussex and that later built in Vaud. The embrasures at Pevensey in Pierre's works share an uncanny resemblance to those found at Yverdon. Specifically sharing, "the use of segmental arches and the stepping in of the jambs at around the mid-point", although we should note here, there are differences "with the treatment of the sill". Sadly, lack of building records for Pevensey precludes confirmation, but it does seem very possible that Pierre had re-employed builders at Yverdon that he'd earlier employed at Pevensey.

In an echo of events that would follow some thirty years into the future, Pierre would soon be accompanying King Henry on an expedition in the summer of 1245 – to Wales. But what in 1245 was Wales? Well, first non-Welsh scribes would have referred to it, most likely, as *Wallia*, Welsh scribes perhaps most likely as Britannia harking back to Welsh origins as the "true Britons". The Welsh had originally called themselves "*Brytanyeit*" or *Britons*, but this had later given way to describing their land as *Cymru* and the language they spoke as *Cymraeg*, but the Welsh themselves described their land as Cymru and the language they spoke as Cymraeg. Geographically speaking, Wales would have encompassed the land pretty much occupied by Wales today. Wales was a geographic, ethnic and linguistic term, but not yet a political term. Politically, Wales was what medieval historian Robert Bartlett called a "half-conquered" country.[98] Interestingly, if the Welsh self-identified as being of *Wallia*, then the invaders from across the Severn estuary could be described as *Franci*.[99, 100, 101]

Since the Norman conquest of England, Wales had been divided into two main regions, *Pura Wallia* and *Marchia Wallie*. The first of these was *Marchia Wallie*, the Welsh Marches, where land had been granted by English kings to control the disputed border lands and to extend Anglo-Norman power into Wales proper. These Welsh Marches, the fief of Marcher lords, extended from Chester in the north, along the border, past Shrewsbury and Hereford and down to the River Wye and Chepstow. The Marcher lords had subsequently extended their territories into South Wales, to such an extent that they held land as far west as Pembroke – thus making the southern lower-lying part of Wales a virtual English fief. The greatest Marcher lords included the earls of Chester, Gloucester, Hereford and Pembroke. The first of these, Chester, was a County Palatinate,[102] which had the power to rule the county largely independently of the king. It should therefore be distinguished from the feudal barony. Hugh d'Avranches, who'd come across with William the Conqueror, was the first influential Earl of Chester; by the beginning of the thirteenth century the county had been in the hands of Ranulf de Blondeville but as we saw was now in Alianor's hands and ultimately Edward's. The Marcher lords themselves had complete temporal jurisdiction over their subjects, without recourse to the King of England. In the words of contemporary writers, the king's writ did not run in the Marches.[103] The king had jurisdiction only in treason cases, though the lords each bore personal allegiance to the king as feudal subjects. In the thirteenth century these powerful lordships had passed to the *Famille de Clare* at Gloucester, the F*amille de Bohun* at Hereford, and the *Famille de Marshal* at Pembroke. Others, the Mortimers, Braoses, Talbots and the LeStrange families, eventually acquired much Welsh blood through politically advantageous marriages with the Welsh nobility.

Chapter Five

The second part of Wales, *Pura Wallia*, the native Welsh lands, were not themselves a united country in the way of England or Scotland at this time. Unlike Scotland, there was no Kingdom of Wales, since the time of Ælfred and Æthelstan native Welsh princes had accepted Kings of England to a varying degree as suzerain. *Pura Wallia* could be subdivided into three main polities: Powys in mid-Wales bordering the Marches, Deheubarth in the south-west of Wales and Gwynedd in the mountainous north-west.[104] In Gwynedd lay the lands of the Gruffydd dynasty, petty princes who often described themselves as "princes of Wales" and held the banner of Welsh independence from the Kingdom of England. The extent to which *seigneuries* in Wales were subject to overlordship from England is the subject of much debate, but the Mabinogion relates a story of Manawydan's journey to Oxford to pay homage and so the concept was deeply rooted.[105] In terms of primary-sourced history, we can date the idea that Welsh princes submitted themselves to English overlordship to before there was even an England, to the time of Ælfred's Wessex. First, Hyfaidd of Dyfed, then Elise ap Tewdyr and more importantly Anarawd ap Rhodri of Gwynedd sought aid from the Viking raids that submission to Wessex brought – the precedent had been set, and the French-speaking dynasties that ruled all England by the thirteenth century would continue to reassert the principle.[106] More recently, King Henry II in England in the twelfth century had been more active in pressing his rights of suzerainty. Welsh historian R. R. Davies described the relationship between the King of England and the Princes of Wales as "elastic", that is it wasn't consistently established, and therefore could be defined by either party in terms of suzerain or vassal how either party wished[107] – an obvious source of conflict. The nature of this independence would be the subject of much conflict throughout the thirteenth century until it was finally snuffed out entirely by Henry's son, Edward.

The lands of Gwynedd might be best described as falling into two halves, divided by the river Conwy: Lower Gwynedd to the east a land of rolling hills, Higher (*Uwch*) Gwynedd Conwy to the west a land of mountains. Gwynedd (*Is*) Conwy or Lower Gwynedd had been contested by the Saxons and subsequently the Normans for some time with the native Welsh. Gwynedd Uwch Conwy or Upper Gwynedd with its impenetrable mountains was the unconquered heart of North Wales. Native Wales was divided into *cantrefi*; each *cantref* had its own court, which was an assembly of the *uchelwyr*, the main landowners of the *cantref*. Uwch Gwynedd was divided into the *cantrefi* of Llyn (the long peninsula stretching out into the Irish Sea), Arfon and Arllechwedd along the north coast, Dunoding and Meirionnydd along Cardigan Bay and lastly on Anglesey were the *cantrefi* of Rhosyr, Cemais and Aberffraw. *Is* Gwynedd was divided into four *cantrefi*, and so became known as the four *cantrefi*, from east to west Tegeingl, Dyffryn Clywd, Rhufoniog and Rhos. These *cantrefi* were subdivided into commotes or *cwmwd*, sometimes spelt in older documents as *cymwd*. Legal control was undertaken from the *llys*, which originally referred to an enclosed open-air space but gradually took on the meaning of a place where legal proceedings took place and was gradually extended to refer to royal "courts".

Gwynedd was a land of high mountains and accordingly, high rainfall, gusty winds and cool temperatures – a maritime climate. This meant that its soil was poor and acidic, not given to the production of wheat, so agriculture was confined to the keeping of animals. Gerald of Wales had noted that there was little bread, but much meat, milk, cheese and butter. The only area that matched in any way the arable produce of lowland England was the isle of Anglesey, the breadbasket, such as it was, of Gwynedd. Towns didn't exist, let alone cities; although trade existed, it played but a small part in the economic life of Gwynedd. At no time did Gwynedd produce its own coinage, that marker of economic activity.[108] Whatever else conquerors came to Gwynedd for, it was not monetary wealth and reward.

Peter of Savoy: The Little Charlemagne

When the Normans had conquered England, they naturally turned their attentions westward to Wales. As mentioned earlier they created marcher lands in mid and south Wales, the more extensive the farther south. But in north Wales it had been more difficult. Hugh d'Avranches, who came from Normandy with William, had been granted the county of Cheshire, centred on the old legionary city of Chester. He'd extended his rule farther west along the coast by means of his cousin Robert, Robert de Roelent, more usually known to us as Robert de Rhuddlan. He was characterised by English monk and chronicler Orderic Vitalis as a man of "pride and greed" and given to "unrestrained plunder and slaughter".[109] Completed in 1086, the Domesday Book entry for Roelent or Rhuddlan reads:

> Earl Hugh [of Chester] holds Roelent of the king. Englefield lay there in the time of King Edward, and it was entirely waste. Earl Edwin held it. When Earl Hugh received it it was still waste. Now he has in demesne half the castle which is called Roelent, and is the caput of this estate. Robert of Roelent holds of Earl Hugh half of the same castle and of the borough, in which Robert has ten burghers' houses and half of the church ... There is a new borough there and eighteen burghers' houses ... In this manor of Roelent a castle has lately been built, which is also called Roelent.[110]

The Domesday Book tells us that what the English called Englefield, what would become Flintshire, had been the pre-Norman conquest land of the Saxon Edwin, who'd had the land since 1063 and the conquest of this part of Gwynedd by Earl Harold. Englefield was the Welsh *cantref* of Tegeingl, but Domesday also tells us that Robert held "Ros and Reweniou" which would be the Welsh *Cantrefs* of Rhos and Rhufoniog, meaning that in 1086 he was in possession of most of lower Gwynedd.[111] Now Robert of Rhuddlan held north-east Wales as a vassal of Hugh d'Avranches, building a motte and bailey castle in lower Gwynedd at Rhuddlan, hence the name. Robert was killed by a Welsh raiding party in 1093; it's unlikely he was missed in north Wales. The castle at Rhuddlan was attacked and destroyed by Gruffydd ap Cynan. Indeed, Gwynedd west of the Conwy had been ultimately defended against Norman incursion by Gruffydd ap Cynan, following futile invasions by William Rufus in 1095 and 1097, and the death of Hugh d'Avranches in 1101. Gruffydd was able to consolidate his position in Gwynedd, as much by diplomacy as by force. He'd met with King Henry I who'd granted him the rule of Llŷn, Eifionydd, Ardudwy and Arllechwedd. The *cantrefi* of Rhos and Rhufoniog were annexed in 1118, and Dyffryn Clwyd in 1124. Another invasion, this time by Henry I of England in 1121, was a military failure. The king had to come to terms with Gruffydd and made no further attempt to invade Gwynedd during Gruffydd's reign. It would be these lands east of the Conwy, which we'll know as the four *cantrefi*, that would be disputed down to the mid-thirteenth century.

Princeps Walliae, Prince of Wales, was a new term in 1245, one Dafydd ap Llywelyn Fawr had begun styling himself thus in 1244. Before the Norman conquest Welsh leaders had sometimes styled themselves "*Reges* or Kings of the Britons" – a reminder if one were needed, that whatever the English and the Normans were – they weren't British. But what was this title *Princeps*? It has been traditionally thought that *Princeps* had begun to be used instead of *Rex* in response to pressure from England to use a more suitable (lower) title. More recently, Llywelyn ap Grufydd's biographer J. Beverley Smith has suggested this may not be so.[112]

The English word we use today by way of translation is *Prince*, but that meant either a close male relative of a monarch or the head of a sovereign entity (neither of which applied). In France and French, the country from whose culture the English monarchy and ruling families originated,

Chapter Five

it meant that too. But in Wales, it had a classical Latin meaning closer to the original, meaning *chief* or *leader*. As evidence of this, Llywelyn Fawr gave himself the title *"Princeps Northwallie"*, more closely defining his territory and meaning more literally "Leader of North Wales".

This is probably because, although the English and Welsh wrote legal texts (and so titles) in Latin, the origins of their Latin were different. The Welsh were descended from the Romanised Britons who occupied Britannia when Classical Latin was the official language of the empire of which they were a part. Whereas the English now wrote a Medieval Latin that had been heavily influenced by the Frankish kingdoms, and these English were for the most part francophones who'd come to England from what are now varying parts of France (Normandy, Anjou, Poitou, Aquitaine, etc.).

In Welsh the title was *Tywysog*, a cognate of the Irish *taoiseach* and the Scots Gaelic *tòiseach*, the source today of the meaning for the Irish head of government or a Scottish clan chieftain. The word *Tywysog* itself comes from the Welsh word *tywys* meaning "to lead", so *Tywysog* means literally "one who leads". As Beverley Smith points out, this meaning attached to the title *Princeps* was "somewhat exceptional among the Christian nations of the Middle Ages"[113] – and as such, I would add, it might generate misunderstanding of meaning on both sides of Offa's Dyke.

Perhaps one of the greatest of these *Princeps* had been the man they called Llywelyn the Great, Llywelyn Fawr or Llywelyn ap Iorwerth. As ruler of Gwynedd for over forty years, he'd come to dominate all Wales, building castles at Dolbadarn, Dolywyddelan and Castel y Bere. Perhaps it had been in 1208 that he'd reached his zenith, when married to King John of England's daughter Joan. He'd been able to take Powys Gwenwynwyn upon the arrest by John of its ruler, Gwenwynwyn ap Owain. When the relationship with John soured, he had allied himself with King Philippe Auguste of France, an earlier example of Celtic alliance with Paris to counter the Plantagenets. Following John's death, he had signed the Treaty of Worcester in 1218 with the young Henry III. This recognised Llywelyn's power in Wales but as Henry's man. Llywelyn suffered a paralytic stroke in 1237, leaving his son Dafydd de facto leader, and when Llywelyn finally died in 1240, Dafydd became sole chieftain. Llywelyn had indeed been a great ruler and was much mourned by the Welsh and laid to rest at the Abbey of Aberconwy. Dafydd challenged Henry, but in return was challenged by his elder illegitimate half-brother Gruffydd ap Llywelyn for at least half of Gwynedd. Dafydd ap Llywelyn Fawr was born in April 1212, the legitimate son of Llywelyn and his wife Joan, daughter of King John of England, whereas his brother, Gruffydd, although older, was the illegitimate son of the woman, Tangwystl. Llywelyn Fawr had decreed in 1220 that his inheritance should pass to Dafydd, but nonetheless this did not stop Gruffydd contesting.[114]

Accordingly, Dafydd had his half-brother imprisoned at his castle at Criccieth. Whether Welsh princes paid homage directly to the King of England or by way of the Princes of Gwynedd became once more a bone of contention, Dafydd began to assert a status which Henry could not accept. Notwithstanding Henry's greater interest in his French lands, he marched an English army, including the newly arrived in England Pierre de Savoie,[115] as far as Rhuddlan before Dafydd yielded. As the chronicler, well informed in north-east Welsh affairs, at Chester, wrote for 1241:

> Also Henry, King of England … having entered Wales at Rhuddlan he remained for eight days. The lord of the land, David son of Llywelyn, came to him there, restoring the land to him, and placing himself at the king's mercy and gave up to him Gruffydd, his brother … Also the king built a castle at Dyserth, and caused the foundations of Mold to be laid.[116]

Dafydd then met met the king at Gwerneigron, near St. Asaph, on the banks of the River Elwy, a small tributary off the River Clwyd, in the *cantref* of Rhos. The resulting settlement, the Treaty of Gwerneigron of 29 August 1241, in which Pierre d'Aigueblanche and Pierre de Savoie, perhaps the first Savoyards to involve themselves in Welsh affairs,[117] returned the cantref of Tegeingl or Englefield to Henry, who began the aforesaid castle at Dyserth.[118] The new castle was just over two miles east of Rhuddlan on the edge of the Clwydian hills, and was intended to replace the castle built by Robert de Rothelan and much disputed by the princes of Gwynedd. As far as Henry was concerned the higher-placed defence of Dyserth was to be the last word on the dispute. The castle would be an extensive affair of two baileys, inner and outer, separated by a bridged dry ditch. The inner bailey, surrounded itself by a dry moat, held the Great Hall protected by a stone curtain wall, stone tower and the bridge guarded by a gatehouse.

There had been a Norman motte and bailey castle at Mold since 1072 when probably built by Robert de Montalt. The name Mold is a modern English rendering of the Latin *Monte Alto* or high mountain. This might seem rather an exaggeration for the motte at Mold, but *Monte Alto* is simply the latinisation of Montaut or Montalt. The family came to north-east Wales with William the Conqueror from Monthault on the Breton–Norman border. It had been destroyed by Gwynedd in the mid-twelfth century and work would now begin again to fortify this outpost just over ten miles (sixteen kilometres) west of Chester.

But the treaty left the remainder of Gwynedd in Dafydd's hands with, however, Henry rebuilding a castle at Deganwy by the Conwy, albeit earth and timber at this stage. Henry accepted Dafydd's position, provided he paid homage for his lands and provided other Welsh rulers paid homage to Henry not Dafydd. Meanwhile, as the Chester chronicler told us, Henry held Gruffydd ap Llywelyn as a hostage to Dafydd's good faith. The luckless Gruffydd traded a prison cell at Criccieth for one in London. The settlement suited both sides – Dafydd retained Gwynedd (save for Tegeingl) and rid himself of the challenge of his brother, Gruffydd, and Henry achieved, at the subsequent Treaty of London, something remarkable: agreement from Dafydd, as follows, that: "Should he die without a legitimate heir, he [Dafydd] grants, of his own free will, all the land of the principality of North Wales, to the king and his heirs."[119] Furthermore, it was agreed by Dafydd that: "If it should happen that they depart from their faithful service to the king, or his heirs, let all their lands be forfeit to the king and his heirs and pass to their use for ever."[120]

This was not the first time an English king had imposed an escheat on a prince of Gwynedd[121], but nevertheless, Beverley Smith, the biographer of Llywelyn ap Gruffydd, describes the Treaty of Gwerneigron as "fiendish" and "excruciating",[122] which means, perhaps, that Henry had bested Dafydd. But as Pope Innocent IV later observed, "every Christian knew that the prince of Wales was no more than a minor *vassalulum* of the King of England."[123] Henry must have thought he'd had the perennial Welsh problem in hand with the settlement of 24 October 1241.

However, Dafydd soon began lobbying the King of France and the Pope for support in gaining greater autonomy. Henry had thought he'd had the perennial Welsh problem in hand with the settlement of 1241 but this was not to be. In one of the more tragicomic episodes in Anglo-Welsh history, on the night of 1 March 1244, Gruffydd ap Llywelyn, being held as a hostage in the Tower of London, died. Gruffydd knotted linen bedsheets and tablecloths together in an endeavour to let himself down from a window, and inevitably they gave way, tumbling a young (perhaps overweight) Gruffydd toward his maker at a rapid rate of untying

Chapter Five

knots. Henry's hostage to Dafydd's good faith was no more. That this might happen on Saint David's Day, Patron Saint of Wales, only adds irony.[124]

Following Gruffydd ap Llywelyn's death, conflict broke out once more in North Wales, under the leadership of Dafydd, now styling himself as Prince of Wales. The nobility of Wales rallied to Dafydd's cause, with the notable exceptions of Gruffydd ap Gwenwynwyn,[125] Lord of Powys Wenwynwyn, and Gruffydd ap Madog, Prince of Powys Fadog: Powys, a longtime rival of Gwynedd, would continue to be a thorn in the side of Gwynedd and a barrier to any Welsh unity. Llywelyn Fawr had, indeed, driven his father, Gwenwynwyn ap Owain, from his lands, along with the young Gruffydd ap Gwenwynwyn, meaning there would be no love lost between Powys and Gwynedd.

Dafydd had agreed just four years earlier "to serve the king and his heirs faithfully".[126] As Paris put it the Welsh went against Henry "forgetting their charters and their oaths".[127] Dafydd must have known he was thus risking Gwynedd. A strongly independent Wales on his western border Henry needed like a hole in the head. Ranulf, the powerful Earl of Chester, had died in 1232. Subsequently, in a process complete by 1241, Henry had brought the county of Cheshire within his royal possession, meaning that the House of Gwynedd now had the King of England for a neighbour, not the Marcher Earl of Cheshire, thus opening the possibility of invasion from Chester.[128] John L'Estrange, Justiciar of Chester, found himself beating off several attacks on Oswestry and sieges at Dyserth and Mold. Indeed, on 28 March 1245, Mold was taken, as the nearby Chester chronicler related, "*Obsessum est castrum de Moalt a David principe Wallie captum,*" that is "the castle of Mold was besieged and taken by Dafydd Prince of Wales."[129] Paris in his inimitable style described the Welsh as "swarming from their lurking-places, like bees, spread[ing] fire and slaughter".[130]

So, in August 1245, Pierre de Savoie found himself as part of another large English army assembled by King Henry, marching westward from Chester to suppress the Welsh.

Historian of the Welsh Wars John E. Morris set out traditional Welsh tactics:

> Time after time they [the Anglo-Normans] penetrated far west. The Welsh retreated upon their natural fortress of Snowdon, restricted themselves to guerrilla warfare, and relied upon the rains and the difficulties presented by the geography of their country. They were easily able to reoccupy whatever land they had temporarily abandoned, for sooner or later the heavy columns of the invaders, wearied out by the bad weather and profitless tramping through pathless forests, had to fall back.[131]

But English tactics this time would be different, as they would be in the later Welsh Wars: first, a march along the coast, establishing strongpoints and fortifications en route, then attacks upon what sustained Welsh resistance there was – destruction and/or confiscation of food production, followed by famine. On Sunday, 13 August Henry and Alianor, along with Richard, Earl of Cornwall, made their way to Chester, with what the watching Chester chronicler called an "*exercitus copiosus*",[132] a "great army". They marched into Wales, first to Coleshill,[133] also known as Ewloe,[134] where a century earlier (1157) Owain ap Gruffydd, also known as Owain Gwynedd, had defeated Henry's grandfather Henry II. But this time there was no Welsh attack; the army continued to Whitford,[135] near Holywell. It had been a site of pilgrimage for nearly six centuries, dedicated to Saint Winifred, who, according to legend, was beheaded there by Caradog who had attempted to attack her. A healing spring had come to life where her head had fallen, which then miraculously rejoined her body. Where Winifred sprung also back into life – Henry and his army were coming into a strange land where myth and legend abounded. We're not told if Henry took the waters, but he was soon on to Rhuddlan and Abergele before the army arrived at the Conwy by 25 August 1245.[136] The previous earth and timber castle at Deganwy would now be rendered in stone, the Chester chronicler confirming that Henry now "*construxisset castrum de Gannoc*", had "built a castle at Gannoc", thus penning Dafydd west of the Conwy back into his Snowdon mountain heartland.[137] The Lord Edward would later take careful note of his father's success of 1245–7.[138]

We saw earlier how the Savoyards, Pierre d'Aigueblanche and Philippe de Savoie had witnessed Henry's passing of the Earldom of Chester to Alianor, rather than as earlier promised to Richard. The cartulary of Pierre de Savoie as transcribed recently by Huw Ridgeway has shed further light on the way Pierre and Alianor acted in concert on Edward's behalf, in this case protecting his interest against those potentially of his Uncle Richard, and the example comes from shortly before Henry and Pierre arrived by the Conwy. It seems that in a campaign tent at Chester, on 20 August 1245, a copy of a grant of Chester to Edward (the scribe likely erroneously wrote Edmund who was then but a newborn baby) was given to Pierre for safekeeping and is now a part of his cartulary in the UK National Archive. Edward would indeed receive Chester from Henry, the hurried erroneously penned document given to Pierre reminds us that as ever he was Alianor's and by extension Edward's protection at court.[139] So, we have the Savoyard Bishop of Hereford, de facto Earl of Richmond and Archbishop of Lyon in both Bordeaux and Chester directing the County Palatine of Chester toward Alianor then Edward and away from Richard.

The army would stay at Deganwy for over two months, guarding the masons and builders as they began work. The site, a natural place to build a castle, sat high over the River Conwy on two volcanic rock outcrops. It had been a defensible position for some time, since the Iron Age in fact, and subsequently the Romans, and the Norman Robert de Rhuddlan had built there.

The main part of the new castle was constructed on the westernmost summit which was crowned with a substantial round tower. A smaller, irregularly shaped structure known as Mansel's Tower was built on the easternmost summit. A bailey was established between the two hilltops. A royal charter of 1252 would seek to establish an English colony by the Conwy as a deterrent to those across the river. Matthew Paris would describe the castle at Deganwy as "impregnable in its walls and position" and "a thorn in the eye of the wretched, yea most wretched Welsh".[140]

There is a story from this time, of the English army at Deganwy in 1245, that illustrates well the sad story of the Welsh experience of English armies in their lands, and of the English experience of their perennial problems in Wales. A boat laden with wine for the English army ran aground in the Conwy, and the Welsh attempted to loot the foundering vessel. English knights rode in pursuit but then continued to plunder the abbey of Aberconwy across the river. As they returned with their ill-gotten gains they were ambushed by the Welsh and captured. In revenge for the earlier killing of a young Welsh nobleman, they were hanged and their decapitated bodies thrown into the Conwy. So perished several of Richard, Earl of Cornwall's household knights and a young Gascon crossbow man by the name of Raymond de Luka: a story that does not reflect well on those either side of the Conwy.[141]

The Welsh would submit on this occasion when Dafydd's death, on 25 February 1246, at Aber, of natural causes, broke their will to fight. Dafydd ap Llywelyn Fawr died, so said Matthew Paris, a "perjured man and fratricide".[142] Welsh chroniclers more kindly mourned

Chapter Five

him as "*Mab Brenin Cymru*", a "son of the king of Wales".[143] Native Wales had always been a tapestry of princelings; slowly they came over to Henry's side before finally Dafydd's nephews, the sons of the ill-fated Gruffydd ap Llywelyn, Llywelyn and Owain Goch, sought terms. A year earlier the name *Lewelino filio Griffini*[144] had appeared for the first time in English archives, amongst a list of Welsh nobles who'd sided against the king. The English would get to know him well. We should note that Llywelyn, the son of Dafydd's late rival Gruffydd, in being added to this January 1245 list, had joined forces with his uncle in rebellion against the king, evidencing the shifting nature of loyalties in Gwynedd and Wales. Indeed, as Llywelyn ap Gruffydd makes his entrance, it's worth remembering the words of Sir James Frederick Rees (1883–1967) on the history of Wales:

> The history of Wales as related by competent historians is well worthy of study: but it is a tangled story and its lessons are not simple. It does not afford a basis for uncritical glorification of the past. Those who seek flame-bearers of Welsh nationhood are apt to burn their fingers. Llywelyn ap Gruffydd, the last Prince of Gwynedd, does not wear the romantic halo of a William Wallace. It has not been possible to promote what a French cynic declared to be the most important element of nationality, a general and unquestioning belief in false notions about the past history of a country.[145]

Duly cautioned, this is to acknowledge that the House of Gwynedd that would give rise to the Princes of Wales, was but one of many competing Welsh princelings and polities. Llywelyn and Owain Goch came to Henry at Woodstock, in Oxfordshire, to agree to the resulting Treaty of Woodstock of 30 April 1247. Henry quashed ideas of a Prince of Wales having jurisdiction over anything other than the mountain fortress of Gwynedd – and most importantly that the ruler of Gwynedd should henceforth submit himself in homage to the English king – that they were in effect feudal tenants, owing military service to their suzerain. By the treaty, the land between the rivers Dee and Conwy, known as the four *cantrefi* or the *Perfeddwlad*,[146] was held to belong to the Crown – and permanently so.[147] As we've seen, securing this annexation of the *cantrefi* was the construction of new castles at Dyserth and overlooking the Conwy at Deganwy.

But it's a little perplexing as to why Henry didn't now press his claim to Gwynedd in its entirety, as Dafydd ap Llywelyn Fawr had died without an heir, which by his seal meant his lands should pass to the Crown. What's more, he'd failed in being "faithful" to the king by his seal, once more meaning his lands should pass to the Crown. Indeed, the House of Gwynedd was twice forfeit, something pointed out by the Bishop of Bangor – so why did Henry not act? As Carpenter rightly suggests, Henry had "the justification, the opportunity and the resources", but he passed.[148] Perhaps if he had acted with greater purpose in 1245–7, then he would have saved his son much time and treasure. Later he would grant the Lord Edward, in 1254, the lands held by the Crown in Wales, the four *cantrefi*, but west of the Conwy remained with Dafydd's nephew, the son of the hapless Gruffydd, Llywelyn ap Gruffydd. However, the Treaty of Woodstock broke with tradition; no longer would Welsh affairs be delegated by the King of England to semi-independent Marcher lords: it would be a matter for the Crown itself – thus setting the Crown ultimately on a collision course with the Princes of Wales.[149]

Chapter Six

So, Pierre de Savoie had, in a few short years, been involved to a significant degree in the affairs of Plantagenet England in the thirteenth century, armed and diplomatic tussles with the Kings of France and Princes of Wales – he was now very much an English noble and indispensable to the realm. Perhaps in reward for services rendered there would be yet more rewards for Pierre de Savoie, who had been in need of a base closer to court for the English end of his virtuous circle of operations; temporary accommodations in London were not fitting for the uncle of the queen and key counsellor to the king. So, in February 1246. he was given land of his own upon which to build a house, some say a palace, to the west of London, not far from Westminster – by a place called the Strand.[1] Pierre was to transform this manor, once owned by one Brian de L'Isle, into one of the finest in the whole of Europe. No record of what once stood there has survived, but we know that in March 1252 he was granted twenty oak trees from the royal forest at Windsor to assist its construction.[2] We also know that he acquired adjacent land for a sweeping garden down to the Thames, one of the related documents even using the title "Earl of Richmond".[3] Sadly, it did not survive the Peasant's Revolt of 1381, but its location has lived on to our own time, in the name of the building that occupies the space on the Strand – The Savoy Hotel. The hotel would in fact grow to such fame that if one googles the word "Savoy" one is apt to find more likely a reference to said hostelry than the lands of the Alps. In reference to its illustrious one-time owner, the hotel has a gilt statue in its courtyard entrance – which is supposed to represent Pierre de Savoie.[4]

In order to imagine the Savoy Palace of the thirteenth century we need to describe the London the Savoyard found. A century earlier William FitzStephen had given us a little of the colour of the London Pierre now called home:

> Moreover, there is in London upon the river's bank, amid the wine that is sold from ships and wine-cellars, a public cook-shop. There daily, according to the season, you may find viands, dishes roast, fried, and boiled, fish great and small, the coarser flesh for the poor, the more delicate for the rich, such as venison and birds both big and small. If friends, weary with travel, should of a sudden come to any of the citizens, and it is not their pleasure to wait fasting till fresh food is bought and cooked.[5]

After describing his favourite eatery, FitzStephen, obviously proud of his city, went on to describe the beating heart of London:

> To this city, from every nation that is under heaven,
> merchants rejoice to bring their trade in ships.
> Gold from Arabia, from Sabaea spice

Chapter Six

> And incense; from the Scythians arms of steel Well-tempered; oil from the rich groves of palm
> That spring from the fat lands of Babylon;
> Fine gems from Nile, f'rom China crimson silks; French wines; and sable, vair and miniver
> From the far lands where Russ and Norsemen dwell.[6]

The London of 1246 stretched only as far as a little to the west of what is now St. Paul's Cathedral. From the city gates, Ludgate, there a road ran west, at first following the course of what is now Fleet Street, named for the river which emptied into the Thames just west of the city, then the Strand to Westminster and its abbey. The road was not the main thoroughfare between London and Westminster – that would have been the river Thames itself. The road, such as it was, followed the course of the river by way of the village of Charing, but set back on higher ground, meaning that there had been available land between road and river. A traveller heading west at the time would have left the city by Ludgate and passed first the two halls of the London headquarters of the Knights Templar before passing St. Clement's Well and arriving at The Savoy. The lands granted to Pierre began a little to the west of what's now Waterloo Bridge, marked by the course of today's Savoy Street that runs from the Strand down to the Embankment, then to the lands of the Bishop of Carlisle once occupied by Beaufort Buildings, encompassing all the land now taken by the Savoy Hotel.[7] We know where Pierre's London house or palace was, but we have no idea of its scope. It's said that it must have been extensive since his name so effectively stuck to the site to our present time. Pierre's palace was destroyed in 1381 during the Peasants' Revolt, and its Tudor-era replacement, the Savoy Hospital, did survive long enough to feature in several illustrations which show an extensive complex, of which the Savoy Chapel remains (see figure 2.0).

Whilst Pierre de Savoie was assisting Henry with his problems in Wales, and being rewarded with lands in London, his brother, Archbishop Boniface, was again the subject of Matthew Paris's righteous indignation:

> At this time [1248] the Archbishop Boniface, oblivious of his church so far as the care of souls was concerned and busy fighting for the pope in the area of Lyons, extorted no small treasure from the vacant churches in his province ... Thus wretched England became like the vineyard wasted "by the boar out of the wood" and plucked "by all they which pass by the way" ... This order published in each and every church in England, roused indignation in the hearts of many, as much because of the greedy, damaging and unprecedented extortion of money, as because of the adulation that went with it, and they heartily cursed the lord king for tolerating and agreeing to such things.[8]

Boniface had stayed with the Pope and neglected England. He'd gone to the First Council of Lyon in June 1245 but did not return to tend his flock until 1249, finally being consecrated Archbishop at Canterbury on 1 November 1249. Worse than a Savoyard with full saddlebags of gold for Paris was an absentee Savoyard landlord. He was to spend nearly fully five years in Europe before coming to England. Along with Boniface in Lyon was that other Savoyard cleric, Pierre d'Aigueblanche of Hereford,[9] another that earned the admonishment of Paris as an absentee. These tirades from Paris earned Boniface and Pierre their bad reputations for centuries until more recently historians like Yates have balanced their accounts by reminding us that "Absenteeism, especially when the bishop was a royal clerk and ambassador, was not unusual in this period, and many bishops were a great deal worse than Aquablanca".[10] We should also remember that Boniface, during his time in Lyon, was working toward the canonisation of his predecessor, Edmund of Abingdon, and had also been one of four archbishops selected by the Pope to codify the privileges of the Church previously accepted by kings and emperors, something you might think that Paris would have approved of.[11] Both Aigueblanche and Boniface were, perhaps harshly, reprimanded by the monk of St. Albans for undertaking precisely the role Henry had brought them to England for.

One of the issues that kept Boniface away from Canterbury was developments surrounding news from Provence. On 19 August 1245 Ramon Berenguer departed this life aged just 47 years. In that time. he had both maintained his fief through difficult years, but most remarkably had sired not one but three queens. He'd suffered a long illness, and at least a year had passed since Béatrice de Savoie, his wife, returned from London to be at his bedside. Matthew Paris dutifully recorded the death of the Count of Provence, "an illustrious and distinguished man, who had been wonderfully tossed about on the wheel of fortune, and who left an unusual source of wonder in the excelling beauty of his daughters."[12] He would be honoured by Henry with the coat of arms of the County of Provence loftily displayed in his rebuilding of Westminster Abbey.[13] But, in his will of 1238 he'd left an unwelcome surprise for Henry and Alianor, and indeed Marguerite and Sanchia too: Ramon Berenguer had bequeathed Provence to his youngest daughter Béatrice, saying in his will that "all my daughters except you alone, are exalted by marriage in a high degree ... To you therefore, at your marriage, I give, and bequeath, by my will, the whole of my land".[14] The finer details of the will left in usufruct[15] the County of Provence to Pierre's sister, Alianor's aunt, Béatrice's mother, the widowed Béatrice de Savoie, for her lifetime. Well, of course, this made young Béatrice suddenly very marriageable indeed. Henry heard of his father-in-law's death whilst with his army in Wales. There was much mourning by Alianor and Sanchia in England, and Marguerite in France, all the more so when they heard their father had left his entire estate to their younger sister Béatrice.

Béatrice, like her mother before her, was now the Countess of Provence. Henry was aggrieved that he'd received neither a dowry for Alianor, nor a return of the 4,000 marks he'd loaned to Ramon, nor the castles in Provence offered as security. The loan to Provence is often cited as an example of Henry's weakness and naivety, but we are looking with hindsight on a failed attempt to protect his position in southern France. Had he succeeded Henry would have been judged differently – 'twas ever thus. Alianor was aggrieved at her younger sister inheriting Provence, but perhaps most of all Marguerite was aggrieved as the eldest daughter. Alianor for one never gave up her right to an interest in Provence, writing later to her son Edward in 1279, "*et se ceste aliance se face, nos porrons bien estre destorbées du droit que nos avons en la quarte partie de Provence,*" translating as, "If this alliance is made, we might well be upset in the right we have to a quarter of Provence."[16]

Apparently, the suddenly very eligible Béatrice was beset with eager suitors. Richard in England offered his son by his first marriage, Henri d'Almayne, as a husband, and even fathers and sons offered themselves. The Kingdom of Aragon dispatched an army for her hand, the Emperor the imperial navy.[17] His navy being unable to land, Frederick II, under threat of deposition by the Pope in Lyon, threatened to bring an imperial army to the Pope's see in Lyon, then on the de facto Franco-Imperial border, to settle with Innocent IV in person and to win Béatrice in one go – the Provençal succession might develop into another round of the wider imperial–papal conflict. So, in the desperate battle for the fair maiden's hand, the Pope in nearby Lyon then came into the fray. Frederick asked Thomas for permission to send his army by way of Savoy to Lyon. Thomas warned Béatrice, in Provence, who in turn made her daughter a ward of the Church to ensure papal protection. The Church and Thomas would decide whom she should marry. Now papal imperial polices decided the matter.

Innocent turned to France. In return for Capetian protection he offered the hand of Béatrice. And so it was that Charles d'Anjou, brother to the King of France, was betrothed to the fair Béatrice, upon the condition that Provence was not to pass to France through the marriage. In the Anglo-French chess game, the last round had gone to the Capetian French – two daughters married to Plantagenets, two daughters to Capetians. As a result, the County of Provence would ultimately fall to Capetian France and as such today is a part of France. The meeting to arrange the marriage took place in the great monastery at Cluny, not far from Lyon. Archbishop Boniface had been instrumental in the match, which is somewhat of a surprise given that as Archbishop of Canterbury he was supposed to be Henry's man and looking after English interests. Both Henry and Richard made a formal protest to Pope Innocent IV "to preserve their right in Provence" but it was to no avail; his answer was that "he would not at present proceed to the required prohibition [of the marriage]" and the protest was thus dismissed.[18] Philippe de Savoie attended the marriage of his niece, Béatrice de Provence, to Charles d'Anjou, which took place on 31 January 1246. Henry, Alianor and England can have had good reason to feel that the Savoyards had not protected their interests. Provençals rightly saw the marriage as the first step into what would prove to be eventual submission to and incorporation into France.[19] Charles marched into Provence without waiting even for the marriage ceremony. Matthew Paris recorded Henry being "disturbed ... in no slight degree" not least because "the queen's mother ... had for five years received annually four thousand marks from the king" for "castles in Provence" – that the castles remained in the mother's name not the father's, daughter's or new son-in-law's did not lessen the fact that the thirteenth-century game of marriage chess had been won by the House of Capet.[20] Many, like Spencer, have seen in the Savoyard connivance in the Capetian encroachment of Provence, a classic example of their putting their own interests ahead of England's;[21] however, others, like Ridgeway, have suggested that they acted to stabilise the south, consistent with their support of Edward's appanage, Gascony.[22] Savoy had, from its beginnings, bestrode the Alps on a narrow ledge of support for the Pope and for the Emperor, not wishing to unduly incur the wrath of either, as that would provide an existential threat to the ruling house. It is in this context that we should understand their actions regarding the Provençal succession, in effect one of self-preservation. In truth, English interests in Provence were seen as less important to the Savoyards than preventing their county being "piggy in the middle" in the conflict between Frederick and Innocent. Henry's southern alliance was no more; the Plantagenets had been outmanoeuvred by the Capetians who held the trump card in protecting the Pope, but it could be convincingly argued that the Provençal affair helped pave the way to the 1259 Treaty of Paris, and in this perhaps Pierre de Savoie was playing a longer game than some have given him credit for.

Just before the marriage of Charles and Béatrice, an agreement brokered by the Bishop of Hereford on the English side and likely Imbert de Seyssel on the Savoyard side of 16 January 1246 brought Amédée IV firmly into the Plantagenet sphere of influence, alongside his brothers Pierre and Boniface.[23] The agreement enfeoffed key Savoyard castles to Henry and should be seen in the light of the Provençal succession. Aigueblanche seemingly sold the idea to Henry in terms of both strengthening familial ties but also of an alliance with Savoy.[24] Amédée became Henry's liege man for castles, a palace and a town in the presence of Boniface and Aigueblanche.[25] For the Savoyards they placed key locations in the hands of a neutral king in terms of the papal–imperial struggle; for the English, it was hoped it would place pressure upon Capetian France to respect Henry and Alianor's interests in the region.

> Grant to Amadeus [Amédée IV de Savoie], Count of Savoy and marquess in Italy, for the homage which he has done to the king for the castle of Avyllan [Avigliana], the town of Susa, with the palace, and castle of Bard and the town of Saint-Maurice [d'Agaune] in Chablais, to hold to him and his heirs of the king and his heirs in perpetual fee of 1,000l at London at the Exchequer, whereof the king has paid 500 marks in hand and will pay 500 marks at Easter next and the remaining 500 marks at Michaelmas following.
> Grant to him also for the said homage and the service which he and his heirs are bound to do the king, of 200 marks a year at London at Michaelmas."[26]

The castle at Bard in the Aosta Valley, sitting atop a *verrou glaciaire*[27] high above the Dora Baltea River, was the very impediment to travellers that Cnut (or Canute) had complained to the emperor back in 1027. It was, in effect, the Savoyard front door, or the Italian front door depending upon which way you were facing: it entirely blocked travel to and from both the Grand- and Petit-Saint-Bernard passes. Not far upstream from Bard lay Aosta, where the Buthier diverged northward from the Dora Baltea. The Buthier took you to the Grand-Saint-Bernard, the Dora Baltea to the Petit-Saint-Bernard. These were routes known to people since Neolithic times and were long vital to trade, pilgrimage and conquest. Indeed, so well did Bard block travel to and from Italy, that an Italian army held up Napoleon's army for so long six centuries later that Bonaparte had the castle destroyed. The small town of Saint-Maurice d'Agaune sat where another *verrou glaciaire* forced the Rhône into a narrow valley, and guarded the northern entrance to the Grand Saint Bernard. The nearby monastery, the Abbey of Saint-Maurice, was built on the ruins of a Roman shrine of the first century BC dedicated to the god Mercury in the Roman staging-post of Agaunum, and the site of the supposed martyrdom of the Theban Legion under Saint Maurice around 285 AD. The monastery, built there, became the property of the Kingdom of Burgundy, until 1033, when it passed to the control of the House of Savoy. From 1128, the community of canons regular lived there under the Rule of St. Augustine. Saint Maurice was and is the patron saint of Savoy; a later Duke of Savoy arranged for the triumphant return of relics: for English readers, paying homage for Saint Maurice was akin to Henry III paying homage for Westminster Abbey, holding as it did the shrine of patron saint of England, Edward the Confessor. Both the castle at Avigliana and the palace at Susa controlled the Valle Di Susa and access to the Mont Cenis pass westward from Turin to Savoy. The Margravial Palace at Susa had been the fief of Adelaide of Susa whose marriage to the Savoyard Count Othon had first brought the Savoyards lands down and into Piedmont. These castles, palace and towns were prized pieces of real estate, indeed of both supreme strategic and cultural value. Perhaps we should also remember that decades later Count Othon of Burgundy would pay homage to Philippe de Savoie who was standing in for King Edward I for the Château de Joux and town of Pontarlier. Taken together, Henry's acquisition of Bard and Saint-Maurice and Edward's of Joux and Pontarlier can be explained

Chapter Six

more easily – they all sit upon that key English pilgrimage road, the *Via Francigena*. We should not dismiss piety as at least a partial motive on Henry's part.

Instrumental in the Anglo-Savoyard alliance had been Pierre d'Aigueblanche, who had moved on to Savoy following his time at the Council of Lyon. Amédée's homage to Henry was taken in Savoy in the presence of his brothers, Archbishop Boniface and Thomas, no longer in Flanders.[28] The alliance, in the view of Wurstemberger, was to be strengthened, not weakened, in the face of the Capetian moves toward Provence.[29] In addition to the castles Henry made marriage proposals of his own, the following grant to Amédée IV:

> Grant to him [Amédée IV] also that the king will marry one of the daughters of the count's daughter [Béatrice de Savoie, Marchioness di Saluzzo], whom he shall send to England, either to John de Warenne, who will be Earl of Warenne, or to Edmund de Lacy, who will be Earl of Lincoln, who are boys in the ward of the king.[30]

For the Savoyards, the attraction of the English alliance was partly in response to the Capetian advance into Provence, and partly to distance Amédée from the imperial–papal conflict as he sat controlling the Alpine passes. For the English the alliance was mostly driven by ties of kinship, but also to prevent what Henry saw as a valuable ally either being drawn into the Capetian fold along with Provence or the region destabilised by papal–imperial conflict. As we've seen, much has been made of Henry's naivety of sending good money after bad in return for castles, towns and a palace of little military use, but history sometimes brings rewards that contemporaries cannot foresee – it would be, after the death of Pierre and Henry, that Edward visited Savoy to receive homage from Philippe for the 1246 castles, palace and towns in the summer of 1273. It would be during this visit that Edward met Maître Jacques de Saint-Georges who'd been building castles for Philippe in the Viennois. The results of the meeting are the UNESCO-listed castles of North Wales. Some investments yield unimagined fruit only in the long term.

The agreement made by Innocent IV with Louis and Charles was that Provence would not become a part of France; Ramon Berenguer's wishes for the independence of his county were to be granted. However, this was not to be: as soon as Charles installed himself, he brought in his own people and Béatrice de Savoie, much to her protests, was denied the administration of Provence guaranteed in her husband's will. Béatrice would eventually be bought out for the price of a pension from Charles, whilst Henry eventually got his 4,000 marks back, apologising for the distress caused to Béatrice.[31] The matter of Provence would bubble on as an issue between the Capetians, the Plantagenets and the Savoyards until the aforesaid rapprochement that ended in 1259, of which more later.

In the meantime, the Capetians had problems of their own in the immediate future. King Louis IX, following his construction of the fabulous Sainte-Chapelle in Paris, had taken up the cross and gone on crusade – what would be known as the Seventh Crusade, departing for the Levant in 1248 from the newly built fortified port of Aigues-Mortes. The port had been built in a corner of the Rhône delta, newly part of the Capetian royal demesne, and though better ports existed, this one was under his direct control. Louis defended his port with extensive fortifications, including the Tour de Constance in 1242, built upon the site of a previous Carolingian defence. These fortifications would be seen by succeeding crusader armies, including the Lord Edward, and the great round donjon proved influential in castle design. Louis sailed with an army of over 15,000 men at a cost of over 1.5 million *livres tournois*. It was an unmitigated disaster. Egypt was the object of the crusade, and he landed in 1249 at Damietta on the Nile. In November, Louis marched towards Cairo, and almost at the same time, the Ayyubid sultan of Egypt, as-Salih, died. A force led by Robert d'Artois, the younger brother of the king, attacked the Egyptian camp at Gideila and advanced to Al Mansurah[32] where they were defeated. Not only did Robert d'Artois perish, so too at the later battle at Fariskur did Hugues XI de Lusignan, another of Henry's Poitevin half-brothers. Meanwhile, Louis' main force was attacked by a Mamluk, who would become the scourge of Outremer, Baibars. Louis was then also defeated and had to return to Damietta and there surrender himself in ignominy. He fell ill with dysentery and was cured by an Arab physician. When Louis returned to Europe it would be after losing his entire army to the Egyptian Mamluks and being freed only upon the payment of a 400,000 *livres tournois* ransom, over £70 million in today's money.

A year earlier than Louis' ill-fated crusade, 1248, Henry decided that it would be a good idea to appoint Simon de Montfort as Seneschal of Gascony, in effect to run the troubled land for him; it would be an unwise choice. Around the same time that Henry had made Simon seneschal in Gascony, he had invited another foreign party into the English court – the Lusignans. Upon the death of his father John, his mother Isabelle d'Angoulême had returned to her native France to remarry, where she married Hugues X de Lusignan. Oddly Isabelle had been betrothed to marry Hugues's father Hugues IX de Lusignan when a girl of 12. Her marriage to John had brought about a rebellion on the part of the Lusignans against the Plantagenets. Marriage to Isabelle had brought Hugh V, Count of La Marche the neighbouring county of Angoulême to the west. However, the family influence had waned somewhat since the Capetians had imposed their man on Poitou, the younger brother of Louis IX, Alphonse, and subsequent revolts had failed, as we saw earlier. The Château de Lusignan was the ancestral home of the House of Lusignan, Poitevin Marcher lords much in the same mould as those that held the border lands between England and Wales. Famous crusaders, one of their clan, Guy de Lusignan, had become King of Jerusalem between 1186 and 1192[33]. Henry still nurtured ambitions for the return of his ancestral lands in Poitou and accordingly favoured the influential Poitevins – to such an extent that he kept over seventy Poitevin knights on his payroll.[34] Isabelle had died in 1246, leaving nothing in her will to Henry and his siblings, and all to the fruit of her second marriage. Despite this, it had been in 1247 that Henry invited to England his half-brothers Geoffrey, Guy and Aymer de Lusignan and Guillaume de Valence.[35] The latter acquired the key Marcher castle at Goodrich in Herefordshire by marriage to heiress Joan de Munchensi. Guillaume soon set about enhancing his new-found status as a Marcher lord by rebuilding the castle.[36] In 1250 Aymer had been proposed for the See of Winchester, following pressure from Henry on the electors, and was not as we saw installed in July 1251. This elevation owed more to nepotism than the illiterate Aymon's ecclesiastical ability. Along too came a sister, Alice de Lusignan, to marry onetime ward of Pierre de Savoie, the young Jean de Warrene, 6th Earl of Surrey, seven years her junior. This largesse showered in the direction of the Lusignans was perhaps to shore up Henry's position in Gascony, but perhaps more because they were family.

In furtherance of the aforesaid January 1246 moves regarding a deepening of the Anglo-Savoyard alliance, Pierre returned to England in February 1247 along with two eligible ladies of noble birth. One of them, Alésia di Saluzzo,[37] was brought to be married to Edmund de Lacy, who held the Honour of Pontefract and the castle there. Their son Henri de Lacy would become a leading knight during Edward's reign. Alésia was the eldest daughter of the late Manfred III di Saluzzo and Béatrice de Savoie, the daughter of Amédée IV de Savoie, and so his granddaughter. The marriage would further bind Saluzzo to Savoy and Savoy to England.

Chapter Six

The other, sadly unnamed, was to be married to Richard de Burgh. The marriages attended by Pierre took place at Woodstock in May 1247.

> Pierre of Savoy, Earl of Richmond, came to the royal court [1247] at London bringing with him some unknown women from his distant homeland in order to marry them to the English nobles who were royal wards. To many native and indigenous Englishmen this seemed unpleasant and absurd, for they felt they were being despised ... Two Provençal girls were married at the instigation of Pierre of Savoy to two young nobles whom the lord king had brought up at court for some years, namely Edmund Earl of Lincoln and Richard de Burgo. These marriages caused considerable murmur and indignation to reverberate round the kingdom for it is said that the women were ignoble, unknown to the nobles, and married to them against their will.[38]

Matthew Paris at his sniffy best. These elegant ladies from Piedmont (not Provence) were far from being ignoble. The marriage of Edmund and Alésia would, despite the chronicler's disapproval, be a successful one. The Anglo-Savoyard couple had a son, Henri de Lacy, who would succeed his father as Earl of Lincoln, and go on to be a chief ally and supporter of Henry's son, Edward, during his reign. As we shall see, Alésia's sister Agnès would also come to England to be married to Jean de Vesci, a knight who despite originally being a Montfortian, would become a lifelong supporter and ally of Edward. Henri de Lacy and Jean de Vesci are good examples, one the son of, the other the husband of granddaughters of the Savoyard comital family, who would go on to be pillars upon which Edward's reign was built. As with the castles in Savoy, so with the marriages. Perhaps if Matthew Paris had lived to see the fruits of 1246–7, he might have taken a less parochial view.

Much has been made of the role of the Savoyards and Poitevins in destabilising Henry III's monarchy, but we should remember that much of the criticism stems from the main source for Henry's reign, our xenophobic friend Matthew Paris. He wrote in 1251:

> At this time, the king day by day lost the affection of his natural subjects, and that now by degrees: for openly following the example of his father, he enticed all the foreigners he could to his side, enriched them, and, despising and despoiling his English subjects, intruded aliens into their place. At one time Earl Richard, at another the Archbishop [Boniface de Savoie], now the bishop of Winchester [Aymer de Lusignan] and his other brothers, now bishop of Hereford [Pierre d'Aigueblanche], and now Peter of Savoy, and others, whom he summoned from all quarters.[39]

Paris obligingly name-checks the leading Savoyards for admonishment, along with the newly arrived Lusignans, making no difference between them, but even singles out Earl Richard of Cornwall, born in Winchester, for criticism as a "foreigner". His likening of Henry to his father John is indicative of a latent xenophobia hanging on from earlier times and present in some parts of the revered *Magna Carta*. The extent to which this perennial English distrust of foreigners existed at all levels of society has been much discussed and is ultimately difficult to judge. Certainly, the English nobility was less than keen on newcomers who might compete for favours and land, as were the higher echelons of the church. The "foreigner" card was progressively played by Montfort for political advantage, which no doubt influenced chroniclers in their attitudes. We should be wary, however, in assuming that the feeling was widespread; there is an assumption made that Henry was overly keen on foreigners, and that this eventually led to the Second Baronial War, but we should challenge this assumption by noting that his son too had his fair share of Savoyards at court without provoking resentment. Perhaps the truth of the matter is that Edward was a little more careful than Henry in not drawing attention to his foreign favourites by not granting them so much land, in this as in many things the son learned from the mistakes of the father.

Wenlock Priory in Shropshire is an interesting case in point in this regard, having as it did a prior from the *Pays de Vaud* for most of the second half of the thirteenth century, through the reigns of both Henry and Edward, with no ill effects that we know of. The Norman knight Roger de Montgomery re-founded the house, on an earlier Saxon site, as part of the Cluniac order between 1079 and 1082. Helpfully, in 1101, the bones of Saint Milburga were discovered in the old church and translated to the new monastery. The influence of the Vaudois was to be felt from 1261 when Aymon de Mont, brother of Ebal II de Mont, was appointed prior.[40] There's nothing unusual in this; his appointment coincides roughly with the resumption of Henry's personal rule following the Provisions of Oxford, and of these provisions we will hear much later. But his arrival in Wenlock helps to illustrate that the events of 1258 were more anti-Lusignan than anti-foreigner as was previously assumed. However, that he should be followed in 1285 by Henri de Bonvillars,[41] the brother of Jean de Bonvillars, Savoyard Constable of Harlech Castle and in 1291 by Jacques de Cossonay[42] illustrates a Savoyard continuity in Wenlock that bestrides the Montfortian rebellion and extends deep into the reign of Edward I.

In his excellent article "King Henry III and the 'Aliens', 1236–1272", Ridgeway finds its significance may have been traditionally overplayed. Ridgeway wrote:

> Henry's love of foreigners is usually just dismissed as a bizarre expression of his artistic and naïve personality, an easily explained cause of his subjects' discontents. This crude picture has only recently, begun to be modified. It has been discovered that Savoyards and Poitevins cannot be lumped together politically.[43]

It was at this time that Henry chose to establish once and for all the validity of his marriage to Alianor. He had, it should be remembered, had an earlier attempt to marry Jeanne de Ponthieu thwarted before marrying Alianor. Such a query was obviously a direct threat to Alianor, and indeed to the wider Savoyard position in England. Accordingly, in 1249, it was Pierre d'Aigueblanche who, along with Archbishop of York, Walter de Gray, was asked to look into the matter. This was something they did at great length, and in some significant detail, and one in which they deployed the prior and abbot of Hautecombe Abbey in Savoy – such was the seriousness of the matter. After some time, in 1252, Pierre d'Aigueblanche pronounced Henry's potential marriage to Jeanne as null, and his marriage to Alianor as valid.[44]

Meanwhile, and only eventually in September 1249, did Boniface come to England, and his See of Canterbury – it would not be a peaceful and calming tenure. In the presence of Henry and Alianor the forty-sixth Archbishop of Canterbury was enthroned with great pomp and ceremony in the great cathedral on All Saints Day, 2 November 1249. Taking the Chair of Saint Augustine, he swore to observe the customs of Canterbury Cathedral on the Canterbury Gospels, said to have been brought to England by the first Archbishop, St. Augustine, in 597[45]. Boniface

Chapter Six

would be styled "Primate of All England", giving him supremacy over the Archbishop of York, Walter de Gray. Following his enthronement, he set off on a tour of his new domain, which wasn't to be a happy promenade. As we know, Matthew Paris is somewhat of an unreliable witness when it comes to Savoyard matters, and there is some doubt as to the veracity of his following account,[46] but it is nonetheless colourful, and if in part true paints a picture of less than harmonious relations between the archbishop and his flock. Paris writes:

> On the fourth of the ides of May, namely the day of St. Pancratius and his companions [12 May 1250], the aforesaid Archbishop of Canterbury B. came to London to visit the bishop and chapter and the monks of that city ... The next day he visited Bishop Fulk. If anyone were to particularize the impudence of the said Archbishop at his place ... it would offend the ears and minds of the hearers, or rather break their hearts ... Going to the chapter of St. Paul's in London, he came to that church in great pomp in order to visit his canons. They were unwilling to admit him, resisting spiritedly, and firmly to the supreme pontiff. When the Archbishop heard this, extremely annoyed and threatening, he precipitately and in a spirit of anger and fury excommunicated the dean [Henry de Cornhill] and some their dignitaries of the church ... And on the following day, still swollen and inflamed with yesterday's anger and according to the testimony of people who saw, wearing a coat of mail under his vestments, he came to the priory of St. Bartholomew to visit the canons there. As he arrived and entered the church, because the prior was away at the time, the subprior came to meet him accompanied by the convent in procession with solemnity and reverence, both in the lighting of numerous candles and in the ringing of bells ... The Archbishop did not care much for the honour thus done to him; he said he had come there to visit the canons. Now all the canons were in the centre of the church ... one of the canons replied to him on behalf of all, saying that they had an experienced and diligent bishop whose task it was to visit them when this was necessary, nor would they, or ought they to, be visited by anyone else ... On hearing this the Archbishop, flying into a more furious rage than he ought or was proper, rushed at the subprior, forgetting his station and the holiness of his predecessors, and impiously struck the holy man, a priest, a monk, with his fist as he stood in the middle of the church, truculently repeating the blows now on the aged breast, now on the venerable face, now on his grey head and yelling 'This is how English traitors should be dealt with!' And, raving horribly with unrepeatable paths he vehemently demanded that his sword be brought to him.
>
> As the tumult increased and the canons tried to rescue the subprior from the hands of the aggressor, the archbishop tore off the precious cope that the subprior was wearing and broke away the clasp ... and it was smashed and lost underfoot in the crowd. That splendid cope, too, trampled on and torn, was irreparably damaged. Nor was the archiepiscopal fury averted even now, for, like a madman, pushing and forcing back that holy man with a violent onslaught, he so crushed the senile body against a pier ... that he shattered his bones to the marrow and caused internal injuries. When the others saw the archbishop's lack of restraint, they managed to rescue the half-dead man from the jaws of

death, after pushing the aggressor back. As he was thrown back his vestments fell aside, his coat of mail was plainly visible to many, who were horrified to see the archbishop in armour ... Meanwhile, his officials, who were impetuous Provençals like himself, truculently assaulted the remaining canons.[47]

Savoyard historian Cox wrote "this lively account ... has been uncritically accepted by all too many subsequent writers" before asserting that "references to the event in less biased contemporary sources make it clear that there was some kind of disorder ... but it is very unclear who was chiefly responsible".[48] Adam Marsh who was travelling with Boniface, wrote that he had conducted himself "in a praiseworthy manner"[49] and that "extremely false accounts have been spread throughout the province both by the clergy and by the populace".[50] And thus is the problem for medieval historians, coping with a paucity of primary sources, and then primary sources that are often so unreliable. However, what this episode does point to is the perceived unpopularity of the Savoyard influence within England and the English court – something that would erupt into violence in the coming decade.

We have couched the words of Matthew Paris several times with the notion that he was and is a partial witness, a witness that too many perhaps have taken too easily to represent Anglo-Savoyard relations. But there is an entry a few short years before the account for Boniface, of 1248, that perhaps very much shows the monk from St. Albans in his true colours. Between the 24th and 25th of November 1248 a massive landslide, an avalanche, from the limestone mountain, Mont Granier, wiped out the villages of Cognin, Saint-André, Vourey, Granier and Saint-Perange, partially destroying Le Murs and Myans, and causing over a thousand casualties. It was common for monks to see natural disasters as the chastening work of the almighty, but Paris's words on one of Europe's greatest medieval natural disasters is perhaps instructive and should colour our view of his chronicles in relation to Savoy and Savoyards.

> In this year [1248] an awful earthquake occurred in Savoy, in the valleys of the Maurienne, by which five villages were overwhelmed ... inasmuch as it destroyed about nine thousand men ... it seems to have been caused by a miracle rather than the common course of events. It was said that the severity of divine judgement justly vented its fury on the abodes of the inhabitants of those parts, because they so shamelessly and indiscriminately practised the shameful art of usury and were so contaminated with the stain of avarice that in order to cover their wickedness with an appearance of virtue that they called themselves money-merchants. They had no horror of simony, and fearlessly and without mercy engaged in theft and pillage. Traders and scholars compelled to go to the Roman court ... they never failed to cut the throats of or to poison."[51]

In the very next account, Paris goes on to give us lurid details of the drunken debauchery of Prior Stephen de Charron at Thetford, before an altercation that led to murder. Paris wastes no time in telling his readers of Stephen's Savoyard origins and of his being a "kinsman of the Queen". Charron was the brother of the Guiscard de Charron who would be Pierre's steward at Richmond and Bernard de Savoie whom we met earlier at Windsor. Chapuisat, reading the relevant assizes, cautions that they do not fully concur with Paris, and that the acts of Stephen, perhaps a relative of Pierre de Savoie, are impossible to judge for certain at this distance. Obviously in 1248 Paris was deep in anti-Savoyard mode as he'd earlier that year recorded a visit by Henry's mother-in-law, Béatrice de Provence, accompanied by her brother Thomas, for the purpose of "filling their empty and gaping saddle-bags at their departure".[52] In this latter case Paris may have had some point,[53] and it may have soured his writing for at least the rest of the year; nonetheless, taken together the three accounts, especially that of Mont Granier, even for a time when disasters were oft taken to be signs of holy displeasure, carry more than a hint of *schadenfreude* and a monk with an axe to grind, which at the very least should render us a little more wary of this testimony than has been the case in the past.[54] Nearly two centuries ago now, Wurstemberger, the Swiss biographer of Pierre de Savoie, sounded a caution toward those who might read too literally the words of Matthew Paris:

> In the British chroniclers of that time, the princes of Savoy, and the Savoy lords of every estate, who followed them to England in quite an abundance of numbers, [are described] now as Provençals, now as Burgundians, less commonly as Savoyards ... Matthew Paris ... often takes poetic occasion ... to portray those princes and their actions in an unfavourable light ... [and so he] cannot remain free from the suspicion of passion and partisanship.[55]

As if to provide further evidence that shows us the folly of taking Matthew Paris at his word regarding Boniface and the wider Savoyard family, is the attack made upon his former priory town of Nantua. We saw earlier that the monks of Nantua had accepted Boniface as their prior to ward off attacks by the Lords of Thoire-Villars. They'd taken Boniface's absence in England between 1249 and 1250 as a signal to attack once more. However, Boniface came to their aid when, as Archbishop of Canterbury, he could have ignored their pleas for help. Paris maliciously dismissed Boniface's defence of Nantua and his monks there, in the face of a siege, as "waging war in Provence like a free-booter".[56]

I hope this book will not be seen too much as a defence of the Savoyards, a revision of English historiography or indeed an overly critical examination of Matthew Paris, but as W. N. Yates eloquently put it, "Unfortunately, Paris's opinions, remarkable in this instance [in this case of Pierre d'Aigueblanche] for their extreme prejudice, have been accepted quite uncritically by most historians of the Hereford diocese in succeeding generations, and by many modern scholars as well."[57] He went on later to add, "It is a great pity that so many historians have been willing to accept at its face value contemporary criticism of Aquablanca, for it disguises the truth."[58] Yates was writing in defence of Aigueblanche specifically but his observations could easily be more widely applied to the view of the Savoyards in England.

Meanwhile, Pierre de Savoie was now dividing his time between England and the *Pays de Vaud*, collecting money and influence in England, and gathering vassals in the *Pays de Vaud*. In 1249, his position in England was further increased, namely by the grant of the castle and Honour of Hastings.[59] The Honour of Hastings had previously been held by the House of Eu in northern France, but like many families in the aftermath of Philippe Auguste's conquest of Normandy, they had had to choose between their English and French possessions, and chose the latter. We saw earlier that the origin of the Honour of Richmond lay in the Norman conquest of England, being granted to kinsman of the Conqueror, Alain le Roux. The Honour of Hastings had similarly been granted by Duke William to another of his kinsmen, Robert d'Eu who held the County of Eu on the northern borders of Normandy. Hastings remained generally within the *Famille d'Eu* until its last holder, Alix, forfeited in 1243 as she chose to remain with her lands in France. The Honour bordered Pevensey to the west, already held by Pierre, and so the conjoining of the territories made sense. The castle at Hastings, high on a promontory above the town facing out to sea, had been slighted by King John when in fear of his realm from French invasion. Pierre put repairs in hand making the castle defensible once more; Henry had granted to Pierre two of the castles vital for the kingdom's defence, Pevensey and now Hastings. This sign of Henry's complete trust in Pierre was also shown by his sending the Savoyard to extend the truce with France, giving him "power to prorogue[60] the said truce, and to swear oh the king's soul that it shall be observed".[61] The grants of Hastings and the power to extend the truce with France are both dated to 2–4 October at Windsor and are clearly related.[62] Before we move on from the acquisition of the Honour of Eu, the recently published cartulary of Pierre de Savoie published by the Pipe Rolls Society, the diligent work of Huw Ridgeway, give us delightful detail of how Pierre might increase his interests. A good example is the purchase of a mill at Maresfield in East Sussex, just over a mile north of Uckfield, one Alexander son of John Syodewell giving up his rights to the mill to Pierre and his heirs – a reminder that history is made up of little details as well as the grand events of the coming Baronial War.[63]

When Boniface came to England, he'd brought news with him of Louis' crusade and apparent victory at Damietta. This spurred Henry to take once more the cross, which he did in March 1250. Accordingly, Henry sent not only Pierre, as above, but his brother Richard to Paris to conclude an enabling truce with France that would facilitate a crusade. We have few details of Pierre at the French court in Paris negotiating the extension of the truce, other than Pierre's envoy was accompanied by Richard, Earl of Cornwall, and in Paris involved Alianor's sister, Marguerite, in Louis' absence, and Pierre's brother Philippe.[64] From Paris, Pierre continued to Lyon, alongside Richard who was travelling to see the Pope with news of Henry taking the cross, and thence to Savoy to begin renewed hostilities with the Count of Geneva in 1250.[65] The prior call in Lyon to visit his brother Philippe is interesting and suggests some degree of collusion, since following the short conflict the resulting arbitration would be imposed by Philippe de Savoie. The arbitration brought the strategically vital castles at Ballaison, Rue and Les Clées into Pierre's hands.[66] Ballaison, now destroyed, lay above Douvaine, dominating the road from Geneva to the Chablais. Also coming to Pierre as vassals would be the Lords of Langin, also in the Chablais and of the Châteaux de Ogoz and Corbières to the north of Lausanne[67] – we will meet these knights later when Pierre is in need of an army that might invade England. Witnessing these acquisitions, we find the ever-loyal lieutenants Henri de Champvent and Pierre de Grandson, both of whom we should remember have children at court in England, Pierre de Champvent and Othon de Grandson.

Amongst these acquisitions was the castle at Rue, where he may have previously been imprisoned. The castle was strategically important, situated north of Lausanne toward Fribourg, just five miles (eight kilometres) south-east of Pierre's regional capital at Moudon. His father-in-law, Aymon de Faucigny, had besieged the castle twice, and later destroyed it. Aymon had since rebuilt the castle, with Rodolphe de Rue a vassal. Now in 1250 the castle passed to his son-in-law, with again Rodolphe the vassal. Several years later, in 1258, he purchased the fief outright from the Counts of Geneva. He installed as his chatelain one Henri de Bonvillars, whose son Jean de Bonvillars would become a Constable of Harlech Castle for Edward I.[68] Another acquisition was the tithe of Avenches, once the important Roman centre of Aventicum and still today the possessor of significant Roman ruins. Lastly, in 1254, Pierre received the homage of another important Vaudois family, that of Aymon de Montagny, another vassal who'd later support his English enterprise in 1264.[69] Jourdan de Montagny would find the aforesaid place in Pierre's army in trying to free a captive King Henry III of

England. Arnold de Montagny would later serve King Edward I of England. In this way, as we've seen many times, acceptance of Pierre de Savoie's suzerainty would involve a Vaudois family in English affairs. It was said that all roads lead to Rome; in the thirteenth century all roads from Savoy to England led through Pierre de Savoie.

Les Clées, meanwhile, meaning *the barrier*, was the front door, so to speak, of the *Pays de Vaud* when coming from the north from Burgundy, France and England along the *Via Francigena*. A little house by the old medieval bridge across the river Orbe still carries the mark of the House of Savoy. An English interest in Pierre de Savoie, de facto Earl of Richmond holding Les Clées, can be discerned from an 1130 edict by the Bishop of Lausanne excommunicating the inhabitants of Les Clées. Apparently, they were fond of robbing travellers along the *Via Francigena*, many of them English.[70] We saw earlier Cnut's concern for pilgrims, Henry II's support for the hospitality offered by the monks of the Grand-Saint-Bernard and that Amédée IV had only recently enfiefed the town of Saint-Maurice and castle of Bard, also along the *Via Francigena*, to Henry III. There was now a chain of English pilgrim-friendly castles through the Alpine region to Italy.

Further conflict, in the autumn of 1250, brought a struggle with the Lords of La-Tour-du-Pin, who sat astride the trade routes from Lyon and Vienne to the Mont Cenis in the hills before those routes reached Savoy. Both Philippe and Pierre were involved in the renewed war when the Genevois were beaten once more. On 29 September 1250 Albert II de la Tour was obliged to pay homage to Pierre for the barony of La-Tour-du-Pin, bringing Savoyard rule down as far as Falavier in the hills above Philippe's See of Lyon.[71] The acquisition of Falavier is a good example of how Pierre de Savoie was using his wealth from England in furthering his position in Savoy. Guillaume de Beauvoir had held the strategically important castle of Falavier from the *Seigneurie La Tour*, having done so since the *Famille de Beauvoir* gave homage to Albert II de la Tour in 1203. In 1250, Pierre de Savoie gave Beauvoir 1,000 marks, enabling Beauvoir to "buy himself out" of his homage to now Albert III de la Tour. In return Beauvoir now paid homage for Falavier to Pierre.[72] This expansive move westward from the mountains to the rolling hills of the Viennois would bring control of the road from Chambéry to Lyon, as the treaty provided for cession of the castle at Bourgoin within three years. Bourgoin lies just to the west of where the road from Lyon divides, the right fork continuing to Grenoble and the Dauphiné and the left to Chambéry and Savoy – this was a prized piece of real estate.[73] Pierre was not alone in extending his regional position: in 1252 Amédée would further enlarge the extent of Archbishop Boniface's estates in Savoy by adding the castle at Tournon on the southern shores of Lac Léman and the town of Saint-Hélène-des-Millières in the Tarentaise to his lands. Both Pierre and Boniface, despite their time in England, never ceased to take care of Savoy, attempting to keep a foot on either side of the Channel, to the increasing disapproval of the English.

This time of diplomacy for Henry, aggrandisement in England and simultaneously in Savoy, bringing advantage to Pierre on both sides of the Channel, meant time away from court. But this was not a good time for Pierre to be absent from the English court. He had been away from England since April 1250 and would not return until January 1252. What's more, his brother Boniface would be similarly absent, as would Bishop of Hereford Pierre d'Aigueblanche. In the absence of the Savoyards, the Lusignans found advancement. Guy and Geoffrey de Lusignan returned from crusade to be met with royal preferment. In July 1251 Aymer de Lusignan was installed as Bishop Elect of Winchester, the very see that Henry had tried to award to the House of Savoy, and Guillaume de Valence was also able to progress his position. After the initial Lusignan arrival of 1247, the year 1251 saw a new increase in arrivals. It was proving difficult for Pierre de Savoie to watch the mice playing in England and the mice playing in Savoy at the same time.

Meanwhile, simmering tensions were beginning to come to a head, culminating in 1252, with a colossal argument between King Henry and his former favourite, Simon de Montfort. The Savoyards and Lusignans had been preceded in the English court by one Simon de Montfort, the younger son of the 5th Earl of Leicester, a Frenchman like many with extensive lands on both sides of the Channel. But, like many, he had been forced to choose on which side of the water he wanted to remain when Philippe Auguste expelled the Plantagenets from much of France – in 1229, his youngest son had come to England to try to claim his land. Henry had granted Simon de Montfort his land in return for his revocation of allegiance to the French king – furthermore, Montfort had become then a favourite of the English king. In 1238, Simon had become one of the family, marrying Henry's sister Eleanor Marshal, who'd previously been married to William II Marshal, Earl of Pembroke. The marriage had indeed caused some notoriety, especially amongst the clergy, since she had previously taken vows of chastity. In January 1248, Henry gave the great castle of Kenilworth to the couple, for so long as Eleanor might live, something Henry would come to bitterly regret.

Henry was not by popular understanding a strong martial king; he was true enough a Plantagenet and thus given to bouts of temper, but he was at heart a pious man. Later centuries would have thought him a good and kind king, but the thirteenth century thought him weak and ineffectual – an unfair description. Dante placed him in purgatory, a king of the simple life sitting silently by himself, his legacy the strong son who followed him.[74] Recent biographers have been kinder to Henry, Stephen Church titling his Penguin Monarchs biography *A Simple and God-Fearing King,* whereas Baker went further, suggesting in his title that Henry was *The Great King England Never Knew It Had*. Whatever we may think now of a good, simple and god-fearing king who left us the beautiful monument of Westminster Abbey, contemporaries of his day, like our friend Matthew Paris, were sometimes less than complimentary – Paris described him as "womanish" and "effeminate".[75] By any stretch of the imagination, as evidenced by his disastrous Poitevin campaign, Henry was not the warrior king embodied by his grandfather Henry II or uncle Richard I.

Before the ill winds that would soon begin to blow around his reign, there was one more moment of pageantry and splendour – a royal wedding. In December 1251, his daughter Margaret, likely named by Alianor for her sister Marguerite, would marry Alexander III of Scotland, thus uniting in marriage the two kingdoms. Alexander was just 10 years, 3 months and 22 days and Margaret not much older, aged just 11 years, 2 months and 28 days. It would not be the first Anglo-Scottish royal marriage union, as Henry's sister Joan had been married to King Alexander II of Scotland until Joan died in 1238. The wedding took place at the great York Minster, with Archbishop Walter de Gray performing the ceremony. Young Alexander was knighted by and paid homage to his new father-in-law amongst great ceremony. Henry tried to get the boy to pay homage for his kingdom, but Alexander stood resolutely to paying homage only for his lands in England – it could have been a quarrel but Henry, unlike his son later, would let it pass. Nothing was to spoil the great day; watching Margaret and Alexander make their vows were her father and mother, Henry and Alianor, her brother Edward, the royal family. Also watching the solemn ceremonial were the newcomers to the kingdom, the Savoyard Ebal II de Mont,[76] and the king's half-brothers, Guy de Lusignan, Guillaume de Valence and Bishop Elect Aymer. In his dealings with Wales and Scotland at this time, the lenient way he dealt with Gwynedd, his unwillingness to press the

Chapter Six

case for overlordship of Scotland – we can say where Henry's priorities lay: it was not in the Celtic fringes of Britain but in his ancestral France. Also watching on, beneath the great roof of York Minster that December day in 1251, was Simon de Montfort, just back from Gascony. The peaceful beauty of the day, the state ceremony, the uniting of two royal families and kingdoms had bubbling away beneath it a growing cancer.

As we saw in 1248, Henry had appointed Simon as seneschal of the last remaining Plantagenet lands in France, Gascony in the south of Aquitaine. Aquitaine had, as mentioned earlier, belonged to Henry's grandparents, Henri d'Anjou and Eleanor d'Aquitaine: the Duchy had encompassed a vast territory. Aquitaine, from the Latin *Aquitainia*, or Old French *Aguyenne*, or the shortened *Guyenne*, literally meant "Land of the Waters", named for the rivers that flowed through it into the vast Atlantic Ocean. From north to south along the Atlantic seaboard there had been the County of Poitou, the County of Saintonge, the Duchy of Gascony, centred on Bordeaux, then the lordships of Tartas and Dax then Labourd, bordering the Kingdom of Navarre. Inland, again north to south, there had been the County of La Marche, Viscounty of Limoges, Périgord, County of Agen, County of Auvergne, County of Quercy, the troublesome Viscounty of Béarn and lastly the County of Bigorre. Much of this Duchy of Aquitaine had been lost to the French king but Gascony itself remained with the Plantagenet Duc d'Aquitaine and its lands down to the Pyrenees. Eleanor d'Aquitaine had brought vast lands to her marriage with Henry's grandfather – and he felt they rightly belonged to him. What is more, Gascony was an allod, not a fiefdom: it was held by Henry as the grandson of Alianor d'Aquitaine, and had never been a fief of the French Crown.[77] As noted earlier, in medieval law, an allod (Old Low Franconian *allōd* or fully owned estate, from all full, entire and *ōd* 'estate', in Medieval Latin *allodium*) was an estate in land over which the allodial landowner (allodiary) had full ownership and right of alienation. The allodial nature of Aquitaine vis-à-vis the French monarchy would be a bone of continual contention throughout the thirteenth and fourteenth centuries.

The region was important to England as it was the source of much of the country's wine since the loss of Anjou and Poitou to France. Gascony was a troubled land, beset by warring families. Simon de Montfort had a name well known in the southern regions of France: his illustrious father, also a Simon de Montfort, had led the Albigensian Crusade against the Cathar heretics. The Earl of Leicester had accepted the role instead of joining Louis IX on crusade, perhaps to emulate the martial fame his father had gained in the south, but perhaps Henry's choice of Simon was to set a bull loose in a china shop. As John Maddicott suggested, his father's "brutality" would "dog his sons' footsteps in that part of France".[78] A citizen of Sault-des-Navailles, a town of which we will come back to later, said of the Montfortian name that "*audiverat sermonem de malo ingenio de familia Montisfortis*" or "he had heard talk of the evil genius of the Montifort family".[79] Simon was not by all accounts a light hand on the tiller and complaints from Gascony soon filled the king's ears. Gascon affairs being all the more important to Henry and Alianor since they would, on 30 September 1249, "Made a gift to Edward, the king's eldest son, of all the land of Gascony",[80] a gift incidentally witnessed by the ever-present Pierre de Savoie.[81] Having previously seen Simon a number of times in England, Henry finally called Montfort back to England again but this time to fully account for his actions, not quite a trial, but one that looked to all who took part like a trial. Pierre de Savoie was also recalled to England, arriving at Dover on 5 March 1252, the recall being obviously in connection with the upcoming Montfort trial. Henry met Pierre at Dover and then both proceeded to Canterbury.[82] Shortly after, on 16 March, a number of arbitrators were chosen, amongst them unsurprisingly, Pierre de Savoie.[83] Simon was affronted at being recalled and even more affronted at being asked to account for his actions – this did not bode well.

As he defended himself before the multitude in the great refectory at Westminster Abbey in May 1252, Simon persuaded many of his innocence of the numerous Gascon complaints, including Pierre de Savoie, Richard, Earl of Cornwall and the Earls of Hereford and Gloucester; however, Henry was less convinced.[84] Matthew Paris gives us his account:

> By shuffling speeches they provoked the anger of each other, and rashly recalled to mind things which had passed long since … And, added he [Simon] "My Lord King, your words should be stable and trustworthy. Keep your agreement with me, or keep your promise to me, in accordance with the tenor of your charter, or repay me the money which I have expended in your service; for it is well known that I have irreparably impoverished my earldom for the sake of your honour." To this the king hastily and ill-advisedly replied: "Be well assured that I will not observe the compact, in regard to any of my promises, with you, an unworthy traitor, who would if you could be the supplanter of your sovereign. For it is allowed one to break his compact, when the other party breaks theirs; and to deal without shame with those who are shameless." The earl on hearing these words was highly incensed, and rising, he loudly declared that the king had clearly lied in this speech, "And" he said, "were it not that he is sheltered by kingly name and dignity, it would have been a bad hour in which he gave utterance to such a speech." At this the king, who could scarcely contain himself for rage, would have ordered him to be seized on the spot, had he not been well assured that such a proceeding would not on any account have been allowed by the nobles. The earl, moreover, added: "Who could believe that thou art a Christian? Hast thou never confessed?" The king answered, "I have." "But" rejoined the count, "what avails confession without repentance and atonement?" As though he meant, "If thou hast confessed, thou hast never been contrite, and never made proper atonement." To which the king, whose anger was more and more inflamed, replied, "I never repented of any act so much as I now repent of ever having permitted you to enter England, or to hold any land or honours in that country, in which you fattened so as to kick against my authority."[85]

There had not been such a public falling out with a Plantagenet king since the days of Henry II and Thomas Becket – and like that previous unpleasantness, this was not to end well. From May 1252 King Henry III and Simon de Montfort were on a collision course that would end very badly for one after nearly losing the kingdom for the other. Of particular concern to Henry was that amongst the nobles who'd witnessed this angry exchange and not leapt to his defence were his brother, Richard of Cornwall, but also notably Pierre de Savoie and Alianor.[86] Historians from the time of Paris have criticised Henry's actions as weak and inconstant; more recently Carpenter has reappraised his actions, suggesting that Henry was quite right to act in such a way. Carpenter points to the level of Gascon criticism of the Earl and the number of times he'd stood by his actions in Gascony before being forced to act.[87]

Nonetheless, the normally loyal Pierre de Savoie had sided with Simon de Montfort, an odd alliance perhaps of Savoyard and the indignant Frenchman. But what had brought about

Chapter Six

this nexus of the interests of the Savoyards and Simon de Montfort? The answer in 1252 as it would be in 1258 was the Lusignans. This temporary alignment of Savoyard and Montfortian interests has been largely overlooked, as it would be later too.[88] But, perhaps Montfort, the son of the leader of the murderous crusade against the Cathars in the south of France, had not been a wise choice as seneschal: the Gascons may well have taken against the very name Montfort.

The foreigners at Henry's court were criticised by contemporary chroniclers, and these criticisms have continued to this day. However, we must be careful to divide these foreigners into two factions, the Savoyards and the Poitevins or Lusignans. Carpenter finds little to find fault in Henry's courting of Savoyard links, that the Savoyard links were not "too disruptive" and that Pierre de Savoie "behaved with caution and sensitivity". He goes further, suggesting that Boniface de Savoie "became a respected and reforming archbishop".[89] The Savoyard faction at court were there primarily at the invitation of Queen Alianor, the Lusignan faction at court at the invitation of King Henry. The Savoyards were after all Alianor's uncles and associates thereof, whereas the Lusignans were Henry's half-brothers and associates thereof – summarised by Paris as the "kingsmen" against the "queensmen".[90] There is no evidence from the archives, marriages or witnessing charters, for example, of any co-operation between the two factions. Having been married to Alice de Lusignan, the young Jean de Warenne joined the unruly Lusignan faction, dissatisfied with his treatment by Pierre. The Warenne wardship was due to expire in 1251, but Pierre was tardy in giving up lands, something that brought clashes between their men between Lewes and Pevensey. There would be further open conflict between the two factions elsewhere: a dispute between the Lusignan Bishop Elect of Winchester, Aymer, and Savoyard Archbishop of Canterbury, in 1252, ended with Aymer's men breaking into Lambeth Palace and making off with jewels, plate and money.[91] Boniface excommunicated some of those involved, men of the household of Guillaume de Valence and Geoffrey de Lusignan.[92]

The queen had, however, been careful to not only surround herself with Savoyards, but she had also taken great care to surround her prized asset with Savoyards: Edward's household was largely from Savoy.[93] Edward's entourage at this time continued to be Savoyard, as his mother surrounded him with her fellow countrymen, Geoffrey de Geneville the brother of Louis IX's chronicler Jean de Joinville and the aforesaid Ebal II de Mont. Michael Fiennes, Edward's first chancellor, also had familial links with Alianor. Ridgeway described the Savoyard surrounding Edward as an "embryonic colonial service".[94] No wonder Paris wasn't happy. Edward's main source of revenue as a boy (until 54) was the Honour of Hastings, often known, as we saw, as the Honour of Eu. A list of names of its custodians is revealing: Bernard de Savoie (1244–7), Pierre de Genève (1247–9) and Pierre de Savoie himself (1249–54).[95] A 1252 issuing of the charter granting Gascony to Edward carries this annotation "*Ista carta missa fuit Petro de Sabaudia*" or "This charter has been sent to Peter of Savoy", confirming that a copy was sent to Pierre by Henry's secretary John Mansel.[96] Mansel had been treated for grievous wounds years earlier by Pierre de Savoie's personal surgeon and had become a key ally of the Savoyard. Similarly a copy of a promise on the part of Guy de Lusignan to restore lands to Edward was marked "transmitted from the wardrobe to Peter de Sabaudia."[97] Cox wrote of the degree to which Pierre de Savoie, as leading the *cordon sanitaire* that surrounded Queen Alianor and Prince Edward, controlled the kingdom: "In February 1254 Pierre also witnessed the act which made Prince Edward Lord of Ireland as well as Lord of Gascony, and the Savoyard seems to have become for a time a kind of regent for his great-nephew." It became normal not only for such acts to be witnessed by the Savoyard, but copies to be sent for safe keeping to Pierre's archives, some of which have survived to the care of the UK National Archive.[98] Witnessing charters might be expected but having copies of these charters made and sent to you for safekeeping was not. The keeping of the charter confirming Edward's appanage in Pierre's drawer, so to speak, confirmed the Savoyard, in Ridgeway's words "as always, as protector of Edward's interests". Whilst Alianor and Henry's brother Richard were left in charge of the kingdom in 1253 as Henry and Pierre voyaged Gascony to suppress revolting barons, a confirming letter was "delivered to P. de Sabaudia".[99] Indeed, we have seen repeatedly Pierre's role as Alianor and Edward's protection.[100] Raised by Savoyards, with a Savoyard mother and uncle close by, surrounded by Savoyard friends such as the ever-present Othon de Grandson, it is no overstatement to suggest that the later King Edward I had "Made in Savoy" stamped somewhere upon his person. A kind of regent are strong words, but given Henry's perceived weakness and perhaps the Lusignan threat, it helps us to understand Alianor's defence of her personal and the wider Savoyard position, as well as the hostility of natives such as Matthew Paris.[101] Pierre de Savoie held the wardship of the heir to the English Crown, Edward was, in the words of Carpenter, "the rock on which Savoyard fortunes were founded".[102]

Notwithstanding the need to differentiate between them, there were now, along with the 300 Savoyard, over 70 Poitevin and assorted French nobles like Simon de Montfort. Perhaps it's not difficult to understand that this may have raised the hackles of xenophobes like Matthew Paris, despite Henry having, as Carpenter once wrote, "no vision of a foreign court dominated by Lusignans and Savoyards".[103] Nonetheless, he later listed for 1252 the number of charters witnessed at Henry's court; the numbers speak for themselves:[104]

Geoffrey de Lusignan	50 (from April)
Pierre de Savoie	45 (from March)
Guillaume de Valence	40
Richard de Clare The Earl of Gloucester	15
Richard, The Earl of Cornwall	14
Roger Bigod, The Earl of Norfolk	12
Humphrey de Bochum, The Earl of Hereford	10

Pierre de Savoie would have witnessed 200 royal charters during his time in England.[105]

During 1252 and the trial of Simon de Montfort, Pierre had been close to the centre of the English government, spending time with Henry at Westminster and Windsor. We know that the ongoing construction of his house on the Strand in London took his attention shortly after arriving there. On 18 March he was granted twenty oaks in the forest of Windsor for the *"operaciones domorum suarum Lond"*.[106] Thereafter he travelled south to await events at Pevensey Castle, his possession on the Sussex coast. His messenger to and from court was yet another Savoyard, indeed a Vaudois, a former valet in Alianor's service, Guillaume de Valereys. Guillaume was a man of Valeyres-sous-Montagny, a small village in the shadow of Yverdon, where Pierre would build a castle, and of Grandson and Champvent, whose Othon and Pierre were with the royal household in England. If one were to throw a net a few kilometres wide across the southern shore of Lac de Neuchâtel, one would capture an awful lot of English history. A document from May 1254 in Vaud attests to Valeyres having been

Chapter Six

enfiefed to Pierre by the offices of his ally or vassal Pierre de Grandson. Another example of how English and Vaudois policy might be combined.[107]

A footnote perhaps to the year 1252 would be the passing of Marguerite de Savoie's mother-in-law, and by whose protective nature of her son Louis IX of France had brought the Savoyards to the English court, not to the French. Blanche de Castille was regent of France at the time of her death, her beloved son Louis being engaged on his ill-fated crusade, which she'd strongly opposed. She never saw Louis again, being buried at Maubuisson Abbey. When Louis heard of his mother's death, he reportedly spoke to no one for two days.[108]

Meanwhile, in England, the rival factions, along with the king, were headed on a collision course with a native nobility looking for reasons to reassert their post-*Magna Carta* authority.

Chapter Seven

On 18 April 1253 Pierre de Savoie put his seal to a charter promising that he would accompany Henry on crusade.[1] But, if wishes were horses beggars would ride;, like for Henry there would be no voyage for Pierre to the Holy Land. Thoughts and intentions of crusade faded: Gascony overtook them. Henry's brother Richard, his son Edward, his brother-in-law Louis, Pierre's fellow Savoyard Othon de Grandson would all be crusaders, but not Henry and Pierre. At the Westminster Parliament of May 1253 Henry sought the money for an expedition to Gascony but was met with significant resistance. The Parliament attended by Pierre de Savoie eventually consented, but only after what was in effect a reissue of *Magna Carta*.[2] The *Great Charter* was the perennial bargaining tool in Henry's relations with Parliament and his efforts to extract funds for his enterprises.[3] On 13 May Archbishop Boniface presided over a solemn ceremony of excommunication, at Westminster Hall, for any that might break with the *Great Charter*. The Savoyard archbishop and an assembly of bishops, including Pierre d'Aigueblanche of Hereford, threw down their lit candles at the climax of the ceremony, promising that those who might break with *Magna Carta* be similarly extinguished and "reek in hell".[4] Pierre de Savoie did not attend the ceremony. Five earls did,[5] but his name was attached to the announcement of the excommunication.[6]

Matthew Paris writes of this time that the Savoyards tried to institute a law in England that had been the custom in Savoy, but that it was resisted by the baronage. The suggested law related to how victims of robbery might be treated, but Paris assures us that whilst the remedy might work in Savoy it could not have possibly worked in England. Responsibility for recompense of the injured and bringing the criminal to justice might be placed on the local landowner. Paris does not give us the name of the Savoyard responsible, but it can only have been Pierre, and if Paris can be believed this is an interesting precursor of the laws and customs he'd later transplant from England to Savoy.[7]

Meanwhile, to secure Pierre's involvement in his forthcoming Gascon expedition, Henry made a gift of some 5,500 marks, including a down payment of £1,000, to be used in Pierre's affairs in Vaud.[8] In response to the Gascon problem created by Simon de Montfort, Henry needed to travel to Gascony – which he did in the summer of 1253, arriving there on 12 August. The Gascons had said that a ducal visitation would resolve matters. He was accompanied on the expedition by a coterie of Savoyards, notably Pierre de Savoie and Pierre d'Aigueblanche, and Savoyard household knights such as Imbert Pugeys and Henry's loyal Savoyard steward, Pierre de Champvent.[9] He'd left England in the care of the queen and his brother Richard as her adviser,[10] and the king's letters patent were handed over to Pierre de Savoie for safekeeping.[11] Pierre, meanwhile, had appointed the Savoyard Ebal II de Mont, Stephen Bauzan and Bartholomew Peche his attorneys to act upon his behalf in England pending his return.[12] Ebal was of the *Famille de Mont* of the castle high above Rolle in Vaud, and had been knighted by Henry's order in 1248,[13] likely at Alianor's request, in whose service he was now a household knight. He had been married to Joan de Somery of the Bohun dynasty, holding the castle of Midhurst in Sussex, just over fifty miles (eighty kilometres) west of Pierre's Pevensey Castle.[14] It would be a step along a distinguished career that would lead him to Windsor Castle and the role of Constable once held by Bernard de Savoie. The Calendar of Patent Rolls is quite clear on the appointment of Alianor as de facto regent:

> Appointment of Queen Eleanor to keep and govern the realm of England and the lands of Wales and Ireland with the counsel of Richard, Earl of Cornwall, the king's brother, until the king's return from Gascony: and mandate to be all intendant to her.[15]

As we noted earlier a letter confirming the arrangement was "delivered to P.de Sabaudia".[16] Historians, perhaps with no little sexism[17], have traditionally held that Richard effectively ruled England in Henry's absence, or at least given Alianor being with child that they were joint rulers, but the mandate is quite clear. I think if Henry had intended there to be joint rule, then he was quite capable of clearly saying so. We should not second guess his intention – for the time being England was in the hands of Alianor de Provence. Despite giving birth to a daughter, Katherine, on 25 November 1253, the government of England was in Alianor's hands from Henry's departure for Gascony on 6 August 1253 until her own on 29 May 1254.

Henry of course was in constant need of finances to fund his ongoing operations in Gascony, and since the *Magna Carta* that had meant calling a parliament and asking it for the money. Something that happened in the spring of 1254 is of great note in the development of parliament as an institution, and it is something in which Alianor had knowledge of and it is just possible may have had a hand in: this is the nature of the Easter Parliament of 1254.[18] As Maddicott has said, it is "curious that contemporaries had so little to say about what seems to us to have been momentous".[19] We are referring to the calling to Parliament of the knights of the shire as representatives of not themselves, but of the shire from which they came.[20] In the event Henry was not granted a tax in 1254; the matter was deferred (kicking problems into the long grass not being a recent innovation), but the prudence of consulting widely when needing the consent of the governed was, with hindsight, an important precedent of "considerable constitutional significance" to have been set.[21]

Much of Gascony was in revolt following the discontent of Montfort's rule as seneschal. The revolt centred upon La Réole. High above the Garonne River, the town was of strategic importance as it governed access to Gascony from the Agenais. On 12 August 1253 Henry and his army made landfall at Bordeaux.[22] Having earlier tried to conciliate the rebels, by early September Henry had moved the forty miles (64 kilometres) upstream and arrived at La Réole on the right bank of the Garonne, besieging the town, but made no progress and gave up the siege after but a week. Elsewhere progress was made: forces under the command of Pierre de Savoie and English nobles such as Bigod, Plessis and Grey took the towns of Saint-Macaire and Meilhan. At Meilhan Pierre left a garrison under Philippe d'Arcy, ensuring that La Réole received no succour from the Agenais.[23] The "English" army in Gascony had had a distinct Savoyard flavour, Swiss architectural historian Louis Blondel identified over ninety "*représentants de familles nobles*" of "*Savoie, du Genevois, de la Tarentaise, du Bugey, de la Franche-Comté, du Pays de Vaud ... et du Val d'Aoste*" amongst Henry's army in the Gascon Rolls,[24] knighting amongst others Jean de Châtillon,[25] Reynaud d'Orbe, Jean Grossi and Guillaume de Pesmes.[26][27] Guillaume de Pesmes returned seemingly to England with the Lord Edward as there is a 1259 confirmation of a charter at Southwark of lands to Ebal II de Mont, which lists him as one of the witnesses, along with, unsurprisingly, Gefferoi de Geneville the brother of Simon, Seigneur de Gex et Marnay and so neighbour in the Franche Comté. We see once more the influence of Pierre de Savoie in the Franche Comté through his familial links with the Famille de Joinville linking in with his interests in surrounding the Lord Edward with Savoyards.[28] Jean de Châtillon's links with Pierre are made by his likely kinsman Imbert de Châtillon who like Jean will serve the crown but mostly remain in Pierre's service in Savoy. Blondel might have added to the list Pierre's kinsman from Geneva, Ebal de Genève whose listed amongst those Englishmen given "protection" for "crossing with the king to Gascony".[29] The Gascon roles also carry the name of a knight from what is now Swiss Germany, Konrad von Kyburg, whose participation is likely through Pierre's sister, Marguerite de Savoie.[30] Jean Grossi was of the *Famille du Châtelard* of the Aosta Valley, he was of the same family as Rodolphe Grossi, Archbishop of Tarentaise, the man who will witness the later 1259 Treaty of Paris for the Plantagenets.[31] That none of these knights appear in the protection lists for those sailing with the King from England to Gascony would seem to suggest perhaps that they joined the English army directly from Savoy and the Jura which would suggest some form of co-ordination with Pierre de Savoie who'd sailed from England. Sadly, the contribution of these knights from Savoy in supporting the Crown in Gascony have been overlooked by historians. Against the ledger of taking advantage of a vineyard without a wall we need to set this help in successfully restoring order to what will become Edward's appanage of Gascony.

Henry's chief adversary in Gascony, had and would be Gaston VII, Viscount of Béarn, a man whom Henry might have thought should have been an ally since Gaston's mother was Garsende de Provence the very sister of his father-in-law Ramon Berenguer. However, Simon de Montfort had in his time as Seneschal made war upon Gaston. In 1248 Gaston had been defeated and taken prisoner by Montfort, taken to London, where in 1250 he'd been vociferous in his complaints against the Earl of Leicester. Now back in Gascony Gaston was prepared to play off the Plantagenets against the Capetians. But the centre of the rebellion wasn't Béarn in the south, but along the Garonne, the very centre of Gascony and key to the Agenais. Leading Gascon noblemen such as Amanieu V d'Albret, Amanieu was Lord of Bazas and Meilhan, and the aforesaid Meilhan and Bernard de Bouville of Benauges had to be dealt with in order to bring order to Gascony. Albret was a good example of the way in which Gascon nobles played the Plantagenets and Capetians off against one another to further their own ends. In 1213–14 Albret had sided with the Plantagenets, but by 1253 he had made his peace with the Capetians. In September a major victory was secured when Bazas, twenty miles (32 kilometres) south of La Réole, was taken and garrisoned. Having bought Albret to terms, the siege of Bouville's castle at Benauges would be the turning point and would see Henry employing two Gascon *ingeniators* (engineers), Master Bertram and Jean Mésoz. We find the first mention of Mésoz, "Johanni de Meysot, Ingeniatori" just a few days after the aforementioned knight Jean de Châtillon.[32] Master Bertram had first appeared in the written record as *Magistro Bertrando de Saltu, ingeniatori* in 1248,[33] Saltu being Sault-de-Navailles,[34] some twenty-plus miles (thirty-two kilometres) north-west of Pau and fifty-odd miles (eighty kilometres) inland, in the shadow of the Pyrenees. Sault lay on the border of the lands of the restive Gaston de Béarn, the castle above the Luy had been recently taken by Montfort in 1249 during his time as Seneschal.

Chapter Seven

The siege of Benauges began on 28 September 1253, the defenders of the castle high on a hill and dominating the surrounding countryside putting up a resolute defence. Throughout October Henry, together with Bertram and Mésoz, encamped in the surrounding fields, now vineyards, but the rebels bombarded them with mill stones. Mésoz appears to have been the senior, in charge of three engines – two mangonels[35] and a belfry.[36&37] Eventually, on 6 November, Benauges fell, eventually to be taken up by a Savoyard appointment as seneschal of Gascony, Jean de Grailly, but not before being granted for a time, as constable, to Alianor and Edward's Savoyard household knight, Ebal II de Mont.[38] Bertram would remain long in Henry's service and continue to serve his son, Edward. Jean de Mésoz would leave Henry's service for that of Pierre de Savoie and in many ways become the mentor of a Maître Jacques in the *Pays de Vaud*. Henry being so pleased with the service of Mésoz, knighted him – we shall meet him again later, but always styled *Dominus*.[39] Whilst Mésoz received his knighthood, Master Bertram was gifted the not inconsiderable sum of £50 (over £36,000 in today's money).[40] It was also at Benauges that Henry reaffirmed his gift of Gascony to Edward "with his hand in the hand" of the Savoyard Bishop of Hereford, Pierre d'Aigueblanche,[41] the Savoyard faction at court, led no doubt by Queen Alianor, once more protecting and ensuring the appanage of Edward. Technically the affirmation at Benauges was that Henry's conquest of Bernard de Bouville and his lands and castle at Benauges formed an inalienable part of the Gascony that would pass to Edward, but that it needed the solemn intervention of Pierre d'Aigueblanche is certainly indicative of Alianor and Pierre de Savoie's fear in 1253 that Henry might be persuaded to pass the fief to either Richard or god forbid the Lusignans.[42]

It was whilst in Gascony, on 7 October, that the prominent noble, lord of the great Northumberland barony centred on Alnwick, William de Vesci, died. The *Famille de Vesci* were of Norman descent, originating in Vassy in the Calvados region. Robert de Vesci had come across with the Conqueror, Ivo [Yves] de Vesci obtaining the important lordship of Alnwick. William's father was the Eustace de Vesci who had been a prominent member of the baronial faction that had forced the *Magna Carta* on John. William de Vesci had only lately taken an oath at Portsmouth, on 22 July (the feast day of Mary Magdalene), in the king's presence as they prepared to sail for Gascony, recorded in the Calendar of Patent Rolls on 25 July, to give his firstborn son, Jean de Vesci's hand in marriage to a daughter of either the "lord of Chambre" or "Vicomte of Aosta". Accordingly, Pierre de Savoie arranged for him to be married to fellow Savoyard Agnès de Saluzzo, the sister of Alésia de Saluzzo, who had been promised by Henry to Edmund de Lacy back in 1246. Agnès and Alésia were the daughters of the late Manfred III di Saluzzo and Béatrice de Savoie, herself a daughter of Count Amédée IV de Savoie – the Savoyard entry into the English nobility continued.[43]

Matthew Paris tells us that "the king gave free possession of them [Bazas and La Réole] to Peter of Savoy".[44] Henry arrived at the cathedral city of Bazas on 19 November, and later he and Pierre held Christmas festivities "with great splendour and solemnity".[45] The city, located on the pilgrimage route to Santiago, at the crossroads of the roads to Bayonne, Bordeaux and La Réole, made an excellent base of operations. It had been just before Christmas that the rebellion effectively ended when Amanieu d'Albret agreed terms and became, once more, the king's man.

It was at Bazas, the following spring, on 12 February, that Henry granted Pierre the ward of the young Jean de Vesci in addition to the aforesaid right to arrange his marriage.[46] In 1252 Pierre's wardship of Jean de Warenne had ended with the coming of age of the 6th Earl of

Surrey, thus Pierre lost the lucrative £1,000 yearly income and castles at Lewes and Reigate. Thus the need for Henry to arrange for the wardship of Jean de Vesci in 1254 provided the timely opportunity to maintain Pierre's income with £625 per annum.[47] The income and marriage of the *Famille de Vesci* might be welcome to Pierre in the short run but the Savoyard interests were perhaps equally served by young Jean going on to be a loyal servant of Edward I and lifelong friend and ally of the Savoyard Othon de Grandson. A good example of Pierre's legacy being both short term and long term.

More importantly perhaps, following the reaffirmation, the charter to grant Edward's appanage was made on 14 February 1254, also at Bazas:

> Charter granting to Edward, the king's firstborn son and heir, the whole land of Ireland ... the whole county of Chester with its castles and towns, with the kings conquest of Wales in these bounds, to wit Rothelan and Gannoc [Deganwy] ... the castles of Mungomery, Karmerdyn [Carmarthen] and Cardigan; the castle of Buelt [Builth]; ... To hold to him and his heirs, on condition that they never be separated from the crown of England ... but that they remain wholly to the kings of England for ever ... Renewal also to him of the gift of Gascony and the Isle of Oleron, on condition that they remain to the lordship of the crown of England.[48]

The witness list is interesting, in order: Pierre d'Aigueblanche, Bishop of Hereford, Jean de Plessis, Earl of Warwick, Geoffrey de Lusignan, Guillaume de Valence and Pierre de Savoie – a very Savoyard–Lusignan set of witnesses. Indeed, holding Henry's hand as he'd sworn the oath to confer the appanage upon Edward, had been Pierre d'Aigueblanche. That Henry "owed a considerable debt" to his foreign relatives for the safe retention of Gascony, contemporary historians like Carpenter have been in little doubt; at the time Matthew Paris simply dismissed it as holding onto something he already had.[49]

Gascony, newly in Edward's hands, was at the time also threatened from the north by the kingdom of France, but also from the south across the Pyrenees by the kingdom of Castile. The newly crowned Castilian king, Alfonso X, was a great-great-grandson of England's King Henry II and so had some reason other than simple greed to claim Gascony. And, as we saw earlier, Gaston VII, Viscount of Béarn, was more than happy to encourage Alfonso in his claim. What's more, the neighbouring kingdom of Navarre had just come into the hands of the 14-year-old Theobald II: an alliance between unmarried Theobald and unmarried 13-year-old half-sister of Alfonso, Leonor, would wed Castile to Navarre and pose a clear and present threat to Gascony.

In order to counter the Castilian threat, Henry offered his son the Lord Edward (to whom he'd granted Gascony in 1249, formalised as we've seen in 1254) to the younger half-sister of Alfonso – Leonor de Castile. In this thirteenth-century web of interrelated monarchies, Alfonso X's father, the late Ferdinand III, had first taken Elizabeth von Hohenstaufen as his wife, the daughter of Philip of Swabia, the Hohenstaufen king of the Germans. When she died, he had next married the lady to which Henry had himself been originally betrothed before marrying Alianor: Jeanne de Ponthieu. This meant of course that Henry's and Alianor's new daughter-in-law was the daughter of the woman he'd once been betrothed to, his "ex" so to speak, and Edward had for a mother and a mother-in-law the two women who'd been at some point betrothed to his father – so again we see the complex familial relationships of the ruling families of Europe. Leonor de Castille would succeed her mother as Countess de Ponthieu,

Chapter Seven

whilst herself then remaining Queen of England, thus for a time, if only by marriage. Henry's family by way of his daughter-in-law acquired Ponthieu after all. This web illustrates well the familial dynastic nature of thirteenth-century politics.

John Mansel and William of Bitton, Bishop of Bath and Wells, were dispatched to open marriage negotiations. In February 1254 Mansel returned with Alfonso's offer; its terms were severe – he wasn't going to give up Gascony without exacting much from Henry. The court that sat at Bazas that early spring was heavily Savoyard and contained no English magnates at all. We should read into the acceptance by Henry of Alfonso's terms the determining of both Alianor and Pierre de Savoie that the Lord Edward receive both Gascony and a good marriage match. Following much negotiation and a treaty offer from Castile that suggested Henry make war on Navarre, John Mansel and finally Pierre d'Aigueblanche concluded negotiations, swearing on behalf of the king on 1 April 1254. Accordingly, Edward set sail from Portsmouth on 29 May for his new realm of Gascony, arriving in Bordeaux on or around 10–12 June, accompanying him, his mother Alianor, his aunt Sanchia, his brother Edmund and Archbishop Boniface. Amongst the panoply of English chivalry bound for Gascony with Edward and Alianor were: William III de Longespée (of the famous Longespée family), John Bek (of the same family as Antony Bek, who would become Bishop of Durham), Edmund de Lacy (Baron of Pontefract, husband to Alésia di Saluzzo and father of Henri de Lacy), Jean de Warenne (6th Earl of Surrey), Roger de Clifford (whose son we'll meet later), Richard de Clare (6th Earl of Gloucester) and the Savoyard Ebal II de Mont, the latter having served Pierre de Savoie in his absence as his attorney.[50] On or about 22 August John Mansel was again sent to Castille to finalise the match of Edward with Leonor de Castile.[51]

An interesting visitor, whilst in Gascony, was Jeanne de Ponthieu, his future mother-in-law and ex-betrothed of his father. She was on her way to Ponthieu having been banished from Castille by Alfonso, as she'd supported a rival, his rebellious brother Enrique. The details of this meeting which would be considered improbable if it formed the plot line of a modern soap opera is not recorded, nor are the thoughts of Alianor at meeting the lady once promised to her husband. As his father and mother were needed in Gascony, and mother-in-law was heading north, Edward would have only his father-in-law present at his wedding.[52]

As mentioned earlier Henry's court that spring was heavily Savoyard in nature. From the witness lists of the English archives we can be sure that Pierre de Savoie and much of his Savoyard coterie, including Imbert Pugeys, Pierre de Champvent and Ebal II de Mont followed the ducal court for much of 1254: we find them at Bazas on 11 February, Meilhan on 3 June, Saint-Macaire on 15 and 16 June, encamped at Bergerac between 28 June and 14 July where Pierre de Savoie was instrumental in the capitulation of the town, back at Saint-Macaire from 18 to 21 July, encamped by the Gironde on 6 and 24 July, Saint-Macaire again on 7 August and Bordeaux on 12 August until at least 11 October.[53] For example, we find a charter of 24 August at Bordeaux witnessed by a list of Savoyards: Pierre d'Aigueblanche, Boniface de Savoie, Pierre de Savoie, Imbert Pugeys and Ebal II de Mont.[54] Ebal got a doubling in pay from 25 to 50 marks annually, whereas the young Champvent, described as the "kings yeoman", was granted the not inconsiderable sum of 60 marks from Henry, almost £30,000 in today's money, both for their ongoing service.[55] Medieval campaigns could be arduous and the Gascon campaign was no exception, Pierre de Champvent himself being recompensed by the Crown for the loss of two horses.[56] Henry was obviously pleased with the boys Pierre de Savoie had brought to England. Ridgeway has suggested, very plausibly, that by this time Ebal II de Mont had left, somewhat, the service of Alianor for the service of the Lord Edward. Certainly Stephen Bauzan, another of the attorneys appointed the previous year in England to act for Pierre de Savoie, is in Gascony, explicitly named as Edward's steward,[57] reminding us once more that the future king was very much in the 1250s in the care of the Savoyard envelope cast by Alianor and Pierre.[58] These were the years of Edward's marriage to his future queen, and of his appanage that included his first attachment to Wales. It was whilst in Bordeaux that on 26 September Henry granted that Pierre could will land as he pleased that he held from the Crown, a notable grant to a noble not yet fifteen years in the realm, and clearly reflecting his service in Gascony and before.[59]

After spending time in Gascony with his father, one assumes coming up to speed with Gascon affairs, Edward travelled south of the mountains to Castile in the autumn of 1254, leaving Bayonne on 9 October, arriving in Burgos on the 18th, there to take his bride. Amidst great splendour, he married Leonor at the abbey of Santa María la Real de Las Huelgas, a mile from Burgos, on 1 November 1254. Las Huelgas, built in the French gothic style, housed the tombs of some of Edward's own family, Leonor of England, the sixth child and second daughter of Henry II and Eleanor d'Aquitaine, and the daughter of Eleanor of England, Berengaria of Navarre. The abbey had indeed been founded at the behest of Leonor of England back in 1187, so was an obvious choice of venue.[60] Marriage of the daughter to the House of Plantagenet was something of a coup for the Castilian monarchy, Alfonso dating his documents henceforth with reference to the year in which his daughter was joined in matrimony with the Lord Edward.[61] As Henry had planned, Alfonso formally renounced claims to Gascony upon the day of the marriage – Edward and Leonor illustrating the way in which marriage was used as a diplomatic weapon in the thirteenth century. But for the 15-year-old Edward and virtually 13-years-old Leonor, the bell tower of Las Huelgas tolled for a new beginning: this was a marriage that would blossom as a love match.

As well as a new, bride Edward received something else from Alfonso, as Matthew Paris records: "At Burgos, he was united in marriage to the king's young sister Alianor, and received the honour of knighthood from the king himself, who was well pleased with the handsome appearance and conduct of the young prince."[62] At this point we should also note that Paris, no lover of Savoyards or Poitevins, was also no lover of Spaniards, calling them "the scum of mankind" and "ugly of face, contemptible in behaviour and detestable in their morals" – at least he was consistent in his dislike of foreigners.[63] Henry, meanwhile, left Edward and Leonor in Gascony for his heir to learn the art of governing amongst the Gascons. In 1254, with his endowment of land, his knighthood and his marriage, the Prince Edward would become the Lord Edward.

At this time another foreign entanglement for Henry that would also damage relations with his nobility first appeared: the matter of Sicily. We should pause at this moment and note the passing four years earlier of the Emperor, Frederick II. On 13 December 1250 the Emperor Frederick II was no more – in the habit of a Cistercian monk the emperor departed this life of that perennial medieval malady, dysentery. He had been on a hunting trip in Apulia and was laid to rest, short of his fifty-sixth year, in Palermo Cathedral, no doubt his soul taking up the struggle with Gregory once more. In Lyon the Pope was less than sympathetic and caring in responding to the passing of the emperor: "Let the Heavens rejoice! Let the Earth be filled with gladness! For the fall of the Tyrant hath changed the Thunderbolts and Tempests which God Almighty held over the Heads into gentle Zephyrs and fecund Dews!" gushed Innocent IV, a man not knowingly underdone when it came to hyperbole then. Frederick had been known to contemporaries as "Stupor Mundi" or the "Bewilderment" or "Wonder of the World". Dante would pass judgement, reserving for him membership of the sixth region of his inferno, that of the heretics who are burned in tombs. With the death of Frederick II, Pope Innocent IV saw an opportunity to prise the Kingdom of Sicily, which encompassed much of southern Italy itself, including Naples, away from the Hohenstaufen dynasty. The empire currently held lands to the north and south of the Papal States within Italy, and he feared being the meat in an imperial sandwich. Accordingly, and taking advantage of the imperial succession, the Pope had been offering around the Sicilian monarchy to the dynasties of Europe. Would it go to a Plantagenet or a Capetian? Henry sought to make it a Plantagenet realm by offering up his younger son Edmund in opposition to a Capetian choice, Charles d'Anjou. So, the eternal chess game between the families would see England embroiled in the unlikely idea of providing a king of Sicily – something the nobility of England thought to be low on the kingdom's priorities, but the king of England thought of high importance. The English nobles, unsettled by much foreign influence, as noted, did not share Henry's dynastic interests and goals in his power-play with the Capetians. Henry's father John had lost Plantagenet lands in France and the nobility simply did not share his enthusiasm for their return or his more extravagant continental ambitions such as Sicily. Henry saw himself as a European prince, not a parochial king, and this conflict of outlook between barons interested in a narrower vision of kingship and a king with a broader perspective recurred throughout his reign.

Carpenter and Chapuisat saw this particular foreign entanglement as a broth cooked up by Savoyard chefs, and they're probably right: certainly, Thomas had a part in its beginnings.[64] Following the death of his wife, Countess of Flanders, in 1244, he had returned to northern Italy to carve out a new role for himself. In 1251, he had remarried, this time into the same family as Innocent IV, the Fieschi family of Genoa, to Béatrice di Fieschi. Apparently, the marriage came with the lifting of an excommunication against Thomas.[65] But, going back to Sicily, in December 1253 papal notary Master Albert received permission from Rome to treat with Henry for the Kingdom of Sicily. In terms of Savoyard responsibility there were certainly few English nobles in Gascony when Henry committed to the enterprise, and Pierre de Savoie and Pierre d'Aigueblanche had the king's ear. The papal envoy who shuttled to and forth between Henry and the papal court was another Savoyard, Jean d'Ambléon, Dean of Saint-André near Chambéry. Another sent as an emissary from Henry to the papal Curia was Savoyard, Guy de Rossillon, whose further service was prevented by his death on 29 August 1254.[66] Guy would later be succeeded in the service of Pierre as a clerk by his relative Thomas de Rossillon.[67] The committee tasked by Henry to negotiate terms with the Pope included the Savoyard brothers, Pierre, Philippe and Thomas, or, as Chapuisat put it, "a preponderance of Savoyards".[68] At the papal court in May, when the Pope ratified his offer, Thomas was there.[69] On 22 May 1254 the Pope wrote from Assisi to Pierre urging him to affirm Henry in the Sicilian affair.[70] So, what did the Savoyards and Thomas in particular, have to gain from such an unlikely enterprise? Carpenter holds the view that it was a regency for Thomas, as Henry was offering Sicily to the underage Edmund.[71] And certainly there exists a record of the aggrandisement of Thomas in Edmund's name, the gift of Capua in Campania, "*Edmondo Re di Sicilia figlio d'Enrico Re d'Inghilterra*" invested "*Conte Tomaso di Savoia di Lui Zio*" as Prince of Capua by order dated "*nella fiesta di S. Dionigio* 1254"[72] – something that was not yet in Edmund's gift. However, one should add that the Savoyard family had an interest in both parties in Sicily. The previously mentioned Agnès and Alésia di Saluzzo were the daughters of Manfred di Saluzzo and Béatrice de Savoie, as mentioned, the daughter of Count Amédée IV de Savoie. On Manfred's death in 1246, Béatrice had been remarried to another Manfred, this time the illegitimate[73] son of Emperor Frederick II. The hand of Amédée is seen in this as a way to strengthen his relationship with the Hohenstaufens. Upon the death of Frederick's only surviving legitimate son,[74] Conrad,[75] in May 1254, the illegitimate Manfred had become the regent ruler of Sicily. So, the House of Savoy did in fact have a foot in both camps, so to speak: Thomas was married into the Pope's Fieschi family and Amédée's daughter Béatrice was now married to Manfred the Hohenstaufen regent of Sicily. But then, as Hilton remarked, "the brilliance of Eleanor's uncles lay in their capacity to engage in apparently conflicting policies whilst simultaneously working for their collective good."[76] One is bound to observe that they were certainly adept at managing the delicate imperial–papal divide and playing both ends to the middle, so to speak. However, in the meantime Anglo–papal negotiations dragged on. How practically was Henry in England to install Edmund in Sicily? It was as if, as Richard of Cornwall remarked, the Pope had offered him the moon and then said now go and get it.[77]

On his way home from his Gascon expedition of 1254, Henry travelled to Paris and met with Louis, himself recently returned from his disastrous crusade – it was the first time the Plantagenet and the Capetian had met. Apparently the two brothers-in-law hit it off and became friends; both shared a value system: a deep and genuine piety. The two men of course shared the Provençals as in-laws and would have been able to converse reasonably easily, albeit Henry speaking Norman-French and Louis the ancestor of what we now call French. Before Paris, Henry and Alianor would visit somewhere very dear to his heart, Fontevraud Abbey – so dear in fact that one day his heart would find its way there to spend eternity. The couple arrived on 15 November 1254, fifty-five years since his father had visited. Buried at Fontevraud was his mother, Isabelle d'Angoulême, his uncle Richard Cœur de Lion, his grandfather Henry II and grandmother Eleanor d'Aquitaine. He found his mother buried, in accordance with her wishes, in a common grave. Isabelle d'Angoulême felt she had much to atone for; nonetheless, Henry reburied her next to his grandparents, carrying her body himself in his arms.[78]

Louis met the couple at Orléans on 24 November. After Henry and Alianor had paid their respects to Archbishop Edmund of Canterbury's tomb at Pontigny[79] (he had after all married them) they met up again with Louis at Chartres and together they made the journey on to Paris. And so it was that eventually, on 9 December 1254, Henry and Alianor entered Paris to be with Louis and Marguerite. The visit was, more than anything, a Provençal family reunion, Alianor and Marguerite joined by their mother, Béatrice de Savoie, and their younger sisters, Sanchia from England and Béatrice married to Charles d'Anjou – they had not seen each other since they were girls in far-off Provence.[80] Matthew Paris described the banquet held as having "eighteen countesses, of whom two were the sisters of the two queens aforesaid; namely, the Countess of Cornwall, the Countess of Anjou, and the Countess of Provence, all of whom were worthy of comparison with queens; also the Countess Béatrice, the mother of them all."[81]

The meeting began something of a temporary accord between the English and French, Plantagenet and Capetian. Paris quotes the French king as declaring, "Have we not married two sisters, and our brothers the others of them? All that shall be born of them, both sons and daughters, will be brothers and sisters."[82] This was a moment in history when the quarrelling dynasties ruling London and Paris might have found peace, through the good offices of the Savoyard and Provençal family that had united them. Alas, with hindsight we know that it was but a temporary lull in hostilities, but that December of 1254 in Paris was filled with what might have been. The next year a truce between the two families would be renewed with

Chapter Seven

the help of negotiators Simon de Montfort and Pierre de Savoie no less. Meanwhile, Henry was taken by Louis to see the beautiful new chapel he'd recently built, the Sainte-Chapelle, there to pray and make offerings. Henry, a lover of beautiful churches, must have been as much in awe of its sumptuous gothic splendour as any modern visitor, a sea of blue glass. Henry visited the monastery of Saint-Denis, just to the north of Paris, and its Merovingian, Carolingian and Capetian tombs. No doubt he quietly resolved within himself to finish his works at Westminster. By way of Amiens and its cathedral, and Boulogne, the royal couple were home just after Christmas. The sojourn had been a success, Gascony retained, Edward married and new bridges built with Louis. So that November, as Edward went to Burgos, and Henry to Fontevraud and England, Pierre de Savoie returned once more to his lands in Savoy, being noted on 29 November at Geneva. Whether Pierre accompanied Henry for part of the journey north is unknown – Chapuisat thought so, but the timeline is tight, Louis meeting Henry at Chartres on 24 November and Pierre being in Geneva on 29 November, it's more likely that the meetings between Henry, Alianor, Louis and Marguerite were purely a family affair. Meanwhile, Pierre returned to Savoy to settle the succession to Amédée, as discussed earlier, that brought him, amongst other things, the Château de Chillon.[83]

Following war with nearby Fribourg, and hostile intentions upon the part of Kyburg, the new King of the Germans, William of Holland, asked Pierre to become the protector of both Morat and Bern on his northern boundary. And so it was that by May of 1255 both Morat and Bern became Savoyard protectorates – albeit retaining titular and nominal independence within the empire (see figure 2.1).[84] However, the new protector would have the full financial rights of the empire within his new protectorates – including the *péage* and mints of Bern. Pierre apparently entered the city in splendour as its protector. He found the city sitting on a finger of land surrounded on three sides by a sharp bend in the River Aar. The citizens had been struggling to obtain permission to bridge the river. Pierre apparently supervised its construction in person, laying the first bridge beam of the *Nydeggbrücke* by hand[85] – a key and often overlooked moment in the history of the Swiss capital.[86] Indeed, so strong was his position in Bern that he became known as the *"zweiter Gründer"* or "second founder", after Berthold V von Zähringen.[87] We should not think of Bern at this point becoming Savoyard, but rather that Pierre had established a relationship with Bern that diminished, for a time, the threat to Vaud from the north. Pierre installed Ulrich de Vuippens to run the city for him. Vuippens was an ally, married to Agnès de Grandson. Their son would be taken, like many, to England by Pierre.[88] There Gérard de Vuippens would become an important diplomat in the service of King Edward I in his negotiations with the duplicitous Philippe IV of France. That Pierre would use Vuippens in Bern and that his children would prosper in England is a familiar theme of this book in terms of the interweaving of his Alpine and English interests. Pierre de Savoie with his income stream from England, was now the dominant power in what is now French-speaking Switzerland and a key influence even in German lands to the north.[89] He would remain de facto ruler of Bern for the rest of his life.[90]

Pierre's extension of power had been at his own volition – without lead from his elder brother Amédée IV, the Count of Savoy – very much the medieval self-made man. As we saw, Amédée had died at Montmélian near Chambéry on 11 June 1253,[91] and was buried 13 July a short distance away at the family abbey of Hautecombe overlooking the beautiful Lac du Bourget.[92] A difficult succession followed in which both Pierre and Philippe made claim over and above Amédée's 8-year-old son Boniface.[93] As we saw, Pierre was to shortly become embroiled in the affairs of Henry in Gascony where the Plantagenet was Duc d'Aquitaine, and may well have heard of his brother's death as he was about to take ship for Bordeaux. If so, the affairs of his nephew Henry took precedence of those of his brothers at this point.

An agreement was reached whereby Boniface, 9-year-old son of Amédée, would become the new Count of Savoy, but in return Pierre and Philippe were granted extensive Savoyard fiefs. For Pierre this meant the acquisition of lands in the Valais and the Chablais, including the castles at Saillon and Chillon.[94] Furthermore, Thomas would act as regent, ruling as Thomas II de Savoie during Boniface's minority. Thomas's wife Joan, Countess of Flandres, had died in 1244 and, since his title was *jure uxoris* (a Latin phrase meaning "by right of (his) wife"), he had returned to the Alps. Thomas later remarried, to Béatrice di Fieschi, in 1245, having sons Thomas, Amédée and Louis. The latter two would serve in England before returning to titles in Savoy – Amédée as Amédée V Count of Savoy and Louis as Baron de Vaud. The 1251 marriage of Thomas and Béatrice tied the Savoyard comital family to the papacy as she was of the Fieschi clan that supplied Popes Innocent IV (until 1254) and Adrian V (from 1276).

So, in the succession arbitration of February 1255, Pierre was granted holdings in the Chablais, the Valais, the great lakeside castle at Chillon but also the new castles in the Valais at Saillon, Conthey and Brignon (see figure 2.2). There had been, thanks to fanciful Savoyard or Vaudois chroniclers, tales of a great battle before Chillon in the 1240s where Pierre was victorious over invading Germans. Historians before and since Wurstenberger give these stories little credence.[95] The Bishop of Sion, Henri de Rarogne, had struggled with Aymon de Savoie before his death nearly two decades earlier, and now another of the Savoyard brothers, one who'd assisted Aymon in those struggles, Pierre, was at his doorstep. This would bring Pierre de Savoie into conflict with a second Alpine adversary – after the House of Geneva it would be the See of Sion. Pierre de Savoie lost little time in strengthening the castles in the Valais, using the engineer he'd met at Benauges a couple of years earlier, Jean de Mézos. Mézos would bring the Plantagenet traditions of castle-building to Savoy, creating the triangle of castle-building influences that would see Gascony and Savoy linked with England to great effect. The movement of castle-building artisans from Gascony to Savoy such as Mézos then the great exodus of Savoyard castle-building artisans to England in the later reign of Edward I that brought about the great castles of north Wales is a direct result of and little-appreciated legacy of the relationship between Pierre de Savoie and King Henry III of England.[96]

Meanwhile, Philippe was granted the castles of Tolvon, Voiron and Bocsozel in the Viennois[97] – thus consolidating Pierre's interest in the upper Rhône against the Bishop of Sion and Philippe's interest in the lower Rhône against the Dauphin. Saillon, Conthey and Brignon sat in the Valais hard by Sion, whereas Tolvon, Voiron and Bocsozel guarded the routes from Lyon and Vienne toward Grenoble. Earlier, in 1242, Philippe had acquired the *seigneury* of a small town in the Viennois, just fifteen or so miles (twenty-four kilometers) to the east, by the name of Saint-Georges-d'Espéranche.[98] It is this Saint-Georges, named for a Viennois bishop not the dragon slayer of legend, that will nurture the castle-building talents of a Jacques or James who will later find fame building castles for Edward I in north Wales. We saw earlier that Henry had granted that Pierre could now will his lands in England as he pleased; accordingly, in the summer of 1255 whilst in Lyon with his brother Philippe, Pierre rewrote his last will and testament. The will, dated 5 June 1255, would leave 5,000 livres Viennois to his daughter Béatrice, his lands in England to his niece Alianor de Provence and his continental lands to his brother Philippe. As for burial, he chose Saint-Maurice d'Agaune should he die in Savoy and London should he die in England.[99] His 1255 will gives us a picture of a man divided equally between England and Savoy, to the English a Savoyard, to later

Chapter Seven

Savoyards "the Englishman". And so it was then that Pierre de Savoie came into the castle by Lac Léman at Chillon, sitting atop its narrow limestone perch. If his palace by the Strand was to be his London base, then the castle by the Léman at Chillon was to be his Alpine base. On 15 August, William of Kilkenny, Lord Chancellor of England,[100] was consecrated as Bishop of Ely, and entertained at Belley by Boniface and Pierre de Savoie. It was unusual for an English bishop to be consecrated in the Alps, something that attracted more grumbles from Matthew Paris, along with the snide remark "that they [the Savoyards] might not seem to be in a state of want in their own country".[101]

Pierre de Savoie had two main projects: first, the aggrandisement of the House of Savoy, and in particular the expansion of his own lands surrounding Geneva and in Vaud, and second, the protection of Alianor and Edward in England. If the beginning of 1255 had seen him devoted to the former, then the second half of the year would see him devoted to the latter – 1255 is a good example of Pierre's dual life. Following his marriage to Leonor de Castille on 1 November 1254 at Burgos, Edward had been cutting his teeth on the administration of Gascony, and all had not been going to plan. Accordingly, Pierre made his way in late August 1255, not to England, but back to Gascony, to set affairs in order and make preparations for the Lord Edward's return to England.[102] We can see from this short missive recorded in the Calendar of Close Rolls in England the sudden departure of Pierre from Vaud to Bordeaux, some 450 miles (724 kilometres). We might pause to imagine his face in Moudon or Bern as the messenger from England arrived, and the realisation that the rest of the year would be in the saddle to Gascony and a boat from there to England, not to mention the ordering of Gascon affairs and the "secret affairs" Henry mentioned in England. Gascony was left for the next two years in the hands of Pierre d'Aigueblanche.[103] The Savoyard Bishop of Hereford would not be the last of his lands to oversee Plantagenet Gascony; following the Baronial War the Savoyard knight of the Pays de Gex, Jean de Grailly, would be seneschal.

Once back in England the Lord Edward made his first visit to his appanage of Chester, and perhaps for the first time met his Welsh subjects that would be so much a vexation to him in years to come. The Chester chronicler wrote, *"Eodem anno in festivitate Sancti Kenelmi dominus Edwardus Comes primum Cestriam,"* that is "In the same year [1256] at the Feast of Saint Kenelmi[104] [17 July] the Lord Edward, Count, first visited Chester." Edward stayed in Chester for three days during which he received the *"hominia et fidelitates tam a nobilibus Cestrisirae et Wallie"* or the "homage and fealty of the nobles of Chester and Wales". Edward's party then rode into the Perfeddwlad for the first time. Whilst there he visited the *"castellas"*, which would have been Deganwy and Dyserth, perhaps his first visit to the banks of the Conwy; it would not be the last.[105] Meanwhile, marriages between the nobility and Savoyards continued – at the instigation of his brother Pierre, Thomas de Savoie's daughter Margaret married Baldwin de Redvers, 7th Earl of Devon in 1257 upon the groom's coming of age. Life appeared to be returning to the normality of recent years.

However, the Sicilian affair would raise its ill-conceived head once more. The original author of the Sicilian offer, Pope Innocent IV, had died in December 1254, and died too as mentioned earlier had Conrad I, Frederick II's only son and incumbent King of Sicily, leaving in his place the illegitimate son Manfred as regent for the young Conradin II. One of Innocent IV's last acts as pope was to excommunicate Manfred – thus the papacy had excommunicated Frederick and his two sons, Conrad and Manfred. Successor, as pope, Alexander IV, in negotiation in Naples with Pierre d'Aigueblanche, renewed the offer to Henry, but this time with a price tag of £90,300, accompanied by excommunication – this was obviously the era in which excommunication was in vogue – and interdict on England if Henry didn't meet the payment. Aigueblanche secured the deal with the down payment of a pledge of funds taken from the tenth tax in England that was to have been used for a crusade to the Holy Land. Henry seems to have been a willing victim of papal bullying, asking Pierre and Thomas de Savoie to find knights for an expedition to Sicily – and yet providing no money. Thus, we meet the gap between Henry's dreams and reality. Henry needed Parliament to authorise his dreams of a Sicilian realm for Edmund, and the October 1255 Parliament said no. Opposition was led by the king's own brother, Richard, who suggested that Henry might have been led astray by the likes of Pierre Aigueblanche, who'd returned from Rome after helping to negotiate the offer. Carpenter suggests that this did much to poison the English against the Bishop of Hereford, who came to regard him with "sulphurous hostility".[106] The origin for this colourful description being English Church not taking well to the Aigueblanche-brokered deal, church funds being diverted from the crusade they'd been gathered for, to the Sicilian expedition by means of blank schedules to be completed by Aigueblanche. Matthew Paris was of course apoplectic and took some delight in relating "these detestable hearings" before gloating two years later of the consequential illness that befell Aigueblanche, who, having "drawn down so many curses on his head", was "punished by the lord in manifold ways".[107]

Indeed, the whole Sicilian enterprise might be seen as a punishment from God. Neither Pierre nor Thomas de Savoie, nor even Archbishop Boniface would now have anything to do with the business: they managed to be elsewhere. The Sicilian affair is the origin of Aigueblanche's unfortunate reputation, but he does seem to have been doing his master, Henry's, bidding. More widely, the Sicilian business is the origin of much of the hostility toward the Savoyards, to Pierre and Thomas in England. They were intimately involved in its origins, but as Carpenter points out, "neither Thomas nor Peter were involved in the second phase of the project … There is no evidence of them at the papal court in 1255."[108] The Savoyard withdrawal from the attempt to make Edmund King of Sicily should have been seen by Henry as a moment to at least reflect upon the wisdom of the enterprise. As we saw earlier, Pierre had other fish to fry at this moment, establishing his protectorate of Bern and Morat, Boniface was away in Savoy and Thomas now had problems much closer to home that proved a distraction to everyone.

In late 1255, Thomas was protecting his lands in Piedmont against the town of Asti. When the Astigiani threatened his castle at Montacalieri, which surrendered on 23 November 1256, Thomas and his ally Tomaso di Saluzzo retreated to Turin. This Tomaso di Saluzzo was brother to Alésia married to Edmund de Lacy and Agnès married to Jean de Vesci – these English marriages had ensured his loyalty to Savoy. But they found Turin in revolt. The two sallied forth and gave battle to the Astigiani at Montebruno but were defeated, returning to Turin to be then taken prisoner. The two Italian cities were seeking to force Thomas to acknowledge their independence from Savoyard control. With one of the Savoyard brothers now in an Italian prison, the family diplomatic support mechanism whirred into action, involving England, France and the papacy. First, Pope Alexander IV placed an interdict against the cities of Turin and Asti. Following a letter from Alexander, in England Henry retaliated by jailing all the Lombards he could lay his hands on. Likewise in France Louis imprisoned over 150 merchants from Asti. We can safely assume both of these acts were instigated by Alianor and Marguerite since their mother Béatrice acted similarly in Provence. Lombard merchants who dwelled in Lyon, Vienne and Valence found themselves in Philippe's dungeons.[109] There are parallels in this to the concerted swiftness of response in recent times to aggression in Ukraine. The economies of Turin and Asti were devastated, and the latter never recovered.

Chapter Seven

The Italians later counted a loss of over £800,000 in lost English, French and Provençal business.[110] One might wonder that the Lombards wished they'd not begun this war, as the thirteenth-century equivalent of sanctions were imposed on the luckless Italians. Pierre[111] and Philippe descended from the Alps with an army in May 1256 and found themselves before the walls of Turin.[112] Details of the war then become unclear, but it seems likely that they began by taking the castle of Montcalieri, to the south of Turin. As Paris has it, "Peter of Savoy, with the nobles of his family, the Archbishop of Canterbury, the bishop elect of Lyon, and other Savoyards most vigorously besieged the city of Turin ... But the more closely they were pressed the more closely they kept Count Thomas confined."[113]

And so, it would not be until 1257 that Thomas was finally freed from the Torinese. He was recorded as visiting London in 1258 following release.[114] As might be expected, Matthew Paris was condemnatory of Thomas, a monk in St. Albans being well acquainted with Piedmontese politics, but also managed snipes at Henry, Richard and Alianor. Paris wrote that Thomas had been "severe and tyrannical" and that "the Savoyards thereupon came with the rapidity of a tempest" as "Pierre possessed an abundance of money" and Boniface and Philippe "large sums of sacred money" – Paris was nothing if not consistent.[115] Henry's brother, Richard, had lent Pierre £1,000,[116] Henry granted the 4,000 marks he was owed by his mother-in-law for the Provençal castles and Alianor had raised some 4,500 marks in the cause of her uncle's Italian tribulations from Florentine merchants, raised in her name (and Pierre's) against a number of religious establishments.[117]

However, the Savoyards, who had done so much to begin the Sicilian affair with the previous Pope Innocent IV, now abandoned the ill-fated enterprise, and what they must have seen as the more onerous terms offered by Pope Alexander IV. The matter became somewhat moot during the Parliament, when news came that a papal army had in any case been defeated by the Hohenstaufen. Despite being rebuffed by Parliament, Henry nonetheless signed up to the papal offer of Sicily, despite having no means to pay for it and potentially facing excommunication.

To add to this, events in Wales would again draw Henry's attention from the continent to the wild lands of Gwynedd, on his north-western border. North Wales had been pacified in 1247: the Treaty of Woodstock had provided for royal dominion of the four *cantrefi*[118] – north Wales east of the river Conwy. Gwynedd itself had been divided between the sons of Gruffydd ap Llywelyn Fawr, Owain ap Gruffydd known as Owain Goch or Owain the Red (parts of Anglesey, the Llyn peninsula and Dunoding in the south) and Llywelyn ap Gruffydd (northern Anglesey, northern and eastern Snowdonia down to the Conwy). Now, another brother, Dafydd ap Gruffydd, joined his brother Owain Goch[119] in asserting what they saw as their rights. Owain Goch had been imprisoned, along with his father Gruffydd ap Llywelyn Fawr, at Criccieth Castle back in 1239, by his uncle Dafydd ap Llywelyn Fawr – this internecine fighting within the ruling family of Gwynedd would eventually bring about its ruin. That the quarrel was "*super terrarum*", that is "over lands", was reported by the chronicler in Chester.[120]

In June 1255 Llywelyn defeated his brothers, Owain Goch and Dafydd, at the Battle of Bryn Derwin[121] in Eifionydd, the northern part of Dunoding, thus becoming sole ruler of Gwynedd. The medieval Welsh chronicle Brut y Tywysogion remembered the struggle:

> In those days great strife was bred at the instigation of the Devil between the sons of Gruffydd ap Llywelyn, Namely Owain Goch and Dafydd on the one side, and Llywelyn on the other. And then Llywelyn and his men, trusting in

God, awaited, unafraid on Bryn Derwin the fierce coming of his brothers, and a mighty host along with them. And before the end of one hour Owain Goch was captured and Dafydd fled, after many of his host had been slain.[122]

Owain Goch, the eldest of the sons of Gruffydd, and Dafydd, the younger, were imprisoned by their brother. Llywelyn was now supreme in Gwynedd – so as their father had been held captive by his own kin, so too would be the grandsons of Llywelyn Fawr.[123] North Wales had been rendered a tinderbox in want of a spark by clumsy English rule east of the Conwy. In Llywelyn the native Welsh found the match with which to light that dry tinder into the flames of rebellion. Carpenter writes that having become secure in his mountain fastness of Gwynedd, he "was encouraged to reach for more".[124] As Matthew Paris relates, "the Welsh, who had been oppressed in manifold ways, were at last so immeasurably oppressed … that they roused themselves for the defence of their country and the observance of their laws."[125] Indeed, Paris goes on once more to pour scorn on the English for allowing foreign influence to pervade their land whilst in comparison the valiant Welsh made a defence of their homeland, writing: "This manly and brave determination might justly shame the English, who lazily bent their necks to foreigners."[126] On his return from Gascony in the summer of 1256, the Lord Edward visited the lands given to him by his father in Wales. It did not help matters; indeed, Welsh historian R. R. Davies believes it "may well have been the spark that lit the tinder of Welsh resentment".[127] A soldier of Breton descent, Alan la Zouche,[128] had been appointed Justiciar at Chester with responsibility for the Perfeddwlad, having boasted that he'd reduced the Welsh to obedience of English laws; his rule proved so heavy-handed that it provoked Henry's censure.[129] Paris ascribed blame for what was soon to come to Edward's man, Geoffrey de Langley.

Whichever royal official carried the blame, early in November 1256[130] there was rebellion. Llywelyn crossed the Conwy and evicted the English rulers of the *cantrefi* and pushed English control back to the border, save for the castles at Dyserth and Deganwy, which stood firm. It had only been a few short months since Edward's first visit to, what he saw as his, his appanage, granted only in 1254 by his father, the king. The Chester chronicler writes that Llywelyn received "*homagia et fidelitates*" or "homage and fealty" from the "*hominibus domini Edwardi*", that is from the men who'd just given the same homage, in July, to the Lord Edward. Herein we see the beginnings of what will be a twenty-and-more-year struggle between the two men. Llywelyn's aims were simple: take back the Perfeddwlad, have the Welsh princes swear allegiance to him, in short tear up the Treaty of Woodstock of 1247. Henry reluctantly sallied forth into Wales in 1257, but as the French had discovered in Poitou, he was no warrior king, and the campaign did nothing to restore his reputation. Paris bemoans that the Welsh "carried fire and slaughter into the provinces of Wales bordering on England".[131] Paris went on to praise the Welsh for standing up to the English, but only as a means to castigate the English for not standing up for themselves, writing in full foreigner bashing mode:

> "Fortune favoured them in this war ; for their cause appeared, even to their enemies, to be just ; and what chiefly supported and encouraged them was the thought that, like the Trojans (from whom they were descended), they were struggling, with a firmness worthy of their descent, for their ancestral laws and liberties. Woe to the wretched English, who, trodden underfoot by every

Chapter Seven

foreigner, allowed the ancient liberties of their kingdom to be extinguished, and were not put to shame by the example of the Welsh."[132]

Edward complained of the loss of his Welsh land to Henry, who Paris quotes as replying: "What is it to me? The land is yours by my gift. Exert your powers for the first time, and arouse fame in your youth, that your enemies may fear you in the future; as for me, I am occupied on other business."[133] One might hear in Henry's words the perennial voice of a father suggesting that his son might stand up for himself – but one might also think that from preceding and ongoing events Henry might take his own advice.

On 2 June a column under Stephen Bauzan, one-time seneschal of Gascony, heading up the Tywi Valley to restore a native Welsh ally to his castle at Dinefwr, were attacked and massacred to a man.[134] On 5 August Henry and Edward arrived at Chester. By 26 August they had marched along the coast to relieve their castle on the Conwy at Deganwy. But then, inexplicably, on 6 September the army turned around and retreated back to England with Llywelyn following. If ever there was a moment that vindicated the tactics employed by the native Welsh and Llywelyn in particular, then this was it. True to previous form an English "grand old duke of York" had "marched his men to the top of the hill, and marched them down again". The Welsh tactic of retreat until such time as an English army grew tired of Wales was once more proven to be effective. Llywelyn ap Gruffydd now stood emboldened and at the peak of his powers. But for young Edward, his own personal humiliation and that of his father was not something he would forgive or forget. In a deliberate challenge to the Crown, on 18 March 1258, Llywelyn applied the following title to himself in an agreement between himself and Scottish lords: "*domino Lewelino filio Griffini principe Wallie*" or "Lord Llywelyn son of Gruffydd, Prince of Wales".[135] A winter's truce expired in April of 1258. Henry would need to reassemble his army for a renewed expedition into Wales. Not for the first time dissensions in the English government would benefit a Prince of Wales; as with Llywelyn Fawr and John, so it would be with Llywelyn ap Grufydd and Henry.

With the English army would be men from the Jura and Savoy, as they had been in Gascony a few short years earlier. We met Guillaume de Pesmes, knighted by the king in Gascony, he had not returned to the Jura but returned to England with the Lord Edward. He'd witnessed two of Edward's charters in England before being added to a list of knights called up from Burgundy by Henry to help with his Welsh campaign. The Calendar of Close Rolls lists "*militibus Burgundie ... Henrico de Peiny, Willelmo de Pemes, Ricardo de Mumbiliard, Simoni de Genvyle, Johanni de Dornay, Guidoni de Rens', Baldewino de Villa, Johanni de Castellione, Petro de Chaunteny, Hugoni Espaulard et Willelmo de Puncayle*" and "*Henrico de Paygerne, Willelmo de Puntyller,. . .Petro, Aymoni et Guidoni de Chaunteny, Galfrido de Bolemont ... Johanni de Dole, Stephano de Bues.*" We can almost certainly ascribe the identity of Simon de Joinville, the *Seigneur de Gex*, half-brother to Pierre de Savoie's wife Agnès de Faucigny to Simoni di Genvyle – especially when we remember that the English rendered Joinville as Geneville. As in Gascony so in Wales, the men of the Jura and Alps had proven loyal to Henry.[136]

Events had developed on the international stage that might change things for Henry and Edmund but were to prove their undoing. Henry's younger brother Richard, Earl of Cornwall, married to Sanchia de Provence, became the next move in the thirteenth-century game of thrones. Henry had previously used marriage to ally himself with the empire: his sister Isabella had been married to the much-excommunicated Frederick II until her early death in 1241, aged just 27 years. So, when the latest King of the Romans, William of Holland, had died 28 January 1256 a vacancy arose in Germany. The King of the Romans or King of the Germans[137] was an elected position in the tradition of the empire. Richard managed to get the votes of Cologne, Mainz, the Palatinate and Bohemia;[138] however, his candidacy was challenged by the half-brother of the lady lately married to his nephew, Edward – King Alfonso X of Castile. Saxony, Brandenburg and Trier had voted for Alfonso; the politics of the empire were nothing if not complicated. The Savoyard came into play at this point; it would after all be of supreme benefit to the House of Savoy to have their niece Sanchia married to the leading role in the empire. Within a few short years the "Eagles of Savoy" would have manoeuvred their nieces into the royal courts of not only Paris and then London, but also Aachen – a quite remarkable and unique achievement. Thus, they persuaded Ottokar II of Bohemia to switch his allegiance to Richard. Thus Richard, Earl of Cornwall, became King of the Romans – being crowned in Aachen on 27 May 1257. The new title remained contested, however, and Richard was to spend but four periods in his new fiefdom. Nonetheless, for the Savoyard uncles this marked the apogee of their rise to European power and influence. Parliament was called at Henry's newly completed and beautiful chapter house at Westminster, where, bathed in light, Henry would present Edmund to the barony as the fully clothed young King of Sicily, Richard attending to say his goodbyes to court. Edward and Edmund's cousin, Richard's son Henry, would soon gain the epithet "d'Almayne" – of Germany. Becoming Emperor of the Holy Roman Empire was in effect a two-stage process: stage one was having oneself elected King of the Romans; stage two being crowned by the Pope in Rome. Sadly for Richard the second stage would never materialise.

Henry had announced Richard's forthcoming ascent of the throne of the Germans on 28 January 1257, a Parliament was called for March 1257 where it might be formalised and Henry hoped the Sicilian business might again be promulgated. On 2 April, amidst the aforesaid splendour of the chapter house at Westminster Abbey, Henry duly presented Edmund to the assembled nobles of England in the finery of a King of Sicily. But on this day that marked the first use of the chapter house for government, fine clothes and indeed words would sadly butter no parsnips – Parliament again said no. What is more the barony drew up a list of logical objections as to why the kingdom ought to be dragged into an impossible imperial enterprise, while the clergy drew up their own list of equally compelling objections. That the barony who drew up these restrictions, of 10 April 1257, on the ability of the king to spend money included Pierre de Savoie and the Poitevins, Guillaume de Valence and Guy de Lusignan is instructive that this precursor to the revolution of 1258 very much included, at this stage, both Savoyards and Poitevins.[139]

Nonetheless, the simmering resentment of the native English nobility at the perceived weakness of Henry's leadership, his continental dynastic interests coupled with his preferment of Savoyard and Lusignans bubbled over even as the kingdom faced new revolt in Wales. Matthew Paris laid the blame for what was to follow firmly at the feet of the Sicilian affair, something Paris thought to be a pipe dream. Contemporary historians have seen the baronial struggle that followed the crisis of 1258 in the light of his father's baronial conflict that led to *Magna Carta*. Carpenter more recently notes that "Llywelyn's triumphs ... helped bring about the revolution of 1258".[140] Henry's embattled kingship has been seen as part of the wider, longer evolution of an autocratic monarchy to a democratic monarchy. In other words, the barons were angry because they were not sufficiently involved in Henry's decision-making. Henry's biographer Church sees the crisis as "a fight for the very soul of Henry's court".[141] A court made up of an English nobility disaffected and marginalised, set alongside

Chapter Seven

the "Kingsmen", the Lusignans, and the "Queensmen", the Savoyard. Henry had thought his "Kingsmen" to be a balance to Alianor's "Queensmen", but events aligned the Savoyard with the nobility against the Lusignans. Indeed, the dispute between Aymer de Lusignan and Boniface de Savoie in 1252 was a precursor to 1258; in it the native nobility largely sided with the Savoyards as forces of law, order and continuity and against the Lusignans, who were seen as newly arrived troublemakers. In 1252, as we shall see in 1258, the retrospective lumping together of foreigners as a cause for the coming baronial war is unhelpful and inaccurate.[142]

Whether it was the Sicilian affair, or the Welsh revolt, or a wider discontent with his kingship will continue to be debated. What is certain is that Henry's hands on the reins of power would soon be loosened. It is remarkable how quickly, following Henry's arrival back from France, events spiralled out of control. Matters had not been helped by an edict issued by Henry in November of 1256 in which he decreed that his brother Richard of Cornwall, Richard de Clare, Pierre de Savoie and all his Lusignan relatives were, in effect, immune from prosecution.[143] For a nobility that had seen the Savoyard and then the Lusignans appropriate so much power and influence this immunity from prosecution was a breach of what they saw as their rights too far. This immunity might have been swallowed for the sake of peace if it wasn't for the plain bad behaviour of the Lusignans. Not only had they come to court and usurped power, the Savoyards had already done that, but they'd been boorish and behaved badly – something the Savoyards (with Boniface's exception) had scrupulously avoided. The nobility felt they had wrung hard-won rights from Henry's father John, and they would be damned if they were going to allow the son to follow the route of the father into tyranny – their very charters of liberties were at stake.

To add to Henry's woes, there was famine, the harvest of 1256 had been poor, in 1257 it had been like a year without summer amidst continual rain, and by 1258 hunger stalked the land. So, with Llywelyn now calling himself Prince of Wales, allying himself with the Scots, the pipe dream of Sicily alienating the barons, and a general resurgence of xenophobic response to Henry's relatives, came the Spring Parliament at Westminster of 1258. Tensions in the chapter house were running high. Guillaume de Valence accused Simon de Montfort of being a traitor and conniving with Llywelyn. Incredibly, Henry tried for a third time to get his nobles to assist in financing the Sicilian project, asking for a tax from Parliament, which again said a firm no. Parliament adjourned without agreement. On Friday, 12 April 1258 the following nobles met to agree a pact of mutual support: Richard de Clare, Earl of Gloucester, Roger Bigod, Earl of Norfolk, Hugh Bigod, Pierre de Savoie, Pierre de Montfort and of course Simon de Montfort, Earl of Leicester – an Anglo-Montfortian-Savoyard alliance designed to defend the king by clipping the wings of the Lusignans. Those at the time outside of this close circle, and those since, have often overlooked, in the simplicity of blaming events to come on the king's patronage of foreigners, that Pierre de Savoie and Simon de Montfort were most definitely not born in England.

So, having come back from his time in Savoy in late 1255, Pierre had returned to England once more, just in time to take part in some of the most tumultuous events in English history, and a reckoning with the Lusignans. At first, as 1256 dawned everything seemed to be continuing normally, Pierre and his followers maintaining their ongoing vigil around Alianor and the Lord Edward. During the beginnings of the problems in his appanage lands of Wales, it was to his Savoyard uncles that Edward had first turned for money to fight Llywelyn: to Pierre and Archbishop Boniface.[144] And, as we saw, it had been to Pierre that the Crown had once more turned for a pool of knights to defend Edward's appanage. Before "coming of age" so to speak, that is acquiring the seisin of his appanage, Edward's household had been an extension of Alianor's. But, from 1254, she was still his guiding hand. Edward's first chancellor was Michel de Fiennes, a kinsman of Alianor's of the *Famille Dammartin*, a position he held from their time in Gascony from 1255 until 1258.[145] Edward's chamberlain and constant companion for all of this time had been the Savoyard knight, Ebal II de Mont.[146] As we saw earlier, the Burgundian associate of Pierre's half-brother-in-law Simon de Joinville, Guillaume de Pesmes, had also been attached as a household knight. However, in late 1257,[147] Edward now a man, was growing tired of being tied to his mother's apron strings, tired of the men who'd surrounded him since birth, and like all young men before and since, he sought to break free, which meant associating himself with the likes of the Lusignans. Amongst his new coterie too was onetime ward of Pierre de Savoie, Jean de Warenne, a young man harbouring much resentment of his treatment by Pierre. Edward's new choices of friends were calculated to irritate his mother and her family. There is also, perhaps, some merit in the assertion that Savoyard funds had been so depleted by the freeing of Thomas from Turin, that when Edward needed funds in Wales the cupboard was bare, thus forcing him into the hands of the Lusignans. Perhaps the Savoyards were beginning to balance too many plates in too many countries all at once. It was at this juncture that diplomatic work for Henry in Paris, and his own visit thence again to Savoy, took Pierre out of the country once more, from June until December 1257.[148]

With Henry in pursuit of the funds to further the Sicilian business, seven earls met on 12 April 1258 and promised to support one another. Matthew Paris seems to be the cause of much of the latter-day confusion of the events of 1258 as being anti-foreigner by writing, "the nobles of England ... leagued themselves together to take precautions; and as they entertained great fears of the crafty plots of foreigners." But the "league" itself included one of the crafty foreigners, Pierre de Savoie. Thus, Pierre de Savoie was from the outset, as Michael Prestwich wrote, "sympathetic to reform in England".[149] Matthew Paris was not the most consistent, or indeed accurate, in identifying the origins of foreigners at court, for "foreigners" he should perhaps have more accurately written "Poitevins". This lumping together of Savoyards with the Poitevins as "foreigners" would lead to much misunderstanding of 1258.[150] The "all for one, one for all" earls included Roger Bigod, 4th Earl of Norfolk, Richard de Clare, 6th Earl of Gloucester, Simon de Montfort, 6th Earl of Leicester, and the de facto Earl of Richmond, Pierre de Savoie. The oath taken was committed to parchment in a solemn document; this was no rash and sudden rush of blood (for a full copy of the oath see appendix). Why, a casual observer might ask, was Pierre de Savoie siding with Simon de Montfort in this enterprise? The answer is often overlooked, but relatively simple: the aim of the oath-takers was to bring about the fall of the Lusignans, and not, as many have assumed since, a general move against aliens at court. As we have seen, alarmingly to Pierre, the Lord Edward had fallen under Lusignan influence, which presented in his mind a threat to both Alianor and his own position in England. His participation in the oath lent the seven earls an eighth silent oath-taker: Alianor de Provence. In the spring of 1258 Simon de Montfort was a colleague in negotiations with Louis IX, Richard de Clare had just lately agreed to the marriage of his daughter, Isabelle, to the Maquis de Montferrand, Guillaume – a marriage that helped the Savoyard position in Piedmont – and Pierre and Alianor were very much a part of the oath-taking group. Pierre and Alianor remained loyal to Henry, but both believed that loyalty now saw its best expression in the demise of the influence held by the king's half-brothers.[151] We should also note with interest the visits of Richard de Clare to Alianor in 1257, relating to the marriage of Isabelle and the Marquis de Montferrand, as it begins what Ridgeway calls a "political co-operation" between the Clares and the Savoyards that will run through to 1260.

Chapter Seven

But we should also note that it would be the Clares who would one day also be instrumental in the outline plot to release Edward from captivity in 1265, a plot behind which Howell sees the hand of Alianor, and, I would venture further, Pierre de Savoie.[152]

On 28 April Henry made a final demand for the new taxes. A response was promised within three days. On 30 April 1258, Roger Bigod, 4th Earl of Norfolk, marched into an unsuspecting Westminster, backed by his co-conspirators, and carried out what can only be described as a coup d'état. We are not certain of who marched with Bigod, as they are not named by the chroniclers, but we are sure they included Clare and Montfort – but so too, likely Pierre de Savoie. So, on 30 April, here was Pierre de Savoie marching in full armour into Westminster alongside Frenchman Simon de Montfort to make demands of the anointed King of England.[153] Henry, fearful that he was about to be arrested, asked if he was now their prisoner. Bigod replied that he was not but demanded the downfall of the Lusignans and reform of the realm by twenty-four men chosen by the baronage. No tax would be imposed, they said, without the twenty-four agreeing. Both Henry and Edward were made to swear oaths upon the tomb of Edward the Confessor to abide by the new arrangements. On 2 May Henry's accession to the demands was made public, twelve appointees of the king, twelve of the barons and a parliament to be held at Oxford in June to agree reform of the realm. However, Henry's nominees to the council drew heavily on the hated Lusignans, including Bishop Elect Aymer, Guy de Lusignan and Guillaume de Valence. The stage was set for a showdown. Pierre de Savoie was, it seems, on neither list, attempting, having helped create the groundwork for the fall of the Lusignans, to step back and adopt an aloof posture – this, he thought now, was a battle for Englishmen. The absence of Pierre from Henry's list was, however, a mark that at this point Pierre de Savoie had met with the displeasure of Henry III of England: following the 30 April events he was obviously seen by Henry as now "one of them" not "one of us".

The Tewkesbury Annalist puts words into Bigod's mouth, that not just the Lusignans, but "*omnes alienigenæ*", all foreigners, should flee.[154] The chronicler Johannes Oxenedes also bemoaned the preferment of Henry's "*fratres suos uterinos*", that is "brothers of the womb" but also that of the "*Reginæ uxoris suæ parentes*", that is the Queen's relatives who'd come to England and become Englishmen.[155] His has been the traditional view of 1258, but standing shoulder to shoulder with Bigod were the "aliens" Simon de Montfort and Pierre de Savoie – it's more than likely the chronicler attributed these words caught up in the wave of xenophobia that came later – he wrote his account after 1263 – or in his own misinterpretation of events, and/or wishful thinking on his part. This conflation on the part of these chroniclers (repeated by others) lent history a false impression of the events of 1258, as we shall see, although it did indeed lead to the flight of foreigners, who were as Pierre and Alianor intended, Lusignans not Savoyards. The April parliament was prorogued until June when it sat again in Oxford. It is in this short period between the April Parliament in London and the June Parliament in Oxford that Henry called up the Burgundian knights mentioned earlier to join him at Oxford, specifically on 25th May 1258. Carpenter asked the question in the newly published second volume of his Henry biography that the king might have been "plotting armed resistance with his Poitevin half-brothers" citing the Burgundian knights as a potential source of armed support. Given that we know Pierre de Savoie was firmly in the baronial camp at this point, his interest being the expulsion of the Lusignans and that not yet accomplished I think we can safely say that the Burgundian knights were not a part of any armed resistance on Henry's part. We can say this because Pierre's half-brother-in-law Simon de Joinville was very much a leader in this group and he as Agnès de Faucigny's "dear brother" and Pierre's vassal as

Seigneur de Gex was very much Pierre de Savoie's man. We saw earlier that Joinville had played a part in bringing the same knights to Gascony in support of Henry but at Pierre's request and that he would later play a likely key role in later freeing Edward from captivity again likely at Pierre's bidding. In short Joinville is very unlikely to have been acting in England in May 1258 contrary to Pierre's wishes. No, the Burgundian knights were almost certainly asked to go to Oxford for the reason stated in the Close Roll, for a Welsh campaign that Henry clearly at this point expected to proceed as planned.[156]

Henry was expecting to submit himself to a baronial council at Oxford as evidenced by a patent roll entry dated to 1st June 1258 in favour of Alésia di Saluzzo. As we saw earlier Alésia was brought to England by Pierre de Savoie to marry Edmund de Lacy, Earl of Lincoln. Edmund had just died and Alésia sought wardship of his lands. Alésia was, as we saw, the daughter of Béatrice de Savoie, daughter of Pierre's late brother Amédée IV de Savoie. Accordingly the widowed Alésia was Pierre's kith and kin. Henry accepted her request but noted that it would be subject to the approval of "the kings council about to meet at Oxford." No doubt Alésia, still but 22 years of age, had every confidence that her grand-uncle Pierre would approve things.[157]

Matthew Paris tells the story of how events, also taking advantage of Richard's absence in Germany, unfolded:

> As the feast of St. Barnabus drew near, the magnates and nobles of the country hastened to the parliament which was to be held at Oxford, and gave orders to all those who owed them knightly service, to accompany them, equipped and prepared as if to defend their persons against the attacks of their enemies. This they accordingly carried into effect, concealing their real reasons for so doing under the pretence that their coming in such a way was to show themselves ready to set out with their united forces against the king's enemies in Wales.[158]

Indeed the assembled knights, including Joinville's Burgundians never made their campaign in Wales, a truce with Llywelyn being agreed on 17th June.[159] So, we have the nobility attending Parliament with an armed retinue of knights, a nobility with deep grievances – this did not bode well. Paris continued:

> At the commencement of the parliament, the proposed plan of the nobles was unalterably decided on; and they most expressly demanded that the king should faithfully keep and observe the conditions of the charter of the liberties of England, which his father, King John, had made and granted to his English subjects, and which he, the said John, had sworn to observe; which said charter, he the present King Henry, had many times granted and sworn to observe.[160]

And so, we have what modern historians have seen as the age-old claim made periodically upon English kings of "the liberties of England", Paris eulogising *Magna Carta*, as would many after him as the foundation stone of liberty. Paris then continued:

> They also made some other demands, in connection with the affairs of the kingdom, tending to promote the welfare, peace and honour, as well of the king as of the kingdom; and they moreover insisted the king should frequently consult them, and listen to their advice in making all necessary provisions.[161]

Chapter Seven

Again, we hear ringing loud and clear from 1258 the age-old English desire to "not be told what to do" but rather be "asked what to do". Henry acquiesced to the demands of his nobility, agreeing to submit himself to a new reforming council, not of the original twenty-four, but of fifteen. This time, belying that what became known as the Provisions of Oxford were anti-Savoyard, two members of this council would be Pierre and Boniface.[162] The Council of Fifteen were: Boniface de Savoie, Pierre de Savoie, Walter de Cantilupe, Bishop of Worcester, Roger Bigod, 4th Earl of Norfolk, Richard de Clare, 6th Earl of Gloucester, Humphrey de Bohun, 2nd Earl of Hereford, John du Plessis, 7th Earl of Warwick, Hugh Bigod, Roger de Mortimer, 1st Baron Mortimer of Wigmore, William de Forz, 4th Earl of Albermarle, John Fitz Geoffrey, James de Audeleye, John Mansel and of course Simon and Peter de Montfort.[163] The council, to serve for twelve years, included none of the fallen Lusignan clan; the revolution of 1258 was most decidedly anti-Lusignan. The revolution of 1258 was a temporary alliance of two parties who had much to fear of the Lusignans, Pierre de Savoie and Simon de Montfort – the crisis in Henry's kingship merely provided the opportunity to act. At Blackfriars Church in Oxford a solemn oath was to be taken to uphold the famed charter of liberties, the council formally instituted and a justiciar, Hugh Bigod, appointed. If we are in any doubt that Pierre de Savoie was central to the reform movement then we are reminded that the oath taken at Oxford was modelled upon that originally sworn by the Savoyard and his fellow oath takers of 12th April. But this time the oath suggested that anyone breaking it might be treated as a "mortal enemy", this clause trapped Pierre from 1263 when he'd turned his back on the reformers in the grip of the xenophobia increasingly gripping England. As the chronicler Thomas Wykes wrote:

> The fifth article was absolutely illegal and particularly detestable, namely, that if anyone presumed to contravene the said provisions, or refused to observe them, he would be considered a public enemy[164]

Simon de Montfort, the son of the Albigensian crusader was not one to either go back on oaths or forgive those that did so themselves. We have in the 1258 oath taken at Oxford the seeds that will later bear a bitter fruit for all concerned.[165]

Parliament, it was decided, would no longer meet when called upon to do so by the king; it would meet regularly every February, June and October. The three main pillars of Plantagenet government: the justiciar, the chancellor and the treasurer all answered to the council. The chancellor couldn't issue, other than routine writs, anything under the royal seal "on the sole command of the king".[166] The king could no longer act without the agreement of the council – he was no longer king by divine right. England would not see its like again until the seventeenth century. Maddicott called the constitutional settlement of 1258 "quasi-republican".[167]

But worse for Henry, he'd lost his Lusignan supporters. Henry and Edward had taken the oath but his half-brothers had not. Matthew Paris wrote:

> Simon, earl of Leicester, addressing himself to William de Valence ... 'You may rest assured that you will either give up the castles which you hold from the king, or you will undoubtedly lose your head'; and the other earls and barons said the same ... The Poitevins were, in consequence, in great alarm, and knew not what to do ... They therefore suddenly and secretly took to flight ... till they reached Winchester ... and thus ended the parliament of Oxford.[168]

By July the Lusignans had fled the country entirely.[169] Amongst all the constitutional novelty of the Provisions of Oxford, which have rightly been the focus of historians since, we should not lose sight of the fact that they also represented a triumph of the Savoyards over the Lusignans. As we've seen, notable amongst the confederation of barons pursuing the reforms was none other than Pierre de Savoie. The reason for Pierre's stance was the need to retain control and influence of the Lord Edward, by now married and 18 years of age. Edward had long been under the wing of the queen and her uncles but had lately begun to move into the Lusignan orbit – this was not something Pierre could allow to happen.[170] Indeed, so far into the Lusignan camp had Edward migrated that when they first fled from Oxford to Winchester, he was with them.

So, Pierre had acted on behalf of Alianor to prevent her precious son falling into what she would have seen as a "bad crowd". The rest of the family swung behind her in Savoyard solidarity. There had been no chance of Archbishop Boniface intervening; he had his own reasons to see the demise of the Lusignans after having clashed with Aymer.[171] Over in France Alianor's sister Queen Marguerite maintained sisterly and Savoyard unity by not allowing the Lusignan fugitives to stay in France, having "shamefully scandalised and defamed" Alianor.[172] As we've noted, the chronicler from Tewkesbury was perhaps being more than a little indiscriminate in his attribution of the target of reform of 1258: not "all foreigners" but solely the Lusignans.[173] So, the idea that what had happened at Oxford was against all foreigners at court, rather than just the Lusignan faction, is a later invention of annalists at Burton and Tewkesbury and the chronicler Walter of Guisborough. What they imagined to be in the Provisions of Oxford was almost certainly not there.[174] In a letter to Pope Alexander IV the English barons sought to justify their actions. They wrote that "the clamour of the poor ascended to the skies against them [the Lusignans]". The barons added, "For their [the Lusignans] ministers and officials, or rather partners in crime and robbers, despoiled the poor, attacked the simple, favoured the impious, oppressed the innocent ... rejoicing in the sufferings of the subject people." This letter bore the seal, amongst the others, on behalf "of all the community" of "*P. de Sabauda.*"[175]

A further example of the revolution of 1258 being anti-Lusignan rather than anti-foreigner is the leaving "in post", so to speak, of Savoyards, such as the long-serving Imbert Pugeys as a steward in Henry's household and Imbert de Montferrand as marshal.[176] True enough, in the surrender of royal castles, Imbert Pugeys gave up the Tower of London, and Ebal de Genève Hadleigh Castle, but as Ridgeway points out, the former is unsurprising given the appointment of a justiciar and in the latter case Ebal de Genève was in any case ill and died the following year in 1259.[177] The Savoyards were not yet "lumped in" with all foreigners in an overarching wave of xenophobia – that was to come, for now – and Pierre and Boniface de Savoie retained both their positions and influence. But, as Carpenter observed, they no doubt felt the xenophobia whipped up in 1258 against the Lusignans might henceforth be less discriminating.[178]

So important were the reforms of 1258 thought to be that the English authorities decided to break with a custom dating back to 1066, nearly 200 years: in addition to the official language of French, and the church language of Latin, news of the reforms were announced in English. Given the alleged anti-foreigner nature of the reforms, which we've since found to be largely in the minds of later chroniclers and Montfortian propagandists, that very archetype "foreigner" Pierre de Savoie found his name rendered into English on the first post-Conquest use of the language – his name was translated as *"Perres of Sauueye"* – his brother Boniface as *"Boneface"*.[179] It is perhaps ironic that the Savoyard brothers found their names attached to the first government document issued in English for nearly two centuries. Given the silence of contemporary chroniclers in the role played by Pierre de Savoie in the revolution of 1258, and one that has subsequently been echoed by historians in north England and Savoy until recently, one can only surmise that his role was subtle; he was after all a diplomat first and foremost, but also there was something else going on. A lead role for a Savoyard in something that was seen by chroniclers as an anti-foreigner revolution was most awkward – better to ignore it in the eulogies to the beginnings of parliament by Englishmen. His part in the revolution of 1258 eluded most commentators in Savoy too, for whom it was both unfathomable and did not fit into their national narratives. And so, the role of Pierre de Savoie in the greatest English constructional novelty since *Magna Carta* fell between the cracks in the pavement of history. As always, he was a pragmatist, not on the side of reform, nor on the royalist side for its own sake: he was on the side of the dynasty as represented by his niece, Alianor, and her son, Edward, even if the latter at this point did not know it. Events would prove him to have been right, and in time Edward would come to understand the wisdom of his great-uncle's actions.

Meanwhile, on 14 July 1258, after first fleeing from Oxford to the castle of Bishop Aymer at Winchester, the Lusignan brothers fled England. But the alliance of interests that had coalesced around the Provisions of Oxford, of the Montfortians, the Marcher lords, the Savoyards and the queen's party were very much together on what they had wanted to rid the realm of, but now a new order had to be created. Perhaps Henry's folly had not been in the preferment of aliens, but in imagining the successful import of Guillaume, Boniface and Pierre de Savoie and the cautious and diplomatic approach of the Savoyards in general might be replicated by his half-brothers from Poitou - it was not to be. In the end the Savoyards formed a coalition with the baronial reform movement to save Henry from himself.[180] How long would this coalition last? But for now, so ended Henry's personal rule.

Chapter Eight

Early in 1259,[1] Pierre and England would have learned of the passing of Thomas II de Savoie in Chambéry. The former Count of Flanders now styled Lord of Piedmont elected for burial in the cathedral at Aosta, where he remains to this day. The elder brother of Pierre, whose assumption of the debt owed by Simon de Montfort and requests for payment from Henry as guarantor had done so much to sour relations between them, was not mourned by Matthew Paris, who wrote that Thomas had "extorted money from the simple-minded king and queen ... as was much other moneys ... seized on by foreigners". Paris noted a report of poisoning before suggesting he'd left this life "to reap the reward of his ways".[2] Perhaps Paris was referring to his one-time excommunication. His death left the 11-year-old son of his late brother Amédée, Boniface, as Count of Savoy. Many historians have confused the young Boniface with his uncle Boniface, Archbishop of Canterbury, Christian names being so often reused by families of the time. The 1246 treaty whereby the Counts of Savoy became vassals to Henry for castles, a palace and town in the Alps came to the fore again in March 1259. Apparently Henry was some 3,000 marks in arrears for payments to the late Amédée IV, Thomas II and young Boniface. Henry made arrangements to pay by way of Pierre, Simon de Montfort refused to have anything to do with it. Therein we see an early breech between the oath takers Simon and Pierre, one that will soon widen further - it had not yet been twelve months since the Provisions of Oxford.[3]

Matthew Paris would not outlast Thomas long, also departing this life in 1259. Perhaps Thomas and Matthew passed the pearly gates together, arguing yet over those full saddlebags. Thomas left two sons, by his wife Béatrice di Fieschi, who would go on to serve the English Crown: Amédée and Louis. Amédée could be found years later leading the English army into Wales to relieve besieged Rhuddlan in the Second Welsh War of 1282. He would eventually become Count of Savoy, being the only man to earn the title *Le Grand* in the process, and Louis would become Baron de Vaud. Interestingly the arbitration between the two brothers as to which should become Count of Savoy would be undertaken by Queen Alianor and her son, by then King Edward I of England. Amédée would name his son Edward.[4] When Edward sought to create a continental alliance against his Capetian opponent, Philippe IV, in 1294, it would be with the help of Amédée V de Savoie, all of which would be unknown to Matthew Paris in 1259. Perhaps his first draft of history was inevitably too hasty – it was contemporary for sure, and invaluable for that – but perhaps events were to prove that he'd been too quick to judgement in assessing who'd been a friend to the English Crown.

In the autumn of 1259, a parliament was held at Westminster, at which the new government attempted to regularise the Provisions of Oxford into what became known as the superseding Provisions of Westminster, which were read out in Westminster Hall on 24 October, in the presence of King Henry III and an assembly of many of his earls and barons, along with many others. The provisions addressed a number of legal and administrative issues of concern to the barons, but also extended reform to the relations between these barons and their own tenants, something which would begin a falling apart of the council.

Chapter Eight

Turning across the Channel, failures of his earlier reign in attempting to reclaim his ancestral lands in France brought about a slow sea change in Henry's relations with his brother-in-law, Louis IX. To what extent the Savoyard sister-queens – Marguerite married to Louis, Alianor married to Henry, Sanchia to Richard and Béatrice to Charles – played a role in this evolution is a matter of conjecture, but Savoyard familial influence is highly likely.[5] We do know that from as early as 10 May 1255 their uncle, Pierre de Savoie, had been asked by Henry to begin negotiations to turn the truce with France into a full-blown treaty.[6] Negotiations began anew on 20 February with the dispatch of Simon de Montfort to Paris.[7] Following Bigod's march into Westminster Hall on 30 April, on 8 May 1258 Pierre de Savoie, Simon de Montfort, Hugh Bigod, Geoffrey and Guy de Lusignan were authorised to extend the truce with Paris, pending a treaty, the text of which was completed by 28 May.[8]

With Henry having to rule by the will of his council, his intention to cut his losses in France and bring to an end what his nobles saw as foreign adventures met with approval – especially as three of the ruling council, Pierre de Savoie, Hugh Bigod and Simon de Montfort, had been involved deeply in negotiations. So, whilst the Welsh prince Llywelyn sought a long-term treaty with Henry, the king's eyes were elsewhere, somewhere much dearer to him than cold and dreary Wales: back to his ancestral homelands in France. When Philippe Auguste had evicted his father John from much of his French lands, he had in effect made the Anglo-Norman nobility choose upon which side of the Channel their allegiance lay – did they owe allegiance to the Plantagenets or the Capetians? The loss of French lands was a double blow to the Plantagenet dynasty; first, it robbed them of a rich source of income – making them perennial paupers in comparison to the newly enriched kings of France. But also, second, it meant that the nobility who'd fallen on the English side of the Channel in terms of their allegiance no longer held extensive land in France – so crucially had no vested interest in supporting their monarch in reclaiming Normandy, Maine, Anjou and Poitou. And so, for Henry it was now a time to face reality, for *realpolitik*. If he was not to recover his lands perhaps it was time to reach an agreement with Louis to protect the remaining French land he did have, Gascony, in return for accepting the fait accompli of 1204. The result was the Treaty of Paris in 1259 (see figure 2.3).

The Treaty of Paris was a reset of Plantagenet–Capetian relations and should have cemented the peace that had descended, especially after Henry and Alianor's visit to Paris in 1254. By the treaty Henry gave up Normandy, Maine, Anjou and his beloved Poitou, and Gascony was no longer an allod but a fief of the King of France. The treaty was held up for a while by the need for his brother Richard's consent – after all he was giving up his rights too – and by his sister Eleanor, wife to Simon de Montfort, who still resented the lack of a dowry.[9] On 10 March 1259 Pierre de Savoie was amongst those asked to persuade the Montforts to come to terms. In this they initially failed, but on 25 June they reported back that Simon de Montfort and Eleanor had finally consented.[10] What Pierre will have seen as an attempt by the Montforts to put a spanner in the works of years of patient diplomacy was the beginning of a parting of the ways between the Savoyard and Montfort. But the Earl of Leicester wasn't to represent the only bone in Pierre's throat regarding the treaty. To cement the alliance Henry's daughter, Béatrice, was to be married to Jean de Dreux, heir to Brittany. The idea itself was likely to have been a Savoyard one, in the person of Marguerite de Provence, the French queen and Alianor's sister.[11] Jean de Dreux chose this very moment to press once more his claims to the Honour of Richmond. After all, if the House of Brittany was to be reconciled with the Plantagenets, should they not be reunited with their lands in England? Pierre obviously thought not, and in a skilful piece of diplomacy persuaded Jean, on 13 December,[12] to renounce his claim to Richmond and in return be rewarded with equivalent lands in the Agenais, newly returned by Louis.[13] Montfort had told Jean that Henry could not award patronage without the agreement of the Council of Fifteen; whether Pierre's solution to the Breton problem had the council's approval is unclear. As always with diplomacy, last-minute objections were raised to further personal interest.[14]

The marriage and act of homage for Gascony meant Henry and Alianor making the journey on 14 November 1259 to join Pierre in Paris. Pierre had taken up residence in Paris at the Hôtel de Nesle,[15] one-time palatial home of Jean de Nesle, but now, after it had passed into the hands of Louis IX, it had been the home of Alianor and Marguerite's mother-in-law, the redoubtable Blanche de Castille, until her death in 1252.[16] On 26 November Henry, Alianor and their entourage of knights and counsellors arrived in Paris to be met by a great reception of the citizens of Paris, and a solemn procession into the great cathedral of Notre Dame.[17] In an orchard two archbishops oversaw the formal act of homage on 4 December 1259.[18] The first was Archbishop Rigaud of Rouen – symbolic because Rouen was of course a Norman archbishopric. But it was the presence of a second archbishop, on Henry's side, that testifies to Pierre de Savoie's key hand in the Treaty of Paris – his name Rodolphe Grossi de Chatelard, the Archbishop of Tarentaise. Chatelard was a small fief of Pierre's at the head of the Aosta Valley, just before the climb to the Petit-Saint-Bernard Pass. Rodolphe was a long-time assistant of Pierre. The name of Jean Grossi, almost certainly a relative, had been amongst the list of knights Pierre had summoned to Gascony to help with Henry's operations there a number of years earlier. When two copies of the treaty were placed for safekeeping in the Temple in Paris, they bore the seals of the Archbishops of Rouen and Tarentaise – that the English representative would be a Savoyard archbishop long in the employ of Pierre de Savoie is instructive.[19] On 6 December at Saint-Germain-des-Prés Henry hosted, what Carpenter noted, was his biggest feast: the new rapprochement between the Plantagenets and Capetians was celebrated to the tune of £178 18s 8d., nearly £130,000 in today's money.[20] Carpenter compares the banqueting to the marriage of Diana and Charles, Prince of Wales, telling of "the knights, barons, earls, dukes, abbots, bishops, archbishops, countesses, queens, and royal princes, with at the very centre Henry and Louis themselves. The feast of 6 December affirmed the family unity at the heart of the Treaty of Paris".[21] Indeed, we should remember that first and foremost this was a peace largely brokered by the uncle of two nieces, married to two kings. It was an attempt to use familial ties to create a bridge between the Plantagenets and Capetians. That this peace may have been flawed, and that ultimately these two families would be ripped apart by over a hundred years of war, does not take anything away from the good intentions of 1259. For Pierre de Savoie the banquet would set the seal on the Treaty of Paris. Of all his achievements in life, this would be the one remembered by the monks of Hautecombe Abbey when they rebuilt his tomb after the French Revolution.[22] In more recent times Carpenter has referred to the treaty as "statesmanlike", if that is so, then one of its great architects Pierre de Savoie, can most definitely be equally so described.[23]

Henry, having been styled from becoming king as "*Henricus Dei gracia rex Anglie, dominus Hibernie, dux Normannie, Aquitanie et comes Andegavie*", was now reduced to "*Henricus Dei gracia rex Anglie, dominus Hybernie, dux Aquitanie*"[24] – but at least Aquitaine had finally been recognised by Paris. Henry, whilst now more secure in his Gascon territory as a fully fledged member of the French nobility, now had to answer for it to Louis and the French *parlement*. The Treaty of Paris received criticism from both sides, then and now, but if there were losses for the Plantagenets – Normandy, Maine, Touraine, Anjou and Poitou – there were gains too, hence the criticism from Jean de Joinville amongst others. We should remember that Henry's brother

Chapter Eight

Richard was now King of the Romans aka Germany and had every prospect of becoming Holy Roman Emperor. From the Capetian perspective in the perennial chess match with the Plantagenets, they now faced the prospect of having hostile neighbours to the north and east, a familiar fear of Frenchmen, of England and Germany uniting against them.[25] No, for Louis, now was the time to bring Henry in from the cold so to speak and to emphasise familial ties and his place as a French noble as well as King of England. Henry's rights in the County of Saintonge, south of the River Charente, were to be recognised. Louis gifted Henry his lands in Cahors, Limoges and Périgueux. It was agreed too that Henry had prior claim to the Agenais should it escheat to the French Crown, which it did in 1271. Similarly treated was the County of Quercy.[26]

Following Christmas in Paris, 'and sadly the funeral of Louis' heir, " Béatrice was married to Jean de Dreux, the heir to the Duchy of Brittany, on 22 January 1260 at Saint-Denis.[27] Watching over the ceremony were Henry and Alianor, Louis IX and Marguerite, Alfonso X of Castile, Jeanne de Ponthieu and of course Pierre de Savoie – then as now royal weddings and funerals occasioned a get-together of Christendom's great and good. Edward, despite the attendance of his parents and his other relatives, was elsewhere: in the newly enfiefed Gascony.[28] As well as recognising the obvious loss of territory and futility of hopes in its recovery, Henry also made an ally of King Louis, which in light of his recent submission to baronial council and in need of support for the Sicilian business, was much needed.

Nevertheless, this represented a colossal submission on Henry's part. His son Edward at first refused to sign – he harboured ideas of reclaiming the lands later as he became king himself. Indeed, despite the Treaty of Paris in 1259, Henry's great-grandson Edward III would again lay claim to the ancestral lands as part of a wider claim to the French throne itself – a claim that would give rise to the Hundred Years' War and not be formally renounced until the nineteenth century, when there was no French monarchy at all to claim.

Pierre de Savoie had been instrumental in the negotiations that had led to the Treaty of Paris, because the settlement of the Anglo-French problem was to be set amidst a wider settlement including the empire and the papacy. Pierre had liaised throughout with his brother Archbishop Boniface, his niece Queen Alianor, his niece Queen Marguerite and sister Béatrice de Provence.[29] The whole affair reminds twenty-first-century readers that in assessing thirteenth-century international affairs we must think of them as family affairs first and foremost – in this case the Houses of Plantagenet, Capet and Savoy. Louis is reported to have said as much when defending the treaty to his nobility, as Cox writes "that he desired peace between his children and Henry's because of their close ties of kinship".[30] Sadly for Henry the treaty had come too late to save the Sicilian business, as Pope Alexander IV had in December 1258 revoked the grant of Sicily to Edmund, upon the grounds that Henry had not fulfilled his financial obligations in the matter. Henry had in effect lost the European game of thrones.

Boniface had officiated at the consecration of the great new cathedral at Salisbury in September 1258, complete in every way save for the incredibly tall spire that would dominate the town in the next century. Storm clouds continued to gather over the kingdom. John Constable would paint the cathedral against the backdrop of a dark and stormy sky, and the scene he painted represents a metaphor for England as 1259 turned into 1260. Simon de Montfort had returned to England from Paris ahead of Henry and was, even now, making trouble for the king there.

In February, after Pierre had left Henry, the king dispensed with the services of a steward, Giles d'Argentan, foisted upon him by the council, leaving Savoyard Imbert Pugeys as his steward, a move that may well have been partly connived between Henry, Alianor and Pierre

119

in Paris.[31] As Henry was returning finally to England from Paris, Pierre de Savoie was furthering his interest in the *Pays de Vaud*. Earlier, whilst with Richard, King of the Germans, at Mere Castle in Wiltshire on 11 December 1259, he had obtained a royal grant for "the place commonly called *Contamina*" between Morat and Bern, now German-speaking and called Gümmenen.[32] This naturally defensible position close to Bern and atop bluffs dominating the crossing of Saane marked the high watermark of Savoyard expansion toward the lands of the German-speakers. He would build there a key castle and walls to defend the frontier, neither of which there remains a trace of today.

Following his attending the marriage of Béatrice and Jean at Saint-Denis, Pierre did not return to London, but headed back to his lands in Savoy. On his return to Vaud he also purchased, for 500 livres Viennois, the *seigneurie* of Yverdon, which was described in the sale as encompassing "a watercourse, with a mill and fishing rights, twenty *livrees* of land, a *péage* and a 'certain man'".[33]

A little earlier, in 1258, he had purchased the fief of Rue from the Count of Geneva, another in the region of Moudon and Romont that saw him strengthen his hold north of Lausanne. First châtelain for Pierre at Rue was a certain Henri de Bonvillars,[34] whose son Jean would marry into the Grandson family and become heavily influential in English affairs in the coming decades.[35] The *Famille de Bonvillars* had been involved with the *Famille de Grandson* for some time, having witnessed charters in the twelfth century.[36]

Yverdon-les-Bains, as it is now known, sits at the very southwestern tip of Lac de Neuchâtel, where the river Thièle empties into the lake on its short journey from Orbe, all of which is overlooked to the north by the Jura mountains. It had been inhabited since the second century BC and been a centre of Roman occupation – its Roman name being *Eburodunum*. The flood plain of the river had been irrigated and become the home to a significant number of Roman villas, the remains of which can be seen to this day. However, by the thirteenth century it had obviously fallen upon hard times, being now just the site of a watercourse, a mill and enigmatically "one man". From the millennium nearby Orbe had been the seat of local government and most recently Amédée III de Montfaucon,[37] Lord of Orbe had held the toll, hunting and mill fees.[38] Wurstenberger cited 26 April 1260 as the date of the acquisition of rights from Montfaucon: "Amédée de Montfaucon cedes to Pierre, for the price of five hundred *livres Viennois*, all his sovereign rights over the castle and the town of Yverdon, on the course of the river and the mills established there."[39] Amédée III de Montfaucon was of the powerful *Sires de Montfaucon* and Counts of Montbéliard, a family that held first rank amongst the nobles of the Free County of Burgundy. Their castle of Montfaucon sat high above the River Doubs close by Besançon and was a key point along the *Via Francigena*, as of course were Les Clées, Orbe, Lausanne and the recently enfeoffed to Henry III Saint-Maurice. We saw earlier that Burgundian knights had served with Pierre in Gascony in 1253-4 and had been summoned to Oxford for the stalled Welsh campaign of 1258. One of their number had been Richard IV de Montfaucon, third son of Richard III de Montfaucon, *Seigneur de Montbéliard*. The acquisition of Yverdon from the *Famille de Montfaucon* and Richard's service for Pierre cannot be unrelated.[40] Nor can we disregard the close relationship that had existed for at least a century between the *Sires de Montfaucon* and the *Sires de Grandson* in Vaud, remembering that, Pierre de Grandson, father of Othon de Grandson at court in England, was along with his cousin Henri de Champvent a loyal lieutenant of Pierre de Savoie in Vaud during Pierre's absences in England.[41]

Chapter Eight

Swiss historiography, based upon Amédée III de Montfaucon's siding with Jean de Cossonay in the bishopric struggle of 1240, has generally taken the view that Amédée had little choice but to sell his rights to Yverdon to such a "formidable competitor" as Pierre de Savoie and it is true that the value of the sale went to arbitration, however they were mostly unaware of the links between the *Famille de Montfaucon* and Pierre de Savoie revealed in both the Gascon roles and English archives. It would seem that by the 1250s the enmity of the 1240s between Amédée and Pierre had been set aside.[42] Finally we should bring to mind once more the pivotal influence of Simon de Joinville, *Seigneur de Gex et Marnay*, half-brother-in-law to Pierre de Savoie. The same Simon de Joinville who'd been, as we've seen, responsible for those Burgundian knights in the service of the English crown. He would be the same Simon de Joinville who was a "nephew by his mother, first cousin of Amédée" [de Montfaucon]. It seems in many ways, and ways that we shall soon see in England Simon de Joinville's name appears over and over again as a hinge by which the affairs of Pierre de Savoie turn.[43]

Going back to Yverdon, Swiss historian Victor van Berchem wrote that Yverdon was "*fermé*" or enclosed by Pierre, confirmed in the aforesaid "*acte du 26 avril 1260*".[44] By 27 May 1260 Pierre had obtained market rights from the Bishop of Lausanne market rights, and begun the construction of his *ville-neuve*, his new town, by the lake.[45] If it had been good enough for the Romans, Pierre might have thought, it would be good enough for him.

Three years later he would consolidate his position in the hinterland just to the south of Yverdon by acquiring three hamlets, including Corcelles-sur-Charvornay and Baulmes, from another Burgundian noble, Amauri IV de Joux. Van Berchem wrote, "*jusqu'au milieu du XIII siècle, Yverdon resta une bourgade peu importante, bâtie dans l'enceinte on au aupres de l'ancien castrum, et dont le caractere ne differait guere de celui d'une simple agglomeration rurale*" translating as "Until the middle of the thirteenth century, Yverdon remained a village of little importance, built inside or next to the ancient Roman fort and of which the character was not very different from that of a simple rural agglomeration."[46] More recent research by another Swiss historian, Justin Favrod, has suggested that reports of the paucity of settlement at Yverdon in 1260 may well have been exaggerated. He notes the existence of a church at Yverdon in 1140 and that the settlement was described as a *villa* later in 1174. He goes on to observe that the wealth of Yverdon reported in 1275 is unlikely to have been accumulated in the fifteen years of Savoyard rule. Favrod writes: "This is evidenced by the founding Act of 1260, which refers to the ancient inhabitants, the men of 'Everdune' and provides that their rights will be respected: it will be for them as it was before 'so as he used it in arrears'."[47] Whether Yverdon was a reinvigorated settlement or one begun anew, it was by Lac de Neuchatel that Pierre de Savoie founded his town.

Nonetheless, Pierre had recognised what the Romans had recognised before him – the strategic importance of Yverdon, commanding as it does routes down either side of Lac de Neuchâtel toward Vaud and Lausanne, but also the point at which the road from Bern turns northward through the Col de Jougne to Burgundy, France and England. Indeed, this route north was the sole north–south traverse of the Jura enabling access from France to the Swiss plateau and thence to the Alps and Italy. The *Via Francigena* passed this way, wending its long way from Canterbury to Rome. Pierre went so far as to extend his suzerainty to the strategically vital La Cluse,[48] and the castle which dominated it over Amauri IV de Joux, the latest of the Lords of Joux.[49] Pierre had in effect tied access to Helvetia from Burgundy and the north, to himself, for the foreseeable future. This route north through the Jura would ultimately see Edward I as suzerain when the County of Burgundy later paid homage for the town of Pontarlier and the Castle de Joux in 1281. We should see this as the logical extension of the 1246 treaty by which the castle of Bard and town of Saint-Maurice similarly became fiefs of King Henry III – Henry and his son had over some forty years established the English crowns rights over the *Via Francigena* in both the Jura and the Alps.[50]

An earlier primitive fortress had been built on the site of Yverdon by Amédée de Montfaucon in 1235, archaeological remains of which had been found in 1943. The fortress had been constructed to withhold Savoyard expansion at the time of the struggle for the bishopric of Lausanne, but destroyed no later than 1252.[51] However, in 1261, Pierre de Savoie rebuilt and significantly augmented the castle at Yverdon (see figure 2.4),[52] as he had done earlier at Pevensey. Indeed, recent visits by the author to both Yverdon and Pevensey have yielded evidence of some similarities the form of the embrasures in Sussex and Vaud; we cannot discount the presence of builders common to both Pierre's works, separated as they were by just six years. The castle at Yverdon would according to Cox transform "the sleepy little fishing village on the southern tip of Lac de Neuchâtel" into "one of the bastions of Savoyard dominion in the Pays de Vaud".[53] Stone for the new castle was *molasse* or sandstone, quarried from the Gros-de-Vaud region, that is the area of rolling hills south and east of Yverdon.[54] Either "la region d'Yvonand ou dans les environs de Suchy" is suggested by Swiss architectural historian Daniel de Raemy, so perhaps Yvonand would have had the advantage of shipment by lake to the construction site.

So, who would build this castle for Pierre? We are indebted to accountants and record keepers for the answer, for they kept records of payments made to the builders of Savoy, and in England and elsewhere – meticulous records of who did what, what they were paid and when. It is from these records, many of which survive in Savoyard records now kept in Turin and Chambéry, in English records held at the National Archive in Kew, that we can trace the story of the great castles. It is upon these primary sources that much of our story is based. The keeping of accurate castle-building records is something that Pierre had learned well of his time in England, and will mark his later period as Count of Savoy, the introduction of what we call in England, Pipe Rolls. We will come to discuss them at greater length in a later chapter on Pierre's administrative reforms in Savoy but the records for Yverdon are an early example which predate his time as Count. They are, of course, written in Latin, not Classical Latin but its later medieval variant from which we can reasonably translate. Archival records discovered by Arnold J. Taylor show that it was "directed by Master James the mason, acting at first under the direction of his father, Master John, and with Peter Mainer, the keeper of the counts works".[55] The Savoyard archive in Turin as transcribed by Mario Chiaudano has the following entry for 1261:

Account of Valeisio and Chablasio of the year 61

> For the discharge of Master John the mason from the day when he came from his home to Yverdon, assuredly the first day of May of this year [1 May 1261] until the
> second Sunday of Lent [5 March 1262] for forty-four weeks who received twelve sol per week. Twenty-six Livres and Eight Sol. For the discharge of his son Master James for same period receiving ten sol and six denier every week. Twenty-three livres and two sol. For his wages and shoes and his linen bandages receiving five sol per month. Fifty-Five sol. For Master

Chapter Eight

James himself, medicine for the time of his illness. Twenty-five Sol. For the discharge of Master Peter Mainier Custodian of the Lord's works for the same period two horses for himself and one for his servant as Master John aforesaid. Twenty-six Livres and Eight Sol.[56]

A further entry for the much later period of 1265–7 simply records:

> In the acquittance [discharge of a debt] of Master James the mason for this year and the year before that ... he James has the fee of Yverdon, 10 *livres Viennois* every year. 15 *Livres*.[57]

One last entry relating to the castle at Yverdon is dated to the period 1 April 1269 to 15 August 1269 and simply reads:

> Master James the mason, 10 *livres*.[58]

Pierre, meanwhile, obtained much of what had been thwarted during the episcopal war twenty years earlier. In August 1260 he persuaded the bishop, Jean de Cossonay, who'd once fought his family for the See of Lausanne, to give him "the illustrious Lord Pierre de Savoie" half of the temporal power over the city of Lausanne.[59] The bishop's concession reflected a *realpolitik*: Pierre pretty much had the power in any case – better to be seen to formally make a grant of it.

Whilst the new castle at Yverdon began to take shape close by the lake, Pierre completed his stranglehold of the region by purchasing, in August 1263, the *péage* of nearby Grandson.[60] The deed of 31 August 1263 survives in an unlikely source: in the records of the British House of Lords. It records the names of the Grandson clan and Othon's absence, presumably in England: "We Agnès, Lady of Grandson, Guardian of our legitimate children Peter and William, Girard, James and Henry, for them and their brother Othon, the sons said Lady."[61]

Now nobody passed from the Swiss plateau, from Neuchâtel, from Bern, from Lausanne, without payment at Les Clées, Yverdon or Grandson – the *Petit Charlemagne* had the Vaud and the wider region in his grip.

Shortly after the acquisition of Yverdon, Pierre formally gained the lands of the *Famille de Mont*, in the shadow of the Jura, just along the lake from Nyon. As we have seen, the family had long had links with the Savoyards; the second son of Ebal I, Ebal II, had gone to England with Pierre and had been appointed his attorney there when Pierre had been out of England. By marriage Ebal had gained Midhurst Castle in Surrey and would become constable of Windsor Castle following the storm that was about to envelop England. The lands above Lac Léman had passed from Ebal I to the eldest brother Henri, who'd died in 1256 to be succeeded by another Ebal, this time Ebal III – the medieval habit of reusing Christian names would confuse many a latter-day historian. In England Ebal II and Joan de Bohun would have a son, yet another Ebal, this time Ebal IV, who would go on to be a household knight for Edward I and play a significant part in the early story of Harlech Castle in Wales. Meanwhile, on 7 May 1260, Pierre bought the lands of of the *Famille de Mont* for twenty *livres Genevois* and enfiefed them back to them.[62] The family would then give up their castle high above the lake and build a new castle by the lake, a much more desirable location on what's now some of the most expensive real estate in Europe by what is now the town of Rolle. With Yverdon and Rolle castles Pierre de Savoie would strengthen his tight grip on the *Pays de Vaud*. That spring another short war with the Count of Geneva resulted in a peace that further denuded the County of Geneva, restricting it to almost the city itself. The cause of the latest altercation with Geneva may well have been the will drawn up in England by Ebal de Genève, one of the two deposed sons of Humbert de Genève taken to England by Pierre de Savoie, whereby Ebal left his rights in Geneva to Pierre. The testament was sealed by those Vaudois in England, Gerard de Grandson (a canon in Lyon), Ebal de Mont, Pierre de Champvent and Simon de Joinville[63] – once more English and Alpine affairs colliding. Indeed Carpenter notes that Pierre was seeing to his affairs in Geneva at the same time as negotiations with France, an indication that his ability to spin plates in both England and Savoy continued unabated by the revolution of 1258.[64]

A war that summer with the Bishop of Sion, Henri de Rarogne, extended Savoyard power down the Valais. An army of Vaudois nobles reinforced from Bern, just done with the Genevois and replete with catapults, made short work of the episcopal forces. By 14 July 1260 a peace was put to the arbitration of the Archbishop of Tarentaise.[65] How Henri de Rarogne expected a fair meditation from the same Archbishop Tarentaise, Rodolfo de Grossi de Chatelard, who'd sealed the Treaty of Paris for the English side and had long been in the employ of Pierre de Savoie, is unclear. The castle at Martigny had fallen after a short siege, its walls so damaged the defenders lost stomach for the fight. There followed an attack on the castle at Crest and another quick capitulation.[66] The peace settlement saw Pierre take three castles from the Bishop of Sion, the Archbishop Tarentaise awarding Crest, Chamson and the aforesaid castle at Martigny in need of repair to Pierre. This last castle was of the utmost strategic importance since it guarded the northern approaches to the Grand-Saint-Bernard Pass and the way to Italy. A substantial portion of the Bishop of Sion's rich wine-growing lands and those of Lausanne and Geneva passed to Pierre. Within a short while of arriving in the region, Pierre had vanquished the Count of Geneva, Bishop of Sion and reached an agreement to secure temporal authority in Lausanne. The *Petit Charlemagne* was now the dominant player in what's now the French-speaking parts of Switzerland.

One of the reasons for the greater attention Pierre lavished upon his homeland from early 1260 was the growing political instability in England – Henry, subject now to his counsellors, sat atop an increasingly emasculated and embattled throne. Even as Pierre returned to Savoy after being with Henry and Alianor in Paris as 1259 became 1260, Simon de Montfort was agitating for his removal from the council. As Henry delayed a return to England in the spring of 1260 there was a threat of civil-war there.[67] Better, Pierre must have thought, to spend time in Savoy, especially as later in 1260 he'd been removed from King Henry's council at Simon de Montfort's behest and Queen Alianor's disgust.[68] Montfort had, as we saw, headed back to England before Henry in the spring of 1260 and called a Parliament without Henry's consent, urging the removal of Pierre de Savoie from the council. When Henry had belatedly returned to England he'd averted a civil war and sought to bring Montfort to book. Montfort's defence was again very much the populist of the "common enterprise" and "common provisions" and that Henry "put his trust more in foreigners than men from his own land." Remarkable criticisms and claims from a natural born Frenchman. But Pierre's removal from the council had laid bare the divisions within the ruling council and ended the 1258 alliance between Montfort and the Savoyards.[69]

Pierre had first sided with the reformers, as a means to rid the court of the Lusignan faction, and in particular the Lusignan influence over Edward, but now the rising tide of xenophobia unleashed particularly by Montfort, himself an alien, was making life in England distinctly uncomfortable for those of foreign birth. Fellow Savoyard council member, Boniface, too faced difficulties in the face of Montfortian expansion. His castles at Canterbury and Rochester were given baronial castellans despite their being within his jurisdiction, his protests coming to nought.[70] If we are to seek the moment when Pierre de Savoie parted company with Simon de Montfort, then it is in two crucial events. First, his removal from the Council of Fifteen: following the Treaty of Paris opposed by Montfort the Earl of Leicester sought and obtained Pierre de Savoie's removal from the council in his absence in Savoy.[71] Second, the death in Paris on 4 December 1260[72] of his adversary, the Lusignan Aymer de Valance, Bishop of Winchester. It had been for Pierre an alliance with Montfort to bring down the Lusignan threat to Alianor's influence at court; with their exile and Aymer's death, the ties which bound Pierre to the reformers fell away. The temporary alliance of Pierre de Savoie and Simon de Montfort was over. With Pierre de Savoie removed from the council during his absence from the kingdom in 1260, and his return to England at Christmas 1260 and access once more to Henry, the stage was set for a reversal of the Provisions of Oxford driven by the Savoyards. Ridgeway noted that with Pierre's return to England in November 1260, there were now "cool relations" between Montfort and the Savoyard, now removed from the council yet still witnessing royal charters.[73] It seems that in December 1260 until February 1261, Montfort inspired the new justiciar, a close ally, Hugh le Despenser, to begin an eyre, or circuit court, investigating cases in Pierre's lands in Sussex. Despenser heard from William Marmion, a lord and later rebel, that a bailiff for Pierre had forced forty shillings from him and his men in Berwick, Surrey, contrary to the Provisions of Westminster.[74] But it was at Pevensey that Despenser heard much complaint, we saw earlier that Pierre had been given free warren there, that is the exclusive right to hunt, but it also included the rights to any wrecks that might wash up upon the shore, these rights were enforced by his bailiff John de la Rede. Pierre's bailiff had been acting vigorously on his behalf, too vigorously for the jurors of Sussex, Rede was fined and gaoled. One of the complainants was John de la Ware, a Montfortian who'd had greyhounds and falcons seized, and had been taking clothes and other things from washed-up bodies, while two casks of his own wine, claimed as wreck, were seized from his cart.[75] It's likely other grievances would have been forthcoming too, as they had been for the eyre of Hugh Bigod who'd found the residents of Witley in Surrey claiming that Pierre had raised their rents which they paid as tenants of the king's demesne unduly.[76] The Franciscan theologian Adam Marsh had written a fervent letter to Pierre, urging the Savoyard to show compassion and generosity and that he should remember "the dread sentence of judgment."[77] Clearly the aim was to discredit the Savoyard. Simon and Pierre, two newcomers to England who'd sworn an oath to remain loyal, one to the other, had now parted ways. Pierre was to forestall Montfort by encouraging Henry in 1261 to throw off the rule of the collapsing council.[78]

Now enter Henry's son at centre stage, first siding against and then with Henry, earning him the later epithet of the *Song of Lewes* in 1264 as Leopard – "Whereunto shall the noble Edward be compared? Perhaps he will be rightly called a leopard. If we divide the name it becomes lion and pard ... a lion by pride and fierceness, he is by inconstancy and changeableness a pard, changing his word and promise, cloaking himself by pleasant speech."[79] A *leo*, strong and brave certainly, but the also *pard* – unpredictable, inconstant and unreliable.[80] Following the Teaty of Paris, As Henry languished in France in the spring of 1260, suffering from tertiary fever, Edward joined Simon de Montfort in what looked to the king like open rebellion. Simon de Montfort had left Paris and the celebrations of the treaty without taking leave of Henry, and on his return to England he'd attempted to call a February parliament despite Henry's absence. Henry returned to England accompanied by a significant number of mercenaries. The king's brother, Richard, saw dynastic disaster ahead and intervened to prevent warfare between father and son. However, the tides in England were shifting this way and then that. Having first sided with Simon, by May 1261, Edward was back with his father's party, and Montfort faced trial before being acquitted in July. The baronial council now collapsed. It looked to all that the baronial democratic experiment was over. Edward's behaviour at this time has often been difficult to understand, that he would at times side with the baronial party and then with his father. What is certainly true is that Edward saw, up close and personal, the perils and travails of medieval kingship – and learned that survival rested upon his ability to not only play the tough leader, but also the unscrupulous politician when it was needed. The political crisis of his youth served him well in later life, for Edward would become a king, if not loved by his people, then certainly respected and feared by his foes. If his father left us Westminster Abbey then Edward would leave us the castle at Caernarfon, both telling monuments to father and son.

In the spring of 1260 Henry had returned and faced down his rebellious son and Simon de Montfort. This might have seen him able to return to personal rule; however, by the autumn of 1260 he was again under the cosh of the council. An example of the continued royal emasculation is a ceremony which took place, before his son Edward and Archbishop Boniface, on 18 October 1260 at Westminster. The royal seal which proclaimed him to be Duke of both Normandy and Aquitaine and Count of Anjou was ceremoniously broken into pieces before him and replaced with one shorn of the ancestral lands lost by the recent Treaty of Paris, and worse, given up into the safekeeping of a chancellor appointed by the council – a new low ebb for the Plantagenet dynasty. The golden years of his grandfather must have seemed light years ago to Henry.[81]

In Wales, more bad news: Llywelyn continued to apply pressure, marching on the castle at Builth in mid-Wales. The Norman, Philip de Braose, had conquered the Welsh borderlands at Builth and Radnor, establishing new Norman lordships over them. At Builth, he had constructed a motte and bailey castle. More recently, as the lands formed part of Edward's appanage, he'd granted custody of the castle to Roger de Mortimer. Whilst Henry was away in France, in January 1260, Llywelyn arrived with siege engines, meaning to take the castle. On his return, Henry had summoned Roger to London. On the day of his arrival there, 17 July, Builth had fallen to Llywelyn. Three of Mortimer's men had opened the gates to Llywelyn during the night.[82] The castle was then destroyed and "not a stone remained upon another".[83] Llywelyn was erasing Edward's holdings in Wales.[84]

In October 1260 Richard returned to England, in November or December he'd be joined by Pierre, but both found an unwelcome change, along with the latters removal from the council they found the Montfortian Hugh Despenser had replaced Hugh Bigod as Justiciar. However, following a Christmas and New Year accompanied by Alianor and Pierre, by January 1261, Henry was beginning to plot new ways to reassert his authority. Pierre and Alianor were now allied with Henry's brother Richard along with royalist lieutenants John Mansel and Robert Walerand.[85] The English court that Christmas had a distinctly Savoyard flavour, along with Pierre and Alianor were Ebal de Mont, Pierre de Champvent and Imbert de Montferrand. Simon de Montfort had also left court for France helping to clear a way for Henry, if Montfort could plot against Pierre whilst he was in Savoy then what was source for the goose, Pierre could now return the compliment. Carpenter makes an excellent point when he writes that it is almost "as though the two men could not bear each others presence." It's with these voices in his ear that Henry would make his move.[86] In order to arrange a papal annulment of the reform provisions, Master John Mansel (not to be confused with

Chapter Eight

Henry's and Pierre's ally John Mansel - Master John was likely a kinsman of the elder Mansel) secretly left for Rome, his task to arrange for an annulment once the king had regained control. Regaining control firstly meant regaining control of the royal seal, perhaps surprisingly this was achieved. In February 1261, so that there would be no repetition of the events of the parliaments of 1258, Henry took himself to the solid refuge of the Tower of London, where in May he made loyal John Mansel the new Constable. Once confident enough Henry, in May, along with Savoyards made for and secured the vital castle at Dover, controlling who could enter or leave his kingdom. This rather careful strategy, had in part, been a scheme devised by what Carpenter, perhaps poetically termed "the fruitful minds" of Richard and Pierre - Pierre de Savoie ever the Machiavellian prince. Sure enough, Henry strove to divest himself of the oath that he'd taken at Oxford; in June he published the absolution he'd obtained from Pope Alexander IV (Alexander died on 25 May). In June–July Henry made public his absolution from the oath of 1258. The absolution extended to Alianor, Pierre and Boniface de Savoie having taken the oath as "magnates" and "clerics" "under the pretext of reforming the kingdom".[87] The association of the Savoyards with Henry's retaking control can only have been strengthened when Boniface published the absolution in August and threatened Bigod with excommunication if he did not return the castles, placed under baronial control in 1258, to royalist control without delay.[88] As a clear sign of Henry's return to power, the Montfortian Justiciar Hugh Despenser was dismissed, to be replaced by Philip Basset, meaning an end to Despenser's eyre and investigations into Pierre's bailiffs in Sussex. In July Henry, accompanied by Alianor, Pierre and other Savoyards felt secure enough to decamp from the Tower to the more congenial Windsor Castle.

Civil war between the king and the barons was only averted when Simon de Montfort went into French exile, nursing grievances a many.[89] Remarkably, the rule of the council melted in the summer of 1261 much as it had boiled in the summer of 1258. We know of no armed opposition to Henry's reimposition of personal rule. The rapprochement between father and son, Henry and Edward, was encouraged, of course, by their uncle Pierre, writing to Henry to advise payment of fees to several of Edward's knights. Pierre wrote, "so that other faithful men may, by this example, be drawn to the strengthening of your side."[90] If the impetus for the restoration of dynastic authority had come from the so-called "queen's party", that is Alianor and Pierre, then the support too of the wider family network which extended to Louis and Marguerite in France was crucial. This placed Henry in a much stronger position vis-à-vis the baronial opposition than his father John had found himself in 1216, when Philippe Auguste had backed the baronial party – in 1261 there would be no French intervention. This familial solidarity of Alianor and Marguerite, Henry and Louis, and Pierre de Savoie, would be something that would prove the rock with which Montfort would eventually collide in 1263 at Amiens, thus bringing on open civil war. Henry was again ruling England as sole ruler, King Henry III again, but it was not to last long. Back to England came Guillaume de Valence, the Lusignan, which did not bode well for Henry's bold return to personal rule. The Savoyards, and in particular Pierre de Savoie and his niece Alianor, the queen, were fundamental to Henry's retaking of power in 1261, support more than understood at the time, notably by the chroniclers, and something that they, the Montfortians more widely, and elements in London more specifically, never forgave them for.[91]

Amidst this political chaos in England, the Savoyard interest in England suffered a further setback: on 9 November 1261 Sanchia de Provence, the wife of Richard, Earl of Cornwall and King of the Romans, passed away. She died at just 33 years of age at Berkhamsted Castle near London, attended by her uncles Archbishop Boniface and Pierre de Savoie; burial was at Hailes Abbey just four days later.⁹² Strangely perhaps, neither the king nor her sister Alianor were there, as they had taken refuge in the troubled times in the safety of the Tower in London. The abbey at Hailes had been dedicated with great ceremony back in the autumn of 1251. Richard had built it at a cost of some 10,000 marks as gratitude for surviving an awful sea voyage from Gascony in 1242. Sadly, Hailes did not survive the reformation, but the ruins still to this day bear the faint outlines of Provence, the far-away county by the Mediterranean from which Sanchia had travelled some twenty years before to marry the richest man in Europe. He'd made her Queen of the Romans. There is still a part of Gloucestershire that remains forever Provence, but for the Savoyard a foundation stone of their power and influence in England had passed.⁹³

The Treaty of Kingston upon Thames of 22 November 1261, just over a week after Sanchia's death, set the seal on King Henry's victory over the council and return to what many of his contemporaries, including the pope, would have seen as his rightful place at the top of the feudal pyramid. On 25 February 1262 Pope Urban IV renewed the absolution of the oaths of 1258, and was laid before Parliament on 23 April, the sheriffs being informed on 2 May.⁹⁴ As Knowles succinctly says, "All promises made by the prelates and magnates contrary to the dignity of the Crown and prejudicial to its rights were declared null and void."⁹⁵ However, in England the genie was out of the bottle; many had rather liked the idea that the king ruled with the consent of his people. The birth of the principle that an English monarch ruled with the consent of the people can be traced to the temporarily suspended Provisions of Oxford; the notion that the king once anointed by God, ruled his kingdom as a personal fief had been challenged.⁹⁶

In June 1262, in a rapprochement between himself and Pierre, the Lord Edward, in need of funds, with an exchange of lands, quitclaimed his rights to the Honour of Hastings, or Honour of Eu, and returned the lands immediately to the east of his uncle's lands at Pevensey to Pierre, who'd previously had custody of them between 1249 and 1254.⁹⁷ Pierre left England for France, his presence in Paris explicitly requested by the king.⁹⁸ He left his affairs in the capable hands of his niece, Alianor, and his trusty steward Guichard de Charron.⁹⁹ Since his arrival at court twenty years earlier in 1241 he had led a life with one foot in England and the other foot in Savoy. For much of this time he'd spent six months of a year in each realm, clocking up a good many horse miles in the process and becoming well known to the boatmen of Dover and Wissant. From the 1250s his absences had grown longer: 1250–1, 1253–6 and 1260, albeit much of the 1253–6 absence was in support of Henry in Gascony. During his time in England, he'd not seen much of the country. He's not known to have spent much time at Richmond; indeed, he may not have visited the Honour of Richmond at all, preferring Sussex or Surrey when not with Henry at court.¹⁰⁰ His only opportunity to visit his northern estates may have been his 1258 diplomatic mission to Scotland.¹⁰¹ Pierre's role in England was, as we have seen, chiefly that of Alianor's and the Lord Edward's protector, and Edward was no longer a boy. Pierre no doubt believed he could safely leave England with Henry safely back at the helm, Edward reconciled and Alianor safely ensconced in a Savoyard court.

Indeed Henry's court during 1262 displays what a distinct Savoyard flavour, as the witness list suggests Imbert Pugeys and Ebal II de Mont were the king's stewards, one of his Marshals was Imbert de Montferrand.¹⁰² His many absences reflected his role as a diplomat in Henry's service, and the need to keep his Alpine plates spinning, countering the efforts of the Count of Geneva and Bishop of Sion. Leaving England in the summer of 1262 he may not have known he'd not see England at peace again, the unexpected death of young Boniface de Savoie in the autumn of 1262 would catapult him into being Count of Savoy, and Henry's kingdom would rapidly unravel around his ears. Nonetheless, Pierre returned to Savoy and Henry embarked on the second period of his personal rule: it would be much shorter than the first.

Again, however, the pious Henry seems to have been his worst enemy: rather than consolidate his position at home, as might have been wise, he once more sailed for France. In the words of Carpenter, it was "difficult to think of a worse time for him to leave the country".[103] On 16 July 1262 he began a six-month leave of absence that would be his undoing, first to visit King Louis, who was now his liege lord for Aquitaine, but also as the pious man he undoubtedly was, to visit the shrines of saints in far-off Burgundy. His stay in Paris at the Abbaye Saint-Germain-des-Prés would be to settle dowry matters for Alianor. A charter bears the usual Savoyard witness list: Imbert Pugeys, Ebal II de Mont, Pierre de Champvent, Imbert de Montferrand and Guillaume de Champvent.[104] Indeed, the Savoyard familial network is noticed once more when hearing that Marguerite had told English envoys earlier in 1262 not to meet Louis until she was at court and could help.[105]

Carpenter relates a story of Henry's time with Louis that says much about the English king, especially given that it occurred whilst his realm was increasingly in peril:

> Henry was summoned to Paris to attend the parlement as duke of Aquitaine, he stayed at Saint-Germain-des-Prés. On the first day of the parlement, however, Henry arrived so late at the royal palace (evidently the *palais de la Cité*) that no business could be done, this because he had dismounted and entered all the churches along the way, remaining in each until mass was completed. On the morrow, despite being urged to be on time, and dutifully getting up before dawn, exactly the same thing happened. Louis and his counsellors now resorted to other measures and ordered all the churches along Henry's route to be shut until he had gone past. This worked and next day Henry was one of the first to arrive.[106]

This passage stands with Westminster Abbey as an insight into Henry's mind, a man so pious churches had to be locked in order for any work to be done. Whilst he was away from England hearing mass in so many French churches, Simon de Montfort returned to England with a stick of political dynamite – he read to the October Parliament Pope Urban IV's bull reversing his predecessor Alexander's decision on the Provisions of Oxford. They were now, it seemed, entirely legal.[107] Interestingly, although we have a copy of Pope Urban's bull supporting Henry, the bull read by Montfort to Parliament confirming the observance of the Oxford Provisions has not survived.[108] Carpenter recently suggested that Montfort's stick of political dynamite may have been at best "a draft of some kind" but then as now people weren't fact-checking a populist. Meanwhile, Pierre de Savoie was implicated in the death of Richard de Clare, Marcher lord and 6th Earl of Gloucester, who'd flip-flopped during recent times, on 14 July 1262. Richard died at John de Criol's manor of Asbenfield in Waltham, near Canterbury, but the anonymous pro-Montfortian Dunstable chronicler suggested there had been *"malefcium"* on the part of the Savoyard, and by implication his niece Queen Alianor.[109] Perhaps the rumour grew from Boniface's seizure of land in Kent, but it was a rumour that may have contributed anti-Savoyard feeling that would soon follow. When Henry returned to England just before Christmas of 1262, he did so to a kingdom once more up in political arms. How should the kingdom be governed, with or without the consent of the people, with or without the baronial council? Following the October parliament Simon had returned to France, as in the spring of 1263 there were calls for him to return – and, with it, England set course for civil war. In the autumn of 1262 the turbulent Prince of Wales, Llywelyn ap Gruffydd had returned to the ways of war by renewing his conquests in the Marches. Maelienydd was a *cantref* in east-central Wales covering the area from the River Teme to Radnor Forest. The area, which is mainly upland, centred around Llandrindod Wells, in what's now Powys, was controlled by a castle at Cefnllys. Like Builth destroyed in 1260, the castle belonged to Roger de Mortimer, and was now a key stronghold for him in the Marches. The castle occupied a fine site high above the River Leithon (Ithon) on a rocky outcrop. Roger de Mortimer was an important Marcher lord, and in the way of the March, whilst he was most likely an Anglo-Norman by language, culture and identity, he was also, as was Llywelyn ap Gruffydd, a grandson of Llywelyn Fawr. On 29 November Llywelyn renewed hostilities with an attack on Cefnllys, which like Builth before was taken and destroyed.[110] Henry and the Marches feared for the future, these fears not being assuaged by a letter from Pierre d'Aigueblanche that spoke of Llywelyn having over 300 horsemen and 30,000 troops in Maelienydd, which would threaten South Wales too.[111] Thankfully for Henry, swift action by Peter de Montfort put this particular Welsh army to flight. However, the following summer, Llywelyn would return to the campaign trail.

Dyserth castle, raised only recently in 1241 as a replacement for Rhuddlan, and completed in 1248, was situated in a naturally defensible strategic location on a mountain ridge at the northern end of the Clwydian hills. On 4 August 1263, after several weeks of a blockade and siege, it too fell and was destroyed by the Welsh Prince, as the Chester chronicler recounted:

> Llwelyn ap Gruffydd and Gruffydd ap Madog . . . besieged the castle of Dyserth for five weeks. Having captured it on the eve of the feast of Saint Oswald, King and Martyr, they razed it to the ground.[112]

Thus we see the alliance of Llywelyn and Gruffydd ap Madog, Lord of Dinas Bran and ruler of Powys Fadog. In late September it was the turn of Deganwy itself, Henry's main defence in North Wales: it was besieged, attacked and destroyed. Deganwy in fact fell even as a truce was being negotiated, on 18 September "that those in the castle of Gannoc [Deganwy] are to furnish themselves with victuals until then [a truce]" but only by "one boat of twelve oars or less".[113] That the truce was to be between Edward and Llywelyn illustrates the extent to which Henry had delegated Edward's appanage to his son.[114] The chronicler in Chester can't hide his contempt for the weakness of the defenders of Deganwy, calling them "*degeneres et imbelles*" or "degenerate and cowardly".[115] Within twelve months, Builth, Cefnllys, Dyserth and Deganwy had all been attacked and erased from the map.

On 6 March 1263 a group of disaffected former supporters of the Lord Edward, of the time he'd been allied to Montfort, returned to England. They were no lovers of the Savoyards since Alianor and Pierre had resumed their control over the heir. The group were Jean de Warenne, Roger de Clifford, Henri d'Almain and Henri de Montfort, the son of the troublesome Earl of Leicester; they joined Jean de Vaux and Hamon Lestrange. Their return proved to be as harbingers of the return of Simon de Montfort as Roger de Clifford, along with Roger Leybourne, called for the return to England of the earl.[116] That summer the barons would make their intention clear to all:

> *Et sciendum, quod talis fuit petitio Baronum ... Item, petunt quod regnum de cetero per indigenas, fideles et utiles sub Domino Rege, gubernetur, et non per alios, sicut fit communiter in omnibus aliis mundi.*[117]

Chapter Eight

> And it should be noted that such was the request of the Barons ... Likewise, they ask that the kingdom will henceforth be governed by natives, faithful and useful under the Lord King, and not by others, as it is commonly done in all other parts of the world.

Montfort had come to defend the Provisions of Oxford, but the 1258 compact had been in part an alliance of reformers and those who wished to see the end of Lusignan influence, this alliance including the Savoyards. In 1263, the association was still of reformers but the aliens in the crosshairs were now the Savoyards themselves. The appeal on the part of the reformers to pandering to the xenophobia of the mid-thirteenth century is the darker side of a genuine reform movement.

Returning in April 1263,[118] Simon de Montfort assembled strong forces to uphold the Provisions of Oxford, including the Welsh, who would take the opportunity to weaken the English monarchy. Likely shortly after, in May, Montfort assembled his supporters in secret to plot their move against the king – their meeting place was with deliberate symbolism, Oxford.[119] The Dunstable chronicler and Thomas Wykes gave us the names of Montfort's allies at this point, they included the group who'd landed ahead of Montfort mentioned above: Jean de Warenne, Henri d'Almain, Roger de Clifford and Henri de Monfort but also Hamo LeStrange, Roger Leybourne, Hugh Despenser, Geoffrey de Lucy, Gilbert de Clare, John Giffard, Nicholas de Segrave, Jean de Vaux, Guillaume de Munchesney, John FitzJohn, Henri de Hastings, Jean de Vesci and others.[120] Also prominent amongst the opposition were the men of London, where by 19th June Henry and Alianor were taking refuge in the Tower, and where close by Edward was based at Windsor (with the royal treasure). Amongst those with Edward at Windsor thar summer of 1263 was Guillaume de Pesmes, the Burgundian knight who'd served in Gascony at the behest of Pierre and likely Wales too. Edward, a one-time ally of Montfort, was now back firmly on the side of the Crown he would inherit. Down at Dover Henry's second son Edmund held the castle, thus the ability to flee to France if need be. With echoes of Thomas Becket, the Savoyard Bishop of Hereford, Pierre d'Aigueblanche, was taken by his own altar and imprisoned, along with his chapter at Eardisley Castle, the possession of Walter de Baskerville,[121] in the Wye Valley, in June 1263. The newly returned Roger de Clifford was aided in his attack on Hereford by the Montfortians Roger de Leybourne and John Giffard, but would later switch back from the baronial party to the royalist side. That Simon de Montfort was behind the attack on an ordained bishop is confirmed by the Merton chronicler of the *Flores Historiarum*.[122] It is notable that the first target of the Montfortians after their secret gathering at Oxford was the Savoyard bishop, this was not to be a move against one group of foreigners but all foreigners, xenophobia was now to be let loose in the land. Archbishop Boniface was in effect exiled, he'd left England on 8 October 1262 on papal business in Rome by way of Savoy.[123] In their absence the Montfortians went on to ravage the lands of both Pierre and Boniface.

Some of the detail of this ravage of Pierre's lands has survived from claims of redress after the war, including the names of some of the Montfortians who'd attacked and robbed the Queen's uncle's lands, men like Jordan de Sackvile, Robert Corbet, Osbert le Hoser, John de Applethon and John de la Haye. In total Pierre complained of 44 pillagers, the attorney presented a claim that:

> "[these men had been guilty of] trespass and robbery whether they together with others came to Pierre's lands . . .and destroyed his goods, chattels, corn

and hay, broke into his forests and parks and took his wild beasts and cut, destroyed and carried away his wood and indeed committed other grace and enormous damage against our peace."[124]

That other Savoyards were targeted in this wave of xenophobia we know from claims for redress following the coming war, claimants included Ebal II de Mont and Imbert de Montferrand. In Dorset it was noted that Roger de Clifford and John Giffard "went with banners flying through the county plundering loyal subjects."[125] Boniface later complained of "the sons of iniquity" who'd attacked Canterbury, by which he named the by now usual suspects: Henri and Simon de Montfort (junior), Leybourne, Clifford, Giffard, LeStrange, Vaux, Hastings and Segrave - all acting on behalf of Simon de Montfort. With these attacks Montfort had clearly declared war upon the Savoyards in England - a Frenchman declaring war upon other aliens in the name of "England for the English."[126] As the xenophobia whipped up by Montfort took hold, he was now demanding that aliens not only be excluded from office, but leave the kingdom never to return, Henry ensconced in the Tower sought to protect those vulnerable in his care. Accordingly on 28th June he sent Marguerite, the widow of the Earl of Devon, a daughter of the late Thomas II de Savoie and so Pierre's niece, along with other foreign women, with his son Edmund and the faithful John Mansel to the safety of Dover. From there they sailed for Wissant, poor Mansel was not to see his homeland again.[127] Not all the Savoyards fled the kingdom. Henry's loyal steward Pierre de Champvent was appointed Keeper of the King's Arms.

Henry was now minded to concede, but Alianor was made of sterner stuff and on 13 July attempted to make for Windsor downriver. Royal historian Lisa Hilton writes: "She was mobbed on London Bridge by a howling, jostling crowd who pelted her with rubbish and pursued her, jeering, back to the Tower."[128] Baker goes further suggesting that the word "whore" was used toward Alianor.[129] The indignity of being pelted with rubbish by Londoners was something the refined queen from Provence would not forgive these peasants. Nor forgive did Lord Edward upon hearing of the treatment of his mother at the rabble's hands. Nor, it seems, did her sister Marguerite and her husband Louis – one simply didn't treat an anointed queen in this way. Thus, the baronial party permanently alienated the royal family not only in England but in France too. However, for the time being, Simon's strong position meant that, holed up in the Tower, Henry had to again accede to Simon's terms – which he did so on 15 July 1263 – fettered once more.

The peace, declared on 16 July 1263, reaffirmed the Provisions of Oxford. Henry's kingship was back in chains. But the baronial council was not the same baronial council to which he'd submitted at Oxford: this was much more the creature of Simon de Montfort. Notably absent was the new Count of Savoy, Pierre II. Simon de Montfort now styled himself Steward, and not the variety that waited upon tables, of the Kingdom. He appointed his own men to key positions, and ensured castles were held by his own castellans. Hugh Despenser was back as Justiciar, Robert Walerand and Ebal II de Mont were removed from Henry's service and replaced by the Montfortians John de la Haye and Roger Leybourne. The new council was radically different from the previous council, just 4 members of the original council remained alive or allied with Montfort - the revolution like many since was eating its own. Henry, Alianor, Edward and Edmund crossed to Boulogne, there to be met by their Savoyard kin, Pierre and Boniface de Savoie along with the now exiled John Mansel, notably Simon de Montfort travelled to Boulogne separately. The first Montfortian council released Savoyard Bishop of Hereford, Pierre d'Aigueblanche, from his captivity – but not before pardons for the barons involved. The Earl of Leicester, the title no longer grand enough for him, was now the de facto ruler of England.

What we now see being proclaimed are the Statute of Aliens of 1263, that some contemporary writers, including Burton, Tewkesbury and Guisborough, mistakenly thought had been a part of the Provisions of Oxford five years earlier. What Carpenter recently termed a policy of "England for the English".[130] The letter patent issued from Westminster of 16 July 1263, and witnessed by Richard, King of the Romans, added that aliens should leave the realm at the earlier request that the kingdom be governed solely by natives. It said:

> That the realm should henceforth be governed by natives, faithful and useful, under the king. and aliens should go forth never to return, except those whom the faithful men of the realm in common will accept.[131]

For the Savoyard too now, as well as the Lusignans, the writing was on the wall: England was closing its doors to "aliens" who should now "go forth never to return", issued in irony of ironies, and to the shame of hypocrisy, by Simon de Montfort, a Frenchman in England. The Dunstable annalist declared that "*Angliam ab alienigenis ex toto mundarent*" or that "England would be totally cleansed of foreigners".[132] With Edward's aliens departed, his former friends Roger de Clifford and company returned to the Edwardian camp that autumn. Such were the shifting alliances. It's not difficult to see in these times echoes of our own uneasy relationship with the continent of Europe.

Biographer of Henry, Baker, writes of the climate within England at the time, comparing it to our own post-Brexit time:

> Whether the English in the mid-thirteenth century hated all foreigners is doubtful, but certainly Matthew Paris, the chronicler who dominates the narrative of the reign of Henry III down to 1259, despised them and was keen to tell his readers what characteristics made Poitevins, Savoyards, Provençals, Flemings, Greeks, Romans, the French, the Welsh and anyone else who came into his sights so loathsome, and in doing so, Matthew captured something of the age. The Sicilian Business, the behaviour of the king's half-brothers, the Lusignans, and the actions of the pope and his representatives pushed the English elite, and, it seems likely, a goodly portion of the county communities of the kingdom, into a Brexit mindset, one which began to see foreigners as the root of the problems that faced the realm.[133]

This comparison to Brexit mentality doesn't seem so fanciful to me; after all, the ill feeling toward foreigners in the thirteenth century came at a time when the English elite and nobility were coming to terms with the loss of lands in France – coming to terms with a realignment of the realm. Whereas it might be argued that Brexit was in part the result of a similar coming to terms with a realignment of the country's place in the world. Certainly, being a foreigner in England was less than comfortable during either period. Baker tells us of the spread of xenophobia:

> The Montfortians originally wanted only the Savoyards and foreign mercenaries out, but discovered that the common people, in joining the

uprising, were venting their frustrations and resentment against Italian clerks, French money-lenders, Flemish merchants, and basically anyone in their neighbourhood who couldn't speak English.[134]

The Pershore continuation of the Flores Historiarum struck a familiar tone that some will imagine they're familiar with in more recent times, he wrote:

> "For whoever did not know how to speak the English language was despised by the common people and held in contempt."[135]

The Waverley annalist, living not but a few miles from Pierre de Savoie's Witley fief, confirms the conflation of Lusignan and Savoyard as:

> Foreigners of different languages [who] had already multiplied in England for many years, and had been enriched with so many incomes, lands, towns, and other resources, that they had the greatest contempt for the English, as if they were their inferiors. It was said by some who knew their secrets, that if their power should proceed, they would extinguish all the nobles of England by poison, and deprive King Henry of his kingdom, and in his place set up another at their discretion, and thus in the end subjugate the whole of England to their dominion for ever.[136]

It seems a sadly recurring truism of history, and particularly of English history, that at times of identity crisis, tolerance and acceptance of foreigners is the first thing to be jettisoned. Farther than England, American readers might well recognise the England First and Make England Great Again slogans of the day – and all recognise the irony that channelling this feeling was one Frenchman, Simon de Montfort. We might even go so far as to say that Simon de Montfort was in effect, if not in intention, the prototype "populist". For the Savoyard Hilton suggests that their power within England had been, perhaps too narrowly focused, built largely around their relationship with King Henry and especially Queen Alianor. She writes, "beyond the Savoyard network Alianor had very little contact with even high-ranking English people."[137] We cannot be sure of the level of genuine xenophobia within England in the mid-thirteenth century, as Matthew Paris didn't speak for everyone, and certainly the prosperity of much of the temporal and spiritual elite rested upon England's place in Europe, but perhaps it's possible to discern a wider non-elite disquiet with what they saw as foreign influence. It's tempting again to read the thirteenth century through the eyes of our own times, a temptation we should perhaps resist taking too far – but I think we can safely say there was considerable ill-feeling toward foreigners, as Carpenter wrote "what unified the English was a hatred of foreigners".[138] For the Savoyards the summer of 1263 marked a low point in their power and influence within England: the queen pelted with rubbish in her own capital, and Pierre and Boniface forced to flee the kingdom.[139] But, the traditional notion that Pierre de Savoie "withdrew from England" due to the increasingly xenophobic climate is a little misleading, as news from Savoy would in any case have pulled him back to the Alps to take on new and greater responsibilities. It is only with Anglocentric eyes that we see his withdrawal from England as "fleeing the kingdom"; in truth he left to take up the reins of something of far greater importance to the House of Savoy: Savoy itself.

Chapter Eight

The summer of 1263 would have one more transforming effect for Pierre de Savoie. As his English world fell into chaos, events "back home" would catapult him into a newly dominant position: at the tender age of just 18, Count Boniface de Savoie died. There is no evidence of how Boniface died. He last appears in archival records in September 1262 receiving the homage of Count Raoul de Genève. On 8 June 1263 Pierre de Savoie was not using the title Count of Savoy; however, three days later he was first recorded as receiving homage as Count Pierre II de Savoie, on 11 June 1263. Pierre's accession violated the will of his deceased brother Amédée IV, in that the County should have passed to the children of his other deceased brother, Thomas. However, they were still minors, and following no objection from Thomas's widow, Béatrice de Fieschi, the obviously stronger claim by Pierre was accepted. French historians have long noted that *"la primogéniture"* had not been *"régulièrement observée"*.[140] Was there a usurpation of comital title? The sons of Boniface's late regent, Thomas, Amédée and Louis, were indeed both children in 1263. Subsequent wills and testaments show that Pierre left the County to his childless brother Philippe, who in turn left the decision as to whether the now adult Amédée and Louis should be Count to his niece Alianor de Provence and her son King Edward I of England. Pierre, as we shall see, attempted to bequeath lands in England to the two sons of his brother Thomas. In the event, Amédée and Louis did indeed spend much time in England, becoming household knights of King Edward I. It looks likely then that Pierre's assumption of the comital title was with the agreement of his brothers Philippe and Archbishop Boniface, pragmatically providing a future pathway for either Amédée or Louis to become Count upon their maturity. Indeed, history records that Amédée V would become one of the great Counts of Savoy from 1285, the only one to be termed *Le Grand*. His brother Louis would inherit much of Pierre's legacy in Vaud, as Baron de Vaud, known to history as Louis de Vaud. So, with hindsight the provisions of 1263 and subsequent wills and testaments look prudent and indeed wise.

Pierre de Savoie, now Count Pierre II de Savoie, was now the third of Thomas I's sons to become Count of Savoy and Marquis of Italy. Pierre came to be Count, an established and rich man of some 60 years. He began to gradually disengage from English affairs that had, to the chagrin of Matthew Paris, brought him fame and fortune. Pierre was never meant to be the Count of Savoy; he was most likely the sixth son of his father, and his nephew, Count Boniface, was a strong, virile 18-year-old, and yet in June 1263 the de facto Earl of Richmond, "the Englishman", found himself Count of Savoy.

In Savoy Pierre took as his preferred residence the imposing castle at Chillon, built on a small island on Lac Léman between Vevey and Villeneuve (see Fig. 1.3). The name itself comes from the Vaudois dialect word for flat stone or platform, upon which the castle is built. An 1195 document called the castle *"Castrum Quilonis"*. The site had been fortified by the Romans as it commanded the road along the lakeside as it ran from the Grand-Saint-Bernard Pass toward Lausanne. Essentially you cannot make your way from Italy via the pass and the valley of the Rhône to Northern Europe without passing within a crossbow shot of its walls. The oldest records of a castle on the site date to 1005, when it was in the care of the Bishop of Sion, but it had already come into Savoyard hands long before Pierre became Count, likely by 1150. The castle featured a strong but square central *donjon* but its walls, which fell sheer to the lake, were in need of work. The defences on the landward side had been strengthened. De Raemy writes that the semi-circular flanking towers were the work of Amédée IV in 1233. Pierre undertook further works between 1260 and 1265, including the newly constructed semi-circular tower (1260–5) at Chillon with similar battlements as those of Yverdon.[141] The use of circular or semi-circular D-shaped towers came to Europe from the Levant in light of battle experience in the crusades. But it would be the windows, from the time of Pierre's works, that would provide a pointer to Arnold Taylor of the Savoyard origins of the castles later built for King Edward I in North Wales. Taylor pointed to the windows later built at Harlech which so closely resemble those built for Pierre at Chillon that he suggested they came from the same pattern book.[142] So, in the works of Pierre at Chillon we find the first traces of the legacy that the Count would bequeath to England and in particular the prince he'd long protected.

The extensive building by Pierre before and after his succession as Count in 1263 are evidence of the need to constrain his main opponent to his east – the Bishop of Sion. There had been a bishopric at Sion since 380 AD in the dog days of the Roman Empire, the first being Theodore – Saint Theodore. It was he who'd discovered the tomb of Saint-Maurice, as mentioned earlier, the patron Saint of Savoy. By the thirteenth century a town astride the *Via Francigena,* that by treaty was fief of the King of England. By the mid-1260s the bishop was Henri de Rarogne, having come to the episcopacy in 1243. As the Bishop held temporal as well as spiritual dominion in the Valais, he was a Prince-Bishop, owing allegiance to both Pope and Holy Roman Emperor – but chiefly himself. The bishopric had had temporal power in the Valais since being granted such by the last King of Burgundy back in 999. This joint spiritual and temporal power would be the source of conflict with the Counts of Savoy in the thirteenth century. Whilst their spiritual power ran throughout the whole of the Rhône Valley above Lac Léman, their temporal power ended in a moving line variously between Conthey, Saillon and Martigny. This lack of temporal power in the western part of Valais was something various bishops tried to change, and the Savoyard resisted.

Accordingly, new Savoyard castles or towers had also been built recently at Conthey and Brignon (1257–8), Saillon (1261) and would be at Martigny (1265). Brignon and Conthey were virtually on either side of the bishop's front door. The castles were a serious provocation to the Bishop of Sion and the people of the Upper Valais. Interestingly, the border between the Upper and Lower Valais still runs where Pierre drew it at Conthey. Saillon's town walls wandering up the hillside had first piqued Arnold Taylor's interests in Savoy, reminding him of Conwy in North Wales. And reminded him with good reason as Savoyard mason Jean Francis, who would later move to Wales with Maître Jacques de Saint-Georges, before building the town walls of Conwy, was involved in the construction of Conthey, Brignon and Saillon. At the latter we know that he was not only paid for his work in raising the tower seventy feet into the air, but was additionally paid by Pierre with two robes.[143] The attribution of his work at Brignon is by association, and accepted as a Mainer–Mézos–Francis combination by Blondel.[144] The small town of Saillon is located on the north bank of the Rhône Valley, just eight miles upstream from Martigny and an ideal location to police the Bishop of Sion. The small town was walled itself; in addition to the tower, work allocated by Gascon mason Jean de Mésoz,[145] was to "settle the form of the tower".[146] Before there would be a Savoyard mason in the service of the English king there would be a mason in the service of the English king who would then serve the Count of Savoy – his name was Jean de Mésoz, the engineer we met earlier in Gascony with Henry at Benauges in 1253.

Mésoz had previously held the title of *magistri ingeniatorum* for King Henry III, working in the Plantaganet territory of Gascony. He was the more senior of the *ingeniators*[147] involved in the siege of Benauges in 1253,[148] working alongside Master Bertram with the two mangonels hurling rocks at the castle of Benauges[149] that was later given to Savoyard Jean de Grailly. His

Chapter Eight

work for Henry, encamped at Loupiac,[150] laying siege to the Gascon rebels, saw him ennobled at Bordeaux, in 1254, by the English king and he is referred to thereafter as *dominus*.[151] Whilst in Gascony he worked alongside fellow Gascon and engineer Master Bertram, who would later work with Maître Jacques in North Wales. Also, at Benauges he would have met Ebal II de Mont who was a Savoyard steward of Henry's. In 1254 Ebal was given charge of Benauges,[152] before returning to England by way of Paris where he was allotted the task of acquiring "*objets précieux*" for Edward to be offered at the Shrine of Saint Edward in Westminster.[153] Indeed, Blondel identified over ninety "*représentants de familles nobles*" of "*Savoie, du Genevois, de la Tarentaise, du Bugey, de la Franche-Comte, du Pays de Vaud ... et du Val d'Aoste*" amongst Henry's army in the Gascon Rolls, knighting amongst others Jean de Châtillon, Reynaud d'Orbe, Jean Grossi and Guillaume de Pesmes.[154] Mésoz would later build a castle for the *Famille de Mont* at Rolle by the shores of Lac Leman. He is first known to have moved to the employ of Pierre de Savoie in 1261.[155] It's possible that reference to "masters" coming from beyond the Jura to repair dykes on the Rhône in the Chablais may refer to Mésoz amongst others;[156] however, to remove any doubt the castellan at Chillon then recorded:

> The expenses of Jean de Mésoz when he was at Saillon for the tower of Saillon. Six sol eight den. Those whom he considers at Saillon.[157]

And later the castellan at Saillon recorded:

> The expenses of Jean de Mésoz to oversee the siting of the tower for three days Six sol six den.[158]

Later in 1266–7 we first find Jean de Mésoz working alongside Maître Jacques at Yverdon:

> The expenses of Jean de Mésoz at Yverdon whilst sick for twenty-eight days, by command of his Lord, six *livre* 12 *den* ... in the acquittance (discharge of a debt) of Master James the mason for this year and the year before that ... he James has the fee of Yverdon, ten livres Vienne every year. xv. *Lib*.[159]

The key to understanding Jean de Mésoz's role at Saillon is the "*supervidendum*". By the thirteenth century this was often written as "*supervis*", from which the English word supervise originates, and the French *superviser*. Medieval Latin took the word from *super*, meaning "over", and *videre*, meaning "to see". Day-to-day construction at Saillon was assigned to a *Magister Franciscus cementarius*, or Francis, Master Mason. As we saw earlier, some Swiss sources continue to misattribute the nineteen-metres-high tower *donjon* to Pierre Mainier, misunderstanding the difference between one who builds and one who pays the bills.[160]

If sadly Conthey is almost no longer with us, Saillon, at least, remains to this day a delightfully medieval island, possessed of peace, charm and idyll and its Bayart Tower a landmark (see Fig. 2.2). Jean de Mésoz would be a key castle-building influence in Savoy, bringing with him Anglo-Norman building styles allied to new styles from Outremer. It would be this blending of the architectural heritage of England and Gascony with the lessons learned on crusade that would influence the building style of the young Maître Jacques. As we have seen, Mésoz was working alongside Jacques from his first project at Yverdon. The seniority between Mésoz and Jacques is most obviously shown by Mésoz's knightly status, but also by the Savoyard archives for the digging of a well at the Château de Melphe at Salins-Les-Thermes in the Tarentaise Valley in 1267–8. The castle, newly acquired by the County of Savoy, guarded the long valley that winds its way towards the strategic Petit-Saint-Bernard Pass and access to the Aosta Valley and Italy. Jean de Mésoz is described as "giving directions" for works including those of Mâitre Jacques.[161] The fruits of Měsoz's mentoring of a young Maître Jacques de Saint-Georges would be felt during Edward's reign in the castles of north Wales – that Pierre brought Mésoz to Savoy setting in motion a chain of consequences that would lead ultimately to Caernarfon is perhaps Pierre's longest lasting legacy in Britain.

The last of the build in Savoy, at Martigny, guarded the entrance to the Grand-Saint-Bernard as it meets the valley of the Rhône. Martigny had also a long past: Gaulish Octodurus had first been conquered by the 5th Legion of the Roman Republic back in 57 BC becoming Roman Forum Claudii Augusti, later renamed Forum Claudii Vallensium – it remained an obvious place too for fortifications. The castle at Martigny, the château de la Bâtiaz, sat high above the town on a suitably rocky outcrop, affording perfect views not only toward the entrance to the Grand-Saint-Bernard but also down the Rhône Valley and Sion – another perfect castle site.

New military building work was also undertaken at Romont (1260), guarding the approach to Lausanne from the north. It too had long been a Savoyard power base – the *Petit Charlemagne* was digging in.[162] Back in 1240 Pierre had sent a castellan to Romont to build a castle and found a village. The Peace of Evian in 1244 had confirmed the Savoyard rights to Romont. The main castle (*Grand Donjon*), with a typical Savoy square floor plan, had been completed much before 1260. The further military work was a second castle with a round tower, formerly known as the *Petit Donjon* but now known as *La tour à Boyer* which may have been built around 1250–60. There is some doubt as to the precise age; Taylor suggested perhaps even 1274–5,[163] and we do have an archival mention for Maître Jacques for Romont in 1275. Further primary source evidence for 1274–5 is provided by an entry in the accounts of the castellan for Romont:

> The same considered to Peter Uldrici the carpenter and his companions who went to Romont for the works of the Lord, for the expenses of their own, with one packhorse who was carrying for ease ... Twenty-five *sol*.[164]

Perhaps works were begun in the earlier period, and modified later.

Jean de Mésoz, *ingénieur*, may well have been responsible for another castle built by Lac Léman, but this time not for the Count of Savoy – at Rolle. The *Castrum de Ruello* was built by the Lords of Mont to rival Saint-Prex and Aubonne. It was built for Ebal III de Mont, the son of Henri de Mont, the eldest brother of Ebal II de Mont, who had left for England with Pierre II de Savoie, there to become a loyal servant of King Henry and eventually Constable of Windsor Castle. Rolle Castle, meanwhile, eventually taken over by the Savoyard, had the newly fashionable round towers. Furthermore, whereas Saint-Prex and Les Clées would, for example, have square towers, those at Yverdon, Saillon and Rolle, begun after 1259–60 and the arrival of Jean de Mésoz, would be round.

We say 'believed' for Jean de Mésoz and his building of Rolle, because the building records are likely to have perished in 1802 when Vaudois peasants burned papers in connection with the French Revolution. Similarly, peasants stormed La Sarraz, Champvent, Yverdon, Grandson and many more, extinguishing much that would have been useful to twenty-first-

Chapter Eight

century historians. We are lucky that much of the records kept by the Count of Savoy had by this time reached Turin and relative safety. English architectural historian Nicola Coldstream has queried the origins of Maître Jacques' building and design skills, looking for sources in England.[165] The true origin of his ability to construct in stone would be his father, Maître Jean, to whom he was apprenticed at Yverdon from 1261, and later Jean de Mésoz. The essential skills of construction would no doubt have passed from the father, but the finer points of more advanced castle architecture, emanating from the Anglo-French world, and possibly *outremer* and Armenia before that, came most likely via the Gascon Jean de Mésoz.

There is one other in this Anglo-Gascon Savoyard milieu we ought to briefly mention, if only to illustrate the connectedness of this triangle. Master Arnaud was a clerk who held a senior position within Pierre de Savoie's court in Savoy and is mentioned in connection with multiple building works including at Chillon.[166] It should be of little surprise that he'd previously been in the employ of Pierre's niece, Béatrice de Savoie, the Countess of Provence (mother to Queen Alianor de Provence and hence mother-in-law of Henry III). Furthermore, it then should come as little surprise that, like Jean de Mézos, he'd previously been employed by the English Crown in Gascony.[167] He's first mentioned in Savoyard accounts at Chambéry in December 1254,[168] and so we can safely conclude that both Master Arnaud and Jean de Mézos accompanied Pierre from Gascony to Savoy in November 1254 following their exploits there. Students of castle history in both the Alpine region and in England should not overlook the triangle thus formed whereby these artisans would travel from Gascony to Savoy, Master Bertram would travel from Gascony to England, and lastly Master James of Saint-George, Jean Francis and many others would travel from Savoy to England.[169]

Meanwhile, in England, the realm was engulfed in what the pope called "a boisterous fluctuation of the storm" spiralling ever downward to a civil war that would establish who ruled: King Henry III or Simon de Montfort.[170]

Chapter Nine

Pierre meanwhile, as the tide of affairs in England ebbed between peace and war, had as the new Count of Savoy new responsibilities. July 1263 found him in Aosta attending to judicial and administrative affairs, in addition to the purchase of *peages* or tolls at the Grand- and Petit-Saint-Bernard passes. Perhaps the ever-astute Savoyard was setting matters to rights at home before he could return to English affairs, certainly the view held by Cox.[1] From Aosta he'd moved on to Faucigny and then Bugey, where at Saint-Rambert in the orchard beneath Pierre's castle, Rudolph de Genève paid homage to him for various assorted fiefs.[2] By September 1263, in Vaud, the new Count of Savoy had completed his tour of the county. As the leaves lost their colour and fell, he made his way northward once more to England and perhaps a reckoning with Montfort.

By the autumn the political climate in England was swinging once more toward Henry and thus Pierre. An offer to arbitrate between the warring factions came from King Louis IX of France. In September 1263 the royal party: Henry, Alianor, Edward and Edmund sailed for Boulogne there to be met by their Savoyard kin Pierre and Boniface de Savoie along with the exiled John Mansel. Boulogne had been agreed as the meeting point as the council didn't trust letting Henry travel to far from England. In October Henry returned to England with Pierre de Savoie, Alianor and Edmund remained in France with Boniface now threatening excommunication on Montfort and his supporters. The Lord Edward began to rally some baronial support to the royalist cause including Jean de Warenne, Roger and Hugh Bigod, Guillaume de Valence, and Roger de Mortimer. At Oxford Edward brought Richard's son Henri d'Almain back to the royalist side. Lines were being drawn, the country heading once more for civil war. Henry (and as he'd returned to England with Henry we must assume Pierre) escaped the Montfortians and joined Edward[3] at Windsor[4] . It is difficult to ascertain Pierre's involvement in the tension that beset England in the autumn of 1263, he appears to have spent some time also at Berkhamsted with Richard - his counsel to Henry and Richard has not survived, it is in any case likely to have been entirely private. But then a truce , and an appeal once more to Louis. Following an inconclusive parliament in England the matter was referred back to Louis for arbitration. Pierre's involvement in the recourse to arbitration will remain unknown, perhaps he advised in its favour, suggesting Henry should put his faith in Marguerite's influence upon her husband. What we do know is that Pierre left England, this time for sure for the last time to join the royal party in Amiens.

Before we pass to Louis' arbitration, the Mise of Amiens, we must pause to reflect upon the afore mentioned move of Jean de Warenne, Earl of Surrey back to the royalist cause. During his minority he had come to resent the control exerted by Pierre de Savoie and the preferment in general of the Savoyards. Accordingly he had been very much a part of the Montfortian party up to this point. Accordingly on 7 August Montfort, in the king's name, had ordered that the castle at Pevensey be granted to Warenne and taken from Pierre, very much the object of Warenne's support for Montfort. However, and within days, the Lord Edward

Chapter Nine

trumped this by offering Warenne Stamford and Grantham, lands that had belonged to his father. Thus when the royalist party regained the ascendancy during the autumn Henry was able to order that Pevensey remained with Pierre who in turn entrusted the castle to the Lord Edward. That Pevensey remained in the hands of the now Count of Savoy would become critical the next year[5]. On the same day that Pevensey was entrusted with the Lord Edward, 25 October, Henry enjoined Pierre to prevail upon his niece, Marguerite, Queen of France to prevail upon her husband to release funds due as part of the 1259 Treaty of Paris. Those involved in the attempts to bolster Henry's funds reveal the usual Savoyard suspects: Pierre de Savoie, Pierre d'Aigueblanche, Marguerite de Provence and her mother, Pierre's sister Beatrice de Savoie, along with as always John Mansel.[6]

Remarkably, both sides of the dispute made it known that they would abide by the result of Louis' intervention, Montfort no doubt feeling that a fellow Frenchmen who'd appeared to side with him during the Boulogne meeting the previous September would find in his favour. However, Montfort was reckoning without the power and influence of the Savoyards, so recently having fled the kingdom. The earl seems to have missed or underestimated a simple fact: Louis was married to Marguerite de Provence, Marguerite's sister was Alianor de Provence, Henry's wife and queen. In simple terms he hadn't accounted for the possibility that familial ties would trump politics. Montfort's confidence in Louis does appear a little puzzling, but along with his experience of the autumn of 1263 we can set simply that, like his father, Montfort was a religious zealot even in an age of religious certainty, he simply could not entertain the idea that the pious Louis could find against the "holy" Provisons of Oxford. Henry would travel to France, it seems, safe in the knowledge that his brother-in-law would find in his favour.[7]

So, in early January 1264, the parties met at Amiens, in northern France, to undergo Louis' arbitration. Pierre d'Aigueblanche crossed with Henry to France, and Savoyard Ebal II de Mont stood as witness for Henry that he would abide by the arbitration. Simon de Montfort was represented by his son Henri, since on leaving Kenilworth for. Amiens, Simon had fallen from his horse and broken his leg - it was not a good omen for the Montfortian party. Sure enough, on 23 January 1264, having reputedly influenced matters, Pierre d'Aigueblanche was amongst those witnessing the judgement of King Louis IV of France, in what became known as the *Mise d'Amiens*, the Settlement of Amiens:

> In the name of the Father, Son and Holy Ghost, by our award or ordinance we quash and annul all the aforesaid provisions, ordinances and obligations by whatever name they are called, and whatever followed from them or was caused by them, especially since it is clear that His Highness the Pope has in writing declared them quashed and void.
>
> We ordain that the said king and the barons and everyone else who agreed to the present compromissum, and in any way bound themselves to abide by the aforesaid, shall wholeheartedly release and absolve themselves of the same.

This absolved Pierre of his involvement in the Provisions of Oxford. Louis, specifically on the matter of aliens, foreigners, be they Poitevin or Savoyard, then said:

> We decree by our award that the foreign-born should be allowed to stay safely in the said kingdom and that the king be allowed to call English and

foreign-born safely to his council, whoever seem useful and faithful to him, as he was able to do before the aforesaid time.

Before going on to confirm his view of medieval kingship:

> We also award and ordain that the said king shall have full power and free authority in his kingdom and over everything that pertains to it; and he shall have the same status and amplitude of power in every way and over everything, just as he did before the aforesaid time.

Louis also qualified the term "full power and free authority". The *Mise d'Amiens* was not to be a revocation of the *Magna Carta*:

> But we do not wish nor do we intend by the present ordinance to derogate in any way from the royal privileges, charters, liberties, statutes and praiseworthy customary laws of the kingdom of England which existed before the time of those provisions.[8]

In the end an anointed king had sided with an anointed king, but as Church notes in his biography of Henry, "It was a comprehensive victory which had undoubtedly been won for Henry by his wife and her supporters."[9] The Savoyard Queen of England had overturned the Provisions of Oxford through her sister and brother-in-laws' good offices. It is perhaps just as well Matthew Paris had died five years earlier, although perhaps all could hear him revolving swiftly in his grave from Amiens. But if Paris was no longer around to condemn Alianor, then the continuer of his chronicle, William Rishanger, did not hold back, writing that Louis had been "seduced, deceived and beguiled by the serpent-like fraud and speech of a woman, that is the Queen of England".[10] Rishanger resorting to misogynistic fury that Louis might listen to his sister-in-law (and his own wife) over the blessed Simon.

Unsurprisingly, the judgement was not accepted by Simon de Montfort or the ruling baronial council – war followed. Before the war began however, Montfort made one last show of peace, he offered to accept Louis' judgement with one primary exception, that foreigners be excluded from the realm. So this is what it had all been about really an attack on not just the Lusignans at court but the Savoyards too, a demand without a hint of irony from a Frenchman living in England.[11] Such a proviso was obviously a non-starter and accordingly King Henry III raised his royal standard at Oxford on 3 April 1264, sending messengers to all parts of the kingdom summoning the feudal host. Once an army had been assembled, he marched toward the Montfortian heartlands of the Midlands.

Pierre and Boniface remained in France with Alianor: this was a quarrel that Englishman was going to have to resolve with Englishman. Before he left for England, Henry had written from Amiens to Guichard de Charron, Pierre's bailiff at Richmond, and John de la Rede at Pevensey, ordering them to forward Pierre's revenues without delay.[12] Henry also asked Alianor and Pierre, along with John Mansel, to go to the Temple in Paris and take possession of the Crown Jewels on deposit there and also monies owed by Louis to Henry.[13] It was obviously a time of gathering one's resources to one's self. The climate of antagonism of 1264 can be seen from the ongoing struggles of Pierre d'Aigueblanche in Hereford with Montfortians, as Barrow colourfully relates:

Chapter Nine

In 1264 Peter's marshal, with a small private army, attacked villages around Hereford to threaten Montfortian supporters in the town. Peter's absences from England did not mean that he was in any way neglectful of his responsibilities there. He simply sent the lads round to sort things out.[14]

Meanwhile, on the national level, Henry began to try to "sort things out" too. Following his raising of the royal standard at Oxford on 3 April 1264, along with Edward and Richard he marched toward Northampton and Simon de Montfort the younger, laying siege to the town on 5 April. The Midlands were of key strategic importance and a Montfortian heartland. Whilst the townspeople were generally Montfortian, the monks of St. Andrews Priory were not, and Prior Guy, apparently a Poitevin, may have been instrumental in the royalists making a breach of the town's walls. Montfort the younger attempted to stem the breach, but managed to fall into a ditch and was taken for ransom. The first military action of the war went to Henry as a day later the castle at Northampton was taken back. Henry then took Montfort's Earldom of Leicester unopposed and then Nottingham too. Meanwhile, Simon de Montfort had left London at the head of a relief column, only to turn back at St. Albans, hearing of a Jewish plot to hand London to Henry. The Montfortians took out their sense of betrayal on London's Jewish community and in so doing no doubt removed all traces of debts they'd owed them.[15] It is difficult to say other than the cold blooded murder of over 500 Jews is a war-crime to be solely attributed to Simon de Montfort. We can mitigate his actions by suggesting that he was a man of the thirteenth-century and that others of his day were equally guilty of such pogroms, nonetheless murder is murder. Montfort had expelled the Jewry of Leicester and now vented his wrath on the Jewry of London, this was entirely consistent with his fathers' actions in southern France against the Cathars.

To draw Henry south, Montfort marched, not northward, but southward to the royalist castle at Rochester where he laid siege from 17 April. Montfort, joined by Gilbert de Clare managed to take the town and thence the castle bailey, but the giant donjon or keep which dominates the scene to this day and had earlier defied King John held out. The challenge could not go unanswered so the king and his army marched south and by 26 April his army were at Aylesbury, just a day's ride from London. Rochester would not fall, but now the two armies began to circle one another. Henry took the castles of Kingston and Tonbridge from the then Montfortian Earl of Gloucester on 27 and 30 April. Henry then made south for the Cinque Ports, there to corral the necessary shipping to take London. On 3 May Henry was at Battle Abbey, scene of the coming of his ancestors to England three centuries earlier. On 6 May Simon de Montfort left London once more, heading south to seek a deciding battle. Thus far Edward acting for Henry had taken Northampton, Leicester, Nottingham, Kingston and Tonbridge from the Montfortians, whereas Montfort had failed in his attempt to take Rochester - now it was time for the renowned martial ability of the Earl of Leicester to teach the young Prince a lesson or two.

The two sides met on the downs above the Sussex town of Lewes on 14 May 1264. Battle was a rare event in the thirteenth century, combat restricted largely to the mock combat of the tournament. Warfare itself, when it did occur, was mostly by besieging an opponent's castle long enough for his food and water to be depleted and a suit of peace requested. A pitched battle, each side having at the other in an open field, was unusual – it was dangerous to the men of power, and worse, its outcome unpredictable. In the days before effective battlefield communication, battle was little more than an uncoordinated mêlée in which much blood was spilled. Therefore, to risk battle, both sides had to be confident of the outcome. Henry was no warrior, still less a leader of men, so we can assume his confidence in victory lay in the numbers at his disposal. For Simon's part he'd seen Henry's lack of martial ability up close in France and was no doubt confident in his own abilities to overcome his deficit in numbers. Baker reminds us that there had not been a battle in England before Lewes, since that at Lincoln in 1217 – nearly fifty years earlier.[16]

Alongside Henry that day were his brother, Richard, Earl of Cornwall and King of the Romans and the Lord Edward, his son – the latter would win his spurs that day. The divided loyalties were best shown by the different sides chosen by two Marcher lords. Gilbert de Clare, Earl of Gloucester, had been knighted by Simon de Montfort a few days before the battle and fought for the rebels. Roger de Mortimer, meanwhile, fought bravely for the royalist army and would be wounded in the fight. Before the battle both sides swore to each other that they had God on their side, Henry of course because he was a king anointed by God, the Montfortians because they upheld the oaths, promises before God, taken in Oxford – the rebels going so far as to affix white crosses to their clothing. On the eve of battle, Walter de Cantilupe, Bishop of Worcester, blessed Montfort's army, elevating them to the status of crusaders. Both sides insisted they fought for the true interests of God, of his king and his realm. The chronicler Johannes Oxenedes gives us Montfort's preaching: "My beloved brothers, nobles and subjects, today we fight for the state of the kingdom of England, for the honour of God and the blessed Mary and of all the saints and the mother church, and we are united to observe our faith."[17] This was to be a battle for the soul of England.

Battle before the town of Lewes began early on the morning of 14 May 1264.[18] Henry commanded the left of his army, Richard the centre and Edward the right. With Edward that day was likely his loyal companion Othon de Grandson, both in their first battle together. If this is so, then it is also likely that with Edward and Othon that day was Jean de Grailly. Like Othon he had come to England with Pierre de Savoie, like Othon he would go on to give Edward long service – but also most importantly, as evidence for their involvement at Lewes, they would later be rewarded by Edward at the end of the baronial revolt. Perhaps at Lewes too was Edward's household knight, the Burgundian Guillaume de Pesmes; he'd been at Windsor the year before but thereafter we have no record of him, suggesting that he may have fallen on the field above Lewes.

In the meantime, the rebels held the high ground, standing along Offham Hill, the River Ouse to their left. The king's army amounted to some 9,000 men, a quarter of them mounted: the rebels could count around half their number. On the rebels' left were Londoners, the very men who'd had the temerity to pelt his mother with rubbish the year before. One can imagine a son's quest for vengeance at his mother's humiliation as Edward sat atop his horse that morning. The Rishanger chronicler writes that Edward was "thirsting like a stag for a spring of water for the blood of his enemies, the Londoners".[19] The royalists had the numbers, the Montfortians crucially the high ground.

Sure enough, at 5 o'clock the eager "stag" gave the order to advance, the Londoners in his sights. To the terrible sound of trumpets, the cry of "*Poignez!*" ("Spur on!") was heard as Edward's charge of armoured knights scattered the rabble of poorly armed men before him. Edward's blood was up as he chased the terrified militia beneath his slashing broadsword from the field.[20] It's very likely that Montfort had "deliberately baited" Edward with the Londoners, knowing that the son would seek to wreak retribution upon his mother's tormentors. If that was the plan then it worked wonderfully for Edward and his charging

Chapter Nine

knights were soon four miles from the battlefield. With Edward gone from the field, Montfort swung his remaining forces down Offham Hill, slamming into the royalist ranks. Henry's centre gave way and fled for the safety of Lewes. Its commander, the King of the Romans, hid in a windmill, Snelling's Mill.[21] This left only Henry in the field against Montfort; The Lewes chronicler wrote that Henry had two horses killed beneath him.[22] He took blow after blow from sword and mace.[23]

Henry, surrounded by his household knights, retreated to the priory as the fighting now spilled into the town of Lewes itself. Meanwhile, far from the battle, Edward had come across Simon de Montfort's baggage train, complete with Simon's coach he had used to travel around in. Of course, the train was sacked, the coach burned (complete with occupants). Only then after sating his revenge on the Londoners and the baggage train did Edward remember to return to the field of battle. When he did so, he returned to a battle lost[24] – it would be a bitter pill for Edward to swallow, and one somewhat of his own making, but a lesson learned.

By noon the battle was over. Edward had reached Henry only to be made a prisoner along with his father[25] in the priory, and Richard was still hiding in the windmill. Some 2,000 men died during the Battle of Lewes, mostly foot soldiers, a mismatch that would be repeated time and time again over the centuries by the "poor bloody infantry". There followed a ritual humiliation of the King of the Germans, as the "wicked miller"[26] of Lewes extricated himself from his refuge. Ironically, taken prisoner that day at Lewes along with Richard, Henry and Edward was none other than Robert de Brus, 5th Lord of Annandale – the grandfather of Robert the Bruce himself.[27]

A number of knights – the chronicler of Guisborough even talks of over 700 armed men – had, however, managed to flee the battle at the moment of royalist capitulation. They made their way through the town of Lewes and across Cliffe bridge over the Ouse, thence the seventeen miles (twenty-seven kilometres) to safe refuge. It's suggested that many drowned in the river, the bridge likely lacked a parapet.[28] They fled through "uproar on every side" and there was "looting, pillaging and catching the horses of the dead".[29] These were mostly men of Edward's, including Savoyards and Poitevins, also Jean de Warenne, 6th Earl of Surrey, Henry's half-brother Guillaume de Valence, 1st Earl of Pembroke and Henry's justicier, Hugh Bigod.[30] They made for the walls of Pierre de Savoie's Pevensey Castle, sitting astride its peninsula abutting the bay and safe harbour. Perhaps as they barred the gates behind them came the exhausted recriminations – most of them had followed Edward after the Londoners, cutting many down, but when they'd returned to Lewes, they'd found a battle lost. Now Edward and the king were prisoners, and soon might they be too, the only recourse was to get notice to Alianor, Pierre and Louis – perhaps something might yet be saved. Following a brief pause to leave a garrison, Warenne, Valence and Bigod took ship to France to spread news of the king's defeat to the queen, her brother-in-law the French king and of course to Pierre de Savoie whose castles were now besieged.[31] The very next day following the Battle of Lewes, on 15 May 1264, Montfort demanded the surrender of Pevensey by the defenders "as they love their bodies and all they hold in the realm".[32] On 8 July the request was made again of "Hanekin de Witsand, constable of the castle of Pevense, John de la Rede and Imbert de Montréal" to accompany "William Maufee" as the king, read Simon de Montfort, "understands that many enormities have been committed by them and others of the munition of that castle".[33] On 18 July the offer was renewed with the addition that "if peace be made with Peter de Sabaudia" then "the goods in it [the castle] shall be reserved for the said Peter".[34] No doubt the "said Peter" was happy that at least he could regain his possessions if not his castle. The once extensive Savoyard position in England was now reduced to a besieged peninsula in Sussex and a lonely castle outpost at Richmond in Yorkshire.

There also followed the inevitable peace treaty, the so-called *"misam Lewensem"* or Mise of Lewes.[35] The king was now back in Simon de Montfort's hands, foreign counsellors again banished and the Provisions of Oxford reinstated. The Mise no longer survives as it was soon overtaken by events, but in essence it confirmed the Provisions of Oxford, albeit subject to possible revision by arbitration, and perhaps French arbitration, though not by Louis.[36] The Lord Edward, as heir to the kingdom, and Henri d'Almayne, as heir to the king's brother, were to be held hostage by Montfort to ensure that, this time, both Henry and Richard would finally succumb to baronial council. A provisional government headed by Montfort, the Earl of Gloucester and Bishop of Chichester was established. In the absence of Archbishop of Canterbury, Boniface de Savoie, the Church coalesced around the Montfortian Bishop of Worcester, Walter de Cantilupe. A Parliament was called for June in which the future government of the kingdom would be settled upon – the settlement of which meant that once more Simon de Montfort was de facto ruler of England.

But in many ways, it was a Pyrrhic victory for Montfort: although he was in effect ruler, his government lacked legitimacy at home and abroad and as such remained fragile despite Lewes. Maddicott summed up the post-Lewes political landscape well, when he wrote:

> His defeat of the king at Lewes had given him no firm basis for his government; rather, it had made that government more difficult. A regime based merely upon coercion, upon the military victory of rebels in a civil war, was likely to be neither stable nor permanent, for it lacked both legitimacy and the consent of the defeated.[37]

The pro-Montfortian writer of the *Song of Lewes* both praised and condemned Edward, writing:

> Whereunto shall the noble Edward be compared? Perhaps he will be rightly called a leopard. If we divide the name, it becomes lion and pard; lion, because we saw that he was not slow to attack the strongest places fearing the onslaught of none, with the boldest valour making a raid amidst the castles ... A lion by pride and fierceness, he is by inconstancy and changeableness a pard, changing his word and promise, cloaking himself by pleasant speech. When he is in a strait he promises whatever you wish, but as soon as he has escaped he renounces his promise.[38]

The criticism of Edward comes from a pro-Montfortian viewpoint, a likely Franciscan prior, but nevertheless it has coloured our view of Edward to this day.

When Henry had returned to England to take up the fight for his crown, Queen Alianor had stayed in France. In June Pierre arranged with Louis for around £12,750 worth of the funds due under the Treaty of Paris to be made over to Alianor.[39] In August 1264 she'd moved from Paris to Boulogne after news reached her from Warenne of the defeat at Lewes. The Savoyard defence sprang immediately into action. Loyal Savoyard knights, Pierre de Champvent, Imbert de Montferrand, Ebal II de Mont and Jean de Grailly, were with Alianor across the Channel in Flanders.[40] Pierre and Alianor began to mobilise their available resources, first at Saint-Omer then Dam (today Damme) in Flanders. Pierre taking out loans with Italian merchants to aid his niece was referenced at Amiens on 6 August, at Saint-Omer on 17 August then Dam on 9 September.[41] Cross-Channel negotiations began with the victorious Montfortians, including, as we shall see, by a legate appointed by the pope. However, hope that they might bear fruit can be seen to have sharply declined as evidenced by documents in Pierre's name, the first of 17 August at Saint-Omer, then the documents in September at Dam. From Saint-Omer a letter sent by Pierre talked of the possibility of "peace" being "restored to England".[42] Whereas in September, from Dam, Pierre was rewriting his will and calling up a feudal host from Savoy.

Uncle and niece gathered an army to them with the purpose of rescuing the captive Henry and Edward. So, Pierre de Savoie, whose rewritten will gives us the names of the aforementioned knights as witnesses,[43] then called up a feudal host from Savoy to join them. Cox writes, "Pierre wrote to Master Arnaud in Savoy ordering him to contact the *baillis* of Savoy, Faucigny, the Pays de Vaud, and the Genevois and command them to dispatch to Flanders as many well-armed warriors as they could."[44] The source of the rewritten will and request for an army from Savoy gives us the likely assembly point for an invasion: the port of Dam in Flanders.[45]

In the thirteenth century Dam was the port for Bruges, and so very well known to English traders. Indeed, it would have been well known too to Pierre de Savoie as his brother Thomas had had a bailiff in the town to deal with aforesaid English traders, a cog in the wool trade shared between the two brothers we discussed earlier.[46] It was a relatively new town, having its origins in a storm surge of 1134 that required a transverse dyke to be created at the mouth of the Zwin, a dam. By the mid-thirteenth century a canal now linked Bruges with Dam, itself now a fishing port. Philippe Auguste had burned Dam to the ground in 1213 but the industrious merchants of Flanders had rebuilt extensively by 1264. The 1213 Battle of Dam had seen an English force under the command of William Longespée, Earl of Salisbury, raid Flanders whilst Philippe was laying siege to nearby Ghent. The English had captured hundreds of French ships and burned many more but the town had paid the price for the victory. Dam and Flanders were no strangers to armies of soldiers.

Whilst Pierre came to the aid of Alianor, the County of Savoy was entrusted to the care of her mother, the redoubtable Béatrice, who since her husband's death had repaired to Les Échelles, and to the Archbishop of Tarentaise, Rodolphe Grossi de Chatelard who'd earlier witnessed the Treaty of Paris for Pierre in 1259.[47] The Savoyard "*clerico domini*", Hugh de Voiron, was involved in raising the necessary finance.[48] A command of 30 September 1264 gives us the names of the nobility of Savoy involved with the potential invasion of England, and thanks to toponymic names we can know something of some of their origins. Traditionally, the army has been called an army of mercenaries, largely because we know so little of its make-up, save the words of English chroniclers who weren't there and often writing retrospectively. The chronicler Thomas Wykes called the army mercenaries "*Teutonicos, Kutarios, Avalenses, Bribantiones, Flandrenses, Normannos, Pictavenses, Wasconenses, Gallicos, et Burgundos*" and there may well have been paid soldiers from Germany, Brabant, Flanders, Normandy, Burgundy, etc. in their number but we can give a name to the Savoyards sent to Flanders by Master Arnaud and Simon de Verters following the feudal summons from Pierre.[49] The St. Albans chronicler was perhaps overlooked when in addition to writing of "*militum stipendiariorum*" or stipendiary knights, mercenaries in our parlance, he also wrote of "*nobilium*" and "*parentes et amici reginæ*", that is relatives and friends of the queen.[50] These relatives and friends of the queen amounted to a feudal muster from Savoy; these men were not mercenaries. The order of 30 September 1264 in Dam, Flanders is described as *"assignat stipendia debita nobilibus et militibus terrarum suarum, quos secum durerat in Flandriam"*, that is that it "assigns the payments due to the nobles and soldiers of his lands, whom he had endured with him in Flanders". The command is mostly to Master Arnaud and Simon de Verters, Pierre's loyal administrators in Savoy. For a full text of this important document see appendix.

There was Guillaume de Saint Laurent, who may be related to a Gerard de Saint Laurent who would later become a key household knight for Edward. They are thought to have come from the Lausanne district of that name. Others named as serving with Pierre in Flanders included Richard de la Balrae from the mountains near Chamonix, and Jourdan de Montagny from close by Pierre's acquisition of Yverdon in Vaud. Also, from the *Pays de Vaud* were Jacques d'Aubonne, a fief definitely acquired by Pierre only three years earlier, and Ferret de Cossonay. From the Pays de Gex came Humbert de Trelay, today's Trelex near Nyon. From the southern shores of Lac Léman came Guillaume d'Allinges, along with a knight and squire, of the castles in the Savoyard Chablais near Thonon; also Guillaume and Jean de Rovéréa of the castle near Yvoire (see figure 2.5). From the Pays de Gex came Pierre de Fernay, whose home would be renamed Fernay Voltaire in latter centuries for its association with the famous writer and philosopher. The Lords of Compeis of the Château de Thorens in the mountains above Lac Annecy sent the brothers Gérard and Pierre de Compeis – the family had links with Nantelme de Cholay and the Lords of Cholay around Geneva. Like many, they had come across their lands guarding the Usillon by way of the falling Second Kingdom of Burgundy and an award of land by the emperor. Originally vassals of the Counts of Geneva, they had more recently, like their neighbours from Faucigny, come into the Savoyard orbit. The regions surrounding Chambéry supplied Guillaume d'Arlod of Pierre's fief on the Rhône, and Guichard de Pontverre of the castle by Lovagny near Annecy. The road from Annecy to Aix sent the neighbours Guillaume de Grézieux of Grésy-sur-Aix and Gérard d'Arbiez of the Château d'Arbiez, now Alby-sur-Chéran. Bugey is likely to have sent Guillaume de Cornillon who is probably named for the Château de Cornillon at Saint-Rambert, Pierre's first castle. Pierre's wife's lands of Faucigny supplied Aymon de Saint Jeoire and Guillaume de Langins, amongst others. The brothers Guillaume and Jean de Ravorée were also from the Chablais adjacent to Faucigny, their feudal manor overlooking Lake Geneva between Yvoire and Excenevex.

Crossing the lake, from the lands to the north of Vaud came Raymond de Corbières, a vassal of Savoy since 1250, and in the lands by the Lac de la Gruyère, neighbours to Pierre's allies, the *Famille de Vuippens*. Others named included Guy d'Agenens, Richard de Saint-Martin, Jean de Berne, Aymon, Conon and Burcard de la Fontenai, Jean de Willayns and Jean de Cernens.[51] Noticeable when plotting these *"nobilibus et militibus"* on a map of Savoy (see figure 2.6) is that they all originate in the personal lands of Pierre de Savoie, from Vaud, Faucigny and Bugey: there are no nobles or knights from the Tarentaise or Maurienne – this is not so much an army of Savoy, but an army of Pierre de Savoie.

Amongst the witnesses of Pierre's will in Flanders was the clerical brother of Othon de Grandson, Gérard de Grandson. Othon would be a loyal servant of Edward throughout his reign; we know he was rewarded for service after the baronial war but we know nothing of his whereabouts, whether he was at the Battle of Lewes, or the siege of Pevensey or with the army in Flanders. Pierre worried that whilst away in Flanders and possibly England that his Alpine rivals might take advantage; accordingly, he ordered Master Arnaud in Savoy to place

Chapter Nine

the Valais on armed alert should the Bishop of Sion choose to take his soldiers westward again.[52] Nonetheless, and remarkably, the Count of Savoy was planning to invade England to rescue their nephew-in-law Henry and restore him to the throne and overthrow the rebels.

But this army would need ships to move it to England, more than the ships available in Flanders. Accordingly, on 24 July, Alianor wrote to Alphonse, Count of Poitiers – as the brother of Louis, Alphonse was her sister's brother-in-law. Alianor asked that her bailiffs be received favourably in La Rochelle with a view to supplying ships for her army.[53] The queen also directed ships to be supplied from Gascony, the Gascons remaining loyal to their duke and duchess, a reminder that they owed no loyalty to England, but rather a loyalty to the descendants of their ducal family. The chronicler Rishanger wrote of "such a multitude of ships that it was scarcely creditable to anyone."[54]

The Montfortian chronicler Rishanger wrote::

> And the whole of that region and land as far as the Alps, at the instigation of the Queen of England, Pierre de Savoie, [Philippe de Savoie] elected to Lyons, Boniface [de Savoie] of Canterbury and the queens of other noble families had conspired against the English, but also against Brittany, Gascony, and Spain.[55]

Here was all the comital family of Savoy coming together in support of the English Crown against "the English", a powerful reminder that kith and kin might be an equal motivation in these times as nascent nationalism. Rishanger may well be suggesting Marguerite de Provence, Alianor's sister, Queen of France, in his writing "queens of other noble families" as we know she too rallied to Alianor's cause. We should also note the support of Gascony, of which Henry was duke and Alianor duchess, the significance of which we will come to. The Dunstable chronicler was also in no doubt as to who led the continental threat, writing "*Petrum de Sabaudia et alios magnates de partibus transmarinis*" or "Peter of Savoy and other great men from beyond the sea" who wanted the "*confusionem et destructionem omnimodam Anglicorum*" or the complete confusion and destruction of the English.[56] There was indignation expressed in Henry's name by Simon de Montfort towards Boniface de Savoie that "the ways to France are not safe for Englishmen at present".[57] The Savoyard Archbishop of Canterbury stubbornly refused to lend the new regime the legitimacy of the See of Saint-Augustine, staying firmly in France and refusing to appoint a deputy or representative.

By the autumn Pierre had built a war chest of some 4,000 *livres viennois* and 2,000 *livres tournois*, and Alianor was recruiting further troops in Gascony. Certainly, Simon de Montfort took the threat of invasion seriously, as he arranged for the southern coasts of England to be well defended that summer and autumn. Simon played for time, feigning to negotiate whilst all the time knowing that finance for Alianor's army would run dry. The attempt at negotiation accepted that the Mise of Lewes was a dead letter, and offered in its stead a Peace of Canterbury. Alianor was being advised by her uncle Philippe, up from Lyon, and together with Pierre and Boniface this was a veritable gathering of the clan in support of Henry and Edward.[58] The papal legate, Guy Foulquois, Guy the Fat, former bishop of Le Puy and archbishop of Narbonne attempted to intercede in vain; he was a Doctor of Civil Law and a renowned jurist and counsellor to King Louis. Pope Urban IV had empowered Guy with the full powers of the church in the overthrow of the unnatural order of things in England including excommunication and even crusade. This would have given Pierre's gathering army in Flanders the status of crusaders invading England in the way of the Duke of

Normandy two centuries earlier in 1066. In return the Montfortian Parliament had threatened beheading to any cleric serving interdict or excommunication. Upon reaching Boulogne, Guy rather prudently sent his chaplain Alan across to Dover to test the water, Alan was told that aliens had destroyed the realm of England, upon hearing the waves of xenophobia Alan advised Guy to stay where he was in Boulogne.[59] When Montfort's terms were offered by way of Foulquois to Louis at Boulogne, Louis had been financing in part Alianor's army. Louis rejected the new terms, saying that "he would prefer to break clods behind the plough than have a rule of that kind". Chief amongst the rules to which Louis objected was the reiteration of the previous year's Statute of Aliens – how could he have such a rule, he was married to a Savoyard queen, whose sister would be enfeebled by such a rule.[60] When on 24 September a delegation of English bishops crossed the channel to bring Montfort's mediation proposals, they brought forth the wrath of Foulquois, but also Philippe de Savoie acting upon Alianor's instruction, that the Montfortians do what they had said they would do and abide by Louis' arbitration latterly given at Amiens.

But earlier by 15 August 1264 an invasion army was assembling at Dam in Flanders where Pierre de Savoie rewrote his will. That he did so tells us that he fully appreciated the dangers of invading England. All his time in England had been to one purpose: the protection of the person and rights of his niece, Alianor, Queen of England. Now in September 1264, with Edward and Henry under the control of Pierre's one-time fellow oath-taker Simon de Montfort, we know that Pierre for the first time came to the realisation that an invasion might fail, and that Alianor may not regain the land of which she'd been crowned as a young girl. In Flanders Pierre de Savoie rewrote his last will and testament to leave the County of Savoy to Alianor.[61] As we saw, in England, meanwhile, the chronicler Rishanger was in no doubt that "all that country and land even to the Alps at the instigation of the Queen of England, P[eter]. Savoy, [Philip] elected Bishop of Lyons, Bonefacius of Cant[erbury]. and the other noble parents of the Queen had conspired against the English".[62] Rishanger suggested that England's invaders came from even the Alps, from Savoy and, one may assume by "parents of the Queen" he was implicating Béatrice, Alianor's mother then "looking after the shop" in Savoy. Rishanger names and blames the entire comital family of Savoy for plotting an invasion of England. But Philippe's counsel to his niece Alianor was constant, that the Mise of Amiens should be upheld, and that any modification thereof should be under the purview of King Louis and Legate Foulquois.[63] In the recently published second volume of his definitive biography of Henry David Carpenter wrote:

> "In all this, Eleanor received considerable help from her uncle, Peter of Savoy. . . Would he [now as Count of Savoy] devote himself entirely to Savoyard affairs, complex and time consuming as they were? But not a bit of it. If ever the patronage bestowed by Henry proved justified it was now.[64]

As we have seen repeatedly and will see again, the Savoyards were loyal to their niece, Queen Alianor and to her son the Lord Edward. This by extension made them loyal servants of the English crown, even though they be aliens, even though they be not "natural born" subjects of the crown. Their loyalty would ultimately be recognised long after Pierre de Savoie had passed from this life, in Edward resting control of his new castles in north Wales in the hands of loyal Savoyard knights, and indeed trusting in the diplomatic and military service of the Savoyard Othon de Grandson just as Henry had done so with Pierre de Savoie. One might

Chapter Nine

argue that some of those accused of taking advantage of the "vineyard without a wall" served the interests of the vineyard better than some of its own vintners. In the summer and autumn of 1264 this newly crowned, so to speak, Count of Savoy was a long way from Savoy, as were the knights of Savoy who answered his call in Flanders, as would be the Savoyard defenders of Pevensey Castle - defence of the Plantagenet dynasty took priority, perhaps indeed Henry knew better than many, then and since, in his years of patronage to the eagles from Savoy.

In England the coast was still be watched. On 18 November the Montfortian government sent two remarkable messages to Flanders, one to Alianor, the other to Pierre de Savoie, saying expressly that "The king and Edward his son are safe and sound".[65] And so it was, with anxious eyes watching the coast, as the last autumn leaves of 1264 fell, the tide inexplicably turned, and no Savoyard invasion of England came – which is perhaps no bad thing. For if England had been invaded by the men of Vaud, Faucigny and Geneva, the xenophobes would have been able to rally all Englishmen to the cause and Simon de Montfort, a Frenchman, would have been able to "wrap himself in the flag" of nascent English patriotism. The remarkable talent for what we might now describe as "populism" on the part of Montfort, had encouraged Englishmen of low birth to rally to his cause in some numbers. Whatever the reality, Englishmen, including the peasantry, in rallying to Montfort thought they were defending their ancient liberties, *Magna Carta*, the Charter of the Forest against alien invasion.[66] Not for nothing did Montfort have Henry reissue *Magna Carta* in the legendary January–March Parliament of 1265.[67] The pro-Montfortian chronicler of Bury St. Edmunds gives us the feeling of the English toward Alianor and Pierre's army in Flanders, writing: "England would have been conquered by foreigners."[68] There are almost countless requests by the Montfortian government, in the king's name, for help from all corners of the kingdom to come to their assistance "against the coming of the aliens".[69] What Michael Wood described as a "nasty tide of jingoism" had been set loose by the Frenchman, Simon de Montfort, who was cheered by the multitude as being "big and strong" and loving "what's right" and hating "what's wrong" along with the boast that he'd always "come out on top". As Wood observes, "the commoners were right with him."[70] For evidence of this "jingoism" we need look no further than the chronicler of St. Albans, who wrote of 1263 that "For whoever did not know how to speak the English language was considered contemptible by the people".[71] Carpenter exposed much detail of the involvement of the English peasantry in supporting Montfort, drawing attention to the many unnamed dead at Lewes as being "almost certainly peasants".[72] Writs had gone out from the Montfortian government "for the defence of the whole kingdom against foreigners", and that:

> You will make from each village to the same village eight or six or more, at least according to the size of the village, with infantry and arms, of the best and most able; well fortified with spears, bows and spears, swords, crossbows and axes.[73]

The response, says Carpenter, was "overwhelming".[74] The chronicler Arnold Fitz Thedmar wrote:

> "After that, by the decree of the aforesaid brief, innumerable people of horse and foot assembled from every county of England, who, well armed, went to the coast of the sea to defend the kingdom against the foreigners, and in like

manner innumerable ships from the Five Ports and other places were put into the sea, with men well-armed to meet the said aliens in a strong hand."[75]

The Montfortian chronicler Rishanger confirmed "all the strength of the kingdom, from all the cities, towns, and villages" was summoned to the new regime's defence.[76] He added:

You would have seen at that time upon Harbledowne, both horse and foot, such a multitude gathered together, as powerful against the aliens of war, as you would not have believed existed in England.[77]

It's perhaps not surprising since the Montfortians claimed that Alianor and Pierre were thirsting for blood and would spare neither man nor woman a cruel death. They wrote of destruction "through the impious hands of those who thirst for our blood, if they are of whatever age or sex, they will by no means be spared, a cruel death".[78]

Unsurprisingly then, the peasants of England joined their feudal lords for a "defence of the whole kingdom", whilst Pierre de Savoie called upon all who owed him service to come to Flanders to the aid of his niece, the Queen of England, and his nephew the captive King of England. The two armies were both acting in, what they thought, was a just cause, but one of entirely different mindsets. What we are witnessing here are the beginnings of the passing of one world, of Alianor and Pierre, in which family and kinship was the overriding concern based upon the age-old feudal system, and the coming of the new world, of nascent nationalism and national identity, involving the wider community, including the peasantry, as the determining motivation.

Not for the first time or last time watch was kept atop the white cliffs of Dover for invasion, not the first or last time an army waited impatiently on the continental shore for the contrary winds of the Channel to show divine favour. That summer and autumn of 1264 watchers on both sides of the channel would have seen the "Great Comet of 1264", but for whom was it an ill omen?

Chapter Ten

However, whilst Montfort's negotiations had successfully wasted time, the winds blew and money for an invasion began to run out, and no invasion came. The watchers waited in vain, the invaders went home. Howell following Maddicott has plausibly suggested that a factor in the delayed invasion was the ongoing negotiations between Montfort and the papal legate, Guy Foulquois.[1] The Montfortian chronicler Rishanger is at this time fulsome in his praise of Alianor and her support for husband and son, writing:

> I would like, however, to join in the praise of the illustrious Queen Alianor, that she perseveres energetically and exhaustedly, to help her lord the king and Edward as energetically and manfully as if she were a brave man.[2]

Whether there was any seriousness on the Montfortian side in coming to terms is debatable[3]; however, Alianor and Pierre would have surrendered moral capital if they had invaded whilst negotiations backed by Rome and Paris were still taking place. However, papal support would soon be wanting. Pope Urban IV departed this life on 2 October 1264, and Foulquois would now return to Rome for the election of his successor. Before departure Foulquois washed his hands of the recalcitrant Montfortians and excommunicated them.[4] His unsuccessful English intervention wouldn't prevent him emerging as Pope Clement IV on 5 February 1265 – Montfort would find no succour in Rome.

In 1066 an earlier invasion by a continental army had been delayed by more than seven weeks by a low-pressure system hovering over the Netherlands, bringing with it northerly winds, rendering any crossing of the Channel impossible. In later centuries Channel winds would favour the English against the armada but favour William of Orange. The Worcester chronicler said, "But the Lord of all, to whom the winds and the sea obey, did not permit the same army to pass into England."[5] Rishanger suggested it was for want of money that an invasion failed to arrive rather than inclement weather.[6]

Nonetheless as the winds blew and money for both armies ran dry, perhaps wiser counsel in Flanders prevailed. It was the renowned historian Carpenter who noted of Pierre that he had "behaved with caution and sensitivity" during his years in England, perhaps it was indeed this sensitivity to nascent English national feeling that now prevailed.[7] Chroniclers such as Arnold Fitz Thedmar give us the names of those around the table, so to speak, counselling Alianor:

> "At that time, because reports came that through the agency of the Queen, Peter de Savoy, John Earl Warenne, Hugh Bigot, William de Valencia, John Mansel, and others then existing in the overseas parts, they wished to bring aliens with arms over the kingdom of England."[8]

Peter of Savoy: The Little Charlemagne

Along with Pierre and Alianor in Flanders was Henry's loyal John Mansel as they prevaricated over plans for invasion.[9] The death of the ever loyal Mansel in Florence early in 1265 raises interesting questions as to the reason for his presence there immediately after being in Flanders. It's difficult to avoid the suspicion that he was engaged either on a mission to the papal Curia, we should recall it was Mansel who had obtained the papal quashing of the Provisions of Oxford, or a money-raising effort with the Florentine merchants on behalf of the army in Flanders. Should the latter have any truth then it would tend to go against the idea that the invasion was abandoned solely for want of funds. If his mission had been financial then notice of his death to Alianor and Pierre could not have arrived earlier than Alianor's adjournment to Gascony and Pierre's need to return urgently to Helvetia. The passing of John Mansel left Pierre in want of his aid and counsel, but much more Henry who had described Mansel as having "always been serviceable and loyal to my affairs and those of my kingdom". Mansel's mission to Italy early in 1265 may be obscure but England lost an able and skilled knight, cleric, diplomat and royal counsellor,[10]

Nonetheless, returning to the north, fear for the hostages was very real, Henry had written to Louis in July of 1264, fearing that the hostages, Edward and Henry of Almain, were in "imminent danger" should the "peace of the kingdom" be "disturbed" by invasion.[11] Alianor's, and therefore Pierre's, overriding concern, as ever, was Edward, and fear that Montfort might act rashly in the event of an invasion no doubt played upon their thoughts. The way to change the nature of this game was to change the circumstances by removing the "imminent danger" to Edward, in short by freeing Edward.

If Henry, and his son Edward, were to be freed from the Montfortians, wrapped as they were in the flag, then maybe there was a better way than by invasion – a way that would not pit Englishman against Savoyard, but one that would free Edward to fight for what would soon be his crown.

Pierre de Savoie, who'd never taken the title Earl of Richmond,[12] to which he was entitled as holder of the Honour of Richmond, and who'd relinquished control of the castle at Dover and the Cinque Ports, was a man particularly conscious of how his "foreign" interventions in England looked to Englishmen. This having been said, he was a man to stand his ground, and to defend vigorously the interest of his niece and great-nephew, to this day a common trait amongst those of the *Suisse Romande*, is what we might call "being given to stubbornness". So having said wiser counsel prevailed in Flanders, this obstinacy had already come to the fore on the part of Pierre's lieutenants in England.

But there is something else we need to consider as the two "oath-takers" faced one another across the English Channel in 1264 and into 1265. Simon de Montfort, in addition to being possessed of the ability to motivate men, had a martial ability second to none: the Earl of Leicester chose again and again to resort to war in achieving his political ends.[13] The Little Charlemagne across the Channel, however, whilst a knight used to much success in war, was possessed of that other necessary attribute of a prince: he had the ability to see the bigger picture and marshal his wide network of associates in achieving his political ends. The two men were very different in character, the Earl of Leicester holding fast by the Provisions of Oxford to the end, a man of firm convictions and contempt for Henry, whereas the de facto Earl of Richmond was the ultimate pragmatist, driven by the protection of his family and its interests in the Plantagenet dynasty. Montfort despised Pierre for turning away from "the common cause", while Pierre de Savoie likely saw Montfort as a real and present danger to Alianor and all he had sought to protect in England. In what surely must have been a vindictive ploy lacking in

Chapter Ten

any form of self doubt, during his Parliament in early 1265 Montfort availed himself of Pierre's Strand Palace, in that moment as he paraded to Westminster from the Savoyard palace Montfort must have felt the victor. Ultimately, however Pierre de Savoie and his family would be left in possession of the field, not the illustrious Earl of Leicester.

Across the Channel in England, in the aftermath of Lewes, three castles held out for the king, their sieges, amongst the longest, by some accounts the longest, in English history are poorly recorded. This has been attributed to the chaos in English governance following Lewes, but contemporary chroniclers also pay little heed to them. These besieged castles became somewhat the orphans of English history because two of them were mostly held not by native-born knights, but by Savoyards holding their castles, as honour and chivalry demanded, for their lord, Pierre de Savoie. Fergus Oakes rightly points to the custom that a constable might be given time to surrender a castle to seek such permission from his lord, and suggests that with Pierre de Savoie most definitively being out of the country, such permission would not be forthcoming. However, given all that we know of the siege at Pevensey, Pierre and Alianor's army in Flanders, and as we shall see an alternative plot to restore Henry and Edward by means of the latter's escape, it's unlikely any permission to surrender would in any case have been forthcoming.[14] Their heroic defence in the face of the forces of Simon de Montfort did not fit into the English narrative, and sadly the efforts of the defenders went unnoticed by later francophone chroniclers of Savoy.

After the surrender demand of 15 May 1264, the Montfortians went after the English possessions of Pierre de Savoie: Richmond and Pevensey castles. Guichard de Charron held Richmond, whilst a concerted effort was made to defend the strategically vital Pevensey. Indeed, by March 1265, of the three castles holding out against Montfort – Bamburgh, Richmond and Pevensey – two were held for Pierre de Savoie on behalf of Henry. Charron was the son of the original Guichard de Charron we met earlier, who'd come to England, along with his brothers Bernard and Stephen, in the 1240s with Pierre, the father having been seneschal of the Honour of Richmond and hereditary constable of Bowes Castle.[15] Charron had been ordered on 15 April 1264, before Lewes, by Henry, to "take into the king's hands all the lands and goods of his said adversaries who hold of the fee of Peter de Sabaudia of the honour of Richmond and keep them until further order", and he was faithful to his order. In his later reign Edward would come to rely upon Savoyards in his Welsh campaigns and elsewhere, the steadfast service of Guichard de Charron being one of many reasons. On 10 July 1264, Montfort issued in Henry's name a mandate to Gilbert de Clare to take into his hands "the castles and lands of Pierre de Savoie in England", the same date a mandate was issued for "Pierre's constable" at Richmond to deliver the castle to Gilbert de Clare.[16] However, Charron was faithful to the lord his father had served before him[17] and continued to hold the castle for Pierre. The Count of Savoy inspired great loyalty in his vassals, as had Ebal II de Mont before him. Guichard de Charron had been given, in 1262, power of granting attorneys to look after Pierre's interests in England during his absence in Savoy – in this Pierre was elevating Charron to the same level of trust as his niece and kin, Alianor de Provence, the queen.[18] Charron was ordered to surrender Richmond on 16 January and again on 5 March 1265;[19] thereafter the picture is unclear following the order of 23 April 1265 to Guillaume de Bossall and Jean d'Eyville to raise the feudal host and "manfully" besiege Richmond,[20] but we have a clearer picture for Pevensey.

As mentioned earlier, the summons of 8 July having failed, on 18 July 1264 Montfort ordered the Sheriff of Surrey and Sussex, Jean D'Abernon, to take control of Pevensey Castle. Those in the castle would be allowed to leave for France beyond the seas. The command included the phrase "if peace be made with Peter de Sabauda" which would imply that Montfortian England now considered itself not at peace with Pierre de Savoie. They were right as the garrison under Hanekin de Wissant, Pierre de Savoie's appointed constable and his steward in Sussex, Jean de la Rede, refused to surrender. What followed at Pevensey would be the longest castle siege in English history.[21] Rede had been assigned Pevensey by Henry on 13 December 1263 and like Charron at Richmond was committed to holding on to Pierre's castle.[22] Hanekin de Wissant was noted as constable of the castle in the earlier 8 July 1264 summons to come to terms; also mentioned were Jean de la Rede and Imbert de Montréal.[23] Montréal and Wissant were later recognised in the last will and testament of Pierre de Savoie.[24] Wissant was a Flemish port across the Channel from Pevensey, much used by those crossing to England from France. It would have been from Wissant that an invasion army amassed by Pierre and Alianor may well have sailed, had the command come. It is also from Wissant that the resupply of the garrison at Pevensey may have originated – it is not then perhaps unsurprising that we find the name of Hamekin de Wissant, constable of Pevensey Castle, in the last will and testament of Pierre de Savoie. That besieged Pevensey was being resupplied by sea from France is alluded to in a plea from the Montfortian government of 3 December 1264 from Oxford which implored the barons of Hastings, Winchelsea and Rye "to keep watch for the capture of certain persons who as the king is informed, are endeavouring by ships to munition the castle of Pevenese with men and victuals to the king's damage".[25] That the defenders were grimly holding out for the king is typical of the doublespeak of the new regime, for "king" we should read "Simon de Montfort". That the Montfortian plea says "men and victuals" suggests that a good many of the Savoyard knights that had come to Flanders may well have crossed the Channel to defend Pevensey.

So, why was Pevensey Castle besieged in the autumn of 1264? First, we should make clear that the sea was nowhere near where it is now; the coastline has changed markedly in the intervening centuries. Instead of the current straight coastline a mile or so distant from Pevensey, we should imagine a great bay, beginning near the existing Cooden railway station and ending near Eastbourne. The bay included many inlets and headlands. This was where William the Conqueror had made landfall and so we know that the bay might hold 700 ships. On the western coast a peninsula jutted into the bay, with many headlands, farthest most a narrow peninsula upon which the Romans had built their fort in the late third century and Robert de Mortain had built the first castle of the Norman Conquest. The narrow peninsula was fed by a Roman road to the western gate of the old Roman fort, still more than extant in 1264. On the landward side of the peninsula lay a harbour, an asset that would prove to be the castle garrison's salvation. As we saw earlier, within the Roman fort lay the castle itself, in the southeast quadrant set against the Roman wall. There was a twin-towered gatehouse and a big Norman keep, held together by the works Pierre de Savoie had set in motion by 1254. Three D-shaped towers mimicked the surrounding Roman towers of antiquity, albeit much broader and to a great height, set into three great walls. Students of castle design in Switzerland and Savoy should recall that Pevensey was the last castle built by Pierre de Savoie before his later castle at Yverdon. Indeed, British students of castle design should recall that Yverdon was the first recorded castle of Maître Jacques de Saint-Georges. In other words, by way of overlapping patron and builder we have a chain of progression that stretches from Pevensey by way of Yverdon to the great castles of north Wales.

As the siege got underway a large ditch was dug around the landward side of the castle to prevent escape and the siege was invested by Simon de Montfort's son, also a Simon.[26] On 18

Chapter Ten

September 1264 a command was issued in captive Henry's name to aid Simon the Younger "in besieging the castle, and in repressing and taking the king's enemies within that castle that are perpetrating homicides, burnings and plundering".[27] On 4 November, with no end in sight, the siege monies were hurriedly dispatched to the younger Simon to bring an end to things, but to no avail.[28] The doublespeak of the Montfortian regime is truly Orwellian in describing those holding Pevensey as "the king's enemies". These "king's enemies" were in fact the men of his kinsman, Pierre de Savoie, and more loyal to Henry's dynasty than Montfort had proven to be. At this point Pevensey was described by Swiss historian Henri Buathier as a *"nid des Savoyards"* or "nest of Savoyards",[29] and Chapuisat as "soldiers of Pierre de Savoie ... who will not capitulate".[30] We know the name of one of these soldiers, not from English records, but from those at Chillon, in Savoy – his name Nantelme de Cholay. The account confirms one name but also that he had others with him, who are described as his *"sociorum"*, the plural masculine of *"socius"* meaning "allies" but also "kindred". So, together with the Montfortian plea to stop men coming to Pevensey by sea, we might reasonably take this to confirm Chapuisat and take it that Nantelme de Cholay was accompanied during the siege of Pevensey by his Savoyard neighbours.

Cholay lay within the parish of Saint-Jean-hors-les-Murs near Geneva; today known as Choulex, it is a small village with just over 1,000 souls six kilometres south of Geneva, just on the Swiss side of the frontier with France, unaware that one of its number once participated in the siege of Pevensey Castle. The later-built castle at nearby Rouelbeau sat on the site of an earlier wooden fortification known as *Bâtie Cholay*; it seems the Lords of Cholay were fellow vassals of Faucigny, and hence Pierre, along with their neighbours at Allinges and Thorens, of which we earlier noted Guillaume d'Allinges Gérard and Pierre de Compei in Flanders with the Savoyards. That Cholay Thorens and Allinges were from Faucigny and not Savoy proper adds weight to the suggestion that the primary reason for their taking part was as vassals personally of Pierre and not any general loyalty to Savoy in itself – this was then perhaps not an army of Savoy, but an army of Pierre de Savoie, rallying in support of his possessions and his kinsfolk, Alianor de Provence, her husband Henry and her son Edward. The Chillon accounts tells us that Cholay and his allies or kindred had been *"stando in munitione in castri de Pevenesea"*, that is "standing in fortification of the castle of Pevensey" or put more simply, defending the castle of Pevensey.[31] Chapuisat put it as *"garnison à Pevensey"*.[32] That Cholay was paid for service in England does pose the question as to whether his neighbours Guillaume d'Allinges, Gérard and Pierre de Compeis and others were ferried to and fro from Flanders to Pevensey during the siege. Was it only supplies that were landed? Or might reinforcements have been made to the "nest of Savoyards"? As we saw, the English mention of "men" as well as "victuals" would suggest more than supplies but reinforcements were landed. Nantelme de Cholay appears later, in 1294–5, as castellan of the Tour-de-Rive, in Nyon in the *Pays de Vaud*. So, we can reasonably suggest that in addition to Nantelme de Cholay, the names of other defenders of Pevensey may well have numbered those from Savoy who witnessed Pierre's will at Dam in Flanders, that they had crossed the Channel to support the castle.

The defenders at Pevensey had the advantage of concentric defence, first the ancient Roman walls of the outer bailey, erected as a Saxon shore-fort in the late third century, but also the stout curtain walls of the inner bailey lately built for Pierre de Savoie. Three D-shaped mural towers enabled the Savoyards to keep a good watch over the increasingly desperate Montfortians surrounding them.

Peter of Savoy: The Little Charlemagne

The besieged garrisons of Richmond and Pevensey continued to hold out, the latter, as we have seen, much aided by receiving reinforcements and supplies from Alianor, Pierre and Louis in France.[33] Today, Pevensey Castle sits just over a mile from the sea, but in the thirteenth century sat upon a natural peninsula with direct, unhindered access to the sea. At Richmond, Jean d'Eyville gave up on the siege and withdrew to Scarborough Castle. At Pevensey, in an effort to break the siege, Simon de Montfort junior brought up massive siege engines, trebuchets, to hurl rocks at the Roman walls.

The counterpoise trebuchet used a counterweight to swing the arm, the only artillery on either side that had not originated with the Romans, making its way west from China borne by the Mongol invasions and taken up first in the Middle East then only recently in Europe. The trebuchet was a compound machine that made use of the mechanical advantage of a lever to throw a missile. They were invariably large constructions, from thirty feet (ten metres) in height to as much as three times that, built mostly of wood, but reinforced with metal, leather, rope and other materials. Counterweight trebuchets used gravity, potential energy stored by slowly raising an extremely heavy box (typically filled with stones, sand or lead) attached to the shorter end of the beam (typically on a hinged connection) and then released on command. The noise of the stones repeatedly crashing against masonry would have been terrifying to those within Pevensey.

However, as many before and since have discovered, the Romans built to last and, save for a section of the northern wall, the 1,000-year-old walls held fast, as did those raised more recently by Pierre.[34] Around eighty years ago Pevensey's moat was dredged and hundreds of catapult balls were recovered.[35] Many can be seen on display in the castle today. The cold dark winter months may have occasioned a lull in the bombardment, and the difficulty of maintaining a long siege come to the fore. In November the Montfortian government gave notice that the local host of Surrey and Sussex be relieved of the burden of military service "against the hostile arrival of foreigners", probably until the spring at least.[36] Christmas passed with neither hope of breaking the siege or the will of the defenders.

One last attempt to implore the defenders to surrender Pevensey was made on 17 March 1265, though sadly it does not name the leaders of the defence, only "two or three of those who are in the castle of Pevenese".[37] But Pierre de Savoie's men held out, and the siege ended when the son was recalled to the Midlands by his father: there had been from the Montfortian side unwelcome developments. Pierre's castles at Richmond and Pevensey had held firm, as Chapuisat said *"ne capituleront pas"*. There is little comment of the siege by Montfortian chroniclers, little mention of the valour of Nantelme de Cholay and his comrades, but we ought to pause to remember knights, a long way from home, who held out for long winter months, not in some great national cause, but merely because they owed allegiance to their lord, Pierre de Savoie. Those keen on projecting ideas of national stories from our own time back to the thirteenth century might reflect that in the past, like another country, they did things differently and that fealty, as that owed by Nantelme, was the glue that held medieval society together.

In mid-February 1265, as she had exhausted the funds to finance her army in the north, Alianor changed tack. We can now see the ghostly outlines of a carefully designed plot that may suggest themselves. First, in Gascony, Duchesse d'Aquitaine Alianor was able to ensure the duchy remained loyal to the duke and cut off the Montfortian government in England. As we have suggested earlier, now was the time for wiser counsel than the blunt instrument of invasion. What follows is entirely the supposition of a necessarily secret plan, that by definition has not survived in the light of day. Details of this plan appear to us now like islands

Freepost Plus RTKE-RGRJ-KTTX
Pen & Sword Books Ltd
47 Church Street
BARNSLEY
S70 2AS

DISCOVER MORE ABOUT PEN & SWORD BOOKS

Pen & Sword Books have over 4000 books currently available, our imprints include; Aviation, Naval, Military, Archaeology, Transport, Frontline, Seaforth and the Battleground series, and we cover all periods of history on land, sea and air.

Can we stay in touch? From time to time we'd like to send you our latest catalogues, promotions and special offers by post. If you would prefer not to receive these, please tick this box. ☐

We also think you'd enjoy some of the latest products and offers by post from our trusted partners: companies operating in the clothing, collectables, food & wine, gardening, gadgets & entertainment, health & beauty, household goods, and home interiors categories. If you would like to receive these by post, please tick this box. ☐

We respect your privacy. We use personal information you provide us with to send you information about our products, maintain records and for marketing purposes. For more information explaining how we use your information please see our privacy policy at www.pen-and-sword.co.uk/privacy. You can opt out of our mailing list at any time via our website or by calling 01226 734222.

Mr/Mrs/Ms ....

Address..................

Postcode.................. Email address..................

Website: www.pen-and-sword.co.uk Email: enquiries@pen-and-sword.co.uk
Telephone: 01226 734555   Fax: 01226 734438
Stay in touch: facebook.com/penandswordbooks or follow us on Twitter @penswordbooks

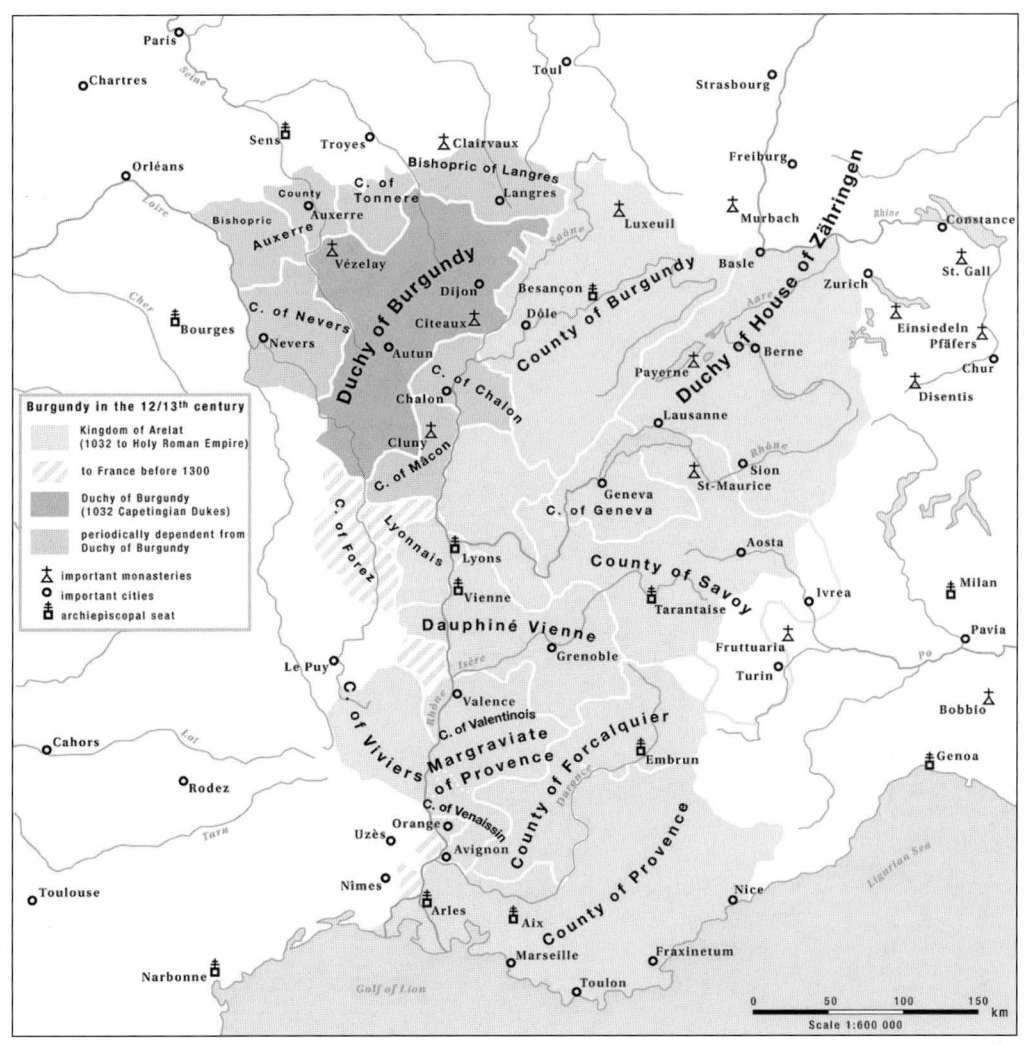

Fig. 1.0. The Second Kingdom of Burgundy, also known as the Kingdom of Arles and Vienne, also as the Arelat. The map illustrates the kingdom during the ninth and tenth centuries. The upper (Transjurane) and lower (Cisjurane) kingdoms would be united as the Second Kingdom of Burgundy. (Wikimedia Commons CC BY-SA 4.0 Marco Zanoli)

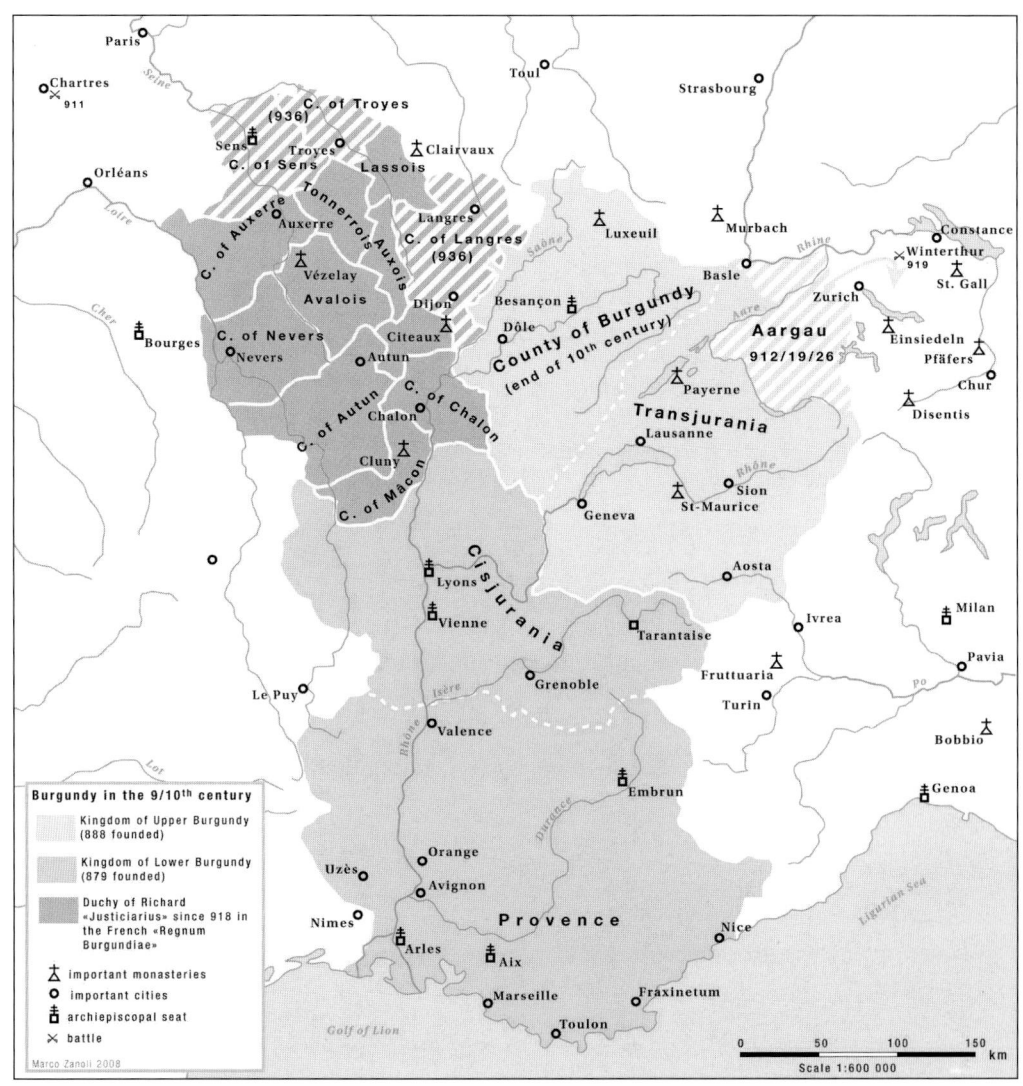

Fig. 1.1. The successors to the Second Kingdom of Burgundy following its absorption into the Holy Roman Empire. The map shows the emerging counties of Albon (Dauphiné Vienne), Burgundy (Franche-Comté or Free County of Burgundy), Provence and Savoy. Forcalquier would become attached to Provence. The German-speaking Zähringen would retreat to its core German lands and Savoy in effect surround the County of Geneva. The map illustrates well the marriage strategy of Count Thomas I de Savoie in marrying his daughters, Béatrice to Provence and Marguerite to the successors to the Zähringen, Kyburg. (Wikimedia Commons CC BY-SA 4.0 Marco Zanoli)

Right: Fig. 1.2. The contemporary statue of Béatrice de Savoie raised in her village of Les Échelles in Savoy. Béatrice was the mother of four queens: Marguerite of France, Alianor of England, Sanchia of Germany and Béatrice of Naples – thus making Béatrice the ancestor of all kings and queens of England and France from the thirteenth century onward. The marriage of her daughter Alianor to King Henry III of England can rightly be said to be act that fundamentally changed the life of Pierre de Savoie.

Below: Fig. 1.3. The Château de Chillon beside Lac Léman (Lake Geneva). Venue for the July 1234 meeting of the sons of Count Thomas I de Savoie, following his death in 1233, at which lands were divided amongst them. The meeting being sponsored by Guillaume de Savoie who would soon become the first son to venture to England. Château de Chillon would later become a residence for Pierre when he became Count Pierre II de Savoie in 1263.

Fig. 1.4. The Château de Cornillon above Saint-Rambert-en-Bugey. The castle first appeared as a watchtower built by the nearby Abbey of Saint-Rambert. It was acquired by Count Thomas I de Savoie in return for his protection of the abbey. Following Thomas's death, it was given to Pierre de Savoie as one of his first castles. His acquisition placed Pierre as a rival to the nearby Count of Geneva.

Fig. 1.5. The town and castle of Romont, a rocky promontory guarding the way northward from Lausanne toward the German lands of the Kyburg, had been acquired earlier by the Savoyard but was acquired by Pierre from his brother Aymon in 1242 just after Pierre had entered English affairs. It is illustrative of the continuing interest Pierre de Savoie took in extending his holdings in Vaud whilst pursuing his career in England.

Fig. 1.6. Count Thomas de Flandres, brother of Pierre de Savoie, often known in Savoy as Thomas Ii to distinguish him from his father, Thomas I. Thomas II never became a Count of Savoy, although he did rule as regent during the minority of Count Boniface de Savoie. It was Thomas's acquisition of a debt owed by Simon de Montfort that began the conflict between Henry and Montfort. Following the death of his first wife, the Countess of Flanders, Thomas was active in Italian politics and particularly the failed attempt to have a Plantagenet on the throne of Sicily. Held prisoner for a time by the inhabitants of Turin, he is today buried in Aosta Cathedral.

Fig. 1.7. Richmond Castle, centre of the Honour of Richmond. Built originally by the Breton compatriot of William the Conqueror, Alain Rufus, it was successively held by Guillaume then Pierre de Savoie. (Sean Marshall)

Fig. 1.8. Pevensey Castle in Sussex, granted to Pierre de Savoie along with the Honour of the Eagle. The Normans had built a castle within the walls of the original Roman-Saxon shore fort. Pierre is then known to have been responsible for the inner castle walls that connected the twin-towered gatehouse to the keep. Embrasures dating from this time have a great similarity with those later built for Pierre at Yverdon in Savoy. Pevensey Castle was the scene of a year-long siege during the Second Baronial War, the castle being described as a "nest of Savoyards" who successfully held the castle for Pierre against the Montfortians.

Fig. 1.9. The hamlet of Charron in the Valromey district of Bugey to the southwest of Geneva. Charron was the very likely origin of Guiscard de Charron and his brothers Bernard and Stephen. Guiscard went on become Pierre's seneschal in Richmond, Bernard constable of Windsor Castle and Stephen Prior of Thetford Priory in Norfolk. The link between Charron and Pierre de Savoie likely came from the 1234 acquisition by Pierre of nearby castles at Saint-Rambert-en-Bugey and Lompnes. Guiscard's son, also a Guiscard, played a leading role in the Second Baronial War defending Richmond for Pierre. Curiously the road from Charron today toward Bellegarde crosses the Col de Richemond (with an English "d" not more usual French "t").

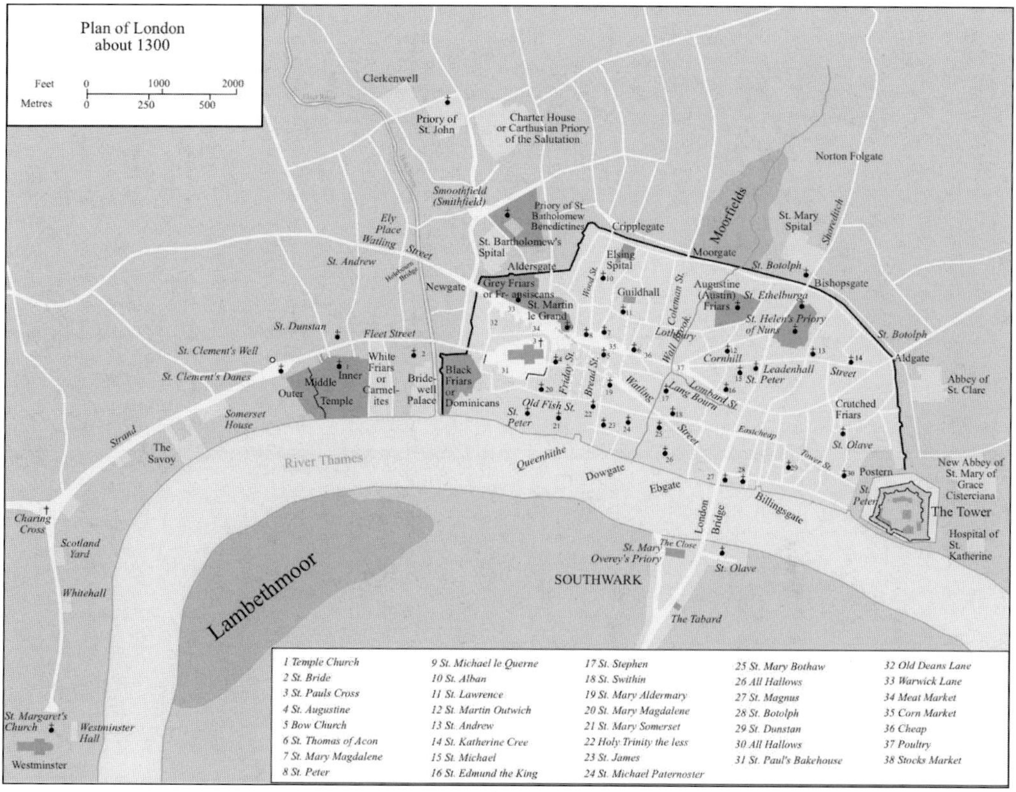

Fig. 2.0. London in the late thirteenth century. Pierre de Savoie's residence was the Savoy Palace built by The Strand on land granted to him by King Henry III. Other Savoyards in London would include Sir Othon de Grandson who was granted a house in Queenhithe following the Second Baronial War and Saint-Martin-le-Grand where first Guillaume de Champvent and then Louis de Vaud were Dean.

Fig. 2.1. Arrival of Pierre de Savoie in Bern. Detail of a miniature from the Chronicle of Diebold Schilling, Library of the Bourgeoisie of Berne, Mss.h.h.I.16 (v. 1485). Pierre is apparently represented wearing the green hat. Pierre de Savoie is regarded in Bern as the "*zweiter Gründer*" or second founder of the city. (Wikimedia Commons)

Above: Fig. 2.2. Saillon in the Upper Rhône Valley, whose walls reminded Arnold Taylor so much of Conwy in North Wales. Pierre de Savoie acquired Saillon in 1255 and as elsewhere undertook works to improve the fortifications, notably with the large round tower built from 1260. Building the tower for Pierre would be the Gascon engineer, Sir Jean de Mézos, whom he'd met whilst on campaign with King Henry III in 1254. Mézos would do much to bring Anglo-Norman castle-building forms to Savoy.

Opposite: Fig. 2.3. The 1259 Treaty of Paris. Pierre de Savoie played a leading role in negotiating the treaty which sought to bring an end to years of Capetian–Plantagenet fighting and regularise relations between the two families. In return for giving up their claims to Normandy, Maine, Anjou and much of Poitou, the Plantagenets were formally recognised as Dukes of Aquitaine retaining Gascony and the Saintonge south of the River Charente. The treaty was much criticised at the time and since by supporters of both parties as giving too much to the other side. However, the monks of Hautecombe Abbey in rebuilding a tomb to Pierre in the nineteenth-century would recognise the Savoyard as a peacemaker. (Wikimedia Commons in the public domain courtesy of the Archives Nationales de France as part of a cooperation project with Wikimédia France. "*Traité de Paris conclu entre la France et l'Angleterre et ratifié à Londres le 13 octobre 1259 par Henri III, roi d'Angleterre, et Louis IX. Acte en français scellé du sceau de Henri III en cire verte sur cordonnets de soie rouge et verte.*")

Fig. 2.4. The Château de Yverdon. Pierre de Savoie acquired the land for a new town at the southern end of the Lac de Neuchâtel, rebuilding the fortification there into a formidable *Carré Savoyard*. The embrasures at Yverdon have recently been found to have similitude with those at Pevensey in Sussex. Pierre employed the services of a *Magistro Jacobo* in building the castle, who would be known in England as Master James of St. George. Yverdon would be the first primary-sourced castle built by Master James. The form of Yverdon would later be replicated at Flint in North Wales.

Fig. 2.5. The Château d'Allinges high above the southern shore of Lac Léman (Lake Geneva). The castle was the fief of Guillaume d'Allinges, one of the Savoyard vassaux of Pierre de Savoie called up to join the army in Flanders in 1264 that sat poised to invade England. Given that a fellow vassal and neighbour, Nantelme de Cholay, was paid for service defending Pevensey Castle, it is quite possible that Guillaume d'Allinges too was one of the defenders of Pevensey.

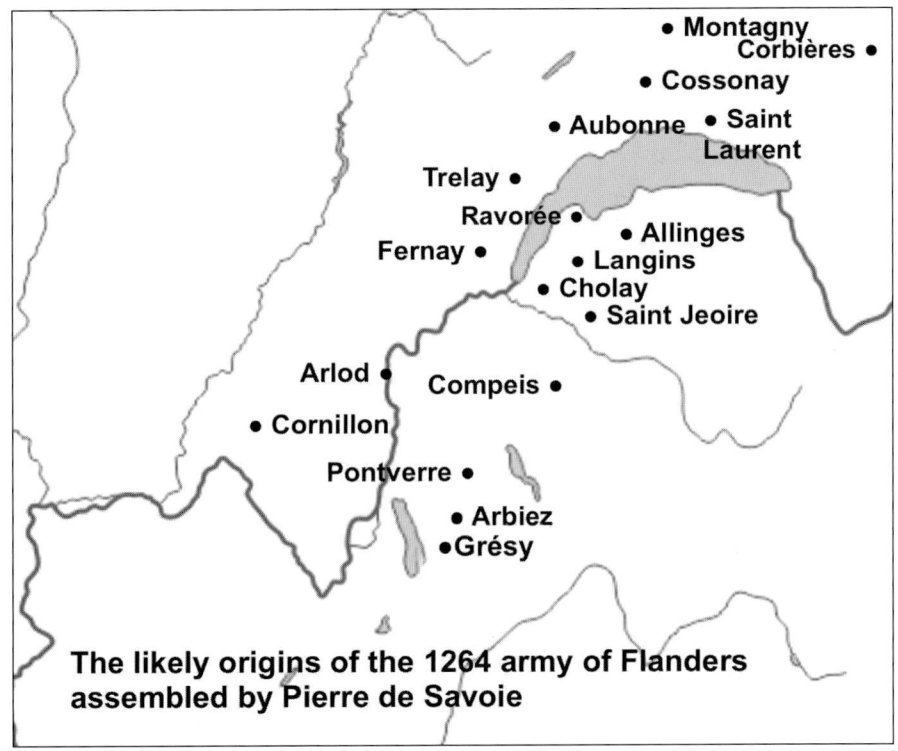

Fig. 2.6. The *nobilibus* and *militibus* who made up some of the army of Pierre de Savoie and Alianor de Provence in Flanders in the autumn of 1264. The names given are French renditions from the Latin of the primary-source document (see appendix) in use in the thirteenth century. It is noticeable from the geographic spread that these nobles and knights came from Pierre de Savoie's fiefs predating his becoming Count of Savoy in 1263. They are men who owed Pierre feudal service. It is noticeable that there are no representatives from either the Tarentaise or Maurienne.

Fig. 2.7. The Bailiffs Tower at Aosta in the Aosta Valley. Pierre purchased the tower from Vuillerme du Palais to accommodate his newly appointed bailiff for Aosta. The tower is still known as the Tour du Bailliage. Pierre had employed bailiffs in his lands before, both in England and in Savoy, but his succession as count saw the widespread introduction of this new means of comital administration.

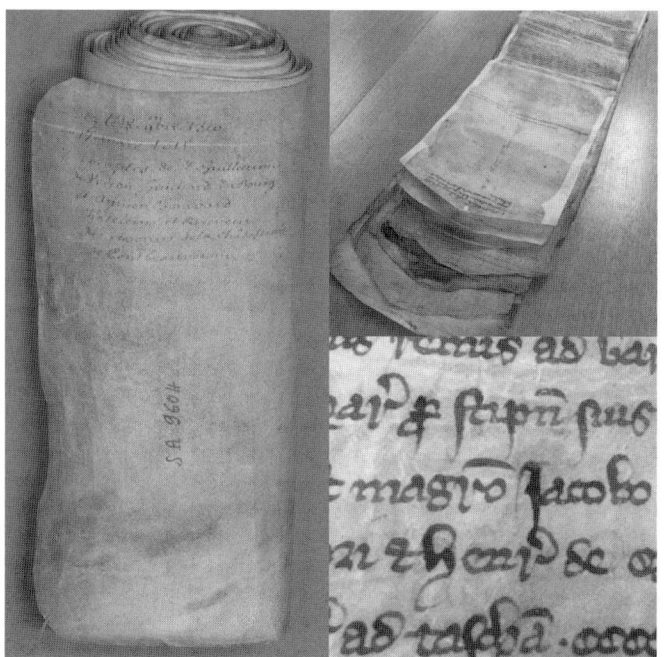

Fig. 2.8. Pipe rolls of Savoy in the care of the Savoyard archives in Chambéry, in comparison with English pipe rolls in the care of the UK National Archive in Kew.

Fig. 2.9. The castle at Pierre-Châtel in Savoy, much modified since the days when Pierre de Savoie died here in 1268. His much-modified last will and testament was written here.

Above and overleaf: Fig. 3.0. The sketches of two tombs at the collegiate church of Saint-Katherine in Aiguebelle made by Thomas Kerrich in 1771. Kerrich took the tombs to be of Pierre d'Aigueblanche and Pierre II de Savoie. He wrote: "The Two first are those of Peter Earl of Richmond, uncle to Queen Eleanor, wife of King Henry III. who died in 1267; and Peter, Bishop of Hereford, who died in the following year: both in the collegiate church of Aquabella in Savoy, where the latter was born, and from which he took his name; which name has been most dismally mangled by our English writers. That supposed to be of the Earl of Richmond is an altar tomb, with an effigy of marble lying upon it, not very different in attitude or habit from those of the same age in England, but perhaps in a rather better style of sculpture. His right-hand is laid upon his breast, and the other rested on the top of his shield; and there are two angels sitting at his head, and a lion couchant at his feet. The figure was a good deal mutilated when I saw it, both the legs broken, and one of them lost … The people of the place seemed to know very well who he was, but called him an Englishman, and insisted upon it that he was related to the bishop buried under the other tomb. Our accounts of him seem to lie very slight: we know that he built the palace in London called from him the Savoy, and that he was much hated here as one of the foreigners attached to the queen … The monument of the Bishop of Hereford is much more important. It consists of a cast statue of bronze laid upon a kind of table with six legs of the same metal, like the monument of the Emperor Charles the Bald at St. Denis, and appeared to me to be a work of considerable intrinsic merit, and not without great beauty, although in a rather dry hard style, such as, if the figure were antique, [it] would be dignified with the title of severe. The whole is executed with the utmost delicacy, and the crosier I thought uncommonly elegant." Kerrich recorded the inscription on the tomb of Pierre d'Aigueblanche: "*Hic jacet venerabilis Pater Dominus Petrus Herefordensis quondam Episcopus, Fundator, Structor & Dotator hujus Ecclesiae. Qui obiit quinto kalendas Decembris anno Domini M.CC.LXVIII. HOC opus fecit Magist. Henricus de Colonia. Anima hujus requiescat in pace. Amen.*" P. The translation of the now-lost inscription is "Here lies the venerable Father Lord Peter of Hereford, formerly Bishop, Founder, Builder, & Endower of this Church. Who died on the fifth of the calendar of December in the year of the Lord A.D. 1268. Master Henry of Colonia did this work. May his soul rest in peace. Amen." Today very little remains of the church. Nicholas Vincent, in the Oxford biography of Aigueblanche, describes the one-time Aiguebelle tomb as a later work of the fifteen-century and of "wishful thinking" upon the part of the canons of Aiguebelle. Certainly, Aigublanche was exhumed at Hereford in 1925 and the body found to be within. So, what were the tombs in Aiguebelle, wishful thinking on the part of a religious house in need of visitors and donations? Or the last resting places of at least part of those described by the residents of Aiguebelle to Kerrich.

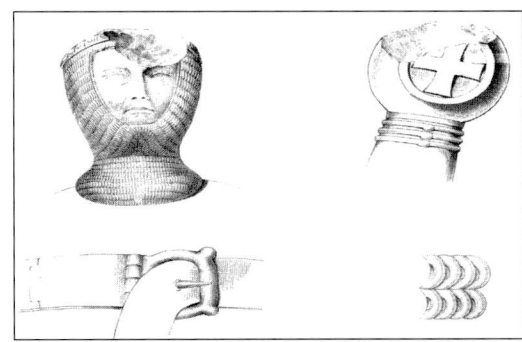

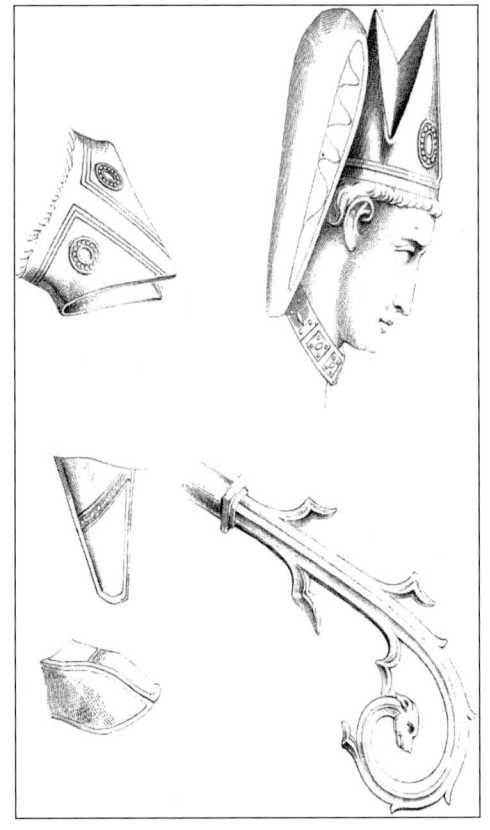

Fig. 3.1. The magnificent towering nineteenth-century tomb of Pierre II de Savoie in Hautecombe Abbey, Savoy. The tomb replaced an earlier tomb lost in the French Revolution. The dedication reads *PETRUS. THOMAE.F. AB. HENRICO III. BRITANNIAE REGE AD. LUDOVICUM. IX INTERPRES. PACIS.IN. GALLIAM. PROFECTUS. BELLUM. ALTERNIS. GLADIBUS. DIU. PRODUCTUM. AUCTORITATE. NOMINIS.COMPONIT.* Which translates as Peter son of Thomas, sent to Gaul as a peace negotiator by Henry III, King of England, to Louis IX, put an end to the war of repeated disasters prolonged for a long time, by the authority of his name." Father Emmanuel of Hautecombe Abbey confirmed to me, "*Les troubles révolutionnaires et la transformation de l'abbaye en usine de faïence, ont détruit toutes les traces des archives médiévales. Le roi Charles Félix de Sardaigne, duc de Savoie et prince de Piémont à voulu reconstituer le plus fidèlement possible le mausolée de sa famille au XIXème siècle. Les corps de tous les princes ertrouvés ont été rassemblés dans le caveau des princes, situé sous la chapelle du transept gauche.*" That is, "The revolutionary troubles and the transformation of the abbey into an earthenware factory destroyed all traces of the medieval archives. King Charles Félix of Sardinia, Duke of Savoy and Prince of Piedmont wanted to reconstruct as faithfully as possible the mausoleum of his family in the nineteenth century. The bodies of all the princes found were collected in the princes' vault, located under the chapel in the left transept." (By kind permission of the Abbaye de Hautecombe)

Fig. 3.2. The 1268 Last Will and Testament of Count Pierre II de Savoie made at Pierre-Châtel on 7 May 1268 as modified by two codicils (see appendix). The original is in the care of the Savoyard Archive in Turin, and was reproduced, untranslated, by Johann Ludwig Wurstemberger. AST/C, Testamenti, m 1, No 6. Wurstemberger, vol 4. No 749. (Archivio di Stato di Torino, Italy)

Chapter Ten

left by a receding tide, yet tide waters still concealing much that connects these islands. But as Carpenter has recently agreed with Howell "the Queen almost certainly played a part in plotting" the arrival in south Wales of Warenne, Valence and Bigod. That this arrival should shortly coincide with the escape of the Lord Edward and that the rendezvous of all be at the castle of Pierre's half-brother-in-law stretches belief in coincidence a long way - to this author past breaking point.[38]

We know from subsequent (1266) records that Alianor was employing at least two Bayonnais shipmasters, and we know their names: Paschasius de Pino and Pelerin de la Poynte.[39] This is most likely to indicate contact with her husband's realm, but with whom and where? There is the distinct possibility of seaborne communication between Gascony and Gefferoi de Geneville in Ireland. We saw that in 1252 Pierre de Savoie had arranged for Gefferoi the half-brother of his wife Agnès, to marry heiress Maud de Lacy, becoming in addition to Lord of Ludlow Castle in the Marches, Lord of Trim in Ireland.

The next part of the puzzle is suggested by Louis IX granting safe conduct through Poitou, neighbouring Gascony, of Guillaume de Valence heading for "England, Wales or Ireland, according to what seems best to him". Guillaume de Valence had taken ship to France from besieged Pevensey Castle; we should recall that the Marcher lord and Lusignan Guillaume de Valence held lands in Ireland and in South Wales.[40] This safe conduct strongly implies that Louis and Marguerite de Provence had knowledge of what was afoot, and therefore it is no leap of the imagination to suggest that her sister Alianor de Provence had too. Indeed, the surviving correspondence of the time between both Alianor and Marguerite on the one hand and Alphonse de Poitiers on the other show a concerted Savoyard familial effort on behalf of the English Crown, one that certainly also involved Pierre de Savoie in the autumn of 1264.[41] We should remember, as Anaïs Waag reminds us, that "family" was paramount in surviving correspondence. Indeed, Carpenter suggests that Marguerite was "very close to Henry".[42] Alianor, Marguerite and their uncle Pierre had but one goal in 1264–5: the release from the control of Montfort of their kin, Henry and Edward.

At some point, likely following Valence's journey across France, his Marshal took twenty men in two ships from Alianor's port of Bordeaux to La Rochelle. Howell reminds us that Alianor herself had ordered such a ship to be fitted out in October 1264. But where might Valence be heading?[43] Sure enough, the whereabouts of Guillaume de Valence soon became very clear. The master of Goodrich Castle landed from French exile at Pembroke with a small army on 10 May 1265, aided by Jean de Warenne and likely also Hugh Bigod. Valence landed with four ships and some 120 men, almost certainly including the two ships that had originated in Alianor's Bordeaux. The small landing group quickly joined forces with Clare and Mortimer.[44] Suddenly Montfort would soon fine himself facing the united challenge of the Marcher lords, and soon the heir to the kingdom too. The opposition to Montfort, the royalist faction,[45] now would have an army and a figurehead around which to unite – something they very quickly did.

Edward, who had been made hostage by Montfort, threw events back into play in the spring of 1265. He'd earlier been held at Wallingford, where an attempt had been made to free him – only to be thwarted when his captors threatened to return Edward to his rescuers by mangonel.[46] However, on 28 May 1265, in a daring escape from those holding him captive, he used a ruse of exercising a horse on Wildemarsh Common, Hereford, to suddenly show them a clean set of hooves. Whilst his captors had tired their horses, and on a fresh horse himself, with a cry of "*aller! aller!*" Edward was away.[47] The metrical chronicler, Robert of Gloucester, imagined the escape a tad more poetically, if not fancifully: "Lordings! I bid you good day! Greet my father the King! And wish him well! And I hope to see him soon and release him from custody!"[48]

As arranged, accompanied by Thomas de Clare he joined with Roger de Mortimer and other horsemen sent by Maud de Braose to ride the twenty-two miles (thirty-five kilometres) to the castle at Wigmore. Edward's flight was, most likely, the idea of husband and wife Roger de Mortimer and Maud de Braose.[49] If the precise escape plan was Maud's, then, Alison Weir sees the long hand of Alianor as the source, writing: "Alianor enlisted her friend, Maud de Braose ... to plot Edward's escape."[50] Powicke had suggested that Edward had escaped into a "family circle of Marchers, bound together by the Braose connection". However, Prestwich found this argument to be "weak". Perhaps this is so, but then Prestwich doesn't comment on the extension of the possible plot from Maud de Braose to Alianor de Provence as do both the later works of Howell, Weir and Hardman and Weir, whose construction of the plot I find to point toward the likely woman to have been at the heart of things, Edward's mother.[51] Especially when we discover that the ultimate destination for Edward will be Ludlow Castle, the home of Pierre's half-brother-in-law, a man who owed his position in England to both Alianor and Pierre. The escape had all the derring-do of later flights to freedom of English heroes such as the "Young Winston", using the ruse of encouraging his captors to exercise and so exhaust their own horses before himself escaping on a fresh steed. It was most likely premeditated and certainly to a purpose, for one of Montfort's ruling council and key fellow rulers was one Gilbert de Clare, another powerful Marcher lord, and elder brother to Edward's escape accomplice Thomas.

The young Gilbert, known as Red Gilbert for his fiery red hair, had succeeded his late father Richard and held Glamorgan in the Welsh Marches. This was some about-face on the part of Clare, who'd fought with (and indeed been knighted by) Montfort at the Battle of Lewes. Clare had been one of nine appointed by Montfort to rule the kingdom following the Battle of Lewes, and indeed had been a leading member. Nonetheless, Gilbert de Clare, Earl of Gloucester had grown increasingly disenchanted with the way in which Montfort was using his position as de facto ruler of the kingdom to enrich himself and his own. Simon had taken the county Palatine of Chester, a part of Edward's appanage, as his own, and the chronicler at Chester records how on 4 January, his son Henri de Montfort had come to Chester to get the "*fidelitates et hominiatam*", "fealty and homage", from the citizens in his father's name.[52] But there was more. Much of Richard's lands in Devon and Cornwall were given to Montfort's fourth son, Guy; another, Amauri, was made treasurer of the church in York. If the land of the Lord Edward was not safe from the reach of Simon de Montfort, how safe was the land of the other Marcher lords? It was a fatal Montfortian mistake. Maddicott saw avarice as a key contradiction in Montfort's character, on the one side deeply religious, wearing a hair shirt and dressing modestly, enjoying close personal relationships with progressive bishops, like Robert Grosseteste of Lincoln and Walter de Cantilupe of Worcester, and yet nursing a deep personal grievance for supposed financial rewards not met by Henry; and as we've seen the outright self-enrichment in taking Chester. Maddicott suggests he "showed a great deal of self-knowledge when, according to a contemporary account, he prayed to be delivered from the sin of avarice".[53]

Meanwhile, for the escaping Edward, from Wigmore it would be on to Ludlow Castle, just ten miles (sixteen kilometres) distant, home of Geoffroi de Geneville, he the brother of Pierre de Savoie's vassal, the Lord of Gex, Simon de Joinville. At Ludlow Edward would rendezvous with Roger de Mortimer and the Earl of Gloucester, aka Red Gilbert.[54] Gefferoi

Chapter Ten

had been brought to England by Pierre de Savoie, and had been a councillor in Edward's service in the years before the baronial unrest, from 1255 until 1257.[55] The wife of Geoffroi de Geneville was another Maud, this time Maud de Lacy, the one-time wife of another Savoyard protégé of Pierre de Savoie, Pierre de Genève. Having married one Savoyard and then another, Ludlow Castle was very much in the Savoyard camp, and the family good friends of Alianor's.[56] So, in terms of our plot we should also remember that Geoffroi's younger brother, Simon de Joinville, had not only served as banneret in Henry's army in Gascony but been instrumental in bringing with him a whole cadre of Burgundian knights to the king's cause. We know that Geneville was in Ireland at the time of consideration, was Alianor and by extension Pierre in touch with Geneville at this time? Was their a plot on the part of Pierre's wider Savoyard network in conjunction with the Marchers to free Edward and change the game? The chroniclers of the time set the escape in the context of the Marcher revolt against Montfort, and this has coloured our thinking to date, but communication betwixt Gascony, Ireland and the Marches would by design have been unknown to them. That Alianor, Pierre and Gefferoi and Simon played a role in Edward's escape is impossible to prove, but it fits entirely with what we know of their relationships one to another, their past behaviour and the context of Edward's escape. As Howell rightly suggests, "it seems inconceivable" that Alianor, and by extension Pierre, had not been "in contact" with Geneville.[57] Beth Hartland agreed with Howell finding that "Gefferoi must have connived" in the escape of the Lord Edward.[58]

If we join the dots of events from Alianor's move to Gascony until Edward's escape, the prime mover of events does indeed seem to be Alianor de Provence and her Anglo-Savoyard royalist network, and pulling the strings, offstage, that Machiavellian maestro, her uncle, Pierre de Savoie. Chapuisat concisely summarises something of Edward's plight after Lewes that is mostly overlooked by English historians: the role of the Savoyards in supporting Edward's cause. He notes the army that *"Pierre prépare en Flandre"* and the defence of *"le château de Pevensey"* and finally that Edward should find *"un refuge sur les terres de Geoffroi de Joinville, à Ludlow"*[59] results in Edward having *"une confiance totale"* in his maternal family.[60] It would be a total confidence that Edward would increasingly turn to and rely upon. Edward never forgot two lessons from the war: first, the example of Pevensey withholding its long siege taught him the advantages of siting castles by the sea for resupply, but most importantly, when the chips were down, kin supported kin, his Savoyard family being people upon whom he could rely. The small army that had landed at Pembroke under Valence, Warenne and Bigod joined forces with Edward, Mortimer and Clare; men rallied to their banner, and all at once Montfort faced an existential threat to his domain and even his life.

There may also be evidence that, as Guillaume de Valence landed in South Wales, Pierre de Savoie joined the defenders at Pevensey. There is a parliamentary summons whereby the Sheriff of Sussex is commanded to summon Pierre de Savoie to a parliament to be held in June 1265.[61] Cox was of the opinion that Pierre had landed "illegally" in Sussex and joined the defenders of Pevensey; despite the scant evidence, it is difficult to imagine another reason the Montfortians would summon Pierre de Savoie to a June Parliament, unless he had in fact landed in Sussex – they could hardly summons him from Flanders.[62] In the event, the summons was ignored and the Montfortian government was to collapse, but if we think of the outline plot to release Edward as outlined by Howell, then a "second front", so to speak, of Pierre joining the defenders of his castle at Pevensey could make sense.

Peter of Savoy: The Little Charlemagne

We should also remember that Gilbert's late father Richard had been an ally of Alianor and Pierre de Savoie between 1258 and 1260, following meetings to arrange the marriage of the Marquis de Montferrand to Gilbert's sister Isabelle in 1257. We should not perhaps be entirely surprised that the relationship between the Savoyards and the Clares might revive itself to mutual advantage in 1265.[63] Carpenter suggests too that Gilbert de Clare "was surely complicit" in the Pembroke landings and thus all that followed.[64] The events of the spring and summer of 1265 are cloaked in mystery. A plot by definition leaves little trace; a plot hatched 700 and more years ago is impossible to prove or disprove, but does seem to fit the known facts rather well. We can summarise by joining the dots accordingly: negotiations with Montfort break down in the autumn of 1264, and bad weather and dwindling funds, together with a fear of harm to Edward render an invasion impossible. Following Alianor's move to Gascony a plot is hatched which is communicated by way of Ireland with Geneville and thence the Marcher lords whereby Edward will escape to Ludlow, and be supported by a change of sides by Gilbert de Clare and the arrival of Guillaume de Valence from Poitou. So we have Alianor acting with Valence, Warenne, Bigod, Clare, Mortimer and Geneville - that Alianor might have acted without Pierre de Savoie's connivance is hard to believe. The *Famille de Savoie's* part in the downfall of Simon de Montfort, cloaked as it was in subtle artifice and design would contrast with Montfort's pomp and triumphant departure from the Savoy Palace just a few short months earlier.

Quickly the apparent strength of Simon de Montfort in the winter of 1264–5 began to evaporate in the early summer of 1265. Simon, having prior to Edward's flight, marched on Gloucester to attempt to settle his differences with Clare, moved to Hereford to quell the flames of rebellion in the Marches. Simon unwisely sought Llywelyn ap Gruffydd as an ally. The Welsh as ever seeking to gain from English weakness, Llywelyn offered soldiers in return for recognition of his title as Prince of Wales. The Chester chronicler has a meeting of 5 January between Simon (presumably Henri) de Montfort and Llywelyn at Hawarden where an "*osculo pacis*" or "kiss of peace" was exchanged.[65] Beverley James in writing his definitive biography of Llywelyn acknowledges that "Llywelyn ap Iorwerth and Llywelyn ap Gruffydd each in turn, derived immense benefit from the internal divisions which affected the realm of England in their time."[66] Certainly, the Agreement of Pipton,[67] agreed by Llywelyn on 19 June[68] and by Henry at Hereford (as forced by Simon) on 22 June,[69] helped increase the hostility of Marcher lords like Mortimer and Clare toward the Montfortians. Of particular alarm to the Marchers would be that amongst other things the agreement conferred upon Llywelyn the castles he likely already held at Hawarden, a Norman motte and bailey castle overlooking Chester, in Tegeingl, and Whittington and Ellesmere in Shropshire.[70] The agreement sought to effectively wipe out Edward's lands in Wales east of the Conwy, reversing all of Henry's earlier gains. As we've seen, taking advantage of English weakness, Llywelyn had besieged and captured the king's castles at Dyserth and Deganwy by the Conwy in 1263. That this agreement is made under the seal of the King of England shows once more how Henry was a humiliated captive of Montfort. The humiliation of his father and the alliance between the Prince of Wales and Simon de Montfort would be added to Edward's tally of grievances against the Welsh. The soldiers would prove of little use to Simon as they broke quickly in the ensuing battle, but Edward's lasting grievance would cost Llywelyn's dynasty deeply.

With Edward's escape the royalists soon had Simon trapped. First, they took the town of Worcester and hearing that Simon's son, Simon junior, had given up the siege of Pevensey Castle, they moved to Kenilworth where the younger Simon was defeated. For the defenders

Chapter Ten

of Pevensey the long siege was over, Montfort junior had vented his frustrations on Winchester en route to Kenilworth, but for Nantelme de Cholay and the gallant defenders of Pevensey the war was as good as over.[71] They had defended their lord's castle; they had fulfilled their feudal obligations.

Meanwhile, Simon de Montfort himself was attempting to move to the east to unite with his son at Kenilworth when he encountered the royalists once more, close to Evesham in Worcestershire. What followed was the Battle of Evesham, although attaching the word battle to what might be best described as a slaughter is perhaps over-dignifying the day – Robert of Gloucester said of it, "murder of Evesham, for battle it was not".[72] Certainly it was Simon de Montfort's nemesis following hard on the heels of his recent hubris. On the night of 3 August, Walter de Cantilupe, Bishop of Worcester heard Simon de Montfort's confession. It would be his last.

Early on 4 August, a dark and stormy morning, an eyewitness recalled, "*le solail retret ... e un vent horrible coveri le firmament*" or "the sun left ... and a terrible wind covered the firmament."[73] Simon's army saw banners coming toward them from the north. They took them to be Simon's son. They were to be disappointed: it was the Lord Edward flying the Montfortian banners captured earlier at Kenilworth. Traditionally, sourced from the likes of Guisborough, Roger de Mortimer had sent his men to block the only possible escape route, at the Bengeworth bridge, but this is now far less certain.[74] Nonetheless, Edward had trapped Simon in the loop of a sharp bend in the River Avon. There was to be no chance of honourable retreat as he took the high ground this time as he deployed on Green Hill above Evesham. A monk dispatched atop of the abbey tower cried out, " We are all dead men, for it is not your son coming as you thought, but the King's son from one side, the Earl of Gloucester from another, and Roger Mortimer from a third."[75] An eyewitness to these moments suggests that it was put to Montfort that the abbey tower might be a defensible position, but Montfort responded, "*Noun, beaus amis, noun, mes homme doit quere chivalers en champs e chapileins a mouster*" or "No, fair friends, no, one ought to seek knights in fields and chaplains in churches."[76] The same eyewitness went on to recall that Montfort had said, "*Sagement vienent. Le corps sunt lour, les almes a Dieu*" or "Wisely they come. Our bodies are theirs, our souls are God's."[77]

By some accounts, Montfort's Welsh soldiers broke and ran for the bridge, where Mortimer awaited them and where they were slaughtered to a man, but the doubt concerning Mortimer's location by the bridge lends doubt to this account. Meanwhile, Edward had learned well from his mistakes at Lewes: this time he knew that in order to win he would have to remove the head from what he saw as the rebellious Montfortian snake. To this end he decided upon what amounted to a "death squad" of knights, who would make it their purpose during the battle to seek out and eliminate Simon de Montfort. The night before at Mosham, Edward and Clare had dubbed several knights, but also:

> Meanwhile Sir Edward had knighted several men in the meadow called Mosham between Craycombe and Evesham and had chosen and designated twelve of the strongest and most intrepid sergeants, and they knew that they were to kill the earl of Leicester, and break through the ranks forcibly and rapidly in such a way that they would look at no one nor let anyone come between them until they reached the person of the Earl.[78]

This they did with bloody efficiency: Simon was brought down in the heat of battle – no ransom for the famed knight – and this time he disappeared under a hail of blows.[79] Roger de

Mortimer led those who applied the coup de grâce. Our eyewitness recalled, "with his lance struck him through the neck, and it was Sir Roger de Mortimer, for he could be recognised by his armour and shield-straps."[80] The one-time ruler of England was decapitated on the spot, shorn of his legs, arms, and having his testicles removed and hung from his nose.[81] The chronicler Thomas Wykes has a full account of the slaughter, writing of Simon's end: "Simon de Montfort, was not only the head that fell beheaded, but his arms and legs were cut off and he sank in pieces, scarcely a stock remained".[82] The ever Montfortian chronicler of Waverley Abbey went so far as to use the word "martyrdom; he was writing some decades after the event and by then the cult of Simon had taken hold.[83]

The dismembered head, complete with appendages, was carried from the battlefield to Wigmore Castle as a gift for the wife of Roger de Mortimer – Rishanger invoked the aid of John the Baptist whose fate at the hands of Salome he compared to Montfort's.[84] It is not recorded what the lady made of Simon's testicles being presented to her, but apparently Maud de Braose was no fan of Montfort.[85] What was left of poor Simon, likely to have been just a rather bloody torso, was buried by the monks of Evesham Abbey. Montfort had brought his other "hostage" Henry with him to the battle. Indeed, the king had almost been killed, taken for a rebel before crying out, "I am Henry of Winchester your King, do not kill me."[86] Remarkably for the time, the rebellious knights were not ransomed. Some forty knights were put to Edward's sword: Henry de Montfort, Hugh Despenser, Peter de Montfort and Roger St. John amongst others.[87] The young Edward was nothing if he wasn't militarily efficient. Gone was the foolhardy excess of Lewes: in its place was a steely determination to obliterate his enemy.

Edward lost little time in reclaiming what he thought to be his, taking back the County palatine of Chester within ten days of Evesham. Following news of his earlier escape, James de Audley and Urian de Saint-Pierre had already moved to retake the key border castle of Beeston for Edward.[88] Accordingly, Llywelyn destroyed the Norman motte and bailey castle he'd only recently taken at Hawarden, preferring his own, more recently constructed castle at Ewloe as a first line of defence for the Perfeddwlad, and withdrew.[89] Following Evesham, Edward retired to Beeston, high atop its rock above the Cheshire plain with some of the few prisoners taken in the battle: the badly injured and soon-to-die Humphrey V de Bohun, Henri de Hastings and Simon's son, the also seriously injured Guy de Montfort.[90]

This would be the Edward Plantagenet that the Celtic regions of the island of Britain would come to know and dread. Edward was to be a Plantagenet in the mould of his great-grandfather, Henry, and of his great-great-uncle Richard, not his pious but militarily incompetent father Henry. Henry's biographer, Church, suggests the reason for the butchery at Evesham was that Simon de Montfort had "committed class treason by encouraging the unworthy to believe that they, too, had a stake in the kingdom".[91]

This is an idea that brings us to a consideration of Simon de Montfort, a man to many who had sown the seeds of modern parliamentary democracy. There have been many that, to use the words of E. F. Jacob, have heard "Big Ben in the thunder of the Battle of Lewes".[92] Remarkably, in 1965, a memorial of stone from Montfort-l'Amauri (de Montfort's family home in France) was laid on the site of the former altar by Speaker of the House of Commons Sir Harry Hylton-Foster and Archbishop of Canterbury Michael Ramsey. The United States House of Representatives has a relief of Simon de Montfort upon its wall. Ironically, Napoleon Bonaparte said of Montfort that he was "one of the greatest Englishmen" – odd really; perhaps the Frenchman didn't realise that Montfort was in fact a fellow countryman of

Chapter Ten

his. Then again, he was of course a Corsican himself. Victorians eulogised Montfort, since for them he had been the prototype democrat, something he himself would not have recognised. Victorian historian James Birchall recounted that "he was regarded as a saint by his own generation and was known by the name of 'Saint Simon the Righteous'".[93] Historians have been divided. Treharne saw the "idealist", Knowles the "opportunist" and Powicke the "dark and destructive force".[94] In our own times the University of Leicester, of which Simon was of course Earl, now proudly carries the title De Montfort University. So why have subsequent generations venerated Simon de Montfort, and not just in England, but in France and in far-away North America? The answer probably lies with the Parliament that Montfort had called in January of 1265 to settle the running of the kingdom. Parliament in the UK, itself describes its ancestor in this way:

> In 1265, Montfort called a ground-breaking Parliament. As well as the Lords, he summoned knights from the shires and representatives from towns, who were known as burgesses. This was the first time that both knights and burgesses – "common men" – had attended Parliament together to discuss national issues and not just consent to taxation.[95]

It is very unlikely Simon de Montfort saw himself in this light. Certainly, he was a very principled man. He continually saw himself as the true upholder of the Provisions of Oxford and, having taken an oath, a man unwilling to break it. And indeed, he had reached out to the peasants of England to broaden his support as it had begun to weaken amongst his peers. True enough, he saw himself as the upholder of *Magna Carta*, on 14 February 1265, as Henry's adherence to the great charter had once more been declared. But as the founder of modern democracy, no. Simon de Montfort was a man of the thirteenth century, not the twentieth or twenty-first century. Gilbert de Clare switched sides, as mentioned earlier, because Montfort was enriching himself at the expense of the realm. He had in 1264 stripped Edward of the valuable palatine earldom of Chester, for one reason – it was incredibly wealthy. However, not only had he stripped Edward of the earldom, he had awarded it to himself – and most importantly he had done so in a way that meant his own heirs would inherit the earldom. On 4 January 1264, the Chester chronicler reported that "*Henricus primogenitus Simonis de Monteforti ... recepit nomine patris sui fidelitates et homiatam*", that "Henry the eldest son of Simon de Montfort ... had received in his father's name the fealty and homage" of both the citizens of the city and county of Chester.[96] Worse perhaps, Henry de Montfort had met with Llywelyn ap Gruffydd at Hawarden to explore mutual spheres of interest and influence.[97] The Chester chronicler gives us the date of the meeting as 5 January, and that in addition to Llywelyn, that Gruffydd ap Madog of Powys Fadog was there also. He goes on to charitably suggest that the meeting was "to some extent" to put an end to the long war between "Cheshire and Wales"[98] – it's doubtful whether Henry or Edward would have cast the meeting in such a charitable light. All of this strongly suggests an attempt to enfeeble the ruling Plantagenet family in favour of the Montfort family – in modern parlance, regime change. Historian Maddicott, author of *The Origins of the English Parliament, 924–1327*, told the BBC:

> The knights and burgesses helped to counterbalance this weakness. They were probably seen as useful emissaries, returning from the parliament to their localities to spread the news of the reforms being undertaken. They could be

used to build support for Montfort beyond their own ranks and throughout the country ... If Montfort was "the father of the House of Commons" he was so only, as it were, by accident. The summoning of knights and burgesses in 1265 was an expedient, not a piece of farsighted constitutional planning.[99]

I would agree entirely with that sentiment: the much-hailed Simon was godfather to the English Parliament, the "mother of parliaments" more by accident of history than by design – he was no freedom fighter. Historian M. T. Clanchy wrote that Simon had "released forces which he could not control", that "his government was as arbitrary as the king's" and that "the rebel barons were not democrats".[100] Carpenter, in a recent edition of *In Our Time* for the BBC, held the view now that any victory for Montfort at Evesham would have inexorably led to King Simon I.[101] And yet the expedient that he had employed in bringing into government for the first time men from outside of the ruling clique let a genie out of the bottle that would forever refuse to be pushed back in, and on battlefields around the English-speaking world from Naseby to Yorktown, the common man would continue to demand a say in his governance – something entirely at odds with feudalism. Simon de Montfort was a man of contradiction, religious and yet given to much avarice. We should not see him as the "founder of Parliament", more as an inadvertent player in a long complex road to parliamentary democracy. As French historian Charles Petit-Dutaillis wrote: "the Parliament called together by Simon de Montfort had been an expedient, and that no one realised at the time that a new institution was being born."[102] His adherence to the oath taken to support the Provisions of Oxford, and refusal to adopt a more pragmatic stance ultimately led to his demise. But in summary there are two stains on Montfort's record that are linked: firstly his treatment of the Jewry of Leicester and London, perhaps mitigated by his being a man of his times, but less easy to excuse is his exploitation of the xenophobia that swept England in the 1260s, something he deliberately encouraged.

For Henry's part, he had seen the man he had welcomed into the kingdom, raised to be earl, married his sister to, made a godfather to his son of, but the same man who had rebelled and nearly destroyed his kingdom and dynasty. He had seen him dead, as Baker recounts:

> There's no record of any last words to pass between these two historic antagonists as they rode off to meet their fates that morning. Probably there weren't any. After thirty years of sharing the world's stage together, they had nothing more to say to each other.[103]

And so passes from our tale Simon de Montfort. But it wasn't the end of the civil war quite yet. Henry and Edward moved on rebellious London by way of Winchester and Windsor. In October 1265, following the arrest of the mayor, who'd sued for peace at Windsor, the king and his son entered the city that had so ill-treated Alianor. The forfeiture of property began immediately, the Montfort Earldom of Leicester would be forfeit to the Crown in 1265, and given by Henry to his second son, Edmund, as a new creation of the earldom in 1267. Edmund also received the title and lands of the rebel Robert de Ferrers, 6th Earl of Derby, in 1266. He'd been arrested following the revolt and languished in first Wallingford and then Windsor Castle. His castle at Tutbury, in the county of Derby, was part of Edmund's new earldom. In 1267, he would also be appointed High Sheriff of Lancaster and later in 1276 add it to a new earldom, that of Lancaster, with Edmund becoming the first Earl of Lancaster and founding a line that would eventually

Chapter Ten

become kings of England and contest the throne with the House of York in what became known as the Wars of the Roses. Edmund's great-granddaughter Blanche de Lancaster married John O'Gaunt, the fourth son of King Edward III, himself a grandson of Edward I – royal lines were both complex and the conflict that so often arose, internecine.

That the Savoyard Othon de Grandson was most probably with Edward, as part of his household knights, is likely from the events following Evesham.[104] Immediately Henry gave orders for land held by the rebels, deceased or otherwise, to be forfeit to the Crown.[105] Savoyard beneficiaries of the post-war land resettlement were the cousins from Lac de Neuchâtel, Pierre de Champvent and Othon de Grandson, both obtaining property in London, Champvent the houses in London of Robert de Montpellier and lands of Guillaume Le Blund, who'd fallen fighting on the Montfortian side at Lewes.[106] Grandson was granted houses at Queenhithe that had belonged to rebel Simon de Hadestok[107] – bustling, noisy Queenhithe, not far from the newly complained St. Paul's Cathedral,[108], was where all cargoes of corn and wool entering the city of London were unloaded. A century earlier William FitzStephen had given us a little of the colour of the London Grandson now called home:

> Moreover there is in London upon the river's bank, amid the wine that is sold from ships and wine-cellars, a public cook-shop. There daily, according to the season, you may find viands, dishes roast, fried, and boiled, fish great and small, the coarser flesh for the poor, the more delicate for the rich, such as venison and birds both big and small. If friends, weary with travel, should of a sudden come to any of the citizens, and it is not their pleasure to wait fasting till fresh food is bought and cooked.[109]

After describing his favourite eatery FitzStephen, obviously proud of his city, went on to describe the beating heart of London:

> To this city, from every nation that is under heaven,
> merchants rejoice to bring their trade in ships.
> Gold from Arabia, from Sabaea spice
> And incense; from the Scythians arms of steel Well-tempered; oil from the rich
>   groves of palm
> That spring from the fat lands of Babylon;
> Fine gems from Nile, f'rom China crimson silks; French wines; and sable,
>   vair and miniver
> From the far lands where Russ and Norsemen dwell.[110]

The house of Othon de Grandson was a long way from the quiet of his birthplace by Lac de Neuchatel; he was now one of the "infinitude of knights or foreigners" that FitzStephen described as treading the streets of a "city older than Rome".[111]

A month later Othon and Pierre de Savoie were granted the lands of William le Blund, who had fallen fighting for Montfort at Lewes.[112] Such a grant of property by the victorious Edward was, of course, for services rendered – and given the proximity of such services rendered to Evesham and Lewes, it's hard not to conclude Othon's participation.[113] More than a year later Othon de Grandson would become Sir Othon de Grandson. It seems likely that his father Pierre de Grandson had died years earlier, in 1258, making Othon the Lord of

Peter of Savoy: The Little Charlemagne

Grandson, but he did not return to Savoy – he would only pay fleeting visits to his home for the next fifty years, each time whilst business for Edward meant he could call in en route.[114] Also at Evesham was fellow Savoyard Jean de Grailly, who'd brought a Gascon contingent to the battle – his reward from Edward, with Alianor's consent, becoming the Viscount of Benauges and the city of Natz, both in Gascony.[115] It seems therefore certain that, although the Savoyard invasion in support of Henry was not to materialise, the victors of Evesham had Savoyard in their midst. Jean de Grailly went on to be Edward's *sénéchal* in Gascony, signing treaties in the king's name with Navarre and France.

From London Edward marched to Dover, there to accept the surrender of his aunt, Simon de Montfort's wife, Eleanor. Also at Dover he welcomed the return of his mother, Queen Alianor, but not of his uncles Pierre or Boniface, who chose for the moment to remain in Savoy; the settlement of the civil war was not yet complete and should be an English affair. It has been implied that Pierre fled the kingdom during the escalating crisis of the civil war, not to return. This is perhaps unfair: he was now the Count of Savoy and had a wide territory to take care of, and increased responsibility to maintain the family's homeland in the mountains. Certainly, Henry restored to Pierre his lands in Richmond and Sussex; a charter dated 10 September gives the post-war settlement as far as Pierre was concerned:

> Whereas by the counsel of the magnates of the council, the king has restored to Peter de Sabaudia his uncle, all his lands, possessions and goods seized by reason of the late disturbance in the realm, he commands the said Peter's tenants of the honours of Laigle and Hastinges to be intendant to Gwichard de Charrun, to whom the king has committed the same in the name of the said Peter ... In like manner it is commanded to the tenants of the honour of Richmond.[116]

There would be the inevitable clean-up at Pevensey. Denise de Pevensey made good the churches of Pevensey and Westham. As for the castle it's possible that Imbert de Montréal may well have had repairs carried out. Montréal, recorded in English archives as Imbert, is almost certainly Humbert de Montréal, for five years later he is remembered in Pierre de Savoie's last will and testament. Pierre remembers to reimburse Humbert for thirty marks in fortifying Pevensey.[117] Sadly, the will doesn't tell us whether the works were during the siege or for repairs made afterward. Montréal also received lands in England following the peace, as we saw with Grandson and Champvent, being granted the lands of the rebel Guillaume de Goldingham.[118]

With all now seemingly restored in England, on his return to Savoy from Flanders, Pierre embarked upon a wide-ranging reform of the county; having seen the sophisticated royal government of England, he had much work to do. In the *Pays de Vaud*, for example, he regrouped administration for the *Pays de Vaud* into one *bailliage*[119] at Moudon, from the previous seventeen *châtellenies*,[120] a bailiwick in English terms, which would roughly correspond to the modern Canton de Vaud.[121] In addition to Moudon, the *bailliages* of Chillon would take care of the Chablais and the Valais, Montmélian controlled Savoy itself, Châtel Argent the Aosta Valley and Avigliana the Susa Valley.[122] Given this reorganisation, moving away from feudal lordships based upon castles towards a wider jurisdiction based upon an appointed bailiff, we can see the first moves toward a modern administration and away from the land-based feudality of previous centuries. In Savoy this marked the return of the paid official as administrator not seen since the dying days of the Carolingian Empire. We will return to Pierre's groundbreaking reforms in Savoy in the next chapter. Furthermore, Pierre was once more acquiring territory, this time

Chapter Ten

in 1266 the tithes for Bière in Vaud from Ebal III de Mont, the nephew of the newly installed Constable of Windsor Castle, Ebal II de Mont. His return from Flanders coincides too with his assignment of work at Chillon to Maître Jacques. No doubt he'd want to feel more secure at Chillon as full-time resident there from this point.

Meanwhile, in England, one of the two main remaining rebel forces (the other in the Isle of Ely) was holed up in the great Montfortian castle of Kenilworth. What followed was one of the few full-scale medieval sieges on English soil, trebuchets and all. The summons to surrender the castle had come in December 1265, but it was not until 21 June 1266 that the great siege began. There were some 1,200 Montfortians within the castle, protected to the south by the great artificial lake or mere, but on all sides by thick curtain walls. The siege would last some 172 days or six months until final surrender in December 1266, the besieged when they came out looking gaunt and pale. The original siege engines had proven inadequate for the work, the weapons on the inside having greater range than those on the outside and Henry had to call up for replacements from London. Trebuchets were hurling stone balls weighing over 300 pounds (140 kilograms) into the walls of the defenders. Additional artillery for the siege were brought to Kenilworth from Nottingham Castle by Pierre de Champvent, "one *ballistam de trullio* and four *balistas ad duas pedes*".[123] Henry brought a papal legate and two bishops to Kenilworth to excommunicate the defenders, who promptly dressed one of their own as a legate and excommunicated the attackers in turn. Two months into the siege Henry celebrated the Assumption of the Virgin Mary with a lavish feast in plain sight of the defenders – psychological warfare designed to drive the starving garrison to surrender. Henry even summoned barges for a waterborne assault across the mere – it failed. Plans to undermine the walls also failed. Archaeologists found a missile thrown some 350 yards (320 metres) by those assaulting the castle – this was a siege in the grand medieval style. Once the siege was finally over, Henry called a parliament, which ended with the Dictum of Kenilworth.[124]

In March 1266, Pierre de Champvent's brother, Guillaume, Dean of St. Martin's Le Grand[125] in London, was entrusted by Henry to travel to Rome to explain events in England to Pope Clement IV. Guillaume was to "lay before him the damages, injuries, oppressions and grievances inflicted upon the king by occasion of the late disturbance in the realm".[126] Guillaume de Champvent would go on to become Bishop of Lausanne whilst retaining a role as envoy and diplomat for the Crown in Edward's reign, a role performed also and to a far greater extent by his cousin Othon de Grandson. Indeed, from 1273 onwards, Savoyards used by Edward in embassies to France included Jean de Grailly, Gefferoi de Joinville, Amédée V de Savoie and Gérard de Vuippens in addition to the ever-present Othon de Grandson.[127] With Pierre de Savoie now focusing on his responsibilities as Count of Savoy, his role of diplomat in the service of the kings of England was passing to a new generation of Savoyards. Normal service was being resumed. If the Montfortians had sought to reduce Savoyard influence upon English diplomacy, they singularly failed. As if to make the point, on 29 May 1266 the Savoyard Archbishop of Canterbury, Boniface de Savoie, returned to his see after nearly four years of de facto exile, his officials having safeguarded his plate and treasure during the civil war.[128] He would leave England for the last time on 14 November 1268, passing away on 14 July 1270 at Saint Hélène-des-Millières in the Tarentaise. He was buried with other members of his family in Hautecombe Abbey, where his current tomb celebrates his stand for church dignities, rights and privileges.

Thomas Wykes wrote of Boniface that he was "a man of astonishing simplicity, although less literate, he lived in sobriety, and ruled himself by the advice of the wisest".[129] Curiously,

Boniface had an after-life of some importance: his tomb became the centre of a cult, and when the grave was opened in 1580, his body was found to be perfectly preserved. Sadly, the tomb and effigy were destroyed in the flames of the French Revolution, but his remains were reburied and a new tomb built in 1839. The archbishop would be beatified by Pope Gregory XVI later that year, and his feast day set as 14 July. So, it turned out the English had, for all those years, been living with a saint. Whilst it's true that Matthew Paris changed his opinion somewhat on Boniface de Savoie, altering some of his more acerbic and provocative descriptions,[130] the beatification of Boniface would have no doubt surprised him. It's not possible, sadly, to guess what Matthew Paris would have made of Saint Boniface, but if you listen very carefully at Hautecombe you can hear the sound of a monk swiftly revolving in a grave in far-off England. As we noted earlier, modern historians such as Carpenter have been kinder to Boniface than was Paris, Carpenter suggesting that "he became a respected and reforming archbishop".[131]

It seems that the final settlement of the English affairs of the Montfort family included Henry's brother-in-law, Louis. The Calendar of Patent Rolls for 25 September 1266, during the period of the siege of Kenilworth, records Henry's receipt of an ambassador from France, Pierre de Cusanc, most likely from the same de Cusanc family of the Franche-Comté that would later serve in England. Henry received Pierre at Kenilworth itself, asking that settlement of the affairs of Simon de Montfort reflect the "damages, trespasses and injuries committed against the king and his faithful subjects". The involvement of the French king reflects the cross-Channel nature of both Henry's and Simon's families.[132]

One last of the Montfortian era relates to Jean de Vesci, the one-time ward of Pierre de Savoie and husband of Savoyard Agnès de Saluzzo. Jean had sided with Simon de Montfort during the recent war, and had been injured at the Battle of Evesham. During 1267 he'd retired to his family castle at Alnwick, in Northumbria, there to begin a revolt of the northern barons. Edward led an army to the northeast and forced Jean de Vesci into submission, but what happened next is a little at odds with the traditional image of Edward. The chronicler Thomas Wykes describes his mercy to the one-time rebel.[133] In return, as we shall see, Jean de Vesci became a lifelong servant of the future king, trusted alongside Edward's lifelong friend Othon de Grandson. The ability of Edward to show clemency and be rewarded with lifelong service thereafter is something often overlooked.

Meanwhile, on 5 January 1266, in Rome, the whole Sicilian business and the Hohenstaufen dispute came to an end, as Charles d'Anjou was crowned King of Naples and Sicily. Thus Béatrice de Provence became also a queen like her three sisters. This was the Hohenstaufen crown hawked around Europe for decades in an attempt (ultimately successful) to clip the wings of the Hohenstaufen eagle. Manfred had ruled his father's kingdom since Frederick's death in 1250, first as regent for the young Conradin, then in his own right from 1258 when he'd usurped the throne. Pope Alexander IV then released Henry and England from their Sicilian entanglement before dying in 1261. He was replaced by Jacques Pantaléon, the son of a French cobbler from Troyes in Champagne, who reigned as Urban IV. Perhaps unsurprisingly, in view of the problems encountered attempting to use the Plantagenets to depose the Hohenstaufen, he turned to his fellow countrymen, the Capetians: the throne was offered once more to Charles d'Anjou. Urban offered the kingdom to Charles for much less than the £90,300 Alexander had asked of Henry: a special cut-price deal for a fellow Frenchman of just 50,000 marks. Given the long animosity between the popes and the Hohenstaufen, the French invasion of Italy would receive the official papal designation of a crusade.[134] Charles led an army of some 30,000 men into Italy. After some minor clashes, the rival armies met at the Battle of Bennevento on 26 February 1266, and

Chapter Ten

Manfred's army was defeated. Manfred fought bravely to save his Hohenstaufen inheritance, but the Capetians were too strong, and he died in battle. We meet Manfred in Dante's *Divine Comedy*, outside the gates of purgatory, where the spirit explains that, although he repented of his sins in *articulo mortis*, he must atone for his contumacy by waiting thirty years for each year he lived as an excommunicate before being admitted to purgatory proper.

Whilst Manfred waited outside of purgatory, the long struggle between the papacy and the Hohenstaufens went into its endgame. Young Conradin, by now all of 16, attempted to win back his grandfather's legacy and invaded Italy from Germany. After losing the Battle of Tagliacozzo on 23 August 1268, he proceeded to Torre Astura in an attempt to sail for Sicily, but here he was arrested and handed over to Charles, who imprisoned him in the Castell dell'Ovo in Naples. He was tried as a traitor, and on 29 October 1268 Charles d'Anjou had the last of the Hohenstaufen line beheaded. The long struggle between the papacy and the Swabian Hohenstaufen had gone to the popes, leaving Charles d'Anjou master of southern Italy and Sicily. But for Henry, Edward, Edmund and the English barons, the Sicilian business that had plagued them for so long and perhaps become the spark that had lit rebellion was now most decisively closed.

Chapter Eleven

Pierre, meanwhile, as we have seen, had returned to Savoy and begun reforms that would lay the foundations for a Savoyard state amidst the Alps – foundations laid upon the administrative practices he'd found in Anglo-Norman England. In this project he was assisted by many of the associates he'd taken from Savoy to England with him, now returned to the towering Alps. *Bailis* were introduced as a means of establishing a local agency for centralised control of the county – Val d'Aosta, Savoy, Viennois, Bugey, Vaud and the Genevois, the Chablais and the Valais. One of his first acts as count had been the purchase of a small castle in Aosta, which still stands at the northeastern corner of the old Roman city close to where the amphitheatre had once stood, for the purpose of accommodating his new bailiff (see figure 2.7).[1] But historians will be most thankful for the introduction by Pierre of the first *chambre des comptes* – the first comprehensive archives for the County of Savoy. In an echo of the earlier conquest by William of Normandy in England, Pierre requested that clerks produce a transcription of hundreds of documents dating from 1218 to 1260 upon a long roll of parchment.

In England an annual audit was recorded on a great roll (the 'pipe roll', as it was later called), a new one being opened for every year. The audit for 1130 is the earliest to survive, it is made up of 16 individual membranes, each around four feet in length and a foot wide and made up of 2 smaller membranes, written on both sides. All 16 were then sewn together at the top so that they could be rolled up into a single roll - hence pipe roll. The roll for 1130 runs to 161 pages in a modern transcribed edition, and records over 300 writs authorising expenditure or pardoning debts, and mentions over 2,000 people and places. A magnificent feat of administrative endeavour, and one which Pierre was mightily impressed with. We should remember at this point that whilst Pierre had extensive contacts, friends and allies within the Plantagenet civil-service and we should be wary in pointing to just one of them as being more influential than the others in exporting this English system, but that John Mansel as Chancellor was at the pyramid of this audit seems instructive. Like English pipe rolls, the purpose of the parchment roll was financial, concerning itself with expenses and revenues. Pierre had no doubt seen Henry III's pipe rolls and taken careful note (see figure 2.8). The alliance between Savoy and England in the thirteenth century had effects in both Britain and the Alpine region. If ultimately the greatest Savoyard legacy in Britain would be the castles of north Wales, then the introduction of pipe rolls to Savoy would be the lasting English legacy in the Alps. As André Perret wrote:

> These itinerant officials, Thomas de Rossillon, Simon de Verters and others, went on site to verify the accounts and wrote them on rolls of parchment, modelled after the rolls of English accounts. It was during their stays in

Chapter Eleven

England that Pierre de Savoie and his advisers came into contact with the highly developed administration of the island kingdom.[2]

The pipe roll was an elaborate means of audit, an audited account of expenditure, for which an official had to render account for expenses incurred. As Perret went on to say, not only were accounts now being kept as in England, but as in England "where the archives of the Crown were carefully kept Pierre took great care of the Savoyard archive".[3] Sadly the French Revolution robbed us of accounts for the Viennois, Bugey and the Tarentaise – all now parts of France – but eleven rolls, containing twenty-eight accounts, do survive for the Aosta and Susa valleys in Italy, Maurienne and Savoy in France and lastly Vaud, Chablais and Valais in Switzerland.[4] These châtelain accounts would prove invaluable to English scholars, such as Arnold Taylor, piecing together the early career of Master James of Saint George who began working for Pierre de Savoie before his reign as count began, in 1260, and whose work at Yverdon is recorded in the châtelain accounts of Chillon. We might say at this point, that not only were the great castles of Edward I's reign made possible by Pierre de Savoie's earlier career in England, but that without Pierre's diligent creation of a Savoyard archive then historians such as Taylor would never have been able to follow the primary-source trail that led from Yverdon to Beaumaris. This focus on record-keeping introduced into Savoy that very English of institutions – a civil service with an administrative bureaucracy. Pierre de Savoie brought the English civil service to the Alps – in spirit if not in materiality. When Pierre had come to England for the first time, he'd inherited, so to speak, a sophisticated administrative system running both the Honours of Richmond and the Eagle, and this he would bring back to Savoy, perhaps with touches of the French royal administration he'd found in his travels to Paris. There was the introduction of clerks to check the accounts of the bailiffs and castellans, men like the aforementioned Thomas de Rossillon and Simon de Verters.[5] Indeed, Rossillon was, like Pierre, more than familiar with the English system from his constant visits to England on Pierre's behalf.

Judicial reform was introduced to the Alpine regions too, as Cox writes, "The judicial authority of the counts of Savoy was at this time almost as varied as the scenery of their transalpine valleys."[6] Pierre issued the *Statuta Petri Comitis Sabaudiae*,[7] creating a new class of judicial officers, creating the first judges in Savoy – the new judges would have a law degree and be salaried judges too.[8] These new judges would hear cases of criminal and civil procedure, with the introduction of *advocati* and notaries. Cox writes, "Parties in a dispute were obliged to take a '*sacamentum calumniae*', an oath that they were acting in all honesty and good faith, and lawyers were permitted to assist them in drawing up a statement of their case."[9] With echoes of the *Magna Carta*, to no one will we .. delay justice, he knew well from England, Pierre promised that cases would be tried "*absque dilatione decidantur et terminentur per iudicem nostrum*", or "without delay they are decided and determined by our judge".[10] Magna Carta was being exported to England's allies in the same century as its birth; its continued hold over the imagination of men would grow ever profound.

These legal reforms followed the pattern established in the century before in England by Henry II, a system that Pierre had grown accustomed to in England and that he'd found to be beneficial in terms of establishing a state. Henry II had institutionalised common law by creating a unified system of law "common" to all England through incorporating and elevating local custom to the national, ending local control and peculiarities, eliminating arbitrary remedies and reinstating a jury system – citizens sworn on oath to investigate reliable criminal accusations and civil claims. This national system would now be applied by Pierre to the County of Savoy. Interestingly, we also hear an echo of the Montfortian reforms in England in Savoy, Pierre having been of course a member of Henry's council established by the Provisions of Oxford in 1258. As Cox again writes, "the influence of Simon de Montfort's regime ... The preamble to the Statutes states that they are being promulgated for the benefit 'of all men, nobles as well as non-nobles, clerics, religious, burghers, rustics, and farmers,' and '*de voluntare et consensu nobilium et innobilum Comitatus Sabaudiae et burgensium*'."[11] Pierre de Savoie, it is oft forgotten, was a fellow oath-taker, along with Simon de Montfort, of 1258, and a fellow member of the Council of Fifteen. That he parted company with Montfort in 1260 and remained loyal to Alianor, Henry and Edward does not detract from his sympathy for the original reforming aims of the baronial faction in England, just that he could not in conscience accompany Montfort all the way to the xenophobia of 1264–5.

So, we see in Pierre's reign in Savoy, and continued with that of his brother Philippe, the arrival of *les baillis* and *les juges territoriaux* – bailiffs and territorial judges – administrators and legal officers of the County of Savoy.[12] Taken together, Pierre's reforms were an important milestone upon the development of a recognisably modern state in the Alpine region. As the English would find, the reforming ideas of Oxford were infectious and difficult to suppress. Henceforth, and perhaps one of Pierre de Savoie's lasting legacies, the County of Savoy was governed by a triad of castellans, bailiffs and judges.[13] The introduction of bailiffs in Savoy had come before Pierre's elevation to count in 1263; he'd introduced them in his lands in Vaud from 1260–1.[14] Eventually Savoy would be served by the baillages of Montmelian for Savoie Propre, Chillon for Chablais, Moudon for Vaud, Avigliana for the Val di Susa, Châtel Argent for the Val d'Aosta, Saint-Georges d'Espéranche for the Viennois and Rossillon for Bugey.[15]

In England there had been bailiffs before the Norman conquest. The Anglo-Saxons had called them *reeves*, from which with the addition of the word *shire* we get *shire reeves*, or conflated to sheriff. The word bailiff had been attached to the role by the Normans, using their Anglo-Norman dialect of French, *bailli* coming from the Latin *bajalus*, which gives us our meaning in Savoy, *bajalus* meaning *manager*. In England Pierre would have been used to the term and operation of bailiffs, and their domain, in English the *bailiwick*, the wick being the addition to *bailli* of the Old English word *wick* for village – in French this would be rendered as *baillage*. To this day, for administrative purposes, the rump of the Norman Duchy of Normandy, the Channel Islands, are divided into the bailiwicks of Jersey and Guernsey. In France, much frequented by Pierre de Savoie in his negotiations with Louis IX, *baillis* had been largely a twelfth-century innovation of Philippe Auguste. The bailiff was then a high-ranking official, representing the king in the fullness of his duties in his constituency.

There was an evolution too in the role of the castellan, from seigneurial, based on the old feudal ideas of fidelity and loyalty, toward a new model of being an officer of the state, of the count. The castellans had been both military governors but also responsible for the collection of the count's revenues and administration of his law.[16] Indeed, the earliest castellan accounts that survive for Savoy predate Savoyard involvement, but only just, and by just one example: 1247 at Falavier, a fief acquired by Pierre de Savoie in 1250[17] – no earlier accounts survive. As Guido Castelnuovo and Christian Guilliéré put it, the castellans "abandoned their seigneurial traits to acquire an ever more administrative character".[18] What we are witnessing in Pierre de Savoie's Savoy is the dissolution of the feudal order of authority, devolved from the centre by means of an award of territory in reward for mostly military service, to a return to a system

Chapter Eleven

the Romans would have better recognised, one of paid governmental officials – paid in salary to hold an office on behalf of the central government.[19]

Also, of pressing need for Pierre on his return to Savoy, were the war clouds gathering to the north with the House of Habsburg, and toward his immediate east with the Bishop of Sion. A four-year struggle between the Savoyard and the Habsburg ensued. Rudolf I von Habsburg had, at his father Albert IV's death in 1239, inherited large estates around the ancestral seat of Habsburg Castle in the Aargau region of present-day Switzerland as well as in Alsace – this would establish him as the main northern rival to the Savoyards in Helvetia.

The Kyburg dynasty that had ruled much of German-speaking Helvetia since the fall of the Zähringen dynasty was itself now on the verge of extinction. The childless Hartmann IV, also known as Hartmann the Younger, had passed much of his lands to his nephew Hartmann V also known as Hartmann the Elder in 1250. By the time Hartmann V von Kyburg died on 3 September 1263, Rudolf von Habsburg was not only the guardian of his only child, a daughter, Anna, but protector of the late Hartmann's wife, Elizabeth de Bourgogne. The Habsburg family, not yet held in check by the not-yet-born Swiss cantons, now held the German lands of Helvetia, the inheritors of the lands of both the Zähringen and Kyburgs. However, Pierre was the protector of the wife of the still-living Hartmann IV von Kyburg, his sister Marguerite de Savoie. It was understood that Hartmann IV was prepared see his lands pass to the House of Savoy.

Pierre moved quickly following news of Hartmann V's death to visit his own nephew, Richard Earl of Cornwall, also overlord of Helvetia as King of the Romans. It was once supposed that the new Count of Savoy would also now be created Imperial Vicar.[20] On 17 October 1263, at Berkamsted, Pierre certainly visited his nephew Richard of Cornwall, now King of the Romans.[21] There he was invested with lands in northern Helvetia belonging to the Kyburgs also claimed by the Habsburgs. Pingon, cited by Wurstemberger and subsequently the artist Angelo Verolengo, took this to be an investiture as Imperial Vicar.[22] Apocryphally, Pierre answered an imperial clerk who questioned his authority by replying "my titles are my sword". The title Imperial Vicar carried with it the ability to administer a part of the empire on behalf of the emperor, in this case Savoy and on behalf of Richard. An imperial vicar, in the words of the Golden Bull, was "the administrator of the empire itself, with the power of passing judgments, of presenting to ecclesiastical benefices, of collecting returns and revenues and investing with fiefs, of receiving oaths of fealty for and in the name of the holy empire". There is the rather fanciful painting of 1863 by Angelo Verolengo that depicts a very renaissance-prince-looking Pierre de Savoie receiving the title from a seated Richard dressed in peach. At the very moment Henry was having his kingship challenged by the Earl of Leicester, Pierre was being reputedly elevated by Richard to almost a kingly state himself.[23] However, the source, Pingon, in this regard may well be exaggerating the grant of imperial fiefs in the possession of the Kyburg dynasty to include Savoy itself. Cox thought this apocryphal as "Pingon is very unreliable" in this regard, and this is now generally taken to be the case. Nonetheless, the Berkhamsted meeting between Pierre and Richard had granted contrary rights over the Kyburg lands of Hartmann V to Pierre over those of Rudolph von Habsburg.[24]

In accordance with the rights granted in England, Pierre sent garrisons to Laupen and Grasburg castles, close to Bern. However, Rudolf in January 1264 became Lord Protector of Fribourg, the town immediately between Bern, where Pierre was Protector, and Lausanne. Rudolf began military operations and expelled the Savoyards from Pierre's castle at Gümmenen threatening Bern.[25] Then Hartmann IV von Kyburg, married so judiciously to Marguerite de Savoie by Thomas I de Savoie to forestall any southward advance by the Germans, died on

27 November 1264. But, not before signing his Kyburg lands, including Winterthur, to his widow Marguerite de Savoie, Pierre's sister. As Rudolf threatened, Marguerite fled to the safety of her brother's castle at Chillon. So, in the space of just over a year between 1263 and 1264, both Hartmanns von Kyburg had passed away, effectively promising their lands to both the Houses of Habsburg and Savoy – and all of this whilst England was in deep crisis, Pierre's castles at Richmond and Pevensey under siege. It is little wonder that Pierre was a little distracted by events in Helvetia whilst supporting Henry in Flanders.

It was at this point that the Bishop of Sion took his chance to overturn the treaty he'd signed with Savoy in 1260 – he invaded the Savoyard Valais. All of this whilst Pierre had been drawn away from his duties as Count of Savoy by affairs in England. The way in which Simon de Montfort, the Hartmanns von Kyburg, Rudolf von Habsburg and even the Bishop of Sion might simultaneously disturb the Count of Savoy's best-laid plans in 1263–5 are a good example of his continuing difficulty in balancing all his plates at once. That winter of 1264–5, just as Pierre and Alianor prepared to invade England in support of Henry and Edward, the extinction of the Kyburg line, and invasion of the Valais by the Bishop of Sion placed Pierre's lands in imminent danger. We should also remember that in Flanders Pierre had gathered much of the nobility and knights of the now-threatened lands. We must then add to the reasons for the lack of an invasion of England that autumn and winter, the real and present danger in Helvetia. That Christmas of 1264 Pierre would have been presented with threats on all fronts, to Henry and Edward in captivity, to the defenders of his castles in Richmond and Pevensey, to his protectorates of Bern and Morat and of Vaud, and of the Valais. Historians in England and Switzerland have hitherto tended to view each of these threats in isolation and as part of their national story, without stepping back and considering the wider picture.

It seems odd to relate to modern readers, but in February 1265 the Bishop of Sion, Henri de Rarogne, broke the truce of 1260 and invaded the lower Valais, as far as Saillon, burning fields and villages as he went. On his hurried arrival from Flanders, Pierre immediately sallied forth into the Valais with an army and put the bishop to flight. One enemy at a time he might have said. Pierre and his army drove the bishop back to Conthey, where the invading ecclesiastical army was defeated. On 17 February, at the conclusion of these brief hostilities a year's truce was agreed. Pierre then strengthened his position in the Valais, and his castles at Saillon, Conthey and Crest were munitioned with crossbowmen.[26] The new Count of Savoy began an inquiry into how his local officers had allowed such an incursion – perhaps defences needed to be strengthened?[27]

The truce expired at Easter 1266, and another short episcopal war broke out, which led to the bishop scuttling back to his palace in Sion. Details of the fighting are inevitably almost non-existent, but it appears the Savoyard army may even have found themselves besieging the bishop in his elevated palace at Sion and his adjacent castle.[28] Perhaps in relation to the earlier inquisition of Valaison defences, Pierre's soldiers occupied and perhaps strengthened the fortifications at Saxon, across the Rhône Valley from Saillon, to provide dual sentry posts that might provide a better warning of any future adventure on the part of the Bishop of Sion. Saxon would again be reconstructed by his brother Philippe a decade later, providing the first origins of Savoyards who'd build castles for Edward I in Wales.[29] But returning to 1266, the bishop was forced to observe a truce to keep the peace, being defeated by Pierre again in May and June.[30] Odd that a man of God ought to break so many truces and be forced to keep the peace. This renewed truce would last the remainder of Pierre's days.

Chapter Eleven

On the northern front, so to speak, the Habsburgs and Savoyards had eyed one another for the remainder of 1265; perhaps Pierre was relieved to hear of the death of his one-time Genevois foe, Rudolph de Genève. His successor Aymon II does not appear to have shared his father's anti-Savoyard inclinations, thus at least removing the threat from Geneva. But in 1266 the armies of the Habsburgs, Savoyards and, as we saw, the Bishop of Sion made war upon one another for western Switzerland once more. Following the end of the episcopal threat in the Valais, the Savoyard unsuccessfully attempted to gain the Habsburg protectorate of Fribourg. In March 1266, Rudolf von Habsburg was called away to the north by the rebellion of Lütold VI and Ulrich von Regensburg. The Savoyard army retook the castles of Laupen and Grasburg near Bern, thus reducing the threat to Pierre's protectorate of Bern. Finally, in September, at Lowenberg a peace treaty was signed – each side keeping what they held; the Savoyards retook possession of Gümmenen. As Cox writes, "The contest between Savoy and Habsburg for control of northwestern Helvetia in 1263–67 thus resulted in a draw."[31] The linguistic division within Switzerland remains mostly where the clash of the House of Savoy with the House of Habsburg left it. There would be no Savoyard expansion northward but no Habsburg expansion into the Suisse Romande. The retaking of Gümmenen is interesting to students of castle-building in Britain, since the Savoyards sent one Maître Jacques de Saint-Georges to work on the castle, and the master mason would later build the great castles of North Wales for Edward.

Meanwhile, on 4 January 1267, at Les Échelles in Savoy, the woman whose daughters had gone on to be queens of France and of England died.[32] Béatrice de Provence, daughter of Thomas, Count of Savoy, in many ways the origin of our story, was no more. Whilst Pierre had been in Flanders readying an army to restore her daughter to the throne of England, her last service to her brother was to look after Savoy. Her brother, *Le Petit Charlemagne*, was, however, not to live much longer. In the autumn of 1267, he fell ill while at his castle of Chillon overlooking Lac Léman. Savoy braced itself for the worst, and the *bailli* reinforced key positions in case of trouble. Pierre made somewhat of a recovery by winter and ventured forth once more, but got no further than Pierre-Châtel, where once more he fell gravely ill. The Château de Pierre-Châtel sat high on a limestone rock above the right-hand bank of the Rhône, by which it got its name "stone castle", dominating the road from Savoy to Bugey, not far from the one-time See of his brother at Belley. The castle site has been described as an "eagle's nest" and indeed Cox gave the name *Eagles of Savoy* to his definitive work on the family. If so, then Pierre-Châtel is the nest to which this eagle found rest.[33] The following century the castle of Pierre-Châtel would be granted by his successor Amédée VI in 1383 to the Carthusian order who rebuilt it as a monastery. The Chartreuse became a high place of both chivalrous ideal and spirituality (see figure 2.9). The founder's will specifies that the monks "would pray to God and celebrate masses every day for the salvation of his soul, and his predecessors". In 1268, Pierre de Savoie would soon be in need of those prayers.

The old man was sufficiently coherent on 7 and 14 May 1268 to write his will. His mind was not gone, but his body was failing him. If we imagine for a moment all those years in the saddle: fighting the Count of Geneva, travelling to and from England, fighting for Henry in Gascony, assembling an invasion army in Flanders, fighting the Bishop of Sion in the Valais and Rudolf von Habsburg around Bern, we can understand that they all began now to tell. Laid up in bed by the Rhône, he began to dictate his will (see appendix), but there was some thinking and rethinking to be done. We have a last will and testament, and it's the two codicils attached that gave rise to Baker's "ingrate" remark.[34] The last will and testament

177

written in May 1268, along with its two codicils, are very different documents than the earlier wills of 1255 and 1264. For the 1255 will Pierre was very much an English nobleman, and whilst the 1264 will was written after becoming Count of Savoy it was given in amidst the tumult of Flanders and the Second Baronial War. The 1268 documents are entirely different, they are of a Count of Savoy, and addressing first and foremost the needs of the County of Savoy. Carpenter recently wrote of the 1268 will that it might show "how little of his heart was in England",[35] this is perhaps a little harsh. Pierre de Savoie still held extensive interests in England at the time of his death, but he was now a Count of Savoy with a Count of Savoy's responsibilities. The will, bur more especially the codicils bear the imprint of his successor Philippe, and can only have been drawn up with his considerable input. The "ingrate" comment along with the need to remind readers that "his heart was in the Alps" is a little Anglo-centric. It's possible to live one's life even today, for decades in another land, and yet have one's heart only for the land of one's birth, Pierre de Savoie was no different.

The 1255 will did indeed leave "all the goods and lands of Peter located in the Kingdom of England" to Alianor. The 7 May 1268 will continued, saying "we give and bequeath to our niece Alianor, Queen of England, the County of Richmond." The codicils to which Baker drew attention do not refer to the Honour of Richmond but to the Honour of the Eagle, and alter the 1255 bequest of this estate from Alianor to the sons of Thomas II, Amédée and Louis. But the validity of Pierre being in a position to grant Richmond to Alianor is in doubt. Whilst in Amiens in January 1264, before the civil war, Henry asked Guichard de Charron, Pierre's steward, to "let the said Peter ... have the issues", likewise for Sussex.[36] And, furthermore, in the aftermath of the "late disturbance in the realm", in September 1265, Henry had expressly "restored" to Pierre "all his lands, possessions and goods" in the "Honours of l'Aigle and Hastinges" and "Richmond".[37] This restoration is cast in some doubt by a further entry for May 1266 which infers that Henry had restored Richmond to Jean II, Duke of Brittany.[38] In a later letter from Henry to Louis requesting payment by him of money to Alianor, regarding the Agenais, previously due to Jean as per the offset agreement that dated back to the 1259 Treaty of Paris, Henry explained

> That whereas Peter de Sauveye, her uncle, devised to her by his will the honour of Richemunt, as he had power to do by charter of the king, and then the king, at Wudestok, gave the said honour to John de Britannia their son, as he was bound to do by his letters.[39]

It seems that Henry had felt bound to restore Jean to Richmond, but that Pierre was within his rights to bequeath the Honour to Alianor. It seems Henry may have promised the land twice. Alianor was thus compensated for the loss of Richmond to her son-in-law early during his reign. This little episode, complex as it is, gives us an insight into how differently matters were viewed in the thirteenth century, matters touching on lands in England and France. Instead of thinking of the Agenais and Honour of Richmond primarily in national terms, as we would now, we need to picture Alianor complaining to her husband that land left to her by her late uncle had been given by her husband also to her son-in-law, and could he in compensation write to their brother-in-law to arrange recompense? Jean II remained in possession of the Honour, despite not providing due support during Edward's Welsh wars as the English king's vassal, until Philippe IV of France made war upon Edward in 1294, at which point the Honour of Richmond was once more confiscated for the Crown of England.

Chapter Eleven

The successor to Pierre in Richmond died in 1305, crushed beneath a collapsing stand of spectators at a papal coronation.

Returning to the will of Pierre de Savoie, the difficulty arose from the many conflicting deserving recipients of his estate, one that had come to him from many sources. From his wife and father-in-law, he'd received Faucigny, from his nephew Boniface and ultimately from his father Thomas I he'd received the County of Savoy, from his nephew by marriage Henry he'd received the Honours of Richmond, the Eagle and his house in London. Surviving him would be his wife Agnès, his daughter Béatrice married to the Dauphin, his brothers Boniface and Philippe, his sister Marguerite von Kyburg, his nieces the surviving daughters of his elder brother Amédée IV, his nephews the surviving sons of Thomas II, and not least his nieces, the surviving daughters of his sister Béatrice, that is Marguerite, Queen of France and Alianor, Queen of England. The division of this estate, which spanned England and the Alps, needed some thought. The original will heavily favoured his daughter Béatrice, quite naturally, but that would have also favoured the Dauphin. The original will passed the County of Savoy to his brother Philippe, who'd now given up on his church career and married the Countess of Burgundy. This would for his lifetime unite much of the former Second Kingdom of Burgundy by reuniting the Free County of Burgundy and Savoy. The sons of Thomas II, Amédée and Louis, were to have lands in the Piedmont and the Honour of the Eagle in England, his niece Alianor de Provence would have the Honour of Richmond, and the monks of Grand-Saint-Bernard his London house.

With such a big and widespread family Pierre thought again. On 11 May he issued a codicil that tidied up some issues regarding his English inheritance before, on 14 May, issuing a second codicil, it seems upon Philippe's advice. The codicil redirected some of his possessions from his daughter Béatrice to his brother Philippe, with the idea of keeping more of the estate together. These possessions passing to Philippe now included the castles at Falavier and Demprézieu in the Viennois and Lompnes in Bugey. However, despite the codicil, the will still passed much Savoyard land to the Dauphin, which led to a century of conflict in the region. Indeed Pierre created Savoyard enclaves in the Dauphin's lands and Dauphiné lands in Savoy - Demprézieu being the scene of incessant Savoyard-Dauphinois wars.

Baker also noted that before his death, Pierre "hadn't bothered to come back to England". With a county to run, reforms to introduce, Rudolf von Habsburg and the Bishop of Sion to keep at bay, I think we might consider that suggestion more than unfair and even anglocentric.[40] Baker, described him in the same paragraph as an "ingrate" and as a "nonentity" at the time of his being granted the Honour of Richmond.[41] This may to some extent have been true, but the description, whilst being anachronistic, something in his time Cox found anglophone historians guilty of,[42] but also entirely misunderstands the potential Henry saw in effectively hiring Pierre in place of his evidentially capable brother Guillaume.

On 16 or 17 May 1268 Pierre II Count of Savoy, the *Petit Charlemagne*, passed from this life at Pierre-Châtel. He was laid to rest, where he likely lies to this day, beside his brothers at Hautecombe Abbey, by the beautiful Lac du Bourget. The tomb beneath which he lies bears the inscription that he made peace between King Henry III of England and King Louis IV of France, and whilst this is true, this is perhaps one of the most understated epitaphs in history, for Pierre de Savoie was so much more than the maker of a temporary peace between the Plantagenets and the Capetians. Even the addition of *"Vir illustris ac srenuissimus*", "the illustrious man, and of great energy" don't go far enough. Pierre de Savoie was one of the key players of his times, the thirteenth century. He'd begun his career as a canon of Geneva and ended it as Earl of Richmond, Baron of Vaud, Faucigny and Chablais, Lord-protector of Morat and Bern, Count of Savoy and Marquis of Italy. But so much more than the titles, Pierre has come down to us in history as the man responsible, more than any other, for a large part of Switzerland speaking French and not German. His intimate relationship with England though is perhaps his greatest legacy, much disparaged by English contemporaries like Matthew Paris, and even later English historians. Pierre left a deep and lasting legacy in England. For it was Pierre who, following his brother Guillaume's lead, introduced so many of his fellow countrymen to England. If we want to see Pierre de Savoie's legacy, we have to go no further than Caernarfon and see the castle there, for it would be in the next generation that the legacy would bear fruit, in men like Othon de Grandson who had been brought to England by Pierre, and in Maître Jacques de Saint-Georges who was brought to England by Othon. Without Pierre de Savoie, King Henry III's son Edward I would not have been able to call upon the array of Savoyard knighthood and castle-building genius that was so to mark his reign. Pierre's legacy is, as he himself would have wished, split between Savoy and Britain, at Chillon and at Caernarfon – just as he'd split his life between the two.

So, the last testament of Pierre de Savoie wills a burial at Hautecombe Abbey, and yet Thomas Kerrich found a sepulchral tomb taken by the locals of Aiguebelle in the eighteenth century to be Pierre de Savoie. Where was Pierre buried? We may never know for certain, as both the original tomb at Hautecombe and at Aiguebelle were destroyed in the French Revolution. Worse, the revolution also destroyed all written records of who might have been originally buried at Hautecombe or the collegiate church founded by Pierre d'Aigueblanche at Aiguebelle. Perhaps, in my view, the way to square the circle, in explaining the two burial sites suggested, is that the body was buried as requested in Hautecombe but what Kerrich found in Aiguebelle was either a memorial tomb or one carrying the heart of Pierre de Savoie. Given the lack of primary-source evidence, we may never know. Certainly, both Hautecombe and Aiguebelle carried great dynastic significance for the comital family – Hautecombe was the last resting place of many of his brothers, Aiguebelle was his father's birthplace. Today, Hautecombe holds a rebuilt tomb of grand proportions, whereas at Aiguebelle little remains of the collegiate church of Saint-Catherine (see figures 3.0 and 3.1).

The will made by Pierre and its two additional codicils was not accepted by his family, as is often the case to this day. First, Pierre left the Barony of Vaud to his daughter Béatrice, his only legitimate child by Agnès de Faucigny. However, his successor and brother Philippe refused to honour the will, the matter eventually reaching the arbitration of King Edward of England's younger brother Edmund Crouchback. Edmund, whilst en route from crusade with his brother in 1272, reached an agreement whereby Philippe's possession of Vaud was limited to the duration of his life, to return to Béatrice upon his death (although this was later ignored) and requiring further arbitration from London, as we shall see later.

In England his bequests were also challenged. First, as we saw, the Honour of Richmond passed to Jean II de Bretagne. But the Honour of the Eagle (Pevensey), did not pass to the sons of Thomas II, Amédée and Louis, as requested in the 1268 will, and as emphasised in the first codicil, although having sued before the king for the lands, they were later compensated with 100 marks per annum,[43] and perhaps more valuably were accepted at court in England as Pierre had requested, going on to serve as household knights for Edward. As if to make our point

Chapter Eleven

regarding young Amédée, the first Savoyard Maître Jacques de Saint-Georges, the builder of Edward's castles in Wales, to meet at the English court in April 1278 would be Amédée de Savoie. David Carpenter asks "What finally of the sons of Thomas of Savoy?" before answering "far from being welcomed in England and given Pevensey: they were fobbed off"[44] with the aforementioned pension. But in reality both Amédée and Louis were welcomed into England, Louis a Dean of St. Martin Le Grand in London, Amédée a household knight and envoy for Edward, upon the death of Philippe, King Edward I would arbitrate between them who would be Count of Savoy, following which Amédée by then Amédée V de Savoie would journey all the way to Berwick to testify on behalf of Edward in matter of the Great Cause in Scotland. In 1299 Amédée was awarded by Edward an income of a thousand marks, over half a million £s in todays money.[45] The first codicil to Pierre's will had followed up his bequest to Amédée and Louis of Pevensey with the request that they be kindly received, and although not as willed with land they had been kindly received at court and in his lifetime well rewarded by his kinsman Edward.

Andenmatten points out correctly that the aim of the codicil was primarily to ensure their future in England than redirect lands from Alianor, and in this Pierre was successful.[46] His lands in the south of England passed instead to the Lord Edward, Pierre's great-nephew, and then after consideration to his niece, Alianor, as Pierre had originally willed, provided that it revert to the Crown on her death. Indeed, Pevensey Castle would pass to Margaret de France, the second wife of Edward I, and to Philippa de Hainaut, the wife of Edward III, becoming a serial part of the estate of Queens of England – something perhaps that as an uncle of a queen of England, Pierre de Savoie might well have approved of.

The Savoy Palace in London, left by Pierre to the monks of the Grand-Saint-Bernard, was likewise granted back to Alianor in 1270 for £200 or £150,000 in today's money, and she in turn gave it to her younger son Edmund in 1284. Thus, the great Savoyard palace of Pierre in London passed into the hands of what would become the House of Lancaster, in whose possession it would remain until torched by the peasants of London and elsewhere in the great revolt of 1381. No doubt Alianor and Pierre looking on from heaven would have been most displeased at their continued ill-use by Londoners. Howell felt that there had been amongst the family in England a wish to prevent the English lands passing "to the counts of Savoy",[47] but save for the codicil regarding the sons of Thomas II, I can find no evidence to support this idea, even then; the first codicil was, as suggested by Andenmatten, a means of ensuring their acceptance at court in England.[48]

There was some symmetry in Pierre leaving his Savoy Palace to the hospice high on the Grand-Saint-Bernard. In endowing the Bernadines with his palace he was no doubt doing so in grateful remembrance of the many times they aided his crossing of the mountains. It had been a century before that Henry II had granted a priory in England to the same brothers of the mountains in return for their aiding his envoys to Italy, thus beginning the Plantagenet entanglement with Savoy. In the end the raison d'etre of Savoy had been the Alpine passes, control and safe passage of them, and recognition of this by Pierre is unsurprising.

Pierre d'Aigueblanche, Bishop of Hereford, would survive his friend by only a few months; he had returned to England in the autumn of 1268 following the Montfortian unpleasantness, but Henry's diplomat from the Tarentaise departed this life on 27 November 1268 at one of his episcopal manors, Sugwas near Hereford. In his will he passed silver basins to Alianor and requested that she might pray for the repose of his soul.[49] His will also requested that his body be returned to his homeland and burial at his foundation church of Catherine and Mary Magdalene at Aiguebelle, but he was buried within his cathedral in Hereford.⁵⁰ It seems likely that his heart was returned to Savoy and remained in the tomb there later discovered by librarian and clergyman from Cambridge University, Thomas Kerrich. It's very possible then that Pierre d'Aigueblanche is at least spending in part his eternity alongside in part his good friend Pierre de Savoie. Kerrich would make a drawing of both tombs before they were destroyed in the early nineteenth century. The locals pointed out the tomb of "the Englishman"; in life both Pierre d'Aigueblanche and Pierre de Savoie had been "foreigners" in England – in death it seems they were foreigners in France.⁵¹

Pierre was survived by but one child, his daughter, known to history as either Béatrice de Faucigny or Béatrice de Savoie. Therein lies the rub: Faucigny or Savoy would give rise to a struggle for her father's lands in Faucigny between the Dauphins and the Counts of Savoy. Pierre's wife, Agnès de Faucigny, had died in the same year as her husband, just a few months later, in August 1268, also at Pierre-Châtel. Agnès was buried at the priory of Contamines-sur-Arve, the necropolis of the *Famille de Faucigny*.⁵² The priory would later be graced by windows in the style of Chillon and Harlech, echoes of the life lived in both England and Savoy. Béatrice had been married in 1253 to Guigues VII, the Dauphin, but her husband outlasted her father and mother but a year, dying in 1269. The Dame de Faucigny remarried in 1273 to Gaston VII, Viscount of Béarn, this the Béarn clan that caused so much trouble for Henry III in Gascony – Gaston rebelled against Edward in 1276 only to find himself imprisoned in Winchester. When Gaston died in 1290, Pierre's daughter Béatrice did not remarry again. Pierre had erected a castle in Faucigny that his daughter Béatrice rebuilt in the *Carre Savoyard* style at Toisinge. Béatrice renamed it *Bona Villa*, her good city, a name as Bonneville that together with her castle survives to this day. Béatrice died on 21 April 1310, being buried at her monastery in Melun. Her various alliances with relatives and clerics in Geneva and the sharing out of her inheritance during and after her life led to conflicts amongst her descendants for generations. The disputes between the House of Savoy and Dauphin over Faucigny ended in 1355 with the Treaty of Paris. The Faucigny of Pierre's wife Agnès became Savoyard once more. However, the Dauphiné had become a part of France, the price of the treaty the ending of the century's old alliance between the Plantagenets and the House of Savoy and a realignment with the France of the Valois. From 1355 Savoy, once allied against Capetian France in 1294, would find itself an ally of France consumed in the Hundred Years' War.

However, that was for the future. Meanwhile, in England, Henry and Richard would outlast their uncle by four years; the first to die was Richard. Edward had left for crusade in 1270 – the crusade was not successful, and his supposed partner Louis had died of dysentery before the walls of Tunis, having been diverted there by his brother Charles, leaving Edward to crusade alone. Just before or during his return Edward would have learned of the passing of his uncle Richard, King of the Romans and erstwhile "Bad Miller" of Lewes. Richard, Earl of Cornwall, perhaps the richest man in all Europe had died at Berkhamsted on 2 April 1272, and was buried alongside his wife Sanchia de Provence at the beautiful Hailes Abbey in the Cotswold hills.⁵³ The Cistercian chronicler at the abbey wrote Richard rather a nice epitaph:

> Here lies Richard, King of Germany, who while living was content with his good fortune. Offspring of the King of the English, formerly Count of Poitou, and later Earl of Cornwall, latterly, by generous gift of the Romans he was honoured with the Golden Crown of Charlemagne. Thus, he displayed the Eagle on his shield with the Lion Rampant. Preeminent among kings of all

Chapter Eleven

races for moderation, worldly wealth, wisdom, goodwill, modesty and in all acts of mediation, all his life a man of probity now exchanging rule of an earthly Kingdom for a better Realm. May he be gathered with honour to the highest place in the Kingdom of Heaven.[54]

Some epitaph, but then Richard had founded the abbey and burial there was an honour reserved by the Cistercians for a privileged few, since it was believed that Richard and before him Sanchia would thereby be granted an assisted passage through purgatory.

A generation was passing away. Richard was followed, as King of the Germans, by Pierre's one-time rival, Rudolf von Habsburg, of a family who would come to dominate European history for centuries. Like Richard, Rudolf would not be crowned emperor, but his coming to the throne in Aachen began the ascendancy of the House of Habsburg. Their upcoming coveting of the Gotthard Pass, between the German and Italian lands of the empire, would lead to the growth from 1291 onward of a new polity to the north and east of the Savoyard: the old Swiss Confederation.

Meanwhile, in England, that autumn of 1272, King Henry III, who'd been gravely ill in February 1271, grew weaker yet. On 16 November 1272 Henry had been confined to his chamber for a fortnight. He called Gilbert de Clare to his bedside and charged him with the good care of the realm until the return of his son. The great and the good gathered around him, along with his wife of thirty-six years, Alianor de Provence. Henry passed away from the kingdom he'd kept together for fifty-six years later that day.

Le Roi est mort, longue vie au Roi, and so passed the days of King Henry the Third of that name. He bequeathed his son a more secure kingdom than his father had given to him – and surely that is the ultimate test of any monarch. Henry had been born into the chaos of his father John's reign, he had been crowned at the tender age of just 10 years in Gloucester not Westminster and yet it would be the great, beautiful, soaring Westminster Abbey that he had lavished so much devotion upon that he would leave his nation. His last resting place was indeed the abbey that became his epitaph in stone, his burial there on 20 November 1272. He had lately transferred his idol, Edward the Confessor, to a new tomb, and Henry was laid to rest in Edward's original tomb. The chronicler Wykes wrote more glowingly of the funeral itself than his reign, *"ampliori splendore decoris effulgebat mortuum, quam prius dum vixerat appa reret"*,[55] "that he'd shone in death with a splendour more amply than had been seen with the eye when he'd lived". Wykes remained critical of Henry, but at least he gives us something of the beauty of the funeral that day in the Abbey. Over the coming centuries his decedents would join him in the Abbey, but for now Henry lay alone in his tomb, in full coronation regalia. *Le Roi est mort, longue vie au Roi* would have echoed around the abbey, except none present would have then known if the new *Roi* had survived his crusade, was amongst the living or the dead. He'd outlived his one-time rival and later friend, Louis of France, he'd outlived his Savoyard in-laws and loyal advisers, Guillaume and Pierre, he'd outlived Archbishop Boniface, his brother Richard, the disapproving Matthew Paris, the upstart Simon de Montfort – Henry was the great survivor. As he passed away that afternoon, no doubt his mind went back to his boyhood coronation, to his wedding and young beautiful bride from exotic Provence, to Oxford, to Lewes and Evesham – he'd outlasted them all.

The chronicler Walter of Guisborough wrote of Henry, "he was an ingenuous man, of peaceful not warlike ways". Certainly he'd not been able to recover his father's lands in

France as he'd dearly wished.[56] One of Henry's latter-day biographers, Baker, wrote, "Henry never outgrew the innocence of the boy who became king."[57] Henry's reputation suffered over the years in comparison to his Uncle Richard and his distant descendants like his namesake Henry V, also in comparison to his rival Simon de Montfort. But this is largely because those who have judged Henry have done so unfairly, and often, as with Simon de Montfort, because they're judging thirteenth-century men with latter-day eyes. A twenty-first-century reader can do no more to reach Henry the king or Henry the man than by going to Westminster to visit his spectacular abbey, a building that has subsequently become part of the very fabric of England – something of which Henry would have been singularly proud. His widow Alianor failed where her sister Marguerite succeeded: Henry was not to be Saint Henry as his friend Louis would become Saint Louis. It's perhaps one of history's unfairnesses that the hapless crusader Louis would be sanctified whereas the equally pious Henry, no warrior himself, would not. I think Baker chose the most suitable epitaph for Henry in the title of his book: *The Great King England Never Knew it Had.*

Henry had also, without knowing it, laid the foundation stones for our story, because through his beloved Queen Alianor, and despite the excesses of his Lusignan half-brothers, he'd not been afraid to call upon advisers and counsellors from beyond the shores of "Little England" – what Victorian historian James Birchall disparaged as "herds of foreigners".[58] Henry had brought to England the talents of men like Guillaume de Savoie, Boniface de Savoie and of course Pierre II de Savoie. Despite the unpopularity it had courted at the time, and in posterity, they brought others in their wake, the loyal Othon de Grandson and Jean de Grailly who would loyally serve his son Edward and of course, as we shall soon see, Maître Jacques de Saint-Georges – the man who would build for Edward the most magnificent castles in all of Europe. Perhaps if our redoubtable chronicler Matthew Paris could have seen Caernarfon or Conwy or Harlech then maybe he might have judged Henry less harshly – perhaps.

Perhaps, because the necessity for the great castles in Wales that were to follow were only a necessity because Henry had not acted more decisively in Wales during the years 1241–7. He'd stopped short of extinguishing the House of Gwynedd, despite having just cause, opportunity and resources. Action then may have saved his son and his kingdom much time and treasure. But that is speculative; he chose to attempt to come to terms with Gwynedd, indeed an agreement short of outright conquest would also be the first preference of his son. The pious Henry had stopped short of a war he did not want and sought to be the peacemaker, but sadly it was a rejected peace not of his doing, and so we cannot entirely reproach him.

For all his love of England and its patron saint, Henry was of the Maison Plantagenet; his body lay at Westminster in the abbey he'd lovingly rebuilt, but his heart was taken across the sea to the lands he'd longed so much to recover, to the ancestral lands of the Loire, and the abbey to Fontevraud.[59] The long days of King Henry were now passed. His wife, Alianor, who'd begun the Savoyard story in England, outlived her uncle, husband and brothers-in-law by some time.

Alianor decided to withdraw from the world, and chose to do so at Amesbury. Alianor, it might fairly be said, began our tale by travelling from far-off Provence to England with a train of Savoyard uncles in tow. Over a decade on from the passing of her husband Henry, Alianor wanted to prepare her soul for the next life. On 7 July 1286, the Feast of the Translation of Saint Thomas the Martyr, Alianor de Provence entered Amesbury Abbey. In the words of

Chapter Eleven

the chronicler Thomas Wykes, she removed her "*diadeamate*", her diadem, and her imperial "*purpura*", her purple robe, and "*velo caput suum cooperuit*", her head was covered with a veil. Alianor "*Regina facta est monialis*", the queen was a nun, although she was to keep in touch with her son Edward and her sister Marguerite.[60] She would now style herself "a humble nun of the Order of Fontevraud of the Convent of Amesbury" and although the Osney chronicler was critical of the financial arrangements for her retreat and her vow of poverty,[61] nevertheless, the Lanercost chronicler at least suggests that she would now lead the life of a good and pious nun. She, according to him, "filled her hands with good works ... spent her whole time in orisons, vigils and works of piety ... was a mother to the neighbouring poor, especially to orphans, widows and monks, and her praise ought to resound above that of all other women".[62]

Whilst Edward was away by the banks of the River Tweed, attempting to resolve the Scottish succession, came back news. In November 1290 he'd been at the bedside of his beloved[63] Queen Leonor de Castile as she passed away at Harby. Now came news, just six months later, that Queen Alianor de Provence had died, on 24 June 1291.

Her funeral would be delayed for the return of her son, but it had been a remarkable journey for the beautiful young girl from Provence. The woman whose marriage to King Henry III of England had begun the deepening of the Anglo-Savoyard relationship for a century to come, perhaps in those final days in the nunnery at Amesbury her mind returned to the journey she'd undertaken north along the Rhône with her uncle Guillaume. She was the third of the four sisters of Ramon Berenguer V and Béatrice de Savoie to pass away, the four sisters who'd all become queens of Europe. Sadly, her queen-ship and marriage to Henry had always been eclipsed by her sister Marguerite's to Louis, the soon-to-be sainted Louis. She had tried to have her late husband, the irredeemably pious Henry, elevated to sainthood, but in this she failed. She'd never quite been accepted by the English, Matthew Paris's contemporaries always distrustful of foreigners – this she shared with her daughter-in-law: both ladies from the sunny, fragrant Mediterranean who'd made their homes in cold, damp, gloomy old England. A more recent reappraisal of Alianor and her daughter-in-law Leonor comes from Hilton. She wrote, "Eleanor of Castille is the better remembered of the two. Yet it is the first of the southern princesses [Alianor] who was the greater English Queen."[64]

Perhaps in her last moments her mind returned, as perhaps Leonor's may have, to her coronation in Westminster Abbey. That was over half a century ago, and she was now almost the only one alive who'd been there. She'd been a Queen of England, Duchess of Aquitaine: it had been a long journey from the Provence of her childhood. She'd known Bordeaux and Gascony, the Paris of her elder sister Marguerite too, Fontevraud, Portigny, Chartres, St. Omer, Bourgogne and Amiens and of course England. Her son had become a great King of England, her daughter Margaret a Queen of Scotland, and her sisters had been Queen of France, another Queen of the Germans and another Queen of Naples – much if not most of this achieved through the family of her mother, Béatrice, and her uncles Guillaume, Pierre, Philippe, Thomas, Amédée and Boniface. She had led a long and fruitful life. With her at the end would have been her granddaughter Mary of Woodstock, Edward and Leonor's seventh daughter and now a nun at Amesbury. She had developed a love for the songs of the troubadours as a child, and perhaps they played once more in her mind, perhaps she heard once more the choir singing at her coronation *Christus vincit, Christus regnat, Christus, Christus imperat.*

Peter of Savoy: The Little Charlemagne

Alianor de Provence, perhaps the central character in forming our story, was laid to rest at Amesbury, not Westminster, on 8 September 1291. It was a quiet affair, not a state funeral. Professed nuns were normally buried in their convents, dressed in the habit of their order, and so it was with Alianor. Edward asked the abbot of nearby Glastonbury to lay to rest his mother. She was placed in a tomb fit for a queen under the high altar; sadly, it has not survived to us, Amesbury Abbey being a casualty of the Reformation. So, the last resting place of Alianor de Provence is unknown; what's more, she is the only queen of England with an unmarked grave. She may lie beneath a beautiful cypress tree within the grounds, and if this be so then it's a fitting memorial of a girl from Provence. Edward brought Master Walter of Hereford from Vale Royal in Cheshire to build her tomb; he's recorded as working on it in 1291 before later going on to complete the castle at Caernarfon for Master James. In November 1871, when the exquisite effigy of King Henry III, crafted in 1292, was lifted for an inspection of the tomb in the Chapel of the Kings at Westminster, a small delicate engraving was found on the underside. The engraver had drawn a crowned and veiled image of a queen, together with a young nun; their hands lifted in prayer to a larger, unfinished figure. We now take this as a representation of Queen Alianor with Mary of Woodstock, and the unfinished figure, the Virgin Mary.

Edward had brought the heart of his beloved Leonor to Amesbury. He continued his mournful journey to London also with his mother's heart *"duarum reginarum"*, the two queens, wrote the Osney chronicler.[65] On Sunday, 6 December Leonor's heart was laid to rest next to that of her son, Alphonso, in the Dominican Priory of the Blackfriars and on the same day Alianor's heart found its resting place in the Franciscan friary of Greyfriars by Newgate. Neither survive to this day, having both being consumed by the flames of the Great Fire of London in 1666.

There is a question as to why Alianor would be buried at Amesbury and her heart in Greyfriars, when her husband had been buried at Westminster Abbey and his heart had gone to Fontevraud, a daughter house of which Amesbury was part. Her granddaughter Eleanor of Brittany had been with her at Amesbury; she was the daughter of Henry and Alianor's daughter Béatrice. In 1290, Eleanor of Brittany had moved to the mother house of Fontevraud and from 1304 she became the abbess there, something that would have made her grandfather Henry especially happy. The nuns of Fontevraud certainly wanted the body of Alianor to find a home in the Plantagenet ancestral abbey. But it was Alianor herself who chose Amesbury and as Powicke noted, that she had "made England her home".[66] Thus in the end, the girl from Provence, who'd been much abused by the Londoners, chose England as her place of eternal rest, which speaks volumes of her nature: she wanted to be close to her family.

In the end, the story of the Savoyards in England, of Pierre de Savoie's role there, and in Savoy, had all been about family. Savoy had long been important to the English, since it lay astride the pilgrimage road to Rome, but the alliance of the thirteenth century between the ruling houses of England and Savoy had been chiefly about family. That Alianor lived such a long life as Queen of England was perhaps Pierre's greatest legacy in England, since his role there was as her protection. That both Alianor and Pierre helped guide the monarchy through the tumultuous later years of Henry's kingship and nurture perhaps one of England's greatest kings, Edward, is a legacy that has been largely ignored.

This brings us to a consideration of the legacy of Pierre de Savoie, *Le Petit Charlemagne*. In his homeland, he is best remembered for extending Savoyard territory into the *Pays de*

Chapter Eleven

Vaud, and ultimately being the reason that the people of western Switzerland speak French to this day. The plaque on the castle of his daughter Béatrice at Bonneville describes him as *"un homme d'état visionnaire"*, that is "a visionary statesman". Indeed, his reforms of Savoy brought from England in 1263 laid the basis for a Savoyard state that continued to prosper for many centuries before in the end being swallowed by its French, Italian and Swiss neighbours. His nineteenth-century tomb in Hautecombe Abbey points toward the Treaty of Paris in 1259 as his greatest legacy, the monks there valuing Pierre de Savoie, the peacemaker, above all others. But his legacy in England will always depend upon your view of this attempt at a lasting peace between the Plantagenets and the Capetians, between England and France. That Philippe IV would destroy the trust fostered by Pierre and Alianor between Henry and Louis by turning on Edward in 1294 and laying the foundations for the Hundred Years' War could not have been known in 1259. Was the Treaty of Paris doomed to fail? Perhaps so, for it rested upon the goodwill of the French Crown, but it was at least worth trying. Carpenter, at least in part, credits Pierre de Savoie with Henry's successful defence of Gascony in 1253-4, a possession solidified by the Treaty of Paris.[67] But, as we said earlier, it's not the Treaty of Paris, or the doomed Sicilian business, or the xenophobia their presence partly provoked in England that would be Pierre de Savoie's greatest legacy in England: that legacy would be one of England's greatest kings, Edward. If we are looking for a legacy of Pierre in England, we would do well to look no further than Caernarfon, and Conwy, and Harlech. For good or ill, King Edward I was a product of Pierre de Savoie and his niece Alianor, who both travelled so far for the sake of family.

We began by comparing English and continental historians' comments on the life of Pierre de Savoie, and we must then find an answer to the differing judgements made of his career. In the end continental authors have taken a more generous view of Pierre de Savoie than English writers - Matthew Paris casts a long shadow. Perhaps the answer is that each has different ideas on what matters in a statesman. Especially a statesman leading much of his career in a land other than of his birth. Upon consideration, I believe the answer lies in what you consider to be the nation state. Nations come to nationhood at varying paces and in varying ways and to a greater or lesser degree. It is worth observing that Pierre de Savoie was born into the County of Savoy, in what is now Italy, but as Count held lands mostly in what's now France and Switzerland.. Whereas the greater part of his career was serving the ruling family of the Kingdom of England, and a King and Queen who are the direct ancestors of King Charles III crowned in the year of this book's publication. It is safe then to say that an English idea of nation and a Savoyard idea of nation might not be the same thing, then or indeed now. As a Savoyard, Pierre was a man whose loyalty was primarily to the family. As we discussed in the consideration of the alliance then rivalry between Pierre de Savoie and Simon de Montfort, the Savoyard's loyalties were to Alianor, Edward and Henry and only then England, and in that order. Whereas Montfort as a populist appealed to the loyalties of an English nation, albeit that he was most definitely a Frenchman. So perhaps, not only did Englishmen unfairly judge him at the time, yes I'm looking at you Mr Paris, as his loyalty was to the dynasty not the nation, but perhaps Englishmen have unfairly judged him since, Cox thought anachronistically[68], taking their lead from thirteenth century chroniclers. Pierre de Savoie was, undeniably in the history of Savoy, an effective and founding figure, but in England too his role was exactly that asked, required and needed by Queen Alianor de Provence and her husband King Henry the third of that name. His life and career prompt us to consider the way in which we judge those coming to our lands and departing having made a career for themselves in the meantime. Hopefully Pierre de Savoie can again prompt us to think.

Think, is it reasonable or unreasonable to expect the stranger to "have his heart in England"? Cox rightly observed that ultimately "his heart was in the Alps, not in England" - and it's reasonable to have one's heart in the land of one's birth. If we hold expectations to the contrary might we risk losing talents that may contribute to our society? If the xenophobia of Pierre de Savoie's day brings to mind the xenophobia of our own day, then that is no bad thing.[69]

Appendix

Key Pierre de Savoie Estate Holdings in England and Savoy

Estate	Dates held where known
Saint Rambert-en-Bugey	1234–1268
Lompnes, Bugey	1234–1268
Faucigny (by marriage)	1234–1268
Romont, Vaud	1240–1268
Honour of Richmond	1241–1268
Honour of the Eagle or Pevensey	1241–1268
Honour of Eu or Hastings	1249–1254 and 1262–1268
Savoy Palace, London	1246–1268
Chablais (Chillon & Saillon)	1255–1268
Yverdon, Vaud	1260–1268

Pierre de Savoie's *Familia* Staff and Vassals in England and Savoy

Knights

Pierre de Grandson	Not recorded as visiting England, witnessed many charters in Savoy, 1245–58. His son, Othon, was in the household of the Lord Edward.
Henri de Champvent	Not recorded as visiting England, witnessed many charters in Savoy. His son, Pierre, was in Henry's and Edward's household.
Ebal II de Mont	
Pierre de Meysins	Emissary to England in 1260, service in Savoy 1253–60.
Ralph de Voiseray	1253.
Geoffrey de Grandmont	Frequent Emissary to England, 1249–60.
Hugh de Grandmont	Frequent Emissary to England, 1254–61.
Gaucher de Gomarcyn	1253.
Imbert de Châtillon	Emissary to England 1254–5, service in Savoy 1254–61.
Geoffrey de Meysins	1259.
Jordan de Montagniaco	Pierre's Yeoman, 1261–4.
Pierre de Casa	1262.
Humbert de Montréal	1261–8.

Physician

Pierre de Mont	1243–59.

Barber
Jaqueto de Bussey   1268.

Clerks
Pierre de Capuz   Rarely in England, service in Savoy 1245–68.

Simon de Vercelli   Noted as clerk in England, parson at Witley.
Thomas de Rossillon   Chief clerk, likely Chancellor. Frequent Emissary to England, 1252–61.
Guillaume de Garneriis   1264.
Maître Arnaud   1264.
Simon de Verters   Possible treasurer 1249–66.
Guy de Montagniaco   1258–9.

Attorneys
Ebal II de Mont   1253.
Guichard II de Charron   1260, and General Steward 1262–6.

Steward of the Honour of Richmond
Guichard I de Charron   1243–50s.
Guichard II de Charron   1250s–68.

Steward of Pevensey
Guichard de Frenes   1241–4.
Geoffrey de Braybouef   1247–53.
Jean de Gaddesden   1257–62.
Jean de la Rede   1263.
Guichard II de Charron   1265.

Constable of Pevensey Castle
Hanekin de Wissant   1263–4.

The Savoyards of the Chapter of Hereford Cathedral

Pierre d'Aigueblanche (Bishop)
Aimon d'Aigueblanche (Precentor)
Jacques d'Aigueblanche (Archdeacon of Shropshire)
Aimeric d'Aigueblanche (Precentor)
Jean d'Aigueblanche (Dean)
Aime de Ponce
Jean de Ambleon
Anthelme de Clermont (Dean)
Anthelme de Conflans
Guillaume de Conflans (Archdeacon of Hereford)
Pierre Eymar

Key Pierre de Savoie Estate Holdings in England and Savoy

Martin de Gex
Alexander de l'Huille
Nicholas de Joinville
Pierre de Langon
Bosom de Macot
Jean de Maurienne
Aimon de Miolans
Richard de Montvernier
Hugues de Moutiers
Gontier de Naves
Jean du Pont
Ponce de Salins
Pierre de Sollieres
Pierre d'Ugine
Humbert de Yenne

Source: Jean-Pierre Chapuisat. 1964. *Le Chapitre Savoyard de Hereford au XIIIe siècle*. In *Actes du Congrès des Sociétés Savantes de la Province de Savoie. Nouvelle Série 1.*

Order from Pierre de Savoie that names the Savoyard knights serving in Flanders with the invasion army of September 1264

Wurstemberger wrote: "*Slor. d. Mon. di Sav. II. App. p. 364. 656. Petrus de Sabaudia Comes, assignat stipendia debita nobilibus et militibus terrarum suarum, quos secum durerat in Flandriam. 1264, Sept. 30. Dam.*"

Which we can translate as "Slor. d. Mon. di Sav. II. App. p. 364. 656. Peter de Savoy, Count, assigns the stipends due to the nobles and soldiers of his lands, whom he had endured with him in Flanders. 1264, Sept. 30. Dam."

Then comes the primary source from the Turin Archive:

"*P. Comes Sabaudie Domino Seuthe* [possibly *Suchet de Féterne*] *Castellano de Cletis Salutem. Mandamus vobis quatinus domino Ricardo de Balma* [**Richard de la Balrae**] *aut certo nuntio suo has literas deferenti in proximis octabis beati hillarij quinquaginta libras viennenses de dono nostro soluatis. Datum apud Dam in fiandria in crastino Sancti Michaelis. Sub eadem formà mandatur eidem ut soluat domino Guidoni de Agenens* [**Guy de Agenens**] *XXX libras Vienn. ad eundem terminum. Datum ut supra.*"

"*Sub eadem forma mandatur magistro Arnaldo* [**Master Arnaud**] *et domino Symoni de Verters* [**Simon de Verters**] *ut soluant domino Ricardo de Sancto Martino* [**Richard de Saint Martin**] *XXV libras vienn. ad eundem terminum. Datum ut supra.*"

"*Sub hac forma mandatur eisdem ut soluant domino Jordano de Montany* [**Jourdain de Montagny**] *XV libras vienn. ad eundem terminum. Datum ut supra.*"

"*Sub eadem forma mandatur eisdem ut soluant domino Willielmo de Sancto Laurentio* [**Guillaume de Saint Laurent**] *XL libras Vienn. ad eundem terminum. Datum ut supra.*"

"*Sub eadem forma mandatur eisdem ut solvant domino Thome et domino Henrico grasset XX libras vienn. ad eundem terminum. Datum ut supra.*"

Sub eadem forma mandatur eisdem ut solvant Raimondo de Corberio [**Raymond de Corbières**] *et socio suo XVI "libras Vienn. ad eundem terminum. Datum ut supra.*

Sub eadem forma mandatur eisdem ut solvant ferret de Cossonay [**Ferret de Cossonay**] *et Guidoni de Morire XIIII libras ad eundem terminum. Datum ut supra.*

Sub eadem forma mandatur eisdem ut solvant libistor et Johanni de berna [**Jean de Berne**] *XX libras Viennenses ad eundem terminum. Datum ut supra.*

Sub eadem forma mandatur eisdem ut solvant Cononi de fonz [**Conon de Fontenai**] *VII libras viennenses ad eundem terminum. Datum ut supra."*

Sub eadem forma mandatur eisdem ut solvant Aymoni de fonz [**Aymon de Fontenai**] *VII libras viennenses ad eundem terminum. Datum ut supra.*

Sub eadem forma mandatur eisdem ut solvant brocardo de fonz [**Burcard de Fontenai**] *VII libras viennenses ad eundem terminum. Datum ut supra.*

Sub eadem forma mandatur eisdem ut solvant Johanni de Willayns [**Jean de Willayns**] *VII libras viennenses ad eundem terminum. Datum ut supra.*

Sub eadem forma mandatur eisdem ut solvant Jacobo de Albona [**Jacques d'Aubonne**] *et socio suo XX libras viennenses ad eundem terminum. Datum ut supra.*

Sub eadem forma mandatur eisdem ut solvant humberto de trelay [**Humbert de Trelay**] *X libras viennenses ad eundem terminum. Datum ut supra.*

Sub eadem forma mandatur eisdem ut solvant domino Willielmo de Alingio [**Guillaume d'Allinges**] *cum uno milite et uno scutifero XXV libras vienn. ad eundem terminum. Datum ut supra. eadem forma m tur eisdem ut solvant domino Willielmo de Rovorea* [**Guillaume de Ravorée**] *XV libras viennenses ad eundem terminum. Datum ut supra.*

Sub eadem forma mandatur eisdem ut solvant Johanni de Rovorea [**Jean de Ravorée**] *centum Solidos ad eundem terminum. Datum ut supra.*

Sub eadem forma mandatur eisdem ut solvant Willielmo de Langins [**Guillaume de Langins**] *et socio suo XXV libras viennenses ad eundem terminum. Datum ut supra.*

Sub eadem forma mandatur eisdem ut solvant Johanni de Cernens [**Jean de Cernens**] *VII libras viennenses ad eundem terminum. Datum ut supra.*

Sub eadem forma mandatur eisdem ut solvant domino Willielmo de Greysiaco [**Guillaume de Grézieux**] *XXX libras viennenses ad eundem terminum. Datum ut supra.*

Sub eadem forma mandatur eisdem ut solvant domino Petro de Compeis [**Pierre de Compeis**] *X libras viennenses ad eundem terminum. Datum ut supra.*

Sub eadem forma mandatur eisdem ut solvant domino Gerardo de Compeis [**Gérard de Compeis**] *X libras viennenses ad eundem terminum. Datum ut supra.*

Sub eadem forma mandatur eisdem ut solvant domino Petro de fernay [**Pierre de Fernay**] *X libras viennenses ad eundem terminum. Datum ut supra*

Sub eadem forma mandatur eisdem ut solvant Gerardo de Arbiez [**Gerard d'Arbiez**] *Centum solidos viennenses ad eundem terminum. Datum ut supra.*

Sub eadem forma mandatur eisdem ut solvant Aymerico de Sancto Jorio [**Aimeric de Saint Jorio**] *X libras viennenses ad eundem terminum. Datum ut supra.*

Sub eadem forma mandatur eisdem ut solvant Willielmo de Cornillini [**Guillaume de Cornillon**] *X libras viennenses ad eundem terminum. Datum ut supra.*

Sub eadem forma mandatur eisdem ut solvant Willielmo de Arlo [**Guillaume [d'Arlod**] *X libras viennenses ad eundem terminum. Datum ut supra.*

Sub eadem forma mandatur eisdem ut solvant domino Guichardo de ponte vitreo [**Guichard de Pontverre**] *et socio suo XV libras viennenses ad eundem terminum. Datum ut supra*

Key Pierre de Savoie Estate Holdings in England and Savoy

Pierre Count of Savoy to [possibly Lord Suchet de Féterne] Châtelain of Les Clées Greetings. We send you as soon as Mr. Richard de la Balrae, or by his sure messenger, conveying these letters, in the last eight weeks of the blessed Hillary, 50 *livres Viennois* paid for our gift. Given at Dam in Flanders on the morrow of St. Michael [30 September 1264].

Under the same form the same is ordered to pay Lord Guy de Agenens 30 *livres Viennois* to the same term. Given as above.

Under the same form, Master Arnaud and Lord Simon de Verters are ordered to pay Lord Richard de Saint Martin 25 *livres Viennois* to the same term. Given as above.

Under this form, they are commanded Master Arnaud and Simon de Verters to pay Lord Jourdain de Montagny 15 *livres Viennois* to the same term. Given as above

Under the same form, the same are ordered to pay Lord Guillaume de Saint Laurent 40 *livres Viennois* to the same term. Given as above.

Under the same form, they are ordered to pay Mr. Thomas and Mr. Henry Grasset *20 livres Viennois* to the same term. Given as above.

Under the same form, they are ordered to pay Raymond de Corbières and his partner 16 *livres Viennois* to the same term. Given as above.

Under the same form, they are ordered to pay the Ferret de Cossonay and Guidon de Morire 14 *Livres* for the same term. Given as above.

Under the same form, they are ordered to pay the libist and Jean de Berne 20 *livres Viennois* at the same term. Given as above.

Under the same form, they are ordered to pay Conon de Fontenai 7 *livres Viennois* for the same term. Given as above.

Under the same form, they are ordered to pay to Aymon de Fontenai 7 *livres Viennois* for the same term. Given as above.

Under the same form, they are ordered to pay the Burcard de Fontenai 7 *livres Viennois* at the same term. Given as above.

Under the same form, they are ordered to pay John de Willayns 7 *livres Viennois* for the same term. Given as above.

Under the same form, they are ordered to pay Jacques d'Aubonne and his partner 20 *livres Viennois* at the same term. Given as above.

Under the same form, they are ordered to pay Humbert de Trelay 10 *livres Viennois* at the same term. Given as above.

Under the same form, they are ordered to pay Lord Guillaume d'Allinges with one knight and one squire 25 *livres Viennois* to the same term. Given as above in the same form, they are to pay to the lord Guillaume de Ravorée 15 *livres Viennois* for the same term. Given as above.

Under the same form, they are ordered to pay Jean de Ravorée 100 *solids* for the same term. Given as above.

Under the same form, they are ordered to pay Guillaume de Langins and his partner 25 *livres Viennois* for the same term. Given as above.

Under the same form, they are ordered to pay Jean de Cernens 7 *livres Viennois* at the same term. Given as above.

Under the same form, they are ordered to pay Sir Guillaume de Grézieux 30 *livres Viennois* for the same term. Given as above.

Under the same form, they are ordered to pay to Lord Pierre de Compeis 10 *livres Viennois* for the same term. Given as above.

Under the same form, they are ordered to pay Lord Gérard de Compeis 10 *livres Viennois* at the same time. Given as above.

Under the same form, they are ordered to pay to Mr. Pierre de Fernay 10 *livres Viennois* at the same term. Given as above

Under the same form, they are ordered to pay to Gerard d'Arbiez 100 *livres Viennois* for the same term. Given as above.

Under the same form, they are ordered to pay Aymeric de Sancto Jorio 10 *livres Viennois* for the same term. Given as above.

Under the same form, they are ordered to pay Guillaume de Cornillon 10 *livres Viennois* at the same term. Given as above.

Under the same form, the same are ordered to pay Guillaume d'Arlod 10 *livres Viennois* at the same term. Given as above.

Under the same form, they are ordered to pay Lord Guichard de Pontverre and his associate 15 *livres Viennois* for the same term. Given as above.

Primary source: *Autenlicum in Archivis cameralibus Taurini : Ex apographe,* that is Authentic in the Chamber Archives of Turin, from a perfect copy or transcript.

Last Wills and Testaments

Pierre II de Savoie, Count of Savoy made four wills during his lifetime, the first relating to his marriage to Agnès de Faucigny thus prior to a career in England, being drawn up at Châtillon-sur-Cluses, the second relating to the addition of his English lands, being drawn up at Lyon. The third relating to the influence of the Second Baronial War, being drawn up at Dam in Flanders, and the fourth and last drawn up on his deathbed at Pierre-Châtel. The fourth and last had two codicils attached to it days after, but before his death. The authenticated parchment originals of all survive, save for the first codicil which is a *vidimus* or attested copy. The original of the first codicil went to London, but was quashed by Henry III.

Number One, 4 February 1234, Châtillon-sur-Cluses
Testamentum Petri de Sabaudia. 1234. Mense Febr.
Ego Petrus filius quondam Thome Comitis Sabaudie notum facio vniuersis presentes litteras inspecturis quod constituo heredem tocius terre mec et omnium bonorum meorum filium vel filiam quam habebo ab Annete filia Nobilis uiri Ay. do mini fuciniaci. quod si forte quod absit contingeret ipsam uiuente me decedere, ad dictum et Arbitrium venerabilis patris et domini Wj Electi Valent. et Ay de Sabaudia fratrum et henrici de Chanuen, domini Willi de Greissie, et domini Jacobi de Albona dicte Anneti dos assignetur. et hec omnia bona fide me seruaturum iuraui. In huius rei testimonium huic carte ad preces meas et instanciam venerabilis pater Episcopus Gebenn. Sigillum suum cum sigillo meo apposuit. Hujus Rei testes sunt petrus abbas de Alpibus. petrus prior Repositorii. W. de Greisie. Rodulfus et Riferius fratres de sancto georio. Actum apud Castellionem Anno domini M°. CC°. XXX°. tertio mense februarii.

Testament of Peter of Savoy 1234. In the month of February.
I, Peter, the son of the late Thomas Count of Savoy, certify to all who shall inspect the present letter that I appoint as heir of all my land and all my property the son or daughter which I shall have by Agnès, daughter of the noble Aymon II, *Seigneur de Faucigny*. But if perhaps it would happen that they should depart while I was alive, to the said and will of the venerable father and lord Guillaume Elect de Valence and that a dowry be assigned to the brothers Aymon de Savoie and Henry de Chanuen, lord Willi de Greissie, and lord Jacques d'Aubonne

Key Pierre de Savoie Estate Holdings in England and Savoy

to Anne and all these things are good I swore that I would keep him in good faith. In testimony of this matter, at my request and at the request of the venerable father, Bishop of Geneva. He affixed his seal with my seal. Witnesses to this event are Peter, abbot of the Alps. Peter prior of the Repository W. de Greisie. Rudolf and Riferius, brothers of Saint George. Enacted at Châtillon-sur-Cluses in the year of our Lord 1234, the third month of February.

Wurstemberger noted that the seals have been destroyed. Pingonius (Zibaldo) describes the seal of Peter, which has not yet been severed in its time: the eagle sitting and looking back, circumscribed: S. PETER DE SAAUDIA. But in another place, in the same book, he describes the same seal in a slightly different way: an eagle sitting, looking back, with the moon above its head, with its horns upturned. AST/C *Testamenti* m 1. No 1. Wurstemberger, vol 4. No 92

Number Two, 8 June 1255, Lyon
Wurstemberger noted Testamentum Petri de Sabaudia. 1255. Junii 8. Lugduni.
Hæredes particulares: Beatrix filia sua in quinque millibus librarum Viennensium. Eleonora, Angliæ Regina, hæres om nium bonorum et terrarum Petri in Regno Angliæ sitarum, sub obligatione solutionis omnium debitorum suorum domesti corum, eleemosynarum et legatorum. Hæredem instituit om nium bonorum et terrarum, quas possedit citra Mare Anglicum, Philippum, Electum Lugdunensem fratrem suum. Agneti vero, Fuciniacensi, uxori suæ, legat mille libras Viennenses. Ecclesia ubi sepeliredur, assignat centum marchas Argenti. Pro sepultura sua, designat, si mori sibi contingeret in Anglia, Monasterium Londinense (Westmonasterium); si vero decederet in Burgundia, monasterium Sancti Mauritii Agaunense, (Augn). Executorem huius testamenti instituit Henricum Angliæ Regem.

In fine testamenti legitur: Ego Petrus de Sabaud testator hanc meam ultimam voluntatem sigillo et subscribo, et septem presentes testes rogo quod idem faciant. In dorso testamenti conspiciun tnr, monogramma ipsius Petri, +, cum punctis in quatuor angulis, et testimonia cum monogrammatibus septem testium. Act. Lugduni VI Idus Junii, A. D. MCCLV. Indict. XIII. Pendent plura Sigilla."

Wurstemberger noted Testament of Peter of Savoy 1255. June 8. Lyon.
Particular heirs: his daughter Béatrice in 5,000 *livres Viennois*. Alianor, Queen of England, heir of all the goods and lands of Peter located in the Kingdom of England, under the obligation of payment of all her debts of her own family, alms and ambassadors. He appointed as heir of all the goods and lands which he possessed on this side of the English Sea, Philippe, his brother-elect of Lyon. But to Agnès, of Faucigny, his wife, he shall bequeath 1,000 *livres Viennois*. The church where we should be buried gives one hundred marks of silver. For his burial, he designates, if he should happen to die in England, the Monastery of London (Westminster); but if he were to die in Burgundy, the monastery of Saint-Maurice d'Agaune. He appointed Henry III King of England as executor of this covenant.

At the end of the testament, we read: I am Peter of Savoy, testator, and I sign this last will with the seal, and I ask the seven present witnesses to do the same. On the back of the testament we see the monogram of Peter himself, + with points in the four corners, and testimonies with the monograms of the seven witnesses. Act. at Lyon Indict. Chapter XIII More seals hang. AST/C. *Testamenti*, m. 1, No 7 and Wurstemberger, vol 4. No 407.

Number Three, September 1264, Dam, Flanders
Wurstemberger noted Testamentum Petri Comitis Sabaudia. 1264. Mense Septembris.
Eligit Sepulturam, moriendo citra Mare, in Abbatia S. Mauricii Agaunensi: si vero decederet in Anglia, vult sepeliri in Ecclesia Londinensi, non accuratius designata. Instituit heredem,

Peter of Savoy: The Little Charlemagne

filiam suam Beatricem, uxorem Guigonis Dalphini in pura legitima sua, quæ assignat in bona sua Comitatus seu honoris Richemundiæ: heredem vero usufructuariam in dicto Comitatu, instituit neptem suam Alienoram Angliæ Re ginam; nec non in honore Aquila, in Castro de Pevenessei et in omnibus aliis possessionibus suis in Anglia. Et casu pramorientis sibi ipsi Alienoræ reginæ, et quando quidem habeat filios, vult ipse quod, tam totus Comitatus Sabaudia, quam omnia quæ legat dictæ reginæ devolvant, sine detractione, Philippo Electo Lugdun. fratri suo, casu, quod sit inter vivos, tempore decessus sui: illo vero præmoriendo sibi, substituitur illi primogenitus filius quondam Thomæ de Sabaudia al, erius fratris sui, vel major natu aliorum filiorum dicti Thoma, tunc superstitum. Legat Agneti, conjugi suæ, locos de Fisterna, Alingio, Versoya et Commugnie et quidquid possidet iuxta Albonam, ad dies vitæ dictæ Agnetis. Legat Abbatiæ Agau nensi CC. Lib. Vienn. pro duobus anniversariis, etc. Ecclesiæ S. Mariæ Augustensis C. Lib. Vienn. pro anima fratris sui Thomæ in illa tumulati et pro anniversario illius ibidem cele brando: Hospitali Montis Jovis legat domum suam Londini. Sequuntur plura legata ad pias causas. Cuique militum, qui extiterit tempore mortis suæ in servitio domus suæ, legat C. Lib. et aliis nobilibus L. lib. Vienn. non nobilibus vero cuique XL libras, Clericis L. lib. Vienn. Et generaliter omnibus se quacibus suis, ad arbitrium Executorum testamenti sui, quos designat in personis Philippi Electi Lugdun. fratris sui, Soffredi de Amaysino, et aliorum quorundam. In dorso testamenti legitur: Nos Petrus Comes Sabaud. hanc nostram vltimam uoluntatem per manum Villi de Aug. capellani nostri subscribi fecimus et sigillari, ac propria manu signauimus Testes, signantes per monogrammata sua, et qui sub scripserunt per manum Will. de Augusta, capellani Comitis, qui solus manu propria subscripsit: Humbertus de Monteferrato, Girardus de Grancione prepositus S. Thomæ de fornerio lug dun. Camillus falasterius miles. Amadeus de Boczesello, petrus de amaysino. Johannes de gllr (?). Ebalus de Montibus, petrus capellanus. Will. de Augusta capellanus propria manu subscripsi.

Appendet Sigillum Petri Comitis, cum leone erecto, ar mato, dextrorsum verso et gradiente pede lævo, stante in dextero. Monogramma Petri: +

Wurstemberger noted Testament of Peter, Earl of Savoy. 1264. In the month of September. He chooses a burial place, dying on this side of the sea, in the abbey of Saint-Maurice d'Agaune. But if he should die in England, he wishes to be buried in the Church of London, not accurately designed. He appoints his heir, his daughter Béatrice, the wife of Guiges VII de Viennois, in his pure lawful rights. He assigns his possessions of the County or Honour of Richmond: and he institutes his niece Alianor, Queen of England, as heir to the usufructuary in the said County; and in the Honour of the Eagle, in the Castle of Pevensey, and in all his other possessions in England. And by the chance of Queen Alianor giving birth to him, and when he has children, he wishes that both the whole County of Savoy and all the said queens roll off, without backing, Philippe Elect of Lyon. to his brother, by chance, that he was among the living at the time of his decease; but that before predeceasing him, the eldest son of the late Thomas of Savoy is replaced by his brother, or the eldest of the other sons of the said Thomas, then surviving. Let him read to Agnès his wife, the places of Fisterna, Allinges, Versoix, and Common, and whatever he has near Aubonne, to the days of the said Agnès's life. Let him read to the abbey of Saint-Maurice d'Agaune, 100 *livres Viennois* for two anniversaries to the church of Saint Mary of Aosta, 100 *livres Viennois* for the soul of his brother Thomas, who was buried in that place, and to celebrate his anniversary there: let him read his home in London at the Hospital of Mount Thursday. There follow several legacies to pious causes. To any one of the soldiers who was at the time of his death in the service of his house, let him have 100 *livres* and the other nobles in 50 *livres Viennois* not to the nobles, but to each 40 *livres Viennois*. And generally he applies himself to all his family, at the will of the executors of his testament, whom he designates in the persons of Philippe Elect Lyon. his brother, Soffred of Amaysinus, and certain others. In the back of the testament we read: We are Peter, Earl of Savoy. This our last will by the hand of Villius de Aug. Our chaplains have caused it to be signed and sealed, and we have sealed it with our own hand. Witnesses, sealing them with their monograms, and those who wrote under Will. from Augusta, chaplain of the Earl, who only subscribed with his own hand: Humbert de Montferrat, Girard de Grancione, provost of Saint-Thomas de fornerio Lyon. Camillus faasterius knight, Amadeus of Boczesello, Peter of Amaysinus. Johannes de Gllr (?). Ebal de Mont, Pierre the chaplain. Will. of Aosta, chaplain, signed with his own hand.

The seal of the Count Peter's is hung, with a lion erect, with ar mato on his right, and with his left foot standing on his right. Peter's monogram: + Testam. Princ. Sab. Fasc. 1. No. 12. 22

Number Four, 7 May 1268, Pierre-Châtel

Testamentum Petri Comitis Sabaudia. 1268. Maii 7.
In nomine Patris, et Filii, et Spiritus Sancti. Amen. Anno Domini millesimo ducentesimo sexagesimo octavo, in crastino B. Joannis Evangeliste ante Portam Latinam, Nos Petrus Comes Sabaudie, sani mente, licet egri corpore, preuidere mortis casus uolentes, nolentes decedere intestati de bonis et rebus nostris, ordinamus et disponimus in hunc modum. In primis uolumus et precipimus debita nostra integraliter persolui et clamores sedari, et emendari per Executores nostros infrascriptos et ad ipsa de bita solvenda, et clamores emendandos et pacificandos ad ar bitrium dictorum Executorum oneramus heredes nostros infras criptos modo et forma infrascriptis: sepulturam nostram eligimus apud Altamcombam. Beatricem Karissimam Filiam nostram, vxorem ill. uiri Dalphini Viennensis et Albon. heredem nostram instituimus in tota terra nostra, quam habemus in Gebennesio et in Uuaudo, usque ad Mosternensem et in Alemania, quo cunque titulo in predictis terris aliquid possideamus, uel quasi, excepto iure quod habemus apud Seyssellum et Montemfalco nem. Item damus et legamus eidem Beatrici filie nostre homagium quo tenetur nobis Albertus Dominus de Turre, cum feudis que a nobis tenet. Item feudum quod a nobis tenet Comes Forensis. Item castra S. Ragimberti et de Lompnes cum mandamentis et pertinenciis vniuersis, et feuda que a nobis tenentur apud Royomont et ipsam heredem instituimus in omnibus et singulis predictis. Item damus et legamus di lectis nepotibus nostris, filiis Dom. Thome de Sabaudia, Ka rissimi fratris nostri, Uillam francham in terra Pedemontis, et ius quod habemus in ipso castro et pertinenciis eiusdem, et terram quam habemus in Essex et in honore Aquile in Anglia. Item Karme Domine nostre Alienore Regine Anglie damus et legamus Comitatum Richemundensem, ita tamen quod ipsa soluat satisfaciat integraliter de omnibus debitis quibus tenemur Mameto Spine et eius sociis civibus et mercatoribus florentinis. In Comitatu autem Sabaudie et in aliis bonis nostris, tam vltra Montes quam citra, vbicumque existentibus heredem nostrum facimus et instituimus Karissimum fratrem nostrum Philippum de Sabaudia Comitem Burgundie, exceptis legatis et eleemosinis que inferius continentur. et si ipsum Comitem decedere contingeret sine liberis masculis. quandocumque sub stituimus eidem in predicto Comitatu et omnibus aliis predictos.

Nepotes nostros, vel ipsorum alii superstiti predicta omnia de voluantur et restituantur, sine restitutione uel diminutione quarte Trebellianice, uel alterius cuiuscumque. Item domino de Turre remittimus et quittamus gageriam quam ab ipso habemus apud Burgundum, et eciam debitum quo nobis pro dicta gageria tenebatur. Item remittimus et quittamus filiis Rodulphi de Gebennis, dil. consanguineis nostris, MM. marcarum, de debito quo nobis tenentur, pro gageria quam habemus ab ipsis. Item turrim de Uiuesio cum omnibus suis pertinenciis damus et legamus dil. et fid. nostro Domino Hugoni de Paleysiux. Item dilecte vxori nostre Agneti Domine Fucigniaci damus et lega mus ad uitam suam Castra de Versoya, de Alingio, de Fisterna, de Charossa, de Albona, cum eorum pertinenciis vniuersis. Item Domine Margarete Comitisse de Quiburgo Karme Sorori notre damus et legamus D libras Vienn. annuas, ad uitam suam percipiendas in pedagio Uille noue pro MM. marchis argenti quas habuimus ab eadem. Item B. filiam Amedei Co mitis Karmi fratris nostri quondam uolumus et precipimus dotari et maritari decenter vsque ad summam VII millium librarum Vienn. per Comitem Burgundie supradictum. Brenue riam uero fructuariam et paleam, quam consueuimus tam nos quam predecessores nostri percipere in Comitatu Sabaudie, totaliter quittamus et remittimus pro nobis et heredibus nostris.

Domui quoque Altecombe pro remedio auime nostre damus et legamus CC. libras Vienn. pro emendis decem libratis terre pro Aniversario ibidem annuo faciendo. Item Ecclesie B. Joannis Baptiste Bellicensis damus et legamus CC. libras Vienn. pro eodem et ad supplendum illud quod per nos iamdiu extitit assignatum ad sustentationem vnius lampadis ante Altare B. Joannis, ibidem damus XV libras Vienn. Item Abbatie S. Sulpicii damus et legamus L libras Vienn. Domui Carthusie LX libras, Domui Arverie XXX lib. Abbatie monialium de Bons L lib. Abbatie Bituminis L lib. Operi pontis Petre Castri XL lib. Hospitali Montis Cenisii XXX lib. hospitali Montis Bernardi Domum nostram de Londonia cum eias pertinenciis. hospitali columne Jouis XX lib. Abbatie S. Mauricii Agaunensis C. lib. hospitali Uille noue XX lib. Item Ecclesie B. Petri de Gebennis XX lib. fratribus predicatoribus ibidem XX lib. fratribus Mino ribus ibidem XX lib. Ecclesie b. Marie Lausann. XXX lib. fratribus predicatoribus ibidem XX lib. fratribus Minoribus ibidem XX lib. Fratribus minoribus de Chamberiaco XX lib. Item Domº. Sofredo de Amaisino CCC lib. Domº. Guigoni de Garnerens C. lib. Domº. Petro de Chassiz C. lib. Domº. Humberto de Montreal L lib. et precipimus sibi solui XXX marchas arg. quas dicit sibi deberi pro quibusdam expensis per eum factis in municione de Peuensey. Domº. Petro Capellano nostro LX lib. Vincencio de Petra Castri LX lib. Hugoni de S. Mauricio L lib. Petro de Secusia XL lib. Roberto de Salins LX lib. et precipimus sibi solui illud quod sibi debemus. Theobaldo de Rotomago soluantur LX lib. quas ei debemus. Roleto de Billens damus et legamus X lib. Lausann. annuas in furnis nostris de Meuduno. Jaqueto de Bussy damus L. lib. barberio nostro XXX lib. Stephano Cotto XXX lib. et precipimus ei solui XLV lib. Lausann. quas sibi debemus. Jaqueto de S. Jorio XXX lib. Petro de Prissio XXX lib. Willermo de Prissio XXX lib. Roleto de Mussie XXX lib. Petro de Meuduno XXX lib. Gerardo de valle Transuersi XL lib. Aymoni de Boza XXX lib. Antelmo de Amaisino XL lib. et emendetur sibi vnus equus quem amisit hoc anno in nostro seruitio. Aymonem de Fucigniaco committimus Sorori sue Domine Fucigniaci quod eidem prouideat competenter. Petro de Frigie XX libras. Ja queto de Sergie XX lib. Putondo XX lib. Gualtero Cotto XL lib. Joanni de S. Eugendo X lib. Sobine scissori X lib. Ver nisto XX lib. Stephano Forratori XV. Willermo de Lucingia X lib. Petro de Valen: X lib. Petro Grossi C. florenos. Joanni de Garderoba XX lib. Galtero Alamanno XXX lib. Omnia autem onera, legata et debita superius contenta, et omnia debita nostra ubique ea debeamus citra mare Anglicum, volumus quod predicti heredes nostri filia et frater, soluant me dietatem omnium quilibet, et pro media parte quilibet ipsorum satisfaciat vniuersis et si quis heredum predictorum partem suam debitorum et clamorum non soluerit, vel de ea satisfacere noluerit, ad arbitrium Executorum infrascriptorum partem non obtemperantis uoluntati et ordinationi nostre huiusmodi ex nunc adimimus, attribuentes

Key Pierre de Savoie Estate Holdings in England and Savoy

eam totaliter alii uolenti et complenti vo luntatem et ordinationem nostram supradictam. De dominio autem, quod petebat a nobis Ven. pater Dominus Aymo Epis copus Gebennensis pro feudo, quod dicit, quod ab ipso tenere debemus, uolumus, quod heredes nostri predicti sibi faciant quod debebunt. Item domo. Petro de Aquablanca remittimus sex viginti libras Vienn. per Executores nostros. Executores autem huius vltime uoluntatis facimus et constituimus Ven. P. in Christo Dom. Tarentasien. Archiepiscopum, Dom. Episcopum Gebenna rum, Abbatem Altecombe, Priorem Lustriaci, Dom. Hugonem de Paleysuel, ballivum nostrum in Vuaudo. Dom. Sofredum de Amaysino ballivum nostrum in Sabaudia, Berlionem de Amay sino et Thomam de Rossillione clientes nostros, et precipimus omnibus nostris fidelibus nobilibus et ignobilibus, sub fide qua nobis tenentur, quod predictis Executoribus nostris ad com plendam hanc nostram vltimam uoluntatem prestent consilium quandocumque poterunt et iuvamen. Hanc autem nostram vltimam uoluntatem ualere uolumus iure testamenti in scriptis, vel nuncupatiui, vel iure cuiuslibet vltime uoluntatis, et iure Codicillorum, et eo melius quo ualere poterit, secundum iura ciuilia, vel canonicas sanctiones, et huic cum subscripcione nostra et testium subscriptorum, sigillum nostrum apponimus in testimonium ueritatis.

In Anglia uero facimus Executores nostros, Karissimam Dominam nostram, ill. Reginam Anglie, et Dom. Guichardum de Charron militem per ordinationem huiusmodi nostram exequendam ibidem, et si qua alia testa menta reperiantur a nobis prius facta, reuocamus ea, et istud testamentum solum valere uolumus vt supra est expressum.

Item uigesimam que leuabatur in mandamento de Montemeliano, ad firmandum castrum ejusdem loci remittimus et quittamus, et precipimus quod ea que iam levata erant, restituantur.

Item Abbatie Stamedei damus et legamus pro remedio anime nostre, L. lib. Item domui Aillonis XXX libras. Item domui de Pomiers, XX lib. Item domui Repositorii XX lib. Item domui de Aujone XX lib. Item domui Mairiaci XX lib. Item domui Portarum XX lib. Abbatie de Cheystri XXX lib. Abbatie Bonimontis XXX lib. Abbatie de Altacrista XXX lib. Domui de Valon XX lib. Item Hugoni Dorchi damus et legamus XX lib. H. Cassino XX libras. Item predicte B. filie nostre damus et legamus cum suprascriptis quidquid habemus apud Dorchiam et in Micalia, tam in dominicaturis quam feudis, homagiis et aliis vniuersis. Item damus et legamus Abbatie S. Michaelis Clusiaci, provno anniversario acquirendo C. libras Vienn. Item domui Vallis S. Benedicti XXX lib. Abbatie S. Iusti Secusie XL. lib. Ecclesie B. Joannis Maurianen. XL. lib. Item Ecclesie S. Petri Tarantasiensis et canonicis et Ecclesie secularibus ibidem L lib. Ecclesie et Capitulo Augustensi L lib. et precipimus quod querelas quas faciebat de nobis Episcopus Augustensis sedare debeat et pacificare Comes Burgundie heres noster, ita quod de eis sine peccato remaneamus. Item Abbatie Alpensi damus et legamus XL lib. Abbatie Abundantie XL. lib. Abbatie Filiaci XXX lib. Sanctimonialibus de Bellaripa XXX lib. Abbatie de Siz XXX lib.

Item ubi supra diximus quod soror nostra Comitissa de Kiburgo habeat ad uitam suam D. libras Vienn. in pedagio nostro Villenoue intendimus et uolumus, quod illi quibus tenemur et quibus suam solutionem assignauimus supra pedagium supradictum prius soluantur integraliter de debito supradicto. Item castra nostra de Falaverio et de Dentesiaco damus et legamus predicte filie nostre cum eorum mandamentis et pertinenciis vniuersis. Quod autem su perius diximus quod heredes nostri predicti, legata debita et clamores debeant soluere quilibet pro dimidia parte. Intelligimus de omnibus debitis et clamoribus, excepto quod Comes Burgundie solus soluere debeat dotem predicte B. filie Comitis Amedei usque ad summam superius dictam et residuum de bebit assignare, si tamen dictus Comes obseruare uoluerit conuentionem seu composicionem factam inter nos et filiam predicti Comitis Amedei. Si vero dictus Comes predicta ob seruare noluerit, predicte fllie in Comitatu Sabaudie ius suum saluum sibi remaneat, sicut ante cessionem, quam nobis dicta filia fecerat de predicto Comitatu. et iuramentum remittimus eidem. Item Ecclesie Paterniaci damus et legamus pro remedio anime nostre L. libras Viennenses.

Nos girardus officialis gebenn. huic testamento tempore aperture et publicationis ipsius sigillum curie nostre apposui mus rogati subscripsimus et signum fecimus (Monogramma, deperditum vero sigillum).

In reasonable translation reads:

Testament of Peter, Count of Savoy. 1268. May 7.
In the name of the Father, and of the Son, and of the Holy Spirit. Amen. In the year of our Lord one thousand two hundred and sixty-eight, on the morrow of Blessed John the Evangelist at the Latin Gate, we, Pierre, Count of Savoy, who are of sound mind, although ill in body, wishing to foresee the cases of death, who will not depart intestate for our goods and goods, order and dispose in this manner. First of all, we will and order our debts to be paid out fully and the cries to be settled and corrected by our undersigned Executors and to be paid out of it and to correct our cries and to be pacified at the hands of the said Executors, we charge our heirs in the manner and form below written: we choose our burial place at Hautecombe. Béatrice our dearest daughter, the wife of the Dauphin of Vienne and Albon. We have appointed our heir in all our land which we have in Geneva and in Uuaudo, as far as Mosternensis and in Germany, in which we possess some title in the aforesaid lands, or, as it were, except the right which we have in Seyssel and Montfaucon. We also give and bequeath to the same Béatrice our daughter, the homage by which Albert IV the Lord of La Tour is bound to us, with the fiefs he holds from us. Also the fee which the Count Renaud of Forez holds from us. We also established the castle of Saint-Rambert[-en-Bugey] and of Lompnes, with all orders and appurtenances, and the fiefs which are held by us at Romont, and as his heir in each and all aforesaid. Likewise, we give and bequeath to our chosen sons, the sons of Lord Thomas de Savoie [Amédée and Louis], our most beloved brother, Villafranca in the land of Piedmont, and the right which we have in that castle and its appurtenances, and the land which we have in Essex and the Honour of the Eagle [Pevensey] in England. Likewise, we give and bequeath to our niece Alianor, Queen of England, the County of Richmond, in such a way that she pays her satisfaction fully of all the debts to which we are bound by Mametus Spine and his allies to the citizens and merchants of Florence. But in the county of Savoy and our other estates, both beyond the mountains and on this side, wherever we reside, we make our heir, and we have established our most dear brother Philippe de Savoie, Count of Burgundy, besides the legacies and alms contained below. and if it would happen that the Count himself should retire without male issue. whenever we have been appointed under the same person in the aforesaid county and all the others aforesaid.

All the aforesaid may be rolled out and restored to our descendants, or any other survivor of them, without restitution or diminution of the fourth Trebellianicus, or of any other. We also send back to the lord of the tower and quit the pledge which we have from him at Burgundy, and also the debt by which he was held by us for the said pledge. We also remit and quit to the sons of Rudolph de Genève, 500 *Livres* to our relatives, 2,000 marks, of the debt which they are bound to us, for the wages which we have from them. We also give and read the tower of Uiusio with all its appurtenances. and fid. to our Lord Hugh of Paleysiux. We also give to our beloved wife Agnès, Dame de Faucigny, and bequeaths to her life the castle of Versoix, of Allinges, of Feternes, of Charosa, of Albon, with all their appurtenances. Likewise, we give and bequeath to our sister Marguerite Countess de Kyburg and bequeath 100 *livres Viennoise* yearly, to receive

Key Pierre de Savoie Estate Holdings in England and Savoy

for life in the toll of Villeneuve for 2000 silver marks which we had from the same. Likewise, we will and order Béatrice the daughter of our late gentle brother Count Amédée IV to be endowed and fittingly married until the sum of 7,000 *livres Viennois* by the aforesaid Philippe I, Count of Burgundy. We completely quit and remit for ourselves and our heirs the short fruit and flour which we have been accustomed both to ourselves and our predecessors in the county of Savoy.

We give and bequeath 200 *livres Viennois* to the house of Hautecombe for our relief for buying ten *Livres* worth of land for the anniversary of the same year. We also give and bequeath 200 *livres Viennois* to the church of Blessed John the Baptist in Belley. for the same and to make up for that which has long been assigned by us for the maintenance of one light at the altar of Blessed John in Belley, we give the same place for 15 *livres Viennois*. We also give and bequeath to the Abbey of Saint Sulpicius [in Bugey] 50 *livres Viennois*. To the House of Chartreuse 60 *Livres*, to the House of Arverie 30 *Livres*. The Abbey of the Nuns of Bons [in Bugey] 50 *Livres*. The Abbey of Betton 50 *Livres*. The work of the bridge of Pierre Castri 40 *Livres*. The Hospital of the Mont Cenis 30 *Livres*. The hospital of the Grand-Saint-Bernard, our house in London with those appurtenances. The hospital of the Petit-Saint-Bernard 20 *Livres*. To the abbey of Saint-Maurice d'Agaune 100 *Livres*. The hospital of Villeneuve 20 *Livres*. Also to the church of Blessed Pierre de Genève to the brothers and to the preachers in the same book. to the brothers of Minus in the same place 20 *Livres* Church of the Blessed Mary, [Cathedral of] Lausanne. 30 *Livres* to the brothers and to the preachers in the same book. To the minor brothers in the same place 20 *Livres*. The Friars Minor of Chamberiaco, Book 20 *Livres*. Likewise, Lord Sofredo de Amaisinus 300 *Livres*. Lord Guigos de Garnerens 100 *Livres*. Lord Petro de Chassiz 100 *Livres*. Lord Humbert de Montréal 50 *Livres* and we order him to be paid 30 marks of silver which he says was due to him for certain expenses incurred by him in the fortification of Pevensey. Lord Pierre our Chaplain 60 *Livres*. Vincent de Petra Castri 60 *Livres*. Hugo de Saint-Maurice 50 *Livres*. Petro de Unlikeia 40 *Livres*. Robert de Salins 60 *Livres* and we order him to be set free from that which we owe to him. Theobald de Rotomago 60 *Livres* which we owe to him. We give and read Rodolphe de Billens 10 *livres Lausanneois*, yearly for our furnaces of Moudon. We give Jaqueto de Bussey 50 *Livres*. Our barber 30 *Livres*. Stephen Cotto and we order him to be paid 45 *livres Lausannois* which we owe to him. Jaqueto de Saint Jorio 30 *Livres*. Petro de Prissio 30 *Livres*. William de Prissio 30 *Livres*. Roleto de Mussie 30 *Livres*. Petro de Meuduno 30 *Livres*. Gerardo de Valle Transuersi 40 *Livres*. Aymoni de Boza 30 *Livres*. Antelmo de Amaisinus 40 *Livres* and let him be improved by one horse, which he lost this year in our service. We entrust Aymon de Faucigny to his sister, *Seigneur de Faucigny*, to provide for her competently. Peter of Frigie 20 *Livres*. Jaqueto de Sergie 20 *Livres*. Putando 20 *Livres*. Gualtero Cotto 40 *Livres*. John of Saint Eugendo 10 *Livres*. Sobine tailoring 10 *Livres*. Veristo 20 *Livres*. Stephano Forratori 15 *Livres*. William of Lucingia Petro de Valen 10 *Livres*. Petro Grossi 100 *Floros*. Jean de Garderobe 20 *Livres*. Galtero Alamanno 30 *Livres*. And all the burdens, legacies, and debts contained above, and all our debts we owe them everywhere on this side of the English Sea, I desire that our aforesaid heirs, daughter and brother, let each and every one of the aforesaid heirs pay me the lordship; he will not pay his debts and claim, or will not be willing to make amends for it, at the will of the executors of the undersigned who does not comply with our will and ordination of this kind, by attributing it entirely to another who wishes and fulfils our wishes and our aforesaid ordination. But of the dominion which he requested from us. Father, Lord Aymon [de Cruseilles], Bishop of Geneva, for the fee, which he says, which we ought to hold from him, we wish that our aforesaid heirs should do to them what they ought to do. Likewise, To Lord Pierre d'Aigueblanche we release six twenty *livres*

Peter of Savoy: The Little Charlemagne

Viennois by our Executors. We make and appoint the executors of this last will. Pierre in Christ Lord Archbishop of Tarentaise. Bishop Geneva, Abbot of Hautecombe, Prior of Lutry, Lord Hugues de Palézieux, our bailiff in Vevey. We allow Sofred de Amaysinus, our bailiff in Savoy, to allow Berlion of Amay and Thomas de Rossillion, our dependents; help. We wish this our last will to be valid by the right of a testament in writing, or by pronouncing, or by the right of any last will, and by the right of the Codicil, and so much the better that it can be valid, according to civil rights or canonical sanctions; we attach ourselves to the testimony of the truth.

In England, indeed, we make our Executors, our Most Dear Lady, Alianor The Queen of England, and Lord Guichard de Charron, a knight, our will be executed there by our order of this kind, and if any other wills are found made by us before, we recall them, and we want this will alone to be valid as has been expressed above.

Likewise, we send back and leave the 200 men who were relieved in order from Montmélian to strengthen the castle of the same place, and order that those who had already been relieved be restored [relieve the special tax imposed in order to pay for the new fortifications at Montmélian].

We also give and read to the Abbaye de Tamié for the relief of our soul 50 *Livres*. Also to the house of Aillo 30 *Livres*. Also to the Chartreuse de Pomiers 20 *Livres*. Also to the house of the Repository. Also to the house of Aujone 20 *Livres*. Also to the house of Mairiacus 20 *Livres*. Also to the house of Portae 20 *Livres*. The Abbey of Cheystri 30 *Livres*. The Abbaye Bonmont 30 *Livres*. The Abbaye Haute-Crêt 30 *Livres*. House of Valon 20 *Livres*. Likewise we give and read to Hugh Dorchus 20 *Livres*. H. Cassino 20 *Livres*. We also give and bequeath to the aforesaid Béatrice, our daughter, with the above mentioned whatever we have at Dorchester and in Micalia, as well on Sundays as feuds, homages, and all other things. We also give and bequeath to the Abbaye Sacrée de San Michele della Chiusa, for one year, by acquiring 100 *livres Viennois*. Likewise, to the house of the Valley of Saint Benedict. To the Abbaye St. Justus de Secusia 40 *Livres*. To the church of the Blessed-Saint-Jean-de-Maurienne [Cathedral] 40 *Livres*. Likewise to the church of Saint-Pierre-de-Tarentaise [Moutiers Cathedral], and to the canons and secular churches in the same place in book 50 *Livres*. Also, to the Church and Chapter of Aosta 50 *Livres* and we order in advance that the Bishop of Aosta ought to settle the complaints which he made against us, and to pacify the Count of Burgundy, our heir, so that we remain of them without sin. We also give to the Abbaye Saint-Marie d'Aulps 40 *Livres*. Abbey of Abundantie 40 *Livres*. To the Abbaye de Filly 30 *Livres*. To the Abbaye de Bellerive 30 *Livres*. The Abbaye de Sixt 30 *Livres*.

Also where we said above that our sister [Marguerite] Countess of Kyburg has for her life 500 *livres Viennois*. We intend our toll at Villeneuve, and we wish that those to whom we are bound and to whom we assigned their payment above the above-named tolls, are to be paid graciously from the above mentioned debt. We also give our castles of Falavier and Demptézieu, and bequeath it to our aforesaid daughter, with all their orders and appurtenances. But what we have said above, that our aforesaid heirs, each ought to pay his debts, legacies and cries for half. We have to understand about all debts and shouts, except that the Count of Burgundy alone ought to pay the dowry to the aforesaid B[eatrice], daughter of the Count Amédée [IV], and assign the remainder of the debt to the aforesaid count. But if the said Count [of Burgundy] will not keep the aforesaid for his sake, let the aforesaid daughter in the County of Savoy remain safe to her, just as before the resignation which the said daughter had made for us of the aforesaid county. and we release the oath to him. We also give and bequeath to the Church of Payerne 50 *livres Viennois* for the relief of our soul.

AST/C, *Testamenti*, m 1, No 6. Wurstemberger, vol 4. No 749.

Key Pierre de Savoie Estate Holdings in England and Savoy

Vidimus of First Codicil to the 1268 Testament
This first codicil to the 1268 will related to the sons of the late Thomas II de Savoie, Amédée and Louis.

Codicillum primum.
1268. Maji 11. Petræcastelli. Legamus vltra legata per nos in primo testamento nepotibus nostris Thome, Amedeo et Ludovico, filiis fratris nostri quondam Thome de Sabaudia Comitis, facta quidquid habemus et tenemus vel habere etc. in Anglia in terra Sussessia cum toto honore Aquile, preter comitatum seu honorem de Richemund, et domum nostram in Londra, que aliis duximus assignandos. Mandatur omnibus suis balliuis, castellanis, senescalcis etc. ut agnoscant dictos nepotes ut heredes sui. „Rogamus autem Regem et Reginam Anglie et Dominos Edwardum et Eadmundum filios Regis, ut amoris sui intuitu et ipsorum, dictos nepotes nostros benigne recipiant, ad predicta, et seisinam eorum eis tradi faciant liberam pacificam et quietam. Testibus, Aymone Episcopo Gebennensi. Berlione de Amasino. Thoma de Rossilione, etc. Actum apud Petracastellum, die Veneris post festum beati Johannis ante portam latinam, Anno Domini Mo. CC. LX. octauo. Invent. Inscriptum.

1268 11 May. Pierre-Châtel. Let us read beyond the legacies by us in the first testament to our nephews of Thomas, Amédée and Louis, to the sons of our brother, formerly Thomas Count of Savoy, whatever we have and hold or have etc. in England in the land of Sussex, with all the Honour of the Eagle, except the county or Honour of Richmond, and our house in London, which we have thought to be assigned to others. He is entrusted to all his bailiffs, castles, stewards etc. that they may acknowledge the said nephews as their heirs. We beg the King and Queen of England and Lord Edward and Edmund, the sons of the King, to receive kindly our said nephews, with regard to their love and theirs, to the aforesaid, and cause their seisin to be delivered to them free, peaceful and quiet. Witnesses: Aymone, Bishop of Geneva. Berlin of Amasino. Thomas de Rossilion, etc. Enacted at Pierre-Châtel, on Friday after the feast of St. John at the Latin Gate, in the year of our Lord 1268.
   Principi di Sangue. Fasc. I. No 9. Ping. Chr. f. 403. Wurstemberger, vol 4. No 750.

Second Codicil to the 1268 Testament
This second codicil to the 1268 will related to Philippe de Savoie.

Codicillum secundum.
1268. Maji 14. Petræcastelli. Nos Petrus Comes Sabaudie notum facimus vniuersis quod nos ad pacem tranquillitatem et concordiam successorum nostrorum et tocius Sabaudie Comitatus pretendentes. uolentes Karissimo fratri nostro ph. de Sabaudia Comiti Burgond. zelum nostrum federis in fine ostendere quod cum ipso habuimus et in uita certi et indubitantes de extrema dispositione nostra in qua Karissimam filiam nostram B. Dalphinam de Vienneisio et ipsum fratrem nostrum heredes instituimus in quibusdam bonis nostris in hac scriptura uel uoluntate nostra alia, sic duximus ordinandum. Videlicet quod si reperiatur dicta filia nostra heres instituta in iure quod habemus in Castro de Gebenn. et in castris de Falauerio et de Dentesiaco et de Sancto Benedicto de Lonnes uel ipsis castris cum eorum pertinenciis et in feudis uel homagiis illustrium uirorum Comitis Foren. et domini de turre et domini de Jez qui "nobis tenentur et predicta bona predicte filie legata seu donata a nobis aliquociens in aliquo testamento seu vltima uoluntate inueniantur. nos ei predicta vniuersa et singula. cum

vniuersis pertinenciis ex toto adimimus et auferimus et uoluntates alias super his reuocamus et ea predicta castra vniuersa et singula et feuda et homagia cum eorum pertinenciis. donamus et legamus predicto harissimo fratri nostro ad habendum tenendum et possidendum sibi et heredibus post decessum meum. uolentes et mandantes et precipientes vniuersis et singulis in predictis castris aliqua de nobis tenentibus uel existentibus in eisdem et pertinenciis ipsoruin et specialiter dicto domino Comiti Foren. et dicto domino de turre et domino de Jez quod predicto fratri nostro sint intendentes et respondentes de predictis omnibus si de nobis contingat humanitus prout nobis respondere aliquatenus tenebantur. Hanc igitur uoluntatem nostram ualere uolumus tam in adimendo quam in legando iure legatorum uel iure codicillorum uel vt donacionem inter uiuos uel eo iure canonico uel ciuili quo melius valere poterit et effectum habere. Testem autem ad hoc aduocauimus dominum Goffredum de Amaisino. dominum de Chassans milites. Thomam de Rossellone. Vincencium de Petracastello clericos et Girardum cochet. et nos predicti testes vna cum sigillo predicti Comitis de Sabaudia sigilla nostra ad instanciam ipsius huic scripto apponenda duximus in testimonium veritatis. Dat. ap. petram castellum die lune Rogal. Anno Domini Mo. CCo. LX0. octauo.

We, Peter, Count of Savoy, certify to all that we are bringing peace, tranquillity, and harmony to our successors and the whole County of Savoy. wishing our dearest brother Philippe of Savoy also the Count of Burgundy. Our zeal for the League is to show at the end what we had with him and in a life assured and unquestioning about our extreme disposition, in which we have established our most beloved daughter, Béatrice, Dalphina of Vienne, and our brother himself, as heirs in some of our goods in this writing or our other will; to arrange. For instance, if our said daughter is found to be the heir established in the law that we have in the castles of Geneva, and in the castles of Falavier and Demptézieu and of Saint Benedict of Lompnes or the castle themselves, with their appurtenances, and in fiefs or homages to the illustrious men of Count Renaud de Forez, and the Lords of La Tour and the lords of Gex who are bound to us and the aforesaid goods bequeathed to the aforesaid daughters or donated by us may sometimes be found in some will or final will, we told him each and every thing aforesaid, when we take away and take away from them all the appurtenances, and call back other wills concerning them, and all that aforesaid camp, and each and all the fiefs and homages with their appurtenances, we grant and bequeath to our most dear brother the aforesaid, to have, to hold, and to possess to him and his heirs after my decease, willing and ordering and ordering to all and each in the aforesaid camp certain things concerning us, tenants or existing in the same and their appurtenances, and specially to the said lord Count Renaud de Forez, and to the said lord of the tower and lord of Gex that our aforesaid brother were attentive and answering about all the aforesaid, if it should happen to us in a humane manner, as they were bound to some extent to respond to us. We want this will to be valid, both in abolishing as well as in legacies, by the right of ambassadors, or by the right of codicils, or as a gift among the living, either by that canon or civil law, so that it may be able to avail and effect better. We have therefore called lord Goffred of Amaisinus as witness to this. master of the Chassans soldiers. Thomas de Rossellone. Vincent de Petracastello and Girard cochet clerics. and we, together with the seal of the aforesaid witnesses, we thought our seals of the aforesaid Earl of Savoy to be attached to this writing at the instance of him as a witness to the truth. He gives at Pierre-Châtel on Monday in Rogal. In the year of our Lord 1268, a week later.

Invent. Teslam. Comil. el Princip. Sabaudiæ, Fasc. 1. No 14. Wurstemberger, vol 4, No 751.

Key Pierre de Savoie Estate Holdings in England and Savoy

Oath of 12 April 1258

> The sworn confederation of seven barons, 12 April 1258
> (Bémont, *Simon de Montfort* (Paris, 1884), App. 30 [French])

Taken from a modern copy in the archives of the Montfort family and now in the Bibliothèque Nationale, Paris:

We, Richard of Clare, earl of Gloucester and Hertford; Roger Bigod, earl marshal and earl of Norfolk; Simon de Montfort, earl of Leicester; Peter of Savoy; Hugh Bigod; John fitz Geoffrey; and Peter of Montfort make known to all people that we have sworn on the holy gospels, and are held together by this oath, and we promise in good faith that each one of us and all of us together will help each other, both ourselves and those belonging to us, against all people, doing right and taking nothing that we cannot take without doing wrong, saving faith to our lord the king of England and to the Crown.

In witness of which thing we have made these letters sealed with our seals ... And this was done at London, on the Friday after the fortnight after Easter, in the year of our Lord twelve hundred and fifty-eight.

Notes

Introduction

1. Jean d'Orville, known as Cabaret, is a Picard, perhaps from Orville, between Amiens and Arras. During his life, he lived in the entourage of several princes. Around 1417–19, he was in the service of Amadeus VIII of Savoy and wrote in ancient French at his request the Chronique de Savoye, a founding text of Savoyard historical literature. Ten years later, he was in Bourbon and wrote the Chronicle of the Good Duke Loys of Bourbon.
2. Jean d'Orville dit Cabaret. 1995. La Chronique de Savoie. Montmélian: La Fontaine de Siloé. 92.
3. Chron. Majora Eng, vol 1. 49. 1 ... 2.
4. Ibid. 122.
5. Darren Baker. 2015. With All for All: The Life of Simon de Montfort. Stroud: Amberley Publishing. 381.
6. Andrew Spencer. 2021. A Vineyard Without a Wall: The Savoyards, John de Warenne and the Failure of Henry III's kingship in Thirteenth Century England XVII: Proceedings of the Cambridge Conference, 2017. Eds. Andrew Spencer & Carl Watkins. (Boydell and Brewer: Woodbridge).
7. André Perret. 1983. *Le comte Pierre II de Savoie. L'expansion savoyarde et l'alliance anglaise au XIIIe siècle. Revue Savoisienne.* 110.
8. Jean-Pierre Chapuisat. 1964. *Le Chapitre Savoyard de Hereford au XIIIe siècle. In Actes du Congrès des Sociétés Savantes de la Province de Savoie. Nouvelle Série* 1. 43.
9. Huw Ridgeway. 2023. *An English Cartulary Roll of Peter of Savoy, Lord of Richmond (1240-1268): Archives, Interests and Servants of an Alien Favourite of Henry III* in forthcoming volume to be edited by Professors Nigel Saul & Nicholas Vincent for the Pipe Roll Society, London. 6. Hereinafter noted as Ridgeway.
10. David Carpenter. 2005. The Meetings of Kings Henry III and Louis IX in Thirteenth Century England X: Proceedings of the Durham Conference, 2003. Eds Michael Prestwich, Michael Britnell & Robin Frame. (Boydell and Brewer: Woodbridge). 1.

Prologue

1. H. F. Westlake. 1923. *Hornchurch Priory: A Kalendar of Documents in the Possession of the Warden and Fellows of New College Oxford.* London: Philip Allan & Co. 45.
2. The story is apocryphal and is alluded to in J Horace Round. 1898. Hornchurch Priory. Transactions of the Essex Archaeological Society VI: 1–12. And also, Perfect. Ye Olde

Village of Hornchurch, Colchester, 1917, 59–60. But the story's historical truth is in doubt, hanging as it does on the dating of the Hornchurch grant by Henry II. H.F. Westlake. 1923. Hornchurch Priory a Kalendar of Documents in the Possession of the Warden and Fellows of New College Oxford. London: Philip Allan & Co. dates the grant to August 1158 prior to Henry's departure for the continent where he would stay until January 1163. If this dating is accurate, then the story is invented. However, the dating of Henry's grants can be difficult. Westlake merely gives the date as "probable". It is possible that Henry made the grant before he despatched his envoys to ensure safe passage, thus rendering the story partly true. St. Andrews church in Hornchurch still relates the story, and it's included here because it's a good story by way of an introduction to English entanglement with Savoy, and as foundation myths go it's as good as any, given that it points toward the *Via Francigena* and the Grand-Saint-Bernard Pass as the origin of the story.

Chapter One

1. *Sapaudia* first appears in Ammianus Marcellinus, who described it as the southern district of *Provincia Maxima Sequanorum*, the land of the *Sequani* enlarged by the Diocletian Reforms. It originally covered the area around *Lac de Neuchâtel*, the land of the ancient *Allobroges*. Its prefect appeared in the late Roman List of Offices. During the 5th century, the Burgundians settled in the area, forming the Kingdom of the Burgundians, the capital of which was *Lugdunum Segusianorum* (Lyon). For centuries thereafter, the names Burgundy and Sapaudia/Savoy became closely linked. In the mid-9th century, *Sapaudia* was ruled by the Bosonid duke Humbert as part of the realm of Upper Burgundy. In 933, it was incorporated into Rudolph II's Kingdom of Arles, the Arelat or Second Kingdom of Burgundy.
2. Canon Jean-Pierre Voutaz & Pierre Rouyer. 2013. Discovering the Great Saint Bernard. Martigny: Les Editions du Grand-Saint-Bernard. 12–13.
3. While the exact origins of the name are unknown, the name Lacus Lemanus was in use during the time of Julius Caesar. Lac Léman was the common name on all local maps and is the customary name in the French language. In contemporary English, the name Lake Geneva has become predominant.
4. The First Kingdom of Burgundy was a successor to the Western Roman Empire in what is now south-eastern Gaul and western Helvetia. The Burgundian tribe had migrated, possibly from Scandinavia, to settle in western Helvetia in the dying years of Rome. Their first king being Gunther in 411 and last Gundomar until his defeat by the Merovingian Franks under Childerbert and Clothar in 534.
5. C. W. Previté-Orton. 1912. The Early History of the House of Savoy (1000–1233). Cambridge: Cambridge University Press. 2. Arpitan is what we used to call Franco-Provençal, but since it's neither French nor Provençal the name was changed. It's a Romance language which grew from Latin as did its neighbours. The names for the towns and cities of the region illustrate the differences with standard French, for example Genève becomes Geneva, Lausanne becomes *Losena*, Aoste becomes *Aousta*, Grenoble becomes *Grenoblo*, Annecy becomes *Enneci*, Chambéry becomes *Chamberi* and Martigny becomes *Martegne*.

6. Peter H. Wilson. 2017. The Holy Roman Empire. Second ed. London: Penguin. 37.
7. Manfred W. Wenner. 1980. The Arab/Muslim Presence in Medieval Central Europe. International Journal of Middle East Studies 12: 59–79.
8. René Poupardin. 1907. *Le Royaume de Bourgogne* (888–1038). Paris: Librairie Honoré Champion. 144. C. W. Previté-Orton. 1912. The Early History of the House of Savoy (1000–1233). Cambridge: Cambridge University Press. 30. King Rudolf III the last independent King of Burgundy died 6 September 1032 and was buried in Lausanne.
9. Norman Davies. 2012. *Vanished Kingdoms: The History of Half-Forgotten Europe.* London: Penguin Books. 110. "*Le Fainéant*" can be translated as "The Lazy".
10. C. W. Previté-Orton. 1912. The Early History of the House of Savoy (1000–1233). Cambridge: Cambridge University Press. 6.
11. Ibid. 5.
12. Ibid. 6. Manfred W. Wenner. 1980. The Arab/Muslim Presence in Medieval Central Europe. International Journal of Middle East Studies 12: 59–79.
13. Peter H. Wilson. 2017. The Holy Roman Empire. Second ed. London: Penguin. 362.
14. Of course, Voltaire was describing the Empire of his time saying "*Ce corps qui s'appelait et qui s'appelle encore le saint empire romain n'était en aucune manière ni saint, ni romain, ni empire*" but the Empire of the thirteenth century could have merited the same epithet. Quoted from *Essai sur l'histoire générale et sur les mœurs et l'esprit des nations*, Chapter 70 (1756).
15. Peter H. Wilson. 2017. The Holy Roman Empire. Second ed. London: Penguin. 196–7.
16. The origins of Humbert I are not entirely clear; several origins have been proposed including descent from Saxony. The book of anniversaries of the church of Aosta includes an entry dated 1040, the dating clause of which says "*regnante et principante in Valle nostra Augustæ Salassorum Umberto P. Maurianensi filio illustris Beroldi de Saxonia*" Also more locally within Burgundy. His appointment as a representative of the Queen of King Rudolf III of Burgundy, Ermengarde, has been taken as possibly indicative of a familial link. A 1033 chapter in her name describes her relationship with Humbert as "*per advocatum meum comitum Humbertum*". The "*comitum*" is also contentious at this point; we are not sure whether the title "count" is honorary as a royal intimate or indicates predating holding of a county, either Maurienne or Aosta or Belley – the charter is unclear. There is also a land transfer from "*Equestricus*" [Nyon] to Romainmotier of 1028 which cites "*Dommus Umbertus comes*" acting as an agent. As we see from the 1027 visit to Rome, Humbert was styled there as Count of Aosta. C. W. Previté-Orton. 1912. The Early History of the House of Savoy (1000–1233). Cambridge: Cambridge University Press (100) summed up his likely land holdings circa 1000AD as "*seigneurs* in the County of Sermorens and also Counts of Belley … the County of Savoy" followed by the acquisition of "the County of Aosta and of the two passes of the St. Bernard [Grand and Petit]" then following the death of Rudolf III the addition of Maurienne and Chablais.
17. There is a charter dated 21 January 1042 describing Humbert as "*Hubertus Comes*" in Carutti (1888), *Documenti del libro primi*, XXVII, 196.
18. It has been suggested though in no way corroborated that Ermengarde was related to Humbert I de Savoie.
19. *Régesete Genevois*. No 185. "Emperor Conrad the Salic went to Burgundy with his army and came to the monastery of Payerne, where he was elected and proclaimed king

of Burgundy on February 2, 1033. Then he besieged the castles held by Eudes; but, given the harshness of winter, he renounced to continue the war, and, by withdrawing through Zurich, he received tributes from Queen Ermengarde, Count Humbert and other greats of Burgundy – in the summer of the same year, he returned to fight the Count of Champagne whose heritage properties he devastated."

20. C. W. Previté-Orton. 1912. The Early History of the House of Savoy (1000–1233). Cambridge: Cambridge University Press. 41.
21. The title was held to signify his generosity but may have been a posthumous confusion of a late medieval record which referred to the walls of his castle as *blancis moenibus*. The reference does not appear until the 14th century.
22. C. W. Previté-Orton. 1912. The Early History of the House of Savoy (1000–1233). Cambridge: Cambridge University Press. 26.
23. M. J. Trow, Cnut: Emperor of the North. Stroud: Sutton Pub Ltd 193.
24. Ibid. Previté-Orton cites William of Malmesbury, Gesta Regnum, L 222 and confirms the tolls of concern to Cnut are at Bard in the Val d'Aoste which would have been within the lands of Humbert.
25. Cædwalla abdicated in 688 to travel to Rome for baptism. He reached Rome in April 689, and was baptised by Pope Sergius I on the Saturday before Easter, dying ten days later on 20 April 689
26. Circa 800 Archbishop Æthelhard went to Rome along with Bishop Cyneberht of Winchester, and carried two letters from Coenwulf to the pope. Æthelhard returned to England in 803.
27. Veronica Ortenberg. 1990. Archbishop Sigeric's Journey to Rome in 990. Anglo-Saxon England 19: 197–200. The itinerary comes from the British Library, London, Cotton Tiberius B. v, 23v–24r. Carrying details of Sigeric's northbound journey through what would become Savoy: "*Agusta* [Aosta] ... *Sancte Maurici* [Saint Maurice d'Agaune] ... *Losanna* [Lausanne] ... *Urba* [Orbe] ... *Punterlin* [Pontarlier]."
28. J Horace Round. 1898. Hornchurch Priory. Transactions of the Essex Archaeological Society VI: 6.
29. Chronicles and Memorials or Rolls Séries, Epistolae Cantuarienses, London, 1865, p. 181. The text of John of Salisbury in full "*Litem instaurarem contra me ipsum, quod varios viarum eventus vobis mandare [negligerem] si me negligentiae arguendum intelligerem. Verum quia multiplex hucusque necessitas calamum cohibuit, dummodo cur non scribam dixerim, mihi indulgendum. In Monte ergo Jovis positus, hinc coelos montium suspiciens, hinc infera vallium abhorrens, coelo jam vicinior et fidentior audiri, << Domine »*, inquam, «< *restitue me fratribus meis ut annunciem illis ne et ipsi veniant in locum hunc tormentorum* ». *Loca namque tormentorum non immerito nuncupaverim, ubi terram saxeam glacierum marmora con sternunt, ubi pedem figere non est, immo nec sine periculo ponere, et mirum in modum cum in lubrico stare non possis, in mortem corruis si labaris. Hic manum in peram conjeci, ut sinceritati vestrae vel syllabas unas exararem, invenique atramentarium a renibus dependens humore sicco repletum et indurato. Sed nec digitos movere potui ad scribendum. Barba quoque gelu rigebat, et de spiritu oris concreto glacies prominebat prolixior. Haec ibi me causa, cum domini prioris nuncius optato advenisset, scripto quod volueram mandare prohibuit. De litteris autem quas ad vos detulit papae Clementis, quae rigoris minus aliquid habere videntur, propositum erat scribere, ne terreremini, quia debile principium, melior prosperabit eventus. Valete.*"

30. H. F. Westlake. 1923. *Hornchurch Priory a Kalendar of Documents in the Possession of the Warden and Fellows of New College Oxford.* London: Philip Allan & Co. 28–9, 40–1 & 44–5. The west window of St.Andrews Church in Havering shows Henry II presenting the charter to the monks of the Grand St. Bernard.
31. Jean-Pierre Chapuisat. 1971. *Les deux faces anglaises du Grand-Saint-Bernard au moyen âge. Vallesia* 26. 5–14. 6–9.
32. The Roman colony of Augusta Praetoria Salassorum
33. Erwin Eugster. "Zähringen, von", in: Historisches Lexikon der Schweiz (HLS), Version vom 03.06.2020. Online: https://hls-dhs-dss.ch/de/articles/019504/2020-06-03/, Consulted 07.10.2020.
34. The Marquisate of Turin had grown out of the March of Arduinic within the Kingdom of Italy in the tenth century. Arduin, Count of Turin from 941 had cleared the Val d'Susa from the Saracens. From the time of Otto the Counts of Maurienne then Savoy began styling themselves Marquis of Susa of the Marquisate of Susa as Turin itself became a prince bishopric.
35. From 1424 the County of Geneva was joined to the House of Savoy.
36. Eugene L. Cox. 1974. *The Eagles of Savoy: The House of Savoy in Thirteenth Century Europe.* Princeton: Princeton University Press. 7.
37. Jean-Pierre Chapuisat. 1960. *A Propos des Relations entre la Savoie et l'Angleterre au XIII siècle. Bulletin Philolgique et Historique* 1: 429.
38. Eugene L. Cox. 1974. *The Eagles of Savoy: The House of Savoy in Thirteenth-Century Europe.* Princeton: Princeton University Press. 7.
39. Jean Pierre Chapuisat. 1989. *De Mont-sur-Rolle à Windsor, de la Dullive à Dumfries. ... La Maison de Savoie et le Pays de Vaud* 97: 118.
40. Norman Davies. 2012. *Vanished Kingdoms: The History of Half-Forgotten Europe.* London: Penguin Books. 339. "Thanks to a common rivalry with France, however, Sabaudia developed a special relationship with England."
41. William Stubbs. 1867. *Gesta Regis Henrici*, the Chronicle of the reigns of Henry II and Richard I, A.D. 1169–1192. London: Longmans, Green, Reader and Dyer. 35–6.
42. Ibid. 41. "*Comes vero Mauriancæ scire voluit apud Limoges quid et quantum prædictus Johannes filius regis, cui filia ipsius, ut supradictum est, data fuerat, haberet de terra patris sui. Et rex voluit ei concedere et dare castellum de Chinone, et castellum de Loudun, et cas tellum de Mirabel cum omnibus pertinentiis suis. Sed rex juvenis contradicebat, et nullo modo hoc fratri suo concedere voluit, nec a patre suo hoc fieri permisit.*" Or "But the Count of Maurienne wanted to know at Limoges what and how much the said John, the king's son, to whom(his daughter had been given, as aforesaid, had of his father's land. And the king wished to grant and give him the castle of Chinon, and the castle of Loudun, and the fortress of Mirabel with all their appurtenances. But the young king [Henry] contradicted him, and in no way wished to grant this to his brother, nor did he allow this to be done by his father." Chinon was the centre of Angevin power, Loudun lay nineteen miles (thirty kilometres) to the south of Chinon, where an enormous tower built by Fulke III Nerra, Count of Anjou in the eleventh century dominated. Mirabeau, another Fulke Nerra castle, lay thirty miles (48 kilometres) south of Chinon. Henry II was in effect handing Anjou, the centre of Angevin power, to John upon Humbert's request, so it is little wonder that Henry the young king resolutely defended his position. While the king was at Limoges he was informed of a conspiracy involving his wife and

sons to overthrow him. Choosing to keep his eldest son by his side, Henry II set off north to Normandy, ensuring along the way that his castles in Aquitaine were prepared for war. En route they stayed at Chinon; under the cover of darkness Henry the Young King escaped and set off to Paris to join the court of Louis VII. Two of Henry the Young King's brothers, Richard and Geoffrey, joined him in rebellion along with the barons of France and some in England. War followed, lasting until 1174, and Chinon and Loudun were key to Henry II's defence.

43. C. W. Previté-Orton. 1912. The Early History of the House of Savoy (1000–1233). Cambridge: Cambridge University Press. 355.
44. Bernard Demotz. 2000. *Le Comté de Savoie du XIe au XVe siècle. Genève: Editions Slatkine*. 26.
45. C. W. Previté-Orton. 1912. The Early History of the House of Savoy (1000–1233). Cambridge: Cambridge University Press.416. n2. Previté-Orton suggests that with this apocryphal story "we seem justified in accepting it" the Hautecombe Chronicle writes that the daughter of the Count de Genève is *"rapta fuit a dicto Thoma"* or "was seized / taken away / dragged away by Thomas".
46. Jean d'Orville dit Cabaret. 1995. *La Chronique de Savoie. Montmélian: La Fontaine de Siloé*. 83
47. Eugene L. Cox. 1974. The Eagles of Savoy: The House of Savoy in Thirteenth Century Europe. Princeton: Princeton University Press. 10–11.
48. The christian name of the wife of Count Thomas de Savoie has been the subject of some contention. As we can see the fifteenth century chronicler gives her the name Béatrice. That she is the daughter of the Count of Geneva is not contested. However, Cox and Previté-Orton before him preferred the – more contemporary chronicler Chronica Albrici Monachi Trium Fontium 1235, MGH SS XXIII, p. 938. *"Margareta filia domni de Fusceneis de matre Guilelmi, filii Humberti comitis Gebenensis"*. That both Marguerite and Béatrice appear in charters appears to support the view that she was known by both names. *"M. comitissa Sabaudie et marchisa in Ytalia et...Amedeus, Aymo, W. electus Valentinus, Thomas, Petrus, Bonifacius et Philippus filii Thome Comitis Sab. et marchionis in Ytalia"* confirmed donations to Hautecombe abbey by charter dated 26 February 1231. *"Beatrix uxor comitis Thomæ, Amadeus primogenitus et Aymo filii eius"* confirmed the purchase of Chambéry by "Thoma comite" by charter dated 1232, with the seal of *"Beatricis comitisse Sabaudie"*. Indeed both Béatrice and Marguerite are used to name her two daughters. For the sake of continuity, we will follow Cox and Previté-Orton in using Marguerite.
49. Despite his surname and his knowledge of French, Matthew Paris was evidently of English birth. He was a Benedictine monk, chronicler and artist based at St Albans Abbey in Hertfordshire. He may have studied in Paris after his early education at the St Albans Abbey school. Active from c.1240–c.1259, he produced the Chronica Majora, a history of the world from the creation of the world until 1259 and much cited herein; the Historia Anglorum, a history of England from the Norman Conquest to 1250; the Gesta abbatum, a history of the abbots of St Albans; two further revisions of the Historia, that is, the Abbreviatio chronicarum and the Flores historiarum; as well as Latin Vitae of the Anglo-Saxon kings Offa I and II, archbishops Edmund Rich, and Stephen Langton of Canterbury; and Anglo-Norman Vitae of Edward the Confessor, Saint Alban, Thomas Becket and Edmund of Canterbury again. Increasingly historians treat his work as

unreliable, as indeed we have, and it may be that Matthew Paris was aware that he'd been a little too purple in his prose, the word "offendiculum", or "cause of offence" appears next to many passages.
50. Chron. Majora Lat, vol 3. 335. "*miræ pulchritudinis mulierem, nomine Beatricis*" or "a woman of wonderful beauty, named Béatrice."
51. Claudius Blanchard. 1875. *Histoire de l'Abbaye d'Hautecombe en Savoie. Chambéry: Imprimerie Chatelain.* 153. n2. "*Courageuse comtesse de la plus haute lignée, nous te tenons pour la plus belle que nous ayons jamais vue au monde: pour la fontaine pure d'où jaillissent toutes les vertus.*"
52. Margaret Howell. 1998. Eleanor of Provence. Oxford: Blackwell Publishers Ltd. 5.
53. Bernard Demotz. 2000. *Le Comté de Savoie du XIe au XVe siècle*. Genève: Editions Slatkine. 30. Saint Anthelme of Belley almost played a key role in English history: Pope Alexander III asked Anthelme to intercede in the dispute between Henry II and Thomas Becket, but sadly Anthelme was too ill to travel.
54. C. W. Previté-Orton. 1912. The Early History of the House of Savoy (1000–1233). Cambridge: Cambridge University Press. 417. Also counts eight sons: Amédée, Humbert, Aymon, Thomas, Guillaume, Pierre, Boniface and Philippe.
55. Eugene L. Cox. 1974. The Eagles of Savoy: The House of Savoy in Thirteenth Century Europe. Princeton: Princeton University Press. 10–11. n1.
56. The dates of birth can only be best estimates. For eight sons and two daughters of Thomas I de Savoie J. Wurstemberger. Vol 1. 97. He cites the *Chronique de Hautecombe* and *Les grans Croniques des gestes... des... ducz et princes... de Savoye et Piemont* complied by Symphorien Champier in 1516 amongst others. Other children have been suggested, Wurstemberger suggested these had been omitted from the primary chronicles as they had been illegitimated. "*Um diese Frage so bestimmt und so kurz als möglich zu lösen, werde bemerkt, dass die, von den alten Chroniken aufgezählten acht Söhne und zwei Töchter, alle, entweder in gleichzeitigen Geschichtwerken, oder in zahlreichen Ur- kunden, als eheliche Kinder des Grafen Thomas von Savoyen.*" Or "In order to resolve this question as definitely and as briefly as possible, it may be observed that the eight sons and two daughters enumerated by the old chronicles, all, either in contemporary histories, or in numerous documents, are legitimate children of Count Thomas of Savoy." Of the potential others, Guichenon suggested two possible daughters: Alix, and Avoye without primary source confirmation, whom Wurstemberger took to be illegitimate. It has been suggested that Bishop Amédée of Maurienne was a further son of Thomas and Marguerite, but C. W. Previté-Orton refutes this citing Carutti. 417. Wurstemberger, vol 1. 98 also pointed to later estate arbitration of February 1255 which listed Amédée, Humbert, Aymon, Thomas, Guillaume, Pierre, Philippe, Boniface, Béatrice and Marguerite. Jean d'Orville dit Cabaret. 1995. *La Chronique de Savoie*. Montmelian: La Fontaine de Siloé. 89–94 also discusses only the following children: Amédée, Humbert, Thomas, Guillaume, Pierre, Boniface, Philippe, Béatrice and Marguerite. André Perret. 1983. *Le comte Pierre II de Savoie. L'expansion savoyarde et l'alliance anglaise au xiiie siècle. Revue Savoisienne* 96–7. "*Nous savons seulement que ses parents étaient déjà mariés en 1191, qu'ils eurent dix enfants, qui parvinrent à l'âge adulte, dont huit fils et deux filles, et que Pierre de Savoie fut l'un des fils. Nous nous bornerons à dire que le futur comte Pierre II est vraisemblablement né dans les toutes premières années du XIIIe siècle et que la date de 1203 ne peut être acceptée qu'en lui*

Notes

laissant un caractère ap proximatif. Il serait vain d'émettre des hypothèses sur le lieu de naissance de Pierre de Savoie." Or "We only know that his parents were already married in 1191, that they had ten children, who reached adulthood, including eight sons and two daughters, and that Pierre de Savoie was one of the sons. We will confine ourselves to saying that the future Count Peter II was probably born in the very first years of the 13th century and that the date of 1203 can only be accepted by leaving it approximate. It would be futile to speculate on the place of birth of Pierre de Savoie."

57. André Perret. 1983. *Le comte Pierre II de Savoie. L'expansion savoyarde et l'alliance anglaise au xiiie siècle. Revue Savoisienne* 97.
58. C. W. Previté-Orton. 1912. *The Early History of the House of Savoy (1000–1233)*. Cambridge: Cambridge University Press. 417.
59. Ibid. 417.
60. Eugene L. Cox. 1974. *The Eagles of Savoy: The House of Savoy in Thirteenth Century Europe*. Princeton: Princeton University Press. 9. Cox tended toward Pierre being the sixth son "as is affirmed by the chronicles of Oronville and Servion", who also assert that he was born in 1203 in the castle of Susa. Earlier Wurstemberger, vol .115. *"steller, die von seiner Geburt han deln, lassen ihn das Licht der Welt im Jahr 1203, auf dem Schlosse zu Susa erblicken."* Or "Authors who deal with his birth let him see the light of day in 1203 at the castle in Susa." and n1 119. Wurstemberger bemoaned the lack of primary sources concerning Pierre's birth. *"Guichenon, I. 281, beruft sich auf Pingons verschiedene Schriften, auch auf Büttet, Papyrius Masson, und auf eine Urk. in der Rechnungskammer, die sich aber nicht mehr finden will. Lavriano in seiner Geschichte des savoyschen Fürstenhauses, nennt das nämliche Jahr. Ritter Domenico Promis, in seiner Numismatik, nimmt, auf jene Schriftsteller hin, auch mit diesem Jahr vorlieb, sagte aber dem Verfasser, dass ihm durchaus kein diplomatischer Beweis für diese Angabe vor die Augen ge kommen sei,"* or 119 Guichenon, I. 281, refers to Pingon's various writings, also to Büttet, Papyrius Masson, and to a document in the Chamber of Accounts, which, however, can no longer be found. Lavriano, in his history of the Savoyard dynasty, mentions the same year. Ritter Domenico Promis, in his Numismatics, makes do with this year based on those writers, but told the author that "he had not seen any diplomatic proof of this statement".
61. Dominico Carutti. 1889. *Regesta comitum Sabaudiae, marchionum in Italia ab ultima stirpis origine ad an. MDCCLIII*. Rome: Fratres Bocca. 169.
62. Wurstemberger, vol 1. 80.
63. Eugene L. Cox. 1974. *The Eagles of Savoy: The House of Savoy in Thirteenth Century Europe*. Princeton: Princeton University Press. 19–20.
64. Wurstemberger, vol 1. 76.
65. C. W. Previté-Orton. 1912. *The Early History of the House of Savoy (1000–1233)*. Cambridge: Cambridge University Press. 373.
66. Ibid. 375.
67. Dominico Carutti. 1889. *Regesta comitum Sabaudiae, marchionum in Italia ab ultima stirpis origine ad an. MDCCLIII*. Rome: Fratres Bocca. 170. Monique Fontannaz & Brigitte Pradervand. 2015. *Les monuments d'art et d'histoire de la Suisse*. Bern: Societe d'histoire de l'art en Suisse SHAS. 21.
68. C. W. Previté-Orton. 1912. *The Early History of the House of Savoy (1000–1233)*. Cambridge: Cambridge University Press. 373.
69. Ibid. 375.

70. Wurstemberger, vol 1. 174. n46.
71. Florian Defferrard: "Romont(FR)", in: Historical Dictionary of Switzerland (DHS), version of 24.05.2012. Online: https://hls-dhs-dss.ch/en/articles/000876/2012-05-24/, consulted on 20.11.2022.
72. Eugene L. Cox. 1974. The Eagles of Savoy: The House of Savoy in Thirteenth Century Europe. Princeton: Princeton University Press. 7.
73. Dominico Carutti. 1889. *Regesta comitum Sabaudiae, marchionum in Italia ab ultima stirpis origine ad an. MDCCLIII.* Rome: Fratres Bocca. 182. An imperial vicar was a prince charged with administering a part of the Holy Roman Empire by the Emperor.
74. Thomas Kerrich. 1817. Observations upon some Sepulchral Monuments in Italy and France. Archaeologia 18: Plate IX.

Chapter Two

1. Gérard Sivèry. 1987. *Marguerite de Provence. Une reine au temps des Cathédrales.* Paris: Fayard. "At the court of Raimond Bérenger and Béatrice de Savoie, these troubadours of great or small birth perpetuate the beautiful tradition of courtly poetry: this sung poetry, accompanied by instruments, celebrates this subtle love which glorifies the woman for herself..".
2. Dominico Carutti. 1889. *Regesta comitum Sabaudiae, marchionum in Italia ab ultima stirpis origine ad an. MDCCLIII.* Rome: Fratres Bocca. 170.
3. The bishops of Die and Antibes.
4. Ramon Berenguer is variously numbered as the 4th or 5th Count of Provence. For consistency we have used the style Ramon Berenguer V Count of Provence as did Margaret Howell in the definitive biography of Alianor de Provence and Gérard Sivèry in his biography of Marguerite de Provence. I have also used the Castilian Ramon in preference to the Anglicised Raymond or Gallicised Raimond.
5. Indeed, Matthew Paris often confused Provence and Savoy.
6. Chron. Majora Eng, vol 1. 7.
7. The precise date of the marriage of Béatrice de Savoie to Ramon Berenguer V de Provence is lost to history. For a fuller commentary see Gérard Sivèry. 1987. *Marguerite de Provence. Une reine au temps des Cathédrales.* Paris: Fayard. 11. "On June 5, 1219, in fact, Thomas I, Count of Savoy, undertook to give a dowry of 2,000 marcs of silver, payable for the first half on February 2, 1220 and for the other at Christmas of the same year, to his eldest daughter Béatrice who married the Count of Provence. However, from September 2, 1220, the inhabitants of Brignoles ceded the consulate of their city to Raimond Bérenger and his wife whom the scribe nicknamed "Lombard lady". Their union had therefore been contracted before this date and, in all likelihood, rather in 1219 than in 1220, since, in a rather usual way, the engagement of the dowry shortly preceded the marriage."
8. C. W. Previté-Orton. 1912. The Early History of the House of Savoy (1000–1233). Cambridge: Cambridge University Press.392. n4. Previté-Orton dated the marriage to "shortly after 5th June 1219".
9. Giovanni Villani, Rose E. Selfe, ed. 1906. Villani's Chronicle, Being Selections from the First Nine Books of the Croniche Fiorentine of Giovanni Villani (London: Archibald Constable & Co.), 196.

Notes

10. Gérard Sivèry. 1987. *Marguerite de Provence. Une reine au temps des Cathédrales.* Paris: Fayard. 11. "[t]he two young spouses should have deplored the loss of two sons, twins no doubt."
11. Margaret Howell. 1998. Eleanor of Provence. Oxford: Blackwell Publishers Ltd. 2. Gérard Sivèry. 1987. Marguerite de Provence. Une reine au temps des Cathédrales. Paris: Fayard. 11–12.
12. Ibid. 1 & Ibid. At the beginning of the marriage, the count family lived in the old castle of the counts of Provence, opposite the church of Saint-Sauveur. Marguerite would therefore have been born in this castle. It was not until 1223 that a new construction, the "Palais deviant", the residence of the comital family when they stay in Brignoles.
13. Alison Weir. 2020. Queens of the Crusades: Eleanor of Aquitaine and her Successors. London: Penguin Random House UK. 453.
14. *La Divina Commedia, Paradiso, Canto* VI; Eugene L. Cox. 1974.
15. Eugene L. Cox. 1974. The Eagles of Savoy: The House of Savoy in Thirteenth Century Europe. Princeton: Princeton University Press. 22. Writes that "The 'Romeo' of whom Dante speaks was Romeo de Villeneuve, grand baile of Provence at the time the marriages were negotiated."
16. Nancy Goldstone. 2010. Four Queens: The Provençal Sisters Who Ruled Europe. London: The Orion Publishing Group. 24.
17. Wurstemberger, vol 1. 83. "*Durch seine ausge zeichnet schöne Beatrix erwarb sich Graf Thomas Stellen in den Stammbäumen der meisten, und zwar der erlauchtesten europäischen Herrschergeschlechter.*" Or "Because of his exceptionally beautiful Beatrix, Count Thomas earned places in the family trees of most, and indeed the most illustrious, European dynasties."
18. Chron. Majora Eng, vol 3. 105. Chron. Majora Lat, vol 5. 477. "*Fuerat autem mater ejus præsens, comitissa vero dicta Provinciae, nomine Beatrix, quæ pignora sua, quasi altera Niobe, glorianda poterat intueri. Nec erat in sexu muliebri mater in mundo, quæ de tali fructu ventris ac tanto, videlicet filiabus, poterat gloriando gratulari.*"
19. Chron. Majora Eng, vol 3. 250. Chron. Majora Lat, vol 5. 654. "*De mirabile fœcunditate ventris comitissa Provinciæ.*"
20. Chron. Majora Eng, vol 2. 113.
21. W. W. Shirley. Ed. Royal and Other Historical Letters. Vol 1. London. 1861. 77–8. No LXVII "*Cum nuncius comitis Sabaudiæ pro filii sui provisione hoc anno venerit ad dominum regem, et ad nos omnes pro eodem portaverit literas suas, et impliciti valde tunc fuerimus quid sibi condigne respondere possemus, communiter tandem sic providimus, ut primi redditus, qui de donatione domini regis occurrerent, assignarentur eidem.*" The 1220 letter is from Pandulf, Bishop of Norwich to Hubert de Burgh, Chief Justiciar of England. Translates as "When the messenger of the count of Savoy [Thomas I] came this year to the lord king for the provision of his son, and brought to us all his letters for the same, and we were then very much at a loss as to what we could answer him in a worthy manner, we finally provided in common in this way, that the first rents, which of the gift of the lord should they meet the king, they would be assigned to him."
22. A benefice was a reward received in exchange for services rendered and/or as a retainer for future services. The practice was prevalent throughout the Middle Ages within the European feudal system, especially within the church. The holder of more than one benefice, as in this case, later known as a pluralist, could keep the revenue to which he

was entitled and pay lesser sums to deputies to carry out the corresponding duties. The benefice system was open to considerable abuse in terms of personal aggrandisement.

23. LF Henry III vol 1, 367.
24. Ibid. 373.
25. Bruno Galland. 1988. *Un Savoyard sur le siège de Lyon au XIIIe siècle: Philippe de Savoie. Bibliothèque de l'école des chartes* 146: 34.
26. Eugene L. Cox. 1974. The Eagles of Savoy: The House of Savoy in Thirteenth Century Europe. Princeton: Princeton University Press. 15.
27. Dominico Carutti. 1889. *Regesta comitum Sabaudiae, marchionum in Italia ab ultima stirpis origine ad an. MDCCLIII.* Rome: Fratres Bocca. 183.
28. Eugene L. Cox. 1974. The Eagles of Savoy: The House of Savoy in Thirteenth Century Europe. Princeton: Princeton University Press. 15.
29. Ibid. 72–3.
30. Ibid. 121.
31. Cart. Lausanne. x. "*prévôt de la Collégiale de Ste - Ourse d'Aoste et de l'église de Genève.*"
32. Dominico Carutti. 1889. *Regesta comitum Sabaudiae, marchionum in Italia ab ultima stirpis origine ad an.* MDCCLIII. Rome: Fratres Bocca. 190. "*P. praepositus Gebennensis, filius comitis Sabaudiae.*"
33. Cart. Lausanne. x.
34. Cart. Lausanne. xi. "*Le prévôt Conon d'Estavayer, qui autrefois avait fait ses études à l'université de Paris, s'était de nouveau rendu dans cette capitale au mois d'octobre 1222 ... Le roi Philippe-Auguste mourut pendant son séjour dans cette capitale. Conon d'Estavayer assista aux funérailles du monarque dans la basilique de St.-Denis.*" Or "The provost Conon d'Estavayer, who formerly had studied at the University of Paris, had again visited this capital in the month of October 1222. . . King Philippe Auguste died during his stay in this capital. Conon d'Estavayer attended the funeral of the monarch in the basilica of St.-Denis."
35. Wurstemberger, vol. 1. 116 "*ipse Thomas comes, Amedeus primogenitus illius, Comitissa uxor Thomæ, eorum quatuor filii clerici...Willelmus, Thomas, Petrus et Bonifacius*" or "Thomas himself, Count Amedeus, his firstborn son, Countess, wife of Thomas, and their four clerical sons...William, Thomas, Peter and Bonifacius" and Dominico Carutti. 1889. *Regesta comitum Sabaudiae, marchionum in Italia ab ultima stirpis origine ad an. MDCCLIII.* Rome: Fratres Bocca. 177.
36. Dominico Carutti. 1889. *Regesta comitum Sabaudiae, marchionum in Italia ab ultima stirpis origine ad an. MDCCLIII.* Rome: Fratres Bocca. 183.
37. Wurstemberger, vol 1. 117.
38. Jean-Daniel Morerod. 2000. Pierre II, Sa mainmise sur l'église de Lausanne. In Pierre II de Savoie 'Le Petit Charlemagne' (+1268), Colloque international Lausanne, 30–31 Mai 1997, Cahiers Lausannois d'Histoire Médiévale. 173.
39. Dominico Carutti. 1889. *Regesta comitum Sabaudiae, marchionum in Italia ab ultima stirpis origine ad an. MDCCLIII.* Rome: Fratres Bocca. 196. "*1233, 1 Martii ... obit Tomas comes Sabaudiæ.*"
40. Eugene L. Cox. 1974. The Eagles of Savoy: The House of Savoy in Thirteenth Century Europe. Princeton: Princeton University Press. 31.
41. Wurstemberger, vol 1. 84.

Notes

42. Eugene L. Cox. 1974. *The Eagles of Savoy: The House of Savoy in Thirteenth Century Europe*. Princeton: Princeton University Press. 34.
43. Wurstemberger, vol 1. 123.
44. Ibid. vol 4. No 91. "*Msc. Febr. Ap. Castellionem. A. D. M. CC. XXXIII. Mense Februarii. Aymo, Dominus Fuciniaci declarat, se instituisse hæredem universalem suam Agnetem filiam suam, quam dederat Petro de Sabaudia, filio, condam Thome Comit. Sabaud. in vxorem, in casu, quo ipsi Aymoni decedere contingeret nullo ex corpore suo hærede masculo relinquente. Reservantur ea, quæ ipse constituerat in gratiam alterius filiarum suarum Beatricis. Si autem filium haberet Aymo ex uxore sua, ille hæres erit ejus, et constituetur Petro dos matrimonii sui, ad arbitrium Willelmi Electi Valentini, et Aymonis de Sabaudia, fratrum dicti Petri, Henrici de Chanvent, Willelmi de Greysi, et Jacobi de Albona. Act. ap.*"
45. Ibid. vol 1. 124. Ibid. "*Willelmi Electi Valentini, et Aymonis de Sabaudia, fratrum dicti Petri, Henrici de Chanvent, Willelmi de Greysi, et Jacobi de Albona.*"
46. Eugene L. Cox. 1974. *The Eagles of Savoy: The House of Savoy in Thirteenth Century Europe*. Princeton: Princeton University Press. 41.
47. Wurstemberger, vol 4. No 96. "1234. *Julii 23 ... Notum sit omnibus presentes ... quod cum inter illustrem uirum amedeum comitem Sabaudie ex vna parte et aymonem et petrum fratres ipsius ex altera super portione hereditatis paterne discordia mota esset tandem per manum venerabilis in Xpo wilielmi valentini electi ... Tota terra citra montem iouis usque ad aruam tam in feodis quam in dominicaturis aymoni remanet supradicto.*" "Or Let it be known to all present. . . that when the illustrious man Amédée, Count of Savoy, on the one hand, and his brothers Aymon and Pierre, on the other, discord having been been stirred is by the hand of the venerable Guillaume in Valence, elected settled amicably . . . All the land on this side of the mount of Jovis as far as Aosta remains in the aforesaid Aymon, both in fees and in dominaries."
48. Dominico Carutti. 1889. *Regesta comitum Sabaudiae, marchionum in Italia ab ultima stirpis origine ad an. MDCCLIII*. Rome: Fratres Bocca. 202. "*Amedeus comes dabit Petro castra de Lunnes et de S. Regneberto et centum marchas argenti.*" Or "Count Amédée will give Peter the castle of Lunnes [Lompnes] and S. Regnebert [Saint-Rambert] and one hundred marks of silver."
49. Bernard Demotz. 2000. *Le Comté de Savoie du XIe au XVe siècle*. Genève: Editions Slatkine. 31.
50. Eugene L. Cox. 1974. *The Eagles of Savoy: The House of Savoy in Thirteenth Century Europe*. Princeton: Princeton University Press. 83.
51. Jean d'Orville dit Cabaret. 1995. *La Chronique de Savoie*. Montmélian: La Fontaine de Siloé, 110.
52. Dominico Carutti. 1889. *Regesta comitum Sabaudiae, marchionum in Italia ab ultima stirpis origine ad an. MDCCLIII*. Rome: Fratres Bocca. 210.
53. Wurstemberger, vol 1. 145. "*Schlug, verwundete, und in einen Kerker warf*" or "Beaten, wounded, and thrown into a dungeon".
54. Jean-Daniel Morerod. 2000. *Pierre II, Sa Mainmise sur l'église de Lausanne*. in *Pierre II de Savoie 'Le Petit Charlemagne' (+1268), Colloque international Lausanne*, 30-1 Mai 1997, *Cahiers Lausannois d'Histoire Médiévale*. 174. "*Une embuscade ... fut tendue à Pierre, pendant une trêve, par Rodolphe de Rue, seigneur vassal des comtes de Genève, et par Rodolphe de Genève, fils du comte Guillaume. Pierre perd des hommes et est retenu prisonnier au Château de Rue. Une coalition – ses frères Amédée et Thomas,*

son beau-père Aymon, les seigneurs de Chalon et de Kibourg – se forma alors et assiège Rue deux fois. Les ravisseurs furent vaincus, le château détruit."

55. As with much of what we know of the conflict between Pierre de Savoie and Guillaume de Genève the truce of 1237 refers. Wurstemberger, vol. 1. 145.n8. Cites Emmanuel-Philibert de Pingon (1525–1582), *Chronique de Savoie* which gives us the truce with details of the kidnapping, which as they are *"Amedeus Comes attestatur, quod tempore induciarum cum comite habennensi quod (sic) petrus prepositus frater suus captus fuisset, verberatus, vulue ratus et in carcere mancipatus."* Or "Count Amedeus attests to the fact that at the time of the truce with the count possessing that (sic) Peter the Provost, his brother, had been arrested, beaten, whipped, and enslaved in prison."
56. Humbert had died in 1223.
57. Eugene L. Cox. 1974. The Eagles of Savoy: The House of Savoy in Thirteenth Century Europe. Princeton: Princeton University Press. 62. And André Perret. 1983. *Le comte Pierre II de Savoie. L'expansion savoyarde et l'alliance anglaise au XIIIe siècle. Revue Savoisienne.* 105. There are some sources that claim Aymon de Savoie died as late as 1242, however the last primary source for him is dated 1 July 1237 in Wurstemberger, vol 4. No 111 ""*1237. Julii 1. ap. Chillon. Aymo, filius quondam Thomæ Comitis Sab. assignat C. Solidos maurisienses, quas pater suus super molendina mauriciensia assignaverat. super redditus de Olone et de Nurie, ad opus unius candele, que debet ardere die ac nocte ante capsam S. Mauritii, in Monast Agaunensi. Hoc fecit de consensu matris suæ Comitissæ et Amedei fratris sui Comit. Sabaudiæ. Sigilla apposuerunt, ipse Aymo, et mater sua, et dil. frater suus Amedeus Com. Sab. Testes: Herluinus Archiepiscopus tharantasiensis. F. abbas de Altocristo. P. capellanus Comitisse Sabaudie. D. Humbertus de vileta. d. Guigo deOmasino. D. P. de Cletis. Act. apud Chillon, Kal. Julii, A. Inc. dom. MCCXXXVII."* Aymon is giving 100 *sol* for a single candle to burn by day and night by the tomb of Saint Maurice. On 30 August Amédée IV is assuming bequests on his behalf, suggestive of a death between 1 July and 30 August 1237. Therefore, I think the 1237 date ascribed by both Cox and Perret is sound.
58. André Perret. 1983. *Le comte Pierre II de Savoie. L'expansion savoyarde et l'alliance anglaise au XIIIe siècle. Revue Savoisienne.* 106.
59. Wurstemberger, vol 1. 171. n29. "Et projecerunt ex utraque parte cum manganellis et trabichetis projecerunt illi de burgo ad monasterium, etc." or "and cast them on both sides with mangonels and trebuchets and cast them from the borough to the monastery."
60. Cart. Lausanne. 66. *"Insustus. Incendia. Dampna. que facta fuerunt ex utra que parte vix possent enumerari. fuerunt ex utraque parte occisi fere."* Or "The Attacks. The Fire. The Damage. Which deeds were done from which side could scarcely be enumerated."
61. Saint Maire in French or Marius Aventicensis as he would have been known was a Gallo Roman of the sixth century. He was venerated in Lausanne as he moved the see of Roman Aventicum (today's Avenches) to Lausanne, becoming its first bishop. He is perhaps best known for his chronicle and being the first to give a name to smallpox.
62. Cart. Lausanne. 66. *"fuerunt ex utraque parte occisi fere .XXX. et vulnerati plus quam. CCC."*
63. Cart. Lausanne. 65–6. *"Fuccignie. Muniuit ciuitatem, et fecit dirui domos prope muros. Muniens ciuitatis. per quas timuit ne ciuitas conbureretur. Non multo post illi de burgo conbusserunt molendina ciuitatis. et eadem nocte appositus fuit ignis sub rupe et conbusta fuit tota villa extra ciuitatem et illis de ciui tate vix se defendentibus, dixerunt illi de Ciuitate quod illi de burgo ignem apposuerant. et illi de burgo dixerunt quod illi de ciuitate fecerant ignem apponi. Non multo post venerunt illi de berna et de VI M auxilium.*

Notes

et fere cum M. armatis et firmauerunt unum castellum prope portam sancti marii scilicet in chablo. et proiecerunt ex utraque parte cum | Manganellis et.... proiecerunt illi de burgo ad monasterium et specialiter ad portale beate marie. Non multo post intrauit. p. filius comitis sabaudie cum M armatorum ciuitatem. Insustus . Incendia . Dampna .que facta fuerunt ex utra que parte vix possent enumerari. fuerunt ex utraque parte occisi fere .XXX. et vulnerati plus quam .CCC. | Non multo post fuit facta pax inter ipsos. per dominum Amedeum de Montfaucon. et dominum Willermum de greisie. et iurata ex utraque parte a multis que vix fuit obseruata. firmauit autem dictus electus | infra dictam pacem castellum ad Sanctum Marium et bastiuit ... hec omnia facta fuerunt Anno ab incarnatione domini $M^o.CC. XL$". Or "[Aymon de] Faucigny, he fortified the city, and destroyed the houses near the walls. defending the city by which he feared lest the city should be burnt. Not long after, those of the *bourg* burned the mills of the *cité* and the same night a fire was set under the rock, and the whole *bourg* outside the *cité* was burnt; and they said of the *cité* that they of the *cité* had set fire to it. Not long after they came from Berne and from Morat for help, and almost with Morat, they armed and fortified one castle near the gate of St. Maire, that is called the Chable. And they threw from both sides with Mangonels and threw them from the city to the monastery and especially to the portal of the blessed Mary [Dominican Monastery of Mary Magdalene]. He entered into the city not long after, Pierre, the son of the count of Savoy with six thousand armed soldiers. The attacks, the fires, the damage, which deeds were done on either side could scarcely be enumerated. there were about 30 killed on both sides. and wounded more than 300. Not long after, peace was made between them. By Amédée de Montfaucon. and Guillaume de Greisie. And the oaths on both sides were sworn by many, which were hardly observed . . . All this was done in the year from the incarnation of the Lord 1240." Cox takes the "P Son of the Count of Savoy" to be Pierre and not Philippe, and given all that we know of the career of both this is convincing. Eugene L. Cox. 1974. The Eagles of Savoy: The House of Savoy in Thirteenth Century Europe. Princeton: Princeton University Press. 91. English readers of this account should not confuse mentions by the chronicler of Saint Maire or Marius, who was a bishop of Avenches (Aventicum) of the sixth century and the Blessed Mary after for which the cathedral of Lausanne was named.

64. Ibid. "*infra dictam pacem castellum ad Sanctum Marium et bastiuit.*"
65. Eugene L. Cox. 1974. The Eagles of Savoy: The House of Savoy in Thirteenth Century Europe. Princeton: Princeton University Press. 93.
66. Ibid.
67. C. W. Previté-Orton. 1912. The Early History of the House of Savoy (1000–1233). Cambridge: Cambridge University Press. 377.
68. Eugene L. Cox. 1974. The Eagles of Savoy: The House of Savoy in Thirteenth Century Europe. Princeton: Princeton University Press. 82.

Chapter Three

1. David Carpenter. 2020. Henry III: The Rise to Power and Personal Rule 1207–1258. New Haven: Yale University Press. 5. "There was also something else about Bishop Peter. He made no secret of his affection for his homeland in the Touraine. His loyalty was to the dynasty not to the land of England."

2. Henry II's son John was father to Henry III, and Henry II's daughter Eleanor was mother to Louis' mother Blanche.
3. Nancy Goldstone. 2010. Four Queens: The Provençal Sisters Who Ruled Europe. London: The Orion Publishing Group. 24.
4. Margaret Howell. 1998. Eleanor of Provence. Oxford: Blackwell Publishers Ltd. 9.
5. Eugene L. Cox. 1974. The Eagles of Savoy: The House of Savoy in Thirteenth Century Europe. Princeton: Princeton University Press. 56. And Alain Marchandisse. 2000. "La Maison de Savoie et les Principalités Belges." In Pierre II de Savoie "Le Petit Charlemagne" ed. Bernard Andenmatten, Agostino Paravicini Bagliani and Eva Pibiri. (Lausanne: Université de Lausanne). 234.
6. Charles Bémont. Simon de Montfort, Comte de Leicester, Sa Vie (120?–1265), Son Role Politique en France et en Angleterre. Paris: Alphonse Picard Libraire. 7.
7. Eugene L. Cox. 1974. The Eagles of Savoy: The House of Savoy in Thirteenth Century Europe. Princeton: Princeton University Press. 44.
8. Ibid. 46.
9. David Carpenter. 2020. Henry III: The Rise to Power and Personal Rule 1207–1258. New Haven: Yale University Press. 4.
10. Chron. Majora Eng i, 397. "When, therefore the king made known to them the irrevocable determination of his heart, namely to cross to the continent"
11. Lisa Hilton. 2008. Queens Consort: England's Medieval Queens. London: Weidenfeld & Nicolson. 218.
12. Björn Weiler. 2001. Henry III and the Sicilian Business: a reinterpretation*. Historical Research 74: 142.
13. Fœdera, vol 1. 217. "Littera Regis comiti Subaudiæ, de matrimonio cum Alianora filid Raymundi comitis Provincia, nepte ejus, contrahendo ... .Eodem modo scribitor W. Valens ecclesiae electo" Or "Letters of the King, to the Count of Savoy, Contracting of the marriage to Alianor, daughter of Count Ramon of Provence, his nièce ... Written in the same way to Guillaume, Bishop Elect of Valence."
14. Fœdera, vol 1. 217. "An. 19 Hen. ill. HENRICUS, DEI gratia, Rex Angliæ, &c. amico suo karissimo nobili viro, A. Subaudiæ, & marchioni Italiæ, salutem. Gratan nimis & acceptam habentes voluntatem, quæ nos inducit ad foedus amicitiæ inter nos & vos ineundum, sicut inter prædecessores nostros & vestros mutuus semper extitit dilectionis affectus, sinceritatem vestram inde co-piosâ prosequimur gratiarum actione; cupientes, quantum in nobis est, quòd contracta dudum inter progenitores nostros amicitia nostris non deficiat temporibus, set potius suscipiat incrementum." Or "in the 19th Year of our reign. Henry III. Henry, by the grace of God, King of England, &c. to his dear friend, a noble, A[médée]. of Savoy, and Marquess of Italy, greeting. Grateful, having an exceedingly and well-accepted will, which induces us to enter into a league of friendship between us and you, just as there has always been a mutual affection between our predecessors and yours, we will pursue your sincerity with pious thanksgiving; desiring, as much as is in us, that a friendship long ago contracted between our ancestors would not fail in our time, but would rather accept an increase." Henry is clearly referencing the contracted marriage between his father, John, and Alais of Savoy.
15. Ibid, 218.
16. Björn Weiler. 2006. Knighting, Homage, and the Meaning of Ritual: The Kings of England and their Neighbours in the Thirteenth Century. Viator 37: 280.

Notes

17. Alison Weir. 2020. Queens of the Crusades: Eleanor of Aquitaine and her Successors. London: Penguin Random House UK. 448.
18. Chron. Majora Lat, vol 3. 335.
19. Ibid. In Latin the feminine genitive / dative of *"venustissimus"'* in French today, *plein d'élégance, plein de charme, plein de grâce* – full of elegance, full of charm, full of grace.
20. Margaret Howell. 1998. Eleanor of Provence. Oxford: Blackwell Publishers Ltd. 5. "Graceful, charming and elegant."
21. Chron. Majora Lat, vol 3. 335. *"viri praclæri et elegantis."*
22. Chron. Majora Eng, vol 1. 7. Chron. Majora Lat, vol 3. 334–5. Of Ramon Berenguer *"Erat autem ille prædictus comes, vir illustris, et in armis strenuus"* Of Béatrice *"miræ pulchritudinis mulierem, nomine Beatricis"* Of Marguerite and Alianor *"decoris expectabilis filias"* Of Alianor *"speciei venustissimæ"*. Of Guillaume de Savoie *"viri præclari et elegantis"*.
23. Alison Weir. 2020. Queens of the Crusades: Eleanor of Aquitaine and her Succesors. London: Penguin Random House UK. 455.
24. Chron. Majora Eng, vol 1. 8.
25. Ann. Cestrienses, 60. *"Henricus Rex Anglie duxit in uxorem filiam comitis de Provincie nomine Alienoram."* Or "Henry III., king of England, took to wife the daughter of the count of Provence, Eleanor by name."
26. Stephen Church. 2017. Henry III: A Simple and God-Fearing King. London: Penguin Random House. 25.
27. Chron. Majora Eng, vol 1. 49.
28. David Carpenter. 2020. Henry III: The Rise to Power and Personal Rule 1207–1258. New Haven: Yale University Press. 187.
29. Nancy Goldstone. 2010. Four Queens: The Provençal Sisters Who Ruled Europe. London: The Orion Publishing Group. 85.
30. CCR Henry III vol 3 1234–7, 300, 325, 405, 409 and 495. David Carpenter wrote a useful explanation of English royal documents contained within the Calendars of Rolls, referred to in these endnotes as CCR, CChR and CPR (see abbreviations). David Carpenter. 2004. The Struggle for Mastery : Britain 1066 - 1284. London: Penguin Books Ltd. 199. "The Anglo-Saxon sealed writ having evolved certainly by 1199 into three distinct types of document, namely charters, writs patent and writs close. The last two in the thirteenth century were equally described as letters patent and letters close. Charters, since they usually conferred rights and properties in perpetuity, were the most solemn documents the chancery issued". They were addressed to all the king's subjects, usually recorded the names of many witnesses and had the seal appended by silken threads. The difference between writs patent and writs close was that the latter were closed, that is folded up, with the seal being broken on opening, while the former were patent or open, the seal being attached to a tongue cut from the bottom of the document. Writs close, usually addressed to a single individual or institution and with a single witness, were used for the mass of routine administrative orders on which government depended, as well as for the writs initiating the comon law legal procedures described later. Writs patent, with a general form of address like charters but usually with a single witness, were used to grant exemptions, make appointments and proclaim a range of government decisions."

31. Chron. Majora Eng, vol 1. 49 in the original Latin it is *"quia clitellis suis refertis et equis oneratis auro et argento et vasis regalibus, transfretavit."*
32. There is some ambiguity regarding whether Peter should be considered duke or count. The duchy was legally held by his wife. The King of France and the Pope (and their courts) always addressed him as count, but Peter in his own charters called himself duke – the English Calendar of Patent Rolls, our source calls him a Count.
33. CPR Henry III vol 3 1232–47, 156. "Aug 22, Nottingham … The King has committed, during pleasure, to W. Bishop elect of Valence, the lands late of the count of Brittany in England … with the crops and stock therein for his sustenance in the king's service."
34. Eugene L. Cox. 1974. The Eagles of Savoy: The House of Savoy in Thirteenth Century Europe. Princeton: Princeton University Press. 34.
35. Chron. Majora Eng, vol 1.49. "He [Henry] also allowed foreigners – Poitevins, Germans, Provençals and Romans – to fatten themselves on the good things of the country, to the injury of his kingdom."
36. H. W. Ridgeway. 1983. The politics of the English royal court, 1247–65, with special reference to the role of aliens. (University of Oxford: Oxford). 235.
37. Jean-Pierre Chapuisat. 1960. *A Propos des Relations entre la Savoie et l'Angleterre au XIII siècle. Bulletin Philolgique et Historique* 1: 430–1.
38. Lawrence, St Edmund, 276; trans. The Life of St Edmund, 160.
39. CCR Henry III vol 2 1231–1234, 135.
40. Darren Baker. 2017. Henry III: The Great King England Never Knew It Had. Stroud: The History Press. 255.
41. CChR Henry III vol 1 1226–57, 225.
42. H. W. Ridgeway, "Henry III (1207–1272), king of England and lord of Ireland, and duke of Aquitaine." Oxford Dictionary of National Biography. 23 Sep. 2004; Accessed 11 May. 2022. "By William of Savoy and Raleigh at a great council at Westminster in January 1237, a large assembly which may also have been attended by representatives of burgesses and knights: Magna Carta was reissued, and recent resumptions of royal demesne were abandoned; three magnate victims of resumptions were even co-opted on to the king's council. In return, Henry III was granted a thirtieth on movables; the last major parliamentary tax for over thirty years, it raised some £22,500." David Carpenter & David Prior. 2015. Magna Carta and Parliament. London: House of Lords. 16. "In England in the thirteenth century there were two great constitutional developments; the establishment of Magna Carta and the emergence of Parliament." Ibid. 17. "The first assembly to be called a parliament in an official document met in 1237, and thereafter the term quickly became established." Ibid. 22. "Henry III never tried to levy a tax without consent. Indeed, he went to parliament again and again asking for it. In 1225 he was successful in return for the issue of what became the definitive *Magna Carta*. In 1237 he was successful again, this time in return for his first confirmation of the Charter as a king of full age (as he had not been in 1225)."
43. The term *Magna Carta* was applied in hindsight to John's charter. The term originally applied to Henry's revised re-confirmation, mostly to differentiate it from Henry's lesser Charter of the Forest. But since the term is now commonly associated with John's charter, we have used it.
44. CPR Henry III vol 3 1232–47, 208–34. "Master Peter de Aqua Blanca, clerk of the [bishop] elect of Valence."

Notes

45. François Mugnier. 1890. *Les Savoyards en Angleterre au XIIIe siècle et Pierre d'Aigueblanche évêque d'Héreford. Chambéry: Imprimerie Ménard*. 21. Today the *Manoir d'Aigueblanche* remains a fortified house, onetime stronghold of the *Sires de Briançon* by the Isère in Aigueblanche.
46. Julia Barrow. 2011. Peter of Aigueblanche's Support Network in Thirteenth Century England XIII: Proceedings of the Paris Conference, 2009. Eds Janet Burton, Frédérique Lachaud & Phillipp Schofield. (Boydell and Brewer: Woodbridge). 30. "Peter had four brothers, Hugh, Aymo, Gonthier and Master Aimeric, and one sister, Agnès."
47. Ibid. 28 *"procurator expensarum"*.
48. Archdeacons: Shropshire', in Fasti Ecclesiae Anglicanae 1066–1300: Volume 8, Hereford, ed. J S Barrow (London, 2002), 26–9.
49. Chron. Majora Eng, vol 1. 290. Parks incorrectly described Aigueblanche as a "Provençal by birth", identification of the differences between Savoyards and Provençals not being his strong point,
50. E. B. Fryde, D. E. Greenway, S. Porter & I. Roy. 1986. Handbook of British Chronology. Third ed. London: Offices of the Royal Historical Society. 229. Chron. Majora Eng, vol 1. 311. CPR Henry III vol 3 1232–47, 238–41 "Dec 14 [1240] Windsor, Dec. 14. Windsor.Exemption of P. bishop elect of Hereford from any account from the time when he received the custody of the king's wardrobe until Easter." And Ibid. "Quit-claim to P bishop elect of Hereford from all account and reckoning which the king might require of him by reason of his custody of the wardrobe from the time when he had that custody." And Ibid. 247–61. "March 18 [1241], Windsor. Mandate to the free tenants of Hereford to make an aid to P. Bishop of Hereford … So that the bishop by their default may not again have recourse to the king."
51. Julia Barrow. 2011. Peter of Aigueblanche's Support Network in Thirteenth Century England XIII: Proceedings of the Paris Conference, 2009. Eds Janet Burton, Frédérique Lachaud & Phillipp Schofield. (Boydell and Brewer: Woodbridge). 28. "Peter made nine trips abroad, the longest lasting three years; the first eight of these largely consisted of diplomatic missions for Henry III."
52. Quoted in Vincent "Aigueblanche, Peter d'" Oxford Dictionary of National Biography.
53. W. N. Yates. 1971. Bishop Peter de Aquablanca (1240–1268): a reconsideration. Journal of Ecclesiastical History 22: 303.
54. Julia Barrow. 2000. Æthelstan to Aigueblanche in Hereford Cathedral. Ed. Gerald Alymer and John Tillier. The Hambledon Press: London. 46. Julia Barrow. 2011. Peter of Aigueblanche's Support Network in Thirteenth Century England XIII: Proceedings of the Paris Conference, 2009. Eds Janet Burton, Frédérique Lachaud & Phillipp Schofield. (Boydell and Brewer: Woodbridge). 31.
55. Ibid. 45–6. Pierre d'Aigueblanche would also be responsible, unsurprisingly as founder, for the Collegiate Church of Saint Catherine in Aiguebelle. Anthelme de Clermont, a member of the Chapter of Hereford Cathedral would also be responsible upon gaining the see of Maurienne for the statutes there in 1267.
56. Julia Barrow. 2011. Peter of Aigueblanche's Support Network in Thirteenth Century England XIII: Proceedings of the Paris Conference, 2009. Eds Janet Burton, Frédérique Lachaud & Phillipp Schofield. (Boydell and Brewer: Woodbridge). 32.
57. Jean-Pierre Chapuisat. 1964. *Le Chapitre Savoyard de Hereford au XIIIe siècle. In Actes du Congrès des Sociétés Savantes de la Province de Savoie. Nouvelle Série* 1. 49. n24.

58. TNA E326/409.
59. W. N. Yates. 1971. Bishop Peter de Aquablanca (1240–1268): a reconsideration. Journal of Ecclesiastical History 22: 311.
60. Jean-Pierre Chapuisat. 1964. *Le Chapitre Savoyard de Hereford au XIIIe siècle. In Actes du Congrès des Sociétés Savantes de la Province de Savoie. Nouvelle Série* 1. 45.
61. Ibid.
62. Margaret Howell. 1998. Eleanor of Provence. Oxford: Blackwell Publishers Ltd. 105. CPR Henry III vol 3 1232–1247 "Lady Gwillelma of the queen's chamber ... Isabel daughter of the said Gwillelma."
63. CPR Henry III vol 3 1232–1247, 290.
64. Lisa Hilton. 2008. Queens Consort: England's Medieval Queens. London: Weidenfeld & Nicolson. 219.
65. The Archbishop of Canterbury officiating the coronation was Edmund of Abingdon who had been appointed just recently in 1233 and would hold the post until his death in 1240; he was canonised in 1246. He rests to this day at the Abbey of Portigny in Burgundy, France.
66. The Bishop of London officiating the coronation was Roger Niger; following his death in 1241 he too was canonised.
67. Chron. Majora Eng, vol 1. 7.
68. David Carpenter. 2020. Henry III: The Rise to Power and Personal Rule 1207–1258. New Haven: Yale University Press. 179.
69. Chron. Majora Eng, vol 1. 10.
70. David Carpenter. 2020. Henry III: The Rise to Power and Personal Rule 1207–1258. New Haven: Yale University Press. 192.
71. Ibid. 328–31.
72. Ann. Dunstable, 145.
73. Chron. Majora Eng, vol 1. 29.
74. Margaret Howell. 1998. Eleanor of Provence. Oxford: Blackwell Publishers Ltd. 25.
75. Chron. Majora Eng, vol 1. 132.
76. Ibid. 133.
77. Ibid. 49.
78. Nancy Goldstone. 2010. Four Queens: The Provençal Sisters Who Ruled Europe. London: The Orion Publishing Group. 54.
79. Michael Prestwich. Medieval People. London: Thames and Hudson. 281.
80. François Mugnier. 1890. *Les Savoyards en Angleterre au XIIIe siècle et Pierre d'Aigueblanche évêque d'Héreford*. Chambéry: Imprimerie Ménard. 20. "*comme sa souer, Marguerite, une Blanche de Castille pour l'éloigner de son époux.*" Or "Unlike her sister, Marguerite, a Blanche de Castille to keep her away from her husband." The overbearing relationship betwixt Blanche and Louis comes from Joinville.
81. David Carpenter. 2023. Henry III : Reform, Rebellion, Civil War, Settlement 12591272. London: Yale Publishing Ltd. "Did he [Henry] also reflect on whether his own mother, had she been around, would have done something to hold Eleanor in check?"
82. Hence Joan or Jeanne being referred to as Joan of Constantinople.
83. Dominico Carutti. 1889. *Regesta comitum Sabaudiae, marchionum in Italia ab ultima stirpis origine ad an. MDCCLIII*. Rome: Fratres Bocca. 211. Guillaume de Savoie is the sixth witness. And E. L. G. Stones, ed. 1964. Anglo-Scottish Relations 1174–1328 London. 19–26.

Notes

84. CPR Henry III vol 3 1232–1247, 208–34. "March 19, Marlborough. Grant to W [bishop] elect of Valence, Henri de Balliol and Jean de Sancto Egidio, executors of the will of J. sometime queen of Scots."
85. Chron. Majora Eng, vol 1. 69–70.
86. CPR Henry III vol 3 1232–1247, 166–72. "16 Nov, Windsor ... it [negotiations with Countess of Flanders] shall be discussed and determined by the decision of W. Bishop elect of Valence." And the same for 3 December, at Woodstock.
87. Charles Bémont. *Simon de Montfort, Comte de Leicester, Sa Vie (120?–1265), Son Role Politique en France et en Angleterre*. Paris: Alphonse Picard Libraire. 1. The son of Simon de Montfort and Alix de Montmorenci.
88. Amice de Beaumont was the Countess de Rochefort and *suo jure* Countess of Leicester; she spent most of her life in France where she married Simon IV de Montfort, their son Simon V de Montfort was the leader of the Albigensian Crusades, in turn their son Simon VI de Montfort is the Simon de Montfort who plays such a role in English history. Once more we see the confusing habit of naming sons for fathers over successive generations.
89. Amauri de Montfort, the eldest of the sons of Simon V de Montfort and Alix de Montmorenci inherited the estate of Montfort-l'Amauri which was subsequently elevated to county status by Louis VIII. He succeeded his uncle Mathieu II de Montmorenci as Constable of France.
90. Charles Bémont. *Simon de Montfort, Comte de Leicester, Sa Vie (120?–1265), Son Role Politique en France et en Angleterre*. Paris: Alphonse Picard Libraire. 2. "*son père ... capitaine ambitieux et fanatique.*" Or "his father ... an ambitious and fanatical captain" and "*et il hérita de leurs rudes vertus.*" Or "and he inherited their harsh virtues." We don't have far to look to find the origins of Earl Simon's character.
91. Ibid. 4.
92. Henry had in 1227 granted Leicester for life to Ranulf of Chester, upon Montfort's claim he granted the lands to the Frenchman upon the death of Ranulf. That Ranulf was a witness to this indicates he immediately acquiesced. In August 1231 Montfort agreed an early transfer of lands and title from Ranulf.
93. Ibid. 333.
94. J. R. Maddicott. 1995. Simon de Montfort. Cambridge: Cambridge University Press. 5.
95. Ibid. "Henry's favours for foreigners were handed out less capriciously than has sometimes been thought, and it is likely that he saw in Montfort both a useful volunteer and a man whose family connections on the borders of Normandy might possibly be turned to advantage."
96. Chron. Majora Eng, vol 1. 117.
97. Ibid. 121. "He [Richard] was on the other hand provoked to anger, on hearing that this marriage was confirmed clandestinely, that is without his knowledge, or the consent of the nobles obtained, he was justly much outraged."
98. Ibid.
99. H. W. Ridgeway. 1983. The politics of the English royal court, 1247–65, with special reference to the role of aliens. University of Oxford. 58.
100. H. W. Ridgeway, "Henry III (1207–1272), king of England and lord of Ireland, and duke of Aquitaine." Oxford Dictionary of National Biography. 23 Sep. 2004; Accessed 11 May. 2022. "This was Henry's sharpest crisis until the 1260s. It was resolved by

William of Savoy." Eugene L. Cox. 1974. The Eagles of Savoy: The House of Savoy in Thirteenth Century Europe. Princeton: Princeton University Press. 61.
101. John Maddicott. 2016. Who was Simon de Montfort, Earl of Leicester. Transactions of the Royal Historical Society 26: 46.
102. Chron. Majora Lat, vol 3, 485. "*Eodem anno statim post Pascha, dominus rex Anglie misit in auxilium domini imperatoris contra rebelles suos in partibus Ytalie, duce Henrico de Trubleville, viro rei militari peritissimo. Cum quibus etiam misit Ioannem Mansel.*" Since Mansel was in Italy from 1238 until 1240 it is difficult to believe he did not meet Pierre de Savoie at this time.
103. John Julius Norwich. 2011. The Popes. London: Chatto & Windus. 363.
104. Chron. Majora Eng, vol 1. 241.
105. Nancy Goldstone. 2010. Four Queens: The Provençal Sisters Who Ruled Europe. London: The Orion Publishing Group. 92.
106. Chron. Majora Eng, vol 1. 241. "A spiritual monster, and a beast with many heads."
107. Jean d'Orville dit Cabaret. 1995. *La Chronique de Savoie*. Montmélian: La Fontaine de Siloé. 91. "*Il était si généreux et prodigue de ses biens que les barons, les chevaliers, les écuyers et les gens d'armes allaient volontiers à lui, de sorte que le pays, fermement tenu, n'avait jamais été mieux dirigé et que les ennemis de l'Eglise furent réduits à l'obéissance. Sa vaillance lui ayant permis de remporter plusieurs batailles, les gens des contrées environnantes le redoutaient et, pour sa largesse, l'appelèrent le petit Alexandre; mais il faisait trop confiance à tout un chacun et on dit que les ennemis de l'Eglise le firent empoisonner.*" Or "He was so generous and lavish with his wealth that barons, knights, squires and men-at-arms willingly went to him, so that the country, firmly held, had never been better run, and enemies of the Church were reduced to obedience. His bravery having enabled him to win several battles, the people of the surrounding countries feared him and, for his generosity, called him little Alexander; but he trusted everyone too much and it is said that the enemies of the Church had him poisoned."
108. Chron. Majora Eng, vol 1. 241.
109. Ibid.
110. Wurstemberger, vol 1. 226. "*Woher Wilhelms kriegerischer Ruf eigentlich rührte, weiss man nicht mehr: es müssen wichtige Thaten von ihm der Vergessenheit anheimgefallen sein. Matthäus von Paris, der alle in England erschienenen Nichtengländer, aber ganz besonders die Verwandten der Königin Alienore bitter hasst, benutzt den kriegerischen Charakter und Ruf Wilhelms, um ein äusserst gehässiges Bild von ihm aufzustellen: er schil dert ihn als blutgierig, und geneigt zu Mord und Brand: auch Todtschlag wirft er ihm vor. Belege hiezu liefert er keine. Dagegen gibt er deren mehrere zu seiner Gewandt heit und Geisteskraft. Matthäus spricht sich zu einseitig und zu leidenschaftlich aus, um als Gewährsmann gelten zu kön nen Wilhelms Geschichte mag sprechen, und in dieser ge reichen die wiederholten Aussöhnungen und Friedensstiftungen zu hoher Ehre für seinen menschlichen und klassenmäßigen Charakter;*" or "It is no longer known where Wilhelm's martial reputation actually came from: important deeds of his must have fallen into oblivion. Matthew of Paris, who bitterly hates all non-Englishmen who have appeared in England, but especially the relatives of Queen Alienore, uses William's warlike character and reputation to paint an extremely spiteful picture of him: he portrays him as bloodthirsty, and inclined to murder and Brand: he also accuses him of manslaughter. He provides no evidence for this. On the other

hand, he gives several of them for his dexterity and intellectual strength. Matthew speaks too one-sidedly and too passionately to be considered a source of authority. Wilhelm's story may speak, and in this the repeated reconciliations and peacemaking are sufficient to high honour for his humanity and class of character."

111. H. W. Ridgeway, "Henry III (1207–1272), king of England and lord of Ireland, and duke of Aquitaine." Oxford Dictionary of National Biography. 23 Sep. 2004; Accessed 11 May. 2022. https://www.oxforddnb.com/view/10.1093/ref:odnb/9780198614128.001.0001/odnb-9780198614128-e-12950
112. Jean d'Orville dit Cabaret. 1995. *La Chronique de Savoie*. Montmelian: La Fontaine de Siloé. 91 And The Chronicle of Hautecombe, Script I Col 673. *"Anno Domini M CCXXXIX delatus fuit de curia romana illustrissimus vir do minus Guillermus de Sabaudia electus Valencie, qui inde Guillermus per inclite ae pie recordationis, «dominus Petrus comes Sabaudie et venerabilis pater Dominus Burchardus abbas Altecumbe tertio nonas Maji fuit hic honorifice sepultus. Requiescat in pace Amen."* Or "In the year of our Lord 239 he was denounced at the Roman Curia, the most illustrious man, Guillaume de Savoie, elected of Valence, who was then of honour and godly memory, By Lord Pierre, comte de Savoie, and venerable father Lord Burchard, abbot of Hautecombe, on the third of May, he was honourably buried. Rest in peace Amen." Also Claudius Blanchard. 1875. Histoire de l'Abbaye d'Hautecombe en Savoie. Chambéry: Imprimerie Chatelain. 142.
113. Michael Prestwich. 1997. Edward I. Yale: Yale University Press. 4. writes "Edward was born at Westminster on the night of 17 June 1239 so it's possible Paris may be quoting an incorrect date."
114. Chron. Majora Eng, vol 1. 172.
115. Stephen Church. 2017. Henry III: A Simple and God-Fearing King. London: Penguin Random House. 3.
116. Chron. Majora Eng, vol 1. 236.
117. Ibid.
118. J. R. Maddicott. 1995. Simon de Montfort. Cambridge: Cambridge University Press. 24–5.
119. Given that a mark constituted approximately two thirds of a pound, we can estimate Simon's debt as £1,320 which adjusted for inflation could have amounted to as much as nearly £1 million.
120. J. R. Maddicott. 1995. Simon de Montfort. Cambridge: Cambridge University Press. 25.
121. Chron. Majora Eng, vol 1. 194.
122. Eugene L. Cox. 1974. The Eagles of Savoy: The House of Savoy in Thirteenth Century Europe. Princeton: Princeton University Press. 154.
123. Chron. Majora Eng, vol 2. 22.
124. Nancy Goldstone. 2010. Four Queens: The Provençal Sisters Who Ruled Europe. London: The Orion Publishing Group. 96.

Chapter Four

1. Wurstemberger, vol 1. 231.
2. Eugene L. Cox. 1974. The Eagles of Savoy: The House of Savoy in Thirteenth Century Europe. Princeton: Princeton University Press. 99. Chron. Majora Eng, vol 1. 268–9.

Paris doesn't date the visit, only saying: "in the course of this year" but Cox estimates the visit as having been "around Easter."
3. Ibid. 107.
4. CChR Henry III vol 1 1226–1257, 252.
5. David Carpenter. 2020. Henry III: The Rise to Power and Personal Rule 1207–1258. New Haven: Yale University Press. 213.
6. Chron. Majora Eng, vol 1. 320. Chron. Majora Lat, vol 4. "*Circa eosdem dies, Petrus de Sabaudia, avunculus reginæ, cui rex comitatum de Richemundia contulerat, venit in Angliam, quam sibi senserat fructuosam. Quem rex adventantem occurrens cum gaudio suscepit incomparabili, se suaque consiliis ejus exponendo, et ipsius terras cum donativis plurimis ampliando.*"
7. Ibid. 241.
8. Andrew M. Spencer. 2021. "'A Vineyard Without a Wall': The Savoyards, John de Warenne and the Failure of Henry III's Kingship." in Thirteenth Century England XVII: Proceedings of the Cambridge Conference, 2017. Eds. Andrew Spencer & Carl Watkins. (Boydell and Brewer: Woodbridge). 43. "As with the heads of the Hydra, the loss of one Savoyard uncle led only to the emergence of two more." Animal metaphors seem to surround the House of Savoy, from Eugene Cox's brood of eagles to Andrew Spencer's hydra. Eugene L. Cox. 1974. The Eagles of Savoy: The House of Savoy in Thirteenth Century Europe. Princeton: Princeton University Press.
9. Ibid. 55.
10. CLR Henry III vol 2 1240–1245, 11–12.
11. Chron. Majora Eng, vol 1. 320. 5 January was the original feast day of the Confessor, but was later overshadowed by his translation feast of 13 October which replaced it as the principal feast. It's likely that Paris may have been referring to the day of death of the Confessor in this case. The 1241 ceremony would have been in the old Confessor's church as Henry III did not start his re-building of the Abbey until 1245. We do not know exactly when the feast day officially changed but it may have been after the 1163 translation of Edward's body to the first shrine a few years after his canonisation. By the time Henry III moved the bones to the new shrine in 1269 he specifically chose 13 October as the feast was obviously normally on that date by then.
12. Chron. Majora Eng, vol 1. 320. Chron. Majora Lat, vol 4. 85–6. "*Idem rex prædicto Petrum de Sabaudia ... in ecclesia Sancti Petri Westmonasterii militari ciiigulo decoravit.*" Paris made clearer in his writing that the ensuing feasting was in honour of Pierre "*propter ipsum P*"
13. Thomas Kerrich. 1817. Observations upon some Sepulchral Monuments in Italy and France. Archaeologia 18: 186–96. Plate IX.
14. Eugene L. Cox. 1974. The Eagles of Savoy: The House of Savoy in Thirteenth Century Europe. Princeton: Princeton University Press. 7.
15. Arnold Taylor. 1985. Studies in Castles and Castle-Building. London: The Hambledon Press. 61. n26.
16. Michael Prestwich. 2010. Knight: The Medieval Warrior's (Unofficial) Guide. London: Thames & Hudson. 45–6.
17. Chron. Majora Eng, vol 1. 322–3.
18. Also inter alia Ibid. 283. CCR Henry III, vol 6: 1247–1251.13, CCR Henry III, vol 7: 1251–1253, 382.

Notes

19. The Honour of Richmond (or English feudal barony of Richmond) in north-west Yorkshire was granted to Count Alan Rufus by King William the Conqueror in 1071. The honour comprised 60 knights' fees and was one of the most important fiefdoms in Norman England.
20. John Goodall. 2016. Richmond Castle and Easby Abbey. London: English Heritage. 10. "Earl Alan of Brittany, struck well with his company. He struck like a baron. Right well the Bretons did. With the King he came to this land to help him in the war. He was the cousin of his lineage, a nobleman of high descent. Much he served and loved the King. And he right well rewarded him. Richmond, he gave him in the north, a good castle fair and strong." Geffrei Gaman, Anglo-Norman Poet, 1136–7.
21. The name Richmond comes from the Old French Riche "splendid" Mont "hill", literally splendid hill. The name would later be applied in imitation in Surrey and Virginia, North America.
22. K. S. B. Keats-Rohan. 1992. The Bretons and Normans of England 1066–1154. Nottingham Mediaeval Studies 36: 42–78. Alan was the grandson of Geoffroi I de Bretagne and Hadvise de Normandie. Hadvise was the daughter of Richard I de Normandie and so the sister of Richard II de Normandie, the grandfather of William the Conqueror. In turn Richard II de Normandie had married Geoffroi's sister, Judith de Bretagne. Their second son had been Robert de Normandie, whose illegitimate son would be Guillaume II de Normandie, known forever to the English as William the Conqueror. The ruling families of Normandy and Brittany were thus intimately linked.
23. John Goodall. 2016. Richmond Castle and Easby Abbey. London: English Heritage. 10.
24. Ibid. 19.
25. Hugh M. Thomas. 1994. Subinfeudation and Alienation of Land, Economic Development, and the Wealth of Nobles on the Honor of Richmond, 1066 to c. 1300. Albion: A Quarterly Journal Concerned with British Studies 26: 399.
26. Lawrence Butler, 2003. "The Origins of the honour of Richmond and its castles" in Anglo Norman Castles ed. Robert Liddiard. (Boydell and Brewer: Woodbridge). 91–5. The Gilling territory consisted mainly of land which lay between the river Tees and the river Swale, with the Tees forming the northern border which separated the land from that granted to the Bishop of Durham. The western border was the watershed of the Pennine hills and the southern border was the watershed between the river Ure and the Swale. The river Wiske formed the eastern border. The manor of Gilling, close to the boundary, was the caput of the barony until Count Alan moved it to Richmond Castle. The division of Hang, or Hangshire, had the river Swale as its northern boundary; its western boundary was the Pennine watershed, and its southern boundary was the watershed with the river Wharfe and the river Nidd. The eastern border followed small streams and minor landmarks from the previous watershed to the Swale. The wapentake meeting place was situated on the Hang Beck in Finghall parish. The third part of the territory, Hallikeld, consisted of the parishes lying between the river Ure and the river Swale until their confluence at Ellenthorpe.
27. According to the 1086 Domesday Book, there had been nine wapentakes making up the North Riding of Yorkshire – three of them belonged to the Honour of Richmond.
28. Malcolm Hislop. 2019. Barnard Castle, Bowes Castle and Egglestone Abbey. London: English Heritage. 37–41.

29. Huw Ridgeway. 2023. *An English Cartulary Roll of Peter of Savoy, Lord of Richmond (1240-1268): Archives, Interests and Servants of an Alien Favourite of Henry III* in forthcoming volume to be edited by Professors Nigel Saul & Nicholas Vincent for the Pipe Roll Society, London. Ridgeway has now "come to the conclusion" that Pierre's income was closer to the £3,000 quoted recently rather than the £2,000 quoted earlier in 1983. *The politics of the English royal court, 1247–65, with special reference to the role of aliens.* (University of Oxford: Oxford). 235.
30. Hugh M. Thomas. 1994. Subinfeudation and Alienation of Land, Economic Development, and the Wealth of Nobles on the Honor of Richmond, 1066 to c. 1300. Albion: A Quarterly Journal Concerned with British Studies 26: 401, Table 1 gives a 1280 summary of income for the Honour of Richmond by county, twenty-first-century equivalents in brackets: Yorkshire £701 (£486,542), Nottinghamshire £1 (£694), Lincolnshire £693 (£480,990), Hertfordshire £81 (£56,219), Cambridgeshire £85 (£58,995), Norfolk £189 (£131,179), Sussex £61 (£42,338) for a total of £1,811 (£1,256,959).
31. Modern equivalent derived from TNA Currency converter 1270 to 2017 values. £1,811 equates to £1,321,715.61.
32. Hugh M. Thomas. 1994. Subinfeudation and Alienation of Land, Economic Development, and the Wealth of Nobles on the Honor of Richmond, 1066 to c. 1300. Albion: A Quarterly Journal Concerned with British Studies 26. 401. In English law, subinfeudation is the practice by which tenants, holding land under the king or other superior lord, carved out new and distinct tenures in their turn by sub-letting or alienating a part of their lands.
33. CPR Henry III vol 3 1232–1247. 268–91. "Feb 16 [1242], Reading. Mandate to the knights and freemen, tenants of the honor of Richmond, when requested by the bailiff of Peter de Sabaudia, the king's uncle, the bearer of these presents, to make oath for an inquisition to be made of the rights belonging to the said Peter by reason of the said honor being in his hands."
34. Catterick, now known mostly for its British Army garrison, lies just over eight miles (12.8 kilometres) from Northallerton in North Yorkshire. The manor of Catterick, with its berewicks of Killerby, Ainderby and Tunstall, was held by Earl Edwin before the Conquest and was valued at £8. It was granted to Count Alan Le Roux, whose successors, lords of Richmond, held it in demesne.
35. The small village of Moulton lies eight miles (12.8 kilometres) east of Richmond, Yorkshire and to the south of Darlington close by the famous Scotch Corner interchange of the A1. Moulton is mentioned in the Domesday Book as the residence of a Saxon named Ulph. After the Norman Conquest the manor was transferred to the Earls of Richmond. Moulton changed hands many times, belonging to the Marshall, Wright, Smithson and Shuttleworth families.
36. Gilling West, not to be confused with Gilling East and Gilling Castle both in Rydale, lies just three and a half miles (5.6 kilometres) north of Richmond. In the Domesday Book, at the time of the acquisition by Alan Le Roux, it was a tiny village with "16 villagers. 3 freemen. 6 smallholders". Gilling was the chief seat of Edwin Earl of Mercia, and indeed in the 1970s a Viking sword was discovered in the beck, the Gilling Sword. Gilling appears to have been the political centre of what would become the Honour of Richmond pre-conquest, Alan Le Roux preferring to move to the more easily defended Richmond.

Notes

37. The hamlet of Forcett lies just eight miles (12.8 kilometres) north of Richmond, Yorkshire. The imposing Forcett Hall would later be built there.
38. The small village of Frampton is three miles (5 kilometres) south of the important medieval port of Boston. The village lies on the edge of one of the great marine creek levees formed during the Bronze Age
39. The manor of Wykes lies on the edge of the village of Donington, itself eight miles (13 kilometres) north of Spalding. The village was the eighteenth-century birthplace of the explorer of Australia, Matthew Flinders.
40. The small village of Washingborough is three miles (5 kilometres) east of Lincoln. Probably the first real account of Washingborough comes from *REGISTRUM HONORIS de RICHMOND* in 1280 AD. The village had 385 acres of arable land with 40 acres of meadow, all rented at a shilling an acre. Through the Middle Ages and up to 1800 village life changed very little. Farming was the main occupation, and this is reflected in entries in White's Directory of Lincolnshire (1826) listing: 6 farmers, 2 wheelwrights, 2 blacksmiths, 1 miller, 2 butchers, 2 publicans (of The Hunters Leap and the Ferry Boat Inn)
41. The important market town of Swaffham is one that was to grow rich on the wool trade. It is situated twelve miles (19 kilometres) east of Kings Lynn on the road to the centre of Norfolk, Norwich. The name is an Old Saxon one, meaning "homestead of the Swabians". It's unlikely that Pierre de Savoie would have made the connection between the distant origins of Swaffham and the Swabian dynasties of the Zahringen and Kyburg, the latter into which his own sister Marguerite had married.
42. The small village of Costessey is four miles (6.4 kilometres) west of Norwich and would now be considered a suburb of Norwich. In Domesday records, the village of Costesela appears in the hundred of Forehoe, with mention of a mill, and of a manor estate across Norfolk, including the only listed hunting park in Norfolk. This formerly belonged to Earl Gyrth Godwinson but was awarded by William the Conqueror to his Breton relative, Count Alan Rufus, along with the rest of the Honour of Richmond. The Manor House of Costessey Hall is now ruined and sits within the Costessey Park Golf Club. The manor had passed to the Breton House of Rohan but had been returned to the demesne of the Honour of Richmond. After Peter's death, however, this manor passed to Queen Alianor rather than to John of Brittany.
43. The small village of Wisset lies two miles (3.2 kilometres) north-east of the East Suffolk town of Halesworth. Wisset Manor predated Richmond in belonging to a Breton family, being held by Ralph the Staller, Baron de Gael in Brittany. The manor soon passed post-conquest to Alan Le Roux and merged into the wider Honour of Richmond.
44. The small village of Kettleburgh in East Suffolk lies close to the towns of Wickham Market and Framingham.
45. The dispersed village of Nettleshead in Mid Suffolk was home to the Chace, Nettleshead Hall which originated in the Honour of Richmond manor.
46. What was the village of Cherry Hinton in Cambridgeshire is now a suburb of ever-expanding Cambridge, three miles (4.8 kilometres) southeast of the city centre. There is an entry relating to Cherry Hinton in the Domesday Book: "Hintone: Count Alan. 4 mills." (The Alan being Alan le Roux or Alan Rufus 'Alan the Red', one of the Counts of Brittany, confiscated Hinton Manor from Edith, the (so-called "common law") first wife of Harold II of England, Edith Swanneck.

47. The manor at Cheshunt in Hertfordshire, in the same way as the manor at Cherry Hinton in Cambridgeshire, originally belonged to Edith, the first wife of King Harold II of England, Edith Swanneck. Like Cherry Hinton it passed post-conquest to Alan Le Roux of Brittany. It was then assessed for 20 hides and had land for thirty-three ploughs. In 1244 Pierre de Savoie received a grant of a weekly market on Monday at his manor of Cheshunt and a yearly fair on the vigil, feast and Assumption of St. Mary (15 August), the days of the fair being changed in 1257 to the morrow of the Exaltation of the Cross (14 September) and the three days following. A mere was also purchased. Ridgeway TNA C/47/9/1 "52. [*undated*] deed: The prior and convent of the New Hospital outside Bishopsgate [St Mary without Bishopsgate] London give in exchange to Peter, for 3s. 4d. (which he has remitted them from 11s. 4d. which they owe him from the manor of Beumund [Beaumond Hall, Cheshunt, co. Herts.]) half the mere of 'Serichemore' to be held by Peter and heirs 'or to whomsoever he wishes to give or assign it'. Peter and heirs are perpetually liable for 12d. payable to Henry fitz Andrew and heirs."
48. CChR Henry III vol 1 (1226–1257), 259. "May 6. Westminster, Gift to the king's uncle, Peter de Sabaudia, for his homage and service, of the towns of Richemund and Bouis, with the castles and wapentakes, and the manors of Cheteriz, Moleton, Gillinges, and Forset, co. Yorks; in co. Lincoln, the soke of Geitun, Boston, with its soke and markets, the manors of Frampton, Wikes, and Walsingburg; and in co. Norfolk, the manor of Swafham, and the manor and soke of Costessey; and in co. Suffolk, the manor and soke of Wischet, the manor and soke of Ketelberge, and the manors of Nettlested and Wikes under Gippeswic; in co. Cambridge, the manors of Bassingburn and Hynton; in co. Hertford, the manor of Cestrehunt; to be held by the said Peter and his heirs or by any of his brothers or kinsmen, to whom he may assign the same, with the forests, woods, knights' fees, wards, reliefs, escheats, marriages, and advow sons and all liberties and free customs belonging to the said manors, castles, sokes, wapentakes, and honour of Richmund, by the service of the fees of five knights; nor shall the king disseise the said Peter, his heirs or assigns, of the foregoing, until he have made a reasonable exchange for the same.Mandate to the barons of the Exchequer to cause this charter to be enrolled."
49. Hugh M. Thomas. 1994. Subinfeudation and Alienation of Land, Economic Development, and the Wealth of Nobles on the Honor of Richmond, 1066 to c. 1300. Albion: A Quarterly Journal Concerned with British Studies 26. 401.
50. John Goodall. 2016. Richmond Castle and Easby Abbey. London: English Heritage. 22–3.
51. Hugh M. Thomas. 1994. Subinfeudation and Alienation of Land, Economic Development, and the Wealth of Nobles on the Honor of Richmond, 1066 to c. 1300. Albion: A Quarterly Journal Concerned with British Studies 26: 405.
52. Ibid. 403.
53. CChR Henry III vol 1 (1226 – 1257), 327. "Nov. 12 [1247]. Windsor..Gift to Peter de Sabaudia of the manor of Aldeburg in Richemundesyr, which the king had of the gift of Roald son of Alan, the younger, saving to the said Roald, and his heirs, the knights' fees, of which Roald his grandfather was seised on the day of his death, to be held by the said Peter, his heirs, assigns or legatees being his brothers or kinsmen, by rendering yearly at the Exchequer of Michaelmas a barbed arrow; nor shall the king disseise the said Peter, his heirs, assigns or legatees, of the said manor, until he have made a reasonable

Notes

exchange therefor; grant also to the same of free warren in the demesne lands of the said manor." Also Ridgeway TNA C47/9/1. "10. Charter of Henry III, 12 November 1247, Windsor: granting Peter and heirs manor of Aldbrough in Richmondshire quitclaimed to the king by Roald fitzAlan junior (saving knights' fees held by his grandfather); also free warren of this manor, trespassers paying the king £10 fine. [MS Dorse note:] *On duplicated charter is added 'Peter of Savoy or any of his brothers or cousins, etc.'* [cf. C 53/40 m. schedule (dated 12 November): 'he may bequeath to *'any of his brothers or kinsmen to whom he may assign them, regardless of whether his own health permitted making this bequest'* (summarised: *CChR 1226-57*, p. 327)]. [There were three versions of this charter: *(a)* a more limited grant dated 10 November, cancelled (*CChR 1226-57*, p. 327); *(b)* this [no. 10] version of 12 November; *(c)* the final, wider grant (noted on the cartulary roll, dorse) also dated 12 November, actually enrolled: *CChR 1226-57,* p. 327, schedule.]"

54. Ridgeway TNA C47/9/1. "9. Charter of Henry III, 20 October 1248, Westminster: After demise of Clemencia countess of Chester [*d.* 1252] Peter and heirs can hold joint manors of Long Bennington and Foston (co. Lincs.) solely by service of a pair of falcons or rendering a penny at Easter, as part of the honor of Richmond conferred on him by the king. Notwithstanding that these manors could, or should, be the king's Norman escheats." And "22. Charter of Henry III, 6 July 1253, Portsmouth: granting Peter and heirs joint manor of Long Bennington and Foston [co. Lincs.], late of Clemencia countess of Chester. No disseisin without exchange; with complete freedom to Peter to bequeath to any of his brothers or cousins *'regardless of whether his own health permitted making this bequest'*. [Extant Charter Roll 37 Hen III actually ends on June 29, last membrane damaged.]" And "42. L.Pat. Henry III, 25 November 1248: to bailiffs of Peter at Richmond. Whereas we granted Peter 'our dear uncle' all Norman escheats holding from the honor of Richmond, you may immediately seize lands of Clemencia countess of Lincoln at Bennington and Foston once she dies."

55. Ridgeway, 13. "how well-placed were his new joint manors of Long Bennington and Foston, Lincs., straddling a road only a few miles off the Great North Road, or the joint manors of Leadenham and Fulbeck (Lincs.) straddling a crossroads near Ermine Street, both connecting to Grantham, Lincoln and Boston?" TNA C47/9/1. 3. L[etters] Pat[ent of] Henry III, 22 February 1247. "The king has sued for Leadenham and Fulbeck [co. Lincs.], with advowson of Fulbeck church, from Warner Engayne as escheats of the Bretons. Warner retains them for life but they revert thereafter to Peter and heirs as purtenant to the honor of Richmond. Peter and heirs immediately obtain advowson of Fulbeck. Similarly, Wensleydale Forest, recovered by the king from Rannulf fitzRobert and Henry fitzRannulf, is confirmed assigned to Peter and heirs." Ibid. 14. "Charter of Henry III, 22 February 1247, Windsor: granting Peter and heirs joint manors of Leadenham and Fulbeck [co. Lincs.], ½ knight's fee, and advowson of Fulbeck church (see no. 3 above), late of Warner Engayne, Breton Escheat, member of honor of Richmond. No disseisin without exchange. [*Not on Charter Roll*, although the roll is complete at that point. Notable declaration of the 'perpetual' grant of Richmond to Peter and its concession allowing him to bequeath Leadenham to 'any of his brothers or cousins at will', *'regardless of whether his own health permitted making this bequest'*.]"

56. Ridgeway TNA C47/9/1. 61. "Final Concord [1258] at king's court in Westminster: 15 days after St John Baptist, 42 Henry III [8 July, 1258] before Robert de Briwes and

Nicholas de Haudlo, Justices. Peter (demandant, via Walter of Bath, his attorney) v. Nicholas de Lenham (tenant) concerning 2 carucates and 1 messuage in Redenhall plus advowson of its church [Norfolk, nr. Diss]. Judgement given for Peter and heirs." Francis Blomefield, 'Hundred of Earsham: Redenhall', in *An Essay Towards A Topographical History of the County of Norfolk: Volume 5* (London, 1806), pp. 358-372. British History Online http://www.british-history.ac.uk/topographical-hist-norfolk/vol 5. 358-372 [accessed 27 February 2023].

57. CPR Henry III vol 3 1232-47, 497. Windsor. Whereas the king sued against Warner Engayne half a knight's fee in Ledenham and Fulebec and the advowson of the church of Fulebec as his escheat of the lands of Bretons, and the said Warner acknowledged these to be the king's right appurtenant to the honor of Richemund and forthwith resigned the said advowson; the king has granted to him that he shall hold the said fee for life, with reversion to Peter de Sabaudia and his heirs, to whom the king has granted the honor of Richemund, and he grants to the latter the said advowson as appurtenant to the honor. He has confirmed also the fine and concord of the plea which was before the king between the king and Randolf son of Robert of the forest of Wendesleydale and between the king and Henry son of Randolf, as enrolled in the rolls of the king's pleas, to the said Peter and his heirs, to whom he has granted the said honor. Also Ridgeway TNA C47/9/1. "3. L[etters] Pat[ent of] Henry III, 22 February 1247. The king has sued for Leadenham and Fulbeck [co. Lincs.], with advowson of Fulbeck church, from Warner Engayne as escheats of the Bretons. Warner retains them for life but they revert thereafter to Peter and heirs as purtenant to the honor of Richmond. Peter and heirs immediately obtain advowson of Fulbeck. Similarly, Wensleydale Forest, recovered by the king from Rannulf fitzRobert and Henry fitzRannulf, is confirmed assigned to Peter and heirs." Originally called *Virosidum*, it was an important centre during Roman times with roads branching off to the south and south-west. The one to the south can be traced for around eight miles, past the slopes of Stake Fell and to the ridges which separates Wharfedale and Wensleydale. The remains of a Roman Fort can be seen at Brough Hill, just across the river from the village. The foundations of the fort cover more than two acres, and while the stones that once stood on the site have long since been removed, the outline of the fort is very visible.

58. Hugh M. Thomas. 1994. Subinfeudation and Alienation of Land, Economic Development, and the Wealth of Nobles on the Honor of Richmond, 1066 to c. 1300. Albion: A Quarterly Journal Concerned with British Studies 26: 406. "A series of lawsuits in the thirteenth century recovered these lands into demesne and it is likely that Peter of Savoy carried out further development. These lands, developed in the period of high farming, were basically large ranches, and were extremely lucrative. The income of just over £214 produced by Bainbridge, like that of Boston, dwarfed the income of any of the traditional manors of the honor."

59. "*Historia Fundationis*" of Jervaulx, in *Monasticon Anglicanuin*, ed. William Dugdale (New ed.: London, 1825), vol 5: 572. The founding monks of Jervaulx talked of Wensleydale in these terms "*Et precipio quod habent pastores ad reprimendum lupos de pascuis suis.*" Or "And I command that the shepherds have to check the wolves from their pastures."

60. Eileen Power. 1941. The Wool Trade in English Medieval History Being The Ford Lectures. Hassell Street Press. 17–19.

Notes

61. Pishey Thompson. 1856. The History and Antiquities of Boston. London: Longman and Co. 37.
In the *quinzeme* or fifteenth tax of 1205 Boston contributed £780 to London's £836 and Lynn's £651 and Southampton's £712.
62. Ibid. 42.
63. Eileen Power. 1941. The Wool Trade in English Medieval History Being The Ford Lectures. Hassell Street Press.
64. Ibid.
65. Alain Marchandisse. 2000. "*La Maison de Savoie et les Principalités Belges.*" in *Pierre II de Savoie "Le Petit Charlemagne"* ed. Bernard Andenmatten, Agostino Paravicini Bagliani and Eva Pibiri. (Lausanne: Université de Lausanne). 238.
66. Hugh M. Thomas. 1994. Subinfeudation and Alienation of Land, Economic Development, and the Wealth of Nobles on the Honor of Richmond, 1066 to c. 1300. Albion: A Quarterly Journal Concerned with British Studies: 408. "£44 from the borough and £289 from the fair".
67. Ibid.
68. Ibid.
69. CPR Henry III vol 4 1247 – 1258, 542. "Feb 20 [1257], Windsor. Grant to Peter de Sabaudia that all merchants coming to Boston fair shall be quit of all prise of wines, cloths and other merchandise except the right and ancient prise of wines, for seven years from Easter so that nothing shall be taken from them for the king's use without his satisfying them for the same."
70. CPR Henry III vol 3 1232–1247, 241–61 "May 23, Westminster. Mandate to the abbot of Gervaus to answer for the fee farm of the manor of Estwyton to the king's uncle Peter de Sabaudia, to whom he has given the honor of Richemund, and not to Peter Boterel as the king remembers he commanded them to do; the latter being now a liege of the count of Brittany."
71. Chron. Majora Eng, vol 3. 8. "Also Peter of Savoy, whose great familiarity with the king supplied him with the horns of presumption ... to disturb ... the holy house of Jervaulx." And W. W. Shirley. 1862. Royal and other historical letters illustrative of the reign of Henry III. From the originals in the Public Record Office. London: Longmans, Green, Longman, and Roberts. 29. "*Possessiones ceteraque bona in comitatu Richemundiae, et præsertim in foresta de Wendeslaydale, a domino P[etro] de Sabaudia et suis minus juste detenta.*" Or "Possessions and other goods in the county of Richmond, and especially in the forest of Wendeslaydale, detained by the lord P[etro] of Savoy and his followers less rightfully."
72. Despite Henry's opposition and Savoyard Henri di Susa's interventions, William de Raley, Bishop of Norwich would eventually in 1244 be translated to Winchester.
73. E. B. Fryde, D. E. Greenway, S. Porter & I. Roy. 1986. Handbook of British Chronology. Third ed. London: Offices of the Royal Historical Society. 210.
74. Chron. Majora Eng, vol 1. 334–6. Despite being ignorant of his origins, Paris declared him to be "totally incompetent." Nonetheless, he describes the monks of Canterbury visit to Rome. Eugene L. Cox. 1974. The Eagles of Savoy: The House of Savoy in Thirteenth Century Europe. Princeton: Princeton University Press. 110. n50. CPR Henry III vol 3 1232–1247, 241–61 March 25 1241 relates to the proctors sent to Rome regarding papal confirmation "in their prosecution of the election of Boniface, proctor of the church of Belley."

75. Eugene L. Cox. 1974. The Eagles of Savoy: The House of Savoy in Thirteenth Century Europe. Princeton: Princeton University Press. 17–18.
76. Clive H. Knowles. "Savoy, Boniface of" Oxford Dictionary of National Biography. 23 Sep. 2004; Accessed 11 May. 2022. "Despite having promised to come as soon as he could, another seven months passed before Boniface travelled to England, probably because of a dispute with Étienne (II) de Thoire-Villars about jurisdiction over the priory of Nantua."
77. Huw Pryce. 2005. The Acts of Welsh Rulers: 1120 to 1283. Cardiff: University of Wales Press. No 294. 462–3.
78. David Carpenter. 2020. Henry III: The Rise to Power and Personal Rule 1207–1258. New Haven: Yale University Press. 215.
79. Ridgeway. 4. "Queen Eleanor and Peter defended Edward's claims against rivals conspiring for land grants from notoriously prodigal Henry III. Peter kept charters as a means of pressurising Henry to honour his promises to Edward until the prince received his estates in February 1254."
80. CChR Henry III vol 1 1226–1257, 252. "Gift to Peter of Sabaudia, and his heirs, the honour of Richemund, with its liberties and free customs, to hold by the service due therefrom."
81. CPR Henry III vol 3 1232–1247, 259-60. "Sept 25 [1241], Westminster. Grant, at leisure, to P. de Sabaudia of the lands of John de Warenna in Sussex and Surrey, and of the honor of Laigle." And "Appointment, during pleasure, of P. de Sabaudia to the custody of the castle of Lewes; and mandate to W. de Munceaus to deliver the castle to him."
82. CPR Henry III vol 3 1232–1247, 265–8. "Sept 28 [1241], Westminster. Appointment during pleasure of P. de Sabaudia to the custody of the castle at Lewes." And Ibid. "Nov 6 [1241], Westminster. Appointment, during pleasure, of Peter de Sabaudia, the king's uncle, to hold the custody of the Cinaque Port; and mandate to the barons thereof to be intendant to him." Ibid. "Sept 28, Westminster. Appointment during pleasure of P. de Sabaudia to the custody of the castle at Lewes."
83. CPR Henry III vol 3 1232–1247, 265–8. "Nov 4 [1241], Westminster. Mandate to John de Cobeham to deliver the castle of Rochester to Peter de Sabaudia, to whose custody the king has committed it, during pleasure; and acquittance to him and his heirs of the said custody." And Ibid. 268–91. "March 12 [1242], Waltham. Mandate to P. de Sabaudia to deliver the king's castles of Dover, Canterbury and Rochester to Bertram de Cryoyl, to keep during pleasure."
84. Nancy Goldstone. 2010. Four Queens: The Provençal Sisters Who Ruled Europe. London: The Orion Publishing Group. 98.
85. André Perret. 1983. *Le comte Pierre II de Savoie. L'expansion savoyarde et l'alliance anglaise au xiiie siècle. Revue Savoisienne.* 110.
86. H. W. Ridgeway. 1983. The politics of the English royal court, 1247–65, with special reference to the role of aliens. University of Oxford. 159.
87. Andrew M. Spencer. 2021. "'A Vineyard Without a Wall': The Savoyards, John de Warenne and the Failure of Henry III's Kingship." in Thirteenth Century England XVII. Proceedings of the Cambridge Conference, 2017. Eds. Andrew Spencer & Carl Watkins. (Boydell and Brewer: Woodbridge). 42.
88. Lisa Hilton. 2008. Queens Consort: England's Medieval Queens. London: Weidenfeld & Nicolson. 218–19.

Notes

89. Franco-Provençal is a separate Gallo-Romance language that transitions into the Oïl languages Morvandiau and Franc-Comtois to the northwest, into Romansh to the east, into the Gallo-Italic Piemontese to the southeast, and finally into the Vivaro-Alpine dialect of Occitan to the southwest. The designation Franco-Provençal (Franco-Provençal: francoprovençâl; French: francoprovençal; Italian: francoprovenzale) dates to the 19th century. In the late 20th century, it was proposed that the language be referred to under the neologism Arpitan (Franco-Provençal: arpetan; Italian: arpitano), and its area as Arpitania.
90. Julia Barrow. 2011. Peter of Aigueblanche's Support Network in Thirteenth Century England XIII: Proceedings of the Paris Conference, 2009. Eds Janet Burton, Frédérique Lachaud & Phillipp Schofield. (Boydell and Brewer: Woodbridge). 28. "Moreover, his [Pierre d'Aigueblanche] mother tongue would presumably have been Franco-Provençal, which would have enabled him to cope with southern forms of French, including the form of Occitanian spoken in Gascony, unlike French-speaking English people, who would be used to northern French in the form of Anglo-Norman. In addition, Franco-Provençal would have been closer than northern French to the Italian and Castilian he would have encountered on some of his embassies."
91. Andrew M. Spencer. 2021. "'A Vineyard Without a Wall': The Savoyards, John de Warenne and the Failure of Henry III's Kingship." in Thirteenth Century England XVII: Proceedings of the Cambridge Conference, 2017. Eds. Andrew Spencer & Carl Watkins. (Boydell and Brewer: Woodbridge). 49–51.
92. H. W. Ridgeway 1988. "King Henry III and the 'Aliens', 1236–1272." in Thirteenth Century England II: Proceedings of the Newcastle Upon Tyne Conference 1987 Ed. Peter R. Coss, P. R. Coss & Simon D. Lloyd. 1988. (Boydell and Brewer: Woodbridge). 82.
93. Ibid. 52–3. Although Spencer does remind us, as did Cox, that this support did not always extend to all of the comital family all of the time, citing Philippe and Boniface's connivance in the marriage of Béatrice de Provence to Charles d'Anjou that led to Provence falling into Capetian hands. This does not, however, discount the efforts on Henry's behalf of Pierre de Savoie, albeit in support primarily of Alianor and Edward. Nor does it discount, not mentioned by Spencer, the benefits of the alliance reaped by Henry's son, Edward, in the loyal service of Savoyards like Othon de Grandson and the castle-building talents of Maître Jacques de Saint-Georges.
94. Alain Marchandisse. 2000. "La Maison de Savoie et les Principalités Belges." in *Pierre II de Savoie "Le Petit Charlemagne"* ed. Bernard Andenmatten, Agostino Paravicini Bagliani and Eva Pibiri. (Lausanne: Université de Lausanne). 235. "*A dire vrai, on ne peut s'emplêcher de tenir les Savoie pour des pions disposés sur un vaste échiquier.*" Or "To tell the truth, one cannot help thinking of the Savoyards as pawns arranged on a vast chessboard."
95. CPR Henry III vol 3 1232–1247, 241–61. "June 23 [1241], Marlborough. Power to the king's uncle Peter de Sabaudia to draw into the king's service the noble men the count of Chabanais (*Cabinonensem*) [Gascony] and William de Vienna [Vienne], and others he may think necessary, and to offer them on the king's behalf a yearly fee for their homage and service."
96. *Fædera*, vol 1. 243. "*REX omnibus, &c. salutem. Sciatis nos concessisse Petro de Sabaudia terras Johannis de Warenna in Sussexia & Surria, REX honorem,de Aquila*

cum pertinentiis, quamdiu nobis placuerit, ad se sustentandum inde in servitio nostro. In cujus, &c. Teste Rege, apud Westm', xxv. die Septembris." Or "King to all, &c. greeting. You may know that we have granted to Peter of Savoy the lands of Jean de Warenne in Sussex and Surrey, the honour of the Eagle with the appurtenances, as long as it pleases us to sustain him in our service thence. In whose, &c. Witness the king at Westminster, 25th day of September."

97. CChR Henry III vol 1 (1226–1257), 296. July 20. Oxford. "Gift to Peter de Sabaudia, his heirs and assigns, of all the honour of Laigle [l'Aigle] in England, which fell to Gilbert de Aquila as his inheritance, with the advowsons of the churches, and the services of the knights and free men; and also of the castle of Peveneshel [Pevensey] with the wards thereof and the services of the knights and free men holding of that castlery; saving the lands, which Gilbert Marshal, late earl of Pembroke, gave from the said honour, which he had of the king's gift, that is the town of Greywell, which was given for 20l. of land to Gilbert Basset in marriage with Isabel, daughter of William de Ferrariis, niece of the said earl, and the town of Ryp, which was given for 15l. of land to Robert de Bruys in marriage with Isabel, daughter of the earl of Gloucester, another niece, and the manor of Westcote given to John de Gatesden for 10l. of land, with 10l. of land in la Dun in the marsh of Peveneshel given to Robert Waleran, and 100s. of land in Waudern given to Nicholas de Wauncy; all which towns and lands shall be held by the said tenants and their heirs of the said earl and his heirs, provided that in case of failure of issue from the aforesaid marriages the towns of Greywell and Ryp shall revert to the said Peter de Sabaudia and his heirs; who shall hold the said honour and castelry by the service of the fees of two knights; nor shall the king dis seise the said Peter, his heirs or assigns, until he have made them a reasonable exchange for the same." CPR Henry III vol 3 1232–1247, 241–61. "Sept 25, Westminster. Grand during pleasure to P. de Sabaudia of of the lands of John de Warenna in Sussex and Surrey and the Honour of L'Aigle." Ibid. "Sept 28, Westminster. Appointment during pleasure of P. de Sabaudia to the custody of the castle at Lewes."

98. *Société D'Histoire D'Archeologie de Genève*, Bulletin 1969. 254–5. "*Pierre est un familier de Pierre de Savoie. Il assiste à la donation faite à ce dernier de l'honneur d'Eagle.*" Or "Pierre is familiar with Pierre de Savoie. He attends the donation made to the latter of the Honour of the Eagle."

99. CCR Henry III vol 12 1261–1264, 19. "*De quercubus datis.- Mandatum est Alano la Zusche, justiciario foreste citra Trentam, quod Petrum de Sabaudia faciat habere in parco regis de Guldeford x. quercus idoneos ex dono regis. Teste rege apud Westmonasterium xiii. Kalendis Ianuariis*" or "Regarding the oaks given.- Alan la Zusche, justiciary of the forest on this side of Trent, was ordered to cause Peter de Savoy to have in the king's park de Guldeford x. suitable oaks from the gift of the king. Witness the king at Westminster xiii. The Kalends of January [1262]."

100. CCR Henry III vol 10 1256-1259, 344. "*Symone de Witeleye, clerico P. de Sabaudia*;"

101. CPR Henry III vol 3 1232–1247, 259–60. "Sept 25 [1241], Westminster. Grant, at leisure, to P. de Sabaudia of the lands of John de Warenna in Sussex and Surrey, and of the honor of Laigle." And "Appointment, during pleasure, of P. de Sabaudia to the custody of the castle of Lewes; and mandate to W. de Munceaus to deliver the castle to him."

102. Isabelle had left England to return to her native France upon the death of her husband, King John of England. There she had married Hugues de Lusignan in 1220.

Notes

103. Alison Weir. 2020. *Queens of the Crusades: Eleanor of Aquitaine and her Successors.* London: Penguin Random House UK. 497.
104. Chron. Majora Eng, vol 1. 404.
105. Darren Baker. 2017. *Henry III: The Great King England Never Knew It Had.* Stroud: The History Press. 349.
106. CPR Henry III vol 3 1232–1247, 274–6. David Carpenter. 2020. *Henry III: The Rise to Power and Personal Rule 1207–1258.* New Haven: Yale University Press. 251.
107. Dominico Carutti. 1889. *Regesta comitum Sabaudiae, marchionum in Italia ab ultima stirpis origine ad an. MDCCLIII.* Rome: Fratres Bocca. 237. *"1242, 19 d. Julii. Apud Tharascon. Petrus de Sabaudia, procurator constitutus a Richardo comite Cor nubino per litteras datas apud Ponz die xxv maii, denuntiat Sanciae, filiae Raimundi Berengarii comitis Provinciae, Richardum illi se tradere in virum; Sancia respondet hanc denuntiationem approbare, recipere et confirmare. Testes fuerunt Philippus Electus Valentinensis, P. Herfordensis epi scopus et alii. Raimundus notarius comitis Provinciae."*
108. Chron. Majora Eng, vol 1. 408.
109. Ibid. 419.
110. Ibid. 420.
111. Ibid. 419–23. David Carpenter. 2020. *Henry III: The Rise to Power and Personal Rule 1207–1258.* New Haven: Yale University Press. 260–2.
112. J. R. Maddicott. 1995. *Simon de Montfort.* Cambridge: Cambridge University Press. 32.
113. Jean de Joinville. 1995. *Vie de saint Louis.* Paris. Garnier. 206–7. *"Le roy d'Angleterre vint en Gascoigne pour guerroier le roy de France. Nostre saint roy a quanque il pot avoir de gent chevaucha pour combatre a li. La vint le roy d'Angleterre et le conte de la Marche pour combatre au roy devant un chastel que en appelle Taillebourc, qui siet sus une male riviere que l'en appelle Tarente, la ou en ne peut passer que a un pont de pierre moult estroit. Si tost comme le roy vint Taillebourc et les hoz virent l'un l'autre, nostre gent, qui avoient le chastel devers eulz, se esforcierent a grant meschief et passerent perilleusement par nez et par pons, et coururent sur les Anglois, et commenca le poingnayz fort et grant. Quant le roy vit ce il se mist ou peril avec les autres, car, pour un homme que le roy avoit quant il fu passe devers les Anglois, les Anglois en avoient mil Toutevoiz avint il, si comme Dieu voult, que quant les Anglois virent le roy passer, il se desconfirent et mistrent dedens la cite de Saintes; et pluseurs de nos gens entrerent en la cite mellez avecques eulz et furent pris."*
114. CPR Henry III vol 3 1232–1247. 399, "April 7th [1242], Bordeaux, Form of the truce between the king and the king of France. The king makes known that he has, for himself and earl Richard his brother, and his adherents and their lands and fees, made truce with Louis, king of France, and his adherents and their lands and fees, from the feast of St. Benedict the abbot in March until five years after next Michaelmas."
115. Dominico Carutti. 1889. *Regesta comitum Sabaudiae, marchionum in Italia ab ultima stirpis origine ad an. MDCCLIII.* Rome: Fratres Bocca. 237. *"1242, 19 d. Julii. Apud Tharascon. Petrus de Sabaudia, procurator constitutus a Richardo comite Cor nubino per litteras datas apud Ponz die xxv maii, denuntiat Sanciae, filiae Raimundi Berengarii comitis Provinciae, Richardum illi se tradere in virum; Sancia respondet hanc denuntiationem approbare, recipere et confirmare. Testes fuerunt Philippus Electus Valentinensis, P. Herfordensis epi scopus et alii. Raimundus notarius comitis Provinciae."*

116. CPR Henry III vol 3 1232–1247, 268–91. "Request to the free men and tenants in socage and burgage as well of the honor of Richmond as of the honor of Laigle and of the lands late of W. earl of Warenne, in the county of Sussex, to make Peter de Sabaudia, the king's uncle, a competent aid, as he is about to cross with the king, where he will have expenses of every kind."
117. H. W. Ridgeway. 1983. The politics of the English royal court, 1247–65, with special reference to the role of aliens. University of Oxford. 44.
118. Pierre de Mont or *Petrus di Montibus* is recorded in Berend Wesperley. Ed 2008. Biographical Index of the Middle Ages: Berlin. K.G. Saur. 877, having an origin as "Savoie" and an occupation as "physician". Certainly, this is the Peter de Montibus referenced in the Calendar of Patent Rolls. His Savoyard origin is also confirmed j. Eugène Olivier. 1962. *Médecine et santé dans le pays de Vaud: ptie. Au XVIIIe siècle*, 1675–1798. 747. "De l'entourage des Princes de Savoie ... vers 1230 ... Médecins appelés en consultation pour Aimon, Sire de Chablais ... Pierre de Montibus, physicien de Pierre de Savoie." Whether he is related to or a part of the *Famille de Mont* is not known. There is no mention of a Pierre in the known family tree, but the connection is likely given that we know Pierre de Savoie brought his namesake Ebal de Mont or Ebulo de Montibus to England. It seems unlikely that a physician from Savoy carrying the name de Montibus must be in some way connected to the *Famille de Mont*. Pierre de Mont had also been identified as Pierre's physician in a papal concession of benefices in England of 1249. Wurstemberger, vol 4. No 237. *"Licentia papalis collata physico Petri de Sabaudia. 1249. Augusti 30. Lugduni. Bulla Innocentii IV Papa, Petro Episcopo Herefordensi perscripta, qua ad intercessionem Philippi, Electi Lugdun. datur licentia, Petro, Physico Petri de Sabaudia comitis Richemundia, ut, præter Ecclesiam Richemundiæ, obtineat et aliud beneficium in provincia Cantuariensi, proviso, quod ecclesia et beneficium non fraudentur obsequiis debitis. Datum Lugduni, III Kalen. Septembris anno septimo pontificatus Innocentii IVI."*
119. Ibid. 377–98. "July 2nd [1243], Bordeaux, Mandate to the archbishop of York to confer the first ecclesiastical benefice of the value of 30 marks upon Master Peter de Montibus, physician of P. de Sabaudia; and at the instance of John Mansel, who is under the care of the said Master, he is to have preference over others who have a like provision." Hui Liu. 2007. "Matthew Paris and John Mansel" in Thirteenth Century XI: Proceedings of the Gregynog Conference, 2005. Eds. Janet Burton, Philipp Schofield & Björn Weiler (Boydell and Brewer: Woodbridge). 162.
120. Ibid. "Wicard de Sabaudia, steward of the Honour of Richmond."
121. John Hodgson. 1893. Vol 9. A History of Northumberland. Newcastle upon Tyne: A Reid and Sons Co. 251. Carries a full family tree for the Charrons in England. Citing Palgrave's Parliamentary Writs, vol i, 416. And Grimaldi's Roll *Collectanea Topograhica et Genealogica.* Vol ii, 327. And Jenyns Ordinary in Walfords Antiquarian vol x. 38.
122. A History of the County of Norfolk: Volume 2, ed. William Page (London, 1906), 364.
123. English Episcopal Acta 29: Durham 1241–1283. ed. Philippa Hoskin, David Michael Smith, British Academy, B. R. Kemp. (Oxford University Press, Oxford). 178.
124. John Hodgson. 1893. vol 9. A History of Northumberland. Newcastle upon Tyne: A Reid and Sons Co. 249–51.

Notes

125. Chron. Majora Eng, vol 2. 275.
126. Wurstemberger, vol 1. 232.
127. Dominico Carutti. 1889. *Regesta comitum Sabaudiae, marchionum in Italia ab ultima stirpis origine ad an. MDCCLIII. Rome: Fratres Bocca.* 236.
128. Wurstemberger, vol 1. 424.
129. Ansgar Wildermann. "d'Aubonne", in: *Historisches Lexikon der Schweiz* (HLS), Version vom 08.10.2009. Online: https://hls-dhs-dss.ch/de/articles/019555/2009-10-08/, Consulted 07.10.2020.
130. Dominico Carutti. 1889. *Regesta comitum Sabaudiae, marchionum in Italia ab ultima stirpis origine ad an. MDCCLIII. Rome: Fratres Bocca.* 238.
131. The Chateau d'Arlod is today a ruin submerged by the great works of the Genissiat Dam which began building just before the Second World War and was at the time of completion in 1949 Europe's largest in terms of capacity.
132. CPR Henry III vol 3 1232–1247, 268–91. "April 25th [1243], Bordeaux, Letters of credit for the *Abbé* [Bouchard] *d'Hautecombe* (*de Alta Cumba*), and Master Henry de Secusia, whom the king sends on his business to the court of Rome, for an amount of 1000 marks."
133. H. W. Ridgeway. 1983. The politics of the English royal court, 1247–65, with special reference to the role of aliens. University of Oxford. 44.
134. G. W. Watson. 1905. The Families of Lacy, Geneva, Joinville and La Marche. The Genealogist XXI: 6.
135. CPR Henry III vol 3 1232–1247, 377. "May 29th [1243]! Bordeaux, Grant to P. son of the count of Geneva of the marriage of Isabel, countess of Arundel, sometime wife of H.earl of Arundel, and grant that if she make fine to marry whom she will, he shall have that fine." Hugh d'Aubigny, 5th Earl of Arundel appears to have died on campaign in France, thus windowing Isabel de Warenne his eligible wife. However, Isabel never remarried, and the Arundel estate passed to John FitzAlan, the son of Hugh's sister Isabel d'Aubigny.
136. CPR Henry III vol 4 1247–1258, 166–7. "Nov 25 [1252], Clarendon. Appointment, during pleasure, of Peter de Sabaudia to the keeping of the castle and honor of Tikehille late of the countess of Eu, in the same manner as Peter de Genevre had the keeping thereof, the king having committed the said keeping to the said Peter de Sabaudia after the death of Peter de Genevre." And "Notification that on 26 October in the thirty-third year the king appointed during pleasure, Peter de Sabaudia to the keeping of the castle and honour of Tikehill late of the countess of Eu, answering at the Exchequer as much as Peter de Genevre used to answer." See also H. W. Ridgeway. 1983. The politics of the English royal court, 1247–65, with special reference to the role of aliens. University of Oxford. 22. Table 1. Also Ridgeway. 4. "Queen Eleanor and Peter defended Edward's claims against rivals conspiring for land grants from notoriously prodigal Henry III. Peter kept charters as a means of pressurising Henry to honour his promises to Edward until the prince received his estates in February 1254."
137. Chron. Majora Eng, vol 2. 322.
138. CChR Henry III vol 1 1227–1256.
139. H. W. Ridgeway. 1983. The politics of the English royal court, 1247–65, with special reference to the role of aliens. University of Oxford. 39–40.
140. CPR Henry III vol 4 1247–1258, 15.

141. H. W. Ridgeway. 1983. The politics of the English royal court, 1247–65, with special reference to the role of aliens. University of Oxford. 39.
142. G. W. Watson. 1905. The Families of Lacy, Geneva, Joinville and La Marche. The Genealogist XXI: 9.
143. Jean-Pierre Chapuisat. 1964. *Au service de deux rois d'Angleterre, au XIIIe siècle: Pierre de Champvent.* Revue historique vaudoise 72: 161.
144. Margaret Howell. 1998. Eleanor of Provence. Oxford: Blackwell Publishers Ltd. 51.
145. Wurstemberger, vol 1. 310.
146. *Regeste Genevois* REG. 0/0/1/1034. "*Testament d'Agnès de Faucigny, veuve du comte Pierre de Savoie. - Elle institue pour son héritière universelle sa fille Béatrix, comtesse de Viennois et d'Albon. Elle lègue à sa soeur Béatrix, dame de Thoire et de Villars, et aux fils de la dite dame, ses châteaux de Crédoz et de Cosimieu (Bresse), sous la condition de les tenir en fief de son héritière. Elle lègue à son frère (fratri meo) Simon de Joinville, seigneur de Gex, soit le château de Versoix, dont elle excepte la villa de Commugny, soit tout ce qu'elle possède dès le dit Commugny jusqu'à la Cluse, près de Collonges, entre le Rhône et le Jura, sous la condition que le tout demeurera du fief de Faucigny, et que le dit Simon de Joinville bâtira près de la Versoix et dotera une maison religieuse (domum Dei). Elle choisit pour lieu de sa sépulture l'église de Contamine en Faucigny, en lui donnant certaines vignes et terres pour qu'il y soit célébré une messe quotidienne. Parmi les legs pies de la testatrice se trouve celui de 30 livres genevoises au chapitre de Genève pour célébrer l'anniversaire de sa mort; elles sont assignées sur les dîmes de l'église de Mieussy, et destinées à distribuer 30 sous à chacun des chanoines qui interviendront à cette célébration.*"

Chapter Five

1. CPR Henry III vol 3 1232–1247, 394. "Aug 17 [1243], Bordeaux. Charter granting to Queen Alianor ... the whole county of Chester." RG ii, no.1143. "*Sciatis nos concessisse et hac carta nostra confirmasse, pro nobis et heredibus nostris, dilecte Regine nostre, Alienore, filie comitis Provincie . . . assignavimus ei totum comitatum Cestrie. . . Testibus: P. Herefordie episcopo, Philippo de Sabaudia, procuratore ecclesie Valentie, Johanne filio Galfridi, Ra- dulpho filio Nicholai, Philippo Basset, Johanne Maunsel, Paulino Peyvre, Roberto de Mucegros. Nicolao de Bolevilla, Waltero de Lutona, et aliis. Datum per manum nostram, apud Burdegalam. wij. die Augusti.*"
2. Chron. Majora. vol 1. 404.
3. David Carpenter. 2020. *Henry III: The Rise to Power and Personal Rule 1207–1258.* New Haven: Yale University Press. 271
4. CPR Henry III vol 3 1232–1247, 353–77. "May 27 [1243], Belin. Presentation to Philip de Sabaudia to the church of Racolvre ... The like to Guy de la Palude to the church of Saltwude." Guy de la Palude no doubt accompanying Philippe de Savoie was a canon and later archdeacon in the church at Lyon, Saltwude being Saltwood also in Kent. Guy was almost granted the pretend of the church of St. Paul in London, but that had already passed to Robert Passelewe, the later Bishop of Chichester. Before becoming an archdeacon at Lyon Palud would serve for a time with Alianor de Provence as guardian of her wardrobe. Ibid. "Sept 27 [1243], Portchester. Presentation of Philip de Sabauda to the church of Wingham."

Notes

5. On a personal note the author's paternal family would hail from the still tiny village of Feckenham.
6. Ibid, 437.
7. The English called Sanchia "Cynthia", Matthew Paris also referring to her as "Cincia".
8. Chron. Majora Eng, vol 1. 459–60.
9. CCR Henry III vol 5 1242–1247, 270, 272, 274. And CPR Henry III vol 3 1232–1247. "Jan 10th [1244]! Westminster. Notification that the king has lent to his father R. Beringer, count and marquess of Provence and count of Forcalquier (Fullk'), 4,000 marks, whereof he will let him have 2,000 at the quinzaine of Easter next and 2,000 at the quinzaine of Michaelmas following, for which loan he has bound in the name of a pledge five castles which the king's assigns shall select, according to the form made between the king and the count's proctor." *Fœdera*, vol 1. 254.
10. Eugene L. Cox. 1974. The Eagles of Savoy: The House of Savoy in Thirteenth Century Europe. Princeton: Princeton University Press. 120.
11. Nancy Goldstone. 2010. Four Queens: The Provençal Sisters Who Ruled Europe. London: The Orion Publishing Group. 132.
12. The castle at Forcalquier lay at the heart of the county of the same name to the north of Provence, of which Ramon Berenguer was also Count.
13. The castle at Volonne lay twenty miles (32 kilometres) north of Forcalquier on the road to Gap.
14. Wurstemberger, vol 2. 62. Guichenon listed the castle as Medes, Wurstemberger as Modes.
15. Ibid.
16. Chron. Majora Eng, vol 1. 7. "He [Ramon Berenguer V] had wasted almost all the money he possessed." Paris recognised the Count of Provence as poor but had his customary lack of sympathy for the causes.
17. J. R. Maddicott. 1995. Simon de Montfort. Cambridge: Cambridge University Press. 32–3.
18. Ibid. And CPR Henry III vol 3 1232–1247, 419.
19. Chron. Majora Eng, vol 1. 479.
20. CPR Henry III vol 3 1232–1247, 414–37. "Feb 4th [1244], Reading. To R. Beringer, count and marquis of Provence and count of Forcalquier. The king is sending to his presence Guy de Russilun, his kinsman, and Nicholas de Bolevill, knight, as his proctors to receive the five castles which he is to deliver to the king according to the covenant made between the king and the bishop of Rodez (Rethensem), the count's proctor."
21. Wurstemberger, vol 4. No 467a. And H. W. Ridgeway. 1983. The politics of the English royal court, 1247–65, with special reference to the role of aliens. University of Oxford. 43.
22. Bruno Galland. 1988. *Un Savoyard sur le siège de Lyon au XIIIe siècle: Philippe de Savoie. In: Bibliothèque de l'école des chartes, tome* 146, livraison 1. 31–67.
23. The Roman Catholic Archdiocese of Embrun was in the County of Forcalquier, a vassal of the County of Provence, in the mountains of the Maritime Alps, on a route that led from Gap by way of Briançon to Turin.
24. Henri di Susa was a canonist and later Archbishop of Embrun; he'd studied canon law in Paris before spending time in England and acting as an envoy for Henry with Pope Innocent IV.

25. Margaret Howell. 1998. *Eleanor of Provence*. Oxford: Blackwell Publishers Ltd. 37–8.
26. Emperor Frederick II was to be excommunicated no less than four times in his life.
27. Eugene L. Cox. 1974. *The Eagles of Savoy: The House of Savoy in Thirteenth Century Europe*. Princeton: Princeton University Press. 132–3.
28. John Julius Norwich. 2011. *The Popes*. London: Chatto & Windus. 365–6.
29. Bruno Galland. 1988. *Un Savoyard sur le siège de Lyon au XIIIe siècle: Philippe de Savoie*. Bibliothèque de L'Ecole des chartes 146.
30. Ibid. 38–9.
31. Ignoring for these purposes the ultra short reign of Celestine IV, who reigned for just sixteen days in 1241.
32. Chron. Majora Eng, vol 1. 458–9.
33. Ann. Waverley, 333. "*Qui sine aliqua mora adiit dominum regem, qui fuit tunc apud Westmonasterium, et ibidem fecit ei homagium suum*" or "He without any delay went to the lord the king, who was then at Westminster, and there paid him his homage."
34. Bruno Galland. 1988. *Un Savoyard sur le siège de Lyon au XIIIe siècle: Philippe de Savoie*. Bibliothèque de l'école des chartes 146: 43.
35. Dominico Carutti. 1889. *Regesta comitum Sabaudiae, marchionum in Italia ab ultima stirpis origine ad an. MDCCLIII*. Rome: Fratres Bocca. 250.
36. Pierre had acquired Moudon from his brother Aymon.
37. Daniel de Raemy. 2004. *Chateaux, donjons et grandes tours dans les Etats de Savoie (1230–1330)*. Lausanne: Cahiers d'archéologie romande 98 et 99. 98–9.
38. Wurstemberger, vol 4. No 178.
39. A charter dated 1244 confirmed the peace agreement reached between the bishop of Lausanne and "*Amadeus comes Sabaudie et in Italia marcho et ... Petrus de Sabaudia ... frater suus*" in Lausanne Bishopric XX, 42.
40. The rivers Glane referred to that which flows into the Sarine at Fribourg and the smaller Glane some fifteen miles to the west that flows northward to Lake Morat.
41. Eugene L. Cox. 1974. *The Eagles of Savoy: The House of Savoy in Thirteenth Century Europe*. Princeton: Princeton University Press. 165–6.
42. Ibid. 167.
43. H. W. Ridgeway. 1983. *The politics of the English royal court, 1247–65, with special reference to the role of aliens*. University of Oxford. 28.
44. CPR Henry III vol 3 1232–1247, 241–61. "June 2 [1241], Windsor. Appointment, during pleasure, of Bernard de Sabauda to the custody of the castle of Reygate, with mandate to William de Munceaus to deliver that castle to him with the two goshawks which are there for mewing."
45. CCR Henry III vol 5 1242–1247, 147. Describes "*Bernardo de Sabaudia*" as "*constabulario*" in 1243.
46. CPR Henry III vol 3 1232–1247. 268. "Dec. 16. Windsor.Appointment, during pleasure, of Bernard de Sabaudia to the custody of the castle and forest of Windlesor [sic]."
47. Ibid. 269 "Jan 2 [1242], Westminster. Appointment, during pleasure, of Bernard de Sabaudia to the custody of the castle of Windlesor[sic]; and grant to him for his custody of the service of the knights' fees which are held of the castellany, with the new purpresture brought into cultivation and 10l. a year, and one tun of wine a year of the king's gift, so long as he keep the said castle."

Notes

48. Michael Prestwich. 1997. Edward I. Yale: Yale University Press. 32.
49. CChR Henry III 1226–1257, 276.
50. CPR Henry III vol 3 1232–1247, 268–91. "April 12ᵗʰ [1242], Westminster. Writ of liberate to the treasurer and chamberlains for 20 marks a year to be paid to Bernard de Sabaudia for the maintenance of Ducelina his wife, who by the king›s special command has come to England, so long as she be in England by the king›s will." Jean-Pierre Chapuisat. 1960. "*A Propos des Relations entre la Savoie et l'Angleterre au XIII siècle. Bulletin Philolgique et Historique* 1: 433. Douceline "tres probablement la femme de Bernard." Or very probably the wife of Bernard [de Savoie]. And Ibid. n1. "*Douceline est un nom particulièrement en Provence*." Or "Douceline is a name particular to Provence."
51. CPR Henry III vol 3 1232–1247, 416. "March 6 [1244], Westminster, Appointment, during pleasure, of Bernard de Sabaudia to the custody of the castle and honor of Tykehull to the use of Edward the king's son, with mandate to the tenants of the honor to be intendant to him."
52. H. W. Ridgeway. 1983. The politics of the English royal court, 1247–65, with special reference to the role of aliens. University of Oxford. 38. n1.
53. CPR Henry III vol 4 1247–258, 166–7. "Nov 25 [1252], Clarendon. Appointment, during pleasure, of Peter de Sabaudia to the keeping of the castle and honor of Tikehille late of the countess of Eu, in the same manner as Peter de Genevre had the keeping thereof, the king having committed the said keeping to the said Peter de Sabaudia after the death of Peter de Genevre." And "Notification that on 26 October in the thirty-third year the king appointed during pleasure, Peter de Sabaudia to the keeping of the castle and honour of Tikehill late of the countess of Eu, answering at the Exchequer as much as Peter de Genevre used to answer." Ibid. 272. "Feb 14 [1254], Bazas. Mandate to Alan de la Zuche, justice of Chester, to give full seisin to Edward, the king's firstborn son and heir, or his attorney, bearer of these letters, of the county of Chester, with all the castles and towns thereof and the castles of Rothelan, Dissard and Gannoc, which the king, by charter, has granted to the said Edward to hold to him and his heirs for ever. The like to the following to give seisin of the following. . . Peter de Sabaudia, the lands late of the countess of Eu." Also Ridgeway. 4. "Queen Eleanor and Peter defended Edward's claims against rivals conspiring for land grants from notoriously prodigal Henry III. Peter kept charters as a means of pressurising Henry to honour his promises to Edward until the prince received his estates in February 1254."
54. Ibid. 44.
55. CPR Henry III vol 3 1232–1247, 238. Imbert Pugeys was in England from at least 28 October 1240 when he is referred to as "*Imbert Pugers*" in a grant of indemnity from Henry III.
56. E. B. Fryde, D. E. Greenway, S. Porter & I. Roy. 1986. Handbook of British Chronology. Third ed. London: Offices of the Royal Historical Society. 75.
57. David Carpenter. 2020. Henry III: The Rise to Power and Personal Rule 1207–1258. New Haven: Yale University Press. 217.
58. Margaret Howell. 1992. "The Children of King Henry III and Eleanor of Provence" in Thirteenth Century England IV: Proceedings of the Newcastle upon Tyne Conference 1991. Woodbridge: Boydell Press.
59. Stephen Church. 2017. Henry III: A Simple and God-Fearing King. London: Penguin Random House. 26.

60. CPR Henry III vol 3 1232–1247, 268–91. "Jan 8 [1242], Westminster. Protection without term for the brethren of the hospital of St. Bernard, Montjoux."
61. Nancy Goldstone. 2010. Four Queens: The Provençal Sisters Who Ruled Europe. eBook ed. London: The Orion Publishing Group. 189.
62. Jean-Pierre Chapuisat. 1960. *A Propos des Relations entre la Savoie et l'Angleterre au XIII siècle. Bulletin Philolgique et Historique* 1: 432.
63. Other estimates include the 170 of David Carpenter. 2020. Henry III: The Rise to Power and Personal Rule 1207–1258. New Haven: Yale University Press. 217.
64. H. W. Ridgeway. 1983. The politics of the English royal court, 1247–65, with special reference to the role of aliens. University of Oxford. 35.
65. Chron. Majora Eng, vol 1. 394.
66. CPR Henry III vol 3 1232–1247, 268–91. "April 8th [1242], Windsor. The like of Bertram de Cryoyl to the custody of the castle of Dover, in this form, that he shall surrender it to no one but the king, and in the case of the king's death, to no one but Eleanor, the queen, to the use of the king's heirs, and if the said Eleanor cannot come personally to receive it, then to no one but one of her uncles, not in the fealty of the king of France, to the use of the said heirs."
67. Eugene L. Cox. 1974. The Eagles of Savoy: The House of Savoy in Thirteenth Century Europe. Princeton: Princeton University Press. 166–7.
68. Bernard Andenmatten. 1989. *La noblesse vaudoise face à la Maison de Savoie au XIII siècle. La Maison de Savoie et le Pays de Vaud* 97: 35.
69. Eugene L. Cox. 1974. The Eagles of Savoy: The House of Savoy in Thirteenth Century Europe. Princeton: Princeton University Press. 166–7.
70. Ebal II de Mont was the son of Ebal I de Mont and Béatrice, their eldest son inheriting their lands in Vaud was Henri de Mont, the second son being Ebal II, their third son was Rudolphe de Mont who followed a career in the church as a Canon of Lausanne before becoming a Dean of Avenches, the youngest child was a daughter, Alice who married Raymond de Montricher.
71. Eugene L. Cox. 1974. The Eagles of Savoy: The House of Savoy in Thirteenth Century Europe. Princeton: Princeton University Press. 167.
72. Ibid. 194. Cox is certain of the vassal nature of the relationship between Grandson, Belmont and La Sarraz, however some have doubted whether Grandson was an ally or vassal. Certainly, Wurstemberger found that Belmont and La Sarraz were duly enfiefed in 1251. Wurstemberger, vol 1. 302–3 n16 and Wurstemberger, vol 4. No 285. Whether Grandson was in actuality a vassal or merely an ally, we can certainly say his actions were those of a vassal, and the vassal nature of the other branches of the *Famille de Grandson* is highly suggestive. Wurstemberger, vol 1. 135. "*Schade, dass die Urkunden nicht mehrere der jenigen Personen nennen, die seine Angelegenheiten so an hänglich und so erfolgreich besorgten: bekannt sind vor nehmlich Wilhelm von Chanvent, Peter von Granson, Wilhelm von Greisy, Humbert von Ferney.*" Or "It is a pity that the documents do not name several of the people who took care of his affairs so devotedly and so successfully: Guillaume de Chanvent, Pierre de Granson, Guillaume de Greisy, Humbert de Ferney are the most well-known." And 264. n22 "*Von Petern von Granson findet sich zwar keine Belehnungs urkunde aber er selbst kömmt so häufig im Gefolge Peters von Savoyen vor, dass sich an seinem Lehensverhältniss*" or "There is no enfeoffment document from Pierre de Grandson, but he appears so often in the entourage of Peter von Savoy that his feudal

Notes

relationship can be inferred." We should also note Bernard Demotz. 2000. *Le Comté de Savoie du XIe au XVe siècle*. Genève: Éditions Slatkine. 27. "*En revanche de nombreux vassaux ont sans doute prête hommage sans que l'on ait trace écrite.*" Or "On the other hand, many vassals have undoubtedly paid homage without a written record."

73. Girart Dorens. 1909. Sir Otho de Grandison 1238?–1328. Transactions of the Royal Historical Society 3: 127.n2.
74. The earliest documented reference we have is from 994 when Adalbert or Lambert II de Grandson had witnessed the election of Saint Odilo or Odilon as abbot of Cluny before King Rudolph III of the Second Kingdom of Burgundy or Arelat. A charter taken from the cartulary of the Romainmôtier and dated 1010 (17th year of reign of King Rudolf III of Burgundy) quotes "*Robertus notarius scripsit, videlicet his presentibus: Anselmo episcopo, Lamberto comite, Willingo, Rodulfo and Adalberto.*"
75. The fourth, Aymon became the Bishop of Geneva, the fifth, Hugues, a monk at Romainmôtier, the others likewise a church career.
76. Pierre I de Grandson himself had English links before Pierre de Savoie took his son there, having been in receipt of a pension from King Henry III. It's not thought, however, that he ever went to England. Maxime Reymond was of the impression he had, but there is no evidence either way. Maxime Reymond. 1920. *Le Chevalier Othon I de Grandson*. *Revue historique vaudoise* 28: 162.
77. Michael Prestwich. 2020. *Othon de Grandson et la Cour d'Edouard I, Othon I de Grandson (vers 1240–1328)*. Lausanne: Cahiers Lausannois d'Histoire Médiévale. Published in French "*C'était donc assurément par le frère de Béatrice [de Savoie] Pierre, qui vint Angleterre en 1240, que les contacts d'Othon de Grandson avec l'Angleterre furent establis.*" Or "It was therefore assuredly through Béatrice [of Savoy] Pierre's brother, who came to England in 1240, that Otho de Grandson's contacts with England were established."
78. Maxime Reymond. 1920. Le Chevalier Othon I de Grandson. Revue historique vaudoise 28: 162. "*Est l'ami de Pierre de Savoie, le chargé d'affaires.*"
79. Aug. Burnand. 1911. *La date de la naissance d'Othon 1er, Sire de Grandson*. *Revue historique vaudoise* 19: 130. Writes: "*Il faut fixer 1238 comme la date de la naissance d'Othon*" Or "we must fix 1238 as the date of the birth of Othon." Later Maxime Reymond. 1920. *Le Chevalier Othon I de Grandson. Revue historique vaudoise* 28: 163. Suggested "*date de naissance d'Othon vers 1240.*"
80. More recently Swiss historiography has cautiously settled on "*vers 1240*" or "around 1240". See Bernard Andenmatten. 2020. *Othon I de Grandson (vers 1240–1328)*. *Lausanne: Cahiers Lausannois d'Histoire Médiévale*. v–vi.
81. Bernard Demotz. 2000. *Le Comté de Savoie du XIe au XVe siècle*. Genève: Editions Slatkine. 41. "*Le revenu de tant de possessions va séduire de très nombreux seigneurs, surtout dans les pays romands, et ceux-ci, moyen-nant finances, vont reprendre de Pierre de Savoie leurs terres en fief.*" Or "The income from so many possessions will seduce many lords, especially in the Suisse Romande, and these, with money, will take back their lands in fief from Pierre de Savoie."
82. In the law of the Middle Ages, and especially within the Holy Roman Empire, an allod (Old Low Franconian allōd or fully owned estate, from all 'full, entire' and ōd 'estate', in Medieval Latin allodium), also allodial land or allodium, is an estate in land over which the allodial landowner (allodiary) had full ownership and right of alienation.

83. Wurstemberger, vol 1. 242. "*Sieht man mächtige Grafen, freie Barone, kleinen Adel, Städteburger, gleichsam um die Wette, ihm zueilen, um ihm ihre freien Herrschaften und Güter zu verkaufen, zu schenken, oder wie sich die Urkunden ausdrücken, zu Lehn aufzugeben, und sich, bisweilen sogar nur ihre Söhne, wieder damit belehnen zu lassen, und ihm dafür die Huldigung zu leisten.*" Or "one sees mighty counts, free barons, small nobility, citizens of towns, as it were in a race, to rush to him to sell or give him their free dominions and goods, or as the documents put it, to give up fiefdom and themselves, sometimes even only their sons to have it enfeoffed again and pay homage to him in return."
84. Bruno Galland. 1988. *Un Savoyard sur le siège de Lyon au XIIIe siècle: Philippe de Savoie. Bibliothèque de l'école des chartes.* 146: 48.
85. H. W. Ridgeway. 1983. The politics of the English royal court, 1247–65, with special reference to the role of aliens. University of Oxford. 42.
86. The compilation '*notitia dignitatum*' (Cnd).
87. CChR Henry III vol 1 1226–1257, 410. "Nov. 24. Clarendon. Pursuant to the finding of an inquisition that from the gate of the Castle of Pevenesh southward to the windmill of the abbot of Begeham on the west side of Westhamme and thence by the old road to la Ruding and thence across the demesne of Wodinton on the north of the court of Geoffrey Falconarius, and thence to the bridge of Chisilford by the old road and thence by the old boundary between Alciston and Sihalmeston and so to Croteberge by the highway and thence to the bridge at Glinde by the highway and thence by the middle of the water (*filum aque*) of Lewes on the South to the sea, and thence along the coast to the gate of Pevensey were the boundaries of the warren of William, count of Mortain, as appurtenant to the barony and honour of Pevenesham; grant to Peter de Sabaudia, and his heirs, of free warren by the afore said bounds, provided that the lands are not within the king's forest."
88. Ibid. 411. "Dec. 8. Gift to Peter de Sabaudia, of the manor of Burne by the castle of Clarendon, Pevenesey, co. Sussex, late of Peter de Croun, to be held by the said Peter and his heirs as freely as he holds the honour of Laigle, by the service due from the said manor." Ridgeway TNA C47/9/1. "4. Charter of Henry III, 2 December 1252: granting Peter and heirs manor and hundred of Eastbourne, co. Sussex, to be held in same way as he holds the barony of Pevensey. [As: C 53/45 m. 18, but this is cancelled (*CChR 1226-57*, p. 412).] [MS Note:] *Two other charters were found granting the manor without the hundred, and with these changes: 'manor of Burn' late of Peter de Croun etc.'* [i.e., as: C 53/45 m. 18, 2 December 1252 (*CChR 1226-57*, p. 411 incorrectly dated 8 December).]"
89. John Goodall. 1999. Pevensey Castle. London: English Heritage. 23.
90. "heckage" being a form of tax whereby a combination of knights' fees, doing suit of court at a castle and being obliged to contribute to specified repairs. L. F. Salzmann in Sussex Archaeological Society. 1906. Sussex Archaeological Collections Relating to the History and Antiquities of the County: Lewes, Farncombe and Co. Ltd. Printers. 3. "Pevensey Castle, besides the service of castle-ward due from a large number of Manors within the Rape, was also provided with certain services called " heckage." The present writer was the first to point out that this was connected with " haga," a hedge, hay or palisade, and implied the obligation of repairing and keeping up a certain portion of the palisade upon the ramparts of Pevensey. The tenure was thus analogous to those by which the tenants are required to keep up a length of the churchyard fence."

Notes

91. Roy Porter. 2020. Pevensey Castle. London: English Heritage. 30.
92. CChR Henry III vol 1 1226–1257, 436–7. "June 24.Siuthwick. Inspeximus and confirmation of a charter whereby Peter de Sabaudia Southwick. for himself, his heirs, and assigns quit-claimed to Ralph de Hays and all other tenants of the castle of Pevensey all the service of heckles (heccagii) due from their holdings and all service due from them for the same; and for this remission the said RalJune 24. Inspeximus and confirmation of a charter whereby Peter de Sabaudia Southwick. for himself, his heirs, and assigns quit-claimed to Ralph de Hays and all other tenants of the castle of Pevensey all the service of heckles (heccagii) due from their holdings and all service due from them for the same; and for this remission the said Ralph and others have paid 12 marksph and others have paid 12 marks for every heckle." L. F. Salzmann in Sussex Archaeological Society. 1906. Sussex Archaeological Collections Relating to the History and Antiquities of the County: Lewes, Farncombe and Co. Ltd. Printers. 3 "At last, in 1254, Peter of Savoy, as Lord of Pevensey, made an agreement with John de Gatesden, Simon de Echingham, William Bardolf, junr., William de Exete, Jordan Sackville, Ralph Harengaud, the Prior of Wilmington, William Maufe of Eckington, John la Ware of Folkington, Ralph de la Haye, Thomas de Audham and others by which they compounded for their heckages at the rate of 12 marcs for each heckage."
93. Ibid. 4.
94. TNA E101/308/1 mm.1,2. And Ridgeway. 11. "[A]nd somewhere 'in Sussex' in June 1252 and January 1253. At about that period that he [Pierre] began works at Hastings, and on a greater scale an inner ward and a new chapel at Pevensey."
95. John Goodall. 1999. Pevensey Castle. London: English Heritage. 6.
96. Ridgeway. TNA C47/9/1. 50. "[*undated*] deed: [March 1245 x April 1253], Aldington: Richard, bishop of Chichester grants Peter 'at his request' license to transfer a chapel at Pevensey within 'the ancient walls of' the vill, so that parishioners may have access 'both in peacetime and war'. Peter will construct the chapel 'at his own expense'."
97. Nicola Coldstream. 2016. *Architects, Advisors and Design at Edward I's Castles in Wales.* Late Medieval Castles. Woodbridge: The Boydell Press. 112.
98. Robert Bartlett. 1993. The Making of Europe: Conquest, Colonization and Cultural Change 950–1350. London: Penguin Books Ltd. 124.
99. Ibid. 164.
100. Huw Pryce. 2005. The Acts of Welsh Rulers: 1120 to 1283. Cardiff: University of Wales Press. n71. 10.
101. Ann. Camb. 1071. "*Franci vastaverunt Keredigiaun.*" Or "Franks ravaged Ceredigion". Cited in Edward Augustus Freeman, 1871. The History of the Norman Conquest of England: Its Causes and Its Results. Cambridge. Cambridge University Press. n4. 501.
102. The name derives from the latin adjective *palātīnus*, "relating to the palace", from the noun *palātium*, "palace".
103. R. R. Davies. 1979. Kings, Lords and Liberties in the March of Wales, 1066–1272. Transactions of the Royal Historical Society 29: 41–61.
104. David Carpenter. 2004. The Struggle for Mastery : Britain 1066 - 1284. London: Penguin Books Ltd. 106.
105. J. Beverley Smith. 2014. Llywellyn ap Gruffudd: Prince of Wales. Cardiff: The University of Wales Press. 51.
106. A. J. Roderick. 1952. The Feudal Relation Between the English Crown and the Welsh Princes. History 37: 202.

107. R.R. Davies. 1987. The Age of Conquest: Wales 1063–1415. Oxford: Oxford University Press. 290.
108. James Given. 1989. The Economic Consequences of the English Conquest of Gwynedd. Speculum 64: 13–14.
109. R. R. Davies. 1979. Kings, Lords and Liberties in the March of Wales, 1066–1272. Transactions of the Royal Historical Society 29: 45.
110. Ella S. Armitage. 1904. The Early Norman Castles of England (Continued). The English Historical Review 19: 420.
111. Ibid. 420. n16.
112. J. Beverley Smith. 2014. Llywellyn ap Gruffudd: Prince of Wales. Cardiff: The University of Wales Press. 468.
113. Ibid. 466.
114. Ibid. 40. Beverley Smith also confirms that Gruffydd was denied inheritance solely on the grounds of his illegitimacy.
115. Wurstemberger, vol 2. 36.
116. Ann. Cestrienses, 62. *"Item Rex Anglie Henricus ... Walliam intrans apud Rothelan per octo dies perhendinavit ubi venit ad eum David filius Lewelini dominus terre reddens ei terram et se ipsum ponens in misericordia sua reddidit et ei Griffinum fratrem suum ... Item Rex construxit castellum apud Disserth fecit et fundare montem altum."* Or "Also Henry [III.], king of England. . . and having entered Wales at Rhuddlan he remained for eight days. The lord of the land, David, son of Llewelin, came to him there, restoring the land to him, and placing himself at the king's mercy; and he gave up to him [Henry], Griffin, his brother [whom he had imprisoned]. . . Also the king built a castle at Disserth, and caused the foundations of Mold to be laid." Also Chron. Majora Eng, vol 1. 371–3.
117. *Fœdera* vol 1. 243. *"Hiis testibus venerabilibus patribus ... P. Herefordensi episcopo . . . Petrus Sabaudiae"*
118. Dyserth is first mentioned in Domesday Book in 1087, as *Dissard.*
119. Huw Pryce. 2005. The Acts of Welsh Rulers: 1120 to 1283. Cardiff: University of Wales Press. 477.
120. Ibid. 473.
121. John had imposed a similar escheat on Llywelyn Fawr in 1211.
122. J. Beverley Smith. 2014. Llywellyn ap Gruffudd: Prince of Wales. Cardiff: The University of Wales Press. 67.
123. Matthew Paris reporting the words of Pope Innocent IV and quoted in J. Beverley Smith. 2014. Llywellyn ap Gruffudd: Prince of Wales. Cardiff: The University of Wales Press. 101.
124. Chron. Majora Eng, vol 1. 487–8.
125. J. Beverley Smith. 2014. Llywellyn ap Gruffudd: Prince of Wales. Cardiff: The University of Wales Press. 94.
126. Huw Pryce. 2005. The Acts of Welsh Rulers: 1120 to 1283. Cardiff: University of Wales Press. 473.
127. Chron. Majora Eng, vol 2. 5.
128. David Carpenter. 2020. Henry III: The Rise to Power and Personal Rule 1207–1258. New Haven: Yale University Press. 233–5.
129. Ann. Cestrienses, 62. *"Obsessum est castrum de Moalt a david principe Wallie captum v kal. Aprilis."* Or "The castle of Mold was besieged and taken by David, prince of Wales, on March 28 [1245]."

Notes

130. Chron. Majora Eng, vol 2. 27.
131. John E. Morris. 1901. The Welsh Wars of Edward I. Oxford: Clarendon Press. 8–9.
132. Ann. Cestrienses, 64. "*Rex Anglic et regina simul venerunt Cestriam idus augusti dominica die et cum eis exercitus copiosus videlicet Ricardus comes cornubie frater Regis, Simon comes Leycestrie Roger comes Wynton W.... comes Habemar.... comes Oxoniae et omnes fere nobiles totius Anglie et ibi morati sunt usque in diem dominicam sequentem et in crastino Sancti Philiberti profectus est Rex cum exercitu suo in Walliam*" Or "The king and queen of England came together to Chester on Sunday, August 13, and with them an abundant army, That is to say, Richard, carl of Cornwall, brother of the king; Simon, earl of Leicester; Roger [de Quincy], earl of Winchester; William, carl of Albemarle; [Hugh], earl of Oxford, and almost all the nobles of the whole of England; and they stayed there until the Sunday following. And on the morrow of S. Philibert the king set out with his army for Wales."
133. Ibid. "*prima nocte apud Coleshul*" Or "the first night at Coleshill."
134. There would be no castle there in 1245; it was not begun until over a decade later in 1257.
135. Ann. Cestrienses, 64. "*secunda et tertia apud Withford*" Or "the second and third at Witford".
136. Ibid. "*iiij apud Rotelan, v apud Abergeleu*" Or "the fourth at Rhuddlan, the fifth at Abergele".
137. Ibid. "*vj apud Gannotum ubi tamdiu moratus est in castris donec construxisset castrum de Gannoc*" Or "the sixth at Gannoch, where he remained a long time encamped, until he had erected the fortifications of Gannoch".
138. R.R. Davies. 1987. The Age of Conquest: Wales 1063–1415. Oxford: Oxford University Press. 300.
139. Ridgeway. TNA C47/9/1. 19. Charter of Henry III, Chester, 20 August 1245: Grant of entire county of Chester to Prince Edmund and his heirs in perpetuity, to be held 'as freely and quit as by Earl Rannulf'. [*Not on Charter Roll*; Transcribed: Appendix no. 3. 'Edmund' is probably a scribal error for 'Edward'.] Ibid. Appendix. C 47/9/1 m. 3 [no. 19] Charter of Henry III granting the Earldom of Chester to his son Edmund (probably a later scribal error for Edward): Appendix 3. Chester. 20 August 1245. "*Henricus dei gratia etc. omnibus presens scriptum visuris vel audituris salutem. Noveritis nos dedisse concessisse et hac presenti carta nostra confirmasse Eadmundo filio nostro totum comitatum Cestr' sine ullo retenemento. Habendum et tenendum de nobis et heredibus nostris eidem Edmundo et heredibus suis adeo libere et quiete sicut nos vel comes Ranulph predictum comitatum unquam melius vel liberius aliquo tempore tenuimus vel haberemus,faciendo nobis et heredibus nostris ipse et heredes sui servicium quod dictus comes Ran' antecessoribus nostris et nobis de dicto comitatu facere consueverunt. Nos vero et heredes nostri eidem Eadmundo et heredibus suis predictum comitatum sicut predictum est contra omnes gentes warrantizabimus. Quare volumus etc. quod idem Ead' et heredes sui habeant et teneant predictum comitatum sicut predictum inperpetuum. Et ut presens scriptum etc. Hiis testibus etc. Datum apud Cestr per manum nostram vicesimo die Augusti anno regni nostri vicesimo nono.*" Also Ridgeway. 4. "Queen Eleanor and Peter defended Edward's claims against rivals conspiring for land grants from notoriously prodigal Henry III. Peter kept charters as a means of pressurising Henry to honour his promises to Edward until the prince received his estates in February 1254."

140. Chron. Majora. vol 2. 109, 115.
141. David Carpenter. 2020. Henry III: The Rise to Power and Personal Rule 1207–1258. New Haven: Yale University Press. 430–1. & Chron. Majora Eng, vol 2. 109–11.
142. Chron. Majora Eng, vol 2. 140.
143. J. Beverley Smith. 2014. Llywellyn ap Gruffudd: Prince of Wales. Cardiff: The University of Wales Press. 103.
144. CCR Henry III vol 3 1242–1247, 347.
145. Sir James Frederick Rees, 1963. The Problem of Wales and Other Essays, Cardiff: University of Wales Press.
146. The Welsh Midlands, Rhos, Rhufoniog, Dyffryn Clwyd and Tegeingl.
147. Llywelyn ap Iorwerth had lately taken back the four cantrefi, for Gwynedd, having lost them to John by Treaty of 1211.
148. David Carpenter. 2020. Henry III: The Rise to Power and Personal Rule 1207–1258. New Haven: Yale University Press. 433.
149. R.R. Davies. 1987. The Age of Conquest: Wales 1063–1415. Oxford: Oxford University Press. 303.

Chapter Six

1. The name is first recorded in 1002 as "*strondway*", then in 1185 as "*Stronde*"and in 1220 as "*la Stranda*", coming from the Old English word "*strond*" meaning appropriately "the edge of a river".
2. CCR Henry III vol 7 1251–1252, 66 "*De quercubus datis.– Mandatum est Godefrido de Lyston', custodi foreste de Windes', quod in eadem foresta faciat habere Petro de Sabaud' xx. quercus cum escaetis ad operaciones domorum suarum Lond', de dono regis. Teste ut supra. Per regem.*" Or "Concerning the given oaks. Godfrey of Lyston, warden of the forest of Winds, was commanded that he should cause Peter of Savoy to have in the same forest 20 an oak with shavings for the operations of his house at London, by the gift of the king. Witness as above. By the king."
3. Ridgeway, TNA C47/9/1. "35. [*undated*] deed: Brothers and sisters of St James' Hospital, London quitclaim to Peter, *earl of Richmond* and heirs all rights in 16 pence revenue from land Peter holds on the south side opposite the Church of Holy Innocents." And "56. [*undated*] deed: Thomas son of Bartholemew 'de Venyc' quitclaims to Peter and heirs ground and garden in Dane Street [London] 'extending south to the Thames' adjacent to property late of Brian de Insula to the east [see: no. 2] and of the Bishop of Carlisle to the west and the 'great street to Westminster' in the north".
4. Eugene L. Cox. 1974. The Eagles of Savoy: The House of Savoy in Thirteenth Century Europe. Princeton: Princeton University Press. 168.
5. Leo T. Gourde, "An Annotated Translation of the Life of St. Thomas Becket by William Fitzstephen" (1943). Master's Theses. 622.
6. Ibid.
7. William John Loftie. 1878. Memorials of the Savoy; the palace: the hospital: the chapel. With an appendix of original documents contributed by Charles Trice Martin and a pref. by Henry White. London: MacMillan and Co. 1-17.

Notes

8. Alan Sutton. 1993. The Illustrated Chronicles of Matthew Paris: Observations of Thirteenth-Century Life. Stroud: Alan Sutton Publishing. 76–7.
9. Ann. Waverley, 335. "*Eodem anno, cum inter dominum Papam Innocentium quartum et dominum Fredericum imperatorem fuisset mota discordia, dictus Papa dicti imperatoris timens insidias, ejectis tamen gentibus dicti Papæ per imperatorem, ab urbe Roma fugit timore perterritus, venitque circa festum Omnium Sanctorum Lugdunum, ibique per multum tempus multa et varia mirabilia faciens perendinavit. Circa festum autem beati Andreæ Apostoli accesserunt ad ipsum ex Anglicanis partibus transfretantes dominus Bonefacius Cantuariæ, et domi- nus episcopus Herefordensis, et dominus Ricardus de Wicio electus Cicestriæ, qui, causa consecrationis dicti electi Cicestrie, ibidem accesserant.*" Or "In the same year, when a discord had arisen between the Lord Pope Innocent the Fourth and the Lord Frederick the Emperor, the said Pope, fearing the intrigues of the said Emperor, being expelled by the said Pope's nations by the emperor, fled from the city of Rome in terror, and came to Lyons about the festival of All Saints, and there by He spent a lot of time doing many and various wonders. And about the feast of the blessed Andrew the Apostles, Lord Boniface of Canterbury, and Lord Bishop of Hereford, and Lord Richard de Wych, Elect of Chichester, came to him crossing from English parts, who, on the occasion of the consecration of the said Elect of Chichester, had come there."
10. W. N. Yates. 1971. Bishop Peter de Aquablanca (1240–1268): a reconsideration. Journal of Ecclesiastical History 22: 307. Yates went on to give the names of some bishops of Hereford, native born, who were a good deal worse in terms of absenteeism than Aigueblanche. "Adam de Orleton (1317–27) and Thomas de Charlton (1327–44)." Orleton was a native of Herefordshire and Charlton of Shropshire.
11. Clive H. Knowles. "Savoy, Boniface of" Oxford Dictionary of National Biography. 23 Sep. 2004; Accessed 11 May. 2022.
12. Chron. Majora Eng, vol 2. 113.
13. C. W. Scott-Giles, O.B.E. Fitzalan Pursuivant Extraordinary. 1962. Coat of Arms nos 51–2, July–Oct. www.theheraldrysociety.com accessed 17 June 2022. "The sculptured and painted shields set up in the nave of Westminster Abbey during its rebuilding by Henry III form a short roll of arms in stone. The sixteen shields originally placed in the spandrels of the wall-arcade bore the arms of Edward the Confessor, Henry III, the Emperor Frederick II, Louis IX of France, Alexander III of Scotland, the Count of Provence, and the Earls of Gloucester, Norfolk, Leicester, Surrey, Hereford, Aumale, Winchester, Lincoln, Cornwall and Ross. Some of these were related to Henry by blood or marriage. The Confessor was included as the Abbey's first founder, and the others are presumed to have been contributors to the cost of rebuilding his church, though this is traditional and there is no actual record of such gifts. Henry began his work at the Abbey with the addition of a Lady Chapel, commenced in 1220. He started to rebuild the Confessor's church in 1245, and the eastern part of the nave, where these shields are found, was erected between 1258 and 1269. Fourteen of these shields remain. Those on the north side are in their original positions, but on the south side part of the wall-arcade has been destroyed, and the shields numbered 1, 2, 4, 5 and 6 below have been reset higher on the wall. All the shields were originally represented as hanging from a guige, or shield-strap, which passed over a head projecting from the wall on each side."

14. Alexandre Teulet. 1866. *Auteur du texte. Layettes du trésor des chartes: de l'année 1224 à l'année 1246 / par M. Alexandre Teulet*. 378–82. No 2719 Sisteron. 1238. 20 Juin. "*Nuncupativum testamentum Raimundi Berengarii Provinciæ comitis ... Beatricem filiam nostram generalem heredem constituimus in omnibus comitatibus nostris Provincie et Folcalcherii.*" Nancy Goldstone. 2010. Four Queens: The Provençal Sisters Who Ruled Europe. London: The Orion Publishing Group. 135.
15. OED. "The right to enjoy the use and advantages of another's property short of the destruction or waste of its substance."
16. *Lettres de Rois, Reines et Autres Personnages des Cours de France et D'Angleterre*, ed. M. Champollion-Figeac (Paris: Imprimerie Royale, 1839), 1.245, ep.191.
17. Nancy Goldstone. 2010. Four Queens: The Provençal Sisters Who Ruled Europe. London: The Orion Publishing Group. 138.
18. '*Regesta 21*: 1243–1247', in Calendar of Papal Registers Relating To Great Britain and Ireland: Volume 1, 1198–1304, ed. W H Bliss (London, 1893), pp. 198–249. British History Online www.british-history.ac.uk/cal-papal-registers/brit-ie/vol 1/pp198-249 [accessed 14 December 2020].
19. Nancy Goldstone. 2010. Four Queens: The Provençal Sisters Who Ruled Europe. London: The Orion Publishing Group. 142–3.
20. Chron. Majora Eng, vol 2. 130.
21. Andrew Spencer. 2021. 'A Vineyard Without a Wall': The Savoyards, John de Warenne and the Failure of Henry III's kingship" in Thirteenth Century England XVII: Proceedings of the Cambridge Conference, 2017. Eds. Andrew Spencer & Carl Watkins. Woodbridge: The Boydell Press. 52. "The House of Savoy was quite prepared to sacrifice Henry III's interests when there were bigger fish to fry."
22. H. W. Ridgeway. 1983. The politics of the English royal court, 1247–65, with special reference to the role of aliens. University of Oxford. 168.
23. Imbert I de Seyssel and Imbert II de Seyssel, father and son, were long-term close allies, vassals (Lords of Aix) and confidants of Thomas I de Savoie then Amédée IV de Savoie, being recorded as witnessing several charters, including the 1244 marriage contract of Amédée. An Imbert de Seyssel appears a number of times in the English archives. CPR Henry III vol 3 1232 – 1247, 497. "Feb 22 [1247] Windsor, Grant to Imbert de Seysel of 30 marks in the name of a fee to be taken yearly at the exchequer of Michaelmas. And he has received his whole fee of Michaelmas term next in the wardrobe." And CLR Henry III 1245-1251, 110. "To the sheriff of Kent. Contrabreve to pay the passage of Imbert de Sessel and his comrades, knights of the count of Provence, returning homewards, and their men whom they are taking with them." Ibid. 227. "Liberate to A. count of Savoy the king's uncle 200 marks for Westminster. Michaelmas term in the 31st year of the 200 marks granted to him yearly at the Exchequer. Liberate to Imbert de Sesell' 30 marks for Michaelmas term in the 32nd year of his yearly fee of 30 marks, and to the Count of Savoy's esquire 100s. of the King's gift for his expenses." I am indebted to Huw Ridgeway for pointing out the CLR references. He writes that the suggestion that Imbert de Seyssel was involved in brokering the 1246 treaty is "very likely".
24. Björn Weiler. 2001. Henry III and the Sicilian Business: a reinterpretation*. Historical Research 74: 143. David Carpenter. 2020. Henry III: The Rise to Power and Personal Rule 1207–1258. New Haven: Yale University Press. 494.

Notes

25. Chron. Majora Lat, vol 4. 550. "*Diebus quoque sub eisdem, comes Sabaudiæ Amedeus, dominum regem Angliæ præcordialiter merito diligens, in præsentia domini archiepiscopi Cantuariensis B[onefacii] et episcopi Herefordiæ P[etri] et aliorum nobilium, tam amicorum et consanguineorum ejusdem comitis quam dicti domini regis, fecit homagium eidem domino regi in^1 manu archiepiscopi, qui supplevit regis absentiam.*" It is notable that Paris had full details of the treaty, presumably from Henry which suggests the king was more than happy with the arrangement. Perhaps evidence from Henry to Paris also of his care for pilgrims on the *Via Francigena* with the acquisition of homage for Saint Maurice.
26. CPR Henry III vol 3 1232–1247, 469. Latin text Wurstemberger, vol 4. No 191. "*Amedeus IV Comes recognoscit in feudum a rege Angliæ castra de Aviliana, de Bardo, et villas Secusiæ et S. Mauritii in Chablasio, pro qua recognitione accipit Comes a rege Mille libras Sterlingorum. 1246. Januarii 16. ap. Westmonasterium. Tria diplomata Heorici Regis, pro Amedeo, Comite Sabaudiæ et Marchione Italiæ. Rex concedit Amedeo, Com. Sab, et March, in Italia, pro homagio quod fecit pro Castro Auyllan et villa Secucie, cum Pallacio et castro de Bardo et villa S. Mauritii in Chablasio, tenendis de Rege et heredibus suis sibi et heredibus suis in feodo imperpetuum, M. libras bonorum Sterlingorum de thesauro suo, percipiendas London. ad Scaccarium Regis de dono suo. De quibus M. libris Rex solvit ei, pro manibus, D. marcas, et ei solvere tenetur D. marcas ad festum Pasche anno regni suo tricesimo; et residua D. marcarum ad festum S. Michaelis anno eodem, preter feodnm suum quod percipere debet ad eundem terminum.*"
27. The English translation of *verrou glaciaire* is glacial lock. It is a phenomenon common to the glaciated alpine valleys, where a hard rocky outcrop is left behind by the glacier. Such *verrou glaciaire* proved excellent places upon which to build medieval castles, to block transit of a valley.
28. The homage made clear that this did not preclude Amédée's pre-existing homage to the Holy Roman Emperor, Frederick II.
29. Wurstemberger, vol 2. 84. "*Raymonds Tod und die dadurch so unglückliche Angevin-Verbindung stärkten die savoyisch-englischen Familienbeziehungen erheblich*" or "Raymon's death and the resulting unfortunate Angevin connection greatly strengthened Savoyard–English family ties."
30. CPR Henry III vol 3 1232–1247, 469.
31. Eugene L. Cox. 1974. The Eagles of Savoy: The House of Savoy in Thirteenth Century Europe. Princeton: Princeton University Press. 282.
32. There was a small English contingent with the Seventh Crusade, led by William Longespée, who also perished at Al Mansurah.
33. Guy de Lusignan will be familiar to filmgoers as the "bad guy" of the Hollywood movie *Kingdom of Heaven*.
34. Stephen Church. 2017. Henry III: A Simple and God-Fearing King. London: Penguin Random House. 33.
35. Guillaume took the name from the Cistercian abbey of Valence near Lusignan; his brother is similarly often referred to as de Valence rather than de Lusignan.
36. Jeremy Ashbee. 2005. Goodrich Castle. London: English Heritage Guidebooks. 32.
37. Also known as Alésia di Saluzzo.
38. Chron. Majora Eng, vol 2. 207, 230.

39. Ibid. 437.
40. CPR Henry III vol 5 1258–1266, 207.
41. CPR Edward I vol 2 1281–1292, 192.
42. Ibid, 367.
43. Huw Ridgeway. 1988. King Henry III and the 'Aliens', 1236–1272 in Thirteenth Century England II: Proceedings of the Newcastle upon Tyne Conference 1987. Woodbridge: Boydell Press. 81.
44. D. L. D'Avray. 2005. Authentication of Marital Status: A Thirteenth-Century English Royal Annulment Process and Late Medieval Cases from the Papal Penitentiary. The English Historical Review 120: 987–1013.
45. These would be the same gospels recently paraded at the coronation of King Charles III in Westminster Abbey.
46. David Carpenter. 2020. Henry III: The Rise to Power and Personal Rule 1207–1258. New Haven: Yale University Press. 557. Carpenter describes it as "grossly exaggerated".
47. Alan Sutton. 1993. The Illustrated Chronicles of Matthew Paris: Observations of Thirteenth-Century Life. Stroud: Alan Sutton Publishing. 147–9.
48. Eugene L. Cox. 1974. The Eagles of Savoy: The House of Savoy in Thirteenth Century Europe. Princeton: Princeton University Press. 178.
49. David Carpenter. 2020. Henry III: The Rise to Power and Personal Rule 1207–1258. New Haven: Yale University Press. 557.
50. Clive H. Knowles. "Savoy, Boniface of" Oxford Dictionary of National Biography. 23 Sep. 2004; Accessed 11 May 2022.
51. Chron. Majora Eng, vol 2. 274–5.
52. Ibid. 253.
53. Eugene L. Cox. 1974. The Eagles of Savoy: The House of Savoy in Thirteenth Century Europe. Princeton: Princeton University Press. 170–1. Cox has the best account of the "novel" financial transaction which attracted the ire of the St. Albans monk but suggests that Béatrice was an innocent party in the matter. Thomas was much in need of a full "saddle-bag" since the death of his wife, Jeanne, Countess of Flanders which robbed him of his County of Flanders, since it was his solely by marriage.
54. Jean-Pierre Chapuisat. 1960. *A Propos des Relations entre la Savoie et l'Angleterre au XIII siècle. Bulletin Philolgique et Historique* 1: 432.
55. Wurstemberger, vol 2. 17. *"Bei den britischen Chronisten jener Zeit, blessen die Fürsten von Savoyen, und die savoyschen Herren Jeden Standes, die ihnen in ziemlicher Anzabi nach England folgten, bald Provincialen, bald Burgunder, seltener Serager ... Matthins von Paris ... nehmen hiußgen, und öfters des age reimtesten Anlass ... jene Fürsten und ihre Handlungen in ge Missigem Lichte darzustellen ... vom Verdacht der Leiden schaft und Partheilichkeit nicht frei bleiben."*
56. Eugene L. Cox. 1974. The Eagles of Savoy: The House of Savoy in Thirteenth Century Europe. Princeton: Princeton University Press. 197–8.
57. W. N. Yates. 1971. Bishop Peter de Aquablanca (1240–1268): a reconsideration. Journal of Ecclesiastical History 22: 305.
58. Ibid. 307.
59. CPR Henry III vol 4 1247–1258, 50.

Notes

60. For this sense of Prorogue see OED – "ORIGIN late Middle English: from Old French proroger, from Latin prorogare 'prolong, extend', from pro- 'in front of, publicly' + rogare 'ask'."
61. CPR Henry III vol 4 1247–1258, 49. "The truce with L. king of France, which should expire at All Saints, 1249, be prorogued until Midsummer, 1250, to swear on the king's soul that it shall be observed. Power to Peter de Sabaudia to prorogue the said truce as above, and to swear on the king's soul that it shall be observed."
62. CPR Henry III vol 4 1247–1258, 49–50. "Grant to P. de Sabaudia of the wardship of the lands and heir of Theobald le Butiler and the marriage of the heir, with all the escheats that can fall in; to fortify with the issues thereof the castle of Hastinges, and with the residue to fortify the castle of La Rye so far as that suffices." And "Grant to Peter de Sabaudia of the castle and honour of Hastinges to hold until out of the issues of the honour, whereby the castle shall be fortified, he have caused it to be fortified. Notification that, whereas the king has committed to the said Peter the issues of the lands late of Theobald le Butiller and Richard de Burgo and the honour of Hastings, with the marriage of the heir of the said Theobald, to fortify the castles of Hastinges and La Rye, he shall not be bound to render account for these. Grant to him of the wardship of the lands and heir of Richard de Burgo, with escheats falling in, to fortify the castle of Hastings out of the issues of the wardship and then the castle of La Rye if anything remains over."
63. Ridgeway, TNA C47/9/1. "40. [*undated*] deed: Alexander son of John de 'Syodewell' quitclaims [sells for unspecified sum] to Peter and heirs a mill at Maresfield [E. Sussex] which mill John was granted by Gilbert de Aquila, former lord of the manor. Gilbert's charter is surrendered."
64. *Fœdera* vol 1. 272. "*De pace & treugis cum Francia. Sciatis quod venerabili O patri Philippo Lugdunensi electo, & dilectis & fide libus nostris Ricardo comiti Cornubiœ, & Petro de Sabaudia plenam dedimus potestatem . . . Habent etiam litteras directas ad reginam Francie, per quam potestas eis data est de pace tractandi et reformandi.*" Or "Know that we have given full authority to our venerable father Philip of Lyon, our chosen and faithful heirs, to Richard, Earl of Cornwall, and Peter of Savoy ... They also have direct letters to the Queen of France, by which authority was given them concerning peace treaty and reform."
65. Wurstemberger, vol 2. 109.
66. Dominico Carutti. 1889. *Regesta comitum Sabaudiae, marchionum in Italia ab ultima stirpis origine ad an. MDCCLIII*. Rome: Fratres Bocca. 285–6.
67. Wurstemberger, vol 4. No 250. "*Nos uero dicti Comes, Rodulphus et Henricus, tradidimus et tradimus ipsi Electo castrum de Ternie et de Cletis in Vaut, et de Rupe.*" No 253. "*Donationes dominiorum de Ponte in Ogo, Petro de Sa*". 254. "*Willelmus de Corbiere cedit partem suam castri de Corberes P. de Sabaudia, qui retrocedit in feudum.*"
68. La *Finanza Sabauda*, vol. 1, 16. " ... domino Enrico de Bono Vilair castellano de Rota"
69. Wurstemberger, vol 4. No 382. "*Homagium Aymonis Domini de Montaniaco Petro de*".
70. D. Martignier. 1867. *Dictionnaire historique, géographique & statistique de canton de Vaud*. Lausanne: Corbaz. 219. "*Au XIIe siècle, le château des Clées était devenu un repaire de brigands qui détroussaient les voyageurs et interceptaient tout commerce. Le mal était devenu si grand que le pape Innocent II en fut touché et adressa, vers 1130,*

à Guy de Merlen, évèque de Lausanne, l'invitation expresse de ne pas permettre que cette ville fût relevée et d'excommunier quiconque tenterait de le faire." Or "In the 12th century, the Château des Clées had become a haunt of brigands who robbed travellers and intercepted all commerce. The evil had become so great that Pope Innocent II was touched by it and addressed, around 1130, to Guy de Merlen, bishop of Lausanne, the express invitation not to allow this city to be relieved and to excommunicate anyone who tried to do so."

71. Eugene L. Cox. 1974. The Eagles of Savoy: The House of Savoy in Thirteenth Century Europe. Princeton: Princeton University Press. 196.
72. Ulysse Chevalier. 1913. *Regeste Dauphinois*, vol 2. 8628. "*Guillaume de Beauvoir, fils de feu Guillaume, donne en toute seigneurie à Pierre de Savoie le château de Falavier (Ffallaverio); il l'a racheté, pour plus de mille marcs d'argent, du seigneur de la Tour et des siens, qui le détenaient injustement. Il s'en dévêt et en investit ledit Pierre, qui le lui rend en fief.*" Or "Guillaume de Beauvoir, son of the late Guillaume, gives in all seigniory to Pierre de Savoie the castle of Falavier (Ffallaverio); he bought it back, for more than a thousand marcs of silver, from the Lord of the Tower and his family, who held it unjustly. He takes it off and invests it in the aforesaid Pierre, who returns it to him as a fief."
73. Ulysse Chevalier. 1913. *Regeste Dauphinois*, vol 2. Nos 8670, 8671, 8681 and 8713.
74. Dante, Divina Commedia, Purgatorio, canto VII, ll. 130–1. "*Vedete il re de la semplice vita seder là solo, Arrigo d'Inghilterra: questi ha ne' rami suoi migliore uscita.*"
75. Darren Baker. 2017. Henry III: The Great King England Never Knew It Had. Stroud: The History Press. 463.
76. Jean Pierre Chapuisat. 1989. *De Mont-sur-Rolle à Windsor, de la Dullive à Dumfries. ... La Maison de Savoie et le Pays de Vaud* 97: 120.
77. Margaret Howell. 1998. Eleanor of Provence. Oxford: Blackwell Publishers Ltd. 10.
78. J. R. Maddicott. 1995. Simon de Montfort. Cambridge: Cambridge University Press. 3.
79. Charles Bémont. *Simon de Montfort, Comte de Leicester, Sa Vie (120?–1265), Son Role Politique en France et en Angleterre.* Paris: Alphonse Picard Libraire. 298.
80. CChR Henry III vol 1 1229–1257, 345. Also recorded in CPR Henry III vol 4 1247–1258, 50.
81. TNA C47/9/1.
82. Jean-Pierre Chapuisat. 2000. "*Pierre de Savoie, Les Affaires Anglaises.*" in *Pierre II de Savoie "Le Petit Charlemagne"* ed. Bernard Andenmatten, Agostino Paravicini Bagliani and Eva Pibiri. (Lausanne: Université de Lausanne). 258.
83. CCR Henry III vol 7 1251–1252, 205–7.
84. David Carpenter. 2020. Henry III: The Rise to Power and Personal Rule 1207–1258. New Haven: Yale University Press. 508.
85. Chron. Majora Eng, vol 2. 488.
86. David Carpenter. 2020. Henry III: The Rise to Power and Personal Rule 1207–1258. New Haven: Yale University Press. 508.
87. Ibid. 507.
88. H. W. Ridgeway. 1983. The politics of the English royal court, 1247–65, with special reference to the role of aliens. University of Oxford. 114–6.
89. David Carpenter. 2004. The Struggle for Mastery: Britain 1066–1284. London: Penguin Books Ltd. 342.

Notes

90. Margaret Howell. 1998. Eleanor of Provence. Oxford: Blackwell Publishers Ltd. 49, 54.
91. David Carpenter. 2020. Henry III: The Rise to Power and Personal Rule 1207–1258. New Haven: Yale University Press. 560.
92. Chron. Majora Eng, vol 3. 1–6.
93. Sara Cockerill. 2014. Eleanor of Castile: The Shadow Queen. Second Edition ed. Stroud: Amberley Publishing. 69.
94. Huw Ridgeway. 1986. "The Lord Edward and the Provisions of Oxford (1258): A Study in Faction" in Thirteenth Century England I: Proceedings of the Newcastle upon Tyne Conference 1985. Ed. Peter R. Coss & S. D. Lloyd. (Woodbridge: Boydell Press). 92.
95. John Robert Maddicott. 1986. *Edward I and the Lessons of Baronial Reform: local government, 1258–1260* in Thirteenth Century England: Proceedings of the Newcastle-upon-Tyne Conference, 1985. Woodbridge: The Boydell Press. 19.
96. CChR Henry III vol 1 1229–1257, 386.
97. CPR Henry III vol 4 1247-1258, 136. "The said letters of Guy were delivered in the wardrobe and transmitted from the wardrobe to Peter de Sabaudia."
98. TNA C47/9/1.
99. CPR Henry III vol 4 1247-1258, 206. "This letter was delivered to P. de Sabaudia by the hands of H. de Wengham. [*Fœdera*.]"
100. H. W. Ridgeway. 1983. The politics of the English royal court, 1247–65, with special reference to the role of aliens. University of Oxford. 133. And also Ridgeway. 4. "Queen Eleanor and Peter defended Edward's claims against rivals conspiring for land grants from notoriously prodigal Henry III. Peter kept charters as a means of pressurising Henry to honour his promises to Edward until the prince received his estates in February 1254."
101. Eugene L. Cox. 1974. The Eagles of Savoy: The House of Savoy in Thirteenth Century Europe. Princeton: Princeton University Press. 241.
102. David Carpenter. 2020. Henry III: The Rise to Power and Personal Rule 1207–1258. New Haven: Yale University Press. 496.
103. David Carpenter. 2004. The Struggle for Mastery: Britain 1066–1284. London: Penguin Books Ltd. 343.
104. David Carpenter. 2020. Henry III: The Rise to Power and Personal Rule 1207–1258. New Haven: Yale University Press. 555.
105. Andrew M. Spencer. 2021. "'A Vineyard Without a Wall': The Savoyards, John de Warenne and the Failure of Henry III's Kingship" in Thirteenth Century England XVII: Proceedings of the Cambridge Conference, 2017. Eds. Andrew Spencer & Carl Watkins. (Boydell and Brewer: Woodbridge). 47. Table 1.
106. CCR Henry III vol 7 1251–1252, 66 "*De quercubus datis.–Mandatum est Godefrido de Lyston', custodi foreste de Windes', quod in eadem foresta faciat habere Petro de Sabaud' xx. Quercus cum escaetis ad operaciones domorum suarum Lond', de dono regis. Teste ut supra. Per regem.*" Or "Concerning the given oaks. Godfrey of Lyston, warden of the forest of Winds, was commanded that he should cause Peter of Savoy to have in the same forest 20 an oak with shavings for the operations of his house at London, by the gift of the king. Witness as above. By the king."
107. Wurstemberger, vol 1. 351.
108. Chron. Majora Eng, vol 3. 6–7.

Chapter Seven

1. *Fœdera* vol 1. 288–90. "*Carta Petri de Sabaudia, de juramento eundi ad Terram Sanctam in comitiva Regis. Omnibus præsentes litteras inspecturis, vel audituris, Petrus de Sabaudia, salutem. Sciatis quod, cum Henricus Rex Anglie, caractere crucis dominicææ insignitus, passagium suum in Terram Sanctam stabilierit in festo sancti Johannis Baptistææ, anno Domini MCCL. nos, ad suum beneplacitum, præstito corporali juramento, tenore litterarum præsentium, protestamur & fideliter promittimus quod, cum idem Dominus noster ad terram prædictam ibit, nos cum ipso proficiscemur corporaliter, DEO nobis vitam & salutem concedente, & prædicto domino nostro Rege sub.*" Or "Charter of Peter of Savoy, on oath of going to the Holy Land in the company of the King. To all who may inspect or hear the present letter, Peter of Savoy, greeting. Know that when King Henry of England, marked with the mark of the cross of the Lord, established his Passage in the Holy Land on the feast of St. John the Baptist, in the year of our Lord 1250 We, at his good pleasure, having taken a corporal oath, by the tenor of the letters presented here, protest and promise faithfully that when our Lord will go to the aforesaid land, we will go with him physically, God granting us life and safety, and under our aforesaid lord King."
2. CCR Henry III vol 7 1251–1253, 482. "*Scias quod ad instanciam prelatorum et magnatum regni nostri concess imus quod magna carta de libertatibus predictis prelatis et magnatibus ac aliis liberis hominibus regni nostri confecta decetero rata et stabilis perseveret et quod omnes articuli in eadem carta contenti et expressi inviolabiter observentur, salvis nobis et heredibus nostris juribus et dingnitatibus corone nostre, et baronibus nostris et magnatibus ac aliis nobis subjectis libertatibus et liberis consuetudinibus prius usitatis non expressis vel concessis in carta predicta: et ideo tibi districte precipimus quod predictam cartam in omnibus et singulis articulis diligenter observes et a prelatis et magnatibus et omnibus aliis predictorum comitatuum firmiter facias observari super gravem forisfacturam nostram.*" Or "You may know that at the instance of the prelates and magnates of our kingdom we have been granted that the great charter concerning the freedoms aforesaid prelates, magnates, and other free men of our kingdom, ended in future, will continue to be ratified and stable the rights and dignities of our crown, and to our barons and nobles and other subjects subject to us freedoms and free customs not previously used, expressed or granted in the aforesaid charter. you shall firmly be observed in all other of the aforesaid counties upon our grievous forfeiture."
3. Björn Weiler. 2001. Henry III and the Sicilian Business: a reinterpretation*. Historical Research 74: 127.
4. Chron. Majora Eng, vol 3. 25–6.
5. J. Brotherton. 1766–84. A Solemn and Public Appeal to Magna Charta, and the Common Law of England, upon the subject of inheritance to the lands of intestates by descent ... By a Gentleman of the Middle Temple. British Library: London, 40. Richard, Earl of Cornwall, Roger Bigod, 4th Earl of Norfolk, Humphrey de Bohun, 2nd Earl of Hereford, Hugh de Vere, 4th Earl of Oxford and Jean de Warenne, 6th Earl of Surrey.
6. Ibid. 42.
7. Chron. Majora Eng, vol 3. 19. "The king, moreover, by advice of the Savoyards, decreed and provided that if anyone on a journey should be robbed, or in anyway injured by the

robbers, those persons on whom the care of that part of the country more particularly depended should give proper and competent satisfaction to the injured, party, and should restore to him what he had lost, according to the Savoyard custom."
8. CPR Henry III vol 4 1247–1258, 188–9.
9. Jean-Pierre Chapuisat. 1964. *Au service de deux rois d'Angleterre, au XIIIe siècle: Pierre de Champvent. Revue historique vaudoise* 72: 159.
10. Chron. Majora Eng, vol 3. 30.
11. Henry left a will at this point, should he not return from Gascony. Its list of executors makes interesting reading; it was of course headed by Queen Alianor, but also included Pierre de Savoie and Boniface de Savoie.
12. CCR Henry III vol 9 1251–1252, 491. "*De attornato – Memorandum quod Ebulo de Montibus, Bartholomeus Pecch'et Stephanus Bauzan, vel unus eorum, habent potestatem a domino rege faciendi attornatum vel attornatos pro P. de Sabaudia in omnibus placitis motis et movendis contra ipsum Petrum usque ad reditum ipsius Petri in Angliam.*" Or "It is noted that Ebal de Mont, Bartholomew Peche and Stephen Bauzan, or one of them, have the power from the lord king to act as attorney or attorneys for P. de Savoy in all pleas filed and moving against Peter himself until Peter's return to England."
13. CCR Henry III vol 8 1247–1251, 56. "*Pro Emerico de Montibus.– Mandatum est eidem Willelmo quod faciat habere Emerico de Montibus, quem hac die Pentecostes milicie cingulo proponimus insignire, ea que sibi necessaria sunt ad dictum honorem recipiendum, de dono regis. Teste ut supra.*" Or "For Ebal de Mont.–It is commanded that William should do to have Ebal de Mont, whom we propose to wear on the day of Pentecost, the girdle of knighthood, those things which are necessary for him to receive the said honour, from the gift of the king. Witness as above."
14. Margaret Howell. 1998. Eleanor of Provence. Oxford: Blackwell Publishers Ltd. 52.
15. CPR Henry III vol 4 1247–1258, 206-7.
16. Ibid. 206. "This letter was delivered to P. de Sabaudia by the hands of H. de Wengham. [*Fœdera*.]"
17. Margaret Howell. 1998. Eleanor of Provence. Oxford: Blackwell Publishers Ltd. 112. Howell is too polite to call it sexism but suggests that Denholm-Young suggesting Richard "bore the brunt of the regency" was suggesting something "simply not true".
18. CPR Henry III vol 4 1247–1258, 370. The name of the Queen is the first mentioned as being present.
19. John Maddicott, The Origins of the English Parliament. http://www.oxford.lu/documents/MaddicottText.doc accessed 6 December 2020.
20. David Carpenter. 2004. The Struggle for Mastery : Britain 1066 - 1284. London: Penguin Books Ltd. 356. "In 1254 the county courts were ordered to elect two knights to come and grant taxation 'on behalf of everyone in the county'. This was the first known occasion when representatives of the shires were summoned to parliament.."
21. David Carpenter. 2020. Henry III: The Rise to Power and Personal Rule 1207–1258. New Haven: Yale University Press. 579–80.
22. Chron. Majora Eng, vol 3. 34.
23. CPR Henry III vol 4 1247–1258. 235. RG i, no.2083. "*Pro Rege. De munitione castri de Millans. Rex omnibus militibus, servientibus, stipen- diariis et omnibus aliis fidelibus suis, cum dilectis et fidelibus suis Petro de Sabaudia et Johanne de Grey, senescallo*

suo Wasconie, salutem. Mandatamus volas in fide qua nobis tenemini, et sicut nos et honoreni nostrum diligitis et omnia que de no- his tenetis, quod hiis que prefati Petrus et senescallus, et dilectus clericus noster Petrus Chacepore, vobis injungent ex parte nostra super munitione castri de Millan, diligenter intendatis, et ea sine dilatione vel dificultate aliqua faciatis; ita quod defectu vestri in hae parte nullum dampuum vel periculum incurramus pro quo ad vos et vestra nos graviter capere debeamus. In cujus, etc. T. etc. uts."

24. RG i. nos. 246, 2337, 2870, 3372, 3447.
25. RG i, no. 3372. "*Pro Johanne de Castillone. Consimiles litteras habent Johannes de Castillone et duo socii sui quod contra idem festum habeant ea que ad miliciam suam pertinent honorifice, videlicet idem Johannes pamos ad aurum, et duo socii sui, sicut Rex aliis novis militibus consuevit invenire. T. R., apud Burdegalam, xij. die Augusti.*" Blondel was identifying Jean de Châtillon as of Châtillon-sur-Cluses in Faucigny, the castle of which was the home of Pierre de Savoie's wife Agnès de Faucigny – in context it's a reasonable identification.
26. RG i, no. 2870. "*. . . et Willielmo de Pesmes et duobus militibus sociis suis robas, scilicet eidem Willielmo tres pecias. et Simoni de Greenvilla et duobus militibus sociis suis robas, scilicet eidem Simoni tres pecias. T. ut s*" The *Famille de Pesmes* would a century later find themselves linked to the Savoyard *Famille de Grandson*. Guillaume's participation in the Gascony expedition would seem to indicate links with Savoy predate this. Pesmes and it's castle sit equidistant north-west of Dole and north-east of Besançon and south of Dijon in what was then the Free County of Burgundy, a part of the Empire.
27. Louis Blondel, "*L'architecture militaire au temps de Pierre II de Savoie: Les donjons circulaires,*" *Genava* XIII (1935): 283. "*Ont été faits chevaliers par le roi à Bordeaux, entr'autres: Jean de Châtillon, Reynaud d'Orbe, Jean Grossi, Conrad de Kiburg, Guillaume de Pesmes.*"
28. CChrR Henry III vol 2 (1257 -1300), 24. "Inspeximus and confirmation of a charter by which Edward, eldest son of the king, gave to Ebulo de Montibus, for his homage and service, all the lands of the late William de Buell in the town of Ketene, to be held by the said Ebulo, his heirs and assigns, of the said Edward, the service of the fourth part of a knight's fees; witnesses, Sir John son of Geoffrey, Sir Humphrey de Boun, the younger, Sir Roger de Monte Alto, Steward of Chester, Sir Geoffrey de Genvile, Sir William de Pemes, Sir William de Wylton, Sir Stephen Bauzan, Sir Geoffrey de Langgele, Sir William de Chaeny, Sir Adam de Jesemue, Sir John Burdet, Sir Eudo la Zuch and Sir Walter de Langele; dated at Suthwerk, March 24" When Guillaume VII de Pesmes dies in 1327 with no male heir, his daughter Jeanne having married Othon II de Grandson the Seigneury de Pesmes will pass to the Famille de Grandson Pesmes. Othon II de Grandson would be the nephew of the Othon I de Grandson that will find fame in the service of King Edward I. The impreximus of 1259 implies strongly that the Familles de Pesmes and Grandson had jointly served the Lord Edward in England as household knights a century before their families will be joined by marriage.
29. CPR Henry III vol 4 1247–1258. 235.
30. RG I, no.3447. "*Pro Conrado de Kiburgo. — Mandatum est Bonacio Lumbardo et tenenti locum Rogeri Scissoris quod, non obstante aliquo mandato, etc., faciant habere sine dilacione Conrado de kiburgo quandam roham militi convenientem. T. ut s*".
31. Gascon Rolls no.3220.

Notes

32. RG i, no.3382.
33. CCR Henry III vol 6 1247–1251, 82. "*Liberate etiam Magistro Bertrando de Saltu, Ingeniator, x liberas.*"
34. Sault-de-Navailles appears in 1273 as Sanctus-Nicolaus de Saltu in the Bordeaux Registers.
35. Traction trebuchet, stone throwing, siege engine. Mangonel is probably derived from the Greek mágganon or mangonon, meaning "engine of war". It could also be derived from mangon, a French hard stone found in the south of France. In Latin it is called a manganum, in French a manganeau, and in English a mangonel.
36. A belfry was a siege tower or wall breaching tower.
37. Arnold Taylor.1989. Master Bertram Ingeniator Regis. Studies in Medieval History presented to R. Allen Brown. Woodbridge: The Boydell Press. 291–2.
38. RG ii, no.4324. "*Pro Ebulone de Montibus – E E., etc., Stephano Bauzanni, etc. Sciatis quod commisimus dilecto et fideli nostro Ebuloni de Montibus castrum nostrum de Benauges, enstodiendum quamdiu no bis placuerit. Et ideo vobis mandamus quod eidem Ebuloni dictum castrum sine dilatione liberetis. In cujus, etc. Datum apud Sanctum Severum .j. die Decembris.*"
39. RG i, no.3462. "*Pro Johanne de Maysoz – Mandatum est eisdem quod Johanni de Maysoz, qui a rege suscepturus est arma militaria apud Burdegalam, sine dilacione habere faciant ea que ad miliciam suam pertinent, sicut alles novis militibus consueverunt invenire. Teste apud supra (apud Burdegallam xxv die Septembris).*"
40. Arnold Taylor. 1989. Master Bertram, Ingeniator Regis. Studies in Medieval History presented to R. Allen Brown. Woodbridge: The Boydell Press. 292.
41. CPR Henry III vol 4 1247–1258, 293.
42. RG i, no.2599. "*Rev omnibus, ete. Sciatis nos dedisse, concessisse, et presenti carta nostro confirmasse Edwardo, filio nostro primogenito, cui dedimus totam terrani Vasconie cum pertinentis, omnes terras et Lencuenta et omnes escaetas que nobis acciderint, vel accidere poterunt, in Wasconia, de Bernardo de Bovilla et de quibuscunque ahis, tam in castris, civitatibus, burgis et villis, quam in omnibus aliis rebus et locis, tam per forisfacturam quam per escactam; ita quod castra illa, terre et tenementa el escaete ille nequeant aliquo tempore alibi conferri vel alienari. Et si quid per nos inde datum fuerit alicui, vel alienatum, volumus quod hoc nullius sit valoris, vel momenti. Et hoe fide nos- tra media in manu venerabilis patris P. Hertelordie episcopi prestita firmiter promisins, quia volumus quod tota terra Vasconie cum omnibus pertinen- tiis suis et escaetis, presentibus et futuris, integre remaneant in perpetuum. In cujus, etc. Teste apud Benaugiam, quarto die Oetobris, anno xxx vij.*"
43. Ibid. 237–8.
44. Chron. Majora Eng, vol 3. 52.
45. Ibid. 60.
46. CPR Henry III vol 4 1247–1258, 268. "Grant to P[eter] de Sabaudia of the wardship of the lands and heirs of William] de Vescy, together with the marriage of the heirs, with the advowsons of churches, liberties and all things belonging to the wardship so that he marry the heirs without disparagement." Also Ridgeway TNA C47/9/1 No. 28, "however [cartulary copy], omits a grant of 'the marriage' of the ward 'without disparagement'."
47. Ridgeway 7–8.
48. Ibid. 270.

49. David Carpenter. 2020. Henry III: The Rise to Power and Personal Rule 1207–1258. New Haven: Yale University Press. 597.
50. CPR Henry III vol 4 1247–1258, 374–7.
51. Ibid. 300–27.
52. Alison Weir. 2020. Queens of the Crusades: Eleanor of Aquitaine and her Successors. London: Penguin Random House UK. 562.
53. CPR Henry III vol 4 1247–1258, 300–27.
54. Ibid.
55. Ibid. "Grant to Peter de Chauvent of 60 marks a year at the exchequer of Easter until the king provide for him to that yearly value in wards or escheats."
56. Jean-Pierre Chapuisat. 1964. *Au service de deux rois d'Angleterre, au XIIIe siècle: Pierre de Champvent*. Revue historique vaudoise 72: 159. Citing TNA Liberate Roll 39 H. III, C 62/31 memb. 6: "*Pro duobus equis suis amissis in servicio nostro ibidem.*" Or "For two of his horses lost in our service there."
57. CPR Henry III vol 4 1247–1258, 300–27.
58. Huw Ridgeway.1983. The politics of the English royal court, 1247–65, with special reference to the role of aliens. Unpublished D. Phil Thesis. Oxford University. 176.
59. CPR Henry III vol 4 1247–1258, 300–27. Grant to Peter de Sabaudia "that he may sell, bequeath or assign, to whomsoever he will all the lands which he holds in fee of the king; and if he happen to be in possession thereof on the day of his death, there shall not on this account be any bar to any gift for assignment he may have made in his lifetime or by his will".
60. Herrero Sanz, María Jesús. 2012. *Guía Santa María la Real de Huelgas*: Madrid: Reales Sitios de España. Patrimonio Nacional. 9.
61. Sara Cockerill. 2014. Eleanor of Castile: The Shadow Queen. Second Edition ed. Stroud: Amberley Publishing. 86.
62. Chron. Majora Eng, vol 3. 83.
63. Ibid. 84.
64. David Carpenter. 2020. Henry III: The Rise to Power and Personal Rule 1207–1258. New Haven: Yale University Press. 586. "To understand the Sicilian affair, one fundamental point needs appreciation: it was an enterprise of the Savoyards." Jean-Pierre Chapuisat. 2000. "*Pierre de Savoie, Les Affaires Anglaises.*" in *Pierre II de Savoie "Le Petit Charlemagne"* ed. Bernard Andenmatten, Agostino Paravicini Bagliani and Eva Pibiri. (Lausanne: Université de Lausanne). 262.
65. Bruno Galland. 1998. *Les papes d'Avignon et la Maison de Savoie (1309–1409)*. Publications de l'École Française de Rome. 247. 41.
66. Bruno Galland. 1988. *Un Savoyard sur le siège de Lyon au XIIIe siècle: Philippe de Savoie*. Bibliothèque de l'école des chartes 146: 48.
67. CCR Henry III vol 8 1259–1261, 357.
68. Jean-Pierre Chapuisat. 2000. "*Pierre de Savoie, Les Affaires Anglaises.*" in *Pierre II de Savoie "Le Petit Charlemagne"* ed. Bernard Andenmatten, Agostino Paravicini Bagliani and Eva Pibiri. (Lausanne: Université de Lausanne). 262.
69. CPR Henry III vol 4 1247–1258, 269.
70. Jean-Pierre Chapuisat. 2000. "*Pierre de Savoie, Les Affaires Anglaises.*" in *Pierre II de Savoie "Le Petit Charlemagne"* ed. Bernard Andenmatten, Agostino Paravicini Bagliani and Eva Pibiri. (Lausanne: Université de Lausanne). 262.

Notes

71. David Carpenter. 2020. Henry III: The Rise to Power and Personal Rule 1207–1258. New Haven: Yale University Press. 586.
72. Italian State Archives, volume 109, page 6, fascicule 6.
73. Manfred was the son of the relationship between Frederick and Bianca Lancia d'Agliano (also called Béatrice and Blanca; c. 1210–c. 1246) who was an Italian noblewoman and Frederick's mistress. Their marriage was conducted while she was on her deathbed, and therefore it was considered non-canonical.
74. Henry, the son of Frederick and Isabella (Henry III's sister) and Henry III's own nephew, had been appointed Governor of Sicily and promised to become King of Jerusalem after his father died, but he, too, died within three years, in May 1253, and was never crowned.
75. Conrad had, like his father, recently been excommunicated.
76. Lisa Hilton. 2008. Queens Consort: England's Medieval Queens. London: Weidenfeld & Nicolson. 222.
77. Chron. Majora Eng, vol 3. 89.
78. Ibid. 104. "On reaching the tomb of his mother which was in the cemetery he caused her body to be removed inside the church." Alison Weir. 2020. Queens of the Crusades: Eleanor of Aquitaine and her Successors. London: Penguin Random House UK. 567.
79. Ann. Waverley, 346. *"cum idem rex ob amorem et devotionem, quam habuit erga beatum Edmundum Cantuariæ archiepiscopum, iter faceret versus Pontiniacum, transitum fecit per civitatem Parisius, ubi ab illustri rege Lodowyco, cum summo honore et solemni processione, præsentibus quatuor episcopis, susceptus est, et ad regis petitionem tribus ibi diebus commoratus."* Or "when the same king, because of the love and devotion which he had for the blessed Edmund, archbishop of Canterbury, was making his way towards Pontigny, he passed through the city of Paris, where he was received by the illustrious king Louis, with great honor and a solemn procession, in the presence of four bishops, and to the king's He stayed there for three days at the request."
80. Chron. Majora Eng, vol 3. 105.
81. Ibid. 108–9.
82. Ibid. 109.
83. Wurstemberger, vol 1. 356.
84. Wurstemberger, vol 4. No 397.
85. The chronicler may have embellished the personal input of Pierre de Savoie, but the bridge, first mentioned in 1265, certainly dates from this tenure as Protector of Bern.
86. Ernst Tremp. 2000. *"Peter II. Und die Nachbarn der Waadt. Bern, Freiburg, Kyburg und Habsburg"* in *Pierre II de Savoie "Le Petit Charlemagne"* ed. Bernard Andenmatten, Agostino Paravicini Bagliani and Eva Pibiri. (Lausanne: Université de Lausanne). 193.
87. Ibid. 192.
88. Ibid. 196. *"das zeitweise ein savoyischer Vogt, Ulrich von Vuippens, den Befehl in der Stadt führte."* Or "that for a time a Savoyard bailiff, Ulrich de Vuippens, was in charge of the city." n13 *"Ulrich von Vuippens ist als advocatus de Berno oder Bernensis belegt für August September 1255 and November/December 1256."* And Wurstemberger, vol 4. No 412.
89. Eugene L. Cox. 1974. The Eagles of Savoy: The House of Savoy in Thirteenth Century Europe. Princeton: Princeton University Press. 203–4.
90. Ernst Tremp. 2000. *"Peter II. Und die Nachbarn der Waadt. Bern, Freiburg, Kyburg und Habsburg."* in *Pierre II de Savoie "Le Petit Charlemagne"* ed. Bernard Andenmatten,

Agostino Paravicini Bagliani and Eva Pibiri. (Lausanne: Université de Lausanne). 198. *"Peter II als de facto Stadthert von Berns von 1255 bis 1268."* Or "Peter II as de facto city leader of Bern from 1255 to 1268."

91. Dominico Carutti. 1889. *Regesta comitum Sabaudiae, marchionum in Italia ab ultima stirpis origine ad an. MDCCLIII.* Rome: Fratres Bocca. 319. *"Anno Domini MCCLIII obiit Amadeus comes Sabadiæ in idus Junii."*
92. Ibid. *"Anno MCCLIII in Idus Julii sepultus hic (Altaecumbae) fuit in clitae recordationis et famosissimus vir dominus Amedeus D. G. comes Sabaudiae."*
93. Wurstemberger, vol 1. 348 n1. Wurstemberger cites Guichenon's date of birth for Count Boniface de Savoie as 1 December 1244.
94. Ibid. 356.
95. Ibid. 241–9.
96. Louis Blondel. 1935. *L'architecture militaire au temps de Pierre II de Savoie: Les donjons circulaires.* André Perret. 1983. *Le comte Pierre II de Savoie. L'expansion savoyarde et l'alliance anglaise au xiiie siècle.* Revue Savoisienne 117.
97. Bruno Galland. 1988. *Un Savoyard sur le siège de Lyon au XIIIe siècle: Philippe de Savoie.* Bibliothèque de l'école des chartes 146: 42.
98. Bruno Galland. 1988. *Un Savoyard sur le siège de Lyon au XIIIe siècle: Philippe de Savoie.* Bibliothèque de l'école des chartes 146: 54.
99. AST/C. *Testamenti*, m. 1, no 7. See Appendix for text.
100. E. B. Fryde, D. E. Greenway, S. Porter & I. Roy. 1986. Handbook of British Chronology. Third ed. London: Offices of the Royal Historical Society. 83. William of Kilkenny had been Controller of the Wardrobe from 1249 until 1252 and previously an archdeacon at Coventry.
101. Chron. Majora Eng, vol 3. 131.
102. CCR Henry III vol 9 1254–1256, 219. *"Et mandatum est eidem Petro quod, si contingat ipsum venire in Wasconiam, statum ipsius terre et recessum Eduuardi filii regis ab eadem et transfretacionem suam in Hiberniam totaliter ordinet, prout melius viderit expedire; et facta illa ordinacione sub omni celeritate qua poterit ad regem veniat in Angliam, cum eo tractaturus super illis secretis negociis, pro quibus venerabilis pater P. Herefordensis episcopus in Curia Romana diligenter et efficaciter laboravit. Teste ut supra."* Or "And it was commanded to Peter that, if it should happen that he should come to Gascony, he should order the state of his land, and the withdrawal of the King's son Edward from the same, and his crossing into Ireland, as he thought it best expedient; and that decree being made, with every speed with which he might be able to come to the king into England, to treat with him on those secret affairs, for which the venerable father, P. Bishop of Hereford, worked diligently and effectively in the Roman Curia. Witness as above."
103. H. W. Ridgeway. 1983. The politics of the English royal court, 1247–65, with special reference to the role of aliens. University of Oxford. 169.
104. Saint Kenelm (or Cynehelm) was an Anglo-Saxon saint venerated throughout medieval England, and mentioned in the Canterbury Tales.
105. Ann. Cestrienses, 72–3. *"Eodem anno in festivitate Sancti Kenelmi dominus Edwardus Comes primum Cestriam veniens procedentibus ei obviam tarn clero quam populo cum quanta decuit receptus est veneracione. Ibique per triduum hominia et fidelitates tarn a nobilibus Cestrisirae quam Wallie recipiens, profectus est in Wallia terras suas et castella videre. rediens die inventionis Sancti Stephani a Cestria recessit et per Darnhall*

Notes

transiens in Anglia remeavit" Or "On the feast of S. Kenelm [July 17] the lord Edward, earl of Chester, entered Chester for the first time, and was received with all due respect, as well the clergy as the laity having gone forth to meet him. Having remained three days to receive the homage and fealty as well of the nobles of Cheshire as of Wales, he set out for Wales to inspect his lands and castles there, and returning on the day of the Invention [or Finding] of [the relics of] S. Stephen [Aug. 3], he left Chester and returned to England, going by the way of Darnall."

106. David Carpenter. 2020. Henry III: The Rise to Power and Personal Rule 1207–1258. New Haven: Yale University Press, 634.
107. Chron. Majora Eng, vol 3. 144, 244.
108. David Carpenter. 2020. Henry III: The Rise to Power and Personal Rule 1207–1258. New Haven: Yale University Press. 635.
109. Chron. Majora Eng, vol 3. 178–9. "We have therefore thought it right to earnestly beg and exhort your serene majesty [Alianor] to seize the persons and property of any of the citizens of Turin and Asti who may be living in the countries subject to your rule and detain them until the aforesaid Count [Thomas] be restored to his former state of freedom." Letter from Pope Alexander to Queen Alianor as recorded by Matthew Paris.
110. Eugene L. Cox. 1974. The Eagles of Savoy: The House of Savoy in Thirteenth Century Europe. Princeton: Princeton University Press. 258.
111. CPR Henry III vol 4 1247–1258, 540–1. "Feb 5th [1257], Westminster. Grant to Peter de Sabaudia [in aid of the deliverance of Thomas de Sabaudia, the count, the king's uncle, brother of the said Peter, who was seditiously taken at Turin—vacated] of 4000 marks which are owing to the king for the loan which the king made to Raymond, sometime count of Provence, and Béatrice the countess, his consort, on the security of four castles in the counties of Provence and Forcalchier, and grant that the king will grant the said money to none but the said Peter."
112. Chron. Majora Eng, vol 3. 165.
113. Ibid. 178.
114. Ibid. 266–7.
115. Ibid. 164.
116. CPR Henry III vol 4 1247–1258, 469. "April 21st [1256], Westminster. Whereas Richard, earl of Cornwall, has lent to Peter de Sabaudia 1000l., the king grants that if Peter die before the money is repaid he will not betake himself to the lands or chattels of Peter until the earl have levied what remains due to him of the said debt."
117. Ibid. 559. "June 4. Westminster. Notification that the king has inspected a letter obligatory of Queen Eleanor and Peter de Sabaudia to the abbot and convent of Cyrencestre touching a loan of 1000 marks made to the queen and Peter by Maynettus Spine and his fellows, merchants of Florence, for which loan the said abbot and convent are bound to the said merchants for the said queen and Peter; and gives his assent to the execution of the same. The abbot and convent of Certeseye have like letters touching a like loan of 1000 marks. The abbot and convent of Abbendon have the like touching a like loan of 1000 marks. The abbot and convent of Hyde have the like touching a like loan of 1000 marks. The abbot and convent of Pershore have the like touching a loan of 500 marks."
118. North Wales east of the Conwy – Rhos, Rhufoniog, Dyffryn Clwyd and Tegeingl.
119. Owain the Red.
120. Ann. Cestrienses, 70. "*Eodem anno orta est dessencio inter filios Griffini filii Lewelini quondam principis Wallie super terrarum participacione, tandem Lewelinus utrumque*

fratrem Oweyn scilicet majorem natu et David juniorem in bello campestri captos incarceravit." Or "In the same year [1255] a dissension sprung up between the sons of Griffin, the son of Llewelin, formerly prince of Wales, concerning the partition of his territories; at length Llewelin, having captured his two brothers, Owen the eldest, and David the younger, in open battle, imprisoned them."

121. This has been interpreted as being near the modern Bwlch Derwyn and Derwyn Fawr, on the borders of the parishes of Clynnog and Dolbenmaen, just east of Bwlch Dau Fynydd (the pass of the two mountains – Drws Daufynydd/the door of the two mountains) (Lloyd, 715). However, fieldwork in this area undertaken in 2014 did not find evidence that could be linked to the battle (Archaeology Wales).
122. Brut. The *Brut y Tywysogion*, in English: *Chronicle of the Princes*, also known as *Brut y Tywysogyon*, is one of the most important primary sources for Welsh history. It is a chronicle that serves as a continuation of Geoffrey of Monmouth's *Historia Regum Britanniae*. *Brut y Tywysogion* has survived as several Welsh translations of an original Latin version, which has not itself survived. The most important versions are the one in Robert Vaughan's *Peniarth MS.20* and the slightly less complete one in the *Red Book of Hengest*. The version entitled *Brenhinoedd y Saeson* (Kings of the English) combines material from the Welsh annals with material from an English source. The Peniarth MS. 20 version begins in 682 with a record of the death of Cadwaladr and ends in 1332.
123. Ann. Cestrienses, 70. "*tandem Lewelinus utrumque fratrem Oweyn scilicet majorem natu et David juniorem in bello campestri captos incarceravit.*" Or "at length Llewelin, having captured his two brothers, Owen the eldest, and David the younger, in open battle, imprisoned them."
124. David Carpenter. 2020. Henry III: The Rise to Power and Personal Rule 1207–1258. New Haven: Yale University Press. 1023.
125. Chron. Majora Eng, vol 3. 200.
126. Ibid. 204.
127. R.R. Davies. 1987. The Age of Conquest: Wales 1063–1415. Oxford: Oxford University Press. 310.
128. The surname la Zouche may have derived from *souch* or *zuche* in Norman French, indicating someone of stocky build. Matthew Paris suggests that he got this office by outbidding his predecessor John de Grey. He offered 1,200 marks for the post instead of 500.
129. CCR Henry III vol 6 1247–1251, 541.
130. The Chester chronicler says "circa festum omnium Sanctorum" or "around the festival of All Saints", 1 November.
131. Chron. Majora Eng, vol 3. 217.
132. Chron. Majora Eng, vol 2. 238.
133. Ibid. 218.
134. As a reminder of the cost of war, there is in CPR Henry III vol 4 1247–1258. 561 consideration given to Agnès the wife of Stephen Bauzan, "of the services of her late husband to the King, and Edward his son".
135. Huw Pryce. 2005. The Acts of Welsh Rulers: 1120 to 1283. Cardiff: University of Wales Press. 499.
136. CR Henry III 1257–1259 223–4, 297.

Notes

137. The title was predominantly a claim to become Holy Roman Emperor and was dependent upon coronation by the Pope. The title originally referred to any elected king who had not yet been granted the Imperial Regalia and title of "Emperor" at the hands of the Pope.
138. King of the Romans was an elected office, elected by the Count Palatine of the Rhine, the archbishop of Cologne, the count of Bohemia, the archbishop of Mainz, the archbishop of Trier (or Treves), the duke of Saxony and the marquis of Brandenburg.
139. H. W. Ridgeway. 1983. The politics of the English royal court, 1247–65, with special reference to the role of aliens. University of Oxford. 259.
140. David Carpenter. 2020. Henry III: The Rise to Power and Personal Rule 1207–1258. New Haven: Yale University Press. 651.
141. Stephen Church. 2017. Henry III: A Simple and God-Fearing King. London: Penguin Random House. 47.
142. H. W. Ridgeway. 1983. The politics of the English royal court, 1247–65, with special reference to the role of aliens. University of Oxford. 133.
143. H. W. Ridgeway. 1983. The politics of the English royal court, 1247–65, with special reference to the role of aliens. University of Oxford. 262. Ridgeway notes that although Paris insisted this exemption extended to Pierre de Savoie, the events of 1258, where he was one of the original seven oath-takers, and later served on the Council of Fifteen, suggest it was the Lusignans who benefited most, or at least were politically damaged by thus benefitting in them: A. H. Hershey, "An Introduction to and an Edition of the Hugh Bigod Eyre Rolls, June 1258–February 1259: PRO Just 1/1187 & Just 1/873" (Univ. of London Ph.D. thesis, 1991). 18. Hershey suggests that Henry in so acting ran counter to Clause 29 of the 1225 reissue of Magna Carta.
144. CPR Henry III vol 4 1247–1258, 554 & 569.
145. RG i, no.4535. "*Memorandum quod xxii die Augusti recepit dominus Michael de Fenes sigillum domini E apud Laureum montem*" or 'It is to be remembered that on the 22nd of August [1255], lord Michael de Fenes received the seal of the lord Edward at Lormont", Lormont now being a suburb of Bordeaux
146. Huw Ridgeway. 1986. "The Lord Edward and the Provisions of Oxford (1258): A Study in Faction." in Thirteenth Century England I: Proceedings of the Newcastle upon Tyne Conference 1985. Ed. Peter R. Coss & S. D. Lloyd. (Woodbridge: Boydell Press). 92.
147. Ibid. 90. Ridgeway cites the following as evidence of the shift CPR Henry III vol 4 1247–1258, 607. "Dec. 12 [1257]. Westminster. Licence for Aymer, [bishop] elect of Winchester, the king's brother, to strengthen the island of Portland, with stone and lime and to crenellate it like a castle, as he shall think most expedient. By K. in the presence of Edward his son." Here Edward is for the first time acting as a witness for a grant to Aymer de Lusignan.
148. CPR Henry III vol 4 1247–1258. 559. Pierre's business with Louis IX of France, alongside Simon de Montfort evidences a departure, on or shortly after 14 June 1257. CChR Henry III Edward I 1257–1300. 3. Pierre has returned to England by at least 18 December 1257, evidenced by the witnessing of a charter with this date.
149. Michael Prestwich. 2005. Plantagenet England 1225–1360. Oxford: Oxford University Press. 296.
150. Chron. Majora Eng, vol 3. 279–80.
151. Margaret Howell. 1998. Eleanor of Provence. Oxford: Blackwell Publishers Ltd.153. "But her [Alianor's] absorbing concern was not with reform, for which she cared little, but with plucking the Lusignans from their influence over her husband and over her son."

152. Ann. Dunstable, 203. H. W. Ridgeway. 1983. The politics of the English royal court, 1247–65, with special reference to the role of aliens. University of Oxford. 280. Margaret Howell. 1998. Eleanor of Provence. Oxford: Blackwell Publishers Ltd. 226.
153. David Carpenter. 2020. Henry III: The Rise to Power and Personal Rule 1207–1258. New Haven: Yale University Press. 696.
154. Ann. Tewkesbury, 164. "*et omnes alienigena*" or "and all foreigners".
155. Chron. Johannes Oxenedes, 203-4. "*Hos fratres suos uterinos dilexit rex Angliæ Henricus. . . Et non solum propriis parentibus donaria plurima tribuit, seipsum depauperando, verum etiam Reginæ uxoris suæ parentes, amotis Angligenis, in Angliam subrogavit.*" Or "King Henry of England loved these brothers of his womb. . . And not only did he bestow many gifts on his own relatives, impoverishing himself, but he also chose the relatives of his wife Queen, who had become Englishmen, in England."
156. CCR Henry III vol 10 1256-1259, 223-4. "*Pro militibus Burgundie.-Mandatum est Philippo Lovel, thesaurario, quod Henrico de Peiny, Willelmo de Pemes, Ricardo de Mumbiliard, Simoni de Genvyle, Johanni de Dornay, Guidoni de Rens', Baldewino de Villa, Johanni de Castellione, Petro de Chaunteny, Hugoni Espaulard et Willelmo de Puncayle, qui jam ad mandatum nostrum venerunt in Angliam pro expedicione nostra Wallie, sine dilacione habere faciat feodum suum quod eis debemus ad scaccarium nostrum, vel saltem medietatem ejusdem feodi, cuilibet eorum modis omnibus persolvi faciat ad expensas suas quibus se preparare possint ad veniendum ad regem ad instans parleamentum Oxonie, sicut rex eis mandavit, exinde cum rege in expedicionem regis Wallie progressuri: et, cum rex sciverit quantum eis liberaverit, faciet eis habere breve de Liberate ubi illud prius non habuerit. Teste rege apud Clarendon XXV. die Maii.*" Or "For the knights of Burgundy. It was ordered to Philip Lovel, the treasurer, that Henry de Peiny, Guillaume de Pesmes, Richard de Mumbiliard, Simon de Joinville, John de Dornay, Guidon de Rens', Baldewin de Villa, John de Castellion, Peter de Chaunteny, Hugh Espoulard and William de Puncayle, who have already come to England for our expedition in Wales, at our command, shall without delay have their fee which we owe them to our treasury, or at least the half of the same fee, to be paid to each of them by all means for their expenses which they that they may prepare to come to the king to the immediate parliament at Oxford, as the king commanded them, and thence to proceed with the king to the expedition of the king to Wales; Witness the king at Clarendon 25th day of May [1258]." Carpenter also notes that a related entry to these Burgundian knights is not annotated "*Pro militibus Burgundie*" but is annotated "*De militibus alieni generis*" CR Henry III vol 4 1256-1258, 297. There is indeed a change of tone, knights of foreign race as opposed to knights of Burgundy. Carpenter reads into this a tone of xenophobia, "hostility to foreigners was even expressed at the heart of the administration" however it is difficult to be certain if such an attitude is responsible for the change of language or merely an administrative style.
157. CPR Henry III vol 4 1247-1258, 632.
158. Chron. Majora Eng, vol 3. 285.
159. CPR Henry III vol 4 1247-1258, 636.
160. Ibid. 286.
161. Ibid.
162. D. A. Carpenter. 1992. King Henry III's 'Statute' Against Aliens: July 1263. The English Historical Review 107: 928.

Notes

163. Chron. Thedmar. 37-38. "*Hoc anno fuit illud insane Parlamentum apud Oxoniam, De parlamento circa festum Sancti Barnabe ; in quo Parlamento provisum fuit et ordinatum per aUquos Comites et Barones Anglie ad abolendum illas malas consuetudines quibus regnum, tempore istius Regis, tamdiu et ultra modum fuerat oppressum et grava- tum, scihcet, per eundem Regem et ahos potentissimos regni. Ad quod idem Rex, et etiam invitus, prebuit assensum et hoc juravit. Et ad hoc negotium ordinandum electi fuerunt Dominus Cantuariensis Archiepiscopus, Dominus Episcopus Wygorniensis, Dominus Rogerus Bigot Marescallus Comes Northffolchie, Dominus Ricardus de Clare Comes Glouvernie, Dominus Simon de Monteforti Comes Leicestrie, Dominus Hunfridus de Boun Comes Herfordie, Comes de Warewyk, Comes de Aibemala, Hugo de Bigot, Petrus de Saveye, Petrus de Monteforti, Rogerus de Mortuo Mari, Jacobus de Audeleye, Johannes Maunsel.*" Or In this year was held that Mad Parliament at Oxford, about the Feast of Saint Barnabas [11 June]; in which Parliament it was provided and ordained by certain Earls and Barons of England, that those bad customs should be abolished, through which the realm, in the time of this King, had been so long and so immoderately oppressed and aggrieved, and that, by this same King and others among the most powerful men in the realm. To which ordinances the King, though reluctantly, gave his assent, and made oath to that effect. And to carry out this matter, there were chosen the Lord Archbishop of Canterbury, the Lord Bishop of Worcester, Sir Roger Bigot, Marshal, [and] Earl of Norfolk, Sir Richard de Clare Earl of Gloucester, Sir Simon de Montfort Earl of Leicester, Sir Humphrey de Bohun Earl of Hereford, the Earl of Warewyk, the Earl of Albemarle, Hugh de Bigot, Peter de Savoy, Peter de Montfort, Roger de Mortimer, James de Audeleye, [and] John Mansel."
164. Chron. Thomas Wykes, 119. "*Quintus articulus omnino illicitus fuit et præcipue detestandus, videlicet, quod si quis dictis provisionibus contraire præsumeret, vel observare recusaret, hostis publicus censeretur, et quia modicum fermentum totam massam corrumpit, articulus iste totum confudit negotium.*"
165. David Carpenter. 2023. Henry III : Reform, Rebellion, Civil War, Settlement 1259-1272. London: Yale Publishing Ltd.
166. David Carpenter. 2023. Henry III : Reform, Rebellion, Civil War, Settlement 1259-1272. London: Yale Publishing Ltd.
167. John Maddicott. 2016. Who was Simon de Montfort, Earl of Leicester. Transactions of the Royal Historical Society 26: 53.
168. Chron. Majora Eng, vol 3. 287–8.
169. Ibid. 291.
170. Darren Baker. 2017. Henry III: The Great King England Never Knew It Had. Stroud: The History Press. 567–8.
171. David Carpenter. 2023. Henry III : Reform, Rebellion, Civil War, Settlement 1259-1272. London: Yale Publishing Ltd.
172. Chron. Majora Eng, vol 3. "But the king of France refused [the Lusignans staying in France], being exasperated by a complaint made against the Poitevins by the Queen of France [Marguerite], to the effect that they had shamefully scandalised and defamed her sister, the queen of England."
173. Lucy Hennings in Thirteenth Century England XVI: Proceedings of the Cambridge Conference, 2015. Eds. Andrew. M Spencer and Carl Watkins, Boydell Press. 143.

Warns against the "capacity of the Tewkesbury analyst to express anti-alien sentiment at the highest register".
174. D. A. Carpenter. 1992. King Henry III's 'Statute' Against Aliens: July 1263. The English Historical Review 107 and 927–8.
175. Chron. Majora Lat, vol 6. 405.
176. D. A. Carpenter. 1992. King Henry III's 'Statute' Against Aliens: July 1263. The English Historical Review 107. 928.
177. H. W. Ridgeway. 1983. The politics of the English royal court, 1247–65, with special reference to the role of aliens. University of Oxford. 293–4.
178. D. A. Carpenter. 1992. King Henry III's 'Statute' Against Aliens: July 1263. The English Historical Review 107. 933. "They [the Savoyards] must have viewed the accompanying xenophobia with acute unease."
179. H. Rothwell. 1975. English Historical Documents vol 3 1189–1327. (Eyre & Spottiswoode Ltd: London).
180. David Carpenter. 2004. The Struggle for Mastery : Britain 1066 - 1284. London: Penguin Books Ltd. 342 "Perhaps encouraged by this success [Pierre and Boniface de Savoie in England], in the late 1240s Henry introduced another wave of foreigners [the Lusignans].

Chapter Eight

1. His date of death is usually given as 7 February 1259, however Swiss historian Jean-Pierre Chapuisat as reported by André Perret may have a more accurate date from a contemporary source. André Perret. 1983. *Le comte Pierre II de Savoie. L'expansion savoyarde et l'alliance anglaise au xiiie siècle. Revue Savoisienne.* 111. n73. "*Thomas de Savoie, frère de Pierre de Savoie, est décédé le 8 janvier 1259 selon une attestation de sa nièce Eléonor de Provence, reine d'Angleterre. Information aimablement communiquée par M. Jean-Pierre Chapuisat d'après une inscription au dos du* Close Roll 51 *Henri III des Arch. d'Angleterre.*" Or "Thomas de Savoie, brother of Pierre de Savoie, died on January 8, 1259 according to an attestation from his niece Eléonor de Provence, Queen of England. Information kindly communicated by Mr. Jean-Pierre Chapuisat according to an inscription on the back of the Close Roll 51 Henri III des Arch. from England."
2. Chron. Majora Eng, vol 3. 324.
3. CPR Henry III vol 5 1258 -1266, 16-7 & 30.
4. Fœdera, vol 1, 237. "*UNIVERSIS CHRISTI fidelibus, praesentes literas. inspecturis vel audituris, Philippus comes Sabaudiae, salutem in Domino sempiternam. . . Quod nos attendentes fidelitatem, industriam, & sinceram dilectionem, quam idem dominus noster Rex Angliae, & domina nostra Regina, mater sua, erga nos & comitatum nostrum Sabaudiae hactenus habuerunt, ut animae nostrae saluti, & securitati corporis nostri, concordiae haeredum nostrorum, ac tranquilitati & paci totius comitatus Sabaudiae consulatur, volumus, concedimus, ac etiam ordinamus ut iidem, dominus noster Rex & domina nostra Regina, mater sua, personam haeredis nostri masculi exprimant & declarent; quem, per ipsos haeredem nostrum nominatum, decernimus fore comitem Sabaudyae post decessum nostrum, qui & nobis succedat in omnibus pleno jure: salvis competentibus portionibus aliis nepotibus nostris masculis, ad quos pertinet aliquid*

ex successione nostra praedicta, prout ipsis domino nostro Regi, & dominae nostrae Reginae, matri suae, videbitur expedire... Dat' apud Russilyon, die Lunae proxima post festem Sancti Lucae Ewangelistae, anno Domini MCCLXXXIV." Or "To all the faithful of Christ, present letters. Philip, count of Savoy, peace in the Lord forever ... Considering us the fidelity, diligence, and sincere love which our lord the King of England, and our lady the Queen, his mother, have hitherto had towards us and our company of Savoy, for the safety of our souls, and the safety of our bodies, the concord of our heirs, and for the tranquility and peace of the whole county of Savoy, we will, grant, and even order that the same, our lord the King and our lady the Queen, their mother, express and declare the person of our male heir; whom, having been named our heir by them, we decree that he shall be the Count of Sabaudia after our decease, who shall succeed us in all things by full right, with the exception of competent portions to our other male nephews, to whom something of our aforesaid succession belongs, according to them, our lord the King, and our lady of our Queen, his mother, it will be seen to be expedien ... Given at Russilyon, on the Monday next after the feast of St. Luke the Evangelist, in the year of the Lord 1284."

5. I. J. Sanders. 1951. The Texts of the Peace of Paris, 1259. The English Historical Review 66: 81. "The background for a peaceful settlement between England and France was created by the marriages which the four daughters of Raymond Berengar IV, count of Provence, made with Henry and his brother Richard of Cornwall, with Louis IX and his brother Charles of Anjou."
6. CCR Henry III vol 9 1254–1256, 196. And I. J. Sanders. 1951. The Texts of the Peace of Paris, 1259. The English Historical Review 66: 84. n2. "As early as 10 May 1255 there were preliminary negotiations for peace with France, for on that date Henry wrote to Peter of Savoy stating that the king of Castile had suggested that peace be made with Louis. Henry said that he was willing to do this and Peter was ordered to join Simon de Montfort in negotiations with the French."
7. CPR Henry III vol 4 1247–1258, 546.
8. I. J. Sanders. 1951. The Texts of the Peace of Paris, 1259. The English Historical Review 66: 84.
9. Chron. Majora Eng, 327.
10. I. J. Sanders. 1951. The Texts of the Peace of Paris, 1259. The English Historical Review 66: 90.
11. CPR Henry III vol 5 1258–1266, 8–29. "May 24. Windsor. Power to Margaret, queen of France, R. earl of Gloucester and Hertford, P. de Sabaudia and J. Mansel to treat of a marriage between John first-born son of J. count of Brittany, and Béatrice the king's daughter; and the king will ratify what they do."
12. Wurstemberger, vol 4. No 527. *"Johannis, Ducis Britannia, renunciatio in Comitatum Richemundia. 1259. Decembris 13. Parisiis. A toz ceaus qui ces letres uerront ou oyrunt Jehan dux de Bretangne saluz Sachent tutt que nos auons quitte et quittons a Henry par la grace de Dieu Roy d'Engletere et a ses hoirs por nos et por nos hoirs tot le droit que nos cla mions on poions clamer par nule maniere de raison en la Conte de Richemund oue ses apertenances. par leschange que le deuant dit Rois de Englete' nos a fait por la deuant dite Conte de Richemund si come il est contenu en lescrit fet entre le deuan dit Rois et nos en forme de Cyrografe que est saele de son seel et dou nostre dont il a lune partie saele de nostre seel et nos lautre saele de son seel et en testmoin de ce nos auons mis nostre seel a cest escrit Ce fu fet a paris le samedi prochain a pres la feste saint*

Nicholas Lan de lincarnation nostre Seignor. mille. CC. Cinquante noef. Invent Chart Sabaud. Fasc. 1. Convol. 4. Ch. N°. 96."
13. Wurstemberger, vol 4. No 531.
14. H. W. Ridgeway. 1983. The politics of the English royal court, 1247–65, with special reference to the role of aliens. University of Oxford. 334.
15. André Perret. 1983. *Le comte Pierre II de Savoie. L'expansion savoyarde et l'alliance anglaise au xiiie siècle. Revue Savoisienne* 111.
16. A. and W. Galignani, 1825. The History of Paris, from the Earliest Period to the Present Day. Vol II. A. and W. Galignani: Paris. 221–2.
17. David Carpenter. 2005. The Meetings of Kings Henry III and Louis IX in Thirteenth Century England X: Proceedings of the Durham Conference, 2003. Eds Michael Prestwich, Michael Britnell & Robin Frame (Boydell and Brewer: Woodbridge). 9.
18. P. Chaplais. 1952. The Making of the Treaty of Paris (1259) and the Royal Style. The English Historical Review 67: 235–53.
19. I. J. Sanders. 1951. The Texts of the Peace of Paris, 1259. The English Historical Review 66: 92. n5. "Clause 1. Louis made a free gift to Henry of all rights which he, Louis, possessed in fief and demesne in the diocese of Cahors, Limoges, and Perigueux. Clause 2. Agenais to be given to Henry if the province escheats to the French Crown on the death of Jeanne, daughter of Raymond VII of Toulouse and wife of Alfonse of Poitiers brother of Louis IX. In the meantime, Louis would pay Henry an annual rent equal to the annual value of the Agenais and if the territory fell to another lord, and not to the French Crown, the rent and the lord's homage would be paid to Henry. Clause 3. Quercy, terms similar to Agenais if Henry could show that Richard I had given this land to his sister Joanna when she married Raymond VI of Toulouse of whom Jeanne, wife of Alfonse of Poitiers, was the heiress. Clause 4. Henry's interest in Saintonge, south of the R. Charente, was recognised and his possession was secured as far as possible after the death of Alfonse of Poitiers. Henry was to do due homage and service as peer of France and as duke of Aquitaine."
20. David Carpenter. 2005. The Meetings of Kings Henry III and Louis IX In Thirteenth Century England X: Proceedings of the Durham Conference, 2003. Eds Michael Prestwich, Michael Britnell & Robin Frame. 12.
21. Ibid. 13.
22. "*Petrus Thomae F. Henrico III Britanniæ Rege ad Ludovicum IX. Interpres Paciis in Galliam Profectus.*" Appears beneath a recreation of the act of homage. Whatever the contemporary thoughts on the Treaty of Paris in 1259 and those of historians since, it is as a man who brought peace to France that Pierre II de Savoie is remembered today at Hautecombe Abbey.
23. David Carpenter. 2004. The Struggle for Mastery : Britain 1066 - 1284. London: Penguin Books Ltd. 338.
24. P. Chaplais. 1952. The Making of the Treaty of Paris (1259) and the Royal Style. The English Historical Review 67: 248.
25. Björn Weiler. 2001. Henry III and the Sicilian Business: a reinterpretation*. Historical Research 74: 137.
26. I. J. Sanders. 1951. The Texts of the Peace of Paris, 1259. The English Historical Review 66: 93.
27. David Carpenter. 2005. The Meetings of Kings Henry III and Louis IX In Thirteenth Century England X: Proceedings of the Durham Conference, 2003. Eds Michael Prestwich, Michael Britnell & Robin Frame. 20.

Notes

28. Alison Weir. 2020. *Queens of the Crusades: Eleanor of Aquitaine and her Successors*. London: Penguin Random House UK. 597.
29. Eugene L. Cox. 1974. *The Eagles of Savoy: The House of Savoy in Thirteenth Century Europe*. Princeton: Princeton University Press. 270.
30. Ibid.
31. add to carpenters book
32. Wurstemberger, vol 4. No 526.
33. Eugene L. Cox. 1974. *The Eagles of Savoy: The House of Savoy in Thirteenth Century Europe*. Princeton: Princeton University Press. 297.
34. *La Finanza Sabauda*, vol 1. 16. "*Domino Enrico de Bono Vilair castellano de Rota.*"
35. Bernard Andenmatten. 2005. *La maison de Savoie et la noblesse vaudoise (XIIIe–XIVe s.), Société d'histoire de la Suisse romande*.
36. P.M.L de Charrière. 1866. *Les Dynastes de Grandson jusqu'au XIIIe siècle* (Lausanne), 109, 111, 116–17 and 119; *Cartulaire de Roumainmôtier (XIIe siècle)*. 1998. ed. A. Pahud, *Cahiers Lausannois d'Histoire Médiévale*, xxi (Lausanne), nos. 73 and 75.
37. Montfaucon lay in the *Franche Comté de Bourgogne* (Free County of Burgundy) just over 4 miles (7 kilometres) southeast of Besançon in the valley of the river Doubs.
38. Eugene Mottaz. 1900. *Note sur la construction du château d'Yverdon. Revue historique vaudoise* 361.
39. Wurstemberger, vol 1. 487. "*Es kam an ein Schiedgericht, in welchem Humbert von Golens und Gottfried von Grand mont, damals Herr von La Sarra, am 26. April 1260 folgen den Entscheid ertheilten. Amadeus von Montfaucon tritt an Petern ab, um den Preis von fünfhundert Vienneserpfunden, all sein herrschaftliches Recht auf Burg und Stadt Iverden, auf den Lauf des Flusses, und die darin befindlichen Mühlen, welche sonst Jordan von Beaumont und dem Grafen von Erlach 2) gehörten: doch soll Peter die Durchfahrt der auf der Zihl von Orbe nach dem Neuenburgersee herunterkom menden Schiffe nicht verhindern dürfen: er mag wohl ein Schleusenthor in den Fluss setzen, das aber eröffnet werden soll, so oft dergleichen Schiffe daher kommen*" Or "It came to an arbitration court, in which Humbert von Golens and Gottfried von Grandmont, then Lord of La Sarra, issued the decision on April 26, 1260. Amadeus of Montfaucon cedes to Peter, for the price of five hundred Livres Viennois, all his sovereign rights to the castle and town of Yverdon, on the course of the river, and the mills located there, which otherwise belonged to Jordan von Beaumont and the Count of Erlach: but Peter should not be allowed to prevent the passage of the ships coming down the Zihl from Orbe to Lake Neuchâtel: he may put a sluice gate in the river, but it should be opened whenever such ships come along.)"
40. RG i No. 2870. "*Pro Ricardo de Muntbeliardo. Mandatum est Rogero Scissori et Bonato Lumbardi quod Ricardo de Munbeliardo et quatuor militibus suis habere faciant robas contra Natale Domini, scilicet eiden Ricardo tres pecias, et Henrico de Paymy et quatuor sociis suis robas: seilicet eidem Henrico tres pecias, et Willielmo de Pesmes et duobus militibus sociis suis robas, scilicet eidem Willielmo tres pecias. of Simoni de Greenvilla et duobus militibus sociis suis robas, scilicet eidem Simoni tres pecias. T. ut s*" Or "2870. For Richard of Muntbeliardo. It was ordered to Roger Scissors and Bonato Lumbardi that Richard de Munbeliardo and four of his soldiers should have clothes against the Christmas of the Lord, that is to say Richard three pieces, and Henry de Paymy and his four companions clothes: immediately the same Henry three pieces, and William de Pesmes and two to the

soldiers of his allies, namely, three pieces of wood for the same William. of Simon de Greenville and two of his fellow soldiers, namely, three pieces of property to the same Simon. T. as s'."

41. M. F. de Gingins La Sarra. 1857. *Recherches Historiques sur les Acquisitions des Sires de Montfaucon et de la Maison de Chalons dans le Pays de Vaud*. Lausanne: Georges Bridel Éditeur. 14-5.

42. M. F. de Gingins La Sarra. 1857. *Recherches Historiques sur les Acquisitions des Sires de Montfaucon et de la Maison de Chalons dans le Pays de Vaud*. Lausanne: Georges Bridel Éditeur. 47. "*L'ascendant grandissant de Pierre de Savoie dans le Pays-de-Vaud et les troubles domestiques qui divisaient la maison souveraine de Franche-Comté laissaient peu de chances au sire de Montfaucon de résister avec succès aux entreprises audacieuses de ce redoutable concurrent. Amédée dut se décider à s'entendre avec lui. Des arbitres ont été nommés de part et d'autre pour régler les conditions d'hébergement.*" Or "The growing ascendancy of Pierre de Savoie in the Pays-de-Vaud and the domestic troubles which divided the sovereign house of Franche-Comté left little chance for the Sire de Montfaucon to successfully resist the audacious undertakings of this formidable competitor. Amédée had to make up his mind to come to terms with him. Arbitrators have been appointed on both sides to settle the accommodation conditions."

43. M. F. de Gingins La Sarra. 1857. *Recherches Historiques sur les Acquisitions des Sires de Montfaucon et de la Maison de Chalons dans le Pays de Vaud*. Lausanne: Georges Bridel Éditeur. 61.

44. Eugene Mottaz. 1900. *Note sur la construction du château d'Yverdon. Revue historique vaudoise*. 216.

45. Wurstemberger, vol 1. 488.

46. Victor Van Bechem. 1913. *La "ville neuve" d'Yverdon: Foundation de Pierre de Savoie. Festgabe fur Gerold Meyer von Kronau*. 213.

47. Justin Favrod. 2000. *La nécropole du Pré de la Cure à Yverdon-Les-Bains. Cahiers d'Archéologie Romande*. "*Nous en voulons pour preuve l'Acte de fondation de 1260 qui évoque les anciens habitants, les «homes de Everdunè et prévoit que leur droits seront respectés: il en sera pour eux comme il en était auparavant, «ensi comme il ont use ca en arriers»*."

48. Cluse translating as transverse valley.

49. Eugene L. Cox. 1974. The Eagles of Savoy: The House of Savoy in Thirteenth Century Europe. Princeton: Princeton University Press.197-8, n69. Cox citing Wurstemberger notes that this suzerainty excepted the valuable péage and castle itself, which Amauri reserved to the Count de Bourgogne but a promise was made that when the count might die, Amauri would have to seek Pierre's permission to do homage to a new count. The position became somewhat moot when Pierre's brother Philippe married the widow of the Count de Bourgogne on his death in any case.

50. Fœdera, 588. *De homagio Othonis com. Palatini Burgundia*. A. D. 1281 . "*Nos Otho comes palatinus Burgondiæ, & dominus Salinen' notum facimus universis præsentas litteras inspecturis, quod nos tenemus, in feodo & in homagio, ab excellentissimo viro, domino Edwardo, divina gratia, Rege Angliæ, Duce Aquitaniæ, & principe Dirlande, pontarliam, & castellaniam, & pediagium ejusdem loci, & totum illud quod habemus en Veras, cum apenditiis eorumdem. Item Calamontem, & Joygne, & la Chandarlie, cum suis pertinentiis*

universis, prout tenet a nobis Johannes de Cabilone, avunculus noster. Item castrum de Jou, cum suis appenditiis, prout dictus Johannes de Cabilone, avunculus noster, tenet a nobilis ariere feodum. Et prædicta omnia confitemur, & recognoscimus nos tenere a dicto domino Rege in feodo & homagio, secundum quod est expressum; salva fidelitate nostrorum dominorum. In quorum testimonium damus & concedimus dicto domino Regi præsentes litteras, nostro sigillo sigillatas. Dat' Lugd' anno Domini MCCLXXXI. Mense Januarii."

51. Daniel de Raemy. 2004. *Châteaux, donjons et grandes tours dans les Etats de Savoie (1230–1330)*. Lausanne: Cahiers d'archéologie romande 98 et 99. 27 & 35.
52. It had been suggested by Eugene Mottaz that the great tower or donjon at Yverdon pre-existed the work carried out for Pierre de Savoie, as cited in Eugene Mottaz. 1900. *Note sur la construction du château d'Yverdon*. Revue historique vaudoise 362. But archaeological work in 1943 has subsequently been discounted as cited in Daniel de Raemy. 2004. *Châteaux, donjons et grandes tours dans les Etats de Savoie (1230–1330)*. Lausanne: Cahiers d'archéologie romande 98 et 99. 27.
53. Ibid, 298.
54. Daniel de Raemy. 2004. *Châteaux, donjons et grandes tours dans les Etats de Savoie (1230–1330)*. Lausanne: Cahiers d'archéologie romande 98 et 99. 42.
55. Arnold Taylor. 1985. Studies in Castles and Castle-Building. London: The Hambledon Press. 39.
56. *La Finanza Sabauda*, vol 1. 63. "*Compotus de Valeisio et Chablasio de anno LXI* "*Item in liberatione magistri Iohannis cementarii a die qua recessit a domo sua veniendo versus Yverdunum, videlicet prima die maii hoc anno [1 May 1261] usque ad secundam dominicam quadragisime, videlicet quintam diem intrante marcio [5 March 1262], per quadraginta et quatuor septimanas, qui cepit duodecim solidos qualibet septimana, xxvj.lib. ij.sol. In liberatione magistri Iacobi filii sui per idem tempus, capientis singulis septimanis decem solidos et sex denarios, xxiij.lib. ij.sol. In vadiis suis et calciatura sua et pannis lineis, capientis quinque solidos per mensem, per dictum tempus .lv.sol. In medicinis ipsius magistri Jacobi tempore egritudinis sue. xxv.sol. In liberatione magistri Petri Mainier custodis operum domini per idem tempus pro se duobus equis et uno valeto suo capientis ut predictus magister Iohannes. Xxvj.lib. viij.sol.*"
57. *La Finanza Sabauda*, vol 1. 118. "*In acquietancia magistri Jacobi cementarii hoc anno preterito ... qui Jacobus percipit [sc apud] Yverdunum de domino in feudo decem libras viannensium singulis annis.xv.lib.*"
58. *La Finanza Sabauda*, vol 1. 73. "*Magistro Jacobo lathomo, .x.lib.*"
59. Eugene L. Cox. 1974. The Eagles of Savoy: The House of Savoy in Thirteenth Century Europe. Princeton: Princeton University Press. 298.
60. Ibid. 298, n69.
61. Minutes of Evidence Taken Before the Committee for Privileges ... to Determine the Abeyance of the Barony of Grandison. 1854. House of Lords: London. 169 "*Nos Agnès, domina de Grandisono, tutrix legitima liberorum nostrorum Petri et Willelini, Girardus, Jaquetus et Henricus, pro se et fratre suo Otonino, filii predicte domine.*"
62. Wurstemberger, vol 1. 489.
63. *Memoires Et Documents de la Societe D'Histoire et D'Archéologie de Genève*. Vol 7. 1849. Genève , Chez Jullien Frères , Libraires - Éditeurs. 312-3. [4th May 1259] . . . "*Actum London . presentibus istis testibus ... Ebalo de Montibus , et Petro Chanvenz militibus , Girardo de Granzano canonico Lugdun . , mag . Grassino , Guidone De*

Montagniaco et Aymone de Vercerio cleri cis , Petro Moutum de Foschie et Hugone de Ferteyns . Et ego Galga nus de Verul ... notarius." And [12th May 1259] "Symonis de Joinvilla Dni . de Jaz , Petri de Chanvenz , Galfredi de Grandimonte et D. Joffredi de Amaisyns militum , et Girardi de Granzon canonici Lug . dun . et Symonis de Vercers canonici Geben . , qui omnes vocati et ro gali interfuerunt omnibus supradictis . Datum London."

64. David Carpenter. 2023. Henry III : Reform, Rebellion, Civil War, Settlement 1259-1272. London: Yale Publishing Ltd.
65. Wurstemberger, vol 1. 510.
66. Ibid. 511.
67. David Carpenter. 2023. Henry III : Reform, Rebellion, Civil War, Settlement 1259-1272. London: Yale Publishing Ltd.
68. Darren Baker. 2017. *Henry III: The Great King England Never Knew It Had.* Stroud: The History Press. 608.
69. David Carpenter. 2023. Henry III : Reform, Rebellion, Civil War, Settlement 1259-1272. London: Yale Publishing Ltd.
70. Clive H. Knowles. "Savoy, Boniface of" Oxford Dictionary of National Biography. 23 Sep. 2004; Accessed 11 May 2022.
71. H. W. Ridgeway. 1983. The politics of the English royal court, 1247–65, with special reference to the role of aliens. University of Oxford. 358.
72. E. B. Fryde, D. E. Greenway, S. Porter & I. Roy. 1986. Handbook of British Chronology. Third ed. London: Offices of the Royal Historical Society. 229. CPR Henry III vol 3 1232–1247, 258.
73. H. W. Ridgeway. 1983. The politics of the English royal court, 1247–65, with special reference to the role of aliens. University of Oxford. 377–8.
74. D. A. Carpenter. 1992. English Peasants in Politics 1258–1267. Past and Present August: 35–6.
75. E. F. Jacob. 1925. Studies in the Period of Baronial Reform and Rebellion 1258-1267. Oxford: Clarendon Press. 355-66.
76. A. H. Hershey, "An Introduction to and an Edition of the Hugh Bigod Eyre Rolls, June 1258–February 1259: PRO Just 1/1187 & Just 1/873" (Univ. of London Ph.D. thesis, 1991). Pierre's defence was that Eudo of Timperley and the other men from the manor of Witley could not have action (*via a querela*) against him as sokeman of ancient demesne (B 105) because the manor was not ancient demesne of the crown but a holding of the barony of Eagle. Ibid. 472. B105.(T, is is to be discussed) Eudo of Timperley and other men of Witley, which was the ancient demesne of the king and his predecessors, kings of England, complain against Peter of Savoy that, after the present king gave him this manor some 5 years ago, Peter unjustly increased their rent by 18 pounds, 7 shillings and 6 pence per year. [This was] more than his ancestors were accustomed to render during the time when the manor was in the hand of the king and his predecessors, kings of England. This is determined by the jurors of the country. Since Peter is not here, so a day is given them on the morrow of the Purification of the Blessed Mary [3 February] at the parliament. Then justice will be done thereon. Afterwards, at the stated term, Peter comes and says that Eudo and his men of Witley are not able to have action against him as sokemen of ancient demesne. Since, he says that the manor of Wiley was never the crown's demesne, rather it belonged to the barony of Eagle which was once the king's

escheat of the lands of the Normans and which the king gave him. On this he places himself on the book called Domesday. The book is examined, in which it is discovered that Gilbert son of Richer del Eagle held Wiley, which [manor] Earl Godwin had held, and was then valued at 20 hides and later in Gilbert's time at 12. There was land for 16 ploughs, two in demesne, 37 villeins and 3 cottars who held the remainder. So it is adjudged that Eudo and the others take nothing by this complaint, but they are in mercy for false claim. Peter is without a day."

77. Adam Marsh (2006–2010). Lawrence, C. H. (ed.). The Letters of Adam Marsh. Oxford University Press. 336-7.
78. H. W. Ridgeway. 1983. The politics of the English royal court, 1247–65, with special reference to the role of aliens. University of Oxford. 379–80.
79. C. L. Kingsford. 2018. The Song of Lewes. Forgotten Books: London.
80. The leopard carried some symbolic meaning; it was thought to be the result of an adulterous union between a lion and a mythical beast called a 'pard' (hence leo-pard).
81. Stephen Church. 2017. Henry III: A Simple and God-Fearing King. London: Penguin Random House. 62–3.
82. C. J. Spurgeon. 1978/79. Builth Castle. Brycheiniog 18: 53.
83. Ibid.
84. J. Beverley Smith. 2014. Llywellyn ap Gruffudd: Prince of Wales. Cardiff: The University of Wales Press. 209–11.
85. Robert C.Stacey. "Mansel, John" Oxford Dictionary of National Biography. 23 Sep. 2004; Accessed 11 Mar. 2023.
86. David Carpenter. 2023. Henry III : Reform, Rebellion, Civil War, Settlement 1259-1272. London: Yale Publishing Ltd.
87. TNA SC 7/3/29.
88. Clive H. Knowles. "Savoy, Boniface of" Oxford Dictionary of National Biography. 23 Sep. 2004; Accessed 11 May 2022.
89. Ann. Dunstable. 217 *"Quo audito, Simon de Monteforti Angliam reliquit, dicens se sine terra malle mori, quam perjurus a veritate recedere."* Or "On hearing this, Simon de Montfort left England, saying that he preferred to die without land, rather than an perjurer to depart from the truth."
90. H. W. Ridgeway. 2016. "What Happened in 1261?" in Baronial Reform and Revolution in England, 1258–1267. Ed. Adrian Jobson. 2016. Baronial Reform and Revolution in England, 1258–1267. (Boydell and Brewer: Woodbridge). 96.
91. H. W. Ridgeway. 1983. The politics of the English royal court, 1247–65, with special reference to the role of aliens. University of Oxford. 390. Chron. Oseney. 128. *"Dissensio inter dominum regem et barones Angliæ, quia rex per consilium Johannis Maunsel et Roberti Walrandi et Petri de Sauveya."* Ann. Londonsienses. 57. *"Quia ab illo tempore Edwardus filius regis blanditus per matrem."*
92. Michael Carter. 2017. Hailes Abbey. London: English Heritage. 10.
93. Nancy Goldstone. 2010. Four Queens: The Provençal Sisters Who Ruled Europe. London: The Orion Publishing Group.
94. William Stubbs. 1896. The Constitutional History of England. Oxford: The Clarendon Press. 88.
95. Clive H. Knowles. "Savoy, Boniface of" Oxford Dictionary of National Biography. 23 Sep. 2004; Accessed 11 May 2022.

96. Stephen Church. 2017. Henry III: A Simple and God-Fearing King. London: Penguin Random House. 67.
97. CChR Henry III Edward I vol 2 1257–1300, 42. "June 8 [1262] Westminster. Whereas Edward, the king's son, in the king's presence, restored to the king for the behoof of Peter de Sabaudia, the king's uncle, the honour, castle and rape of Hastings, co. Sussex, with the lands late of Walter de Scoteny, with the knights' fees and advowsons of churches and prebends, and with the service of the fee of one knight in Turrok, co. Essex, which Bartholomew de Briencun holds of the said honour; gift of the foregoing to the said Peter, his heirs and assigns, in lieu of the manors of Redenhal, co. Norfolk, and Wisset, Ketelberge, Nettlested and Wikes under Ipswich, co. Suffolk, with 4l. 13s. receivable in Ipswich, all part of the honour of Richemund, which the king had given to the said Peter, who has restored them to the king for the behoof of the said Edward; so that the said Peter, his heirs and assigns, shall hold the said honour, castle and rape of Hastings, as above, from the king by the service due therefrom, provided that if the king wish to restore them to the right heirs of his free will or by a peace or in any other way, he shall not disseise the said Peter, his heirs or assigns, until have made a proper exchange to the value of the said honour and rape with any improvement (apropiamento) he may have made therein." H. W. Ridgeway. 2016. "What Happened in 1261." In Baronial Reform and Revolution in England, 1258–1267. Ed. Adrian Jobson. (Boydell and Brewer: Woodbridge). 97. Ridgeway TNA C47/9/1. "12. Charter of Henry III, 15 September 1262, St. Germain, ratification: Lord Edward, in king's presence, quitclaimed to Peter and heirs honor, rape and castle of Hastings, together with escheat late of Walter de Scotney and service of one knight in Thurrock, co. Essex, pertaining to the honor, in exchange for one manor in co. Norfolk and four in Suffolk surrendered by Peter from the honor of Richmond. Tenure of Hastings is guaranteed by the king to Peter and heirs: there will be no disseisin without legal process and reasonable exchange. [Dorse note:] *Duplicate charter found dated St Germain, 18 September 1262, with* [unspecified] *changes.* [Almost certainly as: *CPR 1266-72*, p. 733 which adds details of compensation for Peter's improvements to Hastings castle]."
98. CCR Henry III vol 12 1261–1264, 131. "*Rex dilecto avunculo suo Petro de Sabaudia salutem. Cum pro urgentibus negociis nostris cum illustri rege Francie expediendis, sicut nostis, oporteat nos esse Parisius in festo Beati Petri ad Vincula proximo venturo, ubi presencia vestra plurimum indigemus; vobis mandamus rogantes in fide et dileccione quibus nobis tenemini quod omnibus aliis pretermissis nobis occurratis ibidem. Et hoc sicut de vobis confidimus nullatenus omittatis scituri quod, si hoc faciendum nequaquam duxeritis, statim, cum de hoc nobis constiterit, ad partes Anglie infecto negocio revertemur, aut presenciam vestram in partibus ubi fueritis personaliter requiremus. Teste ut supra.*"
99. CPR Henry III vol 5 1258–1266, 214. "June 2 [1262]. Westminster.The like for Peter de Sabaudia going as the king's envoy beyond seas. June 3. Westminster.Grant to the said Peter that the queen and Gwichard de Charron may nominate attorneys in his name in all pleas moved for or against him before justices in eyre or others; for three years from the feast of Holy Trinity."
100. H. W. Ridgeway. 1983. The politics of the English royal court, 1247–65, with special reference to the role of aliens. University of Oxford. 62. n2.

Notes

101. CCR Henry III vol 10 1256-1259, 329. CPR Henry III vol 4 1247-1258, 645. During Henry's other journeys north (1244, 1251, 1255), Peter was abroad.
102. David Carpenter. 2023. Henry III : Reform, Rebellion, Civil War, Settlement 1259-1272. London: Yale Publishing Ltd.
103. David Carpenter. 2005. The Meetings of Kings Henry III and Louis IX in Thirteenth Century England X: Proceedings of the Durham Conference, 2003. Eds Michael Prestwich, Michael Britnell & Robin Frame. 24.
104. Jean-Pierre Chapuisat. 1964. *Au service de deux rois d'Angleterre, au XIIIe siècle: Pierre de Champvent. Revue Historique Vaudoise* 72: 163. Citing "Calendar of Patent Rolls Henry III C 66/78 memb 1".
105. David Carpenter. 2005. The Meetings of Kings Henry III and Louis IX In Thirteenth Century England X: Proceedings of the Durham Conference, 2003. Eds Michael Prestwich, Michael Britnell & Robin Frame. 24.
106. Ibid. 25–6. And his n 122 relating the story's source to Rymer. "Rymer's copy is BL, Add. MS 4573, fols 57r–58v, a reference I owe to Nicholas Vincent (see his Holy Blood, 36 and n. 18). The story has been printed twice: *Lettres des Rois, Reines ... des Cours de France et Angleterre*, ed. M. Champollion-Figeac (Paris, 1839), 1, 140–2, and '*Historiola de pietate* Regis Henrici, AD 1259', ed. E.A. Bond, Archaeological J. 17 (1860). Champollion-Figeac placed the episode in 1262."
107. William Stubbs. 1896. The Constitutional History of England. Oxford: The Clarendon Press. 89.
108. M.T. Clanchy. 1997. Early Medieval England. Seventh ed. London: The Folio Society.199.
109. Ann. Dunstable, 219.
110. J. Beverley Smith. 2014. Llywellyn ap Gruffudd: Prince of Wales. Cardiff: The University of Wales Press. 248–53.
111. Ibid. 255.
112. Ann. Cestrienses, 84. "*Eodem Lewelinus filius Griffini et G. fil Madoci de mandate baronum castrum de Dissard obsederunt per quinque septimanas. Et pridie festum Sancti Oswaldi regis et martyris illud obtinentes in terram prostrevarunt.*" Or "At [1263] the same time Llewclin, the son of Griffin, by the command of the barons, besieged the castle of Disserth during five weeks, and having captured it the day before the feast of S. Oswald, king and martyr [4 August], they razed it to the ground."
113. CPR Henry III vol 5 1258–1266, 280.
114. Ibid, 276.
115. Ann. Cestrienses, 84. "*Cannocum. Pridie festum Sancti Michaelis majores servientes domini Edwardi degeneres et imbelles castrum Lewelino reddiderunt.*" Or "Gannoch. The day before the feast of S. Michael [28 September 1263] the chief servants of the lord Edward, degenerate and unwarlike men, surrendered the castle [of GannochJ to Llewelin."
116. D. A. Carpenter. 1992. King Henry III's 'Statute' Against Aliens: July 1263. The English Historical Review 107: 929. "According to the chronicle of the London alderman, Arnold fitz Thedmar, 'before Pentecost' [20 May], these dissidents sent a letter to the King, under the seal of Roger of Clifford, asking him (*petentes ipsum*) to keep the Provisions."
117. T. Stapleton Ed. DeAntiquis Legibus Liber. Cronica Maiorum et Vice (Camden Soc., I846), 54. MS: Corporation of London Record Office, Custumal I, fols. 84b–8.

118. Ann. Dunstable, 221. "*Eodem anno, circa festum Sancti Marci evangelistae, venit Simon de Monteforti in Angliam.*" Or "In the same year [1263], about the feast of Saint Mark the Evangelist [25th April], Simon de Montefort came to England."
119. Ibid. "*et congregati sunt ad parliamentum apud Oxoniam, rege et concilio suo ignorantibus*" or and they gathered to the parliament at Oxford, unknown to the king and his council."
120. Ibid. 222. The Royalist leaning chronicler Wykes described this group as "the young boys of England. . . like melting wax, malleable to any form." Chron. Wykes, 133-4. "*junioribus Angliæ ... quos vere et autonomatice pueros nominare possumus, qui tanquam cera liquescens ductiles ad quamlibet formam.*" Or "to the young boys of England ... whom we can truly and autonomously call children, who, like melting wax, are malleable to any form."
121. Julia Barrow. 2000. Æthelstan to Aigueblanche in Hereford Cathedral. Ed. Gerald Alymer and John Tillier. The Hambledon Press: London. 46.
122. Flores Historiarum, 256.
123. Clive H. Knowles. "Savoy, Boniface of" Oxford Dictionary of National Biography. 23 Sep. 2004; Accessed 11 May 2022.
124. Susan Stewart. 2013. Royal Justice in Surrey 1258-1269. Woking: Surrey Record Society. 51. No 89.
125. David Carpenter. 2023. Henry III : Reform, Rebellion, Civil War, Settlement 1259-1272. London: Yale Publishing Ltd.
126. David Carpenter. 2023. Henry III : Reform, Rebellion, Civil War, Settlement 1259-1272. London: Yale Publishing Ltd.
127. David Carpenter. 2023. Henry III : Reform, Rebellion, Civil War, Settlement 1259-1272. London: Yale Publishing Ltd.
128. Lisa Hilton. 2008. Queens Consort: England's Medieval Queens. London: Weidenfeld & Nicolson. 212–13
129. Darren Baker. 2017. Henry III: The Great King England Never Knew It Had. Stroud: The History Press. 659.
130. David Carpenter. 2023. Henry III : Reform, Rebellion, Civil War, Settlement 1259-1272. London: Yale Publishing Ltd.
131. CPR Henry III vol 5 1258–1266, 269–70.
132. Ann. Dunstable, 224.
133. Stephen Church. 2017. Henry III: A Simple and God-Fearing King. London: Penguin Random House. 72.
134. Darren. Baker. 2017. Henry III: The Great King England Never Knew It Had. Stroud: The History Press. 658.
135. Flores Historiarum, ii, 481. "*Nam quicunque Anglicum idioma loqui nesciret, vilipenderetur a vulgo et despectui haberetur.*"
136. Ann. Waverley, 349. "*MCCLVIII. Tot alienigenæ diversarum linguarum jam per plures annos multiplicati erant in Anglia, tot redditibus, terris, villis, et cæteris facultatibus ditati, quod Anglicos, quasi se inferiores, maximo contemptui habebant. Ferebatur vero a nonnullis, qui secreta ipsorum noverant, quod si potestas eorum procederet, omnes majores Angliæ veneno extinguerent, regeque Henrico regno privato, loco ipsius alium ad suum arbitrium constituerent, et sic demum totam Angliam suæ ditioni perpetuo subjugarent.*" Or "1258. So many foreigners of

different languages had already multiplied in England for many years, and had been enriched with so many incomes, lands, towns, and other resources, that they had the greatest contempt for the English, as if they were their inferiors. It was said by some who knew their secrets, that if their power should proceed, they would extinguish all the nobles of England by poison, and deprive King Henry of his kingdom, and in his place set up another at their discretion, and thus in the end subjugate the whole of England to their dominion for ever. Also four brothers of the lord the king, namely Aylmerus elected of Winton, William count of Wales, Guido and Geoffrey, before the rest."

137. Lisa Hilton. 2008. Queens Consort: England's Medieval Queens. London: Weidenfeld & Nicolson. 210.
138. David Carpenter. 2004. The Struggle for Mastery : Britain 1066 - 1284. London: Penguin Books Ltd. 354.
139. Darren Baker. 2017. Henry III: The Great King England Never Knew It Had. Stroud: The History Press. 659.
140. M. Le Gallais. 1860. *Histoire de la Savoie et Piémont. Ad Mame et Cie, Imprimeurs – Librairies.*Tours. 69. "*si la loi d'aînesse avait été régulièrement observée*" Or "if the law of primogeniture had been regularly observed."
141. Daniel de Raemy. 2004. *Châteaux, donjons et grandes tours dans les Etats de Savoie (1230–1330). Lausanne: Cahiers d'archéologie romande* 98 et 99. 172.
142. Arnold Taylor. 1985. Studies in Castles and Castle-Building. London: The Hambledon Press. 9–10.
143. *La Finanza Sabauda.* vol 1. 26. "*Idem libravit Francisco cementario pro tascheria nove camere iuxta turrim et Conteis.*" And 58–9 "*De quibus libravit Francisco cementario de taschia .viii.xx. et .x.librarum et duabus robis de quadraginta sol. pro turre de Sallon facienda de sexaginta et decem pedibus altitudinis tam in grosso muro quam in avante pedibus et in merlis, de duodecim pedibus pissitudinis usque ad primam travaturam et decem pedibus a secunda travatura superius. x. lib.*" And Ibid. 68 "*Idem libravit Francisco ... pro turre de Sallon ... Idem libravit ... apud Brignon.*"
144. Louis Blondel. 1949. *Le Château de Brignon. Vallesia* IV. 19–34.
145. Louis Blondel. 1935. *L'architecture militaire au temps de Pierre II de Savoie: Les donjons circulaires.* 290. Blondel gave Mézos in Gascony as the possible origin for Jean de Mésoz. Subsequently accepted by Arnold Taylor.1989. *Master Bertram, Ingeniator Regis.* Studies in Medieval History presented to R. Allen Brown. (Boydell and Brewer: Woodbridge). 292 n21. Mézos lay on the Via Campino to Santiago de Compostela around midway between Bordeaux and Bayonne.
146. Arnold Taylor. 1985. Studies in Castles and Castle-Building. London: The Hambledon Press. 12. Louis Blondel. 1935. *L'architecture militaire au temps de Pierre II de Savoie: Les donjons circulaires.*290. "*ad turrim de Sallon devisandam*" and "*ad supervidendum ibi situm turris.*"
147. RG i, no.2828. "*Pro Johanne de Mesoz et Bertramo ingeniatore – Mandatum est P. Chacepork' quod, si Johannes de Mesoz, Bertramus Le Engynnur, Geraldus de Winton, Wilhelmis de Nantuyl, Willelmus Le Gelus et Nicholas Anglicus, magistri ingeniorum, nondum habuerint robas suas quas dominus rex eis dedit quando Castrum de Benaug.*"
148. Louis Blondel. 1935. *L'architecture militaire au temps de Pierre II de Savoie: Les donjons circulaires.* Genava xiii: 290.

149. Today the ruins of Benauges lie by the French commune of Arbis in the Gironde department, Nouvelle Aquifer region.
150. RG i, no.2689. *"Teste Rege in castris apud Lupiac".*
151. Arnold Taylor. 1989. Master Bertram, Ingeniator Regis. Studies in Medieval History presented to R. Allen Brown. (Boydell and Brewer: Woodbridge). 292.
152. Jean Pierre Chapuisat. 1989. *De Mont-sur-Rolle à Windsor, de la Dullive à Dumfries. ... La Maison de Savoie et le Pays de Vaud* 97: 120.
153. Ibid.
154. Louis Blondel. 1935. *L'architecture militaire au temps de Pierre II de Savoie: Les donjons circulaires. Genava* xiii: 283.
155. Daniel de Raemy. 2004. *Châteaux, donjons et grandes tours dans les Etats de Savoie (1230–1330). Lausanne: Cahiers d'archéologie romande* 98 et 99. 282–3.
156. Louis Blondel. 1935. *L'architecture militaire au temps de Pierre II de Savoie: Les donjons circulaires.* Genava xiii: 290. *"cum stipendii magistorum venentium de ultra Jurim."*
157. *La Finanza Sabauda*, vol 1. 41. *"In expensis domini Iohannis de Masot euntis apud Sallon ad turrim de Sallon devisandam. .vi. sol. .viii. den. preter illos quos expendit apud Sallon."*
158. Ibid. 68. *"In expensis domini Iohannis de Masot ad supervidendum ibi situm turris per tres dies. Vj.s.vj.d.".*
159. Ibid. 118. *"In expensis domini Iohannis de Masoz apud Yverdunum infirmantis per xxviii dies, de mandato domini, vi lib xii den . . .in acquietancia Magistri Jacobi Cementarii hoc anno et de anno preterito ... qui Jacobus percipit Yverdunum de domino in feudo, decem libras viannensium singulis annis. xv. lib..".*
160. www.martigny-region.ch/tourism/bayart-tower-366.html retrieved 29 April 2021.
161. Arnold Taylor. 1989. Master Bertram, Ingeniator Regis. Studies in Medieval History presented to R. Allen Brown. (Boydell and Brewer: Woodbridge). 294. n31. Jean de Mésoz is described as *"moranti apud Salinas pro dictando opere putei de Salinas"* whilst Master James is *"euntis apud Salinas pro operibus putei per xj. dies, capientis quolibet die 3s. Pro expensis suis."*
162. Eugene L. Cox. 1974. The Eagles of Savoy: The House of Savoy in Thirteenth Century Europe. Princeton: Princeton University Press. 302–3.
163. Arnold Taylor. 1963. Some notes on the Savoyards in North Wales, 1277–1300. With special reference to the Savoyard element in the construction of Harlech Castle. Genava 11: 289–315. 292.
164. Arnold Taylor. 1963. Some notes on the Savoyards in North Wales, 1277–1300. With special reference to the Savoyard element in the construction of Harlech Castle. Genava 11: 292. *"Idem libravit Petro Uldrici carpentario et eius socio euntibus apud Rotundum Montem pro operibus domini, pro expensis ipsorum cum uno runcino qui portabat aysiamentum ipsorum ... xxv.s."*
165. Nicola Coldstream. 2016. *Architects, Advisors and Design at Edward I's Castles in Wales.* In Late Medieval Castles. (Boydell and Brewer: Woodbridge). 100.
166. *La Finanza Sabauda*, vol 1. 63. *"Magistri Arnaundi fossatoris circa opus fossati de Chillon."*
167. Louis Blondel. 1935. *L'architecture militaire au temps de Pierre II de Savoie: Les donjons circulaires.* 289.

Notes

168. Wurstemberger, vol 1. 352.
169. Louis Blondel. 1935. *L'architecture militaire au temps de Pierre II de Savoie: Les donjons circulaires*. André Perret. 1983. *Le comte Pierre II de Savoie. L'expansion savoyarde et l'alliance anglaise au xiiie siècle. Revue Savoisienne* 117.
170. Darren Baker. 2017. Henry III: The Great King England Never Knew It Had. Stroud: The History Press. 666.

Chapter Nine

1. Eugene L. Cox. 1974. The Eagles of Savoy: The House of Savoy in Thirteenth Century Europe. Princeton: Princeton University Press. 305–6.
2. Ibid. 307.
3. CPR Henry III vol 5 1258-1266, 291.
4. Eugene L. Cox. 1974. The Eagles of Savoy: The House of Savoy in Thirteenth Century Europe. Princeton: Princeton University Press. 313.
5. CPR Henry III vol 5 1258-1266, 274 & 295.
6. CPR Henry III vol 5 1258-1266, 295.
7. Stephen Church. 2017. Henry III: A Simple and God-Fearing King. London: Penguin Random House. 75.
8. TNA. E. 36/275. Liber. B, ff. 35–6 (2–3) (O). Printed: Foedera, I. i. 433–4 (refers to Liber B, f. 2).
9. Stephen Church. 2017. Henry III: A Simple and God-Fearing King. London: Penguin Random House. 75.
10. Alison Weir. 2020. Queens of the Crusades: Eleanor of Aquitaine and her Succesors. London: Penguin Random House UK. 619.
11. David Carpenter. 2023. Henry III : Reform, Rebellion, Civil War, Settlement 1259-1272. London: Yale Publishing Ltd.
12. *Fœdera*. vol 1. 776. "A.D. 1264. An. 48. H.3. *REX dilecto & fideli fuo, Wychardo de Charrun, falutem. Cum nuper commiferimus vobis omnes terras & tenementa dilecti & fidelis noftri Petri de Sabaudia, in honore Richemundiæ, cuftodienda, ad opus noftrum, quamdiu nobis placuerit; Vobis mandamus quod omnes exitus, provenientes de terris & tenementis prædictis, eidem Petro, vel fuo certo attornato, fine dilatione, habere faciatis. In cujus, &c. Tefte ut fupra.apud Ambian. duodecimo die Januarii. Confimilem litteram habet Johannes de Rud, de omnibus terris & tenementis pradicti Petri in Comitatu Suffex*" Or "Greetings to his beloved and faithful, Wychardus [Guichard] de Charrun. Since we have lately committed to you all the lands and tenements of our beloved and faithful friend Peter de Savoy, in the honor of Richemond, to be given away for our work as long as it pleases us; We command you to cause all issues arising from the aforesaid lands and tenements to be given to the same Peter, or to my sure attorney, without delay. In whose, &c. Witness as above at Amiens on the twelfth day of January [1264]. Johannes de Rud [John de la Rede] has a letter of trust concerning all the lands and tenements of the said Peter in the county of Sussex."
13. Ibid. 780.

14. Julia Barrow. 2011. Peter of Aigueblanche's Support Network in Thirteenth Century England XIII Proceedings of the Paris Conference, 2009. Eds Janet Burton, Frédérique Lachaud & Phillipp Schofield. (Boydell and Brewer: Woodbridge). 38.
15. Chron. Thedmar. 62. "*Postea, in septimana ante Ramos Palmarum, destructum est Judaismum in Londoniis, et omnia bona ipsorum asportata, et quotquot Judei fuerunt inventi, nudi, dispoliati, et postea de nocte catervatim trucidati, scilicet, numero plusquam quingenti.*" Or "Afterwards, in the week before Palm Branches, Judaism was destroyed in London, and all their goods were carried away, and as many Jews were found, naked, plundered, and afterwards massacred in groups at night, to the number of more than five hundred."
16. Darren Baker. 2017. Henry III: The Great King England Never Knew It Had. Stroud: The History Press. 695.
17. Chron. Johannes Oxenedes, 201. "*Fratres mei dilectissimi proceres et subditi, hodie militamus pro statu regni Anglie, ad honorem Dei et beate Marie ac omnium sanctorum et matris ecclesie, et sumus uniti. fidem nostram observare.*" Or "My beloved brothers, nobles and subjects, today we fight for the state of the kingdom of England, for the honour of God and the blessed Mary and of all the saints and the mother church, and we are united. to observe our faith."
18. Richard Brooks. 2015. Lewes and Evesham 1264–65: Simon de Montfort and the Baron's War. Oxford: Osprey Publishing Ltd. 49. Cites the Worcester Chronicle as Henry's army moving between dawn and 5.30am.
19. Chron. Rishanger, 22. "*Edwardus militis egregii notam adeptus merito, sicut cervus fontes aquarum, sic sitiens sanguinem inimicorum suorum Londoniens.*" Or "Edward, having deservedly acquired the reputation of an excellent soldier, as a stag springs of water, so thirsts for the blood of his enemies, the Londoners."
20. Ann. Waverley, 357. "*Inito autem conflictu Londonienses fugam inierunt, quos Edwardus turba militum magna comitante insequebatur, per quos pars magna fugientium perimebatur.*" Or "At the beginning of the conflict, the Londoners took to flight, and were pursued by Edward with a large company of soldiers, by whom a great part of the fugitives were slain." Richard Brooks. 2015. Lewes and Evesham 1264–65: Simon de Montfort and the Baron's War. Oxford: Osprey Publishing Ltd. 56. Writes that Victorian quarrymen found many of their skeletons in Offham Chalk Pits.
21. Ann. Londonsienses, 64. "*Rex vero Alemanniæ in molendino inventus capitur*" Or "But the king of Alemannia was found in the mill and taken." A plaque denotes the site of the windmill to this day, and site of the "Siege of Snelling's Mill".
22. David Carpenter. 2023. Henry III : Reform, Rebellion, Civil War, Settlement 1259-1272. London: Yale Publishing Ltd.
23. Darren Baker. 2017. Henry III: The Great King England Never Knew It Had. Stroud: The History Press. 702.
24. Ann. Waverley, 357. "*His ita gestis Edwardus desistens ab insectatione Londoniensium revertitur, putans se cum suis obtinuisse triumphum; sed, villa jam flammis tradita, venerunt victores ei obviam*" Or "After these actions, Edward, desisting from the attack of the Londoners, returned, thinking that he had obtained a triumph with his men; but, the town having already been delivered up to the flames, the victors came to meet him." Chron. Rishanger, 34. "*Edwardus a cæde rediens Londoniensium. . . victoria gloriosa*

mirabiliter adepti sunt" Or "Edward returning from the slaughter of the Londoners. . . they [the barons] won a glorious victory in a wonderful way."
25. Chron. Johannes Oxenedes, 23. "*Interim Rex, cum suis complicibus, a capitur, et custodia mancipatus; fugatis igitur Londoniensibus cum dominus Edwardus fessus et fatigatus ad exercitum rediret, comprehensus est.*" Or "In the meantime, the King, with his accomplices, was captured and taken into custody; and when the Lord Edward, tired and weary, had returned to the army, having fled from London, he was arrested."
26. Quoted as such in The Song of Lewes. who thought the sails of the mill were a 'mangonel'.
27. Richard Brooks. 2015. Lewes and Evesham 1264–65: Simon de Montfort and the Baron's War. Oxford: Osprey Publishing Ltd. 56.
28. Ann. Waverley, 357. "*Quidam etiam fugientes per quendam pontem, sic se invicem constrinxerunt, quod multi corruerunt et se submerserunt; evadentes autem partes transmarinas adierunt.*" Or "Even when they were fleeing over a certain bridge, they so straddled each other that many fell down and were drowned; but escaping, they went to overseas parts."
29. Richard Brooks. 2015. Lewes and Evesham 1264–65: Simon de Montfort and the Baron's War. Oxford: Osprey Publishing Ltd. 62.
30. Fergus Oakes. 2015. "King's Men without the King: Royalist Castle garrison resistance between the Battles of Lewes and Evesham" in Thirteenth Century XV Authority and Resistance in the Age of Magna Carta: Proceedings of the Aberystwyth and Lampeter Conference, 2015. Eds. Janet Burton, Philipp Schofield & Björn Weiler (Boydell and Brewer: Woodbridge). 62.
31. Chron. Johannes de Oxenedes. 224. "*Comes vero Warenniæ et dominus Hugo Bigod a bello fugientes cum pluribus nobilium mare transierunt.*" Or "But the Earl of Warrene and lord Hugh Bigod, fleeing from war, crossed the sea with a number of nobles." Ann. Londonsienses, 64. "*Fuerunt igitur, ut supradictum est, quidam fugientes de exercitu regis, de quorum numero fuerunt Johannes comes Warenniæ, et Hugo le Bigot, qui ad castrum Petri de Sabaudia, scilicet de Pevenesheia, lores suas direxerunt; ibique ultra mare occulte transvectu dominum regem Franciæ petierunt, nuntiantes eidem, regem Angliæ in lecto apud Lewes dormientem, non præmunitum, non armatum, a suis baronibus cap- tum esse atque confusum: eo quod idem rex Franciæ pro prædicto rege Angliæ contra barones de statutis Oxoniæ omnino pronunciaverat. Sic itaque prædictum regem Franciæ, nec non etiam quosdam plures Gallise magnates erga barones Angliæ, eorum nephandis mendaciis, ad iram non modicam provocaverunt.*" Or "There were therefore, as aforesaid, some fleeing from the king's army, among whose number were John, count of Warenne, and Hugh de Bigot, who directed their lines to the castle of Peter of Savoy, that is, of Pevenesey; and there, having crossed the sea secretly, they sought the lord king of France, telling him that the king of England, sleeping in his bed at Lewes, unfortified, unarmed, had been captured and confounded by his barons. he had made a complete pronouncement on the statutes of Oxford. And so they provoked the aforesaid King of France, and also some more of the Gallic magnates, to no small anger towards the barons of England, by their nefarious lies." And Chron. Rishanger, 35. "*Eodem tempore, comite Warennie, Hugone Bigot, Willelmo de Valencia, et ceteris fratribus suis, qui cum eis de bello Lewen, ut dictum est, fugerant, et necessitate compulsi et hostiliter perterriti . . .mandavit reginis, qui tunc erant in partibus transmarinis. . . Eodem modo*

regi Francie et domino Karolo fratri suo de captivitate regum Anglie et Alemannie informans eos, auxilium et liberacionem eorum implorans Sed tum, petentibus frustra, discesserunt." Or "At the same time, Earl Warenne, Hugh Bigot, Guillaume de Valence, and the rest of his brothers, who had fled with them from the battle of Lewes, as has been said, and were forced by necessity and terrified by hostility... were commanded by the queen, who was then in overseas parts... In the same way to the king of France [Louis IX] and lord Charles his brother [Charles d'Anjou], informing them of the captivity of the kings of England and Germany, imploring their help and deliverance. But then, having sought in vain, they departed."

32. CPR Henry III vol 5 1258–1266, 318.
33. Ibid. 333. "Safe conduct until Monday after the feast of the Translation of St. Thomas the Martyr and for the whole of that day, for Hanekin de Witsand, constable of the castle of Pevense, John de la Rede and Imbert de Montreal, summoned to come under the conduct of William Maufee, whom the king is sending to bring them, to speak with the king, as the king understands that many enormities have been committed by them and others of the munition of that castle."
34. Ibid. 363. "July 18. St. Paul's, London. Whereas the king, by his council, has provided that the castle of Pevense shall be committed to Ralph de Cameys, during pleasure, but he is prevented at present from coming there to receive the castle, the king has commanded Hanekin de Witsaund, constable of the said castle, John de la Rede and Imbert de Montreal staying in the munition of the said castle, to deliver it, in the name of the said Ralph, to John de Abernun, sheriff of Surrey and Sussex, by indenture, and if peace be made with Peter de Sabaudia, the goods in it shall be reserved for the said Peter. And if the said Hankin, John and Imbert surrender the castle in the form aforesaid, the said sheriff is to let them have the safe conduct which the king is sending to them, to cross beyond seas, and if they will not surrender it to him, he is to let them have safe conduct to come to the king to surrender it to the king, and the king will then let them have safe conduct to go with their horses, goods and harness beyond seas. Mandate in pursuance to the said three. Safe conduct until St. Peter's Chains for them and the others in the munition of the said castle, their households, horses, harness and goods, going beyond seas, or coming to the king and then going beyond seas; and for their greater security the said sheriff will conduct them to the king's presence."
35. Ann. Thomas Wykes, 152.
36. For a full discussion of the Mise of Lewes see J. R. Maddicott. 1983. The Mise of Lewes, 1264. The English Historical Review 98.
37. J. R. Maddicott. 1983. The Mise of Lewes, 1264. The English Historical Review 98: 601.
38. https://archive.org/stream/songlewes00richgoog/songlewes00richgoog_djvu.txt retrieved 23 June 2018.
39. CPR Henry III vol 5 1258-1266, 381. "Appointment of the king's consort Eleanor, queen of England, Peter, count of Savoy, and John Maunsell, treasurer of York, to receive in the king's name the money which Louis, king of France, owes him by the form of the peace; with power to compound and make order with the said Louis touching the said money as they think fit. The like, with this added, whatever they all or two of them, etc"
40. Jean-Pierre Chapuisat. 1964. *Au service de deux rois d'Angleterre, au XIIIe siècle: Pierre de Champvent. Revue Historique Vaudoise* 72: 163–4. We know of there not being in

Notes

England from a document, dated January 1264, in the Vaudois Cantonal Archive that excludes being written in England and to which their seals are attached. ACV C XV 2/2.

41. Wurstemberger. vol 4. No 647 and No 649.
42. Ibid. No 648. *"Si vero auditis pacem in Angliam reformatam"*.
43. Ibid. No 657. *"Testes, signantes per monogrammata sua, et qui sub scripserunt per manum Will. de Augusta, capellani Comitis, qui solus manu propria subscripsit: Humbertus de Monteferrato, Girardus de Grancione prepositus S. Thomæ de fornerio lug dun. Camillus falasterius miles. Amadeus de Boczesello, petrus de amaysino. Johannes de gllr, Ebalus de Montibus, petrus capellanus. Will. de Augusta capellanus propria manu subscripsi."*
44. Eugene L. Cox. 1974. The Eagles of Savoy: The House of Savoy in Thirteenth Century Europe. Princeton: Princeton University Press. 315.
45. Ann. Thomas Wykes, 154. *"in porta quodam Flandriæ qui Dam"*. Wurstemberger, vol 4. No 657 (see appendix). Bernard Andenmatten. 2000. *Les Testaments de Pierre II* in *Pierre II de Savoie "Le Petit Charlemagne"* ed. Bernard Andenmatten, Agostino Paravicini Bagliani and Eva Pibiri. (Lausanne: Université de Lausanne). 287. *"1264 septembre [Dam, Flandres]"*. Damme in the thirteenth century was the port for Bruges. It had been, in 1213, the site of what is considered the first English naval victory. William Longespée had inflicted a defeat on Philippe Auguste, thus ending any prospect of an invasion of England. Therefore, the site of Damme for a prospective 1264 invasion was not without precedent.
46. Eugene L. Cox. 1974. The Eagles of Savoy: The House of Savoy in Thirteenth Century Europe. Princeton: Princeton University Press. 101.
47. Bernard Demotz. 2000. *Le Comté de Savoie du XIe au XVe siècle.* Genève: Editions Slatkine. 257.
48. Jean Pierre Chapuisat. 1978. *Quelques variations sur un thème connu: En relisant certains comptes de châtellenies du XIIIe siècle.* 110. n13 *"Idem libravit Hugoni clerico domini ad expensas cavalcate euntis in Angliam CCC IIIIXX li."*
49. Ann. Thomas Wykes. 154.
50. Flores. 499–500.
51. Wurstemberger, vol 4. No 656. *"Petrus comes Sabaudie nobilibus et militibus terrarum suarum, quos secum in Flandriam attulerat, tributum assignat. 1264 30 [September]. Dam [Flanders] ... assignat stipendia debita nobilibus et militibus terrarum suarum, quos secum durerat in Flandriam"* that is that it "assigns the payments due to the nobles and soldiers of his lands, whom he had endured with him in Flanders." The text begins *"P. Comes Sabaudie Domino Seuthe Castellano Cletis salutem. Mandamus vobis quod dominus Ricardus de Balma, vel eius nuncius, has litteras certitudinaliter afferentes, in crastino octave beati Hilarii quinquaginta libras Viennensis pro nostra donatione persolvissemus. Datum apud Dam in Fandria in crastino sancti Michaelis. Sub eadem formà mandatur eidem ut soluat domino Guidoni de Agenens XXX libras Vienn. ad eundem terminum. Datum ut supra . . . ."* Or "Pierre, Count of Savoy to the castellan of Les Clées, greeting. We order you that Sir Richard de la Balrae, or his messenger, bringing these letters with certainty, that on the morrow, on the eighth day of St. Hilary, we had paid fifty Livres Viennois for our donation. Given at Dam in Flanders on the morrow of St. Michael the Archangel. [30 September]. "Under the same form, the same is ordered to pay Mr. Guidon de Agenens 30 livres Vienn. to the

same term. Given as above." The remainder of the knights they follow. For the full text see appendix.
52. André Perret. 1983. *Le comte Pierre II de Savoie. L'expansion savoyarde et l'alliance anglaise au xiiie siècle. Revue Savoisienne* 113.
53. *Correspondance Administrative d'Alfonse de Poitiers*, ed. Auguste Molinier (Paris: Imprimerie Nationale, 1894), Collection de Documents inédits sur l'Histoire de France, 2.547, ep. 2025.
54. Chron. Rishanger, 35. "*tantam secum multitudinem navium ut vix cuiquam credibile esset.*" Or "He had such a large number of ships with him that it was scarcely credible to any one."
55. Ibid. 36. "*omnis illa regio et terra usque ad Alpes, instinctu reginæ Angliæ, P. de Sabaudia, electi Lugduonensis, Bonefacii Archiepiscopi Cant. et cæterum parentum nobilium reginæ con- tra Anglicos conspiraverant, sed et Britannia minor, Vasconia, et Hispannia*" Or "all that region and land as far as the Alps, by the impulse of the queen of England, Pierre de Savoie, [Philippe de Savoie] the elect of Lyon, Archbishop Boniface of Canterbury. and the queens of other noble families had conspired against the English, but also Brittany, Gascony, and Spain."
56. Ann. Dunstable. 233.
57. CPR Henry III vol 5 1258–1266. 326–56.
58. Chron. Rishanger, 35. "*Regina vero et Bonefacius, archiepiscopus Cantuariensis, Petrus Sabaudie, et ceteri parentes*" Or "But the queen and Boniface, the archbishop of Canterbury, Peter of Savoy, and the rest of their relatives"
59. David Carpenter. 2023. Henry III : Reform, Rebellion, Civil War, Settlement 1259-1272. London: Yale Publishing Ltd.
60. D. A. Carpenter. 1992. King Henry III's 'Statute' Against Aliens: July 1263. The English Historical Review 107: 940.
61. Wurstemberger, vol 4. No 657 (see appendix). Bernard Andenmatten. 2000. *Les Testaments de Pierre II* in *Pierre II de Savoie "Le Petit Charlemagne"* ed. Bernard Andenmatten, Agostino Paravicini Bagliani and Eva Pibiri. (Lausanne: Université de Lausanne). 287. "*1264 septembre [Dam, Flandres] Le comte Pierre de Savoie, sain d'esprit, fait son testament; il élit sépulture auprès de l'abbaye de Saint-Maurice d'Agaune ou de la maison du Temple de Londres, selon son lieu de décès; il institue héritiers sa fille pour sa légitime, sa nièce la reine Aliénor pour le comté de Savoie et la baronnie de l'Aigle, avec substitutions en faveur de son frère Philippe, puis de celui de ses neveux qui semblera le plus capable; il prévoit des legs pieux à des hospices et aux prieurés et abbayes de la province de Tarentaise ainsi que d'importantes donations en faveur des gens de son hôtel.*" Or "September 1264 [Damme, Flanders] Count Pierre de Savoie, of sound mind, made his will; he elects burial near the abbey of Saint-Maurice d'Agaune or the house of the Temple of London, according to his place of death; he institutes his daughter as his legitimate heir, his niece Queen Eleanor for the county of Savoy and the barony of l'Aigle, with substitutions in favour of his brother Philippe, then of that of his nephews who seems the most capable; he foresees pious bequests to hospices and priories and abbeys in the province of Tarentaise as well as important donations in favour of the people of his hotel.". AST/C, *Testamenti*, m. I, no. 12.
62. Chron. Rishanger. 36. "*omnem illam regionem et terram usque ad Alpes instigante Regina Anglie, P. Sabaudia, electus Lugdunensis, Bonefacius Cant. et alii nobiles reginae parentes contra Anglos coniuraverant.*"

Notes

63. Joseph Heidemann. 1903. *Papst Clemens IV* Part 1. Münster: H. Schöningh. 238. 43a *"parati erant tenere dictum verbum, quod rex Francie proposuerat in scuto, et si aliquid mutandum putaretur, stare super eo ad voluntatem et ordinationem ejusdem domini regis vel predicti cardinalis."* Or "they were prepared to hold the said word, which the king of France had proposed under seal, and if anything should be thought to be changed, to stand upon it at the will and order of the same king or of the aforesaid cardinal."
64. David Carpenter. 2023. Henry III : Reform, Rebellion, Civil War, Settlement 1259-1272. London: Yale Publishing Ltd.
65. CPR Henry III vol 5 1258–1266, 473. "Nov 18 [1264], Windsor. To the queen of England. The king and Edward his son are safe and sound .. . .To Peter, count of savoy, the same effect."
66. J. R. Maddicott. 2013. Politics and People in the Thirteenth Century in Thirteenth Century England XIV: Proceedings of the Aberystwyth and Lampeter Conference, 2011. Eds. Janet Burton, Phillipp Schofield & Björn Weiler. (Boydell and Brewer: Woodbridge). 9. "But those of the thirteenth century [revolts including 1258–65] were much more broadly based, and this we can explain by ... and the existence of Magna Carta as a rallying-point."
67. S. T. Ambler. 2015. Magna Carta: Its Confirmation at Simon de Montfort's Parliament of 1265. English Historical Review CXXX: 801–30.
68. Chron. Bury. 32.
69. CPR Henry III vol 5 1258–1266, 326–356. Has over 18 references to Pierre de Savoie's force in Flanders, including "attack by the aliens", "aliens opposing the king", "invasion of aliens", "coming of the aliens", "hostile coming of aliens", "a great multitude of aliens". Ibid 358–85 has a further 17 references.
70. Michael Wood. 2010. The Story of England. Penguin UK. London. 203–4.
71. Chron. Flores. 481. *"Quisquis enim linguam Anglicam loqui nesciebat, a vulgo contemptus habebatur."*
72. D. A. Carpenter. 1992. English Peasants in Politics 1258–1267. Past and Present August: 12. "The pattern of fighting at Lewes, like that in many medieval battles was heavily armoured knights on horseback killing lightly protected peasant foot-soldiers. Thus, the Canterbury/Dover chronicle in its account of Lewes observed that "many foot-soldiers on the side of the barons were killed". Likewise, the Furness chronicle, having given the names of the great men who died, noted that "the others who were killed in that battle were from the masses *(mediocres existerunt de vulgo)*".
73. *Fœdera*, vol 1. 444. *"Facies autem de unaquaque villa ad eandem villam octo vel sex vel plures, ad minus secundum quantitatem oppidi, cum peditibus et armis, scilicet melioris et habilissimi; lanceis, arcubus et lanceis, gladiis, balistis et hackibus bene munitis."* Or "And from each town to the same town you shall make eight or six or more, at least according to the size of the town, with footmen and arms, that is to say, of the best and most skilful; well armed with lances, bows and lances, swords, crossbowmen, and axes."
74. D. A. Carpenter. 1992. English Peasants in Politics 1258–1267. Past and Present August: 12.
75. Chron. Thedmar. 69. *"Postea per preceptum prenotati brevis innumerabiles populi equitum et peditum de singulis comitatibus Anglie convenerunt, qui armis bene muniti,*

profecti sunt ad costam maris ad regnum contra alienigenas defendendum, et similiter innumerabiles naves de Quinque Portubus et de aliis locis posite sunt in mari, cum viris armis bene munitis ad obviandum in manu valida dictis alienigenis."

76. Chron. Rishanger, 35. *"omnes regni robur, ex omnibus urbibus, urbe, oppidis accitis"* or "all the strength of the kingdom, from all the cities, towns, and villages."
77. Ibid. 36. *"Videres eo tempore in Herbaldoune, tam equites quam pedites, tantam multitudinem congregatam, tantamque adversus exteros bellicosos, quantam in Anglia non crederes."* Or "You would have seen at that time in Herbaldoune, both horse and foot, such a multitude assembled, and such a great number against foreign belligerents, as you would not have believed in England." *Herbaldoune* being today's Harbledown just to the west of and contiguous with Canterbury in Kent.
78. *Fœdera*. vol 1. 444. *"per impias eorum manus, qui sanguinem nostrum sitiunt, sexui aut ætati, si prævalere potuerint, minime parcituri, crudelis mortis."* Or "by the impious hands of those who thirst for our blood, sex or age, if they could prevail, would not at all be spared, cruel death."

Chapter Ten

1. Margaret Howell. 1998. Eleanor of Provence. Oxford: Blackwell Publishers Ltd. 218–9.
2. Chron. Rishanger, 36. *"vellem tamen in laude illustris reginae Aleonoris contexere, quod strenue et exhauste perseveret, dominum suum regem et Edouardum tam strenue, tam viriliter adiuvare, ac si esset vir fortis."* Or "I would like, however, to join in the praise of the illustrious Queen Alianor, that she perseveres energetically and exhaustedly, to help her lord the king and Edward as energetically and manfully as if she were a brave man."
3. David Carpenter. 2023. Henry III : Reform, Rebellion, Civil War, Settlement 1259-1272. London: Yale Publishing Ltd.
4. Chron. Rishanger, 38. *"Sententiam excommunicationis fulminavit in comitem Leyc. et ejus filios, Hugonem Dispensatorem, et omnes eis in consilio, auxilio, et favore, habitatores quinque portuum et civitatem London"* Or "He thundered the sentence of excommunication on the Earl of Leicester. and his sons, Hugh Dispenser, and all the inhabitants of the five ports and the city of London in counsel, aid, and favour." Also Joseph Heidemann. 1903. Papst Clemens IV Part 1. Münster: H. Schöningh. 244–7. 50, 51, 52.
5. Ann. Worcester. 453. *"Dominus autem omnium, cui obediunt venti et mare, non permisit eundem exercitum transire in Angliam."* Or "But the Lord of all, to whom the winds and the sea obey, did not permit the same army to pass into England."
6. Chron. Rishanger, 36. *"perdito thesauro suo incomparabili"* Or "[Alianor] lost her incomparable treasure."
7. David Carpenter. 2004. The Struggle for Mastery : Britain 1066 - 1284. London: Penguin Books Ltd. 342.
8. Chron. Thedmar. 67. "Tunc temporis, quia rumores venerunt quod per procura- tionem Regine, Petri de Sauveie, Johannis Comitis Warenne, Hugonis Bigot, Willelmi de Valenciis, Johannis Maunsell et aliorum, tunc existentium in partibus transmarinis, voluerunt alienigene cum armis veniri super regnum Anglie."

Notes

9. Ann. Londonsienses. 64. "*Regina Angliæ, in partibus transmarinis moram faciens, in villa Sancti Omeri de consilio et auxilio Cantuariensis archiepiscopi, Petri de Sabaudia, Johannis de Britannia, Johannis de Warenne, Hugonis Bigot, episcopi Herefordensis, et Johannis Maunsel*" Or "The queen of England, making a stay in overseas parts, in the town of St. Omer, with the advice and assistance of the archbishop of Canterbury, Peter of Savoy, John of Britain, John of Warenne, Hugh Bigot, bishop of Hereford, and John Maunsel", Robert C.Stacey. "Mansel, John" Oxford Dictionary of National Biography. 23 Sep. 2004; Accessed 11 Mar. 2023. John Mansel died shortly after taking part in the deliberations in Flanders; he reportedly died in February 1265 in Florence, Italy. That he was on his way on a matter of finance for Pierre and Alianor or en route to the papal curia cannot be discounted.
10. Ibid. David Carpenter. 2020. Henry III: The Rise to Power and Personal Rule 1207–1258. New Haven: Yale University Press. 220.
11. CCR Henry III vol 12 1261–1264, 390–1. "*Hinc est quod magnificenciam regiam requirendam duximus attentius et rogandam quatinus, cum predicti barones nostri a tempore pacis predicte ad nostrum et regni nostri statum de die in diem meliorandum studiose laborare non cessaverint, ingenio in regno vestro ac provinciis vobis subditis nichil omnino, si placet, fieri permittatis seu in militibus, denariis vel aliis subsidiis quicquam procurari per quod turbata regni nostri pace nobis et regno ipsi dampnum vel jactura sive predictis obsidibus evidens quod absit periculum imminere.*"
12. Wurstemberger, vol 2. 40. n1. "*führt er in keiner einzigen englischen Urkunde, so lange er Richmond besass*" Or "[the title Earl of Richmond] does not appear in a single English document as long as he [Peter of Savoy] owned Richmond."
13. D. A. Carpenter. 1991. Simon de Montfort: The First Leader of a Political Movement in English History. History 76: 6–10.
14. Fergus Oakes. 2015. "King's Men without the King: Royalist Castle garrison resistance between the Battles of Lewes and Evesham." in Thirteenth Century XV Authority and Resistance in the Age of Magna Carta: Proceedings of the Aberystwyth and Lampeter Conference, 2015. Eds. Janet Burton, Philipp Schofield & Björn Weiler (Boydell and Brewer: Woodbridge). 61–2.
15. John Hodgson. 1893. A History of Northumberland. Newcastle upon Tyne: A Reid & Sons Co. 249–51.
16. CPR Henry III vol 5 1258–1266, 326–56. "July 10 [1264]. St. Paul's, London. Commitment during pleasure to Gilbert de Clare, earl of Gloucester and Hertford, of the castles and lands of Peter de Sabaudia in England, so that he answer for the issues at the king's mandate, with mandate to the tenants to be intendant to him. By C. and the justiciary. Mandate to the said Peters constable of his castle of Rich[mond] to deliver the castle to him."
17. Ibid. 591 attests to Guichard de Charron's vassal relationship to Pierre de Savoie "May 5 [1266], Northampton Peter, count of Savoy, lord of Guichard de Charron."
18. Ibid. 213–29. "June 2 [1262], Westminster, … Peter de Sabaudia going as the king's envoy beyond seas." And "3 [1262], Westminster. Grant to the said Peter that the queen and Gwichard de Charron may nominate attorneys in his name in all pleas moved for or against him before justices in eyre or others; for three years from the feast of Holy Trinity."
19. Ibid. 400. "Jan. 16 [1265]. Westminster.Safe conduct until the quinzaine of the Purification for Guichard de Charrun, coming to the king wherever he may be in

England to surrender to him the castle of Richmond, on condition that he do and receive justice if any will impede him of any trespasses; and John de Burgo the elder who is commanded to conduct him." And Ibid. 410. "March 5 [1265], Westminster, Safe conduct until Easter for Guichard de Charrun, coming to the king wherever he may be in England, to surrender the castle of Rychemund; on condition that he do and receive justice in the king's court if any will proceed against him; and mandate to John de Eyvill and William de Boscehale, sheriff of York, to conduct him.." Also CCR Henry III vol 13 1264–1268, 101.

20. CCR Henry III vol 13 1264–1268, 113. "*Rex Johanni de Eyvill' et Willelmo de Bocehal', vicecomiti suo Ebor', salutem. Cum Guiscardus de Charrun nuper ad mandatum nostrum ad nos venire contempserit castrum Richem' nobis redditurus, per quod vobis mandavimus quod assumpto vobiscum toto posse comitatus predicti prefatum castrum expugnaretis prout magis videritis expedire; vobis de consilio magnatum qui sunt de consilio nostro iterato mandamus firmiter injungentes quatinus assumptis (sic) vobiscum toto posse predicto, modis omnibus quibus melius et cautius scieritis et poteritis castrum illud expugnetis, et tam viriliter tamque potenter obsideri faciatis, quod rebelles nostri existentes in municione castri predicti illud exire nequeant ad aliquod dampnum fidelibus nostris partium illarum inferendum. Et, si quos ex eis extra castrum illud intercipere poteritis, eos arestari et salvo custodiri faciatis donec aliud vobis inde significaverimus. Et circa dictam expugnacionem, necnon et conservacionem pacis nostre contra* perturbatores ejusdem ad tuicionem par*tium illarum, tam prudenter et fideliter vos habeatis quod diligenciam et probitatem vestram merito commendare possimus. Teste ut supra.*" Or "The King to John de Eyvill' and William de Bocehal', his sheriff of *Ebor* [York], greeting. Since Guiscard de Charrun has lately disdained to come to us at our command to restore the castle of Richmond to us, by which we have ordered you that assuming with you the whole force of the aforesaid company, you will expediently storm the aforesaid fort as you see fit; We send to you, on the advice of the magnates, who are on our repeated advice, firmly enjoining you to take with you all the aforesaid power, by all the means in which you know better and more cautiously and are able to attack that castle, and to besiege it so manfully and powerfully, that our rebels existing in the fortifications that the aforesaid camp should not be able to go out to do any harm to our faithful in those parts. And if you should be able to intercept any of them outside that castle, cause them to be arrested and kept safe until we have informed you otherwise. And with regard to the said conquest, as well as the preservation of our peace against the disturbers of the same for the protection of those parties, you behave so prudently and faithfully that we can commend your diligence and honesty. Test as above."

21. CPR Henry III vol 5 1258–1266, 363. "July 18 [1264], St. Paul's, London. "The king has commanded Hanekin de Witsaund, constable of the said castle, John de la Rede and Imbert de Montreal staying in the munition of the said castle, to deliver it, in the name of the said Ralph, to John de Abernun, sheriff of Surrey and Sussex, by indenture, and if peace be made with Peter de Sabaudia, the goods in it shall be reserved for the said Peter. And if the said Hankin, John and Imbert surrender the castle in the form aforesaid, the said sheriff is to let them have the safe conduct which the king is sending to them, to cross beyond seas, and if they will not surrender it to him, he is to let them have safe conduct to come to the king to surrender it to the king, and the king will then let them have safe conduct to go with their horses, goods and harness beyond seas."

Notes

22. Ibid. 301. "Dec 13 [1263], Windsor, Commitment during pleasure to John de la Rede of all the lands of Peter de Sabaudia in the county of Sussex; with mandate to the tenants to be intendant to him."
23. Ibid. "July 8 [1264], St Paul's, London ... for Hanekin de Witsand, constable of the castle of Pevense, John de la Rede and Imbert de Montreal, summoned to come under the conduct of William Maufee, whom the king is sending to bring them, to speak with the king, as the king understands that many enormities have been committed by them and others of the munition of that castle."
24. Jean Pierre Chapuisat. 1978. *Quelques variations sur un thème connu: En relisant certains comptes de châtellenies du XIII siècle.* 110. n17. "*Ainsi Hanekin de Wissant; ou Humbert de Montréal, que Pierre de Savoie défraiera pour cette même défense de Pevensey par son testament du 7 mai 1268.*" Or "Thus Hanekin de Wissant; or Humbert de Montreal, whom Pierre de Savoie would pay for this same defence of Pevensey by his will of May 7, 1268."
25. CPR Henry III vol 5 1258–1266, 392.
26. Ann. Thomas Wykes, 164.
27. CPR Henry III vol 5 1258–1266, 371.
28. Ibid. 386. "Nov 4. St. Paul's London. Whereas the king out of the fine which J. bishop of Winchester made with the king for the corn and stock of the said bishopric after the king restored to him the temporalities of the said bishopric, assigned to the king's nephew Simon de Monte Forti, son of Simon de Monte Forti, earl of Leicester, 800l. in part satisfaction of his expenses in the siege of the castle of Pevenese, in part payment whereof the said Simon has already received 500 marks which the bishop lately paid at the Exchequer; the king commands the bishop to pay the remaining 700 marks to the said Simon at the terms at which he is bound to the king; and if anything further of his fine remains to be paid, he is to pay it to the king. By the king, justiciary and council."
29. Henri Buathier. 1995. *JEAN Ier DE GRAILLY un chevalier européen du XIIIe siècle.* 35. Buathier no doubt got this expression from the earlier paper by Jean Pierre Chapuisat. 1978. *Quelques variations sur un thème connu: En relisant certains comptes de châtellenies du XIIIe siècle.* 110. Which discussed in part the siege of Pevensey. "*Une autre conséquence de la guerre anglaise, dite des Barons, surgit dans les comptes de la châtellenie de Chillon. On y paie ce qui est dû à Nantelme de Cholay, soit Choulex, qui avait été en garnison à Pevensey, forteresse de la côte méridionale, en Sussex, restée aux mains de Pierre de Savoie pendant tout le temps du conflit anglais; ce fut un nid de résistance et une excellente tête de pont.*" Or "Another consequence of the English war, known as the Barons [War], arose in the accounts of the châtellenie de Chillon. We [the Savoyards] pay what is due to Nantelme de Cholay, that is to say Choulex, who had been stationed at Pevensey, a fortress on the south coast, in Sussex, which remained in the hands of Pierre de Savoie throughout the time of the English conflict; it was a nest of resistance and an excellent bridgehead."
30. Jean-Pierre Chapuisat. 1960. *A Propos des Relations entre la Savoie et l'Angleterre au XIII siècle. Bulletin Philolgique et Historique* 1: 433. "*les soldats de Pierre de Savoie... ne capituleront pas*" Or "the soldiers of Pierre de Savoie... will not capitulate."
31. Louis Blondel. 1947. *Le château de St-Jean ou du Mont-de-Vence. Annales valaisannes: bulletin trimestriel de la Société d'histoire du Valais romand,* vol. 6, no. 4. 306. Not

reproduced in Chiaudano *La Finanza Sabauda*.. Blondel found the Accounts of Hugues de Grandmont, Châtelain de Chillon, in van Berchem, copies revised by others, from 2 February to 25 November 1266 in the mss. p. 159, in the machine copies. 73. Full Latin text of the 1266 account is *"Item reddit computum de L lb. maur. rec. de P. de Sallion pro redempcione gagerie sue quam tenebat dominus in manu sua preter alias quinquaginta libras maur. quas idem Petrus solvit Nantelmeto de Cholay pro parte solutionis stipendiorum suorum et sociorum suorum de stando in munitione castri de Pevenesea. Et sit quictus Petrus de dicto debito."* The key text obviously being *"Nantelmeto de Cholay pro parte solutionis stipendiorum suorum et sociorum suorum de stando in munitione castri de Pevenesea."* Or "Nantelme de Cholay for part of the payment of his wages and those of his allies for standing in the fortifications of the castle of Pevenesey."

32. Jean Pierre Chapuisat. 1978. *Quelques variations sur un thème connu: En relisant certains comptes de châtellenies du XIII siècle.* 110. *"Une autre conséquence de la guerre anglaise, dite des Barons, surgit dans les comptes de la châtellenie de Chillon. On y paie ce qui est dû à Nantelme de Cholay, soit Choulex, qui avait été en garnison à Pevensey, forteresse de la côte méridionale, en Sussex, restée aux mains de Pierre de Savoie pendant tout le temps du conflit anglais; ce fut un nid de résistance et une excellente tête de pont. On peut supposer qu'une fois les hostilités terminées Nantelme de Cholay est revenu au pays, et sa créance lui est réglée par une châtellenie de celui-ci, là où l'on dispose de liquidités, donc pas forcément en Genevois, la « patrie » du guerrier. L'identification de Pevensey repose sur le fait que cette place forte était partiellement garnie de soldats venus du continent, et écarte l'attribution donnée par Louis Blondel au « Pey de Vense ». Le tiré pour ce paiement fut Pierre de Saillon."* Or "Another consequence of the English war, known as the Barons, arises in the accounts of the castellany of Chillon. They pay there what is due to Nantelme de Cholay, namely Choulex, who had been in garrison at Pevensey, a fortress on the southern coast, in Sussex, which remained in the hands of Pierre de Savoie throughout the English conflict; it was a nest of resistance and an excellent bridgehead. One can suppose that once the hostilities ended Nantelme de Cholay returned to the country, and his debt was settled by a castellany of this one, where one has liquidities, therefore not necessarily in Geneva, the "fatherland of the warrior. The identification of Pevensey is based on the fact that this stronghold was partially filled with soldiers from the continent, and dismisses the attribution given by Louis Blondel to the "Pey de Vense". The drawee for this payment was Pierre de Saillon."

33. Fergus Oakes. 2015. "King's Men without the King: Royalist Castle garrison resistance between the Battles of Lewes and Evesham" in Thirteenth Century XV Authority and Resistance in the Age of Magna Carta: Proceedings of the Aberystwyth and Lampeter Conference, 2015. Eds. Janet Burton, Philipp Schofield & Björn Weiler (Boydell and Brewer: Woodbridge). 63. "Pevensey was receiving assistance from the continent, suggesting that it was both in contact with Peter and receiving aid."

34. Fergus Oakes. 2015. "King's Men without the King: Royalist Castle garrison resistance between the Battles of Lewes and Evesham" in Thirteenth Century XV Authority and Resistance in the Age of Magna Carta: Proceedings of the Aberystwyth and Lampeter Conference, 2015. Eds. Janet Burton, Philipp Schofield & Björn Weiler. (Boydell and Brewer: Woodbridge). 66.

Notes

35. Pevensey Castle has had the benefit of several archaeological excavations; Pevensey Castle – 1852, 1906–8, 1936–9 and 1993–5 in addition to assessments in 1908–10, 1932, 1964 and 1987.
36. CCR Henry III vol 13 1264–1268, 80. "*Rex vicecomiti Surr' et Sussex salutem. Cum homines comitatuum predictorum contra hostilem adventum alienigenarum in regnum nostrum et circa obsidionem castri de Pevenes' laboribus et expensis quamplurimum fuerunt pregravati, et jam assignaverimus dilectum nepotem et fidelem nostrum Simonem de Monte Forti juniorem ad castrum predictum in instanti hieme obsidendum, et ei certam pecuniam providerimus ad certos homines inveniendos ad obsidionem predictam faciendam, ne illi qui sunt in castro predicto nobis adversantes exeant ab eodem; tibi precipimus quod homines comitatuum predictorum ad predictam obsidionem de cetero faciendam nullatenus destringas vel eis super hoc molestiam inferas vel gravamen, set eos inde pacem habere permittas, donec aliud inde tibi preceperimus. Teste me ipso apud Wyndes' xvij. die Novembris. Per regem et justiciarium.*" Or "The King Salutes the viscount of Surrey and Sussex. When the men of the aforesaid companies were greatly burdened with the labours and expenses of the Pevenesey against the hostile arrival of foreigners into our kingdom, and about the siege of the castle, and we had already assigned our beloved and faithful nephew Simon de Montfort, the younger, to the siege of the aforesaid castle in the immediate winter, and to him a certain sum of money we will provide for finding certain men to make the aforesaid siege, lest those who are in the aforesaid camp opposing us should leave the same; We command you that you in no way restrain the men of the aforesaid counties from making the aforesaid a rest of siege, or bring upon them trouble or grievousness over this, but allow them to have peace therefrom, until we have commanded you otherwise. Witness myself at Windsor xvij. on November By the king and the justiciar."
37. CPR Henry III vol 5 1258–1266, 414.
38. David Carpenter. 2023. Henry III : Reform, Rebellion, Civil War, Settlement 1259-1272. London: Yale Publishing Ltd.
39. Ibid. For Paschasius de Pino 641, For Pelerin de la Poynte 583. The latter dated April 1266 describes "his services to the King, Queen and Edward his son, beyond the seas and within".
40. Margaret Howell. 1998. Eleanor of Provence. Oxford: Blackwell Publishers Ltd. 226.
41. Anaïs Waag. 2021. The Letters of Eleanor and Marguerite of Provence in Thirteenth-Century Anglo-French Relations In Thirteenth Century England XVII: Proceedings of the Cambridge Conference, 2017. Eds. Andrew Spencer & Carl Watkins. (Boydell and Brewer: Woodbridge). 113. "Eleanor, playing a more visible role, successfully raised military and financial support, while Marguerite assisted her in securing the necessary ships to transport the royalist army from the Continent to England. Though both women undoubtedly wrote many letters to a number of European rulers and lords in their quest for support for the English Crown, their exchanges with Alphonse are the only letters to survive."
42. David Carpenter. 2005. The Meetings of Kings Henry III and Louis IX In Thirteenth Century England X: Proceedings of the Durham Conference, 2003. Eds Michael Prestwich, Michael Britnell & Robin Frame. 22.
43. Margaret Howell. 1998. Eleanor of Provence. Oxford: Blackwell Publishers Ltd. 226

44. Chron. Rishanger, 42. "*Item, comes Gloverniæ de feroce factus ferocior, memoratos marchiones qui debuerant ut dictum est regnum exivisse, sibi adjunxit in adjutorium, Johannem de Warenna, Willelmum de Walence, qui tunc temporis applicuerunt apud Pembrok*" Or "Likewise, the earl of Gloucester, becoming more ferocious, having mentioned the marquises who should have left the kingdom as has been said, added to him as adjutant Jean de Warenne and Guillaume de Valence, who at that time arrived at Pembroke."
45. The royalist faction was contemporarily known as the *regales* or *reaulx*.
46. Christopher Gravett. 2009. English Castles 1200–1300. Botley: Osprey Publishing Ltd. 96.
47. Chron. Johannes Oxenedes, 206. "*in hebdomada Pentecostes, cum duobus militibus suæ custodia deputatis, illum negligenter et incaute conservantibus, solatii causa in scampum equitare permissus est. Qui ingeniosum ue militum segnitiem considerans, aut ut creditur voluntate eorum gestum est, et consensu, callide artem evadendi finxit. Illis in loco, suæ voluntati opportuno existentibus, rogavit ut equos suorum calcaribus stimulatos currere permitterent. Qui jussis suis obtemperantes, ac equos suos cursu velocissimo fatigantes, ipse freno laxato reliquit eos ad caudam, versus Comitem Gloverniæ*" Or "in the week of Pentecost, with two soldiers deputed to his guard, who guarded him negligently and imprudently, he was allowed to ride on the heath for the sake of comfort. Who, considering the indolence of the soldiers, or, as it is believed, was done by their will, and with their consent, cleverly invented the art of escape. He begged them to allow their horses to run, spurred on by their spurs. Who, obeying his orders, and tiring his horses at a very rapid pace, he himself, with the bridle loosed, left them at the tail, towards the Earl of Gloucester".
48. Chron. Gloucester, 757. "*Louerdinges habbeþ not god dai, & gretep wel mi fader þe king & uf ich mai ise him wel bitime & out of warde him do.*"
49. Cawley, Medieval Lands, Briouse. Records the marriage as "*Rog (secundus)...Radulphi et Gwladusae filius wedded Matildem de Brewys, filiam domini Willielmi de Brewys domini de Breghnoc.*"
50. Alison Weir. 2020. Queens of the Crusades: Eleanor of Aquitaine and her Successors. London: Penguin Random House UK. 633.
51. Michael Prestwich. 1997. Edward I. Yale: Yale University Press. 95. n106.
52. Ann. Cestrienses, 90. "*In octavis Innocentium, Henricus primogenitus Simonis de Montiforti primo Cestriam veniens recepit nomine patris sui fidelitates et hominia tarn a civibus Cestrie, quam etiam a proceribus et libere tenentibus comitatus ejusdem.*" Or "On the octave of the Innocents [January 4 1264] Henry, the eldest son of Simon de Montfort, came for the first time to Chester and received in his father's name the fealty and homage as well of the citizens of Chester, as of the nobles and freeholders of the same county."
53. John Maddicott. 2016. Who was Simon de Montfort, Earl of Leicester. Transactions of the Royal Historical Society 26: 52.
54. Sir Maurice Powicke. 1953. The Thirteenth Century 1216–1307. Oxford: Oxford University Press. 201.
55. H. W. Ridgeway. 1983. The politics of the English royal court, 1247–65, with special reference to the role of aliens. University of Oxford. 40.

56. Margaret Howell. 1998. Eleanor of Provence. Oxford: Blackwell Publishers Ltd. 225–30. Margaret Howell is a supporter of Alianor's key role in the events of 1265.
57. Margaret Howell. 1998. Eleanor of Provence. Oxford: Blackwell Publishers Ltd. 224.
58. Beth Hartland. 2001. Vaucouleurs, Ludlow and Trim: the role of Ireland in the career of Geoffrey de Geneville (c. 1226–13).
59. Jean-Pierre Chapuisat. 1960. *A Propos des Relations entre la Savoie et l'Angleterre au XIII siècle. Bulletin Philolgique et Historique* 1: 433.
60. Ibid.
61. Charles Henry Parry. 1839. The Parliaments and Councils of England (John Murray: London). 46. "June 1. A Parliament" is held at London. The Sheriffs of Sussex and Hertford are commanded to sum mon, by four legal knights of their Counties, Peter of Savoy and others, "*quod sint coram nobis et Concilio nostro in prox imo Parliamento nostro London, primo die Junii, justitiam facturi et recepturi, &c.*" or "that they will be before us and our Council in our next Parliament, London, on the first day of June, they will do justice and receive it, &c."
62. Eugene L. Cox. 1974. The Eagles of Savoy: The House of Savoy in Thirteenth Century Europe. Princeton: Princeton University Press. 317.
63. Ann. Dunstable, 203. H. W. Ridgeway. 1983. The politics of the English royal court, 1247–65, with special reference to the role of aliens. University of Oxford. 280. Margaret Howell. 1998. Eleanor of Provence. Oxford: Blackwell Publishers Ltd. 226.
64. David Carpenter. 2023. Henry III : Reform, Rebellion, Civil War, Settlement 1259-1272. London: Yale Publishing Ltd.
65. Ann. Cestrienses, 90. "*In vigilia Epiphanie Lewelinus films Griffinus films Madoci occurrerunt S.1 de Monteforti apud Hawerdene et guerram que inter Cestrisir et Walliam octo annis et novem mensibus continuata fuerat aliquantulum sedantes, in osculo pacis sese mutuo receperunt.*" Or "On the vigil of the Epiphany [January 5 1264], Llewelin, son of [Griffin], and Griffin, son of Madoc, met Simon [Henry (?)] de Montfort at Hawarden, and to some extent put an end to the war which had continued between Cheshire and Wales for eight years and nine months, mutually giving and receiving the kiss of peace."
66. J. Beverley Smith. 2014. Llywellyn ap Gruffudd: Prince of Wales. Cardiff: The University of Wales Press. 198.
67. Often incorrectly referred to as the Treaty of Pipton.
68. Huw Pryce. 2005. The Acts of Welsh Rulers: 1120 to 1283. Cardiff: University of Wales Press. 533–4.
69. CPR Henry III vol 5 1258–1266, 431.
70. J. Beverley Smith. 2014. Llywellyn ap Gruffudd: Prince of Wales. Cardiff: The University of Wales Press. 278.
71. Ann. Waverley, 363. "*Audito igitur mandato, obsidium de Peveneseye mox deserens, maximum colligens exercitum, xvii. kal. Augusti,[1] vide- licet pridie Sancti Kenelmi martyris, Wyntoniam causa hospitandi venerunt ibidem, ac cives civitatis nolentes eum recipere, sed et quendam de suis coram oculis suis occidendo, introitum negaverunt. Quo prædictus Symon indignatus civitatem incontinenti obsessam hostiliter intravit, ipsam sine misericordia spoliando propter eorundem proterviam, Judæos occidendo, et ad nihilum redigendo. Hinc Oxoniam pacifice veniendo, et ibidem per tres dies moram faciendo, in recessu suo duxit exercitum suum apud Chelinworze.*" Or "Having therefore heard

the command, he [Montfort the Younger] immediately abandoned the siege of Pevensey, and collected the largest army, xvii. cal. Augustus, the day before the martyrdom of St. Kenelm, came there for the purpose of shelter to Winchester, and the citizens of the city, not wanting to receive him, but also killing one of their own before their eyes, denied him entrance. When Simon was indignant at what had been said, he hostilely besieged then entered the incontinent city, plundering it without mercy because of their insolence, killing the Jews, and reducing them to nothing. From thence he came peaceably to Oxford, and tarried there three days, in his retreat he led his army to Kenilworth."

72. Olivier de Laborderie, D. A. Carpenter & J. A. Maddicott. 2000. The Last Hours of Simon de Montfort: A New Account. The English Historical Review 115, 403.
73. Ibid. 407.
74. Ibid. 400–1.
75. Richard Brooks. 2015. Lewes and Evesham 1264–65: Simon de Montfort and the Baron's War. Oxford: Osprey Publishing Ltd. 76.
76. Olivier de Laborderie, D. A. Carpenter & J. A. Maddicott. 2000. The Last Hours of Simon de Montfort: A New Account. The English Historical Review 115: 408.
77. Ibid. And Chron. Rishanger, 45. "*Per brachium Sancti Jacobi sapienter accedunt; nec a se ipsis sed a me modum istum didicerunt; nunc commendemus Deo animas nostras, quia corpora nostra sunt (sic).*" Or "They approach wisely by the arm of Saint James; they learned this method not from themselves but from me; now let us commend our souls to God, because they have our bodies."
78. Ibid. "*Entre ceo, sire Edward e le conte de Glouecestre, sire Gilbert de Clare, avoient les armes a plusours done en le pre qe est apele Mosham entre Craucombe e Evesham, e avoient esleu et assignez dusze serjans, les vigerous e le plus hardis, k'il savoient qe le conte de Leycestre oscireien, e vivement e atasement percereient l'ost, issi qe nulli regardasent ne suffrisent entre eaus venir deskes il venissent al corps le Conte.*"
79. Chron. Johannes Oxenedes, 208. "*et adhuc viriliter defendebat se quousque equus ejus a peditis occisus sub ipso caderet; et adhuc pedestris gloriose pugnavit, seipsum defendendo donec inimici ejus de equis suis descenderent ac ipsum vilissime conculcatum, armis suis expoliarent, et sic eum nudum occiderunt. Qui tam violenter et ignominiose tractatus, nunquam aliquid verbum locutus est, quamvis dicerent ei, "Traditor, redde te" non respondit; sed in ultimo spiritu constitutus, dixit, "Deu merci;" et sic spiritum emisit*" Or "and up to that time he defended himself manfully, until his horse, killed by the foot, fell under him; but he himself fought gloriously on foot, until the enemies, jumping from their horses, trampled him in a most shameful manner, robbed him of their weapons, and thus killed him naked. He who treated him so violently and ignominiously never spoke a word when they said to him, "Treacherous man, give yourself up." he did not answer; but when he had been resolved in his last breath, he said: God bless you; and thus he gave up his breath."
80. Olivier de Laborderie, D. A. Carpenter & J. A. Maddicott. 2000. The Last Hours of Simon de Montfort: A New Account. The English Historical Review 115. 411.
81. Ann. Londonsienses, 69. "*Quidam vero iniquitatis satellites, propria moti voluntate, prædicti comitis, postquam expiraverat, caput, brachia, crura necnon et pudibunda, solo trunco remanente, nequiter amputarunt*" Or "But some of the accomplices of iniquity, of their own accord, cut off the head, arms, legs, as well as the pubic part of the aforesaid count, after he had expired, with only the trunk remaining."

Notes

82. Ann. Thomas Wykes, 174. "*Symon de Monteforti non solum capite detruncatus occubuit, verum etiam brachiis et cruribus amputatis et minuatim in frusta concisis, vix trunco remanente*" Or "Simon de Montfort died not only with his head cut off, but also with his arms and legs amputated and cut into small pieces, scarcely remaining a trunk."
83. Ann. Waverley, 365. "*Dominus vero Symon de Monteforti, capite truncato, membratim decisus, pudibundis suis, proh pudor! ablatis, martyrium pro pace terræ et regni reparatione et matris ecclesiæ, ut credimus, consummavit gloriosum; quia si vellet apud Kenilworze*" Or "Lord Simon de Montfort, with his head cut off, his limbs severed, shameless! taken away, martyrdom for the peace of the earth and the restoration of the kingdom and of the mother church, as we believe, he completed gloriously, for if he would have at Kenilworth"
84. Chron. Rishanger, 46. "*Comes Leyc., capitaneus eorum, capite truncatus, pedibus et manibus amputatis, cujus capud uxori Rogeri de Mortuo Mari, in castro Wigorniæ præsentatur (Animam ipsius adjuvet præcursor Domini! cujus capud saltatrici in convivio offerebatur).*" Or "Earl Leicester, their captain, with his head cut off, his feet and hands amputated, whose head was presented to the wife of Roger de Mortimer, in the castle of Wigmore (May the Lord's forerunner help his soul! whose head was offered to the dancer at the banquet)."
85. M.T. Clanchy. 1997. Early Medieval England. Seventh ed. London: The Folio Society. 201.
86. Stephen Church. 2017. Henry III: A Simple and God-Fearing King. London: Penguin Random House. 83.
87. Darren Baker. 2017. Henry III: The Great King England Never Knew It Had. Stroud: The History Press. 740.
88. Ann. Cestrienses, 94. "*Dominus autem Eadwardus apud Herford die Jovis in Septimana Pentecostes de custodia Domini Simonis de monteforti evasit. Quo audito Jacobus de Audethlegio et V. de Sancto Petro, Sabbato sequenti castrum de Beuston nomine domini Edwardi*" Or "But the lord Edward [the king's son] escaped from the custody of Simon de Montfort at Hereford on the Thursday[May28 1265]in Whit Week. When this was known James de Audley and Urian de Saint Pierre on the following Saturday seized the castle of Beeston in the name of the lord Edward,"
89. J. Beverley Smith. 2014. Llywellyn ap Gruffudd: Prince of Wales. Cardiff: The University of Wales Press. 283.
90. Ann. Cestrienses, 94. "*Winfridum de Bon, Henricum de Hasting, Guydonem de Monte forti in ipso bello captos apud castrum de D. (?) Beuston secum ducendo captivos.*" Or "Humphrey de Bohun, Henry de Hastings, and Guy de Montfort, who were captured in this battle [Evesham], Edward took with him as prisoners to Beeston castle."
91. Stephen Church. 2017. Henry III: A Simple and God-Fearing King. London: Penguin Random House. 83.
92. E. F. Jacob. 1924. What were the "Provisions of Oxford"?. History 9: 188.
93. James Birchall. 1873. England under the Normans and Plantagenets: An Historical Manual. London: Simplin, Marshall & Co. 116.
94. D. A. Carpenter. 1991. Simon de Montfort: The First Leader of a Political Movement in English History. History 76: 3.
95. https://www.parliament.uk/about/living-heritage/evolutionofparliament/2015-parliament-in-the-makin/get-involved1/2015-banners-exhibition/ross-birrell/1265-simon-de-montfort-parliament-gallery/ retrieved 26 June 2018.

96. Ann. Cestrienses, 90. "*In octavis Innocentium, Henricus primogenitus Simonis de Montiforti primo Cestriam veniens recepit nomine patris sui fidelitates et hominia tarn a civibus Cestrie, quam etiam a proceribus et libere tenentibus comitatus ejusdem.*" Or "On the octave of the Innocents [January 4 1264] Henry, the eldest son of Simon de Montfort, came for the first time to Chester and received in his father's name the fealty and homage as well of the citizens of Chester, as of the nobles and freeholders of the same county."
97. J. Beverley Smith. 2014. Llywellyn ap Gruffudd: Prince of Wales. Cardiff: The University of Wales Press. 273.
98. Ann. Cestrienses, 90. "*et guerram que inter Cestrisir et Walliam*" Or "and to some extent put an end to the war which had continued between Cheshire and Wales."
99. https://www.bbc.co.uk/news/magazine-30849472 retrieved 26 June 2018.
100. M.T. Clanchy. 1997. Early Medieval England. Seventh ed. London: The Folio Society. 201.
101. D. A. Carpenter. 2021. "The Second Baronial War." BBC Radio. London, 6 May 2021.
102. Charles Petit-Dutaills. 1936. The Feudal Monarchy in France and England from the Tenth to the Thirteenth Century. New York: Harper and Row. 354.
103. Darren Baker. 2017. Henry III: The Great King England Never Knew It Had. Stroud: The History Press. 740.
104. Maxime Reymond. 1920. *Le Chevalier Othon I de Grandson. Revue historique vaudoise* 28: 163.
105. Michael Prestwich. 1997. Edward I. Yale: Yale University Press. 53.
106. CPR Henry III vol 5 1258–1266, 464–5. "Oct. 16 [1265]. The like to Peter de Chaumpvent of 5 marks of yearly rent in Westminster. Westchepe in the said city late of Thomas de Exeporte, sometime citizen of London, the king's enemy, which the said Thomas used to receive from the stalls of Robert de Muntpelers in Westchepe; to hold by the due and accustomed services." And 465. "Oct. 16. Westminster.Grant to Peter de Chauvent and his heirs of the houses in the city of London late of Robert de Montpelers, sometime citizen of London, the king's enemy." And Ibid. 514. "Grant to Peter de Chaumpvent, to whom with Ottonin de Graunzun the king granted all the lands late of William le Blund the king's enemy, of the goods of the said William, which belong to the king by reason of his forfeiture."
107. Ibid. 465. "The like to the following houses late of the kings enemies in the said city [London] . . .Otoninus de Graunzun, those late of Simon de Hadestok." And Ibid. 467. "The like to the following of like houses in London: Ottonin de Grauncun, those houses with their appurtenances and rents in the street of the Thames by Quenehithe late of Simon de Hadestok."
108. What we now call "Old St Paul's Cathedral", the one lost in the Great Fire of London (1666), had been consecrated as recently as 1240, just some twenty-odd years before.
109. Leo T. Gourde, "An Annotated Translation of the Life of St. Thomas Becket by William Fitzstephen" (1943). Master's Theses. 622.
110. Ibid.
111. Ibid.
112. Esther Rowland Clifford. 1961. A Knight of Great Renown: The Life and Times of Othon de Grandson. Chicago: The University of Chicago Press. 14.

Notes

113. Girart Dorens. 1909. Sir Otho de Grandison 1238?–1328. Transactions of the Royal Historical Society 3: 128. Dorens suggested that Grandson had "no doubt fought under him [Edward] at Lewes and Evesham".
114. Girart Dorens. 1909. Sir Otho de Grandison 1238?–1328. Transactions of the Royal Historical Society 3: 127.
115. Othon de Grandson and Jean de Grailly would be reunited some twenty-six years later on the walls of Acre in 1291.
116. *Fœdera* vol 1. 817. "*De Restitutione, pro Petro Comite Sabaudia. "REX Militibus, liberis hominibus, & omnibus aliis Tenentibus Petri Comitis Sabaudiæ, de honoribus Aquila & Hastings. salutem. Cum, de Consilio Magnatum nostrororum, qui sunt de Concilio nostro, præfato Petro avunculo noftro omnes terras & tenementa, poffeffiones & bona sua, occafione turbationis, habitæ in Regno nostro, a quibufcumque occupata, reddidimus; Vobis mandamus quod Edwardo de Charun, cui custodiam eorumdem com mifimus, in omnibus, quæ ad terras & tenementa prædicta pertinent, nomine præfati Petri, fitis intendentes & respondentes, sicut prius facere consue. Teste Rege apud Winton. duodecimo die Septembris. Eodem modo mandatum est omnibus Tenentibus de honore Richemundia.*" Translation CPR Henry III vol 5 1258–1266, 439–73. "Whereas by the counsel of the magnates of the council, the king has restored to Peter de Sabaudia his uncle, all his lands, possessions and goods seized by reason of the late disturbance in the realm, he commands the said Peter's tenants of the honours of Laigle and Hastinges to be intendant to Gwichard de Charrun, to whom the king has committed the same in the name of the said Peter. In like manner it is commanded to the tenants of the honour of Richmond."
117. AST/C, *Testamenti*, m 1, No 6. Wurstemberger, vol 4. No 749. "*Humberto de Montreal L lib. et precipimus sibi solui XXX marchas arg. quas dicit sibi deberi pro quibusdam expensis per eum factis in municione de Peuensey.*" Or "Humbert de Montreal 50 Livres, and we order him to be paid pay 30 marks of silver. which he says are due to him for certain expenses incurred by him in the defence of Pevensey."
118. L. F. Salzmann. 1906. "Documents Relating to Pevensey Castle" in Sussex Archaeological Collections vol XLIX. The Sussex Archaeological Society. Lewes. 7. "The churches of Pevensey (and Westham) were also at this time much injured and were rebuilt at her own cost by Denise of Pevensey." And "Amongst the Royalists to whom the lands of the rebels were at first granted may be noted Imbert de Montreal, one of the gallant defenders of Pevensey, the recipient of the lands of William de Goldingham."
119. A "*Bailliage*", referred to by Monique Fontannaz (note below), can be translated as a Bailiwick, the jurisdiction of a bailie or bailiff.
120. A "*Châtellenie*", referred to by Monique Fontannaz (note below), can be defined as "*Seigneurie et juridiction d'un seigneur châtelain*", translating as "Lordship and jurisdiction of a chatelain lord".
121. Monique Fontannaz. 2015. *La Ville de Moudon, Les monuments d'art et d'histoire de la Suisse. Tome VI.* Berne: Societe d'histoire de l'art en Suisse SHAS. 33.
122. Louis Blondel. 1935. *L'architecture militaire au temps de Pierre II de Savoie: Les donjons circulaires.* Genava xiii: 274.
123. CPR Henry III vol 5 1258–1266, 632.
124. Richard K. Morris. 2006. Kenilworth Castle. Third Edition ed. London: English Heritage. 40.

125. St Martin Le Grand was a college of secular canons of ancient origin, with a collegiate church dedicated to St Martin of Tours. The church was especially interesting since it was responsible for the sounding of the curfew bell in the evenings, which announced the closing of the city's gates. The college church of St. Martin's Le Grand was not very far from the house granted to Othon de Grandson following the late baronial war. Following Savoyards Guillaume de Champvent and Louis de Vaud as Deacons of St. Martin would be William of Louth, Keeper of the Wardrobe.
126. CPR Henry III vol 5 1258–1266, 566–7. "March 16th [1266], Westminster. Notification to Pope Clement of the appointment of William de Chavent dean of the church of St. Martin, London, and William Bonquer as the king's proctors and special envoys to lay before him the damages, injuries, oppressions and grievances inflicted upon the king by occasion of the late disturbance in the realm, to sue and obtain general and special things for the king and his right, and the advantage and honour of the king's dignity; and to ask and obtain specially graces and indulgences and a timely subsidy for the relief and amelioration of the estate of the king and the realm."
127. Mary C. L. Salt. 1929. List of English Embassies to France, 1272–1307. The English Historical Review 44: 263–78.
128. Clive H. Knowles. "Savoy, Boniface of" Oxford Dictionary of National Biography. 23 Sep. 2004; Accessed 11 May 2022.
129. Ann. Thomas Wykes, 235–6. "*vir mirae simplicitatis, licet minus literatus, sobrietamen degebat, sapientissimorum consilio se regebatIelmus*" Or "a man of wonderful simplicity, though less literate, lived soberly, and governed himself by the counsel of the wisest."
130. Michael Prestwich. Medieval People. London: Thames and Hudson. 271.
131. David Carpenter. 2004. The Struggle for Mastery: Britain 1066–1284. London: Penguin Books Ltd. 342.
132. CPR Henry III vol 5 1258–1266, 678.
133. Ann. Thomas Wykes, 197–8.
134. John Julius Norwich. 2011. The Popes. London: Chatto & Windus. 368.

Chapter Eleven

1. Eugene L. Cox. 1974. The Eagles of Savoy: The House of Savoy in Thirteenth Century Europe. Princeton: Princeton University Press. 306. Purchased from Vuillerme du Palais. The tower is still known as the *"Tour du Bailliage."*
2. André Perret. 1983. *Le comte Pierre II de Savoie. L'expansion savoyarde et l'alliance anglaise au xiiie siècle. Revue Savoisienne.* 116. "*Ces fonctionnaires itinérants, Thomas de Rossillon, Simon de Verters et autres, se rendaient sur place pour vérifier les comptes et les écrivaient sur des rouleaux de parchemin, inspirés des rouleaux de comptes anglais. C'est lors de leurs séjours en Angleterre que Pierre de Savoie et ses conseillers entrent en contact avec l'administration très développée du royaume insulaire.*"
3. Ibid. "*où les archives de la couronne étaient soigneusement gardées*" And "*s'est efforcé de disposer des archives*" Or "where the archives of the crown were carefully kept" And "endeavoured to place the archives in care."
4. Guido Castelnuovo and Christian Guillerë. 2000. "*Les Finances et L'Administration de la Maison de Savoie au XIIIe siècle.*" in Pierre II de Savoie *"Le Petit Charlemagne"*

ed. Bernard Andenmatten, Agostino Paravicini Bagliani and Eva Pibiri. (Lausanne: Université de Lausanne). 48.
5. André Perret. 1983. *Le comte Pierre II de Savoie. L'expansion savoyarde et l'alliance anglaise au xiiie siècle. Revue Savoisienne* 116.
6. Eugene L. Cox. 1974. The Eagles of Savoy: The House of Savoy in Thirteenth Century Europe. Princeton: Princeton University Press. 322.
7. Wurstemberger. Vol 4. No 743. "*Nos Petrus Comes Sabaudie et in italia marchio. Vniuersis presentes litteras inspecturis, rei geste noticiam et salutem. notum cupimus fieri vniuersis tam presentibus quam futuris, quod nos volentes prouidere vtilitati, nec non expensis atque laboribus hominum omnium tam nobilium quam innobilium atque clericorum seu religiosorum, burgensium, rusticorum seu agricolarum et omnium aliorum tocius Comitatus Sabaudie.*" Or "We are Peter, the Count of Savoy and the Marquis in Italy. To all who shall inspect the present letter, have notice of the act and greeting. We desire to be made known to all, both present and future, that we desire to provide for the profit, and not only the expenses and labours of all men, both nobles and nobles and clergy or religious, burgesses, peasants, or peasants, and all others of the whole County of Savoy."
8. André Perret. 1983. *Le comte Pierre II de Savoie. L'expansion savoyarde et l'alliance anglaise au xiiie siècle. Revue Savoisienne.* 116. "*Un juge, diplômé en droit, a été créé dans chacun des bailliages pour juger les affaires qui dépassaient la juridiction des châtelains.*" Or "A judge, with a law degree, was created in each of the bailiwicks to judge cases that went beyond the jurisdiction of the castellans."
9. Eugene L. Cox. 1974. The Eagles of Savoy: The House of Savoy in Thirteenth Century Europe. Princeton: Princeton University Press. 325.
10. Wurstemberger. Vol 4. No 743.
11. Eugene L. Cox. 1974. The Eagles of Savoy: The House of Savoy in Thirteenth Century Europe. Princeton: Princeton University Press. 323. See also Nicholas Vincent. 2004. Oxford National Biography Database. Savoy, Peter of, count of Savoy and de facto earl of Richmond. "Here, ironically, he may well have learned from the reforms attempted by Simon de Montfort and the other baronial rebels against Henry III."
12. Guido Castelnuovo and Christian Guillerë. 2000. "*Les Finances et L'Administration de la Maison de Savoie au XIIIe siècle.*" in *Pierre II de Savoie "Le Petit Charlemagne"* ed. Bernard Andenmatten, Agostino Paravicini Bagliani and Eva Pibiri. (Lausanne: Université de Lausanne). 71.
13. Ibid. 76.
14. Emil Usteri, 1955. *Westschweizer Schiedsurkunden bis zum Jahre 1300*, Zürich, 134. Doc 83.
15. Guido Castelnuovo and Christian Guillerë. 2000. "*Les Finances et L'Administration de la Maison de Savoie au XIIIe siècle.*" in *Pierre II de Savoie "Le Petit Charlemagne"* ed. Bernard Andenmatten, Agostino Paravicini Bagliani and Eva Pibiri. (Lausanne: Université de Lausanne). 80–1. Savoyard *baillages* for the years 1320–30.
16. André Perret. 1983. *Le comte Pierre II de Savoie. L'expansion savoyarde et l'alliance anglaise au xiiie siècle. Revue Savoisienne* 116.
17. Eugene L. Cox. 1974. The Eagles of Savoy: The House of Savoy in Thirteenth Century Europe. Princeton: Princeton University Press. 288.
18. Guido Castelnuovo and Christian Guillerë. 2000. "*Les Finances et L'Administration de la Maison de Savoie au XIIIe siècle.*" in *Pierre II de Savoie "Le Petit Charlemagne"*

ed. Bernard Andenmatten, Agostino Paravicini Bagliani and Eva Pibiri. (Lausanne: Université de Lausanne) 103. *"abadonment leurs anciens trait's seigneuriaux pour acquérit des charactères toujours plus administratifs."*
19. Ibid. 87.
20. The title "Vicar" in this sense needs some explanation for anglophones; it in no way relates to a clerical or church function but originates in the Latin *"vicarius"* meaning substitute or second hand. In the case of an ecclesiastical vicar in England, a substitute for a bishop. In the case of the Holy Roman Empire, it meant a "substitute" for the emperor, or in place of the emperor. One might even say a "vice-roi" or viceroy.
21. Bernard Demotz. 2000. *Le Comté de Savoie du XIe au XVe siècle. Genève: Editions Slatkine.* 41. Demotz doesn't give us his source, his book is not footnoted, but the source is Wurstemberger, vol 4 No 626. *"Ricardus, Romanorum Rex, investit Petrum Comitem Sabaudiæ, avec vicariatu Imperii perpetuo, avec Comitatu Sabaudia et avec ducatibus Chablasii et Augustæ, per tria vexilla. Datum apud Berkamesces, XVII die Octobris, Indictione VIIa. Anno Domini M.CC. LXIII. régna Régis VII."* Or "Richard, king of the Romans, invests Peter, Count of Savoy, avec perpetual vicariate of the Empire, with the county of Savoy and the duke of Chablais and Aosta, with three flags. Given at Berkhamsted, 17 October, 7th Indiction. In the year of our Lord 63 the reign of King VII." His source in turn was the fifteenth-century chronicler Pingon. However, Eugene L. Cox. 1974. The Eagles of Savoy: The House of Savoy in Thirteenth Century Europe. Princeton: Princeton University Press. 363. n99 cast considerable doubt on the validity of this source: "Pingon is very unreliable and the document is usually regarded as apocryphal."
22. Wurstemberger, vol 4. 626. *"Pingonius, Chron. fol. 378. Zibaldone. 626. Petrus Comes Sabaudiæ, a Rege Romanorum investitus,* 1263. Octobris 17. Berkhamstead. *Ricardus, Romanorum Rex, investit Petrum Comitem Sabaudiæ, de vicariatu Imperii perpetuo, de Comitatu Sabaudiæ et de ducatibus Chablasii et Augustæ, per tria vexilla. Datum apud Berkamesces, XVII die Octobris, Indictionc Vila. Anno Domini M. CC. LXIII. regni Regis VII."* Or "Richard, king of the Romans, invests Peter, Count of Savoy, avec perpetual vicariate of the Empire, with the county of Savoy and the duke of Chablais and Aosta, with three flags. Given at Berkhamsted, 17 October, 7th Indiction. In the year of our Lord 63 the reign of King VII."
23. Ibid. *"Le prince a acquis une quasi royauté."* Or "The prince has acquired almost royalty."
24. Wurstemberger, vol 4 No 627. However, Eugene L. Cox. 1974. The Eagles of Savoy: The House of Savoy in Thirteenth Century Europe. Princeton: Princeton University Press. 363. n99 cast some doubt on the validity of this source: "Pingon is very unreliable, and the document is usually regarded as apocryphal."
25. Eugene L. Cox. 1974. The Eagles of Savoy: The House of Savoy in Thirteenth Century Europe. Princeton: Princeton University Press. 364.
26. Victor Van Berchem. 1907. *Les Dernières CampAgnès de Pierre Ii Comte de Savoie èn Valais et en Suisse. Revue historique vaudoise* 15: 322–3.
27. Eugene L. Cox. 1974. The Eagles of Savoy: The House of Savoy in Thirteenth Century Europe. Princeton: Princeton University Press. 365. n2.
28. Victor Van Berchem. 1907. *Les Dernières CampAgnès de Pierre Ii Comte de Savoie en Valais et en Suisse. Revue historique vaudoise* 15: 324. n1.

Notes

29. Louis Blondel. 1954. *Le château de Saxon*. Vallesia IX: 168.
30. Louis Blondel. 1949. *Le Château de Brignon. Vallesia* IV. 31.
31. Eugene L. Cox. 1974. The Eagles of Savoy: The House of Savoy in Thirteenth Century Europe. Princeton: Princeton University Press. 367.
32. Her daughter, Béatrice de Provence, wife of Charles D'Anjou, would not outlast her mother long, passing away on 23 September 1267.
33. www.vtech.fr, V-Technologies / Ligeo-Archives –. "Pierre-Châtel à Virignin – Patrimoine(s) De L'ain." Patrimoine(s) de l'Ain – revenir à l'accueil. Accessed 12 May 2022. https://patrimoines.ain.fr/n/pierre-chatel-a-virignin/n:1045.
34. Darren Baker. 2015. With All for All: The Life of Simon de Montfort. Stroud: Amberley Publishing. 381. "Peter of Savoy had died ... and showed what an ingrate he was by slipping in a codicil to his will." Eugene L. Cox. 1974. The Eagles of Savoy: The House of Savoy in Thirteenth Century Europe. Princeton: Princeton University Press. 368.
35. David Carpenter. 2023. Henry III : Reform, Rebellion, Civil War, Settlement 1259-1272. London: Yale Publishing Ltd.
36. CPR Henry III vol 5 1258–1266, 377. "Mandate to Wychard [Guichard] de Charrun, to whom the king lately committed all the lands of Peter de Sabaudia in the honour of Rychemund during pleasure, to let the said Peter or his attorney have the issues thereof at once. John de Rudes [Jean de la Rede] has a like letter touching the said Peter's lands in Sussex."
37. *Fœdera* vol 1. 817. "*De Restitutione, pro Petro Comite Sabaudia.* "*REX Militibus, liberis hominibus, & omnibus aliis Tenentibus Petri Comitis Sabaudiæ, de honoribus Aquila & Hastings. salutem. Cum, de Consilio Magnatum nostrororum, qui sunt de Concilio nostro, præfato Petro avunculo noftro omnes terras & tenementa, poffeffiones & bona sua, occafione turbationis, habitæ in Regno nostro, a quibufcumque occupata, reddidimus ; Vobis mandamus quod Edwardo de Charun, cui custodiam eorumdem com mifimus, in omnibus, quæ ad terras & tenementa prædicta pertinent, nomine præfati Petri, fitis intendentes & respondentes, sicut prius facere consue. Teste Rege apud Winton. duodecimo die Septembris. Eodem modo mandatum est omnibus Tenentibus de honore Richemundia.*" Translation CPR Henry III vol 5 1258–1266, 439–73. "Whereas by the counsel of the magnates of the council, the king has restored to Peter de Sabaudia his uncle, all his lands, possessions and goods seized by reason of the late disturbance in the realm, he commands the said Peter's tenants of the honours of Laigle and Hastinges to be intendant to Gwichard de Charrun, to whom the king has committed the same in the name of the said Peter. In like manner it is commanded to the tenants of the honour of Richmond."
38. Ibid. 591. "Whereas the king has granted to Peter, count of Savoy, lord of Guichard de Charron, in exchange for the earldom and honour of Richemund, certain lands and manors with which he and his friends ought to be content, and has restored the said earldom and honour to John, duke of Brittany, whereby the king is sending Ralph de Mortein, knight, of the said duke, to the said Guichard to receive the same from him in the name of his said lord; he commands Guichard to deliver the same to the said knight as he will avoid the king's indignation, knowing that if he fail he will be in peril of disherison of his land of the Agenais (Ajanens'); and the king will keep him harmless towards his lord the count of Savoy. Writ de intendendo to the tenants of the said castle (sic), county and honour."

39. CPR Henry III vol 6 1266–1272, 383–4.
40. Darren Baker. 2017. Henry III: The Great King England Never Knew It Had. Stroud: The History Press. 778.
41. Darren Baker. 2015. With All for All: The Life of Simon de Montfort. Stroud: Amberley Publishing. 381.
42. Eugene L. Cox. 1974. The Eagles of Savoy: The House of Savoy in Thirteenth Century Europe. Princeton: Princeton University Press. 371. "English historians have usually, and somewhat anachronistically, condemned that ambition [Henry's continental ambitions], together with Henry's foreign advisers [such as Pierre de Savoie.]"
43. CPR Henry III vol 6 1266–1272, 487. "Whereas Peter de Sabaudia bequeathed the honours of Laigle and Hastings to Thomas de Sabaudia and Amadeus and Lewis his brothers, and these by reason of the bequest sued the said honours before the king; and whereas Edward the king's son, holding the honour of Hastings, is in remote parts, so that the king cannot make any order in this matter; grant to the said Thomas, Amadeus and Lewis of 100 marks a year at the Exchequer until the return of Edward." This settlement appears to be temporary not permanent as it was made during Edward's return. We know thereafter they are both found in the retinue of household knights upon his return. Quite correctly the payment refers to the Honour of Hastings.
44. David Carpenter. 2023. Henry III : Reform, Rebellion, Civil War, Settlement 1259-1272. London: Yale Publishing Ltd.
45. CPR Edward I vol 3 1292-1301, 425.
46. Bernard Andenmatten. 2000. "*Contraintes lignagères et parcours individuel: Les testaments de Pierre II de Savoie*" in *Pierre II de Savoie "Le Petit Charlemagne"* ed. Bernard Andenmatten, Agostino Paravicini Bagliani and Eva Pibiri. (Lausanne: Université de Lausanne). 277. "*Le premier en faveur de ses trois neveux leur confirme les donations en Angleterre et les recommande aux souverains anglais. On peut y voir le souci de leur assurer un avenir à la cour d'Angleterre*" Or "The first [codicil] in favour of his three nephews confirms their donations to England and recommends them to English sovereigns. We can see the concern to ensure them a future at the English court."
47. Margaret Howell. 1998. Eleanor of Provence. Oxford: Blackwell Publishers Ltd. 242–4.
48. Bernard Andenmatten. 2000. "*Contraintes lignagères et parcours individuel: Les testaments de Pierre II de Savoie*" in *Pierre II de Savoie "Le Petit Charlemagne"* ed. Bernard Andenmatten, Agostino Paravicini Bagliani and Eva Pibiri. (Lausanne: Université de Lausanne). 277. "*Le premier en faveur de ses trois neveux leur confirme les donations en Angleterre et les recommande aux souverains anglais. On peut y voir le souci de leur assurer un avenir à la cour d'Angleterre*" Or "The first [codicil] in favour of his three nephews confirms their donations to England and recommends them to English sovereigns. We can see the concern to ensure them a future at the English court."
49. Julia Barrow. 2011. Peter of Aigueblanche's Support Network in Thirteenth Century England XIII: Proceedings of the Paris Conference, 2009. Eds Janet Burton, Frédérique Lachaud & Phillipp Schofield. (Boydell and Brewer: Woodbridge). 29–30.
50. François Mugnier. 1890. *Les Savoyards en Angleterre au XIIIe siècle et Pierre d'Aigueblanche évêque d'Héreford*. Chambéry: Imprimerie Ménard. 308. "*Primo quidem, quia in venerabili ecclesia beate Katherine et Marie Magdalene juxta aquam*

Notes

pulchram, cujus fundatores sumus donatores et patroni, eligimus sepulturam nostram in choro in loco qui est intra ambonem et columnam seu candelabrum."

51. Thomas Kerrich. 1817. Observations upon some Sepulchral Monuments in Italy and France. Archaeologia 18: 188.
52. Nicholas Carrier. 2001. *La vie montagnard en Faucigny à la fin du Moyen Age*, Editions L'Harmattan. 28.
53. Ann. Thomas Wykes, 247.
54. Michael Carter. 2017. Hailes Abbey. London: English Heritage. 5.
55. Ann. Thomas Wykes, 252.
56. Walter of Guisborough quoted in Darren Baker. 2017. Henry III: The Great King England Never Knew It Had. Stroud: The History Press. 803.
57. Ibid. 813.
58. James Birchall. 1873. England under the Normans and Plantagenets: An Historical Manual. London: Simplin, Marshall & Co. 108.
59. Robert Bartlett. 1993. The Making of Europe: Conquest, Colonization and Cultural Change 950–1350. London: Penguin Books Ltd. 404.
60. Ann. Thomas Wykes, 307.
61. Ann. Osney, 329. Criticism stems from her debts on going into Amesbury.
62. Chron. Lanercost cited in Alison Weir. 2020. Queens of the Crusades: Eleanor of Aquitaine and her Successors. London: Penguin Random House UK. 639.
63. Many authors have written of Edward and Eleanor being a true love match, including for example Lisa Hilton. 2008. Queens Consort: England's Medieval Queens. London: Weidenfeld & Nicolson. 20.
64. Lisa Hilton. 2008. Queens Consort: England's Medieval Queens. London: Weidenfeld & Nicolson. 246.
65. Ann. Osney, 330.
66. Sir Maurice Powicke. 1953. The Thirteenth Century 1216–1307. Oxford: Oxford University Press. 73.
67. David Carpenter. 2023. Henry III : Reform, Rebellion, Civil War, Settlement 1259-1272. London: Yale Publishing Ltd
68. Eugene L. Cox. 1974. The Eagles of Savoy: The House of Savoy in Thirteenth Century Europe. Princeton: Princeton University Press. 371. "English historians have usually, and somewhat anachronistically, condemned such ambition, together with Henry's foreign advisers, but Pierre probably enjoyed more respect than did any prominent foreigner at the English court, save for perhaps Simon de Montfort himself."
69. Eugene L. Cox. 1974. The Eagles of Savoy: The House of Savoy in Thirteenth Century Europe. Princeton: Princeton University Press. 371.

Bibliography

Adams, Bernard. 1999. 'János Arany and the Bards of Wales'. *The Slavonic and Eastern European Review* 77: 726–31.
Allen Brown, R. 1970. *English Castles*. London: Chancellor Press.
Allen Brown, R. 1984. *The Architecture of Castles: A Visual Guide*. London: B. T. Batsford Ltd.
Ambler, S. T.. 2015. 'Magna Carta: Its Confirmation at Simon de Montfort's Parliament of 1265'. *English Historical Review* CXXX: 801–30.
Andenmatten, Bernard & Daniel de Raemy. 1990. *La Maison De Savoie En Pays De Vaud*. Lausanne: Editions Payot Lausanne.
Andenmatten, Bernard (ed.). 2020. *Othon I de Grandson (vers 1240–1328)*. Lausanne: Cahiers Lausannois d'Histoire Médiévale.
Andenmatten, Bernard. 1989. *La noblesse vaudoise face à la Maison de Savoie au XIII siècle. La Maison de Savoie et le Pays de Vaud. Bibliothèque historique vaudoise* 97: 35–50.
Arnold Taylor. 1955. 'English Builders in Scotland during the War of Independence: A Record of 1304'. *The Scottish Historical Review* 34: 44–46.
Baker, Darren. 2015. *With All for All: The Life of Simon de Montfort*. Stroud: Amberley Publishing.
Baker, Darren. 2017. *Henry III: The Great King England Never Knew It Had*. Stroud: The History Press.
Baker, Darren. 2019. *The Two Eleanors of Henry III: The Lives of Eleanor of Provence and Eleanor de Montfort*. Barnsley: Pen & Sword Books Limited.
Baker, Darren. 2022. *Richard of Cornwall: The English King of Germany*. Stroud: Amberley Publishing.
Bartlett, Robert. 1993. *The Making of Europe: Conquest, Colonization and Cultural Change 950–1350*. London: Penguin Books Ltd.
Bartlett, Robert. 2020. *Blood Royal: Dynastic Politics in Medieval Europe*. Cambridge: Cambridge University Press.
Bémont, Charles. *Simon de Montfort, Comte de Leicester, Sa Vie (120?–1265), Son Role Politique en France et en Angleterre*. Paris: Alphonse Picard Libraire.
Beverley Smith, J. 1982–3. 'Llywelyn ap Gruffudd and the March of Wales'. *Brycheiniog* XX: 9–22.
Beverley Smith, J. 2014. *Llywellyn ap Gruffudd: Prince of Wales*. Cardiff: The University of Wales Press.
Blanchard, Claudius. 1875. *Histoire de l'Abbaye d'Hautecombe en Savoie*. Chambéry: Imprimerie Chatelain.
Blondel, Louis. 1935. *L'architecture militaire au temps de Pierre II de Savoie: Les donjons circulaires. Genava* XIII: 271–321.
Blondel, Louis. 1949. *Le château de Brignon. Vallesia* IV: 19–34.
Blondel, Louis. 1950. *Le bourg et le château de Saillon. Unsere Kunstdenkmäler* 1: 8–9.

Bibliography

Blondel, Louis. 1954. *Le château de Saxon. Vallesia* IX: 165–74.
Blondel, Louis. 1954. *Le château et le bourg de Conthey. Vallesia* IX: 149–64.
Blondel, Louis. 1955. *Le château de Saxon: Note Complémentaire. Vallesia* X: 87–8.
Borrel, Étienne-Louis. 1884. *Les monuments anciens de la Tarentaise (Savoie).* Paris: Ducher.
Brooks, Richard. 2015. *Lewes and Evesham 1264–65: Simon de Montfort and the Baron's War*. Oxford: Osprey Publishing Ltd.
Buathier, Henri. 1995. *JEAN Ier DE GRAILLY un chevalier européen du XIIIe siècle.* Berne.
Burnand, Aug. 1911. *La date de la naissance d'Othon 1er, Sire de Grandson. Revue historique vaudoise* 19 no 5: 129–35.
Burnand, Aug. 1911. *Vaudois en Angleterre au XIIIe siècle, avec Othon Ier de Grandson: (d'après M.C.-L. Kingsford). Revue historique vaudoise* 19 no 7: 212–18.
Carpenter, David. & David Prior. 2015. *Magna Carta and Parliament.* London: House of Lords.
Carpenter, David. 1985. 'King, Magnates, and Society: The Personal Rule of King Henry III, 1234–1258'. Speculum: 60.
Carpenter, David. 1992. 'English Peasants in Politics 1258–1267'. Past and Present August: 3–42.
Carpenter, David. 1992. 'King Henry III's "Statute" Against Aliens': July 1263. *English Historical Review* 107: 925–44.
Carpenter, David. 2012.. 'The Pershore "Flores Historiarum": An Unrecognised Chronicle from the Period of Reform and Rebellion in England, 1258—65' December 2012. *English Historical Review*. 127: 1343-1366.
Carpenter, David. 2004. *The Struggle for Mastery of Britain 1066–1284.* London: Penguin Books Ltd.
Carpenter, David. 2020. *Henry III: The Rise to Power and Personal Rule 1207–1258.* New Haven: Yale University Press.
Carpenter, David. 2023. *Henry III: Reform, Rebellion, Civil War, Settlement 1259–1272.* New Haven: Yale University Press.
Carter, Michael. 2017. *Hailes Abbey.* London: English Heritage.
Carutti, Dominico. 1889. *Regesta comitum Sabaudiae, marchionum in Italia ab ultima stirpis origine ad an. MDCCLIII.* Rome: Fratres Bocca.
Chaplais, P. 1952. 'The Making of the Treaty of Paris (1259) and the Royal Style'. *English Historical Review* 67: 235–53.
Chapman, Anthony. 2007. *The Gatehouse of Pevensey Castle.* Sussex Archaeological Collections 145: 97–118.
Chapuisat, Jean-Pierre. 1960. *A Propos des Relations entre la Savoie et l'Angleterre au XIII siècle. Bulletin Philolgique et Historique* 1: 29–34.
Chapuisat, Jean-Pierre. 1964. *Au service de deux rois d'Angleterre au XIIIe siècle: Pierre de Champvent. Revue historique vaudoise* 72: 157–75.
Chapuisat, Jean-Pierre. 1964. *Le Chapitre Savoyard de Hereford au XIIIe siècle* in *Actes du Congrès des Sociétés Savantes de la Province de Savoie. Nouvelle Série 1.* 43–50.
Chapuisat, Jean-Pierre. 1971. *Les deux faces anglaises du Grand-Saint-Bernard au moyen age. Valesia* 26: 5–14.
Chapuisat, Jean-Pierre. 1978. *Quelques variations sur un thème connue: En relisant certains comptes de châtellenies du XIII siècle. Vallesia* XXX: 107–14.
Chapuisat, Jean-Pierre. 1989. *De Mont-sur-Rolle à Windsor, de la Dullive à Dumfries ... La Maison de Savoie et le Pays de Vaud. Bibliothèque historique vaudoise* 97: 117–22.

Chapuisat, Jean-Pierre. 1992. *Un cadet vaudois en Gascogne et à Windsor.* Bibliothèque historique vaudoise 105: 27–37.
Chiaudano, Mario. 1933. *La Finanza Sabauda nel sec. XIII.* Turin: Biblioteca Della Societa Storica Subalpina.
Church, Stephen. 2017. *Henry III: A Simple and God-Fearing King.* London: Allen Lane, Penguin Random House.
Citron, Suzanne. 1987. *Le Mythe National: L'histoire de France revisitée.* Paris: Les Éditions de l'Arelier / Éditions Ouvrières.
Clifford, Esther Rowland. 1961. *A Knight of Great Renown: The Life and Times of Othon de Grandson.* Chicago: The University of Chicago Press.
Cockerill, Sara. 2014. *Eleanor of Castile: The Shadow Queen.* 2nd edition. Stroud: Amberley Publishing.
Coldstream, Nicola. 2003. 'Architects, Advisers and Design at Edward I's Castles in Wales. Architectural History'. *Journal of the Society of Architectural Historians of Great Britain* 46: 19–36.
Coss, Peter R., P. R. Coss & Simon D. Lloyd. 1988. *King Henry III and the 'Aliens'*, 1236–1272. Boydell & Brewer.
Cox, Eugene L. 1974. *The Eagles of Savoy: The House of Savoy in Thirteenth Century Europe.* Princeton: Princeton University Press.
D'Avray, D. L. 2005. 'Authentication of Marital Status: A Thirteenth-Century English Royal Annulment Process and Late Medieval Cases from the Papal Penitentiary'. *English Historical Review* 120: 987–1013.
d'Orville dit Cabaret, Jean. 1995. *La Chronique de Savoie.* Montmelian: La Fontaine de Siloé.
Darracott, Ann. 2014. *The Grandisons: Their Built and Chivalric Legacy.* Maidenhead: Maidenhead Civic Society.
Davies, Norman. 2012. *Vanished Kingdoms: The History of Half-Forgotten Europe.* London: Penguin Books.
Davies, R. R. 1979. 'Kings, Lords and Liberties in the March of Wales, 1066–1272'. *Transactions of the Royal Historical Society* 29: 41–61.
Davies, R. R. 1987. *The Age of Conquest: Wales 1063–1415.* Oxford: Oxford University Press.
Davin, Emmanuel. 1963. *Béatrice de Savoie, Comtesse de Provence, mère de quatre reines (1198-1267).* Bulletin de l'Association Guillaume Budé 2: 176–89.
de Laborderie, Olivier, D. A. Carpenter & J. R. Maddicott. 2000. 'The Last Hours of Simon de Montfort: A New Account'. *English Historical Review*: 115
de Raemy, Daniel. 2004. *Châteaux, donjons et grandes tours dans les Etats de Savoie (1230–1330).* Lausanne: Cahiers d'archéologie romande 98 et 99.
de Gingins La Sarra, M.F. 1857. *Recherches Historiques sur les Acquisitions des Sires de Montfaucon et de la Maison de Chalons dans le Pays de Vaud.* Lausanne: Georges Bridel Éditeur.
Demotz, Bernard. 1987. *L'État et le château au Moyen Âge: l'exemple savoyard. Journal des savants:* 27–64.
Demotz, Bernard. 2000. *Le Comté de Savoie du XIe au XVe siècle.* Genève: Editions Slatkine.
di Collegno, Saverio Provana. 1901. *Notizie d'alcune certose del Piemonte,* all'interno di *Miscellanea di Storia Italiana, terza serie, Tomo VI:* Turin. Fratelli Bocca Librai di S.M.
Dipartimento di Lingue e Letterature Straniere e Culture dell'Università degli Studi di Torino (ed.). 2014. 'A Warm Mind-Shake' *Scritti in onore di Paolo Bertinetti.* Turin. *Edizioni Trauben.*

Bibliography

Donnet, André & Louis Blondel. 1963. *Château du Valais*. Olten: Editions Walter.
Dufour, Béatrice, Catherine Santschi, Gustave Deghilage, René Dreyfus, Bernard Golaz & Frank Perroter. 1984. *Saint Prex 1234–1984*. Saint-Prex: Commune de Saint-Prex.
Duncan, A. A. M. 2002. *The Kingship of the Scots 842–1292*. Edinburgh: Edinburgh University Press.
Edwards, J. G. 1935. *Calendar of Ancient Correspondence Concerning Wales*. Cardiff: University Press Board Cardiff.
Edwards, J. G. 1944. 'Edward I's Castle-Building in Wales'. *The Proceedings of the British Academy* XXXII.
Favrod, Justin. 2000. *La nécropole du Pré de la Cure à Yverdon-Les-Bains. Cahiers d'Archéologie Romande*.
Fontannaz, Monique & Brigitte Pradervand. 2015. *Les monuments d'art et d'histoire de la Suisse*. Berne: Société d'histoire de l'art en Suisse SHAS.
Fontannaz, Monique. 2006. *La Ville de Moudon*. Berne: Société D'Histoire de L'Art en Suisse SHAS.
Fryde, E. B, D. E. Greenway, S. Porter & I. Roy. 1986. *Handbook of British Chronology*. 3rd edition. London: Offices of the Royal Historical Society.
Fryde, E. B. 1962. *Book of Prests of the King's Wardrobe for 1294–5*. Oxford: Clarendon Press.
Galland, Bruno. 1988. *Un Savoyard sur le siège de Lyon au XIIIe siècle: Philippe de Savoie*. Bibliothèque de l'école des chartes tome 146 livraison 1. 31–67.
Girart Dorens. 1909. 'Sir Otho de Grandison 1238?–1328'. *Transactions of the Royal Historical Society* 3: 125–95.
Goldstone, Nancy. 2010. *Four Queens: The Provençal Sisters Who Ruled Europe*. London: Orion Publishing Group.
Goodall, John. 1999. *Pevensey Castle*. London: English Heritage.
Gough, Henry. 1900. *Itinerary of King Edward the First throughout his reign, A.D. 1272–1307, exhibiting his movements so far as they are recorded*. Paisley: Alexander Gardner.
Grandjean, Marcel. 1963. *A Propos de la Construction de la Cathédrale de Lausanne (XII-XIIIe Siecle)*. Genava XI: 261–87.
Grandjean, Marcel. 1969. *La 'carentena' du Chapitre de Notre-Dame de Lausanne dans le cloître de la cathédrale*. Revue historique vaudoise 77: 7–13.
Griffiths, J. 1935–7. 'Documents Relating to the Rebellion of Madoc, 1294–5'. *Bulletin of the Board of Celtic Studies* VIII.
Guichenon, Samuel. 1778. *Histoire Généalogique de la Royale Maison de Savoie*. Turin: Chez Jean-Michel Briolo.
Hartland, Beth. 2001. 'Vaucouleurs, Ludlow and Trim: the role of Ireland in the career of Geoffrey de Geneville (c. 1226–1314)'. *Irish Historical Studies* XXXII: 457–77.
Heidemann, Joseph. 1903. *Papst Clemens IV* Part 1. Münster: H. Schöningh.
Hislop, Malcolm. 2019. *Barnard Castle, Bowes Castle and Egglestone Abbey*. London: English Heritage.
Hislop, Malcolm. 2020. *James of St George and the Castles of North Wales*. Barnsley: Pen & Sword Books Ltd.
Hodgson, John. 1893. *A History of Northumberland*. Newcastle upon Tyne: A. Reid & Sons Co.
Howell, Margaret. 1998. *Eleanor of Provence*. Oxford: Blackwell Publishers Ltd.
Jacob, E. F. 1924. 'What were the "Provisions of Oxford"?' *History* 9: 188–200.
Jacob, E. F. 1925. *Studies in the Period of Baronial Reform and Rebellion 1258-1267*. Oxford: Clarendon Press.

Jones, Dan. 2012. *The Plantagenets: The Kings Who Made England*. eBook edition. London: William Collins.
Kaeuper, Richard W. 1973. *Bankers to the Crown: The Lucca and Edward I*. Princeton: Princeton University Press.
Kerrich, Thomas. 1817. 'Observations upon some Sepulchral Monuments in Italy and France'. *Archaeologia*: 18.
Loftie, William John 1878. *Memorials of the Savoy; the palace: the hospital: the chapel. With an appendix of original documents contributed by Charles Trice Martin and a pref. by Henry White*. London: MacMillan & Co.
Maddicott, J. R. 1983. 'The Mise of Lewes, 1264'. *English Historical Review*: 98
Maddicott, J. R. 1995. *Simon de Montfort*. Cambridge: Cambridge University Press.
Maddicott, J. R. 2016. 'Who was Simon de Montfort, Earl of Leicester'. *Transactions of the Royal Historical Society* 26: 43–58.
Marchandisse, Alain. 1997. *Guillaume de Savoie Un Monsfrum Spiiritüelle et Beluá Multorum Capitum sur le Trône de Saint Lambert? Bulletin de la Société Royale le Vieux-Liège* XIII.
Martignier David & Aymon de Crousaz, 1867. *Dictionnaire historique, géographique et statistique de canton de Vaud*, Imprimerie L. Corbaz et compagnie.
Martignier, D. 1867. *Dictionnaire historique, géographique & statistique de canton de Vaud*. Lausanne: Corbaz.
Ménégaldo Silvère & Olivier Bertrand. 2016. *Vocabulaire d'ancien français* 3e édition. (Linguistique) (French edition). Malakoff: Armand Colin.
Morerod, Jean-Daniel. 2012. *La Cathédrale Notre-Dame de Lausanne: Monument européen, temple vaudois*. Lausanne: La Bibliothèque des Arts.
Morris, John E. 1901. *The Welsh Wars of Edward I*. Oxford: Clarendon Press.
Mottaz, Eugene. 1900. *Note sur la construction du château d'Yverdon. Revue historique vaudoise* 8: 359–67.
Mugnier, François. 1890. *Les Savoyards en Angleterre au XIIIe siècle et Pierre d'Aigueblanche évêque d'Héreford*. Chambéry: Imprimerie Ménard.
Ortenberg, Veronica. 1990. 'Archbishop Sigeric's Journey to Rome in 990'. *Anglo-Saxon England* 19: 197–246.
Perret, André, 1983. *Le comte Pierre II de Savoie. L'expansion savoyarde et l'alliance anglaise au xiiie siècle. Revue Savoisienne* 95–119.
Phillips, Charles. 2018. *The Medieval Castle*. Yeovil: Haynes Publishing.
Porter, Roy. 2020. *Pevensey Castle*. London: English Heritage.
Powicke, Sir Maurice. 1953. *The Thirteenth Century 1216–1307*. Oxford: Oxford University Press.
Prestwich, Michael. 1972. 'A New Account of the Welsh Campaign 1294–95'. *Welsh History Review* 6: 89–94.
Prestwich, Michael. 1997. *Edward I*. Yale: Yale University Press.
Prestwich, Michael. 2002. 'Document: Edward I's Wars in the Hagnaby Chronicle'. *Journal of Medieval Military History* X: 197–214.
Prestwich, Michael. 2005. *Plantagenet England 1225–1360*. Oxford: Oxford University Press.
Prestwich, Michael. 2010. *Knight: The Medieval Warrior's (Unofficial) Guide*. London: Thames & Hudson.
Prestwich, Michael. *Medieval People*. London: Thames and Hudson.
Previté-Orton, C. W. 1912. *The Early History of the House of Savoy (1000–1233)*. Cambridge: Cambridge University Press.

Bibliography

Pryce, Huw. 2001. 'National identity in Twelfth-Century Wales'. *English Historical Review*. 116, no. 468: 775–801.

Pryce, Huw. 2005. *The Acts of Welsh Rulers: 1120 to 1283*. Cardiff: University of Wales Press.

Ray, Michael. 2006. 'The Savoyard Cousins: A Comparison of the Careers and Relative Success of the Grandson (Grandison) and Champvent (Chavent) Families in England'. *The Antiquaries Journal* 86.

Ray, Michael. 2017. 'A Vaudois servant of Henry III, Ebal II de Mont (Ebulo de Montibus)'. www.academia.edu/31930999/A_Vaudois_servant_of_Henry_III_Ebal_II_de_Mont_Ebulo_de_Montibus?email_work_card=view-paper.

Renn, D. F. 1971. 'The Turris de Penuesel: A Reappraisal and a Theory'. *Sussex Archaeological Collections* 109: 55–64.

Reymond, Annick Voirol. 2013. *Grandson Castle: 1,000 Years of History*. Grandson: Artgraphic Cavin SA.

Reymond, Maxime. 1920. *Le Chevalier Othon I de Grandson*. Revue historique vaudoise 28, no. 6: 161–79.

Ridgeway, H. W. 1983. 'The Politics of royal court, 1247–65, with special reference to the role of aliens'. University of Oxford.

Ridgeway, H. W. 1989. 'Favourites and Henry III's Problems of Patronage, 1247–1258'. *English Historical Review* 104: 590–610.

Ridgeway. H. W. 2023. 'An English Cartulary Roll of Peter of Savoy, Lord of Richmond (1240–1268): Archives, Interests and Servants of an Alien Favourite of Henry III.' forthcoming in a volume to be edited by Professors Nigel Saul & Nicholas Vincent for the Pipe Roll Society, London 2023.

Rigby. Stephen. H. 2017. Boston, 1086-1225 A Medieval Boom Town. Lincoln: The Society for Lincolnshire History and Archaeology.

Roderick, A. J. 1952. 'The Feudal Relation Between the English Crown and the Welsh Princes'. *History* 37: 201–12.

Roth, Charles. 1948. *Cartulaire du Chapitre de Notre-Dame de Lausanne*. Lausanne: Librairie Payot.

Rothero, Christopher. 1984. *The Scottish and Welsh Wars 1250–1400*. 20th edition. Botley: Osprey Publishing Ltd.

Round, J, Horace. 1898. 'Hornchurch Priory'. *Transactions of the Essex Archaeological Society VI*: 1–12.

Royer, Katherine. 2003. 'The Body in Parts: Reading the Execution Ritual in Late Medieval England'. *Historical Reflections / Réflexions Historiques* 29: 319–39.

Rymer, Thomas. 1816. *Fœdra, Conventiones, Litteræ, et Cujuscunque Generis Acta Publica Inter Reges Angliæ et alios quosvis Imperatores, Reges, Pontifices, bel Communitates*. London.

Salzmann, L. F. 1906. 'Documents Relating to Pevensey Castle'. *Sussex Archaeological Collections* 49: 1–30.

Salzmann, L. F. 1908. 'Excavations at Pevensey'. *Sussex Archaelogical Collections* 51: 99–114.

Sanders, I. J. 1951. 'The Texts of the Peace of Paris, 1259'. *English Historical Review* 66: 81–97.

Shelby, L. R. 1964. 'The Role of the Master Mason in Mediaeval English Building'. *Speculum* 39: 387–403.

Shirley, W. W. 1862. 'Royal and other historical letters illustrative of the reign of Henry III'. From the originals in the Public Record Office. London: Longmans, Green, Longman & Roberts.

Simpson, W. Douglas. 1928. 'James de Sancto Georgio, Master of the Works to King Edward in Wales and Scotland'. *Transactions of the Anglesey Antiquarian and Field Society*: 31–41.

Sivèry, Gérard. 1987. *Marguerite de Provence: Une reine au temps des Cathédrales*. Paris: Fayard.

St. John, Bayle. 1856. *The Subalpine Kingdom: Or, Experiences and Studies in Savoy, Piedmont, and Genoa*. London: Chapman & Hall.

Stevenson, Joseph. 1870. *Documents Illustrative of the History of Scotland* Volume 1. Edinburgh: H. M. General Register House.

Stewart, Susan. 2013. Royal Justice in Surrey 1258-1269. Woking: Surrey Record Society.

Stubbs, William. 1896. *The Constitutional History of England*. Oxford: The Clarendon Press.

Tanquerey, Frédéric Joseph. 1916. *Recueil de Lettres Anglo-Françaises, 1265–1399*. Paris: Librairie Ancienne Honoré Champion.

Taylor, Arnold. 1950. 'Master James of St. George'. *English Historical Review* 65 no. 257: 433–57.

Taylor, Arnold. 1953. 'A Letter from Lewis of Savoy to Edward I'. *English Historical Review* LXVIII: 56–62.

Taylor, Arnold. 1953. 'The Castle of St Georges D'Espéranche'. *The Antiquaries Journal* 33: 33–47.

Taylor, Arnold. 1963. 'Some Notes on the Savoyards in North Wales, 1277–1300. With special reference to the Savoyard element in the construction of Harlech Castle'. *Genava* XI: 289–315.

Taylor, Arnold. 1974. *The King's Works in Wales 1277–1330*. London: Her Majesty's Stationery Office.

Taylor, Arnold. 1976. 'Notes and Documents: Who was "John Pennardd, Leader of the men of Gwynedd?"' *English Historical Review* 91: 79–97.

Taylor, Arnold. 1985. *Studies in Castles and Castle-Building*. London: The Hambledon Press.

Taylor, Arnold. 1986. *The Welsh Castles of King Edward I*. London: The Hambledon Press.

Taylor, Arnold. 1989. *Studies in Medieval History Presented to R. Allen Brown*. Woodbridge: The Boydell Press.

Thomas, Hugh M. 1994. 'Subinfeudation and Alienation of Land, Economic Development, and the Wealth of Nobles on the Honor of Richmond, 1066 to c. 1300'. Albion: *A Quarterly Journal Concerned with British Studies* 26.

Thompson, Kathleen. 1997. 'Lords, castellans, constables and dowagers: The Rape of Pevensey from the 11th to the 13th Century'. *Sussex Archaeological Collections* 135: 209–20.

Toy, Sidney. 1984. *Castles: Their Construction and History*. Mineola: Dover Publications Inc.

Van Bechem, Victor. 1913. *La 'ville neuve' d'Yverdon: Foundation de Pierre de Savoie*. Festgabe für Gerold Meyer von Kronau 205–26.

Voutaz, Canon Jean-Pierre & Pierre Rouyer. 2013. *Discovering the Great Saint Bernard*. Martigny: Les Editions du Grand-Saint-Bernard.

Weiler, Björn. 2006. 'Knighting, Homage, and the Meaning of Ritual: The Kings of England and their Neighbours in the Thirteenth Century'. *Viator* 37: 275–99.

Weir, Alison. 2020. *Queens of the Crusades: Eleanor of Aquitaine and Her Successors*. London: Penguin Random House UK.

Wenner, Manfred W. 1980. 'The Arab/Muslim Presence in Medieval Central Europe'. *International Journal of Middle East Studies*: 12.

Bibliography

Westlake, H. F. 1923. *Hornchurch Priory a Kalendar of Documents in the Possession of the Warden and Fellows of New College Oxford*. London: Philip Allan & Co.

Wheatley, Abigail. 2015. *The Idea of the Castle in Medieval England*. York: York Medieval Press.

William Stubbs. 1867. *Gesta Regis Henrici = the Chronicle of the reigns of Henry II and Richard I, A.D. 1169–1192*. London: Longmans, Green, Reader & Dyer.

Wilson, Christopher. 1990. *The Gothic Cathedral*. London: Thames and Hobson Ltd.

Wilson, Peter H. 2017. The Holy Roman Empire. 2nd edition. London: Penguin.

Wurstemberger, J. Ludwig. 1859. *Pierre II, Comte de Savoie, Marquis en Italie et sa Maison*. Berne: Stæmpfle.

Yates, W. N. 1971. 'Bishop Peter de Aquablanca (1240–1268): a reconsideration'. *Journal of Ecclesiastical History* 22: 303–17.

Index

Aiguebelle, Château, 3, 8–9, 11
Aigueblanche, Pierre de, Bishop of Hereford, 26, 55, 58, 70, 79, 85, 92, 95–6, 130
    Death and Tomb, 38, 180–2
    Diplomacy for Henry III, 26, 46–7, 49, 51, 68, 76, 97, 99, 103–4, 141
    Imprisonment and Baronial War, 131–2, 141–3
    Keeper of the Privy Wardrobe for Henry III, 26
    Matthew Paris Criticism, 26, 73–4, 79, 83, 104
Albon, County of, see Dauphiné
Alexander IV, Pope, 103–5, 114, 119, 127, 129, 170
Alphonse I, Count of Poitiers, 49, 78, 149
Amiens, Mise of, 127, 140–2, 147, 150, 178
Anjou, Charles d', King of Naples, 75, 77, 99–100, 170–1, 182
Angoulême, Isabel de, Queen of England, 22, 30, 49–51, 78, 100
Arlod, Château d', 52, 148
Asti, 10, 104
Auxonne, Béatrice de, Dame de Marnay, 54
Avigliana, Castello di, 8, 64, 76, 168, 174

Bard, Castello di, 64, 76, 85, 122
Baronial War, Second, 28, 34, 46, 48, 62, 80, 84, 103, 109, 143–66 176, 178
    Battle of Evesham, 163–4
    Battle of Lewes, 143–5
    Battle of Northampton, 143
    Siege of Pevensey Castle, 145, 148, 151, 155–9, 161–3, 168, 176
    Siege of Richmond Castle, 155–6, 158, 176
Bazas, 94–7
Béarn, Gaston de, 87, 94, 96, 182
Belley, Bishopric of, 3, 5, 9, 44–5, 47, 53, 59, 103, 177

Benauges, Château, 94–5, 102, 136–7, 168
Berenguer, Ramon, Count of Provence, 12–13, 21, 23, 46–7, 49, 56, 74, 77, 94, 185
Berkhamsted, Castle, 127, 140, 175, 182
Bern, 10, 19–20, 101, 103–4, 120–1, 123–4, 175–7, 180
Bertram, Master, Engineer, 94–5, 136–7, 139
Bigod, Hugh, Justiciar of England, 109, 113, 117, 125–6, 140, 145, 159
Bigod, Roger, 4th Earl of Norfolk, 42, 90, 109–1, 113
Boston, port of, 41–4
Bowes, Castle, 41, 155
Braose, Maud de, Baroness Mortimer of Wigmore, 160, 164
Bryn Derwin, Battle of, 105–6
Bugey, 5, 8, 16–8, 42, 52, 56, 59, 90, 137, 140, 148, 172–4, 177, 179
Burgundy, Free County of, 6, 37, 49, 54, 76, 85, 107, 120–2, 179
Burgundy, Second Kingdom of, 1–3, 12, 21, 61–2, 76, 136, 148, 179

Cantilupe, Walter de, Bishop of Worcester, 113, 144, 146, 160, 163
Castille, Blanche de, Queen of France, 21, 24, 49, 91, 118
Castille, Leonor de, Queen of England, 96–8, 103, 185–6
Chablais, 3, 5, 8, 10, 14–6, 18, 76, 84, 102, 137, 148, 168, 172–4, 180
Chambéry, 9, 26, 85, 99, 101, 116, 122, 139, 148
Champvent, Guillaume de, Bishop of Lausanne, 27, 129, 169
Champvent, Pierre de, Chamberlain of the Household, 54, 59, 61, 84, 92, 97, 124, 126, 129, 132, 146, 167, 169
Champvent, Henri de, 16, 37, 62, 84, 120

Index

Charron, Guichard I de, Steward of the Honour of Richmond, 42, 52, 59, 82, 155
Charron, Guichard II de, Steward of the Honour of Richmond, 42, 52, 128, 142, 155–6, 178
Charron, Stephen de, Prior of Thetford, 52, 82
Châtel Argent, Château, 8, 168, 174
Châtillon-sur-Cluses, Château, 15–6, 194–5, 262
Chillon, Château de, 8–10, 15–6, 18, 101–3, 135–7, 139, 157, 168–9, 173–4, 176–7, 180, 182, 189, 218
Cholay, Nantelme de, 148, 157–8, 163
Clare de, Richard, 6th Earl of Gloucester, 90, 97, 109–10, 113, 129
Clare de, Gilbert, 7th Earl of Gloucester, 131, 143–4, 155, 160, 162, 165, 183
Clement IV, Pope, 153, 169
Conradin, also Conrad III, King of Sicily, 103, 170–1
Constantinople, Jeanne de, Countess of Flanders, 21–2, 30–1, 99
Cornillon, Château de, 16–7, 140, 148
Cossonay, Jean de, Bishop of Lausanne, 19–20, 58, 121, 123

Dam, Flanders, 147–8
Dauphiné, the, 1, 6, 12, 21, 48, 85, 179, 182
Deganwy, Castle, 68, 70–1, 96, 103, 106–7, 130, 162
Despenser, Hugh, Justiciar of England, 125–7, 131–2, 164
Dreux, Jean II de, Duke of Brittany, 117, 119, 178
Dyserth, Castle, 67–9, 71, 103, 106, 130, 162

Eagle, Honour of the, 45, 47–8, 51, 168, 173, 178–80
Edward I, King of England, 26, 28, 37, 47, 61, 65, 74, 76–80, 84–5, 90, 102, 116, 122–3, 135–6, 138, 148, 167, 169, 173, 176–81, 184–7
Edward, The Lord, 62, 64, 77, 86, 92, 94–5, 119, 125, 131–3, 135, 140, 149–51, 153–4, 166, 168, 170–1, 174, 182
  Appanage, 55–6, 70–1, 75, 87, 90, 94–6, 103, 106, 109, 126, 130, 160
  Battle of Evesham, 163–4, 166–8, 170, 183
  Battle of Northampton, 143
  Battle of Lewes, 143–6
  birth, 33–4
  escape from captivity, 147, 154–5, 159–62
  Gascony, 54, 75, 87, 89–90, 94–8, 101, 103
  Lusignans, 110, 113–14, 124
  marriage to Leonor de Castille, 96–8
  Pierre de Savoie, 42, 45–6, 53, 55, 59–60, 70, 87, 89–90, 94, 96–8, 102–3, 109–10, 114, 127–8, 141, 147, 154, 160–1, 176, 186–7
  role of Savoyards, 45–6, 53–5, 59–60, 70, 89–90, 94, 103, 109, 128, 150, 155
  Simon de Montfort, 125–6, 130–1, 160, 162–3, 165
  Wales, 55, 70–1, 96, 103, 106–7, 109–10, 126, 130, 162
Edmund Crouchback, Earl of Lancaster, 62, 70, 97, 99–100, 104, 107–8, 119, 131–2, 140, 166–7, 171, 180–1
Estavayer, Conon d', 14–5
Eu, Honour of, 48, 83–4, 89, 128
Evesham, Battle of, 163–4, 166–8, 170, 183
Evian, Peace of (1244), 58–9, 138

Faucigny, 7, 15–17, 54, 140, 148, 151, 157, 179–80, 182
Faucigny, Agnès de, Countess of Savoy, 15, 54, 107, 111, 180, 182
Faucigny, Aymon II de, Seigneur de Faucigny, 17, 19, 54, 84
Foulquois, Guy, Papal Legate, see also Clement IV, Pope, 149–50, 153
Frederick I Barbarossa, Holy Roman Emperor, 2, 5, 62
Frederick II, Holy Roman Emperor, 2, 5–6, 11, 23, 32, 39, 47, 57–8, 62, 71, 74–5, 98–100, 103, 107

Gascony, 22, 32, 51, 54–5, 78, 87, 90, 92–99, 101, 103, 117, 128, 136–7, 161, 168, 177, 182
Geneville, Geoffrey de, 1st Baron Geneville, 53, 89, 94, 107, 159–62
Genève, Ebal de, 53, 62, 94, 114, 124
Genève, Guillaume II, Count of Geneva, 16, 18, 51, 53–4, 84, 120, 124, 128, 177
Genève, Humbert I, Count of Geneva, 16, 51, 53

319

Genève, Marguerite de, Countess of Savoy, 8, 13, 15–18, 47, 53, 56
Genève, Pierre de, Constable of Windsor Castle, 47, 51, 53–4, 59, 89, 161
Geneville, Gefferoi de, also Joinville, 1st Baron de Geneville, 53–4, 89, 94, 159–62
Grailly, Jean de, Seneschal of Gascony, 95, 103, 136, 144, 146, 168–9, 184
Grandson, Agnès de, 59, 101, 123
Grandson, Château de, 37, 60–2, 90, 123, 138
Grandson, Ebal IV de, Seigneur de Grandson, 61
Grandson, Famille de, 15–6, 59, 61–2, 120, 124, 148
Grandson, Othon de, Justiciar of North Wales, 46–7, 52, 61, 84, 90, 92, 96, 120, 144, 148, 150, 167–70, 180, 184
Grandson, Pierre de, Seigneur de Grandson, 37, 59, 62, 84, 91
Grossi de Chatelard, Rodolphe, Archbishop of Tarentaise, 94, 118, 147
Gruffydd, Llywelyn ap, Prince of Wales, 66, 107–9, 112, 126, 130, 162, 164–5
Guigues VII de Vienne, Dauphin of the Viennois, Count of Albon, 48, 182
Gümmenen, Chateau de, 120, 175, 177
Gwerneigron, Treaty of, 26, 68
Gwenwynwyn, Grufydd ap, Prince of Powys, 67, 69

Habsburg, Rudolf I von, 175–7, 179, 183
Hadleigh, Castle, 54, 59, 114
Hastings, Castle, 63–4, 84
Hastings, Honour of see Honour of Eu
Hautecombe, Abbey, 33, 38, 52–3, 80, 101, 118, 169–70, 179–80, 187
Henry III, Holy Roman Emperor, 13
Henry II, King of England, 2, 5, 7, 21–2, 46, 51, 69, 100
Henry III, King of England, 10, 13, 21, 28, 33, 35–6, 43–4, 48, 52, 59–61, 64, 76, 78, 79, 83, 85–6, 100–1, 105, 108, 115, 117–18, 128–9, 131–2, 134, 136–7, 140–2, 159–60, 165–7, 169, 184, 186
  Anglo-Capetian Relations, 22–3, 31, 46–7, 49, 51, 55–6, 75, 77–8, 87, 99–100, 116–20, 129, 179, 187
  Baronage relations, 25–6, 34, 45, 111–16, 124–32, 140–42, 154, 174
  Baronial War, 142–51, 154–7, 164, 166–7, 169
  Battle of Taillebourg, 50–1, 53
  Boniface de Savoie, 44–5, 47–9, 53, 58, 73–5, 77, 79, 113–4, 116, 119
  coronation, 21
  death, 183
  Evesham, Battle of, 163–4, 166–8, 170, 183
  Gascony, 22, 32, 51, 54–5, 78, 87, 90, 92–99, 101, 103, 117, 128, 136–7, 161, 168, 177, 182
  Gascon Expedition 12, 53–4, 90, 92–6
  Guillaume de Savoie, 24–5, 29–30, 32–3, 38–9, 85
  Lewes, Battle of, 143–5, 148, 160, 164
  Lusignans, 78–9, 89–90, 108–15, 134
  marriage to Alianor, 23–4, 28, 47, 80, 185
  meetings with King Louis IX of France, 100–1, 118–19, 129, 141–2
  Mise of Amiens, 140–2, 150
  patronage, 10, 13, 24–6, 29–31, 36, 39–40, 43–7, 54–6, 60, 78–80, 100–2, 108, 112, 151, 178–9
  Pierre de Aigueblanche, 26, 28, 47, 49, 74, 77, 79–80, 96, 103–4, 130, 141–2, 181
  Pierre de Savoie, 36–40, 43, 47, 49, 51–2, 56, 63–4, 67, 69–70, 78–79, 84, 87–8, 90, 92–7, 99, 101–2, 104–5, 107, 109–15, 117–20, 124, 140–2, 144–5, 147, 150, 154–7, 168, 172–3, 176, 178–80, 187
  Provisions of Oxford, 80, 113–16, 125, 128–9, 131–3, 141–2, 154, 165–6, 174
  Richard, Earl of Cornwall, 32, 34–5, 55, 75, 84, 88, 90, 92, 105, 107, 109, 112, 116, 118, 126, 140, 144–5, 175, 182
  Saintonge War, 49–51, 53, 55, 60
  Savoy, Enfeoffment of Key Castles, Palace and Town, 64, 75–7, 120
  Sicilian Business, 99–100, 103–5, 108–9, 119, 170–71
  Simon de Montfort, 31–2, 34, 50, 56, 78, 86–8, 109–11, 116–17, 124–7, 129, 132, 139, 141–6, 150–1, 155–7, 162, 164, 166, 170, 175

Index

Treaty of Paris 1259, 117–9, 179
Wales, 64–71, 105–9, 112, 126, 130, 162, 184
xenophobia, 25, 79–80, 124, 127–8, 133–4, 174
Hereford, Bishopric of, 26–8, 38, 47, 49, 54, 58, 62, 70, 73, 75, 79, 83, 85, 92, 95–6, 103–4, 131–2, 142–3, 181–2

Iorwerth also Fawr, Llywelyn ap, Prince of Gwynedd, 67, 69, 162

John, King of England, 22, 43, 63, 67, 84, 112, 143
Joinville, Simon de, Seigneur de Gex et Marnay, 54, 94, 107, 110–11, 121, 124, 160–1

Kenilworth, Castle, 56, 86, 141, 162–3, 169–70
Kingston, Treaty of, 128
Konrad II, Holy Roman Emperor, 2–4
Kyburg, Hartmann IV von, 10, 175–6
Kyburg, Hartmann V von, 175–6
Kyburg, Marguerite von, 10, 176, 179

La Bâtiaz, Château de, 138
La Réole, 93–5
Les Échelles, 8, 147, 177
Lacy, Edmund de, 2nd Earl of Lincoln, 77–9, 95, 97, 104, 112
Lacy, Mathilde de, Baroness de Geneville, 53, 159, 161
Lacy, Maud de see Lacy, Mathilde de
Lausanne, Battle of, 18–20
Lausanne, Bishopric of, 7, 10–11, 15–6, 18–20, 55, 85, 121, 169
Lausanne Cathedral, 15, 18–9
Les Clées, Château, 84–5, 120, 123, 138
Lewes, Battle of, 143–5, 148, 160, 164
Lewes, Mise of, 146, 149
Llywelyn Fawr, Dafydd ap, Prince of Gwynedd, 66–71, 105
Llywelyn Fawr, Grufydd ap, 67–9, 71, 105
Lompnes, Château, 8, 16–17, 52, 179
Louis IX, King of France, 21–4, 30, 47, 49, 77, 84, 89, 91–2, 100–1, 104, 110, 116, 127,
132, 140–1, 145–6, 149–50, 154, 158–9, 170, 174, 178
Battle of Taillebourg, 50–1, 53
7th Crusade, 77–8, 84, 87, 91
meetings with King Henry III of England, 100–1, 118–19, 129, 141–2
Mise of Amiens, 140–2, 150
Saintonge War, 49–51, 53, 55, 60
Treaty of Paris 1259, 117–19, 179
Louis, Baron de Vaud, 102, 116, 135, 178–81
Ludlow, Castle, 53–4, 159–62
Lusignan, Alice de, Countess of Surrey, 78, 89
Lusignan, Aymer de, Bishop of Winchester, 79, 85–6, 89, 109, 111, 114–15, 125
Lusignan, Guy de, 78, 86, 89, 108, 111, 117
Lusignan, Hugues X de, Count of La Marche, 30, 49–51, 78

Manfred, King of Sicily, 103, 170–1
Magna Carta, 25–6, 29, 79, 91–3, 95, 108, 112, 115, 142, 151, 165, 173
Mansel, John, Lord Chancellor, 32, 51–2, 70, 89, 97, 113, 126–7, 132, 140–2, 153–4, 172
Maurienne, 3, 5, 7–10, 26–7, 39, 82, 148, 173
Mésoz, Jean de, Engineer, 94–5, 136–9
Mont Cenis, Pass, 3, 5, 10, 76, 85,
Mont, Ebal II de, Constable of Windsor Castle, 52–4, 61, 80, 86, 89, 92, 94–5, 97, 110, 123–4, 126, 128–9, 132, 137–8, 141, 146, 155, 169
Mont-le-Grand, Château, 61, 92
Mont, Pierre de, Physician to Pierre de Savoie, 51–2
Montbéliard, Richard IV de, 120
Montfaucon, Amédée III de, 120–2
Montferrand, Imbert de, 59–60, 114, 126, 128–9, 132, 146
Montfort, Simon de, 6th Earl of Leicester, 21–2, 29, 31, 34, 49, 52, 86, 90, 119, 127, 129–30, 170
Baronial War, Second, 143–66 176, 178
Council of Fifteen, 113
death, 163–4
Evesham, Battle of, 163–4, 166–8, 170
Lewes, Battle of, 143–5, 148, 160, 164
Lewes, Mise of, 146, 149

marriage to Eleanor Marshal, 31–2, 40, 56, 117
Mise of Amiens, 140–2, 147, 150, 178
Murder of London's Jewry, 143
Oath of 1258, 109–10
parliament 1265, 165
Pierre de Savoie, Allies, 88–9, 101, 109, 174
Pierre de Savoie, Enemies, 117, 124–6, 131–2, 140, 150, 154–5, 160, 174, 187
Provisions of Oxford, 113–6, 125, 128–9, 131–3, 141–2, 154, 165–6, 174
Thomas II, Count of Flanders, Debt, 34–5, 116
Revolution of 1258, 110–5
Saintongue War, 50
Seneschal of Gascony, 78, 80, 87, 92–4
Treaty of Paris 1259 Difficulties, 117
trial, 88, 126
xenophobia, 124, 133–4
Montfort, Simon de, the Younger, 132, 143, 157, 162
Montmélian, Château de, 5, 8–9, 101, 168, 174
Montréal, Humbert de, 168
Mortimer, Roger de, Baron of Wigmore, 64, 126, 130, 140, 144, 159–64
Moudon, 11, 19–20, 36, 58–9, 61, 84, 103, 120, 168, 174

Nantua, Priory of, 44–5, 83
Northampton, Battle of, 143

Oxford, Provisions of, 80, 113–6, 125, 128–9, 131–3, 141–2, 154, 165–6, 174

Palud, Guy de la, Keeper of Queen Alianor's Wardrobe, 62
Paris, Matthew, 22, 30, 35, 39, 44–6, 53, 60–1, 70, 75, 86, 88, 90, 92, 96, 98, 100, 103, 106, 108, 110, 112–3, 133, 142, 183–5
Alianor de Provence, 9, 23, 28, 33
Béatrice de Savoie, 8, 13
Boniface de Savoie, 57–8, 73, 81–2, 103, 170
death, 116
Guillaume de Savoie, 14, 24–5, 29, 31–3
Mont Granier Disaster, 82
Pierre d'Aigueblamche, 26, 79, 83, 104

Pierre de Savoie, 37–8, 40, 79, 95, 103, 135, 180, 187
Ramon Berenguer, 12, 74
Stephen de Charron, 52, 82
Thomas II de Savoie, 34, 105, 116
Wurstemberger, 83
xenophobia, 25, 29, 32–3, 37, 79, 82–3, 134
Paris, Treaty of, 117–19, 179
Pesmes, Guillaume de, 94, 107, 110, 131, 137, 144
Pevensey, Castle, 27, 63–4, 90, 93, 145
Pevensey, Honour of see Honour of the Eagle
Pevensey, Siege of, 142, 145–6, 148, 151, 155–9, 161–3
Piedmont, 1, 6, 8, 10, 12, 15, 26, 76, 79, 104–5, 110, 116, 179
Pierre-Châtel, Château, 7–9, 177, 179, 182
Ponthieu, Jeanne de, Countess of Ponthieu, 22, 24, 80, 96–7, 119
Provence, County of, 1–3, 6, 10, 12–14, 21, 23–4, 28, 46–7, 49, 56, 74–5, 77, 104
Provence, Alianor de, Queen of England, 9, 20–1, 39, 42, 45, 47, 49, 56, 58–60, 64, 69, 74–6, 84, 86, 92–3, 95–6, 100–2, 104–5, 110, 116–19, 129, 130–2, 134–5, 139, 140–2, 155, 157, 159–62, 166, 168, 179, 183–5, 187
Attacked by Londoners, 132
birth, 12–3
birth of Edward, 33–4
birth of Edmund, 62
childhood, 13
death, 185–6
escape of the Lord Edward from Captivity, 155, 158–62
Flanders Army, 145–7, 149–56, 158, 176
Lusignans, 89, 95, 109–11, 114, 125
marriage to King Henry III of England, 22–5, 28–9, 80
Pierre de Savoie, 17, 36–8, 46, 48, 53, 55, 59–62, 70, 88–90, 95, 97–8, 103, 109–10, 114–15, 119, 124, 126–8, 142, 145–7, 149–55, 158–62, 168, 174, 178–9, 181
Protection of the Lord Edward, 55–6, 59, 70, 87, 90, 97–8, 103, 111, 114–15, 128, 150, 158–61

Regent, 93
Savoyard Support Network, Queensmen, 30, 33, 35–6, 38, 45–9, 53, 55–6, 59–62, 89–90, 109–10, 114, 127
Wardrobe, 26–8, 60, 62
Siege of Richmond Castle, 155–6, 158, 176
Provence, Marguerite de, Queen of France, 9, 12, 21–2, 24, 30, 47, 49, 74, 84, 86, 100–1, 104, 114, 116–19, 127, 129, 132, 141, 149, 159, 179, 184–5
Provence, Sanchia de, Queen of the Romans, 9, 12, 21, 36, 47–9, 51, 55, 58, 62, 74, 97, 100, 107–8, 116, 127–8, 182–3
Provence, Béatrice de, Queen of Naples, 9, 12, 21, 74, 100, 170
Pugeys, Imbert, 59, 92, 97, 114, 119, 128–9

Rarogne, Henri de, Bishop of Sion, 102, 124, 128, 135–6, 149, 175–7, 179
Rede, John de la, 125, 142, 145
Richard, Earl of Cornwall, King of the Romans, 32, 34–5, 55, 75, 84, 88, 90, 92, 105, 107, 109, 112, 116, 118, 126, 140, 144–5, 175, 182
Richmond, Castle, 27, 40–2, 52, 82, 128, 142, 146, 155–6, 158, 176
Richmond, Honour of, 10, 20, 24–5, 36–7, 40–5, 47–8, 51, 58–60, 63, 70, 72, 79, 82–3, 110, 117, 128, 135, 142, 154–6, 168, 173, 178–9
Rochester, Castle, 45, 125, 143
Richmond, Siege of, 142, 145–6, 155–6, 158
Rolle, Château de, 92, 123, 137–8
Romont, Château, 11, 19–20, 40, 58–9, 61, 63, 84, 120, 138
Rossillon, Thomas de, 56, 99, 172–3
Rudolph or Rudolf III, King of Burgundy, 2–3, 62
Rue, Château de, 18, 84, 120

Saint-Bernard, Grand, Pass, 1–2, 4–5, 14, 60, 76, 85, 124, 135, 138, 140, 179, 181
Saint-Bernard, Petit, Pass, 1–3, 5, 26, 76, 118, 138, 140
Saint-Georges-d'Espéranche, Château, 102, 174
Saint-Georges, Maître Jacques de, 63, 77, 95, 136–9, 156, 169, 177, 180–1, 184

Saint-Maurice, town and monastery of, 2, 4, 8–9, 76, 85, 102, 120, 122
Saint-Rambert-en-Bugey see Cornillon
Saillon, 102, 136–8, 176
Saintonge War, 49–51, 53, 55, 60
Saluzzo, Agnès di, Baroness of Alnwick, 95, 99, 170
Saluzzo, Alésia di, Baroness of Pontefract, 78–9, 95, 97, 9
Savoie, Amédée IV de, Count of Savoy, 8–10, 13–8, 22–3, 25, 47, 52, 57–8, 64, 75–8, 85, 95, 99–102, 112, 135, 179, 185
  Enfeoffment of Key Castles, Palace and Town to King Henry III of England, 64, 75–7, 120
Savoie, Amédée V de, Count of Savoy, 102, 116, 135, 169, 178, 179–81
Savoie, Béatrice de, Countess of Provence, 8–10, 12–3, 21, 23–4, 47, 49, 55–6, 58, 74, 77, 83, 100, 104, 119, 139, 147, 150, 177
Savoie, Béatrice de, Dame de Faucigny, 48, 102, 179–80, 182, 187
Savoie, Bernard de, Constable of Windsor Castle, 52–3, 59, 82, 89, 93
Savoie, Boniface de, Archbishop of Canterbury, 10, 14, 16, 27, 47, 53, 55, 57–8, 76–7, 84–5, 97, 104–5, 126, 135, 140, 183–5
  Alianor de Provence, Queen of England, 45, 60, 62
  birth, 9
  Bishopric of Belley, 44–5, 57, 59, 103
  Bishopric of Canterbury, 44–5, 57, 73–4, 80–3, 89, 116, 129, 131–2, 169–70
  Bishopric of Winchester, 44
  Council of Fifteen, 113, 124
  consecration of Salisbury Cathedral, 119
  death, 169
  De Facto Exile, 131, 134, 146, 149
  Lusignans, 109, 114–15
  Magna Carta, 92
  Marriage of Charles d'Anjou and Béatrice de Provence, 75
  Matthew Paris Criticism, 73–4, 79–83, 170
  Pierre de Savoie, 62, 73–5, 85, 103, 109, 113–5, 119, 124, 127, 140, 142, 149, 168
  Priory of Nantua, 44–5, 83
  Saint Boniface, 170

Savoie, Boniface de, Count of Savoy. 101–2, 116, 128, 135, 179
Savoie, Guillaume de, Bishop Elect of Valemce, 8, 13, 20, 28, 36
- Anglo-Flemish Relations, 31
- Anglo-Scottish Relations, 30–1
- birth, 9
- Bishopric of Valence, 10, 13
- Bishopric of Winchester, 30
- Chief Counsellor to King Henry III of England, 29
- Dean of Vienne, 20
- death, 32, 35–6
- Famille de Savoie Mediator, 15–6
- Honour of Richmond, 25, 40
- marriage of Alianor de Provence and King Henry III of England, 22–5
- marriage of Marguerite de Provence and King Louis IX of France, 21–2
- Matthew Paris Criticism, 23–5, 32–3, 37
- Pierre d'Aigueblanche, 29
- Pierre de Savoie, 15, 20, 23, 32–3, 37–9
- xenophobia, 26

Savoie, Humbert I de, Count of Savoy, 3–4, 7, 10
Savoie, Humbert III de, Count of Savoy, 7, 9, 22
Savoie, Philippe I de, Count of Savoy, 14, 20, 49, 51, 55, 70, 75–7, 84, 105, 149, 176, 179, 181, 185
- Alianor de Provence, Queen of England, 149–50
- Archbishopric of Lyon, 10, 47, 57–8, 62, 85, 104
- birth, 9
- Bishopric of Lausanne, 18–20
- Bishopric of Valence, 55
- Castle Building in the Viennois, 27, 77, 102
- Count of Savoy, 10, 178–80
- Dean of Metz Cathedral, 18
- Dean of Vienne, 20
- Pierre de Savoie, 84–5, 99, 101–2, 135, 174, 178

Savoie, Pierre II de, Count of Savoy, 3, 8, 11, 21, 23, 25, 27, 32, 40, 45–6, 55–6, 60, 64, 72–4, 77, 83, 87, 98, 105, 121, 126, 129, 131–2, 146, 183–8

Arlod, Château d', 52
Battle of Lausanne, 18–20,
Bern and Morat, Lord Protector of, 101, 104, 175–7
birth, 9–10
Bishopric of Lausanne, 18, 58
Boston, Port of, 41–4
Canon, Lausanne Cathedral, 14–5
Charter Witnesses, 90
Chablais and Valais, 102, 136–7, 176
childhood, 9
Chillon, Château de, 102–3, 136
Cholay, Nantelme de, 157–8
Cornillon, Château de, 16–7, 140
conquest of Vaud, 58–9, 61
Constable of Dover Castle, 45, 61
Council of Fifteen, 113
Count of Savoy, 135–6, 139–40, 150, 168–9, 172–6, 179, 187
death, burial and tomb, 177–80
diplomacy for the English Crown, 47, 49, 51, 75, 84, 100–1, 110, 117–19, 128, 179, 187
Eagle, Honour of the, 45, 47–8, 51, 168, 179–81
Edward, The Lord, 42, 45–6, 53, 55, 59–60, 70, 87, 89–90, 94, 96–8, 102–3, 109–10, 114, 127–8, 141, 147, 154, 160–1, 176, 186–7
English and Alpine Career Interlinked, 27, 36, 51–4, 58, 61, 78–9, 83, 85–6, 91, 103
escape of the Lord Edward from Captivity, 155, 158–6
Eu, Honour of, 83–4, 89, 128
Famille de Charron, 52, 82, 128, 142, 155–6, 178
Famille de Grandson, 16, 37, 59, 61–2, 84, 90–2, 96–7, 120, 144, 167
Famille de Joinville, 50, 54, 94, 107, 110–1, 121, 159–60
Flanders Army, 145–7, 149–56, 158, 176
Faucigny de, Béatrice daughter, 48, 182
Gascony Expedition, 90, 92–7, 187
Habsburg, Rudolf I von, 175–6, 183
Henry III, King of England, 36–40, 43, 47, 49, 51–2, 56, 63–4, 67, 69–70, 78–79, 84, 87–8, 90, 92–7, 99, 101–2, 104–5,

Index

107, 109–15, 117–20, 124, 140–2, 144–5, 147, 150, 154–7, 168, 172–3, 176, 178–80, 187
Imperial Vicar, 175
Joinville, Simon de, Seigneur de Gex et Marnay, 53, 94, 107, 110–1, 121, 124, 160–1
knighted, 38–9
Kyburg, Hartmann IV and V von, 175–6
La-Tour-du-Pin, Lords of, 84
Les Clées, Château de, 84–5
Lompnes, Château de, 16–7
Lusignans, 79, 85–6, 89–90, 95, 108–11, 114, 125
Mansel, John, Lord Chancellor, 32, 51–2, 89–90, 126–7, 140, 142, 154, 172
marriage to Agnès de Faucigny, 15–6, 107, 182
Mésoz, Jean de, Engineer, 94–5, 136–9
Mont, Ebal II de, Constable of Windsor Castle and Attorney for Pierre, 52–4, 61, 80, 86, 89, 92, 94–5, 97, 110, 123–4, 126, 128–9, 132, 137–8, 141, 146, 155, 169
Montfort, Simon de, 6th Earl of Leicester, 31, 88–9, 92, 100–1, 109–11, 113, 116, 124–6, 131–2, 140, 150, 154–5, 160, 174, 187
Moudon, 20, 36, 59, 61, 84, 120
Oath of 1258, 109–10
Oxford, Provisions of, 80, 113–6, 128–9, 131–3, 141–2, 154, 165–6, 174
Paris, Matthew, 33, 37–8, 40, 79, 95, 103, 135, 180, 187
Pevensey, Castle, 27, 63–4, 90, 93, 145
Pevensey, Siege of, 142, 145–6, 148, 151, 155–9, 161–3
prisoner of the Count of Geneva, 18
Protection of the Lord Edward, 55–6, 59, 70, 87, 90, 97–8, 103, 111, 114–5, 128, 150, 158–61
Provence de, Alianor, Queen of England, 17, 36–8, 46, 48, 53, 55, 59–62, 70, 88–90, 95, 97–8, 103, 109–10, 114–5, 119, 124, 126–8, 142, 145–7, 149–55, 158–62, 168, 174, 178–9, 181
Rarogne, Henri de, Bishop of Sion, 102, 124, 128, 135–6, 149, 175–7, 179

reforms of Administration and Law in Savoy, 168, 172–5
removal from Ruling Council of England, 124–5
Revolution of 1258, 113–5
Richmond, Honour of, 36, 40–4, 51–2, 58, 142, 154, 168, 178–9
Richmond, Siege of, 142, 145–6, 155–6, 158
rivalry with the Count of Geneva, 16–8, 36, 51–4, 84, 124, 177
Romont, Lord of, 11, 58–9, 61, 120, 138
Rue, Château de, 84, 120
Saint-Georges, Maître Jacques de, 63, 77, 95, 136–9, 156, 169, 177, 180–1, 184
Saillon, 136–7, 176
Saluzzo, Agnès di, Baroness of Alnwick, 95, 99, 170
Saluzzo, Alésia di, Baroness of Pontefract, 78–9, 95, 97, 99
Savoie, Boniface de, 62, 73–5, 85, 103, 109, 113–15, 119, 124, 127, 140, 142, 149, 168
Savoie, Guillaume de, 15, 20, 23, 32–3, 37–9
Savoie, Philippe de, 84–5, 99, 101–2, 135, 174, 178
Savoie, Thomas II de, Count of Flanders and Regent of Savoy, 22, 30–1, 34–6, 43, 47, 77, 99, 102, 104–5, 116, 132, 135, 178–81
Savoy, Palace of, 72–3, 90, 103, 155, 162, 181
Seigneury de Gex, 16, 50, 54, 94, 107, 110–11, 160–1
Sicily Business, 99, 104
Treaty of Paris 1259, 117–19, 179, 187
Via Francigena, 84, 121
Warden of the Cinque Ports, 45
Wales, 64, 67–70, 187
Wardship of Jean de Warenne, 45, 48, 62, 78, 89, 95–6, 110, 130, 140
Wardship of Jean de Vesci, 95
Witley Manor, 4, 125, 134
Yverdon, Château, 63–4, 90, 120–3, 135, 137–9, 148, 156, 173
Savoie, Thomas I de, Count of Savoy, 7, 13, 16, 21, 23, 135, 175, 179

Savoie, Thomas II de, Count of Flanders and Regent of Savoy, 22, 30–1, 34–6, 43, 47, 77, 99, 102, 104, 116, 132, 135, 178–81
  Simon de Montfort debt, 34–5
Savoy, Enfeoffment of Key Castles, Palace and Town to King Henry JJJ of England, 64, 75–7, 120
Savoy, Palace of, 72–3, 90, 103, 155, 162, 181
Sicily, Kingdom of, 99–100, 103–5, 108–9, 119, 170–71
Susa, Margravial Palace of, 6, 8–9, 76

Taillebourg, Battle of, 50–1, 53, 55
Tarentaise, 2–3, 5, 8, 26–7, 85, 93–4, 118, 124, 137–8, 147–8, 169, 173, 181
Tickhill, Castle, 53, 59
Tonbridge, Castle, 143
Turin, 1, 6, 9–10, 32, 39, 76, 104–5, 110, 122, 139

Urban IV, Pope, 128–9, 149, 153

Valence, Bishopric of, 10, 13–4, 20–2, 24–6, 28–9, 32–3, 45, 55, 57
Valence, Guillaume de, 1st Earl of Pembroke, 78, 85–6, 89–90, 96, 108–9, 111, 127, 140, 145, 159, 161–2

Valereys, Guillaume de, 60, 90
Verters, Simon de, 147–8, 172–3
Vesci, Jean de, Baron of Alnwick, 79, 95–6, 104, 131, 170
Via Francigena, 1, 4, 14, 37, 60, 77, 84–5, 120–2, 136
Viennois, The, 8–9, 27, 47–8, 77, 85, 102, 172–4, 179
Vuippens, Gerard de, 47, 101, 169
Vuippens, Ulrich de, 59, 101

Warenne, Jean de, 6th Earl of Surrey, 45, 48, 59, 89, 95, 97, 110, 130–1, 140, 145, 159
Wenlock, Priory, 80
Westminster, Abbey of, 28, 74, 76, 86, 88, 108, 126, 129, 183, 185–6
Westminster, Provisions of, 116, 125
Wigmore, Castle, 113, 160, 164
William of Holland, King of the Germans, 101
Winchester, Bishopric of, 21, 30, 32, 44, 78, 85, 89, 115, 125
Wissant, Hanekin de, 156
Woodstock, Treaty of, 71, 105–6

Yverdon, Château, 63–4, 90, 120–3, 135, 137–9, 148, 156, 173